D1610604

FINAL APPEAL

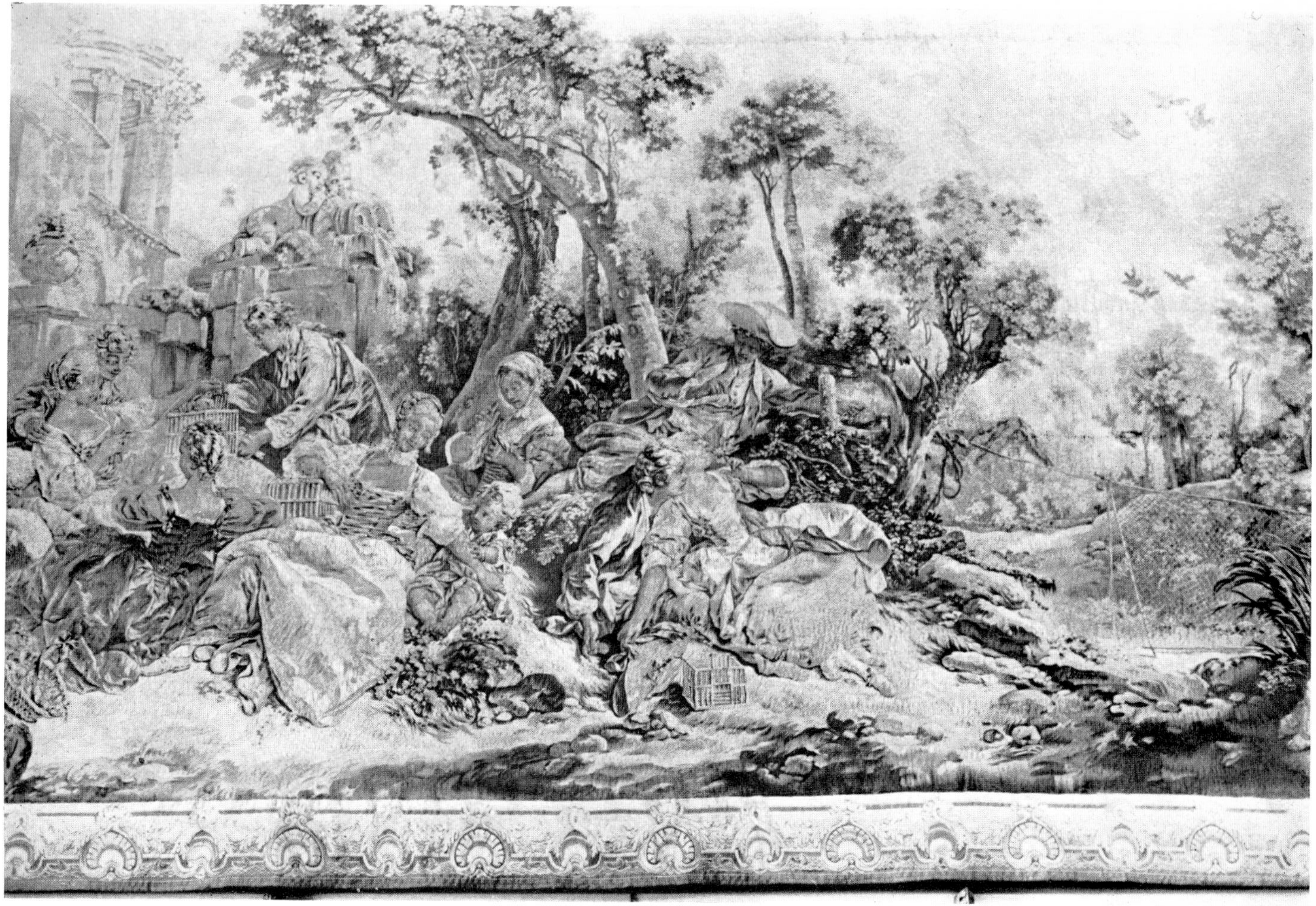

[Jane Bown]

FINAL APPEAL

A STUDY OF THE
HOUSE OF LORDS
IN ITS JUDICIAL CAPACITY

LOUIS BLOM-COOPER, Q.C.

AND

GAVIN DREWRY

CLARENDON PRESS · OXFORD

1972

Oxford University Press, Ely House, London W.1

GLASGOW NEW YORK TORONTO MELBOURNE WELLINGTON
CAPE TOWN IBADAN NAIROBI DAR ES SALAAM LUSAKA ADDIS ABABA
DELHI BOMBAY CALCUTTA MADRAS KARACHI LAHORE DACCA
KUALA LUMPUR SINGAPORE HONG KONG TOKYO

PRINTED IN GREAT BRITAIN
BY WILLIAM CLOWES & SONS, LIMITED
LONDON, BECCLES AND COLCHESTER

TO

The Rt. Hon. the Lord Reid of Drem,
C.H., D.C.L., LL.D., F.R.S.E.

The only ground upon which a suitor ought to be allowed to bring the judgment of one court for examination before the members of another is the certainty or extreme probability of finding in the latter tribunal more wisdom and learning, more maturity of deliberation, and a greater capacity of sound decisions than existed in the court from which the appeal is to proceed. But as every appeal is of necessity attended with the two great and positive evils of expense and delay, it is the bounden duty of every wise and good government to take all possible care that the court of appellate jurisdiction shall possess those advantages, and that superior capacity for wise and impartial adjudication, upon the presumption of possessing which, the public support and the confidence of individual suitors is given to the institution.

> 1832 TRACT:—'Some observations on the necessity of reforming the judicial House of Lords, considered as the court of ultimate appeal in the administration of civil justice'.

The people may be taught to believe in one court of appeal; but where there are two they cannot be blamed if they believe in neither. When a man keeps two clocks which tell the time differently, his fellows will receive with suspicion his weightiest pronouncements upon the hour of the day, even if one of them happens to be right.

A. P. HERBERT, *Uncommon Law*, 3rd ed., 1937, p. 259

ACKNOWLEDGEMENTS

THIS book is based upon research carried out in the Legal Research Unit, Bedford College, University of London, financed by the Joseph Rowntree Memorial Trust. It had a gestation period of five years. That period would have been far longer, and the finished product much the poorer, had we not been assisted and encouraged in a multiplicity of ways by numerous friends and colleagues. To try to list all the people who have so lightened our task would be impossible; often a fruitful train of thought is set in motion by a single chance remark. We are also conscious of our debt to the excellent intellectual environment in which our work has been conducted.

We gratefully acknowledge by name the help of some of the people without whose help and encouragement this study could not have been attempted. We add the customary qualification that those so listed are in no way responsible for the authors' errors of fact or for any of their heresies. We are confident only that we have been rescued from perpetrating errors by the help of others. (This is not to say that those unnamed bear any responsibility; only that we need make no public disclaimer in respect of them.)

First, we owe an immense debt to Mr. Richard Cave, Principal Clerk of the Judicial Office of the House of Lords, whose unique and limitless fund of knowledge about the judicial House of Lords has proved indispensible and who displayed infinite patience in dealing with our many inquiries, both great and small.

Research of this kind requires limitless access to documents of various kinds. In this connection we would like to thank Mr. M. F. Bond, Clerk of the Records, and his colleagues in the House of Lords Record Office, who put up with our presence in their Search Room for so long and who dealt so efficiently with our numerous troublesome requests. Similarly, we would thank Mr. C. A. L. Fisher, Chief Librarian of the Bar Library, Royal Courts of Justice, for his great kindness and patience.

So many professional colleagues have assisted in various ways that it seems invidious to name individuals. But we must make particular mention of Mr. Michael Knight of the Queen's University, Belfast, who gave invaluable help and advice on a wide variety of matters and who generously allowed us to use hitherto unpublished information on the use of full courts in the Court of Criminal Appeal. (See Appendix 6.) Also Mrs. Jenny Brock of the Legal Research Unit, Bedford College, University of London, who did much of the research embodied in Chapter X and who kindly provided, from her own postgraduate thesis, information on the social backgrounds of the Law Lords, used in Chapter VIII.

Professor Delmar Karlen of the Institute of Judicial Administration, New York, supplied information about the appellate systems of the United States; Mr. Sydney Kentridge S.C. of the Johannesburg Bar illumined the South African appellate system for us; Professor T. B. Smith of the University of Edinburgh and his colleagues gave generous and invaluable help on various matters of Scottish law; Mr. Robin Jacob initiated us in the mysteries of patent, trade mark and copyright law; and Mr. E. O. Jackson supplied a vast quantity of expertise and information for our chapter on revenue and rating law. Master Matthews advised us on matters relating to taxation of costs and Master Thompson on several occasions rescued us from our ignorance of procedural technicalities relating to criminal appeals.

Several colleagues and friends, in addition to some of those already mentioned, kindly read through our successive drafts and made numerous suggestions for their improvement. In particular we should mention Professor O. R. McGregor and Dr. Ivor Burton, both of the Department of Sociology, Bedford College; Professor Robert Stevens of the University of Yale; Mrs. Jean Floud of Nuffield College, University of Oxford; and Mr. Anthony Sampson, author of *The New Anatomy of Britain*.

We have had the inestimable benefit of the opinions of some who know the story from the inside but who, for professional reasons, must remain anonymous. We hope that they find some reflection of their words of wisdom in this book. We add a word of thanks to our publishers. Their insistence upon meticulous attention to detail has improved immeasurably any quality our work may have. And we are grateful to them for thinking that our book is worthy of their distinguished imprint.

Finally, we should thank those who from time to time undertook various ancillary tasks on our behalf. Mr Andrew Woodfield collected information about applications for leave to appeal in the Court of Appeal; Mrs. Carol Kitch checked references, read proofs and prepared the first draft of our index. Of the numerous secretaries who have had to contend both with our execrable handwriting and with the vagaries of our moods special mention must be made of Mrs. Ruth Male who typed, and in the course of acting as amanuensis improved our final manuscript by her pertinent observations on syntax and literary style.

NOTE: References to named courts have not taken into account the changes resulting from the Courts Act 1971 which came into force on 1 January 1972. And the important judgments of the Law Lords in *Broome* v. *Cassell and Co. Ltd.* [1972] 2 W.L.R. 645 (23 February 1972) came too late to be discussed in the text.

CONTENTS

FRONTISPIECE

The Bird Catcher. One of the set of three tapestries entitled "La Noble Pastorale" designed by Boucher for Madame de Pompadour, 1755. The tapestry hangs in Committee Room No. 1 where the Appellate Committee of the House of Lords sits regularly to hear appeals. (*Reproduced by kind permission of David Wilkie-Cooper, Esq.*)

LIST OF TABLES

ABBREVIATIONS

A.	[Appeal] Allowed
A.I.P.	[Appeal] Allowed in Part
A.C.	Appeal Cases (Law Reports)
A.L.J.	Australian Law Journal
A.L.J.R.	Australian Law Journal Reports
All E.R.	All England Reports
A.P.	Assisted Person
App. Cas.	Appeal Cases (Law Reports, 1875–1890)
A.T.C.	Annotated Tax Cases
B.	Baron (of the Exchequer)
C.A.	Court of Appeal
Can. Bar. Rev.	Canadian Bar Review
C.B.	Chief Baron (of the Exchequer)
C.C.A.	Court of Criminal Appeal
Ch.	Chancery (Law Reports)
C.I.R.	Commissioners of Inland Revenue
C.L.J.	Cambridge Law Journal
C.L.R.	Commonwealth Law Reports (Australia)
C-M.A.C.	Courts-Martial Appeal Court
C.M.L.R.	Common Market Law Reports
Cox C.C.	Cox's Criminal Cases
Cr. App. R.	Criminal Appeal Reports
Crim. L.R.	Criminal Law Review
C.S.	Court of Session (Scotland)
D.	[Appeal] Dismissed
Div. Ct.	Divisional Court
D.L.R.	Dominion Law Reports (Canada)
E.G.	Estates Gazette
F.S.R.	Fleet Street Patent Law Reports
Harvard L.R.	Harvard Law Review
H.L.	House of Lords
I.L.T.R.	Irish Law Times Reports
In f.p.	*In formâ pauperis*
I.R.	Irish Reports
I.R.C./C.I.R.	Inland Revenue Commissioners
J. or JJ.	Justice(s) (i.e. puisne Judges of the High Court)
J.C.	Justiciary Cases (Scotland)
J.P.	Justice of the Peace Reports
J.P.L.	Journal of Planning and Property Law
J.S.P.T.L.	Journal of the Society of Public Teachers of Law
K.B.	King's Bench (Law Reports)
K.B.D.	King's Bench Division of the High Court
K.I.R.	Knight's Industrial Reports
L.A.	Legal Aid
L.C.	Lord Chancellor

ABBREVIATIONS

L.C.J. or C.J.	Lord Chief Justice
L.J.	Law Journal
L.J. or L.JJ.	Lord(s) Justice(s) of Appeal
L.Q.R.	Law Quarterly Review
L.R.	Law Reports
L.R.[1]R.P.	Law Reports, Restrictive Practices
L.T.	Law Times Reports
Ll. R.	Lloyd's List Reports (1951 onwards)
Ll.L.Rep.	Lloyd's List Reports (before 1951)
M.L.R.	Modern Law Review
M.R.	Master of the Rolls
N.A.P.S.S.	National Association for the Promotion of Social Science
New L.J.	New Law Journal
N.I.	Northern Ireland Law Reports
... (N.I.)	... of Northern Ireland
N.I.L.Q.	Northern Ireland Legal Quarterly
N.Z.L.R.	New Zealand Law Reports
P.	Probate, Divorce and Admiralty (Law Reports)
P.C.	Privy Council
P.L.	Public Law
Q.B.	Queen's Bench (Law Reports)
Q.B.D.	Queen's Bench Division of the High Court
R. and I.T.	Rating and Income Tax Reports
R.P.C.	Reports of Patent, Design and Trade Mark Cases
S. or Scot.	Scotland
S.A.	South African Law Reports
S.C.	Session Cases (Scotland)
Sc. and D.	Scots and Divorce Cases (Law Reports)
S.C. (H.L.)	Session Cases (House of Lords) (Scotland)
S.C. (J.)	Session Cases (High Court of Judiciary) (Scotland)
S.J.	Solicitors' Journal
S.L.T.	Scots Law Times
T.C.	Tax Cases
T.L.R.	Times Law Reports
T.R.	Taxation Reports
U.S.	United States Law Reports
V.O.	Valuation Officer
V.R.	Victorian Law Reports (Australia)
W.L.R.	Weekly Law Reports (since 1953)
W.N.	Weekly Notes
Yale L.J.	Yale Law Journal

PART A

THE BACKGROUND

I

INTRODUCTION

THE scope of this study extends beyond the area of 'lawyers' law'; it is an attempt at an analysis of the role of an important legal institution. That we can claim the study to be unique underlines the lack of empathy which has, at least until very recently, characterized the relationship between the lawyer and the social scientist. With one possible exception, there has hitherto been no attempt to analyse in depth the functions of any British court, employing the increasingly refined methodological and statistical techniques which have been developed and widely used in numerous other areas of social research.

The exception is the book published in 1965 by Professors Yamey and Stevens on the Restrictive Practices Court. That pioneering work surveys an important area of the judicial process in terms of socio-economic theory and, by its very originality, has made a significant contribution to the empirical study of legal institutions. But the scope and purpose of that study bears little resemblance to the present project. The role of the Restrictive Practices Court was, at the time that book was written, essentially confined to interpreting and applying a single statute, the Restrictive Trade Practices Act 1956, though it later acquired a new jurisdiction under the Resale Prices Act 1964. The Court had, moreover, been in existence for only six years at the time of the Yamey–Stevens study, during which period it had delivered twenty-eight decisions.

The importance and diversity of subject-matter in the work of the House of Lords has given us far greater scope for empirical research. Its case-load ranges over the entire field of both the civil and criminal law: and although the court only assumed its present form under the Appellate Jurisdiction Act 1876, its ancestry can be traced at least as far back as the thirteenth century. Quite apart from these factors, the House of Lords is more than a 'court' in the ordinary sense of the word. It is at the apex (or perhaps, more accurately, vortex) of a hierarchy of courts: in a legal system still dominated by the doctrine of *stare decisis*, it exercises an important supervisory role over the entire process of judicial 'law-making'. It was largely our awareness of the importance of this unique duality of function of the House of Lords which prompted the present study.

Courts of law might appear at first sight to be unpromising subjects for empirical study, still less for systematic theoretical generalization. Yet institutions are manifestly of fundamental importance, and as such present a challenging, sometimes elusive, target to the researcher. The task of the present study will be to describe in detail and to arrive at an informed evaluation of the role of the House of Lords in relation to other parts of our legal system.

To this end we have divided this work into three sections: the first describing the context within which the House of Lords operates; the second providing a statistical profile of the Lords 'in action'; and the third analysing the work of the court in various areas of substantive law. We would stress that these divisions have been deployed for the sake of literary clarity rather than with a view to erecting artificial barriers between overlapping aspects of our research.

In undertaking this research we have made at least one fundamental assumption; we have not questioned the notion that a legal system of some description is a concomitant of all developed societies. We have, therefore, assumed that so long as legal institutions exist it is in the interests of society that they should function efficiently and effectively. We may have made, either explicitly or implicitly, incidental criticisms of the socio-legal value system within which the House of Lords operates—in any event this book may provide the launching-pad for further discussion along such lines—but that has not been our primary purpose.

We have confined ourselves to two main tasks. First, we have made a critical assessment of the effectiveness of the House of Lords in terms of the requirements of a *given* socio-legal system. Secondly, we have made an evaluation—inevitably subjective, but backed where possible by empirical evidence—of the role of the House of Lords both in shaping the common law and interpreting the statute law, as compared with the roles of other institutions involved in the numerous ramifications of the law-making process.

This has entailed looking at the House of Lords from four main viewpoints. *Mechanical efficiency:* are there wrinkles and anachronisms in the judicial process and, if so, how best could they be ironed out? *Litigant contentment:* does the individual litigant in the House of Lords get value for money—are House of Lords appeals merely costly replications of proceedings in the lower courts? *Lawyer satisfaction:* does the House of Lords really produce the 'best' law, and play an important part in the development towards a clear, coherent, and consistent legal system? *Social function* (embracing the previous three): what is the relationship of the House of Lords to other legal institutions? The answer to the last question both depends on, and stems from the answer to yet another: whether decisions of the courts, and of the House of Lords in particular, successfully reflect the needs of a rapidly changing industrialized society? The considerable methodological and philosophical difficulties involved in an ambitious exercise of this kind are discussed more fully below.

With a view to providing answers to these questions, our research has involved three distinct, but interrelated operations.

(1) An attempt to place the House of Lords into its proper historical context—first, by reviewing the published literature on the subject, and second, by examining the several series of official judicial statistics published since 1876 and analysing the changing distribution of case-load and variations in the numbers of successful appeals. For easy reference we have concentrated most of the historical material into the next chapter.

(2) To enable the debate about reform or abolition of the House of Lords to proceed on a firm basis of empirical fact, we have attempted to provide a detailed statistical profile of the activities of the House of Lords since 1952. This material is contained in Part B where, in effect, we shall describe the progress of appeals from trial court to House of Lords in the light of certain simple hypotheses about the judicial process. This body of data is designed both to provide a nucleus of empirical information upon which theoretical generalizations can be soundly based and, hopefully, to reveal significant statistical patterns.

(3) Proceeding from our empirical findings, we shall analyse (in Part C) the dual functions of the House of Lords mentioned above—both as an additional tribunal of review in particular litigation and as a court exercising supervision over lower courts.

The bulk of the time occupied by this research was devoted to a systematic empirical survey of the House of Lords in action. Since the variety of subject matter which comes before the House of Lords ranges over the whole field of civil and criminal litigation, and since the number of cases heard annually (approximately thirty-three on average) is relatively small, it was necessary to study appeals over a large number of years. The question was: how many years? It became necessary for some purposes to look at the cases when being determined in the courts *a quo*; some regard, therefore, had to be paid to the availability of records of the case load of the Court of Appeal. Under the direction of the then Master of the Rolls, the late Lord Evershed, every judgment delivered by the civil divisions of the Court of Appeal has been filed in the Bar Library, starting with the new law year in October 1951. This provided us with a convenient and methodologically acceptable period of judicial activity for the purpose of this study.

The seventeen-year period 1952–68 produced some 500 House of Lords decisions on appeal. In addition we have analysed all the petitions for leave to appeal heard by the Appeal Committee of the House of Lords (about 650 cases) and every recorded application for leave to appeal to the House of Lords heard by the Court of Appeal (about 1,900 cases) during the same period.

METHOD OF APPROACH

Social scientists are often accused—and not always unjustly—of collecting empirical data merely for the sake of collecting them: of filling their journals with elaborate but meaningless studies of synthetic social phenomena, to say nothing of their predeliction for theorizing about social noumena. In an attempt to disarm our critics we include an account of the methodology and philosophy of this study, and point to some of the difficulties which arise.

With the status-insecurity which seems to have afflicted students of an academic discipline which is still evolving from its comparatively recent origins, social scientists tend to be very sensitive about the use of adjectives like 'fact-finding' or 'descriptive' when applied to their research enterprises: it is true that social theorists are still at the model-building stage where sophisticated theories of social cause and effect are very much a thing of the future. The real trouble is that in a great many fields we are not even clear as to the nature of the phenomena which require explanation: this stems not only from difficulties of definition, but also from the fact that in many cases little attempt has been made to garner a coherently structured body of empirical data about the phenomena under investigation. There is here a vicious circle: a phenomenon must be defined before it can be studied; definition implies that one is designating the entity defined as meaningful or relevant; this in turn requires us to postulate explanatory hypotheses, based on further definitions. But the chain has to be broken at some point, and the most that one can hope to do in the evolutionary stages of sociological enquiry is to collect a broad range of data on topics which *seem* relevant in terms of existing theory (or, at least, common sense) in the hope that the theoretical foundations of the subject-area will eventually be strengthened *a posteriori* on the basis of the empirical findings. This we have done.

The present study has entered virgin territory: if we cannot always, in terms of coherent socio-legal theory, logically defend the inclusion or omission of specific items of data it is because, in all too many of the areas we are examining, little or none exists. In an exercise of this nature we have felt it necessary to describe and define phenomena before theorizing about them.

If our theoretical foundations are circumscribed by the lack of previous study in the field, this does not mean that we have operated entirely without navigational aids. Although the subject is devoid of rigorous theoretical under-pinnings, students of the judicial process have evolved, largely on an *ad hoc* basis, numerous hypotheses—some demonstrably wild, some eminently plausible—which provide at least a starting-point for systematic empirical study. These low-level hypotheses, supplemented by some of the authors' own hunches, have been implicit in the process by which we have selected questions for inclusion in the questionnaire used, as will be explained later, to extract data from the House of Lords' records.

For example, we decided that it would be relevant to ask questions about the legal backgrounds of the judges—questions to ourselves and not, merci-fully, to the judges—who heard the cases at each stage. It is possible that judges with differing legal experience—common law, chancery, and Scottish judges—might adopt measurably different approaches to legal problems, and we framed the questionnaire accordingly. Similarly we have tried to discover whether legally-aided cases tend to have a higher success rate than non-legally-aided cases, since it seemed a plausible supposition that Legal Aid Area Committees might be loath to allocate public funds to appeals which appear initially to have little chance of success: and such a question ties in with our more general speculations about the functions of legal aid in House of Lords proceedings.

Calling tentative preliminary ideas of this kind 'hypotheses' may appear to endow them with an aura of distinction they do not deserve, but hypotheses of some kind have to be formulated if any questionnaire is to yield meaning-ful results. Taken by themselves our own are too crude to throw much light on a complex multi-variate situation, but they at least provide a starting-point in questionnaire construction. The explanatory role of a survey of this kind is limited, not only by the unfathomable complexity of the relation-ships between the concatenation of factors which relate (or at least appear to relate) to the judicial process, but also by more mundane methodological problems (only too familiar to all social scientists) such as sample size.

Our difficulties of this kind are best highlighted by an example. One of our initial working hypotheses was that judges with (say) Scottish backgrounds might behave differently in their treatment of Scottish appeals from their English colleagues. An attempt to measure this would, however, have been complicated by several factors.

(1) Definition and measurement: what is a 'Scottish judge'? It might well be (as Lord Cockburn once said) that when a Scottish lawyer moves south of the Tweed his Scottish law rapidly 'oozes' out of him. Even an attempt to correct the figures by devising an index of Anglicization (perhaps based upon a proportion of years spent in England to years spent in Scotland, with an upward weighting for English ancestry!) would be defeated by individual personality differences not susceptible to mathematical calculations.

What in any event is a 'Scottish case'? We would start by restricting the definition to cases begun in Scottish courts, but are we justified in treating all such cases on the same basis? There might be a world of difference between a Scottish judge's treatment of a revenue appeal involving the interpretation of a U.K. tax statute or of a provision of a road traffic law enacted at Westminster, and the same judge's reaction to a case involving the finer points of some aspect of peculiarly Scottish land law.

(2) Interfering variables: even accepting the dubious proposition that

'Scottishness' is a definable and inherently meaningful concept, how can we be sure that it is a *causal* factor in a given multi-variate situation, still less that it is the *dominant* factor? The need to confine our study within finite limits has forced us to exclude from our analysis many variables, however relevant in this context, for example, the social backgrounds of the judges. We must be careful to avoid overvaluing the theoretical implications of our correlations: *a fortiori*, we must not fall into the trap of upgrading their significance to accord with our own preliminary hypotheses.

(3) Statistical problems: having taken all the cases decided over a relatively long period of time (seventeen years) we feel we have eliminated the problem of sample bias. But we felt we were on methodologically safe ground only so long as we did not attempt to project our findings too far beyond the boundaries of the actual period of our study.

Our population of 500 appeals was quite large, but we were still faced with the problem of statistical significance. Throughout the study we have had to deal with sub-sets of the main sample; annual totals, totals of Scottish appeals, totals of various subject-categories of appeal, etc.—giving figures very much smaller than 500. The total number of Scottish appeals was not much more than 100: the annual average of Scottish appeals was about six. Only the most superficial conclusions could be drawn from calculations derived from figures of this size.

But having entered this extensive caveat, we would hasten to repeat that these problems are not peculiar to this study: they arise in almost every area of sociological research. So long as we were careful not to overvalue our data, to construct a complex theoretical edifice on the shifting sands of spurious correlation, then this exercise should illumine rather than befog the mechanism of the judicial process—or, as Milton put it, at least make the darkness more visible.

Every one of the 500 appeals included in our study is unique. In order to keep the extent of the research, and of this book, within finite limits, we have sought a compromise between the Herculean, if not Sisyphean, task of writing a substantial essay on every one of these cases (an undertaking which would have highlighted individual trees to the detriment of our principal object of mapping-out the wood) and merely compiling data about such matters as 'how many appeals?', 'how long did they take?' and 'how many involved legal aid?'; information which, taken by itself, provides a skeleton of the legal process stripped of the all-important flesh of substantive law.

Although every appeal is *sui generis*, there is running through the entire case-load of the House of Lords an unbroken thread consisting of rules and conventions of procedural law and practice: added to this, every case has in common certain quantifiable attributes—duration, cost, numbers of personnel involved, etc. In individual cases, and taken item by item, matters of this kind are (except to the litigants themselves) of trifling importance and tell us nothing about the working of the Court; but, taken together and considered in relation to a large number of cases, they constitute both a firm nucleus of factual information about the House of Lords and an invaluable launching-pad for our study of its functions. Answers to questions like 'how long does an appeal take?' or 'how much does it cost?' do not constitute the last word about the social utility of the final appeal court, but considered in conjunction with our considered impressions about the effectiveness of the House of Lords in tackling socio-legal problems, the answers to such questions form a solid basis for an informed judgment. (The problems of marrying hard data of this kind with impressionistic conclusions is discussed later in this chapter.)

In order to accumulate this coherent body of material about the House of Lords we compiled a document[1] (referred to throughout this work as the 'questionnaire', though the questions are addressed to ourselves and not to others) which was used to extract some sixty items of information about every appeal, and rather fewer items for every petition for leave to appeal, during our period of study. The questionnaire was of the pre-coded variety which enabled the information obtained to be transferred to punched cards for the purpose of computer analysis.

Although the questions (based upon working hypotheses as described earlier) were devised after a careful pilot study of thirty cases taken at random, the questionnaire underwent considerable modification as the study proceeded. One or two of the items included proved in practice to be less revealing than had been hoped and were replaced by others; ambiguous wording had to be modified; and new codes had to be inserted to cover unforeseen circumstances. (This brief account of our tribulations will, we suspect, strike a familiar and sympathetic chord among fellow sufferers who have had first-hand acquaintance with imperfect research instruments of this kind.)

The questions ranged widely: the composition of the various courts at each successive stage, the outcome of each hearing, the intervals of time between each successive step from the initiation of proceedings to the final judgment of the House of Lords; questions ranging from matters manifestly fundamental to our study, like subject-matter, costs, the nature and frequency of dissenting judgments, and legal aid, to more technical items such as the use of *amici curiae*, and whether or not the House called upon respondent's counsel to reply to the appellant's opening argument. In addition, on each questionnaire particular points of interest were noted on matters falling outside the range of our pre-coded questions.

The use of a pre-coded questionnaire has the obvious drawback of

---

1 We have refrained from expanding an already bulky book by reproducing a questionnaire which, in any event, is only meaningful in the light of certain interpretative conventions devised as the study proceeded.

inflexibility and it tends to impose a spurious sense of order upon a highly amorphous body of data. Moreover, some questions originally deemed pertinent to the study may turn out in the end to be wholly irrelevant and to have been pursued at the expense of other matters, thought of too late, which have been left out altogether. But pre-coding did have two over-whelming advantages: it has enabled a structured body of 'hard' data to be assembled very rapidly and it permitted analysis to be carried out by com-puter. Technically it would have been possible to have carried out highly sophisticated manipulations of the data so obtained, but as we were working with relatively crude variables we contented ourselves for the most part with simple counts and cross-tabulations: the information yielded by this exer-cise is to be found in Part B.

One of the tasks of this study is to evaluate the functions of the House of Lords in terms of the requirements of contemporary British society: this is one of the principal difficulties which we faced. The House of Lords has a 'creative' role in the sense that it has more scope than the lower courts for developing legal principles; but this is not to say that innovation in a particular case is, by any objective standards, the 'best' possible solution to the problems raised in that case. A decision may seem meritorious from a professional lawyer's point of view because it accords with his fundamental belief in such values as certainty and continuity: a social scientist, judging the decision in terms of broader criteria such as 'social need' (though this of course will *include* the need for coherent law), may see it either as inhumane or as just plain nonsense—in this context, grimgribber nonsense. As Max Weber has said, 'formal rationality' (the systemization of formal procedural rules) may often come into conflict with 'substantive rationality' (the need to approximate the decisions to notions of justice). Conversely a single decision may go a long way towards achieving social justice, but produce legal chaos.

Under such circumstances no objective criteria exist to determine where the line is to be drawn: ultimately the answer depends upon the resolution of a fundamental clash of values between lawyers and social scientists, each re-flecting his own professional ethos. Only a devotee of the orthodox natural law school would attempt to claim that a particular law is 'good' *per se*, and such a person would have great difficulty in persuading a non-believer as to the scientific validity of his criteria: even if a decision ap-pears to fit all the accepted standards of society, it must be remembered that these standards are in a constant state of flux, and can be judged only in sub-jective terms, perhaps by resort to the mythical 'man on the Clapham omni-bus'. And we, as 'objective' researchers, are as committed to our values as anyone else.

This difficulty of assessing merit is of particular importance when we come to consider the role of the House of Lords as an additional revisionary tribunal: unless we can show that a decision by five very senior judges is in some definable way inherently superior to that of three somewhat less senior judges (not necessarily of inferior quality, we hasten to add), then there is a case for arguing that the unfortunate litigant is the victim of unnecessary and costly duplication. It is not sufficient to say that because the House of Lords allows about one in every three appeals which come before it, it is *ipso facto*, performing a useful function: indeed, the fact that this one-in-three success rate seems to occur in a high proportion of appellate systems[1] might only mean that appellate judges subconsciously indulge in role-justification. On the other hand, if very few appeals were allowed we might justifiably challenge the utility of a second appeal, though in the English system the route by which a decision is reached is at least as important as the outcome. A figure of this order, far from demonstrating the virtues of the system, merely illustrates the truism that judges (like other rational decision-makers) cannot always agree among themselves.

The House of Lords is at the top of the judicial promotion ladder; but promotion is not always an indication of ability. In any case, what do we mean by ability: do we mean professional competence or social awareness—or both? If both, mixed in what proportions? Given the present court hierarchy, and a rigid application of the doctrine of *stare decisis*, lawyers are bound to regard decisions of the House of Lords as definitive statements of the law; but it is a moot point whether its superiority in decision-making can be defended in terms of any wider criteria. In later chapters we shall review the activities of the House of Lords in various important areas of substantive law, though our assessments are inevitably impressionistic and subjective, but being based upon the records of the entire case-load of the House of Lords, our value-judgments are at least founded upon cumulative data.

It cannot be emphasized too strongly that there is bound to be a gap between our statistical data, on the one hand, and, on the other, our final evaluation of the system and the proposals for reform. No one piece of data—for example the fact that House of Lords appeals greatly delay the final settlement of litigation—can be conclusive, though it may lead us to make specific recommendations on points of detail. The socio-legal equation which defines the relationship between law and society is far too complex and contains far too many unknown variables to be solved by one or even a dozen research projects. The following chapters are written with an eye to clearing the decks for rational debate to take place—a debate conducted not exclusively among lawyers but among all those concerned with 'government' (using that word in its broadest sense) who will ultimately decide the merits or demerits of a two-tier appellate system.

---

[1] As Lord Atkin once suggested in the *Cambridge Law Journal*, see p. 63, n. 1 below.

LAW-MAKING AND LAW-FINDING

We are concerned in this study both with analysing the functions of various aspects of the legal system and with evaluating the capacity of legal institutions to cope with constant changes in social values and demands. The 'making' and 'finding' of law are ostensibly two entirely different, but by no means unrelated, processes: the dichotomy can be seen historically in the changing role of the courts, and in the changing attitudes of the judges over the centuries. The situation was quite clear so long as the courts (as was the case in medieval times) acted only upon the explicit commission of an absolute sovereign; but increasing diversification of government and of the institutions required to administer its functions resulted in a growing diffusion of legislative and judicial powers. The conflicts between Parliament and the Stuart kings led ultimately to a more or less formal separation of powers, and it became clear (if indeed it had seriously been in doubt) that the courts had no power to question the legislative sovereignty of Parliament.

This basically has remained the position up to the present day, but we have certainly not seen the end of the speculation about the nature and extent of 'judicial legislation'. Even in a codified system the law cannot be finally settled by a single enactment: a code states the law at a given point in time, thereby minimizing the need for the courts to weigh and interpret a multiplicity of statutes and authorities relating to the points raised in litigation. But no code can—nor does it set out to—take account of every possible contingency, of the rapid changes which take place in the structure and the requirements of an industrialized society. What important areas of English commercial law might have been held in suspended animation at a point in the late nineteenth century if the courts had not been permitted to reinterpret the code embodied in the Sale of Goods Act and the Bills of Exchange Act? Even in Continental jurisdictions, where a bureaucratically-structured judiciary is conditioned to treat legal decision-making in a highly formalized way, the original codes have undergone considerable modification by judicial interpretation.

In this country the basic training and ideology of the judges is founded upon common law principles which admit flexibility in interpreting statutes, albeit rationalized in formal and legalistic terms. This does not necessarily mean that British judges perceive their roles very differently from those of their Continental counterparts, since wherever there is a judiciary its professional ethos is based, almost by definition, upon a robust respect for the inherent virtues of 'certainty' and 'rule-following'—and a distinct distaste for the arbitrary solution of problems, and especially for anything which smacks of palm-tree justice. But the common law has been developed by a process of interstitial legislation by the judges, a process which often involves distinguishing or avoiding awkward precedents. Judges themselves are an integral part of society, and it is not in their interests either that the law should lose respect by appearing impervious to social demands or that social development should be hampered by the uncompromising legalism of judges. Such considerations from time to time call for the judge to throw off the shackles of precedent.

The 'declaratory' theory of law whereby judges believed, or affected to believe, that their function was merely to declare existing legal principles enshrined in the customs and rules of society, is as obsolete as the orthodox natural law theory which sees 'right' law as based upon God-given absolute standards. Modern English judges appear to belong to a more positivistic school of thought which, in its most extreme form, sees the solitary criterion by which law should be evaluated as its constitutional source; but the artificiality of such an approach is mitigated by the fact that most judges would probably acknowledge that in situations of ambiguity, or where a legal problem has arisen for the first time, they do exercise a genuine element of creativity in resolving the issues.

In any event the House of Lords is (as we shall see) in a unique position in that it can overrule the decisions of all the courts which are below it in the hierarchy, and even (since the Lord Chancellor's statement in July 1966—see Chapter IV and Appendix 4) review and, if necessary, revise its own previous decisions. It is in a real position to manipulate or even create law on the grand scale, always assuming that it has the mind and the will to do so when occasion arises.

This then is a study of law-making institutions in contemporary British society. The main target for research is of course the judicial House of Lords, but in passing we shall be commenting upon the interrelated roles of various other institutions—the legislature (including the legislative aspects of the House of Lords), the Law Commission (catalysing the process of law reform and acting as a communicating link between courts and legislature), and the lower courts—notably the Court of Appeal—all of which play a part in the creation of law.

Law-making is not the only function of the judicial House of Lords, and conversely, the House of Lords is not the only court involved in law-making. The important point about the House of Lords is that it has a split personality, its creative role in a system dominated by *stare decisis* is one of supervising the judicial process at every level from magistrates' courts, county courts, and sheriff courts, up to the Court of Appeal and the Inner House of the Court of Session. On the other hand, it exercises this supervision by way of conventional appellate review in specific litigation. This dichotomy is one which has given rise to constant confusion in the debate about abolishing or reforming the judicial functions of the House of Lords. Arguments which oppose the retention of a second appeal, as adding to the costs and delays of litigation, take little or no account of the 'public' role of the Law Lords in helping to develop the law.

Finally, the whole picture is clouded (at least in the minds of the lay public) by the fact that the 'House of Lords' is a name which applies equally to a court of law and to the upper chamber of the legislature. It is true that a direct relationship does exist, and can be explained largely in terms of medieval constitutional history. But at the present time the functions are, for most practical purposes, separate. (The overlap will be explained in greater detail in later chapters.)

PRESSURE FOR CHANGE

A court which has existed in one form or another for over six centuries could hardly fail to be caught up in the changes in a constitution evolving from near-absolute feudal monarchy to a modern social democratic state. It would also be remarkable if, in an age of accelerating social change, there had been no contemporary pressure for the reform of legal institutions in general, and of the House of Lords in particular.

During recent years a number of eminent members of the legal profession have called for reform or even outright abolition of the judicial function of the House of Lords. The late Lord Upjohn (a staunch supporter of the view that a second appeal should continue to lie to the House of Lords) recently confessed to 'an uneasy feeling that in twenty or thirty years' time there will not be a second court of appeal'. A modern attempt was made to achieve a one-tier appellate system by the Supreme Court of Judicature Act 1873, but this was thwarted three years later by the Appellate Jurisdiction Act which restored the House of Lords to its present pre-eminence in the judicial hierarchy. (The story of this abortive attempt to decapitate the appellate system is recounted in the next chapter.)

The Evershed Committee in its Report on Supreme Court Practice and Procedure in 1953 suggested a scheme (originally proposed by Lord Greene, Lord Evershed's immediate predecessor as Master of the Rolls) whereby certain categories of appeal would 'leapfrog' from the court of first instance, over the backs of the Lords Justices, directly to the House of Lords. This scheme has much to commend it as a compromise, retaining as it would the House of Lords to deal with cases of great public importance, while eliminating some of the inevitable and costly duplication which must occur in those (comparatively infrequent) cases manifestly destined for the House of Lords from the very outset of the litigation. A modified version of the 'leapfrog' scheme has been introduced in the Administration of Justice Act 1969, which will be discussed in detail in Chapter VII. It is interesting to note that in 1962 Lord Evershed (again in an extra-judicial capacity) modified his views when he advocated the abolition of the House of Lords in favour of an enlarged Court of Appeal composed of five Lords Justices, endowed with the power to reverse previous decisions of the Court.

In a laconic passage in *Law Reform NOW* (published in 1963) Lord

Gardiner, later Lord Chancellor in the 1964–70 Labour Administration, echoed Lord Evershed's sentiments and added his own voice (along with his co-author's) to the cry for a single appeal. The cost of appealing to a second appellate court, they said, was prohibitive to all but the rich and the legally-aided; in any event, one appeal was enough if that one provided judicial calibre commensurate with the present composition of the House of Lords. A strong and final Court of Appeal, with much of the doctrine of precedent relegated to the legal history museum, was all that the country could afford, and all that its citizenry was entitled to expect from the fountain of justice. But when in office, Lord Gardiner no longer displayed such evident hostility to the second appeal. He then asked, '*should* we abolish the House of Lords?' In July 1966 he went a long way towards pre-empting the answer to his own (rhetorical?) question by announcing that the House of Lords would, in certain circumstances, be prepared to reconsider its own previous decisions.

The abolitionist cause received a further jolt with the publication by the Labour Government of the White Paper on House of Lords Reform (Cmnd. 3799 of 1968) which advocated radical changes in the composition and functions of the second chamber. Paragraph 60 of that document (which was embodied in the ill-starred Parliament (No. 2) Bill 1969) specifically excluded the judicial functions of the House of Lords from its proposals. Indeed it suggested strengthening the position of the Law Lords in the reformed House by excluding them from the attendance qualifications and from the provisions for a compulsory retirement age prescribed for every other category of voting peer.

The controversy lives on, if in an attenuated form. In the debate on the second reading of the Administration of Justice Bill 1969 in the House of Lords, Lord Goodman (a solicitor-peer, who should have known better) made a remarkable assertion: 'It is agreed by all lawyers that there is no merit in two appellate processes. We have it as an historical accident [*sic*]. The disadvantage of it is obviously that it is much more costly. If we can reduce the appellate process to one instead of two so much the better.'[1] In the light of such a statement the time is ripe for an investigation of the issues which lie behind the controversy, and we have framed our own inquiry accordingly.

The House of Lords is more vulnerable to attack than most legal institutions by virtue of the fact that it appears to be something of a constitutional anachronism, a feudal relic preserved in the interests of judicial ancestor-worship. From the social scientist's point of view the survival of an appellate court which is so closely associated with the 'aristocratic' chamber of the legislature might even appear to be symptomatic of the continuing dominance of upper- and middle-class values in the judicial process. Courts are strongly class-oriented, but evidence in support of this cannot be found in the formal position of the judicial House of Lords: since 1876 it has become almost separate from both the Upper Chamber and from the hereditary peerage.

[1] H. L. Debs., vol. 297, col. 474, 12 November 1968.

One appeal by litigants can be justified on several grounds. In the first place, it tends to unify and centralize the judicial process; to keep a thread of continuity running through the work of the courts. In the second place, it must be remembered that trial judges have a very hectic life, sitting alone in court, trying to unravel a mass of garbled evidence often with the aid of relatively inexperienced counsel. Out of this morass they are expected to synthesize an *ex tempore* judgment at the conclusion of argument. This being so, it is eminently desirable that the system should provide the defeated litigant with machinery for review, certainly on questions of law.

An appeal court has several advantages over a trial judge. In the first place it deals with material which has been sifted and distilled for it by the trial process; appellate judges have before them the opinion of the trial judge which, even if it is unsound, provides an invaluable point of reference. The evidence has been sieved by one experienced judge, and the judges on appeal can concentrate on the legal principles which underlie the case. Three judges sitting together bring to bear on the case an accumulation of experience absent from the trial court. Finally, it is more acceptable for an appellate court to reserve judgment for more searching consideration.

These are powerful arguments. The question remains: why go through the entire process a second time? Three (or in the Court of Session, four) eminent judges consider an appeal: they review all the authorities, they listen to the arguments of counsel, they may (and in a third of cases do) reserve judgment, and finally they reach a decision which in a remarkably high percentage of cases is unanimous. And, what is more, in most instances they uphold the findings of the trial judge. Why must this process (even if only in a small percentage of the more difficult cases) be repeated with five judges (slightly more eminent) listening to similar—even repetitive—arguments, reviewing the same authorities, invariably reserving judgment (perhaps for a slightly longer period, usually six weeks) and then reaching a conclusion which in about 60 per cent of cases is exactly the same as that of the court below? Why stop here? Why not permit judgments to be reversible *ad infinitum* by slightly larger and more distinguished courts at each successive stage? Before advocating a multiplicity of appeals one is reminded of the remark of A.P. Herbert: 'The institution of one court of appeal may be considered a reasonable precaution: but two suggest panic.'

The present system tends to create an undesirable impression that 'first-class justice' comes from the House of Lords and 'second-class justice' comes from the lower courts. There may indeed be an element of truth in this view, but if the House of Lords is judicially stronger than the Court of Appeal and the Court of Session why not simply strengthen the courts *a quo* and decapitate the present costly hierarchy?

The historical explanation for the present system is that the jurisdiction of the House of Lords was an offshoot of the power of an absolute monarchy.

Far from the House of Lords being *placed* upon the pinnacle of a hierarchy, it was the lower courts which grew outwards from a fountain of judicial authority embodied in the King and his Council and embodied in the House of Lords. Constitutional changes have left the judicial House of Lords as a kind of tributary outside the mainstream of the legal system. But it is in practice still a fulcrum for all British legal institutions.

An attempt to rationalize the existence of a second appeal can be seen ultimately as the solution of a social equation. On the one hand, we may say that the House of Lords is a costly and time-wasting anachronism whose functions could readily be transferred to a strengthened first-tier appeal court. On the other hand, as we shall show, the House of Lords has a number of important points in its favour, particularly in its functions as a supervisory court. It must be confessed that the 'solution' of an equation of this kind depends ultimately upon one's subjective interpretation of the available evidence; evidence which will be examined in detail in subsequent chapters. Thus the purpose of this study is not just to provide an anatomy of our most important legal institution but also to present the relevant data and argumentation for calculating and solving the social equation.

II

A HISTORY OF THE
JUDICIAL HOUSE OF LORDS

THE judicial functions exercised by the House of Lords are as old as Parliament itself. Their primitive origins can be found in the processes whereby medieval kings, unwilling to be burdened by the task of adjudicating personally upon the petitions of supplicant subjects, delegated the task to members of their principal advisory-cum-administrative body, the Great Council. At this stage the process of 'legislating' and 'adjudicating' were indistinguishable.

Certainly it is important to perceive the House of Lords as the still fermenting product of centuries of constitutional and social change; as an institution which has managed to survive, at least in name, by a combination of fortuitous circumstance and shrewd adaptation. But it would not advance our present purpose to delve too deeply into the distant past. We therefore begin our outline of the history of the House of Lords at a point when a recognizable network of legal institutions, manned by professional lawyers and judges, had already come into existence. We propose first to look briefly at the period 1600–1800 when a shadowy picture of the modern jurisdiction can faintly be discerned amid the tumult of constitutional upheaval, as the boundaries of the judicial role exercised by Parliament came to be delineated. We then proceed to examine in greater detail the reforms which took place in the nineteenth century, culminating in the passing of the Appellate Jurisdiction Act 1876, which is the starting point for the development of the present jurisdiction.

The seventeenth century is probably the most eventful era in the development of the House of Lords as a court of appeal—indeed it may well be considered the most important period in English constitutional history. The House of Lords had lain more or less dormant throughout the fifteenth and sixteenth centuries—though in 1585 an Act had been passed confirming its jurisdiction to hear appeals by writ of error in respect of the courts of common law. By 1600 the House enjoyed an undisputed role as a court of appeal: it could hear causes by way of writ of error from the Courts of Exchequer Chamber[1]—which in turn were the tribunals of review in respect of the courts

---

[1] Originally established in the fourteenth century to hear appeals in error in the Exchequer (the latter being a tribunal established originally to deal with fiscal matters).

of common law. Its acknowledged original (as opposed to appellate) jurisdiction was by now confined to the trial of peers for treason or felony (see
below), a jurisdiction which dated back to the thirteenth century, and trials
on impeachment. But as to the extent of its jurisdiction in equity matters—
a branch of the law exercised by the Lord Chancellor, which had not crystal-
lized until the late fifteenth century—no precedent existed.

The appellate remedy provided by the House took the form of the writ of
error, founded originally upon the prerogative of the King in Council to
quash the decision of a subordinate body upon discovery of an 'error on the
face of the record', and dating back to the thirteenth century, almost to the
earliest delegation of judicial power by the King and his Council.[1] The
remedy—in a sense a piece of original litigation against the offending tribunal[2]—was very limited in scope, and symptomatic of what Holdsworth
called 'the extreme technicality and formalism which is always the mark of a
primitive system of law'.[3]

Lawyers played their part in the vicious constitutional upheavals of the
Stuart period. In 1591 the judges had expostulated against the imprisonment
of people by the Court of Star Chamber[4] 'against the laws of the realm'.
In 1610 Coke C.J. won the judicial fight against legislation by royal decree in
the *Case of Proclamations*. In 1641 the Star Chamber was abolished, and in
the same year Charles I, bent as ever upon political suicide, confronted Parliament—and lost—in the *Case of the Five Members*. This was the age of *Bates's
case* and *Ship money*—and above all, it was the era of Civil War, from which
would ultimately emerge parliamentary government, a constitutional monarchy and the various declared constitutional rights and safeguards set out
in the Bill of Rights and the Act of Settlement.

Viewed against this vivid backcloth of bloody revolution and constitu-

---

In 1585 a new Court of Exchequer Chamber had been established for the purpose of dealing
with the errors of the King's Bench, since Parliaments which exercised this jurisdiction were
summoned only occasionally during the sixteenth century. It was provided that the Court
of Exchequer Chamber should consist of the justices of the Common Pleas and the Barons
(i.e. judges) of the Exchequer, or any six of them, and that an appeal to the court was not
to preclude a further appeal to Parliament. The two courts of Exchequer Chamber
were amalgamated in 1830. See William Holdsworth, *A History of English Law*, vol. 1,
pp. 242–5.

[1] In many respects the writ of error resembled the old prerogative writs, particularly
certiorari, which had come into regular use by the thirteenth century. *Certiorari*, however,
was originally a royal demand for information used for numerous administrative purposes.
Certainly this important writ developed into a regular appellate remedy in the hands of the
justices of the King's Bench, but it was always an extraordinary remedy. Unlike the prerogative writs, the writ of error (in civil proceedings at least) was a writ 'of course' and 'an
everyday device whereby the private citizen could impugn the record of a lower court.'
See S. A. de Smith, *Judicial Review of Administrative Action* (2nd ed.), pp. 382–3 (and
Chapter 8 *passim*). Forms of appeal generally are discussed below (Chapter III).

[2] Thus an appellant under this procedure is termed the plaintiff in error.

[3] Op. cit., p. 223.

[4] The judicial arm of the Privy Council.

tional innovation it is hardly surprising to find the House of Lords as part of a Parliament acquiring unheard-of powers, and at the apex of a judicial system which was busy asserting both the sovereignty of Parliament and the independent authority of the courts, caught up in the exhilarating wind of change. It is a paradox, however, that the House of Lords chose to assert itself against the Commons at a time when the latter was pitting its strength against all comers.

The first incident of note during this period occurred in 1621 when in *Floyd's case* the House of Lords laid claim to an original jurisdiction. But, in the same year, a committee of the House itself denied any precedent for appeals in equity.[1] More significantly in *Matthews* v. *Matthews* (1624) the House of Lords, on considering a report from its committee, declined to hear the appeal and asked the King to appoint a commission to review the Chancellor's decision. 'This', remarked Hale, 'is an instance of greater weight against the inherent jurisdiction of the Lords than a cart load of precedents since that time in affirming of their jurisdiction.'[2]

But sixteen years later the Lords renewed their claims to an equity jurisdiction by reversing a decision of the Chancellor. And in the political case of *Lilburne* (1646) and *Maynard* (1647)[3] their further attempts to assert such a jurisdiction were condemned by all the well-known lawyers of the day with the exception of William Prynne. After the Restoration, however, the House of Lords seemed to have acquired a new vigour in its aspirations to acquire wider jurisdiction—it was 'as if there was an unbounded jurisdiction inherent to the peerage, and as if the House of Lords was a forum for all sorts of causes with no other limitation than such as their own choice and moderation for the time should prescribe.'[4]

The argument against the equity jurisdiction of the House of Lords was that, by definition, equity has always been a matter of royal discretion, delegated to the Chancellor. Appeal was by Bill of Review or (ultimately) by an *ad hoc* commission established by the King. Small wonder therefore that lawyers found it difficult to see an anology between the ancient writ of error issued by the House of Lords in respect of the ordinary courts of common law, and a purported right to review this extraordinary jurisdiction of the Chancellor. Pike, however, argues with conviction that 'it does not appear that the King's prerogative suffered more by a petition to the Lords in Parliament than by a petition [i.e. at first instance] to the Chancellor in Chancery.'[5]

---

[1] *Bowchier's case:* this was really only a petition complaining against the Lord Chancellor. (See Holdsworth, op. cit., p. 373.)

[2] Ibid.

[3] Thomas Beven, 'The Appellate Jurisdiction of the House of Lords', 16 L.Q.R. 155 ff. (1901), at pp. 167–8.

[4] Hargreaves's 'Preface' to Hale's *Jurisdiction of the Lords' House*, p. xcl.

[5] Luke Owen Pike, *Constitutional History of the House of Lords* (1894), p. 298.

The issue came to a head in 1675 in the famous case of *Shirley* v. *Fagg*,[1] though, as Beven reminds us, 'other quarrels were raging at the same time and added to the exasperation of both Houses.' The defendant in an action in Chancery, Sir John Fagg (a Member of the House of Commons) was called upon by the Lords to answer a petition presented by the plaintiff, asking for a review of the Chancellor's decision. He protested to the Commons who (in the words of Beven), 'having ascertained that Dr. Shirley persisted in his appeal . . . committed him to custody after voting his appeal a vote of their privileges; they also committed the counsel who ventured to appear at the Lords' bar; and finally Sir John Fagg himself for putting in an answer to the appeal.' Two prorogations of Parliament were needed to quell the unseemly dispute and at one point 'a state of things not very remote from civil war threatened'. But eventually the Lords were left clutching their newly acquired jurisdiction.

Attempts to secure an original jurisdiction were less successful, though equally tempestuous. In the cases of *Fitton* and *Carr* in 1663 the House of Commons declined to intervene when the Lords imprisoned two men for libelling a peer, though it can be argued that this was an issue of privilege. But in *Skinner* v. *East India Co.*[2]—which began in 1666 and dragged on until 1669—the two Houses again came into headlong collision. A merchant called Skinner claimed that he had been assaulted and dispossessed by agents of the East India Company. He petitioned the King who, after consulting the Council, passed the case to the Lords. The latter awarded heavy damages to Skinner, whereupon the company petitioned the Commons, which promptly committed Skinner for breach of privilege. The Lords voted the company's petition 'a scandalous libel', doubled the damages and fined the defendants' deputy director for bringing the petition. The King intervened at this point— and persuaded both Houses to erase the entries of the case from the records. This was the last serious attempt by the House of Lords to assert an original jurisdiction, though in *Bridgeman* v. *Holt* (1693) an original petition was presented, but was withdrawn by the parties on the advice of the judges.

In two important cases decided later in this period the redoubtable Holt C.J. played a part in delineating the Lords' jurisdiction. In 1692 in *Knolly's case* he had come down firmly against their Lordships by asserting that they had no jurisdiction except by writ of error or by reference of the Crown. The case concerned a man purporting to be the Earl of Banbury, who came to be indicted for murder. The Chief Justice objected that, in peremptorily denying the claim of the accused to be tried by his peers, the House was, in effect, adjudicating a peerage claim in a manner contrary to due process. However, twelve years later in *Ashby* v. *White*[3] the Chief Justice came down firmly in

1 See Beven, op. cit., pp. 169–70; 6 Howell, *State Trials*, 1122–88.
2 Beven, op. cit., p. 169; 6 Howell, *State Trials*, 710.
3 Beven, op. cit., p. 359; 4 Howell, *State Trials*, 695.

favour of the House of Lords. A parliamentary election officer had refused to accept the vote of an elector called Ashby: the latter obtained a jury's verdict against the officer, but a majority of the Queen's Bench arrested the judgment on the ground that the determination of election petitions lay with the Commons. In a vigorous dissenting judgment Holt affirmed the jurisdiction of the courts on the grounds that this case raised issues of freehold rights. The Lords thereupon reversed the decision of the Queen's Bench on a writ of error, thereby provoking the Commons to an explosion of protest. Meanwhile, more disenfranchised electors, emboldened by Ashby's success, brought similar actions, and were committed by the Commons for contempt. The prisoners applied for habeas corpus in the Queen's Bench, and on being refused (Holt C.J. again dissenting) they sued for a writ of error to go to the Lords. The Commons petitioned the Queen to refuse the writ; the judges advised her that it lay as of right. Fortunately, the end of a parliamentary session brought this quarrel to an abrupt conclusion: on release the plaintiffs resumed their action and obtained their verdict.

Thus the most stormy era in the House of Lords ended on a note of uneasy calm. The jurisdiction in error had been affirmed and consolidated. The appeal in equity matters had been established. But the assertion of a first instance jurisdiction never got off the ground, largely due to the strength of the courts, and the jealousy of the Commons. A phase began where sheer functional necessity replaced constitutional demarcation disputes as an instrument of reform.

After a cursory glance at this lively epoch in the development of the judicial House of Lords, we must now brake sharply in reviewing the important reforms which took place in the nineteenth century. These reforms completely refurbished an appellate system which had now reached the point of obsolescence.

The development of legal institutions in England, traced back even as far as medieval times, follows a clear pattern. First, the feudal monolithic power structure is fragmented by the pressures for delegation and decentralization. There follows a period of increasing outward growth and institutional independence, even outright rivalry between the courts themselves, and between the courts and the royal Council. A measure of equilibrium is achieved, but this results in stagnation: ancient courts and archaic procedures fail to change with the times. Finally the pressure for reform becomes irresistible: the House of Lords is marked for destruction, but at the eleventh hour is plucked from the furnace to be recast in a completely new shape.

The era of Bagehot and Bentham was marked by a growing awareness of the importance of legislative reform, and by increasing dissatisfaction with obsolescent institutions. The half-century from 1830 to 1881 saw a quite astonishing number of reforms which, taken together, amounted to a complete overhaul of the machinery of justice. Almost at one blow a court structure representing some six hundred years of legal evolution was swept away and a new era ushered in. Today's courts stand as worthy monuments to Victorian reformist zeal.

Thus, in 1830 the two arms of the old Court of Exchequer Chamber (see above) were merged to provide a single appeal by writ of error from all the courts of common law. At the same time the power of the King's Bench to review errors in the Court of Common Pleas was abolished. Three years later came Brougham's reform of the Judicial Committee of the Privy Council, to which we shall allude in Chapter v. In 1834 the Central Criminal Court was established; in 1842 the equitable jurisdiction of the Court of Exchequer was absorbed by the Court of Chancery; in 1846 county courts first appeared on the scene; in 1848 the Court for Crown Cases Reserved was established as an appellate tribunal dealing with criminal causes. In 1851 a more portentous innovation was made: a Court of Appeal in Chancery was established to hear appeals from the Court of Chancery, not by writ of error, but by way of a re-hearing. This was to prove an important model for the appellate reforms of the 1870s. The year 1857 saw the transfer of the divorce jurisdiction from the ecclesiastical courts to secular tribunals—the newly created Probate and Divorce Courts. Finally in 1881—following the momentous reforms of the 1870s which form the main theme of the narrative that follows—the ancient courts of Exchequer and Common Pleas were absorbed into the Queen's Bench Division of the newly created Supreme Court of Judicature. Twentieth-century reformers have made their mark on the legal system, but they barely hold a candle to their energetic Victorian forbears, at least when it comes to refurbishing their institutions. (At the time of writing, the Courts Act 1971 had only just been introduced into Parliament.)

By the end of the eighteenth century, the judicial functions of the House of Lords had reached a sorry state. Although since medieval times the professional judges had been mainstays of the Court—sitting either as assessors or as members of the House itself—it was still possible for lay peers to play a major and sometimes decisive part in judicial proceedings. Thus in 1783 in *Bishop of London* v. *Ffytche*[1] the judges of the Court of Common Pleas and of the King's Bench found for the defendant, as did seven of the eight judges consulted by the House of Lords when the case came before it on a writ of error. But, in the result, the plaintiff-bishop won in the Lords by nineteen votes to eighteen, with thirteen of the bishops voting in support of his cause. Equally blatant partisanship was evident in the case of *Seymour* v. *Lord Euston*[2] in 1806, when the Prince of Wales mustered eighty supporters in the House of Lords to secure a verdict in the interests of Mrs. Fitzherbert in a guardianship appeal.

As late as 1834, twelve judges attended the House to assist in the hearing

---

[1] 2 Bro. Parl. Cas. 211.
[2] See Beven, *op. cit*, p. 368.

of an appeal, but, as no judicially qualified peers were present, the Court had to be constituted with lay peers. But in 1844 in *O'Connell's case*,[1] several lay peers tendered votes opposing the quashing of O'Connell's conviction, contrary to the opinions of the Law Lords. Thereupon, Lord Wharncliffe, the President of the Council said:

> I cannot help suggesting that your lordships should not divide the House upon a question of this kind, when the opinions of the law lords have been already given upon it, and the majority is in favour of reversing the judgment. In point of fact my lords, they constitute the Court of Appeal, and if noble lords unlearned in the law should interfere to decide such questions by their votes instead of leaving them to the decisions of the law lords, I very much fear that the authority of this House as a court of justice would be greatly impaired.

This was virtually the end of lay participation in judicial business.[2] In *Bradlaugh* v. *Clarke*[3] Lord Denman (a barrister), who sat and spoke throughout the hearing, raised his hand to vote, but was completely ignored by Lord Chancellor Selborne. It is interesting to note that the Appellate Jurisdiction Act 1876 did not explicitly exclude lay participation, though the creation of salaried Law Lords was clearly intended to have this effect. The introduction of professional judges also ended the need for the House to call upon the judges to assist it: the last occasion when the judges were so summoned was in the great Irish trade union case of *Allen* v. *Flood*.[4]

Another fly in the appellate ointment at the beginning of the nineteenth century was the plethora of appeals from Scotland.[5] This was due in part to a disastrous ruling to the effect that notice of an appeal to the House of Lords from an interlocutory order of the Court of Session served to stay execution. The Scots exploited this Sassenach weakness to such good effect as to swamp the House with purely time-wasting appeals. In 1808 a Judicature Act eased the position by permitting the Court of Session to enforce execution in such cases, and by making interlocutory appeals subject to the granting of leave by the Court of Session.

In 1811 a Select Committee was appointed to examine the appellate functions of the House of Lords:[6] it suggested a number of procedural reforms

---

[1] 11 Cl. and F. 155, 421–6. (The report cites seven earlier instances of lay peers taking part in judicial decisions between 1695 and 1783.)

[2] Not quite: it appears that Earl Spencer, a lay peer, sat in about 1860, and that there must have been a layman present to make up the quorum with Lord Cairns and Lord Cranworth in *Rylands* v. *Fletcher* (1868) L.R. 3 H.L. 330. (See Hood Phillips, *Constitutional and Administrative Law* (4th Ed.), p. 128.) The mystery of 'the Third Lord in *Rylands* v. *Fletcher*' is discussed, but not entirely solved, by Professor R. F. V. Heuston in 86 L.Q.R. 160 (1970). Several witnesses appearing before the 1877 Select Committee (below) recalled instances of laymen taking part in appeals.

[3] (1883) 8 App. Cas. 354.

[4] [1898] A.C. 1. See R. F. V. Heuston, *Lives of the Lord Chancellors*, pp. 119 ff.

[5] Scottish appeals are discussed in a separate section (below).

[6] Committee to Inspect the Lords' Journals, 1st Report (1811) XI H.C. Sessional Paper 45; 2nd Report (1812) XI H.C. Sessional Paper 343.

particularly in Scottish appeals. In 1823 the report of another Select Commit-tee[1] led to the introduction of a rota for the compulsory attendance of lay peers.

In 1834 Lord Brougham introduced an Appellate Jurisdiction of the House of Lords Bill which would have transferred House of Lords appeals to the newly reformed Judicial Committee of the Privy Council. Eight years later Lord Campbell produced a counter-proposal in the shape of the Appeals (Privy Council) Transfer Bill which would have transferred Privy Council jurisdiction to the House of Lords.

In 1856 came the first and most famous attempt to staff the House of Lords with professional judges, though by now *O'Connell's case* had already sounded the death knell of lay participation. In 1856, during the Chancel-lorship of Lord Cranworth, the Queen was advised to issue letters patent purporting to create Sir James Parke (a Baron of the Exchequer) Baron Wens-leydale 'for and during the term of his natural life'. The letters patent were referred by the House of Lords to its Committee of Privileges which, by a substantial majority, resolved that the issue of these letters patent should not entitle the grantee to sit and vote in Parliament. Eventually the impasse was resolved by the expedient of granting Lord Wensleydale a hereditary peer-age.[2]

Following the *Wensleydale case* a Select Committee was appointed to consider the matter and a Bill was introduced into the House of Lords which would have empowered the Crown to confer life peerages on two persons who had served for five years as judges: these peers would have sat with the Lord Chancellor as Judges of Appeal. The Bill, however, foundered in the House of Commons.[3] A similar but more ambitious Bill, introduced into the Lords by Earl Russell in 1869, failed to pass its third reading in the Lords.[4]

The sequence of events which led up to the passing of the Supreme Court of Judicature Acts 1873–5, and the Appellate Jurisdiction Act 1876, began in 1867 with the establishment by Roundell Palmer (later Lord Chancellor Selborne) of a Royal Commission on the Judicature under the chairmanship of Lord Cairns. This fascinating era of legal and political history has been thoroughly documented by Professor Robert Stevens,[5] and much of what follows is based upon his account.

The Commission's First Report[6] (1869) recommended the absorption of all the old courts of common law, civil law, and equity into a new High Court, and a common appeal to a newly created Court of Appeal: together, the

[1] (1823) X H.L. Sessional Paper 6.
[2] The story is told in greater detail by Pike, op. cit., pp. 376 ff.
[3] Ibid., p. 379. See 143 H.C. Debs. 3rd Ser. *passim.*
[4] Ibid., pp. 379–82.
[5] R. Stevens, 'The Final Appeal: Reform of the House of Lords and Privy Council 1867–1876', 80 L.Q.R. 343 (1964).
[6] (1870) 3 H.L. Sessional Paper 37.

High Court and the Court of Appeal would form a monolithic Supreme Court. Since a Scottish version of the Commission was sitting at the same time, the Report said little about the House of Lords, but it did suggest that 'it may hereafter deserve consideration' that the decisions of the Court of Appeal should be final unless either the Court or the House of Lords gave leave to appeal (a suggestion not taken up till 1934). The Report also anticipated the modern innovation of leapfrogging by suggesting that cases involving a point of law might, with the consent of the respondent, proceed directly from the trial court to the House of Lords. It further recommended that the practice already adopted in Chancery cases of appeals by rehearing rather than by writ of error should be extended to all House of Lords appeals.[1]

In 1870, Lord Chancellor Hatherley introduced an Appellate Jurisdiction Bill to implement the Commission's proposals. A new Court of Appeal would absorb the Courts of Exchequer Chamber, the Court of Appeal in Chancery and the Court for Crown Cases Reserved. Appeals to the Lords would be heard by a 'Judicial Committee' (which could contain members of the Privy Council, so long as peers were always in the majority). The latter proposal, however, provoked the opposition of the peers and (decisively) of the judges. The Bill was dropped, but another was introduced in the same year to strengthen the Judicial Committee of the Privy Council, whose backlog of cases was far more serious than that of the House of Lords. This measure too made scant progress.

In 1871 a House of Lords Appellate Jurisdiction Bill was introduced: this would have confined House of Lords appeals to matters involving £1,000 or more (with certain minor exceptions), and eliminated appeal in cases where the court *a quo* had agreed with the decision of the trial judge, unless the appeal court gave leave, or a divorce were involved. Although this measure was no more successful than its predecessors, the Judicial Committee of the Privy Council Act, passed in the same year, provided for four paid judges to lighten the burden of the Privy Council: section 1 of the Act provided that 'they shall hold their offices subject to such arrangements as may be hereafter made by Parliament for the constitution of a supreme court of appellate jurisdiction.' 'Suddenly', Stevens says, 'everyone had ideas for reforming the final court of appeal.'[2] Among the most vociferous of the reformers was Lord Westbury who proposed the merger of the House of Lords and the Privy Council into a final Imperial Court of Appeal.

---

[1] Despite the historical importance of the writ of error in the jurisdiction of the House of Lords, it must not be supposed that this procedure completely dominated the work of the Court. Causes from Chancery and from Scotland were by way of appeal. Thus during the period 1833–65, only 12·1 per cent of causes heard by the House of Lords (more than half the cases during the period being from Scotland) were by way of error or by case stated, and the corresponding proportion for the period 1866–71 was 17·4 per cent. (Figures obtained from minutes of evidence to 1872 Select Committee, p. 109—see below.)

[2] Stevens, op. cit., p. 348.

The following year saw more jostling for reform: a Select Committee was established to study the work of the House of Lords and of the Privy Council. The Report and minutes of evidence[1] provide interesting illustrations of the work of both tribunals during the middle part of the nineteenth century, backed up by useful statistical evidence.[2] At this time, the number of judicially qualified peers had increased considerably, but the judges were still consulted, on an average, about three times a year in causes in error;[3] and appeals, if still expensive,[4] were dealt with more quickly than had previously been the case. (Almost 80 per cent of appeals heard during the period 1866–71 were disposed of either in the session in which they were set down, or in the following session.) A fair proportion of appeals were frivolous or hopeless: 22 per cent of the 1866–71 appeals were dismissed without the respondent's counsel being heard. Scots litigants earned the reputation for being particularly guilty in this respect, though all the Scots witnesses appearing before the Committee unequivocally condemned any prospect of Scottish appeals going to an English tribunal.

In the result the Committee recommended (by a narrow majority) the establishment of a joint Judicial Committee of the House of Lords and the Privy Council, staffed by the Lord Chancellor and four salaried Lords of Appeal who would be both life peers and Privy Councillors, supplemented by various ex-officio members.

When in 1872 Lord Selborne (formerly Sir Roundell Palmer) succeeded Lord Hatherley as Lord Chancellor in Gladstone's administration the stage was set for major reform of the appellate system. The reforms proposed by the 1869 Royal Commission were substantially incorporated into a Judicature Bill: English appeals would go no further than a new Court of Appeal, and the House of Lords would entirely lose its jurisdiction. Exceptional cases would be referred to a full court of the Court of Appeal, and this full court would ultimately hear all appeals from Scotland and Ireland, and from the colonies. The Bill was widely supported by the legal profession, and received the general blessing of the Conservative majority in the Lords led by Lord Cairns. There was some opposition from Conservative backwoodsmen in the Lords, and a little more from Conservatives in the Commons, though at this stage the retentionists were holding their fire, and indeed they had little ammunition. The progress of the Bill was threatened only by Gladstone's abortive move to have Irish and Scottish appeals transferred at once to the Court of Appeal. He gave way to protest, and the Bill received the Royal Assent on 7 August 1873: it was set to come into force in November 1874.

1 Report of H.L. Select Committee on the Appellate Jurisdiction, 9 July (1872) 9 H.L. Sessional Papers.
2 Some of this statistical material is set out as an annex to this chapter at pp. 39–43.
3 And, according to one witness, the need for the judges to be present was responsible for the inordinate delay in hearing many of the appeals.
4 The average cost of an English Appeal was about £400.

Shortly after the passing of the Act, Gladstone's administration fell and was replaced by a Conservative government led by Disraeli, with Lord Cairns as Lord Chancellor. The latter had given his general support to Selborne's Bill, and now showed himself prepared to go even further and abolish all appeals to the Lords. He introduced a new Bill[1] which provided for Scottish and Irish appeals to go to the Court of Appeal, now to be styled 'The Imperial Court of Appeal' where they would be heard by a First Division containing five appeal judges. This Division would also rehear all cases where the judges of the ordinary divisions disagreed: thus a limited form of second appeal was ingeniously retained.

But opposition had begun to harden. The peers were realizing that the abolition of the appeal to the Lords might be a threat to the second chamber itself. The Scots and Irish lawyers voiced strong objections to appeals from their courts going to an English court of appeal. Although in the result this bipartisan Bill passed quite easily through the Lords and reached its report stage in the Commons, Disraeli began to hearken to the strident voices of the growing retentionist lobby: Cairns was overruled in the Cabinet, and the Bill was dropped. A new Bill[2] to postpone for one year the coming into effect of the 1873 Act was rushed through all its stages in both Houses.

Meanwhile a pressure group[3] was organized by William Charley M.P. to ensure that there would be no backsliding, and he and his fellow retentionists busied themselves in organizing petitions among members of all branches of the legal profession. Despite this, Cairns was allowed to reintroduce his earlier Bill, but the lobby had done a thorough job. Disraeli—not altogether reluctantly—bowed to the strong pressure from Charley and the peers, and the Bill was again withdrawn.

On 9 April 1875 yet another Bill[4] was introduced to postpone the implementation of those parts of the 1873 Act which had abolished appeals to the Lords, and to affirm the principle of a second appeal: accordingly, it also reduced the number of judges to be appointed to the new Court of Appeal. The political climate dictated that the second appeal must be to the House of Lords—subject to the ironing-out of some constitutional anachronisms, and the provision of a permanent complement of paid judges. Cairns wished to see a joint Judicial Committee of the House of Lords and the Privy Council, staffed by salaried Law Lords and sitting all the year round in a courtroom separate from the Chamber of the House. This idea likewise fell by the wayside.

The Appellate Jurisdiction Bill 1876 (see Appendix 1(i)) passed through all its stages without untoward incident, though the abolitionists grumbled

---

[1] The Supreme Court of Judicature Act (1873) Amendment Bill 1874.
[2] The Supreme Court of Judicature Act (1873) Suspension Bill 1874.
[3] See Stevens, op. cit., pp. 362 ff.
[4] The Supreme Court of Judicature Act (1873) Amendment Bill 1875.

mightily. The new judicial House of Lords began its life in 1877. Thus, after a saga of political intrigue, the final appeal was preserved from destruction at the joint hands of the Liberal Selborne and the Conservative Cairns. Nominally it remained in the hands of the hereditary chamber, but in reality it was transferred to a court of law under the control of a professional judiciary.

THE HOUSE OF LORDS AND CRIMINAL APPEALS[1]

Hitherto our account of the history of the Lords' jurisdiction has been confined largely to civil litigation. It must be remembered that in the earliest days, when the King's Courts and the House of Lords were developing jurisdictions distinct from each other and from the Council, the modern distinction between civil and criminal appeals did not arise. In modern times the criminal jurisdiction of the House of Lords had been reduced to dwindling-point, until it was expanded by the Administration of Justice Act 1960.

Gone forever is the power of Kings to accuse great offenders in Parliament (a practice declared illegal in the *Case of the Five Members* in 1641).[2] Gone too is the ancient right of a subject to invoke the procedure of 'appealing' against another by standing before the Lords and accusing him of felony, a popular technique at the time of the Wars of the Roses, the last recorded instance being in 1819.

The unwaivable right of peers to be tried for felony or treason by their fellow peers, which can be traced back to the twelfth century, proved to be a more robust phenomenon in the history of the Lords' jurisdiction: in this at least there was no doubt as to the existence of an original jurisdiction. Such trials were presided over by the Lord High Steward (in modern times by the Lord Chancellor). The case was heard by the whole House, except when Parliament was not sitting, in which case the Lord High Steward sat as judge with a jury of peers. The last occasion on which this clumsy and expensive piece of legal machinery ground into action was in the trial and acquittal of Lord de Clifford for manslaughter in 1935. The right of trial by peers was abolished by section 30 of the Criminal Justice Act 1948, the clause having been inserted into the Bill by the Lords themselves.

Two further archaic features of the criminal jurisdiction of the House of Lords should be mentioned. Both, technically, are still in existence, but neither is likely to be revived. First, Acts of Attainder,[3] which were a popular device during the Wars of the Roses and during the reign of the Tudors. By some authorities they are regarded as being tantamount to 'judgments' of the full Parliament: as their name suggests, they amounted to a vicious species of private legislation. Impeachments, on the other hand, take a more judicial

1 The modern criminal jurisdiction is discussed below at pp. 270–282.
2 See Holdsworth, op. cit., p. 378.
3 See Lord Justice Somervell, 'Acts of Attainder', 67 L.Q.R. 306 (1951). They are not unknown in some countries even today: see *Kariapper* v. *Wijesinha* [1968] A.C. 717. (Ceylon)

form: they involve an accusation by the House of Commons against any person alleged to have committed a high crime beyond the reach of the law, or in which no other authority in the state will prosecute.[1] The cause is tried by the House of Lords. Impeachment dates back to 1376[2] and reached its zenith during the period 1621–1715 when there were fifty impeachments, but since then there have been only four. It was last used in the cases of *Warren Hastings* in 1781 and *Lord Melville* in 1805, both of whom were acquitted. (The last judge to be impeached was the Lord Chancellor, Lord Macclesfield, in 1720 for abuses relating to the sale of Chancery Masterships.)[3] Even today the glorious prospect of impeaching a miscreant minister is sometimes raised by a member of the Opposition, but in an age of collective responsibility, and with ministers answerable to the ordinary criminal law, the possibility of a modern revival of the procedure is negligible.[4] We come now to the modern criminal jurisdiction of the House of Lords.

An appeal by writ of error was always available in criminal proceedings: before 1705 the writ issued only under the fiat of the Attorney-General, and when this was forthcoming the court automatically accepted the Crown's 'confession' of error. But in 1705 it was held that the writ issued as of right and that it lay within the discretion of the courts to determine the error, though the former practice continued in cases of treason or felony. (In practice the Attorney-General never refused his fiat in cases of "probable" error.)

As we have said elsewhere, the writ of error was never a satisfactory remedy: this was especially true in criminal proceedings where the record took no account either of the evidence or of the judge's summing-up to the jury. Holdsworth[5] records three methods whereby the rigours and the limitations of the procedure were mitigated. First, in the seventeenth century there developed a procedure for retrial of misdemeanours, 'on the grounds of misreception of evidence, misdirection of the judge, or because the verdict was against the weight of evidence'. Second, a jury might find a special verdict upon the facts, and leave it to the court to make a finding of guilt or innocence upon these facts. Finally there were those cases where the judge felt sufficiently doubtful of the law as to feel constrained to consult with his brother judges: a process analogous to that employed in the Court of Exchequer Chambers in civil matters. Eventually the latter procedure was formalized by the establishment of the Court for Crown Cases Reserved in 1848, though the discretion for referring cases to this Court still lay entirely with the judge or chairman of Quarter Sessions who tried the case.

The jurisdiction in error of the House of Lords extended in theory to criminal causes, but until the passing of the Criminal Appeal Act 1907 this jurisdiction was almost defunct. That Act abolished writ of error in criminal

---

[1] See Hood Phillips, op. cit., p. 97.   [2] See Holdsworth, op. cit., p. 380.
[3] Henry Cecil, *Tipping the Scales* (1964), pp. 113–26.
[4] Holdsworth, *op. cit.*, p. 215.   [5] Ibid., at pp. 216–17.

appeals, and established a right of appeal on the fiat of the Attorney-General. The fiat was abolished by the Administration of Justice Act 1960, and the House of Lords now has a case-load of criminal appeals which is numerically of the same order of magnitude as in civil appeals from Scotland: a fact which clearly illuminates the impact of reforms during the last hundred years.

THE HOUSE OF LORDS AS A SCOTTISH COURT

Today it is hard to believe that the House of Lords was once to all intents and purposes a Scottish Court. At the beginning of the last century, nearly 80 per cent of the House of Lords' business came from Scotland. Now the position is reversed: Scottish appeals are outnumbered four to one by causes from England, reflecting more accurately the relative litigiousness of disparate populations.

The origins of the Scottish jurisdiction of the House of Lords are inextricably linked with the more general process whereby that country was united with England. The Court of Session itself is (by English standards) a comparatively modern court: it was established in 1532, 'and like the civil law it administered it was Roman in conception'.[1] Until the early 19th Century the Court invariably sat in banc.

In the seventeenth century the Scottish Faculty of Advocates raised the question of a possible appeal from the Court of Session to the Parliament of Scotland. The idea was opposed by Charles II and the matter was dropped, albeit reluctantly; but in 1690 a decree of the Court of Session was heard and reversed by Parliament. 'Several others followed,' remarks Beven, 'but it is said that the judgments of the Parliament of Scotland were not held in particular esteem.'[2]

Article III of the Act of Union 1707 provided 'that the united kingdom of Great Britain be represented by one and the same Parliament'. And Article XIX, while affirming the powers of the Scottish Courts and rendering them subject to regulation by Parliament, continued by saying that 'no causes in Scotland shall be cogniscible by the Courts of Chancery, Queen's Bench, Common Pleas or any other court in Westminster Hall; and that the said courts or any other of the like nature after the union shall have no power to cognosce, review, or alter the acts or sentences of the judicators within Scotland, or stop the execution of the same'. These two Articles are the essence of the relationship between the House of Lords and the courts of Scotland: the Scottish Parliament was absorbed by the English Parliament, and since the latter could hardly be described as 'of the like nature' to the

1 N. T. Phillipson, 'The Scottish Whigs and the Reform of the Court of Session 1785–1830' (unpublished doctoral thesis, University of Cambridge).
2 Beven, op. cit., p. 363.

courts in Westminster Hall there was no serious obstacle to the House of Lords acquiring the jurisdiction for 'remeide of law' possessed by the Scottish Parliament. (The exclusion of appeals to English courts was to prove a potent weapon in the hands of those Scots who opposed the 'Imperial Court of Appeal' in the 1870s. See above.)

In 1707–8 the Earl of Rosebery entered a test appeal from the Court of Session to the House of Lords, and the jurisdiction was quickly established. But in the early days the system had serious blemishes. This was partly a reflection of the unsatisfactory state of affairs which prevailed in the Scottish courts:[1] the judges were hampered by procedural anomalies, and often by a plethora of written pleadings, the procedure for taking oral evidence was thoroughly unsatisfactory and, worse, while there was no proper appellate process, the courts had the power to review their own interlocutors almost *ad infinitum*. Moreover, early in the eighteenth century it was laid down that the service of an order upon a respondent to answer an appeal to the House of Lords served to stay execution, thereby enabling litigation to be dragged out for years. It was not until the passing of an Act in 1808, giving the Court of Session the power to enforce execution notwithstanding an appeal to the Lords, and making interlocutory appeals subject to the leave of the Court of Session, that the tide was stemmed. Meanwhile, nearly three hundred appeals had accumulated in the cause list, and in December 1812 the arrears of appeals and writs of error still amounted to more than 276 cases, 'four-fifths of the whole arrear consisting of Scottish appeals upon questions of fact'.[2] During the period 1794–1807, 419 out of 501 appeals had been Scottish.

Despite important reforms which took place in the Court of Session at the beginning of the nineteenth century[3]—the advent of a limited jury trial, the introduction of a closed record and the splitting of the Court of Session into two Divisions—Scots appeals to the House of Lords continued to proliferate. According to Phillipson, between 1835 and 1855 Scottish appeals never represented less than 30 per cent, and the usual proportion was 60 per cent of House of Lords business.

Whether or not the judgments of the House of Lords were generally held in high esteem by those north of the Border (whose feelings upon the matter seem to have been mixed) the uneven quality of performance of the Scottish courts rendered imperative the appeal to a distinguished tribunal. Lord Eldon once remarked that 'appeals were often made from Scotland to their Lordships in order to discover the reasons on which the judgments rested in the courts below.'[4] In any event, the Lords was not by any means exclusively a Sassenach tribunal: several Lord Chancellors and Law Lords of the period

---

[1] See Phillipson, op. cit., *passim*.
[2] Twiss, *Life of Lord Eldon*, vol. 2, pp. 238–40.   [3] Phillipson, op. cit., *passim*.
[4] Judges of the eighteenth-century Court of Session seldom gave reasons for their decisions: when they did so they forbade publication upon pain of contempt.

were eminent Scots, by origin if not in every case by legal training: Mansfield, Loughborough, Erskine, Brougham, and Campbell, a veritable procession of able Scotsmen to hear the pleas of their litigating fellow countrymen. And many English judges proved competent in Scottish appeals: in 1728 Lord Hardwicke overruled the unanimous judgment of the Court of Session in the *Gordon of Parke case*, and although criticized at the time this judgment has been vindicated by subsequent opinion. Scots lawyers also owe much to Lord Eldon who, among other things, did much to reform the Scottish law of entail.

But the fact remains that up to the middle of the nineteenth century many appeals—not only from Scotland—were heard by the Lord Chancellor (the only peer with a positive duty to attend) or a single Law Lord sitting with two lay peers to make up a quorum.[1] In 1827 two deputy speakers were commissioned to assist Lord Lyndhurst in disposing of the backlog of Scottish appeals: both were Englishmen, Lord Alexander C.B. and Sir John Leach M.R. In 1867 the distinguished Scots lawyer, Lord Colonsay, was added to the judicial strength, to the almost universal applause of the Scottish legal profession.[2] Since that time at least one Scots lawyer has always been available to hear appeals in the House.[3]

In the latter part of the nineteenth century Scots appeals had been brought within reasonable proportions by the combined weight of the reforms already mentioned. But as late as 1870 several instances can be found where their Lordships grumbled mightily at the triviality of some of the issues raised in appeals from Scotland.

Thus three cases (all reported in one volume of the Law Reports) can be cited by way of example. In *Reid* v. *Keith*,[4] Lord Hatherley C. remarked:

My Lords, that your Lordships' time should have been occupied to the great detriment to other suitors is perhaps one of the least grievances of a litigation which has been going on now for about seven years and a half. . . . I can therefore, my Lords, only say that this lady [the respondent/pursuer] is greatly to be pitied for the course into which she has been dragged—evidently without any consciousness on her part of the extreme folly of these proceedings.

These sentiments were echoed by Lord Westbury, whom we have already encountered as one of the leading agitators for reform of the appellate system:

1 See Minutes of Evidence to the 1872 Select Committee, *passim*, and p. 24 above.

2 Though Professor Heuston remarks in 86 L.Q.R. 165 that 'Lord Colonsay's reported judgments do not suggest unusual juristic capacities.'

3 Some Scots feared that a lone Scottish judge would be left entirely to his own devices when a Scottish appeal came before the House, and that the English Law Lords would rely entirely on him to decide questions of Scots law instead of broadening their own expertise on the subject. Cf. the views of James Anderson Q.C., 'On the Appellate Jurisdiction of the House of Lords from the Courts of Scotland', *Transactions of the National Association for the Promotion of Social Science* (1860), pp. 239, 248.

4 (1870) L.R. 2 Sc. and D. 39 (the appeal was allowed).

'It may be instructive to the people of Scotland to examine this case a little further in order that they may see the lamentable consequences which arise from the state of the procedure in their law courts, and the abuses in that procedure which take place.'

In *Fraser* v. *Crawford*[1] Lord Westbury again took up the cudgels, saying: 'This litigation, at the end of I do not know how many years, has terminated in an appeal to this House. A controversy so exceedingly minute in point of value[2] would naturally excite one's indignation if it were not that such things occur in the appeals from Scotland day by day: and it appears useless to complain.' His Lordship continued his lament in *Gray* v. *Turnbull*:[3]

It is to me a constant source of grief that there should be in Scotland the power of litigants of coming on the most trifling matters to your Lordships' House. The result is that the time of the greatest tribunal in the land is occupied with the most insignificant matters, and further the expense and misery are augmented indefinitely by this prolonged litigation.

We must not pass from the Scottish appeals of this period without referring to a case which must rank as one of the most bizarre ever heard by their Lordships. *Shedden* v. *Patrick and the Attorney-General*[4] proceeded to the House of Lords on no fewer than three separate occasions over a period of nearly seventy years. The final stage was conducted by the garrulous appellant, Mrs. Shedden, appearing in person before the House. Judgments were eventually delivered amid a barrage of interruption and correction by the redoubtable lady (all duly recorded in the Law Report) who all but succeeded in putting the Lord Chancellor completely off his stroke. (On one occasion the Lord Chancellor had unwillingly to concede that Mrs. Shedden had pointed out a factual error in his judgment.)

But, to be fair, the situation with regard to Scots appeals had by this time improved considerably, and not all appeals from England could be described as of shattering importance. The 1872 Select Committee on the Appellate Jurisdiction heard evidence from a procession of Scots witnesses who testified that they had no recollection of appeals involving trivial subject matter. One witness, however, did admit that he recalled a case heard in 1849 which involved the sale of an ox valued at three guineas, the animal having died before the appeal was heard.[5] Another witness was of the opinion that as the House of Lords had reduced the backlog of appeals, and hence the delay, this had discouraged many litigants who would otherwise have appealed to the House merely to postpone final judgment.[6]

---

[1] (1870) L.R. 2 Sc. and D. 42.
[2] It involved arbitration about a disputed sum of £80.
[3] (1870) L.R. 2 Sc. and D. 53.   [4] (1869) L.R. 1 Sc. and D. 470.
[5] Evidence of J. G. S. Lefevre, Report and Minutes, p. 106.
[6] Evidence of Dougald Maclarin, ibid., at p. 80.

Statistics presented to the Committee[1] showed that during the period 1865–1871 nearly half the appeals and writs of error presented to the House of Lords came from the Court of Session: 42 per cent of these were withdrawn before hearing or dismissed for want of prosecution, as compared with 30 per cent of English appeals. The Scots might have been guilty of abusing the system of appeals, but at least the problem eventually reached manageable proportions. By 1880[2] only one-third of appeals came from Scotland; in 1900[3] only ten out of seventy-nine; and in 1910[4] eighteen out of eighty-nine. The present proportion has remained fairly steady at one in five.

THE HOUSE OF LORDS AS AN IRISH COURT

English rule in Ireland dates back to the twelfth century, and until 1920 all English kings since Henry VIII were styled Kings of Ireland. In the case of the *Prior of Lanthony*,[5] decided in the reign of Henry VI, it was established that an appeal in error lay from the King's Bench in Ireland, either to the English King's Bench or to the Irish House of Lords. In both cases a further appeal lay to the English House of Lords.

But the unruly Irish quickly tried to throw off the shackles of an appeal to an English Parliament: arguing on the basis of the denial of the Lords' equity jurisdiction in *Shirley* v. *Fagg* (see above) the Irish House of Lords went so far as to imprison an appellant who had the temerity to serve an order of the English House upon the Bishop of Derry. But two years after a later judicial skirmish in *Annisley* v. *Sherlock* (1717) the English Parliament passed an Act abolishing the jurisdiction of the Irish House of Lords altogether and empowering the English Parliament to enact laws binding in Ireland. This Act was repealed in 1783, to be replaced by what Pike justly calls 'a very remarkable Act'[6] which prevented any writ of error from the courts of Ireland being considered in England. Thus, for the remaining seventeen years up to the Act of Union, the Irish enjoyed the privilege of an appeal to their own House of Lords.

Although the Irish courts are geographically no less remote than those of Scotland, Irish law has conformed to the pattern of English common law. Indeed from the earliest times, in theory at least, English laws prevailed in Ireland, and Irish courts were subordinate to those of England. Thus there

---

1 Ibid., at pp. 123–6. See Statistical Annex to the present chapter, pp. 39–43.
2 *Judicial Statistics* (1880) C. 3088, p. 44. (See Annex below.)
3 *Civil Judicial Statistics* (1900) Cd. 1115.
4 *Civil Judicial Statistics* (1910) Cd. 6047.
5 See Beven, op. cit., p. 361.
6 Pike, op. cit., p. 303. 'The effect of this very remarkable Act was, to place the Kingdom of Ireland in a position as independent as that enjoyed by the Kingdom of Scotland, between the accession of James I and the Act of Union with Scotland in 1707. There was a difference in that the laws of Scotland were different from those of England, while those of Ireland were the same, but in each case the administration was independent, and subject only to the same Crown.'

has never been any real conflict between disparate systems of jurisprudence. Even the system of courts in Ireland has tended to mirror that of England: for example, in 1856 an Irish Court of Appeal in Chancery was formed, close upon the heels of its English counterpart established in 1851, and the Court of Appeal in Ireland (Court of Appeal in Northern Ireland since partition in 1920) was established in 1877 soon after the corresponding English reforms earlier in the same decade.

Certainly during the period leading up to the reforms of the 1870s, the extent of the Irish jurisdiction of the House of Lords was very much greater than it is today in respect of Northern Ireland. Of 1,076 appeals and causes in error presented to the House during the period 1833–65, 134 (12·3 per cent) were from Ireland. During 1866–71, 21 causes out of 230 (9·1 per cent) were Irish.[1] In 1880, 5 appeals out of 48 presented were Irish, in 1900, 10 out of 79, and in 1910 only 7 out of 89.[2] The modern figure is almost negligible, around 3 per cent, and this in spite of the fact that only since 1962 have appeals from Northern Ireland been curbed by the necessity of obtaining leave to appeal. Unlike the situation in Scotland, criminal appeals lie from the Court of Criminal Appeal in Northern Ireland to the House of Lords, but these are very few in number.

With constitutional upheaval in Northern Ireland very much a matter of current concern, one aspect of the Lords' jurisdiction, recently abolished, merits special mention. Sections 49 and 50 of the Government of Ireland Act 1920 provided an appeal to the House of Lords from the courts of Northern Ireland, not merely in matters which had been within the jurisdiction of the House prior to 1920, but also in all matters arising in the course of ordinary litigation concerning the constitutional validity of legislation passed by the Northern Ireland legislature.[3] This gave rise to several important appeals involving section 5 (1) of the 1920 Act. This prescribed any legislation which provided for the taking of any property 'without compensation'.[4] This is perhaps the nearest that we have come in the United Kingdom to emulating the constitutional jurisdiction of the United States Supreme Court: the right of appeal was amended by the Northern Ireland Act 1962[5] to bring Northern Irish appeals into line with English procedure: thereafter leave to appeal was necessary.

The decline in the number of Irish appeals during this century is explained largely by the shrinkage in the geographical extent of the jurisdiction follow-

---

[1] Minutes of Evidence to 1872 Select Committee (above), p. 109. (See Statistical Appendix below.)

[2] These figures were obtained from the appropriate volumes of *Judicial Statistics*.

[3] See Lord MacDermott, 'The Supreme Court of Northern Ireland: Two Unusual Jurisdictions', 2 J.S.P.T.L. (N.S.) 201 (1952). Some interesting aspects of the right of appeal are discussed by Professor F. J. Newark in 6 N.I.L.Q. at pp. 102 ff.

[4] See p. 261 below, for a discussion of some cases arising under s. 5 (1).

[5] s. 14.

ing partition. A case could be made out to the effect that the smaller the population from which the judges of the courts *a quo* are drawn, the more necessity there is for its decisions to be supervised by a strong court of last resort. This argument is weakened in the case of the contemporary courts of Northern Ireland by the presence there since 1951 (until his retirement in 1971) of a strong and able Lord Chief Justice (Lord MacDermott), himself a former Lord of Appeal in Ordinary.

EPILOGUE: THE HOUSE OF LORDS IN THE TWENTIETH CENTURY

The jurisdiction of the contemporary House of Lords is a product of many centuries of constitutional development. Some of its procedural rules and conventions, and its terminology—its 'petitions', 'speeches', and 'votes'—are redolent of an epoch when the final appeal really was to Parliament, when the appeal to 'the King and his Council in Parliament' was more than mere rhetoric.

We might argue, Bagehot fashion, that gracing the modern final appeal court with the name of 'Parliament' serves a useful function by erecting a dignified façade behind which an ordinary court of law can carry out mundane tasks of adjudication under an aura of public deference conferring special weight upon its pronouncements. But, while the 1873 Act abolished the House of Lords in its judicial capacity, the phoenix which arose from the ashes was something completely new, resembling the former tribunal only in name and venue. The change was an inevitable result of changing social demands: an age of deference to supposed hereditary excellence had to give way to the need for increasing professionalism and differentiation of function. As law became more complex, in response to the increasing complexity of social life, judicial functions were transferred from the peers into the hands of professional judges. To make the change more palatable the old name of the final appeal court was retained, but the change was fundamental, inevitable and irreversible.

The Bagehotian thesis would carry greater conviction if the façade really did enhance the status of the court. But in fact the Parliamentary mumbo-jumbo surrounding the judicial House of Lords deceives none of those involved professionally with it; at worst, some of the quaint archaisms which characterize its procedure are regarded with irritation; at best there is a toleration of all things traditional. When they become a positive nuisance—for example, speeches had to be read in full when judgment was delivered—the procedure is reformed. Some laymen may not be able to grasp the fact that the judicial House of Lords is detached from Parliament, and this is a pity. But ultimately the quality of the House of Lords is to be judged by its performance and not by any harking back to its ancient role as the High Court of Parliament.

The Act of 1876 was not a genesis: it was more of an exodus from the captivity of archaism. But when a reform of this magnitude takes place, the situation tends to reach a temporary plateau of stability while the former agitators for reform sit back on their haunches and admire their handiwork. Further changes tend to be confined to sanding down any rough edges.

The reforms which have taken place since 1876 superficially have the appearance of *ad hoc* tinkerings, but, taken together, they are as momentous as the Appellate Jurisdiction Act itself. In rationalizing the court system the Victorian reformers laid the foundations for a new era of functional utility in legal institutions. At least seven major changes have taken place since 1900, quite apart from the growth in the actual size of the final appeal court: changes which represent an attempt to build something new upon these foundations. (All are discussed elsewhere in the text.)

(1) The Criminal Appeal Act 1907 created a genuine (if limited) form of appeal, and extended the supervisory jurisdiction of the House of Lords over the higher criminal courts.

(2) The Administration of Justice (Appeals) Act 1934 (similarly enacted for Northern Ireland in 1962) qualified the ancient right of an aggrieved litigant to petition the King in Parliament by imposing the functional-legal requirement of leave to appeal granted by the judges themselves. In effect this was a logical development from the nineteenth-century principle whereby appeals came to be heard only by professionally qualified Law Lords: thus, the judges themselves came to control their own case-load as well as to determine the appeals.

(3) The establishment of the Appellate Committee in 1948: this marked the end of the fiction of appeals to the 'whole House'—in spite of protestations to the contrary on the part of the then Lord Chancellor.

(4) The Administration of Justice Act 1960: extended the criminal jurisdiction of the House of Lords, so that (as regards leave to appeal) criminal appeals are only slightly less stringently restricted than civil appeals. Magistrates' courts come for the first time within the supervisory jurisdiction by virtue of appeals to the Divisional Court of the Queen's Bench Division and from there to the House of Lords. And one of the last relics of the royal prerogative in appellate jurisdiction disappeared with the abolition of the Attorney-General's fiat.

(5) Extension of legal aid to House of Lords appeals in 1960: more a social reform than a constitutional revolution, but one which (potentially, if not in practice) opened the doors of the House of Lords to a much wider cross-section of the litigating population.

(6) The House of Lords ceased to be bound inevitably by its own previous decisions in 1966: a technical reform which acknowledged the creativity of judges, and gave an added impetus to the supervisory role of the House of Lords: a profound psychological, if not a practical, change.

(7) Administration of Justice Act 1969: the introduction of 'leapfrogging', marking a marginal attempt to achieve a compromise in the question of a second appeal. In theory at least, this reform entrenched more firmly the role of the House of Lords as part of the ordinary court hierarchy.

This then has been the saga of the judicial House of Lords. Inevitably, much has been left unsaid, and we have circumnavigated controversial issues which we (as non-historians) have felt unqualified to tackle. What has emerged is that while the House of Lords of today little resembles its sixteenth-century counterpart, its development represents a continuous process of dynamic interaction with its environment dating back to feudal times. We trust that some of the more obscure corners of the present system have been illuminated by our account, and that would-be reformers will think long and hard before brushing aside six hundred years of evolution and change merely to satisfy a momentary whim or a political ideology.

STATISTICAL ANNEX

No study of the House of Lords in its judicial capacity would be complete without some account of the changes in the case load of the court which have accompanied (and in some cases stimulated) the reforms already discussed in the main body of this chapter. The tables set out in this annex have been adapted from two principal sources. First, the statistical information (covering the period 1833 to 1871) set out in the Report of the 1871 Select Committee on the Appellate Jurisdiction.[1] Second, the relevant tables included in the annual volumes of *Civil Judicial Statistics*, published annually[2] since 1858.

In some respects these tables might have been more appropriately sited with the main body of statistics included in later chapters and appendices, but we have included them here for two reasons. First they are not part of our main statistical analysis, and as they cover one of the periods discussed earlier in the chapter it seems appropriate to set them out here as an appendix. Second, the bases on which the official returns are calculated are different from that employed by us. The most important difference is that some of the official statistics count consolidated appeals separately while we, being more interested in appeal *hearings*, have counted consolidated appeals as a single item.[3] This explains why many of the official tables arrive at higher totals than ours.

In using the official statistics we have attempted to summarize in statistical terms the work of the House of Lords at the turn of every decade from 1860 to date. This has involved two further problems. First some of the volume of statistics is more comprehensive than others, and more reliable. Thus those produced during the period 1894 to 1920 were edited by the redoubtable Sir John Macdonnel, and con-

---

[1] Discussed above.

[2] Except for the decade following the outbreak of the Second World War, when publication was suspended on the grounds of economy.

[3] Our concern with 'hearings' breaks down however when we come to cross appeals. Like the official statistics our tables count appeals and cross appeals as separate items since the issues involved—and the outcomes—are often very different, even though only one hearing takes place.

tain wealth of detail.[1] Those for other years are much more sketchy, and vary from year to year in such matters as distinguishing different types of outcome on appeal. This variation presents us with a dilemma. If we reduce all the statistics to a lowest common denominator, in order to obtain a uniform picture over the entire period, much of the detail in the more comprehensive volumes will be lost. On the other hand, this is essentially a supplement to a chapter, and we do not wish to lose both ourselves and the reader in a mass of superfluity. We have decided, therefore, to provide tabular summary of some of the more important information covering the whole period, and to note some of the other information (e.g. relating to costs) in the appropriate sections of the book.

A second difficulty arises from the years which we have chosen. In two instances it proved impossible to use the appropriate decennial year. The table in the 1860 statistics dealing with the House of Lords is set out in such a curious way that we suspect the total number of appeals given (108) to be double the true total for the year. We have, therefore, substituted figures for 1861. In 1940 no official statistics were published owing to wartime economy: we have therefore used the last of the pre-war volumes, that for 1938.

[1] For a short history of the *Civil Judicial Statistics* see the Report of the Adams Committee (1968) Cmnd. 3684, paras. 8 to 13.

TABLE 1

House of Lords Appeals, 1833–1871ᵃ

Year(s)	Causes Heard	English	Scottish	Irish	Affirmed		Reversed		Varied	Other	Dismissed as Incompetent	Session when Heard		
					With Costs	No costs (or Special Order)	Wholly	In Part				Same Session as set Down	One Session after Setting Down	Only Appellant Heard
Total 1833–65	946 [130]	270 [99]	573	103 [31]	444 [78]	194 [17]	212 [30]	44	20		32 [5]	147	537	117
1866	37 [5]	23 [5]	12	2 [—]	18 [5]	6 [—]	9 [—]	2	1	1	—	16 [—]	17 [2]	9 [—]
1867	31 [10]	10 [9]	19	2 [1]	16 [7]	3 [1]	7 [3]	—	2	—	3	12 [2]	18 [4]	4 [1]
1868	31 [6]	9 [4]	18	4 [2]	15 [4]	6 [1]	7 [1]	1	2	—	—	2 [1]	26 [4]	4 [2]
1869	18 [6]	6 [6]	8	4 [—]	11 [3]	3 [1]	2 [1]	—	2	—	—	— [1]	17 [1]	9 [1]
1870	45 [6]	13 [6]	31	1 [—]	21 [3]	5 [—]	8 [3]	4	7	—	—	1 [1]	36 [4]	12 [1]
1871	28 [7]	10 [5]	15	3 [2]	18 [5]	— [5]	6 [1]	—	3	—	1	3 [1]	12 [4]	4 [3]
Total 1866–71	190 [40]	71 [35]	103	16 [5]	99 [27]	23 [3]	39 [10]	7	17	1	4	34 [5]	126 [19]	43 [8]

ᵃ Adapted from Tables A and B in the appendix to the Report of the 1872 Select Committee (above).
Note: Figures in square brackets refer to causes in error and appeals by case stated.

Commentary on Table 1

During the period 1833–65 an average of 28·7 appeals and 3·9 causes in error were heard annually by the House of Lords. The corresponding figures for the period 1866–71 were 31·7 appeals and 6·7 causes in error. (We do not know to what extent these figures are augmented by consolidated appeals and by cross appeals.)

Between 1833 and 1865 Scottish appeals constituted 52·8 per cent of the causes heard and Irish appeals and causes in error amounted to 12·5 per cent of the total. By the period 1866–71 the percentage of Scottish appeals had declined to 44·8 per cent and Irish appeals to 9·1 per cent. Thus the proportion of English causes rose sharply from 34·7 per cent to 46·1 per cent.

Of all the causes heard during the period 1833–65, 66·0 per cent of causes were dismissed (plus a number dismissed as incompetent). Only 22·5 per cent were wholly allowed. During 1866–71, 66·0 per cent of causes were dismissed and 21·3 per cent wholly allowed. (Unfortunately there is no breakdown of the success rates in the different types of appeal.)

No fewer than 36·4 per cent of the 1833–65 appeals were heard *later* than the year after the appeal was sent down: this proportion had dropped to 20 per cent by the 1866–71 period.

During 1833–65, 10·9 per cent of appeals were disposed of without the respondent or his counsel being called upon to reply. This figure doubled to 22·2 per cent by 1866–71.

In 92 of the 132 causes in error heard between 1833 and 1865 (i.e. 69·6 per cent) the judges were summoned to assist the House. The judges were called upon in only 15 of the 40 causes (i.e. 37·5 per cent) heard between 1866 and 1871.

TABLE 2A

Appeals Presented, 1861–1968

Courts *a quo*

Year	Total Presented	Chancery England	Chancery Ireland	Exchequer England	Chamber Ireland	Ct. of Session	English Court of Probate	Court of Divorce	Court of Appeal England	Court of Appeal Ireland	Ct. of Crim. App. England	Ct. of Crim. App. Ireland	Q.B. Div. Ct.	Ct.-M.A.C.
1861	64	16	10	2	2	30	3	1						
1870	48	17	2	4	1	22	—	2						
1880	48					10			15	3				
1890	57					14			43	—				
1900	79					10			59	10				
1910	89					18			62	7				
1920	93					26			55	11	2			
1930	74					27			46	1	1			
1938	43					10			32	1	—			
1950	43					10			33	—	—	—		
1960	48					6			38	2	2	—	—	—
1968	52					9			35	2	1	—	4	1

Commentary[a]

The case-load of the House of Lords appears to have reached a peak during the period 1900–30 after which there is a marked decline, probably due partly to the shrinkage of the Irish jurisdiction in 1920, and to the curbing of the right of appeal in English appeals in 1934. (Though Scottish appeals, which were unaffected by the 1934 Act, showed an even more rapid decline after 1930.)

[a] Both Tables 2A and 2B were compiled from the following volumes of judicial statistics: 1861 (1862, LVI Sessional Papers, 491); 1870 (1871, LXIV, 1); 1880 (1881, XCV, 1); 1890 (1890–1, XCIII, 1); 1900 (1902, CXVII, 191); 1910 (1912–13, CX, 187); 1920 (Home Office publication, H.M.S.O.); 1930 (1930–1, XXXII, 231); 1938 (1938–9, XXV, 731); 1950 (1951–2, XXIV, 561); 1960 (1960–1, XXVII, 407); 1968 (July 1969, Cmnd. 4112).

TABLE 2B

Appeals Heard, 1861–1968, by Success Rate and Nationality of Court a quo

Year	Total Appeals Heard	Total from England	No. and % Successful[a]	Total from Scotland	No. and % Successful	Total from Ireland	No. and % Successful
1861	45	22	5 (22·8)	17	6 (35·3)	6	5 (83·4)
1870	51	19	8 (42·0)	31	14 (45·2)	1	—
1880	36	22	5 (22·7)	12	2 (16·7)	2	1[b]
1890	47	30	9 (30·0)	16	6 (37·5)	1	—
1900	67	56	13 (23·2)	8	5 (62·5)	3	—
1910	74	59	18 (30·5)	13	4 (30·8)	2	—
1920	74	45	18 (40·0)	23	12 (52·3)	6	3 (50·0)
1930	50	38	14 (36·9)	11	3 (27·3)	1	1[b]
1938	42	36	12 (33·3)	4	2[b]	—	—
1950	31	31	12 (38·7)	—	—	—	—
1960	38	29	14 (48·3)	9	2 (22·2)	—	—
1968	33	31	13 (42·0)	2	1[b]	—	—

Commentary

Both this table and Table 2A confirm the decline both in the overall case-load and in the proportion of appeals from Scotland and Ireland. In as much as one is justified in calculating 'averages' for twelve arbitrarily selected years it is interesting to note the discrepancies between the success rates of appeals from the different courts *a quo*: 45·5 per cent of Irish appeals, 39·1 per cent of Scottish appeals, and 33·8 per cent of English appeals enjoyed at least a measure of success in the House of Lords.

[a] i.e. Causes heard which resulted in a reversal in whole or in part of the judgment below, or in a variation of the judgment.
[b] Numbers too small to justify the calculation of a percentage.

III

THE NATURE OF THE
APPELLATE PROCESS

IN the course of saying a great deal about various aspects of the judicial process we make extensive and somewhat indiscriminate use of the word 'appeal'. But what does 'appeal' really mean: indeed, is it a meaningful term at all in any universal sense? The word is in fact merely a term of convenient usage, part of a system of linguistic shorthand which accepts the need for a penumbra of uncertainty in order to achieve universal comprehensibility at a very low level of exactitude. Thus, while 'appeal' is a generic term broadly meaningful to all lawyers in describing a feature common to a wide range of legal systems, it would be misleading to impute a precise meaning to the term, or to assume, on the grounds that the word (or its translated equivalent) has international currency, that the concept of an appeal means the same thing in a wide range of systems.

On any orthodox definition, an appeal includes three basic elements: a decision (usually the judgment of a court or the ruling of an administrative body) from which an appeal is made; a person or persons aggrieved by the decision (who is often, though by no means necessarily, party to the original proceedings), and a reviewing body ready and willing to entertain the appeal. Thus the essence of an appeal is a request to a competent tribunal to reconsider a decision arrived at by another body, or a request to the same body to review its own decision. This definition leaves much unsaid: how formal must the machinery for review be to fit the definition; does, for example, a letter to a head of state asking for the exercise of executive clemency count as an appeal? Does the consideration of an abstract point of law in isolation from the operation of that law in particular litigation (e.g. by 'Special Reference' to the Judicial Committee of the Privy Council) fit into our model? Probably it does not matter; our definition is stipulative and elastic. 'Appeals' can be arranged along a continuum of increasingly formalized procedure, ranging from a condemned man in supplication before his tribal chief to something as jurisprudentially sophisticated as appeal by *certiorari* to the Supreme Court of the United States. Like Aneurin Bevan's elephant, an appeal can only be described when it walks through the courtroom door. The purpose of the present chapter is to isolate various specific types of appeal which lie along, or at least adjacent to, this definitional continuum.

The nature of a particular appellate process—indeed the character of an entire legal system—depends upon a multiplicity of interrelated (though largely imponderable) factors operating within the system. The structure of the courts; the status and role (both objectively and subjectively perceived) of judges and lawyers, the form of law itself—whether, for example, it is derived from a code or from judicial precedent modified by statute; the attitude of the courts to the authority of decided cases; the political and administrative structure of the country concerned—whether for example its internal sovereignty is limited by its allegiance to a colonizing power. The list of possible factors is endless, and their weight and function in the social equation defy precise analysis. Indeed we might as well attribute the character of the legal system at any given point of time to 'historical accident', a term whose use excuses the scholar from seeking more sophisticated answers. The complexity of the relationships involved has already become apparent in looking (in the preceding chapters) at the historical development of the appellate process in Britain—and, in the present chapter, at some of the systems which have evolved in other countries.

Appeal, as we have stressed, covers a multitude of jurisprudential ideas. It means different things to different men, in different places at different times. The layman's expectation of an appeal is very often quite different from that of the lawyer and many an aggrieved plaintiff denied his 'just' remedy by judge or jury has come upon the disturbing reality that in England a disputed finding of fact can seldom, if ever, form the basis of an appeal. Similarly, a Frenchman accustomed to a narrowly legalistic appeal in cassation, subject to subsequent reargument in a court below, would find little familiarity in the ponderous finality of the judgment of the House of Lords. And a seventeenth-century lawyer accustomed to a painstaking search for trivial mistakes in the court record, which formed the basis of the appeal by writ of error, would be bewildered by the greater flexibility and increased sophistication of jurisprudential argument which characterize a modern appeal.

In examining the development of appellate machinery in England since feudal times we discover an amoeboid judicial process which has reshaped itself in response to changing social and constitutional conditions, and, even today, is still in a state of flux. Under the early feudal monarchy, before anything resembling a coherent legal system (in the modern sense) came into being, might was right, and the mightiest sword was wielded by the King who was able thereby to secure a virtual monopoly in dispensing justice. He strove to maintain this monopoly, not out of a sense of obligation stemming from a social contract, nor because of feelings of philanthropic paternalism towards his serfs, but for two more mundane reasons. First the courts were a valuable source of revenue, and second the notion of the 'King's peace' was central to monarchical authority; the enforcement of justice by the King was a self-satisfying symptom of his power over his vassals. Appeal in this one-man judicial system meant little more than trying to catch the King in a more benign mood, or by seeking the intercession of a favourite courtier. (In invoking this *ad hoc* procedure the hapless suppliant might discover that further representation served only to aggravate the royal wrath, an occurrence which, until recently, found a faint echo in the former power of the Court of Criminal Appeal to increase sentences.)

The growing complexity of government made differentiation of functions and delegation of authority essential; separate and increasingly formalized judicial institutions and procedures came into being, but ultimately the King remained the fountain of justice. It is here that we come upon the foetus of a modern appeal; a litigant dissatisfied with the decision of the courts petitioned the sovereign. Eventually, as we have seen, the busy (or bored) monarch came to delegate even his powers of review to his Council (in which, at first, he retained a substantial voice), a body which soon split up into two parts, Parliament and the Privy Council. Something akin to a 'judicial committee' of the Council came to deal with all appellate business and a hierarchy of courts—fundamental to the modern notion of appeal—thus came into existence. In fact there were several hierarchies as courts proliferated and fought both for increased jurisdiction and for enhanced status; the situation was further complicated by the growth of a separate system of equity jurisprudence, administered by the courts of chancery. Decisions frequently oscillated for years between different courts administering different systems of law.

Appeal in those days, and until the mid-nineteenth century, was a very limited procedure; initially a cause of action had to be framed within one of the existing rigidly stereotyped writs. If the facts were proved and the case correctly pleaded then that was the end of the matter for the dissatisfied litigant. If, however, a technical error—however small or incidental to the substance of the litigation—could be found on the face of the record of the proceedings the decision would be reviewed on a writ of error in the superior courts, and quashed, regardless of the justice of such a result.

The modern English appellate system emerged from the need to rationalize a hotch-potch of conflicting jurisdictions. Elimination of the narrowly based appeal by writ of error also followed as a logical consequence of an increasing concern for substantive legal content rather than for procedural form in the judicial process. Once this step had been taken (and it was no more than a corollary of the growing acceptance of the law-making role of judges) the way became open for the emergence of a supervisory role, exercised by the court at the apex of the hierarchy—alongside its more mundane function as second appellate court in particular litigation.

There are two, mutually complementary, ways in which we can explore the application of our general model of appeal to specific instances. In the first place we can set out a number of known procedures in paradigm form (or as Weberian 'ideal types') and discuss their relationship to each other and to the general notion of an appeal. Second, we can proceed geographically by examining appellate procedures in various overseas countries, paying particular attention to Anglo-Saxon legal systems which have relevance in illuminating the role of the House of Lords.

SPECIES OF APPEAL

1. *The appeal by writ of error*[1] This archaic and unsatisfactory procedure (now mercifully living on only in attenuated form by virtue of the prerogative orders) depended, as we have seen, upon the existence of an error on the record of proceedings in the lower court. Points arising outside the narrow confines of the 'record' were unimpeachable, while many sensible decisions were quashed on a mere verbal quibble resulting from a slip of the clerk's pen. Historically, the procedure does qualify as an 'appeal', albeit a very limited one. When the Court of Appeal was established by the Judicature Act 1873 the method of appeal prescribed was a 're-hearing' along the lines of the procedure adopted for the Court of Appeal in Chancery, and the same form of appeal was provided for by the reformed House of Lords in 1876. In criminal appeals, writ of error was abolished by the Criminal Appeal Act 1907 which set up the Court of Criminal Appeal in place of the Court for Crown Cases Reserved.

The procedure is of considerable historical interest in considering the House of Lords whose appellate jurisdiction up to the passing of the Appellate Jurisdiction Act was founded largely upon writ of error: by that Act, the modern jurisdiction of the House is confined to cases which would have lain on appeal or in error before the Act was passed.

2. *Appeal by Rehearing* This procedure is the essence of the modern British appellate system, though its name is ill-conceived. The only true 'rehearings' are the appeals to Quarter Sessions from a determination of a magistrates' court made on the hearing of an information or complaint and on appeal from Supreme Court Master to Judge in interlocutory civil proceedings.[2] In all other cases (for example in a civil appeal from the High Court to the Court of Appeal, and to the House of Lords) the 're-hearing' is limited to an examination by the appeal court of transcripts of the proceedings below and other documents relating to the case, supplemented by the arguments of counsel. It is the rare exception rather than the rule, both in England and in Scotland, for fresh evidence to be heard on appeal, or for witnesses to be examined or re-examined by the appeal court.

---

[1] Discussed more fully in Chapter II above, at pp. 19, n. 1, 26, n. 1, and 30.
[2] And cf. County Court Rules, Ord. 37, r. 1, empowering a county court judge to order a new trial. In effect, this enables the judge to review his own decision in order to rectify a mistake, or to hear a case which he has struck out in the erroneous belief that he has no jurisdiction.

3. *Appeal by Case Stated* This method of judicial review is provided by
various statutes which require an inferior tribunal, on request by one of the
litigants, to state a case: this takes the form of a question upon a point of
law. Thus a losing party to any proceedings (mainly criminal) before a
magistrates' court may request the bench to state a case for consideration by
a Divisional Court of the Queen's Bench Division of the High Court: thence
further appeal lies to the House of Lords, provided that a point of law is
certified by the Divisional Court, and that either that Court or the House of
Lords gives leave to appeal. At each stage, argument is confined to the point
of law raised in the case stated, and a successful appeal results in the case
being sent back to the justices with a direction to convict (or to acquit, as the
case may be).

The same procedure also applies to some categories of civil proceeding,
particularly in appeals to the courts from the ever growing body of special
tribunals. Thus an appeal by case stated lies from the Income Tax Commissioners to a single Chancery judge in the High Court (though in some
cases there is an intermediate appeal to the Board of Referees).[1] Under the
Arbitration Act 1950 an arbitrator or umpire may state an award in the form
of a special case for decision of the High Court.

The procedure reflects the obsession of lawyers with keeping fact separate
from law in the appellate process (if such a distinction is ever wholly valid).
This is particularly evident in appeals from statutory tribunals, set up with
the intention that they will build up a body of expertise and experience in a
narrow field which cannot be rivalled by the courts; an appeal on a question
of fact from such bodies would be otiose.

4. *Appeal by way of prerogative order* It is here that we begin to encounter
real difficulties in adapting our definition of 'appeal' to a procedure which
certainly involves judicial review, but which questions the legality of proceedings while leaving unsullied the decision on the merits. In other words, a
person can *appeal* by stating a case to the Divisional Court of the Queen's
Bench Division against his conviction by a magistrates' court on the grounds
that the decision was wrong in law. Alternatively, he can *appeal* to Quarter
Sessions on a matter of fact. But if the real issue is, for example, whether or
not the justices were acting within their jurisdiction in trying a particular type
of case, then the appellant would apply to the Divisional Court for an order of
certiorari quashing the decision.

The distinction may be a fine one, but it is more than a semantic quibble.
The supervision of inferior tribunals, exercised by the courts through the

---

[1] Thus the procedure is of particular importance *vis-à-vis* the House of Lords, since a
very high proportion of the latter's case-load consists of tax appeals by case stated.

prerogative orders,[1] is of fundamental importance, particularly in administrative law.[2] The orders of *certiorari, prohibition,* and *mandamus*—coupled with the comparatively recent development of the declaratory judgment[3]— enable the courts to supervise the decision-making process in numerous statutory bodies acting in a judicial or a quasi-judicial manner. Thus the work of local authorities, statutory tribunals, disciplinary bodies—even government departments and non-statutory bodies[4]—are brought within the power of the courts.

The prerogative order—formerly prerogative writ[5]—dates back to the feudal days when the courts required a means of keeping a grip upon any possible rival centres of judicial power. In some respects, their ancestry is closely linked with the writ of error,[6] at least as regards procedure. Thus *certiorari* may be issued for 'error of law on the face of the record' of the lower court's proceedings. Although in some contexts it is valuable to retain a distinction between 'appeal' and 'review', it is probably correct to consider the exercise of prerogative orders as a particular species of appeal. In recent years the House of Lords and the courts in general have played an increasingly active part in shaping principles of administrative law by exercise of the prerogative orders.

5. *Appeal to a Full Court*   This procedure takes many different forms: thus the primitive review provided during the last century by the Court for Crown Cases Reserved (and, before this court was established, in a less formalized manner), whereby points of law were reserved by the trial judge for consideration by his brethren,[7] falls into this category. This procedure is too limited to fall squarely within our definition of appeal, since its effectiveness depends entirely upon the predilections of the trial judge; its real function is to act as a judicial safety net rather than to supply a readily available remedy to the aggrieved and mesmerized litigant at the ringside.

More usually, however, a full court procedure exists *within* the normal appellate machinery. Thus the House of Lords, the Court of Appeal (both civil and criminal divisions), the Court of Session, and Divisional Courts of the High Court are all empowered to convene a full court (see Appendix 6).

---

1 The other prerogative orders are *prohibition* (preventing a future *ultra vires* act) and *mandamus* (compelling the inferior body to exercise its obligatory powers).

2 See the comments of Professor Wade, *Administrative Law* (2nd ed.), pp. 47 ff.

3 See Zamir, *The Declaratory Judgment* (1962).

4 e.g. the Criminal Injuries Compensation Board: see R. v. *Criminal Injuries Compensation Board; ex p. Lain* [1967] 2 Q.B. 864.

5 Prerogative 'writs' (which involved an archaic procedure) were abolished by the Administration of Justice (Miscellaneous Provisions) Act 1938, with the exception of the writ of habeas corpus.

6 See Chapter II, pp. 19, n. 1, 26, n. 2, and 30.

7 See below (Chapter IV).

Two appeals during our period of study were heard by a House of Lords containing more than five judges.[1] In 1898, the trade union case of *Allen* v. *Flood*[2] was initially heard by seven Law Lords, but Lord Halsbury, well-known for his anti-union sentiments, arranged for the case to be re-argued before nine Law Lords and eight High Court Judges, who 'sat in their red robes on either side of a narrow table, looking rather like an omnibus full of old ladies'. Lord Halsbury still found himself in a minority, and there has been no subsequent repetition of this plenary convocation of the judges. Numerous examples could be cited of full courts of the Court of Appeal or formerly the Court of Criminal Appeal (and there are several instances in the early years of the latter court's life)[3] but all these examples merely concern the procedure and composition of a tribunal conducting an orthodox appeal by way of a re-hearing. Perhaps in the Court of Session,[4] which still retains much of its collegiate character, a plenary sitting resembles more closely the 'reference' procedure than does an English appeal to a full court.

6. *Cassation* We conclude this parade of appeal-types with a form of procedure totally alien (in theory at least) to common law systems—the continental process of cassation. (The procedure of the French Cour de Cassation is considered below.)

Almost every feature of the code-oriented legal system of France militates against the existence of an Anglo-Saxon appeal system. French judges (at every level of the hierarchy) have, in effect, the role and status of civil servants applying known rules and regulations to established facts; judges are recruited directly into the lower levels of the judicial hierarchy, without having previously engaged in legal practice. Judicial creativity is largely precluded by adherence to the Code and (to quote Sir Carleton Allen) 'a judgment of a French court is, as we should expect of the Gallic genius, a meticulously constructed piece of logic—a pared and polished judicial syllogism.'[5] Thus the Code Napoleon, the structure and role of the judiciary, allied with the highly decentralized character of the courts, all combine to discourage the development of anything resembling *stare decisis*.

[1] *B.T.C.* v. *Gourley* [1956] A.C. 185 and *Ross Smith* v. *Ross Smith* [1963] A.C. 280. And see Appendix 6, below at pp. 523–4.
[2] [1898] A.C. 1. See Heuston, *Lives of the Lord Chancellors*, pp. 119 ff. Lord Macmillan cites a later instance where Lord Loreburn C. ordered a rehearing of a Scottish case, in which four Law Lords were equally divided, by a court of seven judges. See *A Man of Law's Tale*, p. 117 (also 1908 S.C. (H.L.) 10).
[3] See Michael Knight, 'The Court of Criminal Appeal and Binding Precedent', 113 L.J. 589 (1963), also Appendix 6 below.
[4] See T. B. Smith, *Scotland: the Development of its Laws and Constitution*, p. 91. Cf. also the procedure in Australian courts.
[5] Allen, *Law in the Making*, 7th ed. (1964) p. 180. Cf. D. Lloyd, *Introduction to Jurisprudence*, 2nd ed. (1965) p. 392. For a more general discussion of styles of judgments see J. G. Wetter, *The Styles of Appellate Judicial Opinions* (1960).

Yet, are those processes of law so very alien to our own system? Judges who purport to 'find' rules are a familiar feature of most legal systems. And while no formal doctrine of *stare decisis* exists in France, we still find the French judge seeking *la jurisprudence* underlying a decision, including the evaluation of a line of previous authorities. Although a judge in a lower court may not be strictly bound by a superior court's judgment, like any civil servant he will be loath to question decisions of senior judges who are not only more experienced but are also his superiors in the judicial-bureaucratic hierarchy.[1]

The prerequisites of a conventional appeal system are there. There exists an element of hierarchy, a watered-down notion of precedent, and reasoned decisions to form a basis for judicial review. The French may pay regard to the 'thereness' of codified law but they too have been obliged to acknowledge the fallibility of judges, the rapid changes in modern social conditions, and the universal need for supervision and review within the judicial process. Review by way of cassation in the French court of last resort recognizes this need.

APPEALS OUTSIDE THE UNITED KINGDOM[2]

So far we have (with the exception of a note on cassation) confined our discussion of the appellate process to the domestic scene, in an attempt to fit our rather crude definitional model of appeals to various types of judicial review which operate in the United Kingdom. To explore the general character of appeals it is necessary to range more widely and look at systems operating elsewhere. More specifically, we are concerned with evaluating the social utility of a final court of appeal and with the question of whether a modern industrialized society not given to excessive litigiousness should provide one, two, or more appeals to those of its citizens who wish to avail themselves of the judicial process. A clue to this question—and not much more than a clue—can be found in an examination of other contemporary legal systems. If we find that our double-appeal system is not unique then we can at least content ourselves with the knowledge of being in good company—or, with innate British conservatism, take refuge behind the *status quo*.

But before undertaking the survey, a word of warning is called for. Simple comparative analyses of constitutional and procedural rules can be only of limited value in assessing the respective *merits* of the legal systems involved. The criteria which would have to be employed in any comprehensive comparative study of widely diversified institutional structures are dauntingly numerous and confusedly complex: the pattern of institutional development within a given system is merely a single aspect of its general socio-legal

---

1 See H. C. Gutteridge, *Comparative Law* (2nd ed.), pp. 89–93. But note the warning by Professor R. Cross against the danger of carrying these comparisons between the two systems too far, *Precedent in English Law* (2nd ed.), pp. 10–15.
2 The substance of this section was published as an article in 32 M.L.R. 262 (1969).

development. Thus, while it is permissible to note the existence of two-tier appellate systems in countries as geographically separate and culturally diverse as Canada, France, and Norway, as an interesting sociological phenomenon, it would be quite irresponsible, if not irrational, to point to this fact as evidence of some kind of universal law, or to attribute some kind of intrinsic merit to a second appellate tribunal.

On logical grounds, David Hume's 'is/ought' distinction must be borne in mind: one cannot infer that a type of institution is functionally indispensable merely because the same institutional pattern is endemic in a large number of systems. It should be remembered, moreover, that institutions cannot be treated as autonomous entities standing aloof from the main system of which they are merely components, and we have already mentioned some of the social determinants which operate to shape a given legal system at a particular point of time. We have also discussed the generic nature of the word 'appeal' which precludes its general application in any rigorous sense, to a multiplicity of systems.

It is even more difficult to make any objective assessment of the *merits* of particular institutions in particular systems, since we are faced with the insuperable problem of evaluating the differing value-systems which characterize each society. It would be wholly impermissible to say, for instance, that the United States Supreme Court is in any generic sense 'better' than the French Cour de Cassation when the two institutions are products of wholly incomparable historical and social circumstances, and indeed, perform wholly different judicial functions within those societies. We could perhaps say that one system achieves 'quicker justice' than the other (even supposing that speed is a virtue in the legal process) or that the costs incurred by litigants are lower, but to go beyond superficial assessments of this kind is to exceed the bounds of what is acceptable in a scientific social analysis. It may be true to say that the task of evaluation is best entrusted to those who operate within the legal systems concerned—judges, lawyers, or academics—but to achieve the degree of detachment essential for satisfactory comparative study is a tall order, even (or perhaps especially) for those within the legal profession.

But having entered this extensive caveat, we hasten to add that this aspect of the exercise is far from valueless. In the last analysis a decision as to the number of appeals within a given system must depend upon whether the more authoritative adjudication of litigious issues accruing from the provision of a multi-tier appellate structure is thought to be justified in terms of delays and expense in protracted litigation. We do not suggest that governments and constitutional draftsmen consciously attempt to solve this social equation, but merely that the existence of such an equation (albeit with different sets of variables) is a common factor in every legal system. It is for this reason that a comparison of this kind should prove valuable. We shall now proceed to look at the systems of ten countries, starting with three interesting variants of Anglo-Saxon systems, the United States, South Africa, and Australia.[1]

The United States of America

The complexity of the court structure of the U.S.A. stems largely from the multiplicity of more or less autonomous state jurisdictions which overlap the federal legal system. Although the American legal system was originally founded upon English common law, the written Constitution (in effecting a more or less rigid separation of powers, and with its entrenched libertarian provisions such as 'due process'), coupled with nearly two centuries of independence, has resulted in the evolution of a system which bears little resemblance to that of contemporary Britain. The differences can perhaps be seen most clearly in the Constitution-orientation of the work of the Supreme Court, and in a wholly different approach to the doctrine of *stare decisis*.

So far as state jurisdictions are concerned, only eighteen of the fifty states have two appellate tiers;[2] but it should be borne in mind that all the principal states have a two-tier system and that the eighteen states mentioned contain no less than 70 per cent of the United States population. Survey data (available for only eleven of the three-tier states) shows that in five states appeal to the second-tier appellate court in all categories of cases lies as of right, and in two other states all final appeals are subject to the granting of leave, while in four states appeal only in certain categories of cases lies as of right.

The federal appellate system is also basically two-tiered. The first tier of appellate jurisdiction is exercised by eleven district federal Courts of Appeal. The final appeal[3] lies to the U.S. Supreme Court which has jurisdiction in respect not only of appeals from federal courts but also of appeals from state courts in cases which involve a substantial federal element.

Appeal to the Supreme Court does not generally lie as of right but is subject to the granting of *certiorari* by the court; exceptions (which do lie as of

---

[1] The material for this section was gleaned mainly from the following sources: the series British Commonwealth—the Development of its Laws and Constitutions: vol. 4, *New Zealand*, by J. L. Robson (1967); vol. 5, *Union of South Africa*, by H. R. Hahlo and E. Kahn (1960); vol. 2, *Commonwealth of Australia*, by G. W. Paton (1952); *Appellate Courts in the United States and England*, by D. Karlen; *Comparative Federalism*, by E. McWhinney (1962); *Comparative Law*, by H. C. Gutteridge (1949); *Administration of Justice in Norway*, ed. Royal Norwegian Ministry of Justice (1957); *The French Judicial System*, published by the French Embassy; *The Italian Constitution* (translation published by the Italian Embassy); *The Legal System of Israel*, by H. E. Baker (1961). We are also indebted to Professor Delmar Karlen of the New York Institute of Judicial Administration for supplying us with material relating to state appellate systems in the U.S.A., and Mr. Sydney Kentridge S.C., for guidance on South African appellate procedure.

[2] The states with two appellate courts are: Alabama, Arizona, California, Florida, Georgia, Illinois, Indiana, Louisiana, Michigan, Missouri, New Jersey, New Mexico, New York, Ohio, Oklahoma (criminal appeals only), Pennsylvania, Tennessee and Texas.

[3] There is a provision for a petition to the Supreme Court for a rehearing, but this is rarely granted.

right) include cases where a state statute is said to be 'repugnant to the Constitution, treaties or laws of the United States', but even these cases are carefully 'screened' by the court before it will grant a hearing.

The rules governing presentation of argument to the court provide an interesting contrast to the procedure in the House of Lords. The emphasis is upon the argument presented by both sides in an elaborate (and costly) printed brief, a far more elaborate document than the 'case' used in the House of Lords. Almost invariably the oral argument supplementing the brief is confined to one hour on each side; exceptionally the court may allow additional time, or schedule the case for summary argument, in which case each side will be allowed thirty minutes. Whereas much of the protracted oral argument of the House of Lords is devoted to the reading of authorities and statutes, the Supreme Court frowns heavily upon advocates who read prepared material. In any event, the emphasis placed upon case law is less marked in the jurisprudence of the United States.

Finally, we should mention the mechanics of judgment preparation. Whereas the Law Lords produce highly individualized opinions which are circulated among their brother judges, the procedure adopted by the U.S. Supreme Court involves formalized judicial conferences, and largely collective judgments. At those conferences tentative conclusions are reached on the most recent cases, and the task of writing the judgment of the court is assigned to a particular Associate Justice or even the Chief Justice himself; judgment already drafted and circulated will be formally approved for publication. Although a single judgment is prepared (the Justice concerned working in close collaboration with those of his brethren who share the majority opinion) it is open to any judge, or groups of judges, to prepare separate assenting or dissenting opinions, and unanimous opinions are reached in only about 25 per cent of the cases considered on their merits by the court.[1]

South Africa

The Republic of South Africa abolished appeals to the Privy Council in 1950 and seceded from the Commonwealth in 1961. Its legal system, however, displays a measure of British influence.

At the apex of the basically two-tiered South African Supreme Court hierarchy is the Appellate Division of the Supreme Court which exercises an appellate jurisdiction in respect of the decisions of the Provincial and Local Divisions of the Supreme Court. The six Provincial Divisions and the three Local Divisions are basically civil and criminal courts of first instance, but the Provincial Divisions also sit (with a quorum of two judges) to hear appeals from inferior courts in both civil and criminal cases. Appeals to the Provincial

---

[1] See Karlen, op. cit., p. 74. The general question of dissenting judgments is considered in a later chapter.

Divisions from inferior courts can only proceed to the Appellate Division by special leave, either of the Provincial Division or of the Chief Justice.

Appeals to the Appellate Division lie as of right from final judgments given in civil actions. But in some important classes of case, particularly motions heard by a single judge, an appeal lies to a full court (three judges) of the Provincial Division and thence by leave to the Appellate Division. However, even in those cases an appeal may be brought direct to the Appellate Division by consent of both parties.

In Supreme Court criminal cases, an appeal lies direct to the Appellate Division, but only by leave of the court *a quo* or of the Chief Justice, the test being whether there is 'a reasonable prospect of success on appeal'.

The quorum for the Appellate Division in civil appeals is five, and in criminal appeals, three. Since 1955 (following the 'entrenched clauses' controversy) a quorum of eleven is required in the rare cases in which the constitutional validity of an Act of Parliament is considered.

The procedure for argument is an interesting compromise between the English system and that adopted by the U.S. Supreme Court. Four days before the hearing of an appeal by the Appellate Division, counsel must submit 'heads of argument' which contain a full précis of propositions and authorities to be relied upon. There is no time limit to oral argument, but counsel are expected to confine themselves to supplementing the material in the heads of argument, and are not permitted to adduce additional arguments without the leave of the court.[1]

Australia

Two factors must be borne in mind in looking at the court structure of Australia. In the first place, the complexity of the system is attributable largely to the federal character of the country. In the second place, Australia is a Commonwealth country which has inherited (basically) the English legal system and which has opted to retain an appeal to the Judical Committee of the Privy Council, albeit in an attenuated form.[2]

Internally, the States of Australia each have two tiers of appeal (although this becomes three if we include an extra-territorial appeal to the Privy Council). Each State has a Supreme Court which exercises original state jurisdiction and, in contrast to state courts in the United States federal jurisdiction, State Supreme Courts also possess an appellate jurisdiction in respect of the decisions of state intermediate courts and justices' courts. Appeals lie from a Supreme Court in original jurisdiction to a full court of the Supreme Court.

---

1 We feel that this procedure might with advantage be adopted by the House of Lords: see chapter XIX, pp. 403–4.

2 In the four-year period 1965–8, eight such appeals were entered from the High Court of Australia, eight from New South Wales, and two from Queensland. This represents 13 per cent of the case-load of the Judicial Committee during the period.

The final appellate court within the territory is the High Court of Australia. This court possesses original jurisdiction in a wide range of public law matters, for example, cases arising out of a treaty, cases to which the Commonwealth of Australia is a party or in which a prerogative order is sought against an officer of the Commonwealth (i.e. the Australian Federal Legislature), and in litigation between two or more states. Section 73 of the Constitution provides that appeals lie to the High Court from four categories of tribunal: a single judge of the High Court; any other Federal court (*viz.* the Commonwealth Industrial Court and the Federal Court of Bankruptcy); a court exercising federal jurisdiction (such a jurisdiction is bestowed upon State Supreme Courts by enactments of the Federal Legislature); and a State Supreme Court (in practice such appeal is limited to final judgments, and lies as of right only if the amount at issue exceeds a certain sum).

The Constitution states that a High Court judgment on appeal shall be final and conclusive, but this only precludes appeals as of right to the Privy Council. Until recently, an appeal lay to the Judicial Committee by special leave, subject to the important constitutional restriction which denies an appeal upon any question 'as to the limits *inter se* of the constitutional powers of the Commonwealth and those of any State or States, or as to the limits *inter se* of the constitutional powers of any two or more States . . .', unless the High Court certifies that the question is one which ought to be determined by the Queen in Council. Only one such certificate has ever been issued.[1]

By the Privy Council (Limitation of Appeals) Act 1968 the Australian Parliament exercised its constitutional power (which is subject to Royal Assent) to limit 'the matters in which such [Special] Leave may be asked'. Section 3 of this Act provides that Special Leave to appeal from a decision of the High Court may be asked only where the High Court's decision was on appeal from a State Supreme Court not exercising federal jurisdiction, and the decision of the Supreme Court did not involve interpretation or application of the Constitution, or a Commonwealth law or instrument. By section 4, leave to appeal shall not be asked from the decision of a federal court (other than the High Court) or of the Supreme Court of a territory. The Act came into effect on 1 September 1968.

New Zealand

The neighbouring territory of New Zealand is a unitary state with a very small population and with a relatively simple court structure: it thus provides in some respects a more valid comparison with Great Britain than does Australia. Like Australia, it has inherited the English common law system and has retained the appeal to the Privy Council.[2]

New Zealand has a single (internal) appellate court, the Court of Appeal,

[1] *Colonial Sugar Refining Co.* v. *Attorney-General for the Commonwealth* (1912) 15 C.L.R. 182.

[2] In the period 1965–8, five such appeals were entered.

which was established as a permanent appellate court only in 1957. (Previously a Court of Appeal sat *ad hoc* and was composed of Supreme Court judges.) The Court hears appeals from the first-instance decisions of the Supreme Court and also exercises an original jurisdiction where the Supreme Court has ordered a case to be removed to the Court of Appeal. The Supreme Court exercises original jurisdiction in both civil and criminal causes.

An appeal lies as of right to the Privy Council from the Court of Appeal in all cases involving subject-matter valued at £500 or more. All other appeals require the leave of the court appealed from, or of the Judicial Committee.

Canada

The Canadian court structure reflects the somewhat amorphous composition of the Federation. It also differs from the two preceding examples in that since 1949 there has been no provision for appeal to the Privy Council.

The appellate structure is essentially two-tiered. All the provinces and territories have superior courts with original and appellate divisions. At the apex of the hierarchy, the Supreme Court of Canada exercises a civil and criminal appellate jurisdiction throughout the country; it also has jurisdiction to determine important constitutional questions referred to it by the Governor-General in Council.

France

Moving now from English-rooted common law systems to European civil law, epitomized in the legal system of France, we find a wholly different approach to final judicial review in the notion of cassation (discussed above) coupled with (and, indeed, largely stemming from) a judicial approach which attempts to mitigate the rigour of its legal code by search for the 'jurisprudence' underlying the decision.

First-instance jurisdiction (civil and criminal) is in the hands of tribunaux d'instance and tribunaux de grande instance. From here, there is an unqualified right of appeal (in the English sense of the word) to regional Cours d'Appel (of which there are twenty-seven in all). The final tier is the Cour de Cassation, which differs from the English pattern for an appellate court in that it cannot substitute its own decision for that of the lower court. It can merely refer the case back to a Cour d'Appel in a district other than that where the appeal was originally heard. It is open to this second Cour d'Appel (sitting as a full court) to reject the finding of the Cour de Cassation and in the latter event the case would be reheard by the Cour de Cassation sitting in banc, and its decision would this time be final.

The Cour de Cassation is divided into a number of Chambers, each of which exercises jurisdiction in a particular area of law—commercial, social, criminal etc.—defined by statute. Before 1947, cases were given a preliminary screening by a Chambre de Requêtes which decided whether the case should be referred to one of the principal chambers for a full hearing. Since the abolition of the Chambre de Requêtes the preliminary vetting is carried out by the chamber into whose jurisdiction the case falls.

Italy

The most interesting feature of the Italian court system lies in the existence of separate institutions for dealing with judicial cassation (as in France) and the constitutional legitimacy of legislation. Following the French pattern, the court system is in three tiers, but a constitutional court lies alongside the civil and criminal judicial systems.

First instance civil and criminal jurisdiction lies with local magistrates and pretors in minor matters, and with three-judge tribunals (of which there are 150 in all) in more substantial litigation. Serious criminal cases are tried by assize courts. Appeal lies to the appropriate Court of Appeal (twenty-three in all) situated in most regional capitals and in a number of other major towns: these courts normally sit with a chairman and four additional judges.

The ultimate tier of the hierarchy is the Supreme Court of Cassation which is situated in Rome and deals (like its French counterpart) solely with points of law. It consists of six civil and ten penal sections manned by career judges promoted from the Court of Appeal: the divisions have occasionally sat 'Seizioni Uniti' in cases of outstanding importance.

The Constitutional Court came into existence in 1955 and consists of fifteen members, one-third of whom are nominated (for twelve-year terms) by the Head of State, one-third by the legislature, and one-third by the judiciary: all the judges are senior magistrates or academics. In practice its chief function is to determine the constitutionality of state and regional laws, and to resolve conflicts of competence between state and region, and between regions. It also has powers relating to the impeachment of the Head of State and to the admissibility of constitutional referenda.

If a question of constitutional legitimacy is raised by the parties to legal proceedings, the proceedings will be suspended while the case is considered by the Constitutional Court. The trial judge may decline to refer the question if he is not satisfied that a prima facie conflict with the Constitution is involved, or if he considers that the question is irrelevant to the decision in the case. If the Constitutional Court upholds the claim its ruling is published in the Official Gazette and the law concerned is thereby invalidated.[1]

The Netherlands

In the Dutch system we find, once again, the French pattern of cassation, coupled with a codified legal system. First-instance jurisdiction is shared between sixty-two cantonal courts and nineteen district ones, the latter dealing

[1] e.g. the recent consideration by the Court of divorce legislation which was said to contravene the constitutional-legal status of married women.

with more substantial civil and criminal cases, and with divorce and bank-ruptcy proceedings. District courts also exercise appellate jurisdiction in re-spect of the proceedings in cantonal courts.

Appeal lies from a district court to one of five courts of appeal: these sit in divisions of three, except for the fiscal divisions which consist of a single judge. There is also a separate tenancy division which sits in Arnhem to hear appeals from the tenancy divisions of cantonal courts throughout the country.

Finally, the Supreme Court has jurisdiction in cassation over all inferior courts. It consists of twenty judges divided into divisions of five, and follows the conventional pattern of confining its jurisdiction to points of law. One interesting feature is the power of the Supreme Court to deal with cases 'in the interests of law' when appeal in cassation is not brought: in this event the decision in the case under consideration cannot be affected. Finally, the Supreme Court has certain constitutional powers: for example, it acts as a special court to deal with charges against members of the executive.

Norway

We move in a north-easterly direction to Scandinavia where, in Norway, we find a system which resembles the English rather than the Continental pattern of appeal.

Norway has two tiers of review, but the picture is complicated by the fact that appeal lies directly to the Supreme Court from the final judgments of a court of first instance when the latter has sat with three judges: leave of the Select Appeals Committee of the Supreme Court (see below) is required in such cases. When (as is more usual) the first instance proceedings have taken place before a single judge (and in all interlocutory proceedings) there is an intermediate appeal to the Court of Appeals. Such an appeal lies as of right unless the sum at issue is less than a certain monetary value, in which case the leave of the trial judge must be obtained.

From the Court of Appeals an appeal lies as of right to the Supreme Court if the amount involved exceeds a certain value, otherwise an aspiring appellant must obtain leave to appeal from the Select Appeal Committee of the Supreme Court. Whether or not leave is required, all appeals go first of all to the Select Appeals Committee, a body consisting of three judges and having the power to refer the decision back to the lower court if it (unanimously) holds that there has been a serious error in the latter's decision, or to quash the appeal if it decides (and again it must be a unanimous decision) that the appeal is hopeless. If the appeal is not finally decided by the Committee the latter refers it to a five-judge division of the Supreme Court for a full hearing.

Israel

A State newly created in the mid-twentieth century, whose background was the unique and fortunate alchemy of separate European legal systems, was likely to adopt a hierarchy of courts reflecting a composite form of its legal forbears. In the event Israel's judicial system is neither wholly a one- nor a two-tier appeal system.

At the heart of the court structure are the four District Courts, in Jerusalem, Tel Aviv, Jaffa, and Haifa, each having unlimited jurisdiction as courts of first instance in all civil and criminal matters not within the limited criminal and civil jurisdiction of the magistrates' courts, in two of the six administrative districts into which the country is subdivided. Appeals from the twenty-four magistrates' courts lie to the District Court. Below the magistrates' courts lie the municipal courts dealing with petty crime: the maximum sentence such courts may impose is a fine of I£750 or fifteen days' imprisonment. Members of these courts are laymen, save that a stipendiary magistrate sits in a few major centres.

At the apex of the court hierarchy sits the Supreme Court of Israel having jurisdiction as an appellate court from the District Courts in all matters, both civil and criminal, as well as possessing a residual original jurisdiction in matters in which it considers it necessary to grant relief in the interests of justice and which are not within the jurisdiction of any other court or tribunal. It has original jurisdiction (a) to make habeas corpus orders; (b) to make orders directed to State authorities, local authorities and their officials and to other bodies and persons performing public functions under the law, requiring them to do or refrain from doing any act in the performance of their functions according to law, and if they were unlawfully elected or appointed, to refrain from acting (in other words the Supreme Court exercises an original and exclusive jurisdiction in the issuance of prerogative orders); and (c) to make orders in the nature of *certiorari, mandamus* or *prohibition* against inferior courts and tribunals, including the religious courts.

Thus the Supreme Court sits in a variety of capacities; sometimes handing down the first and final judicial word; sometimes as a court of last resort in appeals which have come from a magistrates' court via a District Court, and most frequently in appeals where the trial court has been the District Court itself. The preponderance of appeals in the latter category lends the appearance of a single-appeal system.

APPEALS: ONE, TWO, OR NONE?

This cursory glance at a selection of non-English appellate systems has shown the diversity which exists, even within Commonwealth countries. Some basic factors underlying this diversity are not hard to find: we must not ignore the influence of Montesquieu's political philosophy in shaping the role of the U.S. Supreme Court, or of the Code Napoleon in relation to the French system; nor must we forget that smallness of population goes a long way towards explaining the simplicity of the New Zealand system. But more detailed solutions of the various 'social equations' are defeated by the complexity of the variables concerned.

But so far, of course, we have side-stepped the main contentious issue, central to the present study: why two appeals? Why is one not enough? And if two are needed, why not three, four—or as many as will neither exhaust the most tenacious litigant nor strain the resources of the state responsible for staffing appellate courts? By what criteria can we determine the 'right' number of appeals for a given system?

Appellate review depends upon a reasoned judgment of the court *a quo*, and reasoned opinions and appellate review are concomitants of procedural law. An appeal presupposes dissatisfaction and even censure of the decision appealed against, and appeal is hardly conceivable when the ratiocination of the judgment at first instance is not articulated. This has been specifically recognized by the courts in making available the remedy of the prerogative orders only against the 'speaking order', i.e. an order which on its face indicates how it was arrived at. This factor also explains the absence of a true appellate system in the jury-based criminal law of England. A jury's verdict is unreasoned (if not unreasoning) and there can thus be no means of attacking such a decision short of declaring it 'unsafe or unsatisfactory' (the phrase used in the Criminal Appeal Act 1966).[1] Unlike a judge, jurors are not required, and indeed could not be expected, to clothe in cold syllogism the impulses of sentiment tempered, one hopes, with common sense which, we suspect, are often the basis of their decisions. In areas of law where jury trial has been abandoned, the urge to challenge and to have reversed the adverse decision has impelled the state to establish machinery for appeal.

But in this element of criticism inherent in an appeal lies a factor which acts as a constraint upon the possible proliferation of appeals. While judges sensibly acknowledge the need for review and correction of lower courts' decisions by an eminent body of appeal judges, to carry this process too far might be thought an insulting encroachment upon the functions of the trial courts, or even a reflection upon their competence. The combined forces of judicial *amour-propre* and a need for public confidence in the quality of courts of first instance (coupled with the social cost of appeals) has tended to narrow the scope of the judicial review. Just as the traditional sanctity of a jury verdict is preserved by appeal courts, so the appellate process seldom extends to reversing a finding of fact by a judge, or a legitimate exercise of his discretion. As Barry J. remarked in a powerful judgment in the Full Court of the State of Victoria: 'Certainty and predictability are eminently desirable features in a legal system, and they are not likely to be achieved if an appellate court is astute to substitute its subjective notions of what is just and reasonable for the conclusion of the judge who saw and heard the parties.'[2] Thus appeal courts

[1] Section 4 (1), now replaced by s. 2 (1) (a), Criminal Appeal Act 1968.
[2] *Atkinson* v. *Atkinson* [1969] V.R. 278, 279.

generally (and *a fortiori* the House of Lords, except in a small percentage of Scottish appeals which lie as of right) confine themselves to questions of law. In practice, however, this is not as constricting as it sounds: appeal judges have always retained the power to question *inferences* from ('primary') facts.[1] An appeal court would never question a finding by a trial judge that a machine was unfenced, but it might question his inference that the failure to fence either constituted a breach of statutory duty or caused the accident for which the plaintiff sought damages.

The composition of the court *a quo* is a vital determinant of the structure of the appellate system. The decision of a single judge, unaided or uncorrected by his brethren, ought not to be allowed finality. But what if the trial court itself is a composite body of three or more judges? It is interesting to note that when the International Court of Justice was established, the architects of that court felt that an appeal from a body of fifteen judges was superfluous:[2] and so it would be where questions of law alone are concerned. But when the court of first instance is the judge of both fact and law, a calm review based on the cold formalism of a printed record, unencumbered by emotional reaction at the more personal level of the trial, is called for. A measure of isolation from the dust raised by forensic combat is the hallmark of the appellate court, and this is increasingly important at the higher levels of the appellate hierarchy. So long as due regard is paid to the value of oral testimony heard by the trial court, the appellate court need not fear any adverse consequences of judicial remoteness from litigious contest.

Then, if one appeal, why two? Logically, once fallibility is accorded to the judicial process the only rational ground for restricting the number of appeals lies in the need for finality. But where along the appellate highway should there be a road-block? Experience in other states, as we have seen, seems to disclose a choice between one or two appeals, or—exceptionally—three.

The British system is also, of course, essentially three-tiered. This fact is not explained in terms of a conscious constitutional choice as in France or in the U.S.A.; nor is it a system imposed by a colonizing power. Historically, the basis of the evolution of the British court structure is one of outward growth by delegation and subdelegation of the overriding and centralized judicial powers of the Sovereign. Centuries before Parliament achieved independence of the monarchy in the legislative field, the House of Lords (which gradually became distinct from the medieval King's Council) had gained *de facto* control of the judicial process—albeit subject to varying degrees of royal interference. The only real question of positive constitutional choice arose when the judicial functions of the House of Lords were threatened with extinction during the 1870s. Far from the House of Lords being in any sense imposed

---

[1] See *Benmax* v. *Austin Motor Co. Ltd.* [1955] A.C. 370; also Barry J. in *Atkinson* v. *Atkinson* (above).

[2] See S. Rosenne, *The International Court of Justice*.

upon an existing structure of inferior courts, it was the latter which developed and multiplied as organs administering the justice which emanated originally from the King in Council.

It is in this factor that we find the real clue to the present functions of the House of Lords. The existence of a second appellate court can be defended in terms of the 'social equation' already mentioned, that is to say, the benefits accruing from the provision of detached, rigorous and intellectually sophisticated appellate procedures may be thought to outweigh the 'cost' of protracted litigation. The House of Lords, furthermore, still has a general supervisory role over the judicial process which is analogous to its medieval position as council to the royal 'fountain of justice'. In effect it is the *alter ego* of a sovereign legislature which does not merely hand down statute law but also exercises a considerable measure of control over the manner in which judges interpret and apply that law. (A similar argument could be applied to the common law which can be treated as 'judicial legislation' bearing the tacit approval of the legislature.)

It is perhaps paradoxical that the House of Commons (which petitioned to be relieved of the burden of judicial business in 1400, and, as we have seen, tried unsuccessfully to regain these functions during the seventeenth century) should have gained legislative pre-eminence, while the House of Lords has retained its position at the apex of the judicial system, but is in constant peril of being shorn of what little remains of its legislative power. The separation of judicial and legislative powers has become virtually complete during this century, though the Law Lords remain as a unique, if tenuous link between the two sectors of the Constitution.

It still remains to consider whether two appeals are sufficient. It can be argued that a continuous process of review results in a valuable refinement of legal principle as cases are sifted by increasingly eminent tribunals. There is an element of truth in this, but counter-argument may be founded upon a jurisprudential law of diminishing returns. Each appeal has its price, both to litigant and State: the marginal utility of providing a third appeal would be heavily outweighed by the disadvantages of expensive and protracted litigation.

There can be little doubt, however that a third court of appeal would often reverse the House of Lords: Lord Atkin once remarked extra-judicially that, since all appeal courts allow an average of about one-third of appeals, he saw no reason why this phenomenon should not extend to a court hearing appeals from the House of Lords.[1] This might well be so, but it is a very insubstantial argument for providing a further appeal. The fact that a court allows about one-third of appeals—particularly at these rarified judicial altitudes—simply reflects the truism that judges are decision-makers, and that law itself (not-

---

1 'Appeal in English Law', 1 C.L.J., at p. 9.

withstanding the legalistic ethic of certainty) is very often a matter of personal opinion.[1]

Thus the entire appellate system in Great Britain can be summarized, not so much in terms of a hierarchy of increasing judicial authority, but as a series of concentric spheres of influence. The essence of the problem is 'bulk' versus 'sophistication'. In England the Divisional Courts and the Court of Appeal supervise the work of lower courts which deal with an infinite variety and a huge bulk of litigation, necessarily in a somewhat summary and perfunctory way. Thus these intermediate courts of appeal have relatively large case-loads, and perform an invaluable function in correcting judicial fallibility and bringing an element of consistency to the grass-roots of the judicial process. The House of Lords is at the centre of the system: its small case-load, while in some respects a crippling handicap,[2] includes only the *crème de la crème* of legal conundra (ranging over the entire field of civil and criminal law) which require the most weighty consideration and which have the widest implications in raising issues of general public importance.

Whatever we understand by the word 'appeal', whether we deal with Anglo-Saxon or with Civilian law systems, this hierarchical progression from adjudication of particular litigation to enunciation of general legal principles is a feature common to all the systems we have considered. Anyone contemplating the reform or abolition of the House of Lords should bear in mind the dangers of upsetting the equilibrium of this delicately balanced and highly complex socio-legal mechanism.

[1] An alternative hypothesis which we might call 'the [Parkinsonian] law of one-third reversal' is that subconscious motivation may be at work in producing this seemingly recurrent proportion of successful appeals. A higher percentage (say 50 per cent) would undermine public confidence in the courts *a quo*, while a lower percentage (say 20–25 per cent) would call into question the need for an appellate court. (This is a good illustration of what sociologists call role justification.) We suggest this as a possible line of inquiry for those souls less timorous than ourselves who dare to sound the unplumbed depths of judicial psychology.

[2] See below, pp. 399–400.

IV

JUDICIAL REVIEW AND 'STARE DECISIS'

A DETAILED description of the complex institutional edifice incorporating the House of Lords lies completely outside the terms of reference of the present study, but one aspect of the system does merit detailed examination. At the heart of the British appellate system—or, perhaps, hovering over it—like a 'brooding omnipresence' is *stare decisis*: a doctrine which compels judges to synthesize present decisions (or at least articulate the reasons for such decisions) out of the accumulated wisdom (or folly) of their judicial forebears. Both in England and, to a lesser extent, in Scotland, though only of course in a jurisdictionally anglicized Scotland, *stare decisis* represents the apotheosis of a legalistic ideology which expresses a profound belief that law should be founded upon such values as certainty, consistency, and continuity, a belief that the judicial process is concerned with rule-*following* as opposed to the more arbitrary (and inherently unjudicial) process of rule-*making*. The doctrine of judicial precedent is one of the foundations of the supervisory jurisdiction of the House of Lords, and, indeed, is the very essence of the English common law system.

Sir Carleton Allen[1] distinguishes between two distinctive approaches to judicial decision-making. First, *deductive* decision-making, which he associates with a codified legal system, 'assumes that the legal rule applicable to any particular case is fixed and certain from the beginning of time', and the sole task of the judge is to select the rule or rules applicable to the case in hand. Second, with *inductive* decision-making, which characterises the English judicial process, the judge 'has to search for [his "master principle"] in the learning and dialectic which have been applied to particular facts'. At first sight, these approaches might appear to be irreconcilable, but, as Sir Carleton Allen himself admits, the real difference is merely one of emphasis. English judges rationalize their decisions in terms of the *rationes decidendi* of past decisions: they are, in theory, 'bound' by authorities and statutes—but in practice these can usually be adapted to meet each individual case. Justice according to strict law can be tempered, if not with mercy, at least with common sense. The French judge purports to extract his rules from a code, but in practice, as we saw in the preceding chapter, relies heavily upon *la jurisprudence*—the mass of case law and dicta in which analogous problems have been considered—and upon *la*

---

[1] Allen, *Law in the Making*, 7th ed. (1966), pp. 181–2.

doctrine which consists of authoritative academic commentaries upon the Code. The Cour de Cassation—the supreme judicial tribunal in France—is always loath to depart from principles applied in previous cases.

In both countries the judges have been obliged to accept a compromise between two extreme positions. Complete adherence to the rigorous canons of deductive decision making would inevitably render the law over-inflexible. On the other hand, in terms of what Professor Lon Fuller describes as the 'internal morality'[1] of law, and what Professor Judith Shklar calls 'legalism',[2] both of which attribute basic and definitive characteristics such as 'consistency' to the processes of law, the introduction of any arbitrary element in the form of wide judicial discretion would be to weaken the essentially 'legal' quality of the system.

The compromise has involved a more or less universal (if tacit)[3] acceptance by judges that some degree of judicial legislation is inevitable, and indeed necessary; but that it must always be rationalized in terms of the 'rule-finding' ideology.

The doctrine of precedent has had its virtues trumpeted to the point of tedious repetition. Those appellate judges who, even when free to discard outdated or illogical decisions, indulge in reasoning away the earlier case almost to vanishing point, do no service to the aim of certainty. They dilute the authority of the case distinguished but leave it lingering as an authority binding upon future courts in respect of the part left intact. Legal advisers and their clients are thus left to wade through a morass of case law, only to sink into a quicksand of uncertainty,[4] until, hopefully, the legislature rescues them, the courts having stood by, helpless spectators of the engulfed citizen's struggles. As Mr. Justice Holmes said in a case decided by the U.S. Supreme Court in 1917, 'I recognize without hesitation that judges do and must legislate, but they can do so only interstitially: they are confined from molar to molecular motion. A common law judge could not say, I think the doctrine of consideration a piece of historical nonsense and I shall not enforce it in my court.'[5] Aspiring judicial legislators also face a practical limitation in that each specific case is decided upon a narrow rule and a unique set of facts: parliamentary legislators can pick and choose their subject-matter, judges must confine their creative talents to the case in hand, and in the House of Lords cases in many areas are few and far between.

Medieval English courts were dominated by the forms and procedures relating to 'pleading' a case in court, and bringing the case within one of the

---

[1] Lon L. Fuller, *The Morality of Law*, Chapter 11.

[2] Judith Shklar, *Legalism* (1966).

[3] Sometimes this recognition is more explicit: see for example *Indyka* v. *Indyka* [1969] 1 A.C. 33, 65.

[4] Cf. the remarks of Judge Cuthbert Pound, quoted by Jerome Frank, *Courts on Trial*, p. 283.

[5] *South Pacific Co.* v. *Jensen* 244 U.S. 205 (1917).

existing writs which inflexibly circumscribed the forms of action. The seeds of the modern doctrine of *stare decisis* were sown by Bracton whose *Treatise* (written in the late thirteenth century) included the following passage. 'If anything analogous has happened before, let the case be judged in like manner, since it is a good opportunity for proceeding *a similibus ad similia.*'[1] Bracton himself played a part in facilitating this process by producing the earliest forerunner of modern law reports in the form of a notebook of decided cases garnered from the plea rolls of the courts. As recourse to decided cases became more common, Year Books (essentially students' and practitioners' notes of practical pleading) came into widespread use, and this in turn encouraged the judges to seek analogies in previous cases. In 1454 in *Windham* v. *Felbridge* it was said:

... And, Sir, if this be now adjudged 'no plea', as you vainly contend, it will be a bad example (*mal ensample*) for the young apprentices who are keeping their terms; for they will never be willing to trust their books (*doner credence a lour livres*) if a judgment like this, which has been so many times laid down in their books, is now to be reversed (*ajuge le contrary*).

This reciprocal development of records of the proceedings and the use of precedent continued until, by the sixteenth century, a coherent body of law reports (albeit of widely varying quality) began to be produced, though the emphasis was still upon the niceties of the rules of pleading.

The turning-point in the process was marked by the appearance, at the end of the seventeenth century, of Coke's Reports which served as a model for subsequent series: Coke himself was a powerful exponent of the case for developing a coherent doctrine of precedent. The issue was far from settled however: in 1673 in the case of *Bole* v. *Horton* the reporter remarks that

... if a court give judgment judicially, another court is not bound to give like judgment, unless it thinks that judgment given in another court to be erroneous, he being sworn to judge according to law, that is, in his conscience, ought not to give the like judgment, for that were to wrong every man having a like cause, because another was wronged before ...[2].

This was the beginning of an era dominated largely by a declaratory theory of precedent, a doctrine which held previous decisions to be, at best, evidence of what the established law 'is'. This philosophy, which attracted such eminent disciples as Sir Matthew Hale and Sir William Blackstone, is redolent of the approach of modern Continental judges to the authority of decided cases. Even as late as 1892 the Master of the Rolls, Lord Esher, remarked that, 'judges do not make the law though they frequently have to apply existing law to circumstances as to which it has not previously been authoritatively laid down that such law is applicable.'[3]

---

[1] Quoted in Allen, op. cit., p. 188.   [2] Vaugh. 382.
[3] *Willis* v. *Baddeley* [1892] 2 Q.B. 324, 326.

As Professor Cross remarks, the strict doctrine of precedent 'is the creature of the nineteenth and twentieth centuries. It could only come into being when law reporting had reached its present high standard, when the hierarchy of courts assumed something like its present shape, and when the judicial functions of the House of Lords were placed in the hands of eminent lawyers as they are today.' Even as late as 1869, he points out, 'a judge of first instance seems to have had no compunction in delivering a judgment in which he did no more than say that a decision of the Court of Appeal in Chancery was clearly mistaken and that he must therefore decline to follow it.'[1]

The contemporary position—certainly in England, if not in Scotland—is that the formal doctrine of *stare decisis* is deeply entrenched; but most judges are percipient enough to admit that there are occasions when authorities must be side-stepped in the interests of maintaining some sort of parity between law and the requirements of society, and certainly in those rare instances where an earlier decision was reached *per incuriam* or was based upon a palpable logical fallacy. The judiciary has a vested interest in ensuring that the law does not make too much of an ass of itself by appearing to be stubbornly adhering to past errors.

What is the extent of *stare decisis* in British courts, and how far does the doctrine govern the workings of the House of Lords? In any hierarchical system it is generally true that the decisions of higher courts bind the lower courts unless the decisions are distinguishable. Lower courts, however, regard House of Lords' decisions with particular reverence and application; for even though the binding authority is distinguishable it will often be followed if the case is analogous, so long as it is not erroneously decided.[2]

Two problems remain unsolved. First, what is a 'higher court'? The Court of Appeal is said to be of higher standing than a Divisional Court of the Queen's Bench Division, but would a decision of the Court of Appeal in a civil case be binding upon the Divisional Court in a criminal case? Is a decision of the House of Lords in an English appeal binding upon the Court of Session? To what extent are decisions of the Judicial Committee of the Privy Council binding upon the House of Lords—and vice versa? These are problems arising from decisions of courts of concurrent or collateral jurisdiction, but they are not directly germane to a discussion about the House of Lords, since it has no rival court. Second, to what extent are courts, particularly appellate courts, bound by their *own* previous decisions? This problem has profoundly affected, if not afflicted, the House of Lords in exercising its jurisdiction. The House of Lords in 1861 in *Beamish* v. *Beamish*[3] was invited to reconsider a doctrine laid

---

[1] Cross, *Precedent in English Law*, 2nd ed., p. 20. And see *Collins* v. *Lewis* (1869) L.R. 8 Eq. 78.

[2] *Re House Property and Investment Co. Ltd.* [1954] Ch. 576, 601; *Broome* v. *Cassell & Co. Ltd.* [1971] 2 Q.B. 354.

[3] (1861) 9 H.L. Cas. 274, 338.

down in *R. v. Millis*[1] by a House equally divided in its opinion (the appeal was dismissed on the principle, *semper praesumitur pro negante*).[2] Lord Campbell who had dissented in *R. v. Millis* nevertheless spoke firmly against reversing the decision:

> ... it is my duty to say that your Lordships are bound by this decision as much as if it had been pronounced *nemine dissentiente*, and that the rule of law which your Lordships lay down as the ground of your judgment, sitting judicially, as the last and supreme Court of Appeal for this Empire, must be taken for law until altered by an Act of Parliament agreed to by the Commons and the Crown, as well as by your Lordships. The law laid down as your *ratio decidendi*, being clearly binding on all inferior tribunals, and on all the rest of the Queen's subjects, if it were not considered as equally binding upon your Lordships, this House would be arrogating to itself the right of altering the law and legislating by its own separate authority.[3]

The doctrine in *Beamish* v. *Beamish* was laid down before the statutory rationalization of the position of the House of Lords during the 1870s, and the more recent case of *London Street Tramways* v. *L.C.C.*[4] is generally regarded as laying down the modern rule in the House of Lords: a rule which survived until 1966. In this case, which involved the interpretation of a statute which had been considered by the House four years earlier in a Scottish appeal (and the principle adopted had also been considered by the House in a subsequent English appeal) Lord Halsbury firmly stated that the House was bound by the principles laid down in the previous cases.

> Of course I do not deny that cases of individual hardship may arise, and there may be a current of opinion in the profession that such and such an opinion was erroneous; but what is that occasional interference with what is perhaps abstract justice, as compared with the inconvenience—the disastrous inconvenience—of having each case subject to being reargued and the dealings of mankind rendered doubtful by reason of different decisions, so that in truth and in fact there would be no real final court of appeal.

Writing in the 1962 volume of the *Modern Law Review*,[5] Mr. (now Professor) Gerald Dworkin has documented a number of recent instances in which members of the House have indicated circumstances in which a precedent might be avoided. These include cases where there are two conflicting decisions of the House of Lords and where the previous decision of the House was delivered *per incuriam* (i.e. in ignorance of a previous binding decision of the House of Lords, or of a relevant statutory provision). He also cites more dubious judicial rationalizations to the effect that a previous decision might be ignored if the principle laid down is 'too wide' or (more curiously)

---

[1] (1844) 10 Cl & F. 534.   [2] See Appendix 6, pp. 521–32.

[3] In contrast to this view, see the remark of Lord Cohen at 11 C.L.J. 11 that: 'This House, being a part of Parliament is not in theory so strictly bound by precedent as is the Court of Appeal, though it naturally treats with great respect earlier decisions of its own.'

[4] [1898] A.C. 375.

[5] '*Stare Decisis* in the House of Lords', 25 M.L.R. 163 (1962).

where it conflicts with a 'fundamental principle'. There has, however, never been anything in the House of Lords corresponding to the tariff of exceptions laid down by the Court of Appeal for itself in *Young* v. *Bristol Aeroplane Co.*, which is discussed below.

In a final (as opposed to an intermediate) court of appeal, whose task it is to lay down the guide lines for the development of sound legal principles, there should be no need for the judges to resort to self-deceiving rationalizations to escape the previous errors, or in order to adapt the law to conform to changes in society. This was recognized in the Lord Chancellor's extra-judicial practice statement[1] in the House of Lords in July, 1966, announcing the intention of their Lordships 'to modify their present practice and, while treating former decisions of the House as normally binding, to depart from previous decisions when it appears right to do so'.[2] To place the position of the House of Lords in its proper perspective relative to the hierarchy of courts, it is necessary to review the operation of *stare decisis* throughout the system. We hope, therefore, that the reader will bear with us in the following, necessarily rather lengthy, digression from the principal subject of our study.

Notwithstanding Lord Denning's attempt in *Gallie* v. *Lee*[3] to extend the relaxation of *stare decisis* to previous decisions of the Court of Appeal, that Court is still firmly bound by its own previous decisions. Until 1944 there was some doubt in the matter, and in *Wynne-Finch* v. *Chaytor*[4] the Court had declined to be bound by an earlier decision. Then came the case of *Young* v. *Bristol Aeroplane Co.*[5] in which it was established that the Court of Appeal is bound by its own previous decisions and by decisions of other courts with co-ordinate jurisdiction, such as the Court of Exchequer Chamber. Lord Greene M.R. laid down three exceptions to the rule which he summarized as follows:

(1) The Court is entitled and bound to decide which of two conflicting decisions of its own it will follow. (2) The Court is bound to refuse to follow a decision of its

[1] Set out at Appendix 4, p. 517.

[2] In *Conway* v. *Rimmer* [1968] A.C. 910, their Lordships might be said to have exercised this power, though there was some judicial disagreement whether the authority in question (*Duncan* v. *Cammell, Laird and Co.* [1942] A.C. 624) was being 'departed from' or merely 'distinguished'. In *Beswick* v. *Beswick* [1968] A.C. 58, the House was presented with a golden opportunity to reconsider the long-established, but much criticised, judge-made doctrine of *jus quaesitum tertio*. Instead their Lordships chose to allow the appeal on narrower grounds, and to leave the issue of reform to the Law Commission and to Parliament. In *Owen* v. *Pook* [1970] A.C. 244, of the three Law Lords in favour of allowing the appeal, only Lord Pearce was prepared explicitly to grasp the nettle of overruling the earlier decision in question (*Ricketts* v. *Colquhoun* [1926] A.C. 1). Lords Guest and Wilberforce merely distinguished the two decisions. Their Lordships, when minded to reverse one of their own previous decisions (particularly a recent one) may resort to the device of reconstituting the Appellate Committee into seven or nine Law Lords: *Jones* v. *Secretary of State for Social Services* [1972] 1 All E.R. 145; and *Cassell & Co. Ltd.* v. *Broome* (December 1971).

[3] [1969] 2 Ch. 17.   [4] [1914] 3 K.B. 448.   [5] [1944] K.B. 718.

own which, though not expressly overruled, cannot, in its opinion, stand with a decision of the House of Lords. (3) The Court is not bound to follow a decision of its own if it is satisfied that the decision was given *per incuriam* . . . .[1]

Why should there be one rule for the House of Lords and another for the Court of Appeal? The answer lies partly in finality and partly in the status of the two courts: so long as the House of Lords is retained to supervise 'judicial legislation', and is unencumbered by the burden of previous decisions —or decisions arrived at in a different social context—there is hope that some of this flexibility may permeate downwards through all the lower courts. The alternative would be to extend the use of Parliament as a long-stop for the House of Lords: but on-the-spot first aid is often more satisfactory than belated surgery by an overworked team of surgeons who, with the best will in the world, cannot know everything of the patient's history.[2] The Court of Appeal can expect (and even encourage, by granting leave to appeal) that the malady can receive curative treatment from the Law Lords.

The present position as regards *stare decisis* in English courts is that (to quote Professor Cross) 'every court is bound to follow any case decided by a court above it in the hierarchy, and appellate courts (other than the House of Lords) are bound by their own previous decisions.'[3] There is an exception to this rule in that decisions of Quarter Sessions, acting as an appellate court in summary proceedings, do not bind magistrates' courts in subsequent cases, nor are Quarter Sessions themselves bound by their own previous decisions. (Law reports which are an integral part of a system of *stare decisis* do not normally cover proceedings in courts of inferior jurisdiction—Quarter Sessions, county courts, and magistrates' courts: thus there are no records of their own decisions to enable them to be followed. In contrast to this, proceedings in higher appellate courts are given extensive coverage: some 25 per cent of Court of Appeal decisions and 95 per cent of House of Lords decisions find their way into one of the several series of reports, see pp. 250–1, below.)

A distinction should be drawn (but not overemphasized) between the application of precedent in civil and in criminal proceedings. First, it may be argued that in criminal cases, 'certainty' of outcome should to some extent be subordinated to the need for flexibility in order to achieve a just and sensible result in cases involving the liberty of the subject; although if any branch of the law should be clear and simple it is the criminal law. The law must not be enforced so logically as to arrive at unjust solutions. Second, one of the primary functions of civil law is to enable parties to order their affairs according to well-settled principles of conduct. While criminal law plays some part

---

[1] Exceptions to *stare decisis* in the Court of Appeal are discussed in detail by Cross, op. cit., at pp. 128–37.

[2] Lord Simon of Glaisdale in *Jones* v. *Secretary of State for Social Services* [1972] 1 All E.R. 145, 198, suggests that the House of Lords should possess the power to overrule prospectively a previous decision but so as not to affect necessarily the parties before the court.

[3] Ibid., p. 6.

in establishing behavioural norms, and in defining the penalties which may accompany their violation, it would be inaccurate to suggest that even a small minority of citizens order its affairs in accordance with settled principles of criminal law: the burglar armed with a jemmy and a copy of the Theft Act is a product of the cartoonist's productive imagination. (The nearest we come to a conscious ordering of penal affairs in accordance with statutory criminal law is in the shady area of white collar offences, such as tax evasion.) Third, it might also be argued that public mores in areas of particular concern to the criminal courts[1] are in a constant state of flux, and that this should be reflected by permitting these courts greater flexibility.

In practice, the modern criminal law itself, with its presumption of innocence favouring the accused even at the expense of a few unmerited acquittals, has always been disposed to recognize that hard cases make bad law in an era of rapidly changing social attitudes to crime and morality. On the other hand, the case for greater flexibility is undermined by the need for overt uniformity of approach in the criminal courts: in the minds of many people 'criminal justice' is synonymous with consistency in matters such as sentencing. Paradoxically, the criminal's own demand for a fair deal is one of the most substantial obstacles to increased judicial flexibility.

Bearing in mind these preliminary points, we can summarize the position as regards the application of *stare decisis* to the hierarchy of English courts. The Court of Appeal (Civil Division) is bound to follow its own previous decisions,[2] apart from the exceptions discussed in *Young* v. *Bristol Aeroplane Co.* Unlike a full court of the Court of Appeal in its criminal jurisdiction (when it can and does reverse its own previous decisions) or a plenum of the Court of Session, a full court of the Court of Appeal (Civil Division) is in no special position to overrule decisions of the ordinary divisions of the Court.

In 1966 the Court of Criminal Appeal was superseded by the Court of Appeal as a separate Criminal Division of the Court of Appeal, but for all practical purposes (save the injection of Lords Justices of Appeal into membership of the court) it remains the same tribunal as that set up in 1907, as a successor to the Court for Crown Cases Reserved. Like the latter, the Court of Criminal Appeal made a general practice of following its own previous

---

[1] Viz. the remarks of Lord Simonds in *Shaw* v. *D.P.P.* [1962] A.C. 220, 226, in which he reaffirmed the role of the court as 'the *custos morum* of the people'.

[2] The Master of the Rolls, Lord Denning (never an ardent admirer of *stare decisis*) has other ideas. In *Gallie* v. *Lee* [1969] 2 Ch. 17 he said, in a dissenting judgment, that the Court of Appeal (like the House of Lords) could overrule its own previous decisions. His brethren begged to differ. Nearly a year later, in *Hanning* v. *Maitland (No. 2)* [1970] 1 Q.B. 580, his Lordship elevated his earlier dissentient dictum to the level of unanimous judicial dogma; his brethren did not allude to the question of precedent, but contented themselves with distinguishing the earlier case. In *Broome* v. *Cassell & Co. Ltd.* [1971] 2 Q.B. 354, Lord Denning claimed that the Court of Appeal is not required to follow a decision of the House of Lords reached *per incuriam* (in the sense that the House had not considered an earlier decision of its own which might, before 1966, have been binding on it).

decisions, though examples may be cited where earlier decisions have been overruled by the device of convening a full court of five or seven judges,[1] and there are no unequivocal judicial statements on the point. In general, however, *stare decisis* tends to be applied less rigidly in criminal courts, and the exceptions listed in *Bristol Aeroplane* would certainly apply in the Criminal Division.

A conflict of authority may sometimes arise between a civil and a criminal court. In *Hardie & Lane* v. *Chilton*[2] the Court of Appeal refused to be bound by a decision given two years previously by the Court of Criminal Appeal. Lord Hewart C.J. later said in the Court of Criminal Appeal[3] that the Court would continue to be bound by its own decision until such time as it might be overruled by the House of Lords. A clash of this nature has seldom arisen, but it might well be that the combined civil and criminal jurisdiction of the House of Lords could be the crucial factor in resolving any such dispute.

The third category of superior appellate courts consists of the Divisional Court of the Queen's Bench Division (which has both a civil and a criminal jurisdiction); of the Probate, Divorce, and Admiralty Division; and of the Chancery Division. In *Police Authority for Huddersfield* v. *Watson*,[4] a civil appeal, Lord Goddard C.J. stated that Divisional Courts were bound by their own previous decisions, a practice which has extended, in modern times, to criminal appeals. Divisional Courts are bound by the decisions of the Court of Appeal, probably regardless of whether they come from the Civil or from the Criminal Division.

The Divisional Court of the Queen's Bench Division, led by Lord Goddard, has shown itself anxious to take advantage of the exception clauses prescribed for the Court of Appeal in the *Bristol Aeroplane* case. In *Nicholas* v. *Penny*[5] the Court refused to follow one of its earlier decisions in which two material authorities (also of the Divisional Court) had not been cited. In *R.* v. *Northumberland Rent Tribunal*[6] the Court went one step further and declined to follow a decision of the Court of Appeal inconsistent with earlier House of Lords decisions which had not been cited. A logical extension of the *Bristol Aeroplane* doctrine, one might think; but legal minds would surely boggle at the prospect of (say) a High Court Judge ruling that two decisions of the House of Lords were in conflict and that it was open to him to decide which to follow.

The final class of tribunal to be considered is the single High Court Judge. A judge sitting alone at first instance is bound by the decisions of all superior appellate courts, but not by the decisions of his fellow High Court Judges: the latter are, however, persuasive authorities.

---

[1] e.g. *R.* v. *Norman* [1924] 2 K.B. 315, decided by a court ultimately composed of thirteen judges. See also *R.* v. *Newsome* [1970] 2 Q.B. 711, discussed more fully in Appendix 6.
[2] [1928] 2 K.B. 306.   [3] *R.* v. *Denyer* [1926] 2 K.B. 258.
[4] [1947] K.B. 842.   [5] [1950] 2 K.B. 466.
[6] [1951] 1 K.B. 711. And see *Broome* v. *Cassell & Co. Ltd.* [1971] 2 Q.B. 354 (p. 72, n. 2).

It should be stressed that the 'binding' nature of decisions at any level is only one factor (admittedly an important one) in the development of case law. If a High Court Judge is faced with a relevant decision of (say) the House of Lords, the strict doctrine of precedent should, in theory, compel him to adopt and apply the *ratio decidendi* of that case. In practice, however, things may not be so simple: the authority may overlap, or even conflict with another of equal weight; subsequent dicta of the Court of Appeal may imply that the authority is open to a narrow interpretation; the judge may doubt the relevance of the authority to the circumstances of the present case. In such circumstances what does *stare decisis* really mean? In practice the judge enjoys considerable latitude of approach.[1] Conversely, while the decisions of higher courts are said to be binding upon a judge of first instance, in practice the judgments of the latter are accorded considerable weight in appellate courts as persuasive authority. To admit this degree of flexibility in an outwardly rigid hierarchy, or to lay down a tariff of exceptions on the *Bristol Aeroplane* pattern surely highlights the fact that *stare decisis* is merely the name given to a general principle, a judicial philosophy, which refers to the form rather than to the precise content of the judicial decision-making process. The common law cannot escape from its precedents any more than an individual can deny his own ancestry; but the individual tribunal can, in specific instances, often disregard the more pernicious manifestations of judicial ancestor-worship. It can do this confident in the knowledge that the entire process is supervised and co-ordinated by the House of Lords—a tribunal which has taken a significant psychological, if not profoundly practical, step towards loosening the shackles of judicial precedent.

The history of the doctrine of precedent in Scotland reflects the Civilian ancestry of the Scottish legal system. This gave rise, at least until quite recently, to something resembling a Continental approach to the authority of decided cases, placing reliance upon the law evolved from a sequence of authorities rather than acknowledging the strictly binding character of single precedents. To quote Professor T. B. Smith:

Regard for the rules of *stare decisis* applicable in normal circumstances has crept in imperceptibly; and modern doctrines of precedent seem to be due principally to the influence during the nineteenth century of the appellate jurisdiction of the House of Lords, to improved methods of law reporting, and to the reorganisation of the Court of Session.[2]

The Scottish attitude to precedent is, even today, more flexible than that of the English. Again quoting Professor Smith: '. . . there is nothing to compel the Scottish judges to accept any rule which offends their sense of justice, or which would subject them to servile compliance with recognised errors in

---

[1] See, for example, the approach adopted by Megarry J. in *Cordell* v. *Second Clanfield Properties Ltd.* [1969] 2 Ch. 9.
[2] Smith, *Scotland: the Development of its Laws and Constitution* (1962), p. 34.

policy or interpretation propounded by those who may now—too late—repent of them in the light of fuller understanding.'[1] Even allowing for the emancipation of the modern English judge from the classical declaratory theory of precedent, these words have an alien—even a heretical—ring in English ears.

The structure of Scottish civil courts is centred upon the collegiate Court of Session, which is organized into an Outer House consisting of eight Lords Ordinary who sit singly at first instance, and an Inner House consisting of two divisions, each of four judges. The Lord President presides in the First Division and the Lord Justice-Clerk in the Second Division: there is no formal distinction between the respective jurisdictions of the two Divisions, though in practice most 'chancery' business is handled by the First Division, and the majority of appeals from Sheriff Courts are heard by the Second Division. The Inner House, in addition to an original jurisdiction, hears civil appeals from Sheriff Courts (which, roughly, combine the jurisdictions of English county courts and Quarter Sessions) and from the Outer House. Appeal lies from the Inner House to the House of Lords. In criminal causes no appeal lies to the House of Lords, the final appellate tribunal being the High Court of Justiciary, which consists of the Lord Justice-General (who in the civil jurisdiction is the Lord President) and the Lord Justice-Clerk, plus all other judges of the Court of Session.

It has long been a matter for complaint of Scottish lawyers that the House of Lords has adulterated well-established principles of Scottish law by haphazardly applying English law to Scottish appeals.[2] While the force of this grievance is to some extent weakened by virtue of the presence of two Scottish Law Lords in the House, some Scottish authorities suspect that these anglicized Scots[3] (or judicial Sassenachs?) may themselves be the true culprits.

The doctrine of precedent in Scotland differs from that in England, largely because the underlying philosophies of the two legal systems are historically so very different. This has obliged the House of Lords to keep the two systems of jurisprudence in separate compartments—though even the most rabid Scottish—or English—nationalist would be forced to admit that the two systems have quite a lot to teach one another.

[1] Ibid.

[2] e.g. D. M. Walker, 'Some Characteristics of Scots Law', 18 M.L.R. 321 (1955). This process of adulteration was far more marked during the nineteenth century—see for example *Bartonshill Coal Co.* v. *Reid* (1858) 3 Macq. 266.

[3] Cf. Lord Cockburn's remarks in 1852 objecting to the migration of Scots judges to Westminster: 'The transplanted Scotsman must lose his Scotch [*sic*] law. Nothing oozes out of a man so fast as law.' 11 *Cockburn's Journal* 278 (1874). And as Professor Hunter observed: 'It would be a fascinating pursuit to discover how many false doctrines . . . that is, false so far as the law of Scotland is concerned—have had their origin in that august assembly, i.e. the House of Lords, and also, which is more shameful, how many of these false doctrines have been fathered or preached by peers and Lords of Appeal of Scottish origin who have crossed the Border and found in the metropolis of London their spiritual home.' 6 *Accountants' Magazine* 238 (quoted by Smith, op. cit., p. 88).

As regards *stare decisis*, House of Lords decisions in Scottish appeals bind both the Court of Session and Sheriff Courts: but decisions of the House in English and in Northern Irish appeals are not strictly binding upon the Scottish courts,[1] though where the principle of law involved is comparable as between the two systems decisions of the House are treated as having very strong persuasive authority. It is unlikely, moreover, that the Court of Session would dispute a ruling of the House of Lords in an English appeal on, for example, the interpretation of a statute which had common application in both England and Scotland. As regards the binding quality of previous decisions of the House of Lords itself, there is no ruling of the House relating to Scottish appeals comparable to *London Street Tramways*, and if Scottish practice generally were to be followed, it would seem that the House might have a positive duty to reconsider its previous decisions in Scottish appeals where they seemed inappropriate, or incompatible with established principles. However, the whole position has been rationalized by the Lord Chancellor's practice direction which makes no distinction between the practice of the House in Scottish and in English appeals.

The position within the other Scottish courts is that the collegiate basis of the Court of Session has survived: decisions of each Division of the Inner House bind the other Division and conflicts are resolved and anomalous precedents overruled by convening a full court of seven or sixteen judges (the whole bench of the Court of Session).[2] There is, however, no Scottish equivalent to *Young* v. *Bristol Aeroplane Co.* which would conclusively bind the Court of Session to follow previous decisions of a single judge. A Lord Ordinary cannot bind either his fellow Lords Ordinary or the Sheriff Courts.

The Judicial Committee of the Privy Council is in a curious position in its relationship to other British courts. Conducting its proceedings in London, and manned largely, but not exclusively, by Law Lords, one would expect its pronouncements to carry considerable weight in British courts. On the other hand it is almost exclusively a Commonwealth tribunal (though many Commonwealth countries have taken advantage of their power under the Statute of Westminster to decree that their indigenous appeal courts should be the final court of appeal). Questioning the desirability of a uniform 'Commonwealth common law', Professor Cross remarks: 'For historical reasons Australian and Canadian judges may, *faute de mieux*, have to start their thinking with English law, but there is no obvious merit in their binding themselves to adopt the English solution.'[3] And Australian judges have often displayed a vigorous independence from the influence of English decisions.[4]

---

[1] See, for example, the decision of the House of Lords in *Glasgow Corporation* v. *The Central Land Board* 1956 S.L.T. 41.

[2] See p. 523, n. 1., *infra*.

[3] Cross, op. cit., p. 19.

[4] See for example Dixon C.J. in *Parker* v. The *Queen* (1963) 111 C.L.R. 610, 632.

Decisions of the Board (as the Judicial Committee is often called) are binding upon all courts within its jurisdiction and not just courts of the territory whence the particular appeal came, and are of a strong persuasive authority in British courts. Equally, House of Lords decisions are only of persuasive authority in Commonwealth courts. The unique constitutional position of the Judicial Committee in giving 'advice' rather than judgment militates against a rigid adherence to previous decisions, and several instances exist (even outside the field of constitutional law) where the Board has gone back on earlier advice.[1] On the whole, however, it has shown itself to be loath to reverse earlier decisions.[2]

Another factor which is relevant in this context is the Special Reference procedure provided by section 4 of the Judicial Committee Act 1833. This provides that the Crown may refer any question for the opinion of the Judicial Committee and,

there is no inherent incompetency in ordering a re-hearing of a case already decided, even where a question on property is involved, but such an indulgence will be granted in very exceptional cases only. But expedience (not competency) requires the avoidance of the great public mischief which would arise on any doubt being thrown on the finality of the decisions of the Judicial Committee.[3]

This possibility of their Lordships being commanded to have second thoughts about advice given after inquiry in Council implies a non-adherence to the rigid application of the doctrine of precedent. In *Re Irish Civil Servants*[4] Lord Reading said:

It may well be that the Board would hesitate long before disturbing a solemn decision by a previous Board, which raises an identical or similar issue for determination. But for the proposition that the Board is in all circumstances bound to follow a previous decision, as it were blindfolded, their Lordships are unable to discover an adequate authority.

Lord Reading concluded that it was 'repugnant to good sense' to attribute to the Board as a court of last resort, 'an impotence which would be deplorable'.[5] In *A.G. for Ontario* v. *Canadian Temperance Federation*[6] Lord Simon said 'Their Lordships do not doubt that in tendering humble advice to His Majesty they are not absolutely bound by previous decisions of the Board, as is the House of Lords by its own judgments.' If Lord Simonds's pronouncement in *Bakhshuwen* v. *Bakhshuwen*,[7] that for all practical purposes the doctrine of *stare decisis* is as 'effective in the Privy Council as it is in the House of Lords', were ever the guiding rule, the Lord Chancellor's pronouncement of 1966 serves to allay any fears of a reversion to an orgy of strict precedent-following.

---

[1] e.g. *Gideon Nkambule* v. *R.* [1950] A.C. 379; and *Schaefer* v. *Schuhmann* [1972] 2 W.L.R. 481.

[2] See *Bakhshuwen* v. *Bakhshuwen* [1952] A.C. 1.

[3] *Hebbert* v. *Purchas* (1871) L.R. 3 P.C. 684.   [4] [1929] A.C. 242.

[5] See also the remarks of Lord Porter in *Gideon Nkambule* v. *R.*, above.

[6] [1946] A.C. 193.   [7] [1952] A.C. 1.

Thus these two courts of last resort—an ultimate court of competence, an American cynic once observed of the U.S. Supreme Court—are no longer hidebound by precedent. Mr. Justice Cardozo, an unrelenting advocate of the sensible application of precedent, condemned the 'sterility of ignoble ease' which characterizes judges so enslaved by precedent that they can be compared with those medical practitioners of whom John Stuart Mill said 'would rather the patient died by rule than lived contrary to it'. It is only a weak and unimaginative judge today who would make himself a slave of the past and a despot of the future. The precedent-seekers have had their comfortable prop taken away from them, at least in the House of Lords. Judicial reasoning, not antique decisions, governs pronouncements of the court of last resort. But reasoning can properly look to precedent for guidance, by which legalistic requirements of certainty implicit in any developed jurisprudence cohere.

V

JUDICIAL INDIVIDUALISM

WHILE *stare decisis* epitomizes the legalistic ethos underlying the judicial process, individuality remains the essential characteristic of the English judicial function. Although certainty and uniformity are the desiderata of all legal systems, in any appellate system based upon the interaction of three or more independent judicial minds, the only certainty which arises is the certainty of at least occasional disagreement. Such disagreement may merely be between the trio of appeal judges and the trial judge, in which case reversal of the latter's decision is the sole consequence. But disagreement is fairly common among the appellate judges themselves. It may reveal itself in outright dissent, or be camouflaged by spurious expression of solidarity concealing the doubter's true opinion. There may also be, and often is, concurrence in the result but disagreement on the appropriate legal route to reach it.[1] This practice does little to advance the cause of legal certainty.

The appellate judge in the Anglo-Saxon legal system is not required to submerge his views in the composite judgment of the court; he is free to give full expression to his own reasoning. If he wholeheartedly endorses the presiding judge's reasons for judgment, he will normally deliver a formal concurrence ('I agree and have nothing to add').[2] But there are broadly three other situations in which the appellate judge may find himself. First, he may have lingering doubts but, being prepared to bow to his brethren's greater legal acumen, will capitulate (gracefully or otherwise) and formally concur in the decision. Second, his doubts may amount to outright disagreement, in which case he will wish to stand up and be counted; he will deliver a reasoned dissenting judgment. Third, there is the case where differing legal arguments may lead to the same conclusion; a preference for a line of reasoning other than that adopted by the other judges may impel the delivery of an assenting judgment.

The assenting and dissenting judgment have much in common. A dissenting

---

[1] In *Morris* v. *C. W. Martin & Sons Limited* [1966] 1 Q.B. 716, 730, Lord (then Lord Justice) Diplock explained the more devious route he had taken to arrive at the same destination as the Master of the Rolls, by claiming that the beauty of the English Common Law was that 'it is a maze and not a motorway.'

[2] There is an apocryphal story of the appeal court judge who, in following the presiding judge's judgment, said: 'I agree and have nothing useful to add', to which the third member of the court quickly chirped, 'I agree.'

judgment may very well express agreement with the basic rule of law expressed by the majority but reveal disagreement only in its application to the instant case. An assenting judgment may, on the other hand, disagree fundamentally with the proposition of law, but find the result reached by the majority acceptable on other grounds. In each instance the separate judgment reflects the individual judge's personal attention to the points at issue and thereby provides evidence to the world at large of a proper discharge of his judicial responsibility. In a system dominated by *stare decisis* the dissenting judgment may be cheerfully ignored, though it may sometimes be of academic interest in foreshadowing the course of subsequent legal development. The assenting judgment, on the contrary, commands attention, if only because it is a concurrence in the result. The successful litigant may be happily unconcerned with how the forensic battle was won; but his legal adviser may wistfully seek clear guidelines to future judicial behaviour from the diverse reasoning of assenting judgments. In the battle of independent judicial minds the ultimate loser is that doctrine of legal certainty which is the essence of any rational jurisprudence.

These reflections apply to the final appellate court more than to any intermediate court of appeal where a division of opinion may become submerged more or less quickly in a ruling of the higher court. To most lawyers a final court of appeal achieves its maximum authority as the final arbiter of the law if it speaks loudly and clearly—and with a single voice: hence Continental courts invariably hand down a single reasoned judgment. But if the hallowed individualism of English judges has precluded the imposition of a single judgment system in appeal courts, judicial unanimity as a legal desideratum is not entirely an alien concept; it had its early advocates among the English judiciary.

Lord Mansfield in the great eighteenth-century copyright case of *Millar* v. *Taylor*[1] claimed that the hitherto untarnished unanimity of his court 'gives weight and dispatch to the decisions, certainty to the law and infinite satisfaction to the suitors; and the effect is seen by that immense business which flows from all parts into this channel'. But on this occasion Lord Mansfield was forced to admit the open division among the judges: 'We have all equally tried to convince or be convinced but in vain. We continue to differ. And *who ever is right, each is bound to abide by and deliver that opinion which he has formed upon the fullest examination.*' (Our italics.)

During the first few years of the United States Supreme Court's existence, the justices tended to deliver opinions *seriatim*, the first reported opinion of a justice in 1792 in fact being a dissent delivered in this manner.[2] Though not himself originating the change, Chief Justice Marshall, chief architect of the Court's constitutional role, is generally credited with establishing the rule

---

[1] (1769) 4 Burrows 2303, 2395.
[2] *State of Georgia* v. *Brailsford* 2 Dalles 402, 403 (1792).

that there should be a single opinion of the Court representing the views of the various justices. With few exceptions, this pattern has been maintained, although Mr. Justice Frankfurter, that tireless Anglophile, once prefaced his concurrence by saying: 'I join in the Court's opinion but deem it appropriate to add a few remarks. The volume of the Court's business has long since made impossible the early healthy practice whereby the Justices gave expression to individual opinions.'[1] The Supreme Court now generally avoids separate concurring judgments, if for no better reason than that its case-load precludes the time-consuming practice of handing down multiple opinions which are invariably reserved. But separate (or, more usually, joint) dissenting opinions, which were accepted early in the life of the Court, are still not infrequent features of its judgments.

In English criminal appeals, it has long been regarded as imperative that the discomfiture of the unsuccessful appellant should not be aggravated by an overt division of opinion among the judges. To the criminal, punishment itself is bitter enough, without the salt of a favourable but impotent dissenting judgment being rubbed into the wound. This was recognized in section 1 (5) of the Criminal Appeal Act 1907 which precluded separate judgments in the Court of Criminal Appeal without the leave of the presiding judge. This rule was perpetuated (though with different wording) in the Criminal Appeal Act 1966 which excludes separate judgments, unless the presiding judge considers that it is convenient that separate judgments should be pronounced.[2]

Unanimity by a single composite judgment is not possible under the existing procedure of the House of Lords. When an appeal is concluded and ready to be publicly announced the Appellate Committee has to report to the full House, which on these occasions is simply the Law Lords, who heard argument sitting *qua* the full House of Lords. The presiding Law Lord puts the various questions—'that the report of the Appellate Committee be agreed to', 'that the Order appealed from be reversed (or affirmed)', etc.—to which each Law Lord has a vote, and on that vote the presiding Law Lord declares: 'the contents have it.' The individual judgment of the Law Lord is (in terms of strict

---

[1] *Graves* v. *New York; ex rel. O'Keefe* 306 U.S. 466, 487 (1900). Thomas Jefferson, in particular, had assailed the early practice of the single judgment. He disliked the notion of an opinion arrived at by justices 'huddled up in a conclave, perhaps by a majority of one, delivered as if unanimous, and with the silent acquiescence of lazy or timid associates, by a crafty Chief Judge, who sophisticates the law to his own mind by the turn of his own reasoning'. He thought there should be a rule requiring the judges to announce *seriatim* their opinions in each case; thus each judge would take his position, 'throw himself in every case on God and his country; both will excuse him for error and value him for his honesty'. *Jefferson's Works*, vol. 7, p. 191, letter to Thomas Ritchie, 25 December 1820, and p. 276, letter to William Johnson, 4 March 1823.

[2] S. 2(4): *Commissioners of Customs and Excise* v. *Harz and Power* [1969] 1 A.C. 760, is one of the few cases in the Court of Criminal Appeal involving separate judgments. The majority was upheld unanimously in the House of Lords in two complementary judgments. (See p. 90, n. 1.) The Divisional Court of the Queen's Bench Division (which hears appeals by way of case stated from magistrates' courts) has never excluded separate judgments.

constitutional theory) a 'speech' delivered in the upper chamber of Parliament. Thus in form, the individuality of the Law Lord is preserved, to the point where a submergence of his identity in a composite judgment would be unthinkable, if not constitutionally improper.

Unanimity in the House of Lords' judgments can be sustained in practice only by the individual Law Lords declaring their formal concurrence in the result. There is no means of suppressing either a dissenting or an assenting judgment giving reasons for supporting the unanimous or majority verdict. The assenting judgment is in practice the most common form of judgment, though occasionally there is a single judgment to which all other four Law Lords subscribe without more ado (see Chapter VIII).

Law Lords, however, are familiar with the single-judgment technique since this was the invariable practice of the Judicial Committee of the Privy Council until 1966.[1] As long ago as 1627, by an order of the Privy Council (and continued by the Judicial Committee of the Privy Council, when it was statutorily created in 1833), it was provided: 'When the business is carried according to the most voices, no publication is afterwards to be made by any man, how the particular voices and opinions went.' This effectively stifled both the dissenting and the assenting judgment, although there were a few cases in the middle of the last century when it was published that the Board had not been unanimous.[2]

The theory behind this practice was that, unlike the House of Lords, the Judicial Committee of the Privy Council was advising the Sovereign and that therefore the members of the Judicial Committee had necessarily to give united counsel. This theoretical justification was sustained, even though the Board itself had declared on a number of occasions that it was in everything but form a court of law whose judgments and orders were to be directly obeyed by the courts from whom appeals lay.[3] The Board's judgments (until 1966) have always been unanimous, although there can be no doubt that the seeming unanimity often covered up either actual dissent from the advice given to the Sovereign or basic differences of reasoning among the members of the Board.

Whatever the merits of the notion of the advice to the Crown as a historical reason for the single judgment system, it hardly offers a satisfactory explanation for the continuation of the practice in modern times. The presumption against violating a historical tradition was no doubt reinforced by policy considerations in the heyday of Imperial power which dictated a single clear pronouncement for subject peoples not attuned to the institutions and conventions of their Imperial masters. The historical justification was breached

---

[1] *The Judicial Committee (Dissenting Opinions) Order 1966*. (See Chapter VI.)
[2] e.g., *Sheppard* v. *Bennett* (1870) L.R. 4 P.C. 350, 415.
[3] *British Coal Corporation* v. *The King* [1935] A.C. 500; *Ibralebbe* v. *The Queen* [1964] A.C. 900.

by the principles of the Statute of Westminster 1931, further eroded in 1966 by the allowance of dissenting judgments, and sapped of any logical reason by the retention of the Judicial Committee as the final court of appeal for Singapore (on its secession from the Federation of Malaysia) whose judgments were directly enforceable without advice to the Head of State (as in the case of appeals from Malaysia).

The cloak of anonymity may have given a depersonalized objectivity and certainty to Commonwealth systems of law in their early development. But in the constitutional cases between the wars, resolving the federal problems of Australia and Canada, the individualized approaches of members of the Board percolated through in successive cases. In any event the countries of the Commonwealth, either while they still retained the Judicial Committee of the Privy Council as their final court of appeal, or when they had established their own indigenous final supreme courts, did not adopt the practice of single judgments but left their appellate judges to express their opinions *seriatim*.[1] There seems little point at this twilight stage in the life of the Judicial Committee in suggesting any extensions of the reform permitting dissenting judgments. The present practice of one majority judgment with one single dissent or one joint dissent by two judges will see out the remaining years of the fast-dwindling jurisdiction of this Commonwealth court.

But if there were to be any merger of the House of Lords and the Judicial Committee of the Privy Council,[2] consideration would necessarily have to be given to the form of the delivery of judgments. Since English appeals would dominate the work of the new final court of appeal, the practice of the Law Lords of delivering separate opinions would be likely to prevail for all appeals. But it is worth considering now whether there ought to be any modification of current practice.

The various types of judgment delivered by the House of Lords can be arranged along a continuum. At one end we have the comparatively rare single judgment already discussed. In the middle, and probably the most common category, is the leading judgment which is supported by one or more assenting opinions following similar lines of reasoning—the other member(s) of the court indicating a formal concurrence in the result. Third, there is the judgment which appears on the surface to be unanimous, but which conceals the diversity of routes by which each judge reached the same result: this we shall discuss later in the chapter. Finally, the most apparently poignant judicial tragedy in a legal system founded upon the dramatic conventions of certainty and unanimity, is the formal dissenting judgment.

---

[1] The High Court of Australia started its life in 1901 with the practice of separate opinions. In the first two cases before it there were three separate assenting opinions: *Tasmania* v. *Commonwealth* (1904) 1 C.L.R. 329 and *Deakin* v. *Webb* (1904) 1 C.L.R. 585. See generally, McWhinney, 'Judicial Concurrences and Dissents: a Comparative View of Opinion Writing in Final Appellate Tribunals', 31 Can. B. Rev. 595–625 (1953).

[2] See pp. 411–2 below.

The nature of the processes by which judgments are produced is of great importance in the study of a multi-judge court, but it is in the field of dissenting judgments that the present authors have suffered the greatest pangs of self-restraint, since the endless and fascinating statistical ramifications of this subject require a separate thesis.

The crucial question arising out of dissenting judgments is the nature of the substantive grounds which give rise to a dissent. If (as we shall argue later) a dissent is to be reserved for a really worthwhile legal cause we should ask how far the Law Lords adhere to this maxim in practice. Evaluating the importance of a judgment is not so easy as it sounds, since objective criteria are hard to find: one judge's 'worthy cause' may look to another judge like disgruntlement with the majority view or downright hair-splitting. Dissenting judgments, like those of Lord Atkin in *Liversidge* v. *Anderson*, of Lord Reid in *Shaw* v. *D.P.P.*, of Lord Porter in *Joyce* v *D.P.P.*, of Lord Denning in *London Transport Executive* v. *Betts*, or of Lord Hodson in *Gollins* and in *Williams*, may bear the clear imprint of fundamentalism. But the bulk of dissents fall into a more indeterminate category, defensible in terms of strict legal logic, but achieving only short-term impact in ventilating the dissenter's interpretation of the case in terms of his personal ideology and social perception. In evaluating the importance of any particular dissent we must remember that even a straightforward issue of statutory construction has to be interpreted in the light of the history of the legislation concerned and a particular judge's past reaction to it. A seemingly petty dissent may in fact be an uncontrollable expostulation against a whole line of cases in which the dissenter has hitherto concealed his disagreement.

Dissenting judgments, as a species of judicial activity, have variously been acclaimed and disapproved of, though acclamation has usually been reserved for a specific dissent reflecting the commentator's own views. The most general complaint has been the dissent's debilitating effect on the united judicial front. Lord Mansfield's suggestion that dissents should be very sparingly employed stemmed from a strong fear that disunity on the Bench would keep commercial litigants away from the courts of law. Perhaps the fear of waning public confidence in the judiciary, rather than of the staying-away of the litigating public, still lurks behind the expression of regret so often prefacing a dissenting judgment? But why does a dissenter look upon his disagreement with his brother judges as a misfortune? Is it because he is forced to acknowledge his own inability to convince his brethren, the essence of appellate work being for the judge to influence and lead the court rather than to behave like a book-end, propping up the presiding judge? Or is the professed distaste for a dissent a tacit recognition that separate judgments produce fissiparous law?

Dissent, as we have indicated, signifies a rift in the court's unanimity. The norm is for judges to cohere in decision-making, since the suspicion still lingers that the judicial process involves 'finding' unique principles of law which are somehow 'there' in the accumulated wisdom of the common law; but even though English judges, peculiarly, are from similar social and educational backgrounds, they are imbued as much with intellectual integrity as with the unique judicial ideology which serves to unify attitudes towards the law. Thus where there is conflict, judges tend to prefer sincere dissent to insincere and sullen concurrence. But what are the factors that prompt the abandonment of unanimity?

Our search for the factors which underlie the recurrence of dissenting judgments is, to some extent, an exercise in individual psychology. Any analysis discloses that some judges are more prone to indulge in dissents than others; and it is not always the great judges who are the most frequent dissenters. Mr. Justice Holmes, justifiably dubbed 'The Great Dissenter', in fact dissented much less often than most of his colleagues on the Supreme Court of the United States. Lord Atkin, who might justly be compared with Mr. Justice Holmes, was a sparing dissenter. But when he did dissent, it was with a real sense of purpose: proclaiming his protest at the majority decision, exposing the fallacy in the majority's reasoning and issuing a clarion call to the public of threats to the rule of law. We are disposed to think that Lords Reid, Radcliffe, and Pearce have been more effective dissenters than those of their brethren who have dissented more frequently; but we reserve a more detailed discussion of contemporary dissenters to a later chapter (Chapter VIII).

The strongly cohesive ideology which makes judges adopt a common standpoint cannot be equated with a sheep-like uniformity of approach. It is one thing to say that most judges are actively conservative, in the sense that they see their role in terms of rule-finding, rationalizing deviations from established principles by purporting to 'find' the appropriate rule in an ambiguous series of authorities. It is another thing altogether to say that there is no room for individuality in the particular case.

Individual psychology doubtless plays its part both in the fact of dissent and in the manner of its expression. But it can provide only a clue to answering the question: why dissent? To understand the rationale of dissent entails a review not only of the attitudes of individual judges but also of the nature of judicial decision-making as a whole and particularly the doctrines of *stare decisis*, both in its pristine form and, since 1966, when their Lordships were unshackled from the albatross of their own previous decisions. We do not pause here to reconsider the effect of that doctrine, except to state that the nature of the judicial process impels a judge (who is unwilling to break the fundamental rules governing that process) to stand by precedent. Only the maverick judge will, in the face of clear authority to the contrary, side-step the rules and rationalize his dissenting judgment. It is when judicial authority is not unequivocal that the door is left open to dissent. Indeed it is only then that the truly great dissenter permit such self-indulgence.

Thus there are dissents, and dissents. An outward appearance of unanimity when judges are not really unanimous is incompatible with the vigorous intellectual integrity of those who compose the tribunal and who will continue to sit together on countless future occasions; nor can it foster that degree of confidence which the public looks for in its highest judiciary. If ever the public suspects latent dissent, it will want it brought out into the open, though probably the public is ill-equipped to decipher the nuances of judicial argument since the law does little to foster public awareness of its internal processes. But it is the legal profession, quick to detect the underlying disagreement, which will dictate the public unease.

But does a declared dissent demand a reasoned dissenting judgement? There is merit surely in the unreasoned dissent once uttered by Mr. Justice Jackson of the U.S. Supreme Court: 'I give up. Now I realize what Mark Twain meant when he said "the more you explain it, the more I don't understand".' Judicial confusion was thus avoided without the dissenter acceding to the majority view; but when a dissent is stated in this terse and arrogant form, professional and thus public confidence in judicial certainty can hardly be enhanced.

English judges, used to behaving more decorously towards their brother judges, often indulge in a polite *dubitante*, a useful device which both assuages the judicial conscience and avoids legal disunity by the reasoned dissent. This was a device much favoured by Mr. Justice Holmes.[1] Rarely is judicial controversy brought into the open in England. Personal attacks are

---

[1] In *Richardson* v. *Shaw* 209 U.S. 365, 385 (1908) he said: 'A just deference to the views of my brethren prevents my dissenting from the conclusion reached, although I cannot but feel a lingering doubt', and in *Bernheimer* v. *Conwase* 206 U.S. 516, 535 (1907) he said that 'under the circumstances I shall say no more than that I doubt the result.'

A similar and healthy practice has emerged in the House of Lords in recent years. In *University of Strathclyde* v. *Carnegie Trustees*, 1968 S.C. (H.L.) 27, 47, Lord Wilberforce said, '. . . as the point is one of construction and as the arguments in favour of the limitation to the four old Universities have been clearly and forcefully put in the unanimous judgments of the First Division, now to be overruled, I see no purpose in diluting them by observations of my own. I must however rank myself as *dubitans*.' In *C.I.R.* v. *Carron Co.* 1967 S.C. (H.L.) 47, 61 Lord Upjohn said, '. . . as it is a most difficult and border-line case, depending largely upon the facts, and in the unanimous opinion of your Lordship, of the judges of the First Division and of the Special Commissioners as they may otherwise be described, I shall concur in dismissing this appeal.' In *Pickering* v. *John Tye & Son Ltd.* (unreported) Lord Donovan said, 'I have had some doubts about this case. But your Lordships, with greater experience of these cases than I possess, have reached the conclusion that these omissions are inadequate grounds upon which to reject the Respondent's argument; and in the circumstances I do not feel so firmly attached to my doubts as to press them to the point of dissent. I must therefore concur in the dismissal of the appeal.'

Lord Reid, in *Vandervell Trustees Ltd.* v. *White* (1970) 46 T.C. 341 succumbed to a dour Scottish approach when he prefaced his judgment thus: 'I am under the disadvantage that I am not familiar with the practical operation of the English Rules of Court. Treating the matter as an ordinary question of construction, I would have been inclined to agree with the decision of the Court of Appeal. But if your Lordships think otherwise I am not prepared to dissent on this matter.'

politely concealed, unlike Chief Justice Fuld of the New York Court of Appeals who once wrote: 'It is perfectly apparent that the majority here have failed to read either the record on appeal or the reported decisions.'

There is the apocryphal story of another American judge who cryptically dissented 'for the reasons so ably expressed in the majority opinion'. This is matched by the authentic dissent of Lord (then Lord Justice) Diplock in a case[1] where he sat in the Court of Appeal as the junior Lord Justice of Appeal to the Master of the Rolls and Lord Justice Harman, both of whom favoured allowing an appeal. Lord Justice Diplock laconically added: 'For the reasons given by my brother Harman, I would dismiss this appeal.' Such a terse judicial observation at least has the merit of permitting dissent (and of venting the dissenter's spleen) without producing uncertainty in the principles of law.

The tradition of separate judgments in Anglo-Saxon systems springs, as we have seen, from the historical position of the House of Lords, but they have acquired a justification quite apart from that. Any attempt by misguided but well-meaning reformers to suppress the judicial right to dissent would be met with howls of traditionalist protest, rationalized by claims that dissenting judgments are an aspect of freedom of speech, a doctrine which extends to judges as much as to anyone else.

Indiscriminate encomia of dissenting judgments have been prompted by the assumption that they sharpen the issues before the court, and in the result clarify the majority decision. Sometimes, however, the reverse happens. The technique of some dissenters is to exaggerate the finding of the court beyond the meaning of the majority and then to blast away at the alleged excess. There is then a confusion whether the majority meant what it seemed to say or what the minority said it meant to say. Dissenters would do well to heed the practice which that masterly but sparing dissenter, Mr. Justice Holmes adopted: 'When I am going to dissent I almost always make such adjustments as to bring out discussion *ad idem*—which I think is the decent way, but which is not practiced.'[2]

The eulogizing of dissenting judgments has had the additional effect of endowing them with a spurious aura of importance. Most dissenting judgments have an initial impact; but, with a few exceptions, the attention they receive is short-lived. For an advocate to cite in a later case a dissenting judgment is usually to concede that he is scraping the barrel of judicial authority to support his proposition of law. The active practitioner is concerned with *lege lata* not *lege ferenda*; a dissenting judgment by definition reflects desired rather than declared law; the legal practitioner, if not the lawyer-administrator, pays little heed to a shrill or feeble shriek as to what the law ought to be.[3]

---

[1] *Hughes* v. *Hughes*, 28 April 1966, Bar Library Transcript 117A/1966.

[2] *Holmes–Laski Letters*, vol. 1, p. 240.

[3] See Carson, 'Great Dissenting Opinions', 50 Alb. L.J. 120; 22 Wash. L. Rep. 585 cited by Simpson, 'Dissenting Opinions', 71 *Univ. of Pennsylvania Law Review* p. 205 (1923).

If dissents are designed to induce fellow judges to embrace the dissenter's views, their efforts are usually futile. Once delivered, they have palpably failed to convince the majority on the court. Even with *stare decisis* modified to allow reversal of earlier decisions, the likelihood of early reversal and acceptance of a previous dissent is small indeed. Rarely will the experience of Chief Justice Stone of the U.S. Supreme Court be repeated. His pungent dissent in the *Gobitis case*[1] in 1940 (the first 'flag salute' case) coupled with a barrage of public criticisms of the majority decision[2] brought about the overthrow of the decision within the space of three years in *West Virginia Board of Education* v. *Barnette*. English judges would be likely to echo the strong dissent of Mr. Justice Frankfurter in the *Barnette case*[3] which castigated the majority for their rapid *volte face*. It is such violent switches in judicial opinion that have done much to pitchfork the Supreme Court into the arena of political controversy.[4]

Judges in lower courts bound by the *ratio decidendi* of the majority decision may look fleetingly and enviously at a dissent, but will have largely to ignore it. If designed to induce law-makers outside the judiciary to give statutory force to judicially dissentient views, the efforts may be more successful; more often, however, it is unanimous judgments that the legislature finds most unacceptable,[5] though occasionally Parliament favours the dissenter.[6] Save for the few outstanding exceptions, dissents may be read more or less eagerly by law students but very soon become at best an inert segment of legal literature and at worst as the posturings of vain judges. It was Mr. Justice Holmes himself in a dissent, who stated paradoxically but accurately, that 'it is useless and undesirable, as a rule, to express dissent.'[7]

If the dissent has little direct influence on the law, what part does it or can it play in a modern legal system? While its appeal lies outside practical law, the notable dissent can properly claim the accolade of scholarship, a place in legal history and be regarded as an appeal to reason. The business of judging is an intellectual process and is entitled to be itself so judged. Chief

---

[1] *Minersville School District* v. *Gobitis* 310 U.S. 586 (1940) in which Mr. Justice Frankfurter delivered the court's judgment; Mr. Justice Stone (not then Chief Justice) was the lone dissenter.

[2] See McWhinney, *Comparative Federalism*, p. 612. [3] 319 U.S. 624, 646 (1943).

[4] Moreover, such occurrences as the resignation of Mr. Justice Fortas for 'wheeler-dealing' in private commercial affairs and the threat to impeach Mr. Justice Douglas (which failed) are damaging, to say the least, to the favourable public image of the judiciary.

[5] *D.P.P.* v. *Smith* [1961] A.C. 290, after much public vilification by the legal profession, was reversed by s. 8, Criminal Justice Act 1967.

[6] War Damage Act 1965, enacting the minority views of Lord Radcliffe and Lord Hodson in *Burmah Oil Co. Ltd.* v. *Lord Advocate* [1965] A.C. 75; the dissenting views of Lord Pearce and Lord Donovan in *Myers* v. *D.P.P.* [1965] A.C. 1001 were enacted, although it is fair to say that the majority invited reversal of the decision which they felt bound to give (the appellant's argument availed him nought, since the appeal was dismissed as disclosing no substantial miscarriage of justice).

[7] *Northern Securities Co.* v. *U.S.* 193 U.S. 197, 400 (1904).

Justice Stone, himself a bold and not infrequent dissenter, put it picturesquely in a letter of 1928 to Columbia University. 'A dissent in a court of last resort', he said, 'is an appeal to the brooding spirit of the law, to the intelligence of a future day, when a later decision may possibly correct the error in which the dissenting judge believes the court to have been betrayed.' This sentiment presupposes an issue of more than momentary significance for which a judge should reserve his powers of dissent. It argues strongly for judicial self-restraint. To cry wolf is to invite public apathy for a valid protest, and in the process to debase generally the coinage of dissent. Mr. Justice Brandeis is said to have written a number of dissenting opinions, many of which he never published, preferring to sit silently until there arose an issue compelling a judicial riposte to the majority view.

There are, however, three minor practical advantages to be derived from a dissent. First, judges *a quo* like to feel that there is some support from above for their overturned decision. Public relations are as important within the judiciary as between the judges and the public. A contented trial judge is a better and more confident judge than one who experiences nothing but discouragement from the appellate courts. Second, the losing litigant likes to know that someone would have found for him. Any advocate will testify to the contentment of a litigant who comes away from the forensic foray with the consolation prize of at least one judicial vote, though this can have the converse effect of increasing frustration and encouraging false hopes of success on further appeal—if such exists. Third, it may be important for future policy-making and projected legislation that Government departments should know the strength of a minority view. (See *Home Office* v. *Dorset Yacht Co.*)[1]

The plea then is for a more moderate use of the dissent, not because present practice falls foul of any of the canons of judicial propriety but because legal development can so easily become bogged down in a morass of dissents. Dissenting judgments do not, we think, tarnish the aura of judicial omnipotence; rather (if sparingly used) they enhance respect for honest intellectual differences. In a sophisticated society few can any longer believe in the myth of judicial omnipotence, so that judicial fallibility (*pace* Lord Justice Mackinnon who quipped that the Law Lords represented 'the infallible voices') is better out in the open than concealed, however ingeniously.

It remains for us to consider the value of the dissent before public issuance as a factor in moulding the majority view of the court. Because a dissent goes against the grain of the judicial ethic of unanimity, when it does rear its head it induces caution and care in those of a contrary view. If, as Mr. Justice Holmes enjoined, a proposed dissent is calibrated to the wavelength of the other judges, the issues are both sharpened and neatly exposed, while the real grounds of the majority judgments are pointed up, and the decision

1 [1970] A.C. 1004.

considerably illumined. But these considerations could equally well argue in favour of dissents to be frequently withdrawn before judgment is publicly declared. Having once failed to persuade, the dissenter might as well concede his defeat with as good grace as he can muster.

If the dissenting judgment can for all practical purposes be consigned to the attention of scholars, legal historians, and jurisprudents, the same cannot be said of the reasoned judgment assenting in the result. In a multi-judge court with each individual judgment carrying equal weight, the English lawyer has often to pick his way through as many as five judgments to find the highest common factor binding on lower courts. The very notion of a hierarchy of courts presupposes stronger and usually larger courts at each successive stage. The undoubted benefit accruing from an increasingly authoritative adjudication of litigious issues in a multi-tier system is to some extent offset by the need to interpret a larger number of judgments. It is not uncommon for difficulties to arise in unravelling three assenting judgments in the Court of Appeal; this difficulty is heightened in the House of Lords where five separate judgments are often delivered, added to which, the issues raised in House of Lords appeals are always of a high order of intrinsic complexity. It is not as if assenters complement each other, splitting up the court's decision into two or more distinct parts, although this is sometimes done;[1] they cover usually the same ground, but in overlapping they introduce some line of reasoning not deployed by others and omit reasoning used by one or more of the others. If the judgments are truly complementary and not conflicting no great harm is done.[2] We propose to give just four recent examples of House of Lords appeals which illustrate this problem.

(a) *Ross Smith* v. *Ross Smith* [1963] A.C. 280

The issue argued before seven members of the House of Lords was whether

---

[1] In *Commissioner of Customs & Excise* v. *Harz & Power* [1967] 1 A.C. 760. Lord Reid gave the leading judgment, declaring the answer to a compulsory interrogation inadmissible, while Lord Morris of Borth-y-Gest gave the reasons why it was thought improper to apply the proviso to s. 4, Criminal Appeal Act 1966, which permits upholding a conviction if no substantial miscarriage of justice occurred. The other three Law Lords entered formal concurrences to the complementary judgments.

[2] Lord Reid's prefatory observations on multiple judgments in the Lords in *Gallie* v. *Lee* [1971] A.C. 1004, 1015, strike a not very convincing note of apologia. He said that whenever the Lords were trying to extract principles on which decisions were based 'there are dangers in there being only one speech in this House. Then statements in it [the singular judgment] have often tended to be treated as definitions and it is not the function of a court or of this House to frame definitions: some latitude should be left for future developments. The true *ratio* of a decision generally appears more clearly from a comparison of two or more statements in different words which are intended to supplement each other.'
If the pronouncements by each assenting Law Lord were indeed complementary and not, as so often in the recent past, irreconcilable or at least conflicting, the *ratio* will emerge clearly enough. *Gallie* v. *Lee* is a good example of the emergence from five assenting judgments of a set of flexible principles. But cases, such as we have cited in the text, have not complied with the prerequisite of complementary or even supplementary statements. Nothing but confusion and hence uncertainty has emerged from multiplication of judicial utterances.

an English court had jurisdiction to annul a marriage on the grounds that the marriage had been celebrated in England. By five to one—Lord Merriman died on the day judgment was delivered and his speech was read as part of Lord Hodson's dissent—the House held that there was no jurisdiction in respect of a voidable marriage, in this case wilful refusal to consummate the marriage. The question left open was: did the same rule apply to void marriages? Lord Reid thought that a decision in 1860[1] conferring jurisdiction should be overruled, 'but I shall not pursue that because I understand your Lordships are equally divided on this matter' (it is a little difficult to see how the division was equal). Lord Morton of Henryton agreed entirely with Lord Reid in a formal concurrence read by Lord Reid. Lord Cohen thought that it was too late in the day to reverse the 1860 case. Lord Morris of Borth-y-Gest thought it unnecessary to overrule the case, although he acknowledged the difficulties of supporting it. Lord Hodson, the dissenter on the issue relating to the voidable marriage, not unnaturally thought that the 1860 case was good law, as would have Lord Merriman. Lord Guest thought the 1860 case wrong, but in view of the fact that 'your Lordships are equally divided on the matter' he proceeded to deal only with the voidable marriage. Out of this welter of judicial utterances, what would a House of Lords do today if faced with a case involving jurisdiction of a void marriage? Three would cheerfully have disposed of the 1860 case, enough to be effective if they all sat in a five-judge House of Lords. In the event it took the imperious and elegant judgment of Sir Jocelyn Simon P. (as he then was) in *Padolecchia* v. *Padolecchia*[2] to confound any predictor, by holding that there were valid distinctions between a court accepting jurisdiction over a void marriage on the basis of the ceremony of marriage having been performed in England, and accepting jurisdiction over a voidable marriage on so tenuous a link as the place of the marriage ceremony.

(b) *Rondel* v. *Worsley* [1969] 1 A.C. 191

Barristers were held immune from suit for professional negligence in respect of their work as advocates. Where did advisory work end and advocacy begin, and were solicitor-advocates covered by the special privilege? Lord Upjohn opined that the litigious process began with the letter before action; thereafter the cloak of immunity fell around counsels' shoulders. He clearly would not extend the immunity to non-litigious work, such as tax advising, drafting of commercial contracts, or conveyancing. Lord Pearce disagreed fundamentally: for him the immunity was a blanket one over all the barrister's professional work. Lords Reid and Morris of Borth-y-Gest expressed agree-

---

[1] *Simonin* v. *Mallac* (1860) 2 Sw. & Tr. 67.

[2] [1968] P. 314. Of their Lordship's treatment of *Simonin* v. *Mallac*, the President remarked that 'none of this is, in my view, the language in which the House of Lords overrules a decision.'

ment that paper work was not protected, but they declined to draw any line, though Lord Reid seemed to suggest that the immunity might operate only in or about the courtroom. Lord Pearson thought only that 'it is doubtful whether barristers have any immunity from liability for negligence in doing pure paper-work.' On the immunity of solicitor-advocates, all of their Lordships, with a non-commital expression of view by Lord Pearson, thought that what was sauce for the barrister-gander was sauce for the solicitor-goose. The case confirmed what had always been accepted as the law, namely the barrister's anomalous immunity. But at what price of uncertainty in the precise ambit of the barrister's liability for professional negligence was the confirmation of his limited immunity bought?

(c) *Koufos* v. *C. Czarnikow Ltd.* [1969] 1 A.C. 350

The thorny issue of the remoteness of damage in contract was thrashed out at length. The Law Lords all upheld the rule that a party was entitled to such damages 'as might naturally and usually arise from the breach of contract'. But what did that nebulous phrase cover? A number of formulae were considered without receiving express approval. Some no less indistinct formulae were rejected. All the Law Lords rejected the colloquialism 'on the cards'. 'A serious possibility' and 'a real danger' were generally acceptable. Lord Reid went so far as to quantify the degree of seriousness: a one-in-three chance was not too remote; one-in-fifty was. He personally did not like 'a real danger', on the basis that all dangers are real. 'Liable to result' was another formula kicked around the forensic arena. Lords Morris of Borth-y-Gest and Hodson nodded approval: Lords Reid and Upjohn turned their thumbs down. Where does the law really stand after this inelegant judicial caper with semantics?

It is no doubt good to see the Law Lords ceasing to limit themselves to precise issues and reviewing a branch of law in general terms. But in the multiplicity of judicial utterances the advantage gained by subject-review is almost wholly lost in the lack of uniformity produced by separate minds, as reflected in written judgments. Differences in expression and in reasoning may obscure rather than yield clear new propositions of law.

(d) *Pook* v. *Owen* [1970] A.C. 244

The hapless citizen often has cause to complain that the complexity of modern fiscal legislation sets numerous snares for the unwary taxpayer. While the courts have never regarded it as their duty to iron out the creases in the legislation, there can be no excuse for making confusion worse confounded, particularly fiscal confusion. This case concerned the taxability of certain travelling expenses payable to a doctor in respect of his work in carrying out a part-time hospital appointment. Lord Wilberforce and Lord Pearson agreed with the judges in the Court of Appeal that the expenses payable were a taxable emolument, particularly since the expenses were paid regardless of the actual travelling cost. But five judicial heads (three in the Court of Appeal and two in the Lords) counted for nought; Lords Guest, Pearce and Donovan were in the majority in the Lords, and their view, that these payments were not an emolument, won the day for the taxpayer.

The second point arose from the fact that the appellant had been called upon to pay part of the cost of travel out of his own pocket. Did these payments qualify as admissible deductions from taxable income under Schedule E? To satisfy the statutory criteria for deductability the appellant must have incurred the expenses 'wholly, exclusively and necessarily in the performance of his duties'. As in *Ross Smith*, their Lordships were faced with an authority germane to the point at issue,[1] but unlike its earlier counterpart, the 1968 House of Lords had the power to overrule the previous case if it thought it advantageous to do so. The authority in question had been much criticized, yet only Lord Pearce grasped the nettle and uprooted it: Lords Guest and Wilberforce reached the same result as Lord Pearce, but by the less robust expedient of distinguishing the earlier case. Since Lords Pearson and Donovan dissented from the majority view on this point, the earlier case remains intact, to the detriment of legal rationality, and at the expense of the long-suffering taxpayer and of his legal and financial advisers.

Assenting judgments, by not *ex facie* opposing the majority view, are deceptive. They purport to traverse the same ground using different language and emphasizing this rather than that part of the legal problem posed. They may do no more than give credence to the cult of judicial prolixity;[2] not infrequently they serve only to fudge the areas of real agreement, and sometimes in the interstices of an apparent assent there lurk all the signs of partial dissent without the benefit of the clear hallmark of a dissenting judgment. As such, they are insidious to the two valuable criteria for evaluating the product of a final court of appeal, clarity and certainty in the law. There is, moreover, a real human (judicial) problem with the assenting judgment. A Law Lord may write a judgment first, and having had it circulated may find that it influences his brethren who proceed to follow precisely the same line of reasoning. In the interests of reducing multiplicity a more junior Law Lord may suppress his opinion. This is frustrating enough. To be accused subsequently, by authors such as we, of inactivism is galling. Law Lords must sometimes feel that they can never win. We would applaud the withdrawal of unnecessary assenting judgments, and hope that *amour-propre* is

---

1 *Ricketts* v. *Colquhoun* [1926] A.C. 1.

2 There is the harsh, but justifiable, remark of McWhinney, op. cit., p. 604, that 'the five dreary repetitive Gothic opinions written by the judges of High Court of Australia in the Bank Nationalization case, gain . . . little by comparison with the Privy Council's single opinion in the same case: *Commonwealth of Australia* v. *Bank of New South Wales* [1950] A.C. 235.

not too severely dented. A self-denying ordinance on the part of senior Law Lords in favour of an influential judgment of a junior colleague would provide an answer.

Assenting judgments—like dissents—nevertheless have a part to play in the process. Unlike dissents, they make less pretence to fame as legal historical milestones, although their authors might wish (and often deserve) to have them accredited as pieces of scholarship and perhaps to be more widely cited than other judgments in the case. Again, unlike dissents, they play a vital role in the legal process, for they form an integral part of declared law. Assenting judgments should never be superfluous. To traverse the ground afresh only adds verbiage and may unwittingly confuse: hence the incentive to withdraw an opinion that is merely repetitive. They should be used, but almost as sparingly as a dissent. Where a judge has some special contribution to make to the decision he should readily resort to the device. Mr. Justice van den Heever's judgment in the South African constitutional case, *Harris* v. *Minister of the Interior*[1] in the Appellate Division of the Supreme Court of South Africa, strengthened that Court's hand in its tussle with a government not overfond of the rule of law, by providing an authoritative Roman–Dutch basis for the court's decision, hand in hand with the purely English precedents used by the rest of the court.

To summarize our conclusions: the responsibilities of the House of Lords as the final appellate tribunal would seem to indicate that it could, with distinct advantage, continue to allow the individual Law Lords the right of separate judgments. Dissents present no practical problem; they can be left to the individual judicial conscience to decide if and when they can usefully be employed. If they are over-indulged in, the main sufferer will be the perpetual dissenter; no great harm will come to the legal system.

Multiple judgments concurring (other than formally) in the decision do present a growing obstacle to sound law-making. The compromise formula, if and when the Law Lords are shorn of the incubus of formal attachment to Parliament, is to insist in most cases on one majority judgment which binds all lower courts. Assenting judgments would be permissible, but would have no greater status than a dissent. To the extent that they varied from the majority judgment they would cease to be treated as forming any part of the *rationes decidendi* of the case. In special cases the presiding judge might permit reversion to the judgments of Law Lords being delivered *seriatim*, but this would be exceptional. It should be allowed where the views of the majority were so divergent that a composite judgment would emasculate the varied reasoning.[2]

---

[1] 1952 (4) S.A. 769, 789.

[2] This is a variation on a theme propounded by Lord Diplock in a public lecture at King's College, University of London in November 1969, where he recommended a composite judgment in cases involving statutory construction.

This is more than just an issue of single versus multiple judgments. It is a concern with the nature and content of individual judgments, when actually written and handed down. If one could be sure that more attention was paid by judges themselves to the disadvantages of multiple assenting judgments, there would be less need for reforming the procedure and of limiting the individuality of judges. The crusade should be more against the assenter who brings obscurity to the law than against the dissenter whose quixotic tilt at the windmill of unanimity hardly upsets the legal equilibrium and may even act as a catalyst to subsequent legal reform.

The plea is for an Occam's razor in the judicial field. To translate the philosopher's canon of parsimony into legal language, the law will suffer if the final appellate court does with many judgments what can better be done with few.

VI

THE FORMAL POSITION

THIS study is concerned largely with theories about the working and functioning of the appellate process; yet it would be quite impossible to exclude a substantial element of descriptive material. Indeed, description, in the sense of collecting and recording a mass of related data on the workings of the House of Lords, is the very essence of a study attempting to break new ground. We have, however, tried to go behind the constitutional façade, the formal framework of rules and regulations which circumscribe the functions of the House of Lords, since the overt characteristics of an institution often conceal important latent functions. This concealment is seldom a conscious process: many a researcher has had to face hostility, even ridicule, for attempting to investigate functions of an institution which are not apparent even (or perhaps especially) to those involved in its day-to-day workings. This does not mean, however, that formal rules can be ignored; merely that they must not be regarded as the anatomy of the House of Lords. Here then we set out the relevant rules, both statutory and non-statutory.

The modern position of the House of Lords in its civil jurisdiction is defined in the Appellate Jurisdiction Act 1876, which placed it at the summit of the newly established hierarchy of the Supreme Court judiciary.[1] The Act of 1876[2] provides that an appeal shall lie to the House of Lords from the English Court of Appeal, and from any court in Scotland or Ireland 'from which error or an appeal at or immediately before the commencement of this Act lay to the House of Lords by common law or by statute'.[3] Later sections of the Act prescribe the quorum of peers for judicial business: the House in its judical capacity must include at least three members drawn from three categories of peer, the Lord Chancellor, the Lords of Appeal in Ordinary, and holders and former holders of high judicial office (including ex-Lord Chancellors). Holders of the newly created office of Lord of Appeal in Ordinary were to be appointed from the ranks of those who had held high judicial office for at least fifteen years. Commoners appointed to the office would receive

---

[1] See above, pp. 27–29. The House has, however, never been an integral part of the ordinary network of courts, and, even today, an appellant who is successful in his appeal to the House of Lords must, as a matter of form, go back to the court *a quo* to obtain an enforceable order against the respondent (Rules of the Supreme Court, Order 32, rule 10: see *Barnes* v. *Hampshire County Council (Practice Note)* [1971] 1 W.L.R. 892.).

[2] See Appendix 2.   [3] Section 3.

a life barony, though the right to sit and vote as full members of the House of Lords was to continue only as long as they held office as Lords of Appeal.[1]

Criminal appeals to the House of Lords have a quite separate history. The crucial section of the 1876 Act—section 10—provides: 'An appeal shall not be entertained by the House of Lords without the consent of the Attorney General or other Law Officer of the Crown in any case where proceedings in error or on appeal could not hitherto have been heard in the House of Lords without the fiat or consent of such officer.' As we have seen, the House had hitherto acted as a criminal court only to a very limited extent.[2] English law had never been sympathetic to defiling the sanctity of the jury trial by permitting any appeals in criminal cases, let alone to the House of Lords. In theory, a writ of error (itself a very restricted means of judicial review) could lie from a criminal trial, but this issued only by leave of the Crown, which as prosecutor, was an interested party. The judges of the King's Bench had long been uneasy about this dubious and dangerous tribute to their infallibility, and often took the precaution of reserving important points of law for discussion among their colleagues at Sergeants' Inn: this procedure— only a very limited form of appeal since it was dependent upon the willingness of the trial judge in each case to reserve the point for discussion by his brother judges in banc—was formalized in 1848 by the establishment of the Court for Crown Cases Reserved. But a criminal appeal, in the modern sense, was not introduced until the establishment of the Court of Criminal Appeal in 1907, and even then only in a limited form.[3] At the same time a further appeal was provided to the House of Lords to those fortunate enough to be granted the fiat of the Attorney-General, who is of course the Crown's chief Law Officer and prosecuting counsel.[4]

---

[1] This was amended by s. 2 of the Appellate Jurisdiction Act 1887 which provided that Lords of Appeal should be entitled to sit in the House for life. s. 5 of the same Act included the office of Lord of Appeal in the definition of 'high judicial office': thus retired Lords of Appeal became eligible to participate in judicial business.

[2] See pp. 29 ff, above.   [3] Criminal Appeal Act 1907. See pp. 30–1, above.

[4] Section 1 (6) is reproduced in Appendix 1(iii) below, on p. 433. In practice, this certificate was only rarely granted. There were in fact only twenty-three such cases, of which seven fall within our period of study. The full list is:

R. v. *Ball* [1911] A.C. 47	*Mancini* v. *D.P.P.* [1942] A.C. 1
Leach v. *R.* [1912] A.C. 305	*Stirland* v. *D.P.P.* [1944] A.C. 315
Felstead v. *R.* [1914] A.C. 534	*Joyce* v. *D.P.P.* [1946] A.C. 347
R. v. *Christie* [1914] A.C. 545	*Holmes* v. *D.P.P.* [1946] A.C. 588
Thompson v. *R.* [1918] A.C. 221	*Wicks* v. *D.P.P.* [1947] A.C. 363
D.P.P. v. *Beard* [1920] A.C. 479	*Harris* v. *D.P.P.* [1952] A.C. 694
Crane v. *D.P.P.* [1921] 2 A.C. 299	*Davies* v. *D.P.P.* [1954] A.C. 378
Maxwell v. *D.P.P.* [1935] A.C. 309	*Bedder* v. *D.P.P.* [1954] 1 W.L.R. 1119
Woolmington v. *D.P.P.* [1935] A.C. 462	*Board of Trade* v. *Owen* [1957] A.C. 602
Andrews v. *D.P.P.* [1937] A.C. 576	*D.P.P.* v. *Head* [1959] A.C. 83
Milne v. *Commissioner of Metropolitan Police* [1940] A.C. 1	*Welham* v. *D.P.P.* [1961] A.C. 103
	D.P.P. v. *Smith* [1961] A.C. 290

The position was altered fundamentally by the provisions of the Administration of Justice Act 1960[1] which provided for appeals to the House of Lords both from the Court of Criminal Appeal (since 1966, the Court of Appeal, Criminal Division) and from the Divisional Court of the Queen's Bench Division in its criminal jurisdiction. This has resulted in the House of Lords acquiring a significant criminal jurisdiction. The introduction of appeals from the Divisional Court meant that, for the first time, the supervisory jurisdiction of the House of Lords could permeate directly downwards to the work of the magistrates' courts, which includes the vast bulk of criminal trials. The fiat procedure was abolished and replaced by a requirement that an aspiring appellant must apply to the court *a quo* for a certificate that the case involved a point of law of general public importance. On obtaining the certificate, the applicant must obtain leave to appeal from the court *a quo* or, failing that, ask for leave from the Appeal Committee of the House of Lords. It is not open to the Appeal Committee to entertain an application for leave if the certificate has been refused by the court below,[2] nor can it grant a certificate itself. Even if a certificate is granted in respect of a point of law relating to conviction, there is still no jurisdiction to entertain an appeal on questions of sentence.[3] Criminal cases in Scotland have never been subject to review by the House of Lords, the final criminal appellate court in Scotland being the High Court of Justiciary.

In civil appeals from the courts of England and of Northern Ireland the right of appeal is subject to the important restriction that permission to appeal is a prerequisite to appealing. Section 1 of the Administration of Justice (Appeals) Act 1934 provides that English appellants must first obtain leave to appeal, either from the Court of Appeal or from an Appeal Committee of the House of Lords. Section 1 (2) of the Northern Ireland Act 1962 makes the same provision for appeals from the Court of Appeal in Northern Ireland: section 1 (3) makes the further important qualification that orders stated by statute to be 'final' are not appealable to the House of Lords unless the issue involved is the validity of a statute of the Northern Ireland Parliament. Scottish appellants may proceed to the House of Lords as of right in all final appeals. In Scottish interlocutory appeals,[4] however, the position is more complicated: if the judges of the Inner House of the Court of Session are divided in their opinion, appeal to the House of Lords is as of right;[5] if they are unanimous then the appellant must obtain leave to appeal from the Court

---

[1] See Appendix 2. The statutes relating to criminal appeals have been consolidated in the Criminal Appeal Act 1968.

[2] *Gelberg* v. *Miller* [1961] 1 W.L.R. 459.

[3] *Jones* v. *D.P.P.* [1962] A.C. 635.

[4] Scottish procedure makes considerable use of 'relevancy' (analogous to the demurrer in English law). This is used to test whether a remedy would be available if the facts alleged were proved to be true.

[5] *Argyll* v. *Argyll*, The Times, 10 April 1962.

of Session. In appeals which lie as of right, Standing Order III of the House of Lords requires that all petitions of appeals 'be signed and the reasonableness thereof certified by two counsel'. These restrictions on the right of appeal are examined at length in a later chapter, together with the 'leapfrogging' provisions of the Administration of Justice Act 1969, which permit certain categories of civil appeal from the English and Northern Irish courts to proceed directly to the House of Lords, bypassing the Court of Appeal.

The status and conditions of service of the Law Lords (a generic term, used to refer to all peers qualified to participate in the judicial business of the House) are also defined by statute. The 1876 Act[1] provided in the first instance for the appointment of two (plus a further two, when necessary) Lords of Appeal in Ordinary. Subsequent Appellate Jurisdiction Acts of 1913, 1929, and 1947 raised the maximum to six, seven, and nine respectively. Section 1 (1) of the Administration of Justice Act 1968 raised the maximum to eleven,[2] while section 1 (2) permits this limit to be further increased in future by Order in Council. Pensions and salaries were originally fixed by section 7 of the 1876 Act. The original salary of £6,000 has crept up to its present level of £15,500, with £14,000 for judges of the High Court and of the Court of Appeal: by no means a pittance, but hardly an increase which reflects the inflationary trend and fiscal erosion accelerating over nine decades. Formerly overpaid, even most senior judges are now priced only a little higher than top civil servants, and at considerably less than the chairmen of nationalized industries.

Lords of Appeal in Ordinary fall within the provisions of the Judicial Pensions Act 1959 which came into effect on 17 December of that year. After that date all newly appointed judges (promotion *within* the judicial hierarchy does not count as a new appointment) became subject to a compulsory retirement age of seventy-five and a pension of half salary for service of fifteen years or more; one-quarter salary for five years' service or less, plus one-fortieth for every year of service in excess of five and up to fifteen. Since the Act need only affect judges appointed since the relevant date (those appointed earlier may opt to come under the scheme) it is mainly the next generation of Law Lords who will be affected by these provisions; although a half of the present Law Lords, Lords Wilberforce, Dilhorne, Simon of Glaisdale, Cross of Chelsea and Kilbrandon were appointed since 1959 to their *first* judicial appointments.

There is another area in which statute law has, less directly, affected the functions of the House of Lords. The House of Lords is sometimes accused, and not without justification, of being a rich man's court concerned primarily with the affairs of wealthy individuals and corporations. Until 1960, impecunious litigants might avail themselves of the archaic *in forma pauperis* procedure, whereby, on swearing an affidavit as to their lack of

[1] Sections 6 and 14.   [2] There are ten at the time of writing.

means (and convincing the Appeal Committee that they had a *prima facie* case) litigants might be exempted from the requirements of printing a 'case', from providing security for costs, and from the payment of certain court fees: most important of all, if unsuccessful they did not face the usual order to pay their opponents' costs. In 1960 legal aid was extended to House of Lords appeals and petitions, a reform which has, rather surprisingly, made little difference either to the number or to the distribution of cases heard in the House, a fact to which we shall allude hereafter.

Apart from these statutes, the judicial business of the House of Lords is governed by a formidable list of standing orders.[1] These concern such matters as the form and content of petitions to the House, the court fees payable, the time-limit for lodging both petitions for leave to appeal and the petitions of appeal themselves, procedure for lodging incidental petitions (such as those asking for further time in which to prepare the bound 'case'), and taxation of costs. One provision which merits special mention is Standing Order VI which relates to security for costs. An important deterrent against frivolous appeals (quite apart from the need, in most cases, to obtain leave to appeal) is the provision that all appellants, except those who are legally aided, and those granted exemption by the House (with the consent of the respondent), must lodge the sum of £1,000[2] with the Judicial Office as security for costs. One can only speculate as to how many potential appellants have been halted in their litigious tracks on being confronted with this unpleasant prospect of costly reality.

This outline of the framework of rules reveals only the bare bones of an institution at work. The flesh of the House of Lords is to be found in such factors as the intellectual qualities, biases, and interrelationships of the Law Lords; the relationships between the House of Lords and other legal, political and administrative institutions, plus the climate of politics and public opinion at any given point in time. Acknowledging the importance of these factors is one thing, measuring them is another.

Even the most comprehensive analysis of statistical factors cannot properly convey to a reader unacquainted with the House of Lords how this institution looks when at work as a final court of appeal: one would not attempt to assess a work of art by a scientific analysis of the distribution of colour tones over the surface of the canvas. Such an analysis might be interesting; in some circumstances even valuable—but only as a supplement to a more impressionistic evaluation based upon subjective aesthetics. An analysis of a social institution in these terms is perhaps not as fanciful as it might sound, since social systems may be seen as possessing such aesthetically pleasing characteristics as order, symmetry, and a neat dove-tailing of interdependent functions. While not wishing to pursue this analogy too far, we believe that external appearance is a vital part of our study, since most of the litigants,

[1] Set out in Appendix 3.   [2] This was raised from £700 in 1962.

and probably some of the lawyers, who have dealings with the House of Lords are in a position to perceive its functions only in terms of their superficial first, and sometimes lasting, impressions. We conclude this survey, therefore, with a short description of the House of Lords in action, based upon little more than non-participant observations of its proceedings. (Although one of us has, on a number of occasions, appeared before the institution as advocate).

An illustration of the feudal origins of the House of Lords as an offshoot of the monarch's justice-dispensing Council is found in the fact that all appeals and applications to the House take the form of petitions. Appeal, however, is by the customary method of 'rehearing', a somewhat misleading term since it does not involve a reintroduction of oral evidence. It is in fact based upon a review of the documents in the case, together with the transcripts of the proceedings in the courts *a quo*, supplemented by extensive, and sometimes exhaustive oral arguments by counsel. Parties must collaborate in supplying the House with typed (until 1962 they had to be printed) and bound 'cases' consisting of summaries of the argument to be advanced by each party, the formal petition of appeal, and appendices setting out the judgments below and (unless reported) copies of the principal documents in the case. Oral argument by counsel (occasionally an appellant or respondent, and frequently a petitioner for leave to appeal, may present his case in person) is in theory confined to the points raised in the bound case.

The Appellate Committee normally sits in a Parliamentary Committee room (Committee Room No. 1). The room is large, half-panelled, oblong, with large windows overlooking the Thames. Hanging in the room are three 18th-century tapestries, designed by Boucher for Madame de Pompadour and depicting lighthearted pastoral scenes—a background which some (though not the authors) might feel was ill-suited to such august proceedings. Proceedings are surprisingly relaxed and informal. The Law Lords (usually five for the hearing of an appeal, three for an Appeal Committee) are not robed, as they would be in the lower courts, but wearing ordinary dress (seldom even donning the penguin-like outfit of most barristers). They sit at a semi-circular table, with the presiding judge (the Lord Chancellor, on the relatively rare occasions that he sits, otherwise the senior Lord of Appeal present) in the centre chair. Counsel, robed and wigged (solicitors are not permitted to appear on appeal, though they may be heard on a petition for leave to appeal) address their Lordships from a lectern. When the Court sits in the Chamber, counsel stand at the bar of the House wearing full-bottomed wigs: the Chamber, however, is notoriously ill-suited to forensic proceedings. The advocates are cooped up in a pen below the bar of the House and there is little room for books, still less for human bodies.[1] But

1 On the occasion of the Committee's twenty-first birthday the late Sir Milner Holland Q.C. remarked that 'there is in your Lordships' House that extreme risk to life and limb to which counsel are exposed if they take one step backwards from the Bar.' (See p. 112, n. 3 below.)

wherever the Court is physically sited, the ambience of the proceedings assumes more the air of an academic seminar than the gladiatorial aspects of the normal English forensic process; the rigour of intellectual exactitude imposed by the Law Lords is invariably tempered by an unhurried and amiable audition. Procedure is similar to that adopted by the lower courts: argument is opened by appellant's counsel. In the days (prior to 1934) when all appeals lay as of right, it was not uncommon for hopeless appeals to be dismissed following argument, but today's screening process has all but eliminated *ex tempore* judgments. A more summary fate is reserved for petitions for leave heard by the Appeal Committee[1] which gives no reasons.

Judgments are invariably delivered in a quaint ceremony on the floor of the Chamber of the House at 10.30 in the morning, before the Chamber is used for legislative business, whereby the five Law Lords *qua* the Appellate Committee report back to themselves as the House of Lords proper, and take a 'vote' on the outcome of the appeal. It is in every sense a sitting of the House. The Mace is on the Woolsack and prayers have been read, usually by a bishop, who in all probability is seated on the spiritual side of the House. Prior to 1963 each Law Lord would slowly read his printed opinion (or 'speech') aloud and in full before handing it down to counsel, and in some cases the proceedings took several hours to complete.[2] Now the printed opinions are handed to counsel about an hour before formal judgment is given, and each Law Lord stands up (in order of seniority) and says merely that he would either allow or dismiss the appeal 'for the reasons given in my printed speech'. In some cases each judge will write a fully argued opinion: in others only one or two full opinions will be delivered, the other judges merely indicating formal concurrence.[3] Dissenting judgments are not infrequent; indeed they have become almost common (this is not the case in the Privy Council which, until recently, adhered firmly to the fiction that, since their Lordships were advising the monarch, they should speak with one voice: the decision was

---

[1] See Chapter VII.

[2] In *Ross* v. *Ross Smith* [1963] A.C. 280, a case in which five separate opinions were delivered and a sixth (that of Lord Merriman who had heard argument and prepared a dissenting speech, but died on the morning of the day judgment was delivered) was incorporated into the other dissenting speech delivered by Lord Hodson, the speeches took three and a half hours to deliver. The practice of one Law Lord adopting a deceased Law Lord's prepared opinion appears to have been dropped; see, Lord Donovan's posthumous opinion in *Ealing London Borough Council* v. *Race Relations Board* [1972] 2 W.L.R. 71, 74.

[3] In one recent case, *Onassis* v. *Vergottis* [1968] 2 Ll.R. 403, Lord Wilberforce in formally concurring said that since preparing an opinion of his own he had read the speech of Lord Pearce, and 'with that opinion find myself so broadly in agreement that, this being a case in which the issues are essentially factual, I do not think that any benefit would be delivered from presenting a further discussion of them.' This matter is discussed more fully in Chapters V and VIII.

reached by a simple majority vote which remained unexpressed.)[1] Perhaps United Kingdom litigants were regarded as sufficiently sophisticated (or perhaps phlegmatic) to suffer their marginal defeats to the accompaniment of openly declared votes for and against.

No description of the Law Lords in action is complete without some reference to the Judicial Committee of the Privy Council. Almost every court-sitting day of the legal year at least two and usually three Law Lords are to be found, not at the Palace of Westminster, but in an elegant and spacious room in a building on the corner of Downing Street and Whitehall. They will be sitting there as the Judicial Committee of the Privy Council, mainly to hear appeals from the courts of Commonwealth countries. (Space and time have prevented us carrying out a fully-fledged study of the Judicial Committee in action: it would be necessary in order to gain a complete picture of the work of the House of Lords to consider in detail the distribution of work between the two tribunals.)

The Bagehotian concept of a fusion of the legislative and executive powers of government, epitomized in the modern Cabinet, is something of a cliché in British constitutional theory. More remarkable is the common membership (with only minor and occasional exceptions) of the Appellate Committee, the House of Lords and the Judicial Committee of the Privy Council. Historically the sovereign is the fountain of all justice, and today, in two legal institutions ultimate justice is dispensed, on behalf of Her Majesty's subjects in the United Kingdom by the House of Lords, and on behalf of those in the territories of the Commonwealth by the Judicial Committee. Both sprang from the same source; indeed the entire history of judicial institutions in this country can be traced through the origins of the Privy Council and the remarkable genealogy of its offspring.

The House of Lords itself is a direct descendant the judicial and legislative powers originally vested exclusively in the King in Council. Monarchs quarrelled incessantly with Parliament, and the latter became increasingly assertive of its autonomy from royal influence, and jealous of the prerogatives retained by the Council. As Parliament wrested itself free from the Crown's prerogative power, so its judicial arm was similarly emancipated to fill the role of the court of last resort. But the dependent peoples of the Imperial power still looked to the Sovereign in Council for their remedies, both political and judicial.[2] During the seventeenth century the foundation of the British colonial empire was laid in North America and in the West

---

[1] This means that 'if, for example, two Law Lords dissent from a majority view that the Court of Appeal decision should be reversed, and the Court of Appeal had unanimously upheld the trial judge, then in the result, on a counting of judicial heads, the appeal is allowed by a *minority* of 3:6. This question of minority decisions is discussed more fully in a later chapter.

[2] For the history pre-1833 see Bentwich, *Privy Council Practice*. Also Baldwin, *The King's Council*.

Indies, and the Sovereign's subject peoples began in ever-increasing numbers to present petitions about a multitude of problems affecting their lives. In 1681 an Order in Council provided that certain members of the Privy Council were to deal with any matters concerning the plantations and with appeals from the Channel Islands. The growth of strictly legal problems forced the Imperial Government ultimately to set up by statute a judicial body equipped to handle these cases. The Judicial Committee Act 1833 created the Judicial Committee of the Privy Council to 'report and recommend' on all appeals from decisions of courts in the Sovereign's territories, and it is this Act which principally establishes the jurisdiction of the Court today. If the Judicial Committee's power has ebbed and flowed with the tide of Imperial power, it is still both an important link with those territories from whose courts appeals still lie and is a powerful voice in the jurisprudence of the English common law. Its *raison d'être* is on the wane but the Committee's influence will long outlive its natural life.

The common ancestry of the Judicial Committee and the House of Lords is significant, and their relationship is of fundamental importance. The Judicial Committee is in reality the Commonwealth arm of the House of Lords (though historically it would be more accurate to describe the House of Lords as the domestic arm of the Privy Council). Both tribunals combine 'review' and 'supervisory' functions relative to a plurality of lower courts; both apply the Common Law of England, except that in appeals from some territories the Judicial Committee must apply Roman–Dutch law.[1] (Some Scottish Nationalists might claim that the House of Lords has paid scanter attention to the Civilian system of law in Scottish appeals than have their Lordships in the Judicial Committee hearing appeals from Ceylon or Rhodesia.)

The one distinguishing feature that marks out the work of the Judicial Committee from its counterpart on the home front is the former's involvement with constitutional issues. English lawyers as a rule take a fierce, almost unreasoning pride in an unwritten constitution, and the judges in the Judicial Committee have shown little taste for constitutional instruments, in spite of the fact that more written constitutions for dependent territories achieving degrees of autonomy and finally independence have been written in Whitehall than anywhere else in man's history. Yet decisions on constitutional matters, particularly dealing with the federal structure of government in Australia and Canada, did much to discredit the Judicial Committee. For example, the much criticized decision in 1947 whereby the Banking Act 1947, passed by the Labour Government in Australia, under which private banking in the

---

[1] South Africa (until appeals were abolished in 1950), Rhodesia (see for example *Mapolisa v. R.* [1965] A.C. 840), Ceylon and Guyana (where, as from 1917, Roman-Dutch law was virtually substituted by English law). See, T. B. Smith, Studies Critical and Comparative (1962) pp. xxvii to xxxvii.

various states was to be prohibited, was declared unconstitutional.[1] Few lawyers felt that the Judicial Committee acquitted itself sensibly.

Many Commonwealth countries have welcomed the Olympian aloofness of the Board and its freedom from political pressure. Its decisions in times of acute political controversy have sometimes brought a calming influence to constitutional problems. The decision in *Liyanage* v. *R*.[2] where the assumption by the Ceylon Government of judicial powers (in a Constitution establishing a separation of powers) was recognized, has restored some lost faith in the value of the Judicial Committee to independent Commonwealth countries.

Lack of judicial involvement in the local affairs of geographically remote territories and an unawareness by judges of political realities have their pitfalls. The inept handling of a series of cases in the 1930s concerning the distribution of political power in Canada between the Federal Government in Ottawa and the provincial governments, led directly in 1948 to Canada abolishing all appeals to London. While English lawyers might recoil at the thought of their judges ever being embroiled, like the Justices of the United States Supreme Court, in political issues, disavowal by the Judicial Committee of its politico-legal influence has done much towards stripping it of its jurisdiction. If a denial of its constitutional role has raised the phoenix of a truly Commonwealth court from the ashes of the former judicial tribunal, an acknowledgment that judges can no longer insulate themselves from political issues will help to preserve what is left of the Judicial Committee. Moreover, as there is a growing clamour for a Bill of Rights for the United Kingdom, or even a written Constitution, the House of Lords may well be forced into an even more vital role in government, though one which might be incompatible with its present formal position as part of the legislature. The experience of their Lordships in handling constitutional problems of the Commonwealth may yet provide them with a significant insight into such problems nearer to home.

For these reasons it is not unreasonable to divert some attention to details of composition and powers of the Judicial Committee of the Privy Council.

The main jurisdiction of the modern Judicial Committee is in hearing appeals from Commonwealth courts, though in 1833 (when the Committee was first established) it was given statutory power to determine appeals from Ecclesiastical courts (including matrimonial causes), from the Court of Admiralty, and from the Vice-Admiralty Courts of the Colonies. By later statutes,[3] appeals from the disciplinary boards of the General Medical Council and other similar medical bodies were added.

Apart from appeals from the Commonwealth various oddments of jurisdiction used to be vested in the Judicial Committee. Most of them have been

[1] *Commonwealth of Australia* v. *Bank of New South Wales* [1950] A.C. 235.
[2] [1967] 1 A.C. 259; there was a partial retraction from this realistic interpretation of the Ceylon Constitution in *Kariapper* v. *Wijesinha* [1968] A.C. 717.
[3] The Medical Act 1956; The Dentists Act 1957.

swept away, save that the Committee retains a jurisdiction in certain appeals from English Ecclesiastical Courts,[1] and a mere shadow of its extensive nineteenth-century Admiralty jurisdiction in hearing appeals from Prize Courts throughout the Commonwealth. This seemingly indigestible *potpourri* in practice adds very little to the annual case-load of Commonwealth appeals to the Judicial Committee.

Its composition and jurisdiction are defined mainly in the Judicial Committee Acts 1833 and 1844 which established a Judicial Committee consisting of members of the higher judiciary, and which provided for the making of Orders in Council to extend the Committee's jurisdiction to the hearing of appeals from any British Colony or overseas possession. Although in form the decision is advice to the sovereign,[2] it is judicial in character and directly binds the judges of the courts *a quo*.[3] The *ex-officio* head of the Judicial Committee is the Lord President of the Council, who now never sits; the Lord Chancellor is entitled to sit[4] but seldom does so. The same applies to the Lords Justices of Appeal, retired or while still on the Bench, all of whom are now automatically appointed as Privy Councillors.[5] The nucleus of the Committee is provided by the Lords of Appeal in Ordinary: the introduction of the office of Lord of Appeal by the Appellate Jurisdiction Act 1876 superseded the provision of four paid members of the Committee by the Judicial Committee Act 1871. As in the House of Lords, ex-Lord Chancellors and ex-Lords of Appeal may be asked to sit, and in addition, the Court may contain senior judges and ex-judges of Australia, New Zealand and other independent Commonwealth countries.[6] Finally, the right of bishops to participate in the proceedings of the Committee was abolished in 1876, but they may still sit as assessors in ecclesiastical appeals.

As further acknowledgment of the role of the Committee as a Commonwealth court of appeal, it is interesting to note that counsel from Commonwealth countries can, and frequently do, appear before the Committee. This is particularly so in Australian cases; sometimes in cases from New Zealand and Ceylon and rarely in cases from Malaysia, West Indies or any of the dependent territories.

---

[1] e.g., The Pastoral Measures Act 1968 replaced appeals from schemes formulated under the Union of Benefices Measures 1923–1936.

[2] In the case of Malaysia to the Yang di-Pertuan Agong, the Head of the Federation.

[3] *Ibrallebe* v. *R.* [1964] A.C. 900.   [4] e.g. *Walters* v. *R.* [1969] 2 A.C. 26.

[5] See e.g. Sir Frederic Sellers in *Lopes* v. *Chettiar* [1968] A.C. 887, and in *Osman* v. *Public Prosecutor* [1967] 1 A.C. 233, Sir Charles Russell in *Tan Chye Choo and Others* v. *Chong Kew Moi* [1970] 1 W.L.R. 147.

[6] There has been a conscious attempt in recent years both to extend the membership of Commonwealth judges on the Board and to have them sitting. Some idea of the extent to which Commonwealth judges have sat recently is given by the following (not exhaustive) list of appeals reported in 1967, 1968, 1969, 1970 and 1971 Appeal Cases and Weekly Law Reports:

Since the enactment of the Statute of Westminster there has been a marked contraction of the geographical extent of the jurisdiction of the Judicial Committee as former colonies and dependencies have become increasingly independent both in status and in their attitude to the laws and institutions of the former colonizing power. New Zealand and Australia have opted to retain the appeal, though generally only appeals from the Australian State Courts are permissible. Canada and India opted out in 1949, followed by South Africa and Pakistan in 1950, Cyprus and Ghana in 1960, Tanganyika in 1962, Nigeria and Zanzibar in 1963, and Kenya and Zambia in 1964. The Malaysian legislature recently considered a Bill to exclude appeals in constitutional and in criminal cases.

During the last five years of our study the appeals recorded in the *Civil Judicial Statistics* were 60 (1964), 39 (1965), 34 (1966), 40 (1967), and 37

Jeffs v. *N.Z. Dairy Production & Marketing Board* [1967] 1 A.C. 551 (from New Zealand)—Sir Garfield Barwick C.J. of Australia.

Frazer v. *Walker* [1967] 1 A.C. 569 (from New Zealand)—ditto.

C.I.R. v. *Mutual Investment Ltd.* [1967] 1 A.C. 587 (from Hong Kong)—ditto. (Sir Garfield Barwick delivered the judgment of the Board.)

Lee Kar Choo v. *Lee Lian Choon* [1967] 1 A.C. 602 (from Malaysia)—ditto.

Dharmasena v. *Inspector of Police, Kegalla* [1967] 2 A.C. 330 (from Ceylon)—Sir Hugh Wooding C.J. of Trinidad and Tobago.

Chin Keow v. *Government of Malaysia* [1967] 1 W.L.R. 813 (from Malaysia)—Sir Hugh Wooding, who delivered judgment.

Moller v. *Commissioner of Estate Duty* [1967] 1 W.L.R. 1022 (from Hong Kong)—Sir Hugh Wooding.

Lau Liat Meng v. *Disciplinary Committee* [1968] A.C. 391 (from Singapore)—Sir Hugh Wooding.

Kanayson v. *Rasiah* [1968] A.C. 746 (from Ceylon)—Sir Douglas Menzies, High Court of Australia (who delivered judgment), Sir Alfred North, President of N.Z. Court of Appeal.

Kepong Prospecting Ltd. v. *Schmidt* [1968] A.C. 810 (from Malaysia)—ditto.

Public Prosecutor v. *Oie Hee Koi* [1968] A.C. 829 (from Malaysia)—Sir Douglas Menzies and Sir Garfield Barwick. (*N.B.* Menzies took precedent over Barwick on the Board, although in the High Court of Australia Barwick presides as Chief Justice. In this case Barwick was a joint dissenter with Lord Guest.)

Peiris v. *Appu* [1968] A.C. 869 (from Ceylon)—Sir Alan Taylor, High Court of Australia.

Aik Hoe & Co. Ltd. v. *Superintendent of Lands & Surveys* [1969] 1 A.C. 1 (from Malaysia)—ditto.

Woolworths Ltd. v. *Stirling* [1969] 1 A.C. 113 (from New South Wales)—Sir Alfred North.

More recently Sir Richard Wild, Chief Justice of New Zealand has sat, *Collymore* v. *A.-G.* [1970] A.C. 538, as has Sir Thaddeus McCarthy, a Judge of Appeal in New Zealand. See also:

Borneo Airways Ltd., Kuching v. *C.I.R., Kuching* [1970] A.C. 929 (from Malaysia)—Sir Garfield Barwick.

Sim Lim Investments Ltd. v. *A.-G., Singapore* [1970] A.C. 923 (from Singapore)—ditto.

Williams v. *Govt. of St. Lucia* [1970] A.C. 935 (from St. Lucia)—ditto.

Mangin v. *C.I.R.* [1971] A.C. 739 and *C.I.R.* v. *Europa Oil (N.Z.) Ltd.* [1971] A.C. 760 (from New Zealand)—Sir Frank Kitto.

Irving v. *The Queen* and *Palmer* v. *The Queen* [1971] A.C. 814 (from Jamaica)—Lord Avonside, a judge of the Scottish Court of Session.

I.R.C. v. *Associated Motorists Petrol Co. Ltd.* [1971] A.C. 784 (from New Zealand)—Sir Frank Kitto.

(1968), one-third of which came from Malaysia[1] and Ceylon.[2] Appeals lie to the Judicial Committee from all H.M. Dominions (by virtue of the citizen's right to petition the Sovereign) and from the Channel Islands, the Isle of Man, and the Colonies: also, by virtue of section 1 of the Foreign Jurisdiction Act, 1890, from Protectorates and Protected States. Appeal may lie in some circumstances by right of grant (defined in each case by statute or Order in Council) which applies in practice only to civil appeals. Generally speaking, appeal by right of grant is as of right (in the sense that the court *a quo* must give leave to appeal if certain preliminary conditions are fulfilled)[3] in final appeals, so long as the subject matter in dispute is worth at least a specified sum (usually £500). Alternatively, if the conditions are not fulfilled (for example, if the appeal is interlocutory, or the sum involved is less than the minimum figure, or the application is made out of time) the court below may have discretion to grant leave to appeal if such a course is warranted by the importance of the question involved: security for costs is normally imposed as a condition of leave.

Alternatively, appeal may lie by special leave of the Judicial Committee in instances where the local court has no power to grant leave (generally in criminal cases) or where a court has declined to exercise its power to grant leave. (Leave to appeal *in formâ pauperis* is granted only by the Judicial Committee.) It also applies in cases where an appeal lies directly to the Judicial Committee from a court of first instance, under the provisions of the Judicial Committee Act 1844. The power to grant special leave cannot be restricted or abolished by the legislature of the dependent territory.

It was laid down in *Prince* v. *Gagnon*[4] that special leave will be granted in civil appeals only 'where the case of gravity involving a matter of public interest or some important question of law, or affecting property of considerable amount, or where the case is otherwise of some public importance or of a very substantial character'. (This has been held not to extend to abstract or academic questions, nor to findings of fact.) The power of the Judicial Committee to grant special leave in criminal appeals has been exercised very sparingly: the principles to be applied have been repeatedly re-stated. They were expressed in the following statement in *Arnold* v. *King-Emperor*:[5]

This Committee will not interfere with the course of the criminal law unless there has been such an interference with the elementary rights of an accused as has placed him outside the pale of regular law, or unless, within that pale, there has been such

---

[1] Unique among countries within the ambit of the Judicial Committee, in being a monarchy whose Head of State bears no allegiance to the Crown.
[2] Ceylon abolished appeals at the end of 1971, the last two judgments being handed down on 11 January 1972 at which there was a ceremony to commemorate the ending of the jurisdiction, The Times, 12. i. 1972.
[3] See *Lopes* v. *Chettiar* [1968] A.C. 887, and *Madzimbamuto* v. *Lardner-Burke* [1969] 1 A.C. 645.
[4] (1882) 8 App. Cas. 103, 105.   [5] [1949] A.C. 644.

a violation of the natural principles of justice so demonstrably manifest as to convince their Lordships, first, that the result arrived at was opposite to the result which their Lordships would themselves have reached, and, secondly, that the same result would have been reached by the local tribunal also if the alleged defect or misdirection had been avoided.

This uncompromising statement does not exaggerate the inflexible attitude of the Board towards criminal appeals (although, from time to time, as the result of the changing composition of the Board, the attitude is a little less inflexible). Special leave is granted only in cases of either gross injustice, coupled with manifest procedural irregularity, or misdirection, or a case of exceptional public importance; certainly it is never extended to issues of fact. In cases where special leave is refused, the Judicial Committee could always draw the attention of the Crown to any feature of the case affecting, for example, the exercise of the Royal Prerogative of Mercy.

One important feature of the jurisdiction which has no parallel in British domestic courts is the 'Special Reference' procedure under section 4 of the Judicial Committee Act 1833, which provides that the Crown may refer any question of law (not necessarily arising out of litigation) to the Committee for its opinion. Thus in 1924 the provisions of the 1921 Anglo-Irish Treaty which related to the settlement of the boundary between Northern Ireland and Eire were referred to the Board for decision.[1] In another instance, the Supreme Court of Hong Kong wrongly acquitted certain defendants of piracy, and reference was made to the Committee to define the extent of this crime.[2] (In this case there was no appeal from the acquittal.) A recent instance was the Strauss Parliamentary Privilege case.[3]

Nothing remotely resembling this phenomenon of Special Reference is found in the functions of the House of Lords: but in some respects the procedure is reminiscent of the role of some Continental constitutional courts. It is of particular relevance to our basic assumption that there is a meaningful distinction between the 'private' function of appellate courts in adjudicating in particular litigation and the 'public' function in relation to the development of coherent and socially realistic principles of law by 'judicial legislation'. Only by way of something akin to Special Reference can the two roles be separated: English courts can function only by consideration of specific litigious issues presented to them via an adversary procedure. In Special Reference we have the nearest approach to a pure process of judicial supervision liberated from the litigious process.[4]

---

[1] (1924) Cmd. 2214.   [2] Re *Piracy Jure Gentium* [1934] A.C. 584.
[3] Re *Parliamentary Privilege Act 1770* [1958] A.C. 331; (1958) Cmnd. 431.
[4] A provision in the current Criminal Justice Bill will give the prosecution the power to appeal against an acquittal in certain circumstances if the Attorney-General can be induced to refer the matter to the Court of Appeal, from which court there would be the possibility of a reference to the House of Lords.

Apart from a different venue the outward appearance of the Judicial Committee closely resembles that of the House of Lords. The Committee conducts its proceedings in a room at No. 1 Downing Street, off Whitehall, a singularly appropriate address for the judicial arm of an institution which has so many traditional links with the executive and administrative institutions of government, though such links have little' practical significance in modern times. The room in which the appeals are heard lacks the ornate tapestries of Committee Room No. 1 at Westminster, but is altogether larger and airier, with half-panelled walls; in its simplicity it gains in impressiveness. The provisions for accommodating their Lordships out of court are, however, even less commodious than their very modest accommodation at Westminster, there being no separate rooms for them to work in, although there are a few rooms in which to sit and confer.[1]

As in the Appellate Committee, the judges are neither wigged nor robed. Appeals are heard by three or five judges. For a court of a dependent country three is the norm, but five if an independent country (e.g. Australia, New Zealand, Ceylon), and occasionally five judges sit in other cases where a matter of importance is involved. Five is the almost invariable rule in the Appellate Committee. The same rules of seniority apply in determining the order of precedence on the Bench, with appropriate adjustments to take account of the seniority of any Commonwealth judges who may be sitting.[2]

The Board employs no Appeal Committee to consider applications for leave to appeal; it acts as its own sieve. In both appeals and petitions for leave to appeal, only counsel or litigants are permitted to appear: the right of audience is extended to barristers from the countries in which the litigation originated. As in the House of Lords, a bound 'case' must be submitted by the parties prior to the hearing: again, oral argument is unrestricted in time.

The Board has until recently tendered its advice to the Sovereign in the form of a single judgment concealing any dissenting voice; the judgment is distilled from the collective view of the majority in favour of the decision. The decision is translated into the form of an Order in Council made by the Sovereign in Council, which is then transmitted to the governmental authority responsible for the administration of justice in the territory concerned. The fiction that the judges were simply giving advice to the sovereign was abandoned when dissenting judgments were allowed for the first time by the Judicial Committee (Dissenting Opinion) Order in Council 1966. This did not however, confer any power on the judges to deliver assenting judgments as is the practice in the House of Lords. Hence there is, American-style, a majority judgment;

---

1 One Law Lord successfully applied to be excused from service on the Judicial Committee during a period of heavy extra-judicial public duty on the ground that at Westminster he would at least have access to a telephone.
2 See *Public Prosecutor* v. *Oie Hee Koi*, p. 106, n. 5 above.

and if required, a separate judgment is delivered by one judge, or two judges jointly dissenting.[1] The implications of such a practice are discussed elsewhere (pp. 401–2).

Historically the judicial arm of the House of Lords is the High Court of Parliament: the ultimate repository of royal justice—where the King and his advisers both made and applied rules of law. But the decline of monarchical authority and the growing separation of judicial and legislative power have brought about a metamorphosis of the court of last resort, accelerated by a series of statutes, beginning with the Appellate Jurisdiction Act 1876.

But lawyers as a breed tend to be enamoured of tradition: perhaps the pivotal role of the doctrine of *stare decisis* in English jurisprudence is a constant reminder to judges of the enduring wisdom of their ancestors. And hell knows no fury like a judge who suspects that his most cherished traditions and long-established institutions are being defaced by the scorn of reformers or iconoclasts: this was certainly the reaction of some Law Lords (especially Viscount Simon) to the setting up of the Appellate Committee itself.[2]

In 1948 Parliament was operating under a serious physical handicap. The roof of the Commons Chamber having been demolished by enemy action in

---

[1] There have been fourteen instances of the use of dissenting judgments up to the end of 1971:

National and Grindlay's Bank Ltd. v. *Dharamsh Vallabhji* [1967] 1 A.C. 207—Lord Morris of Borth-y-Gest.

Peate v. *Commissioner of Taxation of the Commonwealth of Australia* [1967] 1 A.C. 308—Lord Donovan.

United Engineering Workers Union v. *Devanayagam* [1968] A.C. 356—Lord Guest and Lord Devlin.

Public Prosecutor v. *Oie Hee Koi* [1968] A.C. 829—Lord Guest and Sir Garfield Barwick. (*N.B.* This was only a nominal dissent since the joint 'dissenters' did not favour the losing party to the appeal, but would have advised the head of the Malaysian Federation that a more stringent order in favour of the successful appellant Government should be made.)

Madzimbamuto v. *Lardner-Burke* [1969] 1 A.C. 645—Lord Pearce.

Dullewe v. *Dullewe* [1969] 2 A.C. 313—Lord Donovan.

Ranaweera v. *Ramachandran* [1970] A.C. 962—Lord Diplock.

McClelland v. *The Commissioner of Taxation for the Commonwealth of Australia* [1971] 1 W.L.R. 191—Lord Pearson, with whom Lord MacDermott concurred.

Mangin v. *C.I.R.* [1971] A.C. 739—Lord Wilberforce.

C.I.R. v. *Europa Oil (N.Z.) Ltd.* [1971] A.C. 760—Lord Donovan and Viscount Dilhorne.

Mutual Life Assurance Ltd. v. *Evatt* [1971] A.C. 793—Lord Reid and Lord Morris of Borth-y-Gest.

Aquilina v. *Depasquale* [1971] A.C. 728—Viscount Dilhorne.

Government of the State of Penang v. *Beng Hong Oon* [1972] 2 W.L.R. 1—Viscount Dilhorne.

Schaefer v. *Schuhmann* [1972] 2 W.L.R. 481—Lord Simon of Glaisdale.

[2] Our history of the Appellate Committee has been gleaned principally from the following sources: 'Appellate Committee' by Patrick Purpoole, 118 N.L.J. 1160 (5 December 1968); 'Appellate Jurisdiction of the House of Lords' by Sir Victor Goodman, *Parliamentary Affairs* vol. 7 (1954); 'The Judicial Jurisdiction of the House of Lords' by Francis Cowper, *Burke's Peerage* (1953) pp. cxxvii ff.

1941, the Lords had graciously relinquished their own Chamber to the Commons and retired to makeshift accommodation in the King's Robing Room. Here judicial proceedings were conducted to the occasional accompaniment of air-raid warnings, and were regularly interrupted on Tuesday and Wednesday afternoons when legislative sittings took place. Until this time legislative business had commenced at 4.30, but now it was moved back to 2.30 because of the blackout, thereby curtailing judicial sittings.

After the war the damage to the Palace of Westminster had to be repaired. Among the building operations which took place was the installation of central heating in a part of the building adjacent to the King's Robing Room. The noise of pile-driving brooked no competition from even the most stentorian advocate. The builders forced the Law Lords to retreat from the Chamber to a committee room: the constitutional split between judicial and legislative functions, which had occurred during the nineteenth century, was translated into a physical division. As Francis Cowper (a distinguished law reporter in the Lords) wrote: 'It is not out of harmony with the temper of English history that the chance location of a building operation should have had such far-reaching effects.'

The change did not come about without much gnashing of judicial teeth. On 11 May 1948[1] the Lord Chancellor, Lord Jowitt, proposed a motion to establish an Appellate Committee, though he did so with a great show of reluctance, and emphasized the temporary nature of the change. His predecessor in office, Lord Simon, was still more uneasy: he feared that the change would mark a departure from the time-honoured role of the final appellate court as an *alter ego* of Parliament. His Lordship was also concerned about the effect on the office of Lord Chancellor: was there not a risk that future Lord Chancellors would concentrate upon their legislative role to the exclusion of their traditional task of presiding in appeals? And would this not subsequently handicap the Lord Chancellor in his task of making judicial appointments by isolating him from the world of counsel and judges, and possibly even lead to the end of the practice of appointing Lord Chancellors from the ranks of eminent barristers? In the event it has turned out that Lord Simon's point was well made. Lord Chancellors rarely sit judicially nowadays, and their contact with leading practitioners at the Bar is accordingly decreased.[2]

The Appellate Committee was duly appointed, and sat for the first time on 26 May 1948.[3] The move was an enduring one. The convenience of having

[1] H.L. Debs. cols. 737–47.
[2] Cf. Lord Gardiner's more recent comments on this matter in H.L. Debs., vol. 302, cols. 469–70, 22 May 1969.
[3] On 26 May 1969 a little-publicized ceremony took place in the Committee Room. At the conclusion of the day's argument on an appeal, the late Sir Milner Holland Q.C. moved the formal congratulations of the Bar on the 'coming of age' of the Appellate Committee and made a brief speech about its history. After expressing their Lordships' appreciation,

judicial business transacted according to a continuous timetable, which was
not subject to legislative sittings of the House, was overwhelming. Moreover,
the constitutionalists could at least content themselves with the knowledge
that the Committee's function was only to hear argument: final decisions are
formally voted upon and speeches handed down in the Chamber of the House
—even if on such occasions the Law Lords on the Committee are the only
members present. Notwithstanding further complaint by Lord Simon,[1] the
Appellate Committee has been reappointed annually since 1948. Even when,
in the middle of 1951, the Lords returned to their former Chamber, the Appellate Committee continued to function.[2] And in November 1960 a further
motion was agreed upon to enable two Appellate Committees to sit simultaneously,[3] a phenomenon which has become increasingly common now
that the number of Lords of Appeal has been increased to ten. It seems clear
that with an ever-increasing pressure of litigation, the Appellate Committee
is here to stay.

No court could operate effectively, if at all, without the support of well-
oiled administrative machinery. In the House of Lords this machinery
is in the hands of the Judicial Office, which, in turn, is a branch of the Office
of the Clerk of the Parliaments: the latter is the Registrar of the Court.
The part played by this small department in ministering to the needs of
the court of last resort cannot be over-emphasized. It is responsible for clerk-
ing arrangements in the Appellate Committee and in the Appeal Committee;
it organizes the considerable volume of paperwork generated by the appellate
process; and, as the repository for all judicial petitions, it acts as a buffer
between Law Lords and litigants, and sometimes even as an *ex-officio* advice
bureau for litigants and petitioners in person. The Judicial Office is also responsible for organizing the lists so as to optimize the smooth flow of business
through the House—though it is the Lord Chancellor's Department which
arranges for individual Law Lords to sit in particular cases.

The staff of the Judicial Office are servants of Parliament: they are not
appointed in the first instance to deal exclusively with judicial business, and
do not necessarily have any previous legal experience or training. Normally
they serve for successive periods in each of the sub-departments of the Clerk
of the Parliaments Office. At the present time the Judicial Office is staffed by
the Principal Clerk,[4] assisted by two clerks, one personal assistant to their

Lord Reid cryptically added: 'Whether this is an occasion for rejoicing, I am not quite sure;
but having come of age, I hope we shall behave accordingly in future.'

[1] See H.L. Debs. vol. 169, cols. 19–25, 1 November 1950. As Patrick Purpoole remarked:
'despite . . . soothing reassurances in 1948 Lord Simon remained recalcitrant and virtually
entered on a grève de zèle. Thereafter he scarcely ever participated in judicial business.'

[2] See H.L. Debs. vol. 174, cols. 21–5, 13 November 1951.

[3] See H.L. Debs. vol. 226, cols. 27–8, 2 November 1960.

[4] The present Principal Clerk is Mr. Richard Cave (a member of the Judicial Office since
1945) whose invaluable assistance we have gatefully acknowledged elsewhere. On 29

Lordships (aided by three typists), three office assistants and one typist. The Principal Clerk is also Taxing Officer of Judicial Costs, in which capacity he is assisted by the House of Lords Accountant.

The administrative arrangements in the Judicial Committee of the Privy Council are entirely separate from those in the House of Lords. Again it is the Lord Chancellor who determines the composition of the Board in each case. Both bodies have equal claims upon the services of the Law Lords, though in practice the latter spend most of their time in the Palace of Westminster since House of Lords appeals are slightly more numerous and take longer to hear than Privy Council cases: moreover, five judge courts are by no means the exclusive rule in the Judicial Committee, as they are in the Lords.

The Law Lords themselves share one personal assistant and have the services of one full-time and one part-time typist: these staffing arrangements seem quite adequate to serve their needs. Their Lordships do not even employ individual clerks to organize their personal business as do judges of the High Court and the Court of Appeal, a fact which probably reflects the leisurely (but by comparison with courts abroad, speedy) and predictable timetable of judicial business in the House of Lords. Certainly the Law Lords do not have the services of 'law clerks' to assist with judgment-drafting and research, as do the Associate Justices of the United States Supreme Court.

The Law Lords are victims of the notorious accommodation problem which afflicts nearly all occupants of the Palace of Westminster. We are told that since their numbers were increased to ten, only five Lords of Appeal retain separate rooms on one floor in a corridor off the Peers' Lobby, while the other five occupy rooms on two floors above.[1] The phrase 'judicial hierarchy' thus assumes a novel and unexpected connotation.

November 1963 the Solicitors' Journal paid cryptic tribute to the Judicial Office and to its Principal Clerk by remarking: 'To those who work on the outer circumference of its approaches, the oracular pronouncements which spasmodically emerge from that cave of mystery, the Judicial Department of the House of Lords, always provide material for interesting meditations.'

[1] After October 1972 all the Law Lords will be accommodated in the new State Officers' Court block which will form part of the newly constructed administrative wing of the Palace of Westminster.

PART B

LAW LORDS IN ACTION
1952–1968

VII

THE RIGHT OF APPEAL

To devote an entire chapter—and a long one at that—to the litigant's right of appeal to the House of Lords might appear to be overemphasizing the importance of, what is, at best, a fringe issue. But the question of the right of appeal is anything but peripheral: indeed it is central to the problem with which the present study is concerned—the function of a second-tier appellate court.

The arguments against retention of the House of Lords as a final court of appeal can be reduced to two essential elements. First, the extra burden, both financial and psychological, which must be borne by litigants, and particularly (since the loser generally pays all the costs) by unsuccessful parties, in the Lords. And, second the danger of duplication, not merely of the functions of the courts *a quo* but also of Parliament and of the agencies of law reform.

Neither of these arguments can be dismissed by appealing to rationality or empiricism since, in the last analysis, they turn solely on one's highly subjective ideas about the rationale of the judicial process: they also involve the imponderable moral question: how far the individual litigant is or should be a pawn in the cause of socio-legal development. If, however, it can be shown that

(a) trivial litigation is effectively siphoned off, at least before the second-appellate stage;
(b) bona fide litigants are not excluded from the Court solely on the grounds of impecuniosity; and
(c) the machinery, whereby appeals from the Court of Appeal are sifted before being granted a hearing in the House, is working smoothly and with minimum wastage of judicial time;

then clearly the arguments put forward by the abolitionists tend to lose much of their force.

Inherent in litigation is the fact that each case produces at least one defeated (although not necessarily disgruntled) party. But in practice very few litigants go to the trouble and expense of appealing, even to the appropriate first-tier court of appeal. In 1968, for example, more than a million and three-quarter civil actions were started in England and Wales—the vast bulk of these being in county courts.[1] In contrast to this figure, only 679 appeals were heard by

1 *Civil Judicial Statistics* 1968.

the Court of Appeal and 391 by the appellate divisions of the High Court.[1] In other words, only 0·06 per cent of actions climb even to the first rung of the appellate hierarchy, and the percentage of cases which go to the House of Lords is even smaller. In 1968 only thirty-five appeals were heard by the House of Lords—twenty-five of them coming from the English Court of Appeal.

The primary reason for the relatively small number of appeals is simply that the vast majority of actions never come to trial,[2] with the result that, in most cases, there is no judgment or order from which to appeal. The subsidiary reason is that, even if the action is one of those rare cases which actually reaches trial, many defeated litigants feel (or are advised) that an appeal would be hopeless, or that the very small chance of getting the trial decision reversed would not justify the high cost of an appeal. Closely allied to this is the fact that Legal Aid Local and Area Committees, while prepared to finance a litigant in bringing or defending an action, are not empowered to allocate public funds to an appeal which is likely to be nothing more than an endorsement of the trial verdict.[3] A third factor which serves to restrict both the number and the character of appeals is that, in many types of case, appellate courts are not automatically open to every litigant who wishes to have his case reviewed. For example, if a litigant wishes to appeal to the Court of Appeal in an interlocutory matter, he must first obtain leave either from the court below or from the Court of Appeal; the leave of the Court of Appeal is also required for the hearing of an appeal which is lodged outside the time limit specified in the Rules of the Supreme Court. It should be emphasized, however, that generally civil appeals to the Court of Appeal lie as of right; but a very different situation exists *vis-à-vis* the House of Lords. Since 1934 it has been necessary for an aspiring appellant to obtain leave to appeal, either from the Court of Appeal or, failing that, from the House of Lords itself.

We have already argued that, among the various species of judicial institution, the House of Lords is a court apart. Over and above its role as a tribunal of review, it performs the vital task of supervising the process of judicial law-making which is such an integral part of our common law system. An analogy between the House of Lords and the U.S. Supreme Court is in many respects a misleading one since, apart from numerous procedural differences and a substantially different approach to the doctrine of *stare decisis,* the latter institution, operating in a federal system, has a function totally alien to our unitary system of government. However, Mr. Justice

---

[1] Ibid.

[2] Of about 1½ million actions commenced in county courts in 1968, only about 140,000 got as far as being tried or heard by a judge or a registrar.

[3] In 1968 only 1,066 of 132,686 legally-aided persons were receiving legal aid in respect of appellate proceedings, though in proportionate terms this reflects the relatively very small number of cases which reach appellate courts.

Frankfurter's words[1] concerning the right of appeal to the Supreme Court apply with equal force, in principle at least, to the House of Lords:

... the judgments of this Court are collective judgments.[2] Such judgments presuppose ample time and freshness of mind for private study and reflection in preparation for discussion at conference. Without adequate study there cannot be adequate reflection; without adequate reflection there cannot be adequate discussion; without adequate discussion there cannot be that fruitful interchange of minds which is indispensable to thoughtful unhurried decision and its formulation in learned and impressive decisions. It is, therefore, imperative that the docket [i.e. list of cases for hearing] be kept down so that its volume does not preclude wide adjudication. This can be avoided only if the Court rigorously excludes any case from coming here that does not rise to the significance of inevitability in meeting the responsibilities vested in this Court.

What is the situation with regard to appeals to the U.S. Supreme Court (always recognizing the federal and constitutional nature of that court)? At one time most of the appeals heard by the Supreme Court came to it as of right, but by various enactments[3] the types of appeal which fall into this category have been restricted. An unrestricted right of appeal applies today only to cases from Federal courts of appeal and from state courts of appeal which involve the constitutionality of a state or Federal statute, or where the lower court's decision has infringed a statute or U.S. treaty. And even in these cases a claim that the appeal lies as of right is carefully scrutinized by the Court. In all other cases, an aspiring appellant must file a petition for *certiorari*, and the petition is considered by the full Court in private conference; if at least four of the nine judges are in favour of granting *certiorari* then the petition is granted.

The position of the House of Lords is far from being identical with that of the U.S. Supreme Court. There is, however, an essential similarity of status, and of role in articulating social demands via the judicial process. At least the dignity, if not the efficiency of the two bodies would be immeasurably impaired if they were to be constantly beleagured by appeals of little or no social or legal significance. But, whereas there is always a danger of the U.S.

---

[1] *Dick* v. *New York Life Insurance Co.*, 359 U.S. 437, 458–9 (1959).

[2] It would certainly not be correct to suggest that House of Lords judgments are 'collective' in quite the same sense as those of the U.S. Supreme Court. The latter reaches tentative decisions at formal conference of the full Court, and one judge is given the task of writing the judgment of the Court; dissenting opinions (if there are any) may or may not be written jointly, but in any event an individual judge is always at liberty simply to concur in a dissenting opinion. The judgment of the court will attempt to amalgamate the views of the judges on whose behalf it is being written, although, again, there is nothing to prevent other judges writing individual opinions. In the House of Lords the procedure is more individualistic. There is no formal conference as such, but there is much prior consultation before opinions are finalized. Very often, only one or two of the Law Lords deliver full opinions, the others being content to deliver formal concurrence with one or more of their brethren. (See Chapter V, above.)

[3] Culminating in the Judicature Act 1925.

Supreme Court being inundated with appeals,[1] the House of Lords has hither-to been, if anything, supplied with too few. Bearing in mind what has been said about the creative functions of the House of Lords in the British judicial system, we shall now consider the ways in which the number (and character) of appeals constituting its case-load are kept within manageable proportions.

In 1933 the Business of Courts Committee under the chairmanship of Lord Hanworth, Master of the Rolls, produced a second Interim Report[2] which con-tained the following proposal on appeals to the House of Lords:

> With regard to appeals from the Court of Appeal to the House of Lords, we are of opinion that such appeals should in no case lie as of right. At present save for some cases in bankruptcy in which the right of appeal is either non-existent or is only with the leave of the Court of Appeal (see Bankruptcy Act 1914, section 108 (2) (b)), appeals to the House of Lords are as of right.
>
> In our opinion restrictions should be imposed on all appeals from the Court of Appeal to the House of Lords. There should be an appeal only with the leave of the Court of Appeal or if refused there, of the House of Lords. Probably this latter leave could be applied for to, and granted by, the Appeal Committee of the House of Lords and any great expense avoided.
>
> We also think that both the Court of Appeal and the House of Lords, when giving leave to appeal, should be empowered to impose conditions on the appellant.[3]

The Appellate Jurisdiction Act 1876, the relevant Act then in force, placed no explicit restriction on the right of appeal from the courts specified in the Act. Subject to any subsequent statutory exception or to any procedural rule laid down by the House, the litigant's right of appeal to the House of Lords prior to 1876 remained unimpaired. However, the Standing Orders[4] of the House as regards appeals had always been (and are to this day) stringent. For example, since 1876 there has been a time limit for the lodging of peti-tions of appeal. And, in respect of Scottish appeals only, a provision that petitions of appeal (except where leave is required) must be certified as reason-able by two counsel (S.O. X). There have been rules requiring that an ap-pellant must lodge a substantial sum of money (increased from £700 to £1,000 in 1962) as security for costs,[5] unless the respondent gives his consent to the rule being waived. Other Standing Orders have been drawn up to regulate the procedure for the lodging of the printed cases and for the taxation of costs.

These and other regulations, particularly those requiring the signatures of counsel in Scottish appeals and security for costs, helped to keep the number

---

[1] Recently the Chief Justice, Mr. Warren Burger, warned that there was a danger of the Supreme Court becoming swamped by a deluge of appeals; *The Guardian*, 7 December 1970.

[2] December 1933, Cmd. 4471.

[3] See p. 131, n. 2 below. The Act of 1934 had nothing to say about conditions.

[4] The Standing Orders are set out at Appendix 3.

[5] One recent appeal where the condition was waived was *Rondel* v. *Worsley* [1969] 1 A.C. 191; see *R.* v. *Legal Aid Committee No.* 1 (*London*) *Legal Aid area, Ex parte Rondel* [1967] 2 Q.B. 482, 492–3.

of appeals within reasonable bounds; yet there remained an anxiety about the number and appropriateness of appeals. This anxiety was part of a more general concern about the structure of the courts in England since, apart from minor, piecemeal reforms, the judicial system in the early 1930s had changed little since the Judicature Act of 1875. The reforms of the 1870s had introduced an element of order where before there was chaos—but innovations which had so beneficially transformed the situation in the late nineteenth century now needed refurbishing to meet the increasing pressures of twentieth-century litigation.

The Government's response to the problem was to appoint the Hanworth Committee to consider the vast field of the 'Business of Court': the terms of reference of the Committee were, *inter alia*, to find ways of effecting a speedier and more economical despatch of business in the Supreme Court. One of the suggestions for achieving this was, to quote the terms of reference, '. . . by the elimination or restriction of the right of appeal to, within, or from the Supreme Court'.

The Committee devoted considerable time to considering the anomalous situation whereby a county court action involving only £25 could go first to the Divisional Court, thence with leave to the Court of Appeal, and thence by right to the House of Lords.[1] It also considered the right of appeal to the House of Lords. And in June 1934 the Administration of Justice (Appeals) Bill, based upon the Committee's report, was introduced into the House of Lords.[2] Introducing the Bill the Lord Chancellor (Viscount Sankey) commented upon the widespread dissatisfaction among members of the legal profession regarding the multiplicity of opportunities for appealing. The present system, he pointed out, operated both to the detriment of the poor litigant and against 'economy and expedition in the administration of the law'. The Lord Chancellor continued:

There are some who would like to lay the axe to the root and to abolish either the Court of Appeal or your Lordships' House. Whatever the future may have in store for us, that method is not at the moment practical politics. It is not our way to make violent changes in the administration of the law. At present the Court of Appeal acts as a sieve for the House of Lords.

Taking the average for the last three years, the number of appeals heard annually in the Court of Appeal has been 424, of which 124 were wholly successful and in 19 the judgment was varied. To abolish the Court of Appeal would be to throw such an amount of work on the House as would necessitate alterations too drastic to be carried out at one and the same time. With regard to the judicial side of your Lordships' House, may I be permitted to say that, although I have received many deputations and suggestions with regard to legal reform, there were very few indeed who advocated that the appeal to your Lordships' House should be abolished. On the other hand, there seems to be a very general desire for some check to be placed upon appeals to this House. The cost of such an appeal is high. The fact that there

[1] Hanworth Report, op. cit., pp. 17–27.
[2] H.L. Debs., vol. 92, cols. 789–801, 5 June 1934.

is an unrestricted right is not seldom held *in terrorem* over the head of an intending litigant, especially in Revenue cases. The present Bill proposes as a remedy that there should be no appeal to this House without the leave of the Court of Appeal or of the House itself.

I do not prophesy that this Bill will mean a great saving in judicial time, but it will save great anxiety to many a litigant.

This speech is notable for its unequivocal acceptance of the judicial House of Lords, indeed, generally, for its unconcealed conservatism. The squabbles of the 1870s, when the fate of the institution hung in the balance, had been quietly forgotten.

The subsequent speakers in the House of Lords did little more than echo the words from the Woolsack. Lord Atkin was at pains (as had been the Lord Chancellor) to point out that the measure was aimed primarily at eliminating the threat of irresponsible appeals at the expense of poor litigants) rather than at effecting any significant reduction in the number of actual appeals:

Speaking for myself, after five or six years of experience of this House, I must say that very few cases have, in fact, come before your Lordships' House which were not suitable for appeal and in which, in all probability, leave would not have been given. There have been a few cases, but I agree with what has been said by the Lord Chancellor: the great importance of this reform is this, that a rich corporation—or perhaps I might say, a strong government department—will not for the future be able in any way to terrorise the person with whom they have a dispute by a threat that the case will probably be taken to the House of Lords.

Predictably, Lord Hanworth, who, apart from Lord Merrivale, was the only other speaker in the debate, gave unreserved support for a Bill which substantially enacted the recommendations of his Committee. It duly passed through its remaining stages without amendment.

Much the same approach emerged in the debate on the second reading of the Bill in the House of Commons.[1] Sir Donald (later Lord) Somervell, the Solicitor-General, commended the Bill in terms similar to those adopted by the Lord Chancellor. The only sour note was struck by Mr. Milne (Unionist M.P. for West Fife) who wanted to know why the Bill did not apply to Scotland where the appellate system suffered from defects similar to those the Bill was intended to remedy in England. He was told that reforms for Scotland were under consideration but that it would not be possible to include them in the present Bill.[2] The Bill passed through its remaining stages without incident and received the Royal Assent on 25 July 1934. (Its text is included in Appendix 1.)

There was an element of irony in this legislative attempt to eliminate a situation whereby an appeal to the supreme tribunal might be a veiled at-

[1] H.C. Debs., vol. 291, cols. 1528 ff.
[2] Scotland never has been included; nor has leapfrogging been extended to the Court of Session.

tempt either to intimidate an impecunious litigant or to delay the execution of a judgment. The change simply threw up another problem, the enormous amount of judicial and administrative time which was until recently, and to some extent still is, expended in sheltering the House of Lords from frivolous appeals. As we shall show, the Appeal Committee which is constituted to hear petitions for leave to appeal had, during our period of study, to deal with increasing numbers of petitioners in person who, in a vast majority of cases, indulged in an exercise far removed from the recognized forensic rules. What is more, such petitioners (where their opponents felt obliged to enter an appearance) ran up costs which the successful respondent had little or no hope of recovering. Mercifully, common sense has prevailed, if somewhat belatedly, and as a result of a practice direction in July 1970 their Lordships are now effectively armed to deal peremptorily with most of these frivolous petitions.

The 1934 Act took a statutory sledgehammer to crack a very tiny litigious nut: such marginal benefits as may initially have accrued from the Act were more than nullified by subsequent abuse of the procedure. Since 1952, 32 per cent of substantive English civil appeals heard by the House of Lords have been revenue cases,[1] and in these cases leave is granted so freely as to be tantamount to an unqualified right of appeal. In practice, a taxpayer who has the temerity to engage in litigation against the Inland Revenue receives little protection under the provisions of the 1934 Act. The plight of the taxpayer has, however, been mitigated by the policy of the courts in granting *unconditional* leave to the Revenue sparingly:[2] the Revenue is not infrequently put on terms as to costs, with the result that unsuccessful respondent-taxpayers rarely have to shoulder this burden in full.

The rules relating to security for costs and the convention that costs must normally follow the event combine to deter the frivolous appellant and to safeguard the impecunious respondent from financial ruin at the hands of an appellant with a weak case but a long purse. The problem has been partly solved by the extension in 1960 of legal aid to House of Lords appeals. And if the criteria applied by Area Committees in relation to the granting of certificates were statutorily extended, it would be wholly solved.

The Appeal Committee of the House—which dates back to 1812—meets in one of the Committee Rooms to consider various categories of petition presented to the Lords in their judicial capacity: during the period 1952–68 it met on average about ten times a year. It considers all petitions for leave to appeal in civil causes where leave has been refused by the English or (since 1962) by the Northern Irish Court of Appeal,[3] and (since 1960) in criminal causes in which a point of law has been certified by the Court of Appeal, Criminal Division, or by the Queen's Bench Divisional Court, or by the

---

[1] These are discussed in Chapter xv.   [2] See below.
[3] Most Scottish Appeals lie as of right, but leave is required in certain appeals.

Courts-Martial Appeal Court. The Committee also deals with such inter-locutory matters as applications for further time in which to lodge the bound cases[1] (where the respondents have not consented to such an extension): and under the old *in formâ pauperis* procedure (which still applies to Northern Ireland) it examines the affidavits of poverty and determines whether the prima facie case, required under the rules of this procedure, has been made out.[2] Under the Administration of Justice Act 1969 the Committee is entrusted with the task of considering applications for leave to leapfrog, though it does so on the documents of the case, without a formal hearing.[3]

In dealing with petitions for leave to appeal under the rules that prevailed until July 1970 the Appeal Committee generally disposed of between three and six petitions at a single sitting: leave was granted only in about 18 per cent of cases though for reasons which will be discussed this percentage will almost certainly increase in the future. Exceptionally, a Committee was convened to consider a single petition and, with equal rarity, eight or nine petitions were sometimes disposed of at one sitting. Normally the Com-mittee consists of three Law Lords, but occasionally the number is increased to five.

Since 1956 the Committee has usually conducted its proceedings publicly.[4] Petitioners may appear in person or be represented by counsel or by an agent. This procedure thus provides an occasional confrontation between members of the higher judiciary and solicitor-advocates. (Devotees of fusion of the two branches of the profession might care to note that no harm appears to result from this tiny inroad into the Bar's monopoly.) Exceptionally, a friend of a petitioner in person may be allowed to contribute to the argument. It has not been uncommon, particularly with petitioners in person, for a petition to be dismissed without the respondent (if indeed he has gone to the trouble of entering an appearance) being called upon to reply; sometimes, however, counsel briefed for the respondent may be called upon by their Lordships less to oppose an unintelligible application by a petitioner in person than to explain what it is all about.

Proceedings vary considerably in length. Occasionally (particularly if a petition has been demonstrably out of order because the House has no jurisdiction to entertain the application) the petition has been dismissed in a very few minutes. (Now such cases should never reach the point of a hear-ing.) On the other hand, a single petition may occupy the best part of a day. A realistic average over the period studied would probably work out at about one hour in cases which are argued by counsel and (judging from the relative lengths of the transcripts) about one-third of that time for petitions which are argued in person. This means that, at one end of the scale, half-a-dozen hope-less petitions in person may have been dealt with in less than two hours, and,

[1] Applications for further time are discussed in Chapter XI.   [2] Ibid.
[3] Discussed more fully below.   [4] *Blackburn* v. *Attorney-General* [1956] 1 W.L.R. 1501.

at the other extreme, two difficult cases could (very rarely) take the proceedings into a second day.

The proceedings are only superficially judicial in form. Although staffed by Law Lords, the Committee is only an administrative arm of the House of Lords in its judicial capacity. The petition is (or should be) directed not so much at the merits of the case—although this may in fact have a bearing on the outcome of the application—as on the degree of public importance involved and on the necessity of the legal issue being finally resolved by the House of Lords, though in petitions for leave in criminal cases the public importance of the case has already been acknowledged by the court *a quo* issuing its certificate. Either at the conclusion of argument or when their Lordships could tolerate a garrulous petitioner no longer, the parties have usually been asked to withdraw: the Committee's decision is announced by the presiding judge, no reasons being given, save in circumstances (by no means exceptional) where their Lordships considered that they had no jurisdiction to entertain the petition.

The fact that application for leave to appeal is by way of petition to the whole House (which thereupon refers it automatically to its Appeal Committee) can give rise to difficulty, since petitions can only officially be dealt with when Parliament is in session. In the Christmas vacation of 1967, for example, it proved necessary to hold over eight petitions until the New Year since, to the extent that the parliamentary recess coincided with the law vacation, it would have been impossible to have dealt with the petitions.[1] This is an example of the efficient running of the final court of appeal being impaired (albeit marginally) by an attachment to parliamentary convention and to the traditional law terms.

As indicated in Table 3, the Appeal Committee of the House of Lords heard 639 petitions[2] for leave to appeal during the period 1952–68, an average of 37·5 a year. However, the year 1961 saw a sharp increase in the numbers. The annual average for the period 1952–60 was 25·2 and for 1961–8 it was 51·5. This twofold increase is explained in part by the extension of the criminal jurisdiction of the House in 1960 and by the advent of legal aid in respect of House of Lords proceedings in December of the same year. But even if we subtract the fifty criminal petitioners and the twenty legally-aided civil petitioners from the 1960–8 aggregate, the average is reduced only to 42·5: and, of course, some or all of the legally-aided petitioners might have pur-

---

1 But, very exceptionally, as where an appellant was under sentence of death, an Appellate Committee is convened in vacation. In *Bratty* v. *Attorney-General for Northern Ireland* [1963] A.C. 386, their Lordships sat for three days in the first week of September 1961.

2 Once again we encounter the problem of definition: sometimes several petitions are lodged by one petitioner, or by a group of petitioners, and dealt with at one hearing. Sometimes a petitioner may present several petitions raising different issues so that the Appeal Committee gives a separate ruling on each petition. In the latter case we have counted the petitions separately, but in the former we have counted them as one.

TABLE 3

Petitions for Leave to Appeal heard by the Appeal Committee, 1952–1968

Year	Total no. Petitions Heard[a]	No. of Times Appeal Committee sat	Civil Petitions		Eventual Outcome of Successful Petitions			Criminal Petitions[f]		Eventual Outcome of Successful Petitions		
			Refused	Granted	Appeal allowed wholly or in part	Appeal dismissed	Appeal withdrawn	Refused	Granted	Appeal allowed wholly or in part	Appeal dismissed	Appeal withdrawn, etc.
1952	16	6	11	5	0	4	1					
1953	19	6	13	6	3	2	1					
1954	31	5	20	11	3	5	3					
1955	26	9	21	5	2	2	1					
1956	25	9	19	6	2	4	—					
1957	21	6	16	5	2	3	2					
1958	23	8	19	4	1	1	—					
1959	31	14	29	2	2	0	1					
1960	35	11	27	8	2	5	—					
1961	54[b]	20	43	6	2	4	—	3	2	1	1	—
1962	49[c]	20	42	3	1	2	—	3	1	—	1	—
1963	44	20	35	2	1	1	—	7	—	—	—	—
1964	51	20	38	4	2	2	2	5	4	2	2	—
1965	50	17	36	8	2	4	2	4	2	—	2	—
1966	49[d]	15	39	6	1	3	—	4	—	—	—	—
1967	57[e]	18	40	9	3	6	2	4	4	1	3	—
1968	58	13	43	8	3	3	—	7	—	—	—	—
	639	171	491	98	32	51	15	37	13	4	9	—

[a] These totals do not include applications for leave to appeal *in formâ pauperis* where an appeal lies as of right or where leave to appeal has already been given; nor do they include proceedings which were adjourned.

[b] The total for 1961 includes one successful petition from the Court of Criminal Appeal in Northern Ireland and one unsuccessful petition from the Court of Appeal in Northern Ireland.

[c] The total for 1962 includes one case (*Duchess of Argyll v. Duke of Argyll*) where the Appeal Committee ruled that the House could not entertain an appeal against a unanimous interlocutory judgment of the Court of Session, (1962) The Times, 10.iv.1962.

[d] The total for 1966 includes one unsuccessful petition from the Court of Appeal in Northern Ireland.

[e] The total for 1967 includes two petitions from Scotland: one was dismissed as incompetent to be heard, in the other (*Lord Advocate v. Reliant Tool Co.* [1968] 1 W.L.R. 205), in which there was a statutory requirement of leave to appeal, leave was granted.

[f] Totals of criminal petitions include cases involving habeas corpus and applications for bail...

sued their application in person, or have taken advantage of the *in formâ pauperis* procedure, had legal aid not been available.

Table 3 also shows the increasing number of Appeal Committees which have had to be convened in recent years to tackle this increase in business, though Committees do deal with matters other than petitions for leave to appeal. The average number of petitions heard by each Committee is rather less than four, though the figure was as high as 6 in 1954 and as low as 2·2 in 1963. (See p. 145 for subject-matter of petitions.)

We have already alluded to the problem of petitioners in person, and Table 4 deals with the representation of the petitioner before the Appeal Committee, and the degree of success enjoyed by petitioners represented in different ways:

TABLE 4

*Representation of Petitioners for Leave to Appeal before the
Appeal Committee, 1952–1968*

Representation	Total	Petitions Refused	Petitions Granted	% Successful
Queen's Counsel	182	117	65	35·9
Junior Counsel only	158	115	43	27·2
Agent	9	7	2	22·2
In person	279	278	1	0·4
Petitioner absent	11	11	—	—
	639	528	111	

53·2 per cent of petitioners were represented by counsel, 43·7 per cent appeared in person; a very small number, nine (1·4 per cent), were represented by an agent and in eleven cases the petition was dismissed in the petitioner's absence, a course which the Committee takes only after ascertaining that the petitioner is unlikely to appear, and that the petition is manifestly incompetent to be heard, or wholly devoid of merit. It is interesting to note that no fewer than 53·5 per cent of petitioners electing to appear by counsel went to the expense of briefing a Silk, and that these were markedly more successful than junior counsel in obtaining leave: it is not clear, however, whether the latter fact is due to any superior advocacy on the part of the Queen's Counsel or to the fact that the kinds of case *inherently* more likely to obtain leave (revenue, contract, patents, etc.) are promoted by wealthy individual and corporate litigants who can afford the more costly services of a Silk. (The cost involved in petitioning for leave is analysed at pp. 225–6, below.) Only one petitioner in person obtained leave to appeal during our period of study, *Moore* v. *Lea* (1962): he also conducted his appeal in person,[1] and lost.

[1] Seven other appeals were conducted in person, four of them by appellants (*Bennett* v. *Rowse* (1959) 38 T.C. 476; *Malloch* v. *Aberdeen Corporation* [1971] 1 W.L.R. 1578; *Wintle* v. *Nye* [1959] 1 W.L.R. 284; and *Warden* v. *Warden* (1961)) and three by respondents (*Braithwaite & Co. (Structural) Ltd.* v. *Caulfield* (1961); *Koppelman* v. *Kopel* (1958); and *London Clinic* v. *Hoare* (1960)).

In seventy-five cases (26·9 per cent) argued in person, the respondent did not enter an appearance, as compared with ten cases (2·9 per cent) argued by counsel or by an agent. This means that in nearly three-quarters of cases argued in person (a large proportion of which were manifestly hopeless) the respondent felt obliged to incur costs which he can often have had little hope of recovering. In a substantial proportion of the 543 cases in which both parties were present at the hearing, the respondent was not called upon to reply to the petitioner: this occurred in 101 petitions (36·2 per cent) presented in person and in 128 petitions (36·7 per cent) presented by counsel or by an agent. Relevant here is the fact that the Committee often called upon counsel to elucidate an argument which the petitioner in person was unable to present coherently. Four petitions were granted without the petitioner being heard, the respondent being called upon to justify dismissal of the application.

Except where the competence of the Appeal Committee to entertain the application is raised as a preliminary issue by the respondent, it is almost unheard of for their Lordships to give reasons for refusing leave, though in the course of argument they may indicate to the petitioner any special points of difficulty which he may have to overcome, or some of the general criteria which must be satisfied before leave can be granted.[1] One special exception to this is the so-called *Lane* v. *Esdaile*[2] rule. In *Lane* v. *Esdaile*, a decision of the House of Lords in 1891, it was laid down that no appeal can lie to the House of Lords from the Court of Appeal's refusal of leave to appeal *to itself*, since such a refusal does not constitute a 'judgment or order' within the meaning of the Appellate Jurisdiction Act 1876. (Leave to appeal is required, for example, in order to appeal to the Court of Appeal from the interlocutory ruling of a Judge in Chambers or, as in *Lane* v. *Esdaile* itself, when an appeal is out of time.)

For many years *Lane* v. *Esdaile* seems to have lain fallow in the law reports, though during the early part of the 1950s the Appeal Committee (without expressly alluding to the case) excluded a few applications on similar grounds[3]. Then in 1960, in the case of *Whitehouse* v. *The Board of Control*,[4] this useful addition to the Committee's armoury against incompetent petitions was re-discovered[5] and extended to cases where the Court of Appeal's refusal of leave to appeal *to itself* was *within* time. And during our period of study a substantial proportion of petitions in person (perhaps as many as a quarter) foundered upon the rocks of *Lane* v. *Esdaile*. Thus between 1960 and 1968, 204 petitions presented in person were rejected by the Appeal Committee: of

---

[1] See, for example, Lord Reid's revealing observation to counsel in *Wednesbury Corporation* v. *Ministry of Housing and Local Government* (1965): 'I think the public importance of it is very clear, but you have also got, of course, to establish that there is a point of general importance to put before the House, and that you have a prima facie case for success.'

[2] [1891] A.C. 210.   [3] e.g. *Hatherly* v. *Crofts* (1956).   [4] [1960] 1 W.L.R. 1093.

[5] We understand that this came about through the researches of Mr. Richard Cave, Principal Clerk of the Judicial Office.

these, no fewer than 54 (26·4 per cent) fell more or less squarely within the rule in *Lane* v. *Esdaile*, and a further 9, in which litigants had sought to reverse orders striking out their actions or declaring them to be vexatious litigants, had all the symptoms of the *Lane* v. *Esdaile* syndrome, though the scanty record of the proceedings makes accurate diagnosis uncertain. In any event such actions clearly fell outside the criteria of general public importance demanded by the final court of appeal.

Apart from *Lane* v. *Esdaile* cases, there are several instances every year of petitions being brought which are clearly outside the competence of the House. Again considering only petitions argued in person, during 1960–8 there were seven bankruptcy cases (in which appeal is excluded by statute); three criminal cases in which no certificate had been granted by the court *a quo*; two petitions dismissed expressly on the grounds that they were appeals from county courts involving trivial subject-matter (these probably fell within the rule in *Lane* v. *Esdaile*); one petition from Scotland; and nine cases in which the only contentious issue was an order for costs or one requiring security for costs. In addition there were two appeals in lunacy, both of which (like *Whitehouse* v. *The Board of Control*, which was itself a lunacy case) were probably incompetent to be heard.

This left 118 petitions brought in person (56·7 per cent) which did not clearly fall within these clearly designated categories of incompetence. The operative word here is 'clearly': the taciturnity of the Appeal Committee in revealing its reasons for dismissing a petition was matched only by the unintelligibility of most of the petitions themselves and of the oral argument the petitioners adduced before the Committee, and we are confident that the figure of 43·3 per cent of petitions as incompetent is a considerable under-estimate. For one thing it takes no account of matrimonial proceedings in which appeals are statute-barred unless the appellant is given leave to appeal by the Court of Appeal: we have noted eight petitions (other than ones expressly dismissed as incompetent) which appear to fall into this category.

Apart from this, no fewer than twenty-eight petitions presented during the period completely defied our attempt at classification: it proved quite impossible, with the best will in the world, to see a glimmering of sense either in the petitions themselves or in the oral arguments presented. Of the remainder we would estimate that a very large proportion were hopeless in a less tangible respect: although competent to be heard and more or less intelligible their subject-matter put them well outside either of the basic criteria for success, general public importance and a fighting chance of reversal on appeal.

Finally we must mention the question of the time limits prescribed by Standing Orders I and II. As we have already mentioned, no petitions are rejected solely on the ground of being out of time under S. O. II (i.e. presented between one and three months of the ruling of the court *a quo*), though S. O.

1, which lays down a three-month limit for presenting an appeal to the House, is very strictly interpreted. Some 16 per cent of unsuccessful petitions for leave heard during our period of study were out of time.

To sum up, we would argue that, on the basis of the petitions heard during the period 1960–8 (i.e. after *Whitehouse* had heralded a tightening-up of the rules for dismissing incompetent petitions) at least half of the petitions presented in person were incompetent to be heard and at least three-quarters of the remainder were palpably hopeless. This leaves a residue of about 10 per cent which appear to have merited an expenditure of valuable judicial time.

Our evidence shows that the procedure for dealing with petitions for leave, bequeathed by the 1934 Act and perpetuated by some measure of over-indulgence on the part of their Lordships towards incompetent petitions, resulted in considerable waste of the resources of the Appeal Committee.

Happily the situation has now been remedied. On 23 July 1970 a practice direction was issued, headed 'Incompetent Petitions for Leave to Appeal'. It reads as follows:[1]

As from 1st October 1970, Petitions for leave to appeal to the House of Lords which appear to be incompetent, in that they fall under the following headings, will be considered without a hearing by three Lords of Appeal who, if they are satisfied that the Petition is incompetent to be received by the House, will certify accordingly and the Clerk of the Parliaments will then notify the parties:

    (1) Criminal Petitions for leave to appeal to the House of Lords in respect of which no certificate has been granted by the Court below under section 1 (2) of the Administration of Justice Act 1960;

    (2) Petitions for leave to appeal to the House of Lords against a refusal of the Court of Appeal to grant leave to appeal to that Court from the judgment of the High Court.

    (3) Petitions for leave to appeal to the House of Lords barred by section 108 (2) (b) of the Bankruptcy Act 1914.

In the event of one or more of the three Lords of Appeal expressing a doubt as to whether the Petition in question is incompetent to be received by the House, it will be referred to the Appeal Committee for a hearing in the normal manner.

On 20 May 1971 a further practice direction was issued, adding a fourth category of incompetent petition to be subject to the new procedures:

    (4) Petitions for leave to appeal to the House of Lords barred by paragraph 4 of the Fourth Schedule to the Housing Act 1957.

And on 29 July another category was added:

    (5) Petitions for leave to appeal to the House of Lords brought by a Petitioner in respect of whom the High Court has made an Order under section 51 of the Supreme Court of Judicature (Consolidation) Act, 1925 as amended by the Supreme Court of Judicature (Amendment) Act 1959, unless leave to present such a Petition has been granted by the High Court or a Judge thereof pursuant to that section.

If the pattern of petitions revealed by our analysis is continued into the

---

[1] Practice Direction (House of Lords: Petitions) [1970] 1 W.L.R. 1218.

1970s then it seems clear that the Appeal Committee will be relieved of the burden of about 40 per cent of petitions presented in person, and possibly substantially more, since the three Law Lords concerned will now be directing their minds exclusively to the issue of competency. Certainly this is a sensible, if belated innovation, though the amount of *time* saved will be very small, since the categories of petition now to be excluded often involved very little oral argument, and judicial time will still have to be spent in conducting the preliminary scrutiny. But although there will still be a hard core of petitioners in person appearing before the Appeal Committee, an aspect of the work of the Law Lords which did much to impair the dignity of the judicial process will now be curtailed.

All English appeals to the House of Lords as we have observed, require leave to appeal, either from the court *a quo* or from the Appeal Committee, and the same has been true for Northern Irish Appeals since 1962. Criminal appeals, since 1960, have been subject to the granting of a certificate of public importance by the lower court, and to the granting of leave either by the court *a quo* or by the Appeal Committee. Scottish appeals still generally lie as of right, except in interlocutory proceedings where the judges of the Court of Session are unanimous when leave is required from the Inner House. There are also certain statutory provisions[1] in the field of administrative law where leave to appeal is required, though the number of such cases heard by the Appeal Committee is very small.

Table 5 shows the route by which *civil* appeals reached the House of Lords in each of the years 1952–68.

Of the appeals, 21·4 per cent—nearly all Scottish—came to the House of Lords as of right. Of the 366 appeals which came by leave, 78·1 per cent came by leave of the court *a quo*, and 21·9 per cent by leave of the Appeal Committee. The courts *a quo* imposed conditions in 12·4 per cent of cases where they granted leave,[2] and the Appeal Committee in 33·8 per cent of cases. (In nearly all cases the conditions related to costs, but sometimes the appellant was required to present the petition without undue delay.)

---

[1] The Electricity Act 1947, the Tribunals and Inquiries Act 1958, the Transport Act 1962, and the Iron and Steel Act 1967. There have been only two instances of petitions for leave, both under the Tribunals and Inquiries Act 1958. The first was *Lord Advocate* v. *the Reliant Tool Co.* in which the Appeal Committee gave leave on 12 June 1967. The second was *Williamson* v. *N.C.B.* in which the Committee refused leave on 16 October 1969.

[2] Lord Evershed M.R. felt at one time that it would be improper for the Court of Appeal to impose conditions, but in *Rennell* v. *C.I.R.* [1961] 3 All E.R. 1028, 1041 he announced a change of practice: 'The House of Lords has recently let us know that it is regarded as competent for this Court to impose conditions in giving leave to appeal. Hitherto we felt we could not impose conditions. Any party who is given leave on a condition is entitled to take that as a refusal and go to the Appeal Committee.' (There is a difference between a party agreeing in advance to pay his opponents' costs and a party being presented with terms on a take it or leave it basis by the Court. Sometimes, however, it is difficult to tell whether counsel is being invited to make an offer to the other party or whether he is being put on terms: we have therefore not distinguished between these two sets of circumstances in our tables.)

TABLE 5

Source of Leave: Civil Appeals, 1952–1968

	By Leave of Court *a quo*		By Leave of Appeal Cttee.		As of Right[b]
	con-dITIONAL	uncon-ditional[a]	con-ditional	uncon-ditional	
1952	4	8	3	1	8
1953	1	10	—	3	2
1954	1	8	1	4	4
1955	4	22	4	4	1
1956	2	18	2	5	6
1957	1	14	3	2	5
1958	2	12	3	—	4
1959	3	19	1	1	13
1960	4	15	1	4	8
1961	2	13	3	5[c]	9
1962	2	18	—	3	5
1963	3	20	—	3[c]	6
1964	1	13	2	3	9
1965	2	20	—	1	3
1966	2	15	1	5	4
1967	1	12	2	4	11
1968	—	14	1	5	2
(Total appeals, 466)	35	251	27	53	100

[a] Includes twelve Scottish interlocutory appeals, and five post-1962 Northern Irish appeals.

[b] Includes ten pre-1962 Northern Irish appeals.

[c] Includes one case where conditions imposed below were waived by the Appeal Committee.

The corresponding figures for post-1960 criminal appeals are shown in Table 6. (Pre-1960 criminal appeals were subject to the fiat procedure which is discussed elsewhere.)

In all, fourteen out of thirty-seven appeals (37·8 per cent) came by leave of the Appeal Committee. Separating those cases which originated in the Court of Appeal and the Courts-Martial Appeal Court from those coming from the Divisional Court, we find that the Divisional Court seems much more reluctant to give leave in 'appealable' cases than is the Court of Appeal. This may be because the provision of an appeal from the Divisional Court (in cases involving the relatively humble jurisdiction of magistrates' courts) is still something of a novelty, and it is felt, therefore, desirable for the Law Lords themselves to decide the question of leave in such cases.

Does the source of leave to appeal play a significant part in determining the success-rates of appeals? In another context we draw attention to the fact that Scottish appeals are significantly more successful than English.

TABLE 6

Source of Leave: Criminal Appeals, 1961–1968

Court *a quo*	C.C.A., etc.		Div. Ct.	
Leave:	C.C.A.	A.C.	Div. Ct.	A.C.
1961	3[a]	1[a]	1	—
1962	3[b]	1	1	1
1963	2[c]	—	—	—
1964	2	—	1	3
1965	2	1	2	1
1966	2	—	—	1
1967	1	—	1	1
1968	3[b]	1	1	3
(Total Appeals, 39)	18	4	7	10

[a] Each includes one case from C.C.A. (N.I.)
[b] Includes one case from C-M.A.C.
[c] One appeal and cross-appeal.

This is surprising since, assuming that likelihood of success is at least a marginal factor in granting leave (viz. Lord Reid's remarks in the *Wednesbury* case: see footnote 1, page 128) one would expect that appeals which lie as of right would contain a percentage which were *less* likely to succeed in the Lords. As regards English appeals, the relative success-rates are set out in Table 7.

TABLE 7

Success-Rates of English Appeals according to Source of Leave to Appeal, 1952–1968

	Civil Appeals		Criminal Appeals	
Leave given by	successful	unsuccessful	successful	unsuccessful
Court *a quo*	98	175	6	19
Appeal Committee	27	49	4	10

Thus 34·9 per cent of all appeals (civil and criminal) given leave by the court *a quo* were successful, and those given leave by the Appeal Committee enjoyed an almost identical rate of success. There may be two counteracting factors at work here. On the one hand, most of the obviously appealable cases are given leave by the lower court which is the first hurdle, but the members of the Appeal Committee may have a closer awareness of the kinds of case which they and their brethren are likely to reverse on appeal.

Further statistics make it clear how far the 'obvious' cases are creamed off by the granting of leave to appeal by the lower court without the matter having to come before the Appeal Committee. One criterion of 'appealability' is the existence of a division of opinion in the court below. One would anticipate that many of the appeals eventually reaching the Lords have already given rise to controversy, and that part of the reason for giving leave was to have the conflict resolved at the highest possible level. Of 349 English civil appeals heard by the House of Lords during the period 1952–68 no fewer than 232 (66·5 per cent) involved an element of disagreement below: i.e. either a dissenting judgment in the Court of Appeal, or a reversal (complete or partial) of the trial judge's decision, or both. Of the 273 cases which obtained leave from the Court of Appeal, 184 (67·4 per cent) involved disagreement, as compared with 45 of the 76 cases (59·2 per cent) where leave came from the Appeal Committee. Clearly, even when the judges below are divided, the Court of Appeal often does not regard this in itself as sufficient grounds for leave. In criminal cases these considerations do not apply since a dissentient judgment is permissible only with the leave of the presiding judge.

But this overlooks one very significant factor: the judges of the court below may very well attach greater weight to a division among *themselves* than to disagreement with the trial judge. This is borne out by the statistics. Altogether, eighty English appeals had involved a full dissenting judgment in the Court of Appeal: In seventy-six of these cases the Court of Appeal itself gave leave, and in only four instances was the decision left to the Appeal Committee. Putting it another way: 27·8 per cent of cases by leave of the Court of Appeal had involved a dissent below, as compared with 5·3 per cent of those given leave by the Appeal Committee. It is thus frequently left to the Appeal Committee to scrutinize a difference of opinion between the court below and the trial judge.

The Act of 1934 undoubtedly relieved the House of Lords of the burden of hearing a few unimportant cases each year. But at the same time it burdened their Lordships with the not inconsiderable task of acting as their own sieve. If Appeal Committees consisting of three Law Lords are convened fifteen times a year, and sit for an average of three hours, then 135 judicial man-hours are expended annually, not to mention considerable expenditure of administrative time and effort. (The Appellate Committee usually occupies 87½ judge-hours in a week's business in hearing full appeals.)

In recent years (certainly after 1960) the number of petitions for leave to appeal rose sharply (Table 3 above). But certainly the most prominent feature of the period was the high proportion of cases, many of them completely hopeless and quite beyond the help of the courts, which were argued in person. No fewer than 45·4 per cent of petitioners either appeared in person or did not appear at all: the extension of legal aid to House of Lords proceedings in 1960 appeared to have no effect in stemming this flow of unrepresented petitioners, though the practice direction of July 1970 seems likely to have a salutary effect.

The Law Lords who sat to hear these petitions must often have echoed the sentiments of Tom Thumb, 'Petition me no petitions' (Fielding, *Tom Thumb*, I. ii). Although reasons are not given for refusals of leave, it seems clear that at least half of the petitions presented in person were outside the jurisdiction of the House, either because they fell within statutory provisions making the Court of Appeal the final appeal tribunal, or because they came under the rule in *Lane* v. *Esdaile*.

The Law Lords doubtless feel in duty bound to give a hearing even to these inherently hopeless petitions: in consequence they exhibit extraordinary tolerance towards petitioners. A few of those who appear before the Committee are quite clearly mentally deranged: others suffer from what might be called litigation neurosis, symptomized by an ever-increasing sense of grievance which brings the sufferer repeatedly before the courts, adding useless embellishments to bolster a non-existent case. A glance at the list of petitions reveals the same petitioner returning again and again to the Appeal Committee, condemned, like the Wandering Jew, to find no haven of rest in any tribunal.

Their Lordships are occasionally subjected to abuse or even belligerence which would ordinarily constitute contempt of court: at the very least they have to listen to a series of rambling and vaguely coherent utterances from garrulous petitioners. The fact that a petitioner appears in person militates against, rather than prompts, peremptory dismissal of the petition by the Appeal Committee. Up to a point this is justified in terms of the universal rule that justice should be seen to be done, but in the result petitioners are allowed to wander well beyond the usual limits of permissible legal argument, to the detriment of an orderly legal process and to no objectively discernible advantage to themselves. Patience is a judicial virtue, and the proceedings may even be of therapeutic value to the neurotic litigant, but it can hardly be the purpose of the judicial process to indulge in psychotherapy.[1]

The position was aptly described by Lord Pearce in his speech in *Rondel* v. *Worsley*:[2]

The history of this case has, in its general lines, followed a pattern which is not unfamiliar. Even in your Lordships' House many hours are spent each year (and in the Court of Appeal the numbers are naturally larger) in listening to wholly unbalanced attempts to re-open, without justification, a case which a party has lost and which, by brooding over it, he can no longer see in an objective light. Disgruntled by a decision, he reflects on various side-issues (often quite irrelevant or at least not matters of decisive importance) of which he now considers that the judge

[1] We are reminded of the incident of a litigant in person appearing before that model of judicial behaviour, Lord Denning M.R. After the hearing of a motion the litigant said: 'You, my Lord, are the person who makes the lives of plaintiffs in person possible.'
[2] [1969] 1 A.C. 191, 257.

failed to take any account or any sufficient account. Two frequent symptoms of such cases are that they are brought forward years after the event and that the strength of the complaint increases as the years go by. . . . Another frequent symptom of such cases is that a plaintiff seeks to give additional momentum to his complaints by throwing in charges of 'fraud' and 'conspiracy'.

Armed with firm evidence about the defects in the system for dealing with the plethora of incompetent petitions for leave to appeal, the present authors prepared a number of proposals for tackling the problem. To some extent, however, the impetus for recommending substantial changes was reduced by the 1970 Practice Direction restricting incompetent petitions. The probable effects of this innovation have already been discussed: if the new procedure is strictly applied (and there is every reason to think that it will be) then the number of petitions for leave to appeal will be substantially reduced. The saving of judicial man-hours will be slight, but certainly the change will benefit many respondents (often innocent victims of a vendetta conceived by a deranged mind) who, under the pre-1970 rules, would have been involved in irrecoverable expense[1] and inconvenience in opposing incompetent petitions. Their Lordships too may still have to cope with garrulous and sometimes abusive petitioners, but, one hopes, not nearly so often.

Notwithstanding the importance of this reform we would argue that it probably does not go far enough: indeed, it is open to argument whether the present sieve constitutes the most effective means of securing an orderly and efficient legal process in the final appeal court, and at the same time of securing the important rights of private litigants. In the first place a public hearing in which their Lordships are seen to be bending over backwards in the latitude they give to petitioners in person, is to be replaced by justice behind closed doors. We would not question for one moment that incompetent petitions should be given short shrift, but it must be remembered that many of these petitions are the last hope of litigants already thoroughly disillusioned with the machinery which (in their eyes) has failed to give them justice. One feels that a letter from the Judicial Office announcing yet another judicial rebuff, however felicitously phrased, is a poor substitute for a few sympathetically worded sentences from a judge explaining why the petition has been adjudged incompetent.[2]

There remains too the problem of legal aid. Even the most deserving, but impecunious, litigant may not be able to afford an appeal after being granted

---

[1] These amount, on an average, to about £40 for every civil petition (see p. 226).

[2] See Practice Direction of 28 June 1966, [1966] 1 W.L.R. 1084: 'In cases where an appeal is offered for presentation outside the time limit imposed by Standing Order I owing to a misunderstanding or a technicality, provided that the consent of the respondents is obtained to the presentation of the appeal out of time, the petition for leave to present an appeal out of time will be considered in private by three Lords of Appeal. Their Lordships' decision will be conveyed to the parties by the Clerk of the Parliaments.' (This replaced the old Practice whereby the agents of the parties were required to attend and be heard by the Appeal Committee.)

leave to appeal because of the present deficiency in the power of Legal Aid Area Committees to grant legal aid. Moreover, the Legal Aid Act 1964 has no application to petitions for leave to appeal and this means that respondents successfully opposing a legally-aided petitioner cannot be reimbursed by the Legal Aid Fund.

There are various methods by which the present system could be further tightened up. It might, for example, be expedient to impose security for costs to a limited amount (say £40) as prerequisite to lodging a petition for leave as a safeguard for respondents and as a deterrent to frivolous petitioners. It might be possible to save time by rationing the time of a petitioner in his opening address to the Appeal Committee to (say) thirty minutes, though such a rule would be regarded as alien to English forensic practice.

Our remedy to the problem of the right to appeal is more radical. We have already argued that the culprit for the present situation is the Administration of Justice (Appeals) Act 1934 itself, and we would question the basic assumptions that lay behind that piece of legislation. Paradoxically, the most practicable solution to the problem of frivolous and time-consuming petitions would be to revert to the pre-1934 position. This would involve giving a right of appeal, subject only to those specific statutory provisions taking away the right of appeal other than on points of law for which leave to appeal has been granted. (These statutory exceptions should be reviewed and extended in the light of current experience.) The practice of certifying that selected types of case raised important points of law, as is done in *criminal* appeals under the 1960 Administration of Justice Act, could be copied.[1] The majority of cases would not require any leave, but would call into play the rule requiring £1,000 security for costs, except in those cases where the appellant was granted a legal aid certificate or where the respondent gave his consent to the security being waived. Our findings on costs indicate that security might well be raised to an even higher level, say £1,500.

The requirement of security would discourage most, if not all, hopeless appeals. Litigants unable to afford the deposit of £1,500 would, of course, have the right to apply for legal aid. The unique role of the House of Lords as supreme appellate court and court of supervision demands that legal aid should be awarded more or less automatically to both parties (except for government departments and corporate bodies) where there is any substantial point of law to be argued. The problem of deciding which cases raise such points (and hence should go to the House of Lords) would be shifted from the Appeal Committee of the House of Lords to the courts *a quo*. In those cases where the right of appeal was not excluded by statute, legal aid should be granted more or less automatically for the appeal whenever

[1] See *Gelberg* v. *Miller* [1961] 1 W.L.R. 459; and *Gallagher* v. *Attorney-General for Northern Ireland* [1963] A.C. 349.
[2] See p. 401, *post*.

the Court of Appeal has certified that a point of law of general importance is involved, and for any petition for leave required by statute.

The advantage derived from a general right of appeal would be that ostensibly a litigant would be given something which, at present, he does not
have. The financial disincentive to exercise that right would be overcome if
legal aid were made much more readily available. The dual control of security
for costs and the requirement of a certificate from the court *a quo*, coupled
with the function of legal aid would ensure that very few cases unsuitable
for appeal would ever trouble the Appellate Committee. The caseload of
the Appeal Committee would be limited to criminal petitions under the
1960 Act and a few civil petitions in, for example, bankruptcy cases where
a point of law of general public importance had been certified by the Court of
Appeal, but leave from the court *a quo* had been withheld.

APPLICATIONS FOR LEAVE IN THE COURT OF APPEAL

The sieve for English civil appeals to the House of Lords operates at two
levels: in the Court of Appeal and in the House of Lords itself. It is necessary,
therefore, to complement the material in the earlier part of this chapter by
examining applications for leave heard by the Court of Appeal.

There is, however, an important factor which must be borne in mind before any attempt is made to compare the data from the two studies. Our
analysis of petitions in the House of Lords was based on the total case-load
over the period of study, for the simple reason that *all* the 639 petitions presented to the House during our period of study were systematically lodged
in a well-organized repository and could readily be traced via the House of
Lords Journals. The procedure for dealing with applications for leave in civil
appeals in the Court of Appeal is far less formalized than that of the Appeal
Committee. In the Court of Appeal applications are treated very much as a
footnote to the main appeal proceedings. The Court Associates note when
applications for leave are made, but their notes are not intended (as are the
Lords' Journals) to constitute a permanent record of the proceedings of the
Court.

For this reason we have been obliged to rely on the transcripts of Court of
Appeal proceedings prepared by the Association of Official Shorthand-
Writers and lodged in the Bar Library. When an application for leave is made
at the end of the appeal hearing, a note of the outcome of the application
appears on the transcript of the judgments. Unfortunately, notwithstanding
the difficulty which may be involved in reconstituting the identical court to
hear a late application, an appreciable number of such applications are in
fact made at a date subsequent to that when judgment was delivered. When
this happens, it is largely a matter of chance whether the same shorthand-
writer who heard the original appeal is present at the hearing of the applica-

tion. If he is present, he will probably append a note to the transcript; otherwise it is only the Associate who notes the application.

Since we have been compelled to rely on the Bar Library transcripts, our sample is less than 100 per cent. More accurately, we are taking a 100 per cent sample of a particular and unrepresentative category of case, namely, all those applications which are recorded in the transcripts. From our point of view this clearly raises difficulties. In the first place, our data are incomplete: our figures are bound to be deficient to the extent of the unrecorded applications. In the second place, our 'sample' is far from being a random one: it has been forced upon us by the limitations inherent in our source of data, and we do not even know how near it is in size to the total number of applications. Such a sample may well be unrepresentative: 'late' applications may achieve a smaller success rate. They may very well include, for example, a higher proportion of appellants in person who are not acquainted with the correct procedure for applying for leave.

Unfortunately it is not possible to measure the extent of any error. It would be possible (but laborious) to trace back all the House of Lords appeals and petitions for leave (all of which must, at some time, in theory at least, have involved an application to the Court of Appeal) and discover how many did not appear on our list derived from the transcripts. This, however, would still leave those cases where leave was granted or refused in the Court of Appeal on a late application, but where the party applying did not take the case to the House of Lords. We have chosen simply to accept the data as it is, bearing in mind its limitations. The bias is, we think, likely in any event to be quite small.

Table 8 sets out the overall total of applications for each year. In interpreting this table we must bear several points in mind:

(1) The 'total appeals' column refers to the number of *hearings* (i.e., separate transcripts). We have not followed the practice of the Civil Judicial Statistics and counted conjoined appeals and cross-appeals as separate cases. Among the transcripts are a few unsuccessful applications for leave to appeal to the Court of Appeal: these are so few in number that we have not excluded them, particularly as a few of them include an application for leave to appeal to the Lords.

(2) The 'year' column refers to the calendar year in which the appeal was heard.

(3) The 'total applications' column includes cases in which both parties to the appeal apply for leave (a fairly rare occurrence). This means that the 'percentage applications' column is fractionally weighted on the side of applications since some single appeals involve two separately recorded applications.

The figures show no particularly noteworthy trends. The ratio of applications to appeals rose appreciably, reaching a peak (29·6 per cent) for each of the three years 1962–4, but declined slightly during the last four years. The average success rate attained a peak of 40 per cent in 1959, but has dropped steadily to an all-time low of 17·9 per cent in 1968. One might expect the success ratio to vary inversely with the percentage of applications since it is reasonable to assume that a higher level of applications will contain a larger proportion of unsuccessful 'long shots'. A glance at the figures, however, suffices to show that this is not strictly the case.

TABLE 8

Applications to the Court of Appeal for Leave to Appeal to the House of Lords, 1951–1968

Year	Total Appeals	Total Applications	% applications per appeal	Applications Granted			% Successful Applications
				Uncon-ditionally	With conditions re costs	With other conditions	
1951	331	60	18·1	15	3	0	30·0
1952	502	98	19·5	26	2	0	28·6
1953	482	94	19·5	30	0	0	32·0
1954	462	84	18·2	22	2	0	28·6
1955	425	87	20·4	22	5	1	32·2
1956	418	87	20·8	32	2	0	39·1
1957	403	87	21·6	28	6	0	39·1
1958	383	98	25·6	28	6	1	35·7
1959	334	80	24·0	23	9	0	40·0
1960	432	119	27·6	29	5	1	29·4
1961	475	125	26·3	38	3	2	34·4
1962	486	144	29·6	33	8	0	28·5
1963	405	120	29·6	26	3	0	24·2
1964	378	112	29·6	23	4	2	25·9
1965	442	111	25·1	26	4	0	27·0
1966	456	101	22·2	18	5	0	22·8
1967	428	109	25·4	19	3	0	20·1
1968	550	117	21·3	19	1	1	17·9
Totals:	7,792	1,833		457	71	8	
	Average 432 p.a.	Average 102 p.a.	Average 23·6%				

Total 536 successful.
14·8% of successful applicants   Average
were put on terms.   29·2%

7·1% of all appeals get leave from the C.A. to proceed further.

The table can be summarized briefly as follows. The mean number of applications over the period of our study was 102 per annum, which is 23·6 per cent of the total number of appeals. Of these applications, 29·2 per cent were granted leave, 14·8 per cent subject to conditions. (The 'other conditions' column refers to those applications where leave is granted subject to the petition of appeal being lodged within a stipulated period, or where, for example, some provision is made requiring the payment of damages into court.)

We decided to carry out a detailed analysis of applications for leave in revenue appeals, for a number of reasons. In the first place revenue cases constitute about 30 per cent of the total case-load of the House of Lords, a fact which led us to suspect that leave is granted almost automatically in such cases. In the second place, revenue cases are one of a number of categories of litigation in which the executive confront the private citizen: perhaps we might find some indications of the 'executive-mindedness' of the judiciary in such cases in giving preference to applications for leave by the Crown. Finally, we were interested to find out something about the extent to which the Court of Appeal were prepared to make use of their power to impose on the Crown terms regarding the payment of costs in the House of Lords. (It was not really worth doing this for revenue petitions before the Appeal Committee because the number of such cases is too small.)

To facilitate our analysis we extracted from the data-recording forms details of every appeal which came under the heading 'revenue', i.e. income tax, estate duty, profits tax, surtax, purchase tax, stamp duty, and excise duty. These cases were then sub-divided into five categories, as follows:

TABLE 9

Applications for Leave to Appeal in Revenue Cases

Applications by the Taxpayer:	successful	81
	unsuccessful	42
Applications by the Revenue:	successful	30
	successful, but subject to terms	24
	unsuccessful	28
	Total	205

Thus, revenue appeals constitute 11·2 per cent of the total number of applications. The overall success ratio for revenue appeals was 66 per cent (as compared with 29·2 per cent for *all* classes of appeals).

This high success rate (66 per cent) confirms our hypothesis that a relatively very large proportion of applicants in revenue appeals are successful in obtaining leave from the Court of Appeal. The success rate for the Crown (65·8 per cent) is identical with that for the taxpayer, but in 44·5 per cent of the cases in which leave is granted to the Crown it was made subject to terms as to costs.

The next step was to break down the data under the five sub-categories in Table 10 as follows:

TABLE 10

Results of Revenue Appeals

Successful applications by the taxpayer (total 81)
  58 (71·9%) were ultimately heard by the Appellate Committee
  20 (24%) were not presented to the House
   3 (3·7%) were presented, but withdrawn before hearing.
Of the 58 which were heard:
  14 (24·1%) were allowed (8 by a majority)
  44 (75%) were dismissed (11 by a majority)

Unconditionally successful applications by the Crown (total 30)
  25 (83·4%) were ultimately heard by the Appellate Committee.
   5 (16·6%) were not presented to the House.
Of the 25 which were heard:
  10 were allowed (4 by a majority)
  15 were dismissed (6 by a majority)

Successful applications by the Crown, subject to conditions (total 24)
  11 (46%) were ultimately heard by the Appellate Committee[a]
  12 (50%) were not presented to the House
   1 was presented but withdrawn before hearing.
[a] N.B. In one of these appeals, the conditions imposed by the Court of Appeal were waived
by the Appeal Committee.
Of the 11 which were heard:
  5 were allowed (1 by a majority)
  6 were dismissed (1 by a majority)

Unsuccessful applications by the taxpayer (total 42)
  18 (43%) petitioned the Appeal Committee
  24 (57%) did not proceed further
Of the 18 heard by the Appeal Committee:
  In 14 leave to appeal was refused
  In 4 leave to appeal was granted
Of the 4 in which leave to appeal was granted:
  1 case, the appeal was never presented for hearing
  3 cases, the appeals were heard by the House, all were dismissed.

Unsuccessful applications by the Crown (total 28)
  10 (35·7%) petitioned the Appeal Committee
  18 (63·3%) did not proceed further
Of the 10 heard by the Appeal Committee:
  In 3 leave to appeal was refused
  In 7 leave to appeal was granted
Of the 7 in which leave to appeal was granted, all were heard on appeal
  2 were allowed
  5 were dismissed (2 by a majority)

To summarize the main points which emerge from this analysis:

(1) Of the 205 applications for leave to appeal in revenue cases, 104 (51 per cent) were ultimately heard by the House of Lords, 94 by leave of the Court of Appeal and 10 by leave of the Appeal Committee.

(2) 60 per cent of applications for leave come from the taxpayer and 40 per cent from the Crown: there is no appreciable difference between the success rates of the two categories of applicant.

(3) Having failed to get leave in the Court of Appeal, 43 per cent of taxpayers and 36 per cent of Revenue applicants petition the Appeal Committee. On the small numbers of cases involved, the Crown seems more likely than the taxpayer to be granted leave by the Appeal Committee.

(4) When placed on terms as to costs, the Crown frequently abandoned the appeal. Only 11 out of 24 such cases went to the House of Lords (and in one of these the conditions had been waived by the Appeal Committee). When the leave was unconditional, 25 out of 30 went to the House of Lords. Thus placing the Crown on terms acts not just as a safeguard for the respondent but also as a real deterrent to the appellant.

Just as we know that revenue appeals constitute 30 per cent of the case-load of the House of Lords, we are also aware that at the other extreme some categories of case very seldom obtain leave to appeal. Appeals from county courts, because of the relatively trivial nature of their subject-matter, seldom involve important points of law, although several important cases in the field of landlord and tenant law and the law relating to hire purchase have originated in county courts. Altogether, however, only 10 of the 349 English civil appeals decided in the House of Lords during the period 1952–68 originated in county courts. With appeals in interlocutory matters (including decisions on preliminary points of law) very much the same situation has arisen, with only 13 such appeals heard by the House of Lords during the same period. The Court of Appeal frequently has expressed its reluctance to delay the final trial of actions by granting leave to appeal, even in cases where the point raised is of general importance.

The outcome of applications for leave in county courts, and in interlocutory appeals is as follows:

Interlocutory appeals:
    Total applications   171 (9·4 per cent of all applications)
    Applications successful   11 (6·4 per cent)
County court appeals:
    Total applications   225 (12·3 per cent of all applications)
    Applications successful   24 (10·7 per cent) including 5 on terms.

In Table 8 the 'total appeals' column recorded the total number of appeal transcripts in each year. From this we can calculate the ratio of applications to appeals, but it does not enable us to relate the various categories of case in which there were applications to the overall distribution of cases heard by the Court. To have undertaken a full analysis of the 7,242 appeals heard by the Court of Appeal during the period of our study would have been an immense task, but by confining our detailed analysis to the appeals heard in a single year, 1967, we have been able to keep it within manageable limits. As with any kind of sampling, particularly of the non-random variety, we cannot be sure that the sample which we have selected in this arbitrary manner is wholly representative of the entire case-load. On the other hand, we have no evidence to suggest that the year which we have chosen is atypic, and this procedure probably gives at least a fair indication of the figures involved.

The results of our analysis are set out in Table 11. The first two columns represent a breakdown into case categories of the 109 applications for leave to appeal heard by the Court in 1967, divided into successful and unsuccessful applications. The table indicates that the success rate in fault liability, practice, and property and family law appeals was very low, while the rate was comparatively high in revenue and defamation appeals, and above average in contract cases.

The third column breaks down all the *appeals* heard by the Court of Appeal during 1967. Juxtaposing this column with the first two columns, the ratios of applications to appeals have been calculated and expressed as percentages in the fourth column. It will be seen that the percentage of applications is very high in revenue, defamation and patent appeals, and very low in family law, practice and fault liability appeals. In fact there seems to be a very strong positive correlation between probability of success and rate of application, as one might expect.

The last three columns in Table 11 are added purely for convenience in order to relate this study to our earlier section on the Appeal Committee. They represent breakdowns of 584 English civil petitions heard by the Appeal Committee of the House of Lords during the period 1952–68 derived from our earlier study. The final column represents all English civil appeals heard by the House of Lords during 1952–68. (It must be remembered that these columns cover different periods of time and that the total figures are therefore not strictly comparable.) It is interesting to note that while revenue appeals account for 30 per cent of the case-load of the House of Lords they accounted for only 2·8 per cent of the 1967 appeals in the Court of Appeal. Conversely, appeals on points of practice and on family law together constituted nearly one third of appeals in the Court of Appeal, but only 5·5 per cent in the House of Lords.

It seems reasonable to assume that the majority of cases in which there is a division of opinion in the Court of Appeal involve intricate points of law (not exceptionally obstinate judges): if this is true, we would expect to find that a higher than average proportion of such cases would satisfy the basic criteria for the granting of leave. This hypothesis is borne out by our data.

Of the 1,833 applications, 199 (10·8 per cent) were in appeals in which there was a division of opinion among the judges of the Court of Appeal. Of these, 122 were successful, a rate of 61 per cent as compared with 29·2 per cent for

TABLE 11

Subject-Matter of Appeals and Applications and Petitions for Leave to Appeal to the House of Lords, 1952–1968

Category[a]	Applications for Leave in the C.A. 1967 only[b]		All Appeals in the C.A. 1967[b]	Ratio of applications to appeals (%)	English Civil Petitions to the Appeal Committee (1952–68)		All English Civil Appeals heard by the House of Lords 1952–68
	Successful	Unsuccessful			Successful	Unsuccessful	
Revenue	6	5	12 (2.8%)	92	14	20	106 (30·4%)
Fault Liability	3	20	118 (27·6%)	19·5	25	81	54 (15·5%)
Contract	6	12	55 (11·7%)	33	8	63	42 (12·0%)
Trade Union/R-P	1	0	3 (0·7%)	33	0	5	6 (1·7%)
Master and Servant	0	3	4 (1·0%)	75	0	10	2 (0·6%)
Property	2	16	62 (14·5%)	29	15	63	57 (16·3%)
Company	0	2	6 (1·4%)	33	2	14	3 (0·9%)
Defamation	0	2	4 (1·0%)	50	1	16	4 (1·2%)
Patent	1	6	10 (2·3%)	70	14	15	28 (8·1%)
Practice	0	15	71 (16·6%)	21	4	50	8 (2·3%)
Administrative	2	0	2 (0·5%)	100	8	11	10 (2·9%)
Family	0	4	69 (16·1%)	6	2	41	10 (2·9%)
International	1	0	1 (0·2%)	100	—	—	9 (2·6%)
Constitutional	0	0	0	—	2	5	4 (1·2%)
Transport	0	0	0	—	—	—	1 (0·3%)
Miscellaneous or Unidentified	0	2	11 (2·6%)	—	1	93	5 (1·4%)
Totals	22	87	428		96	488	349

Note: Figures in brackets indicate percentage of total appeals.

[a] These categories conform to the classification we have used throughout this study (see below, pp. 244–5).
[b] 1967 was adopted as a 'specimen' year (see text).

all types of application. Returning to our sample of the 428 appeals and 108 applications heard in 1967, only 21 appeals (4·9 per cent) resulted in a division of opinion, but in 14 of these appeals there was an application for leave, and eight were successful. The high proportion of applications in non-unanimous cases may imply that counsel are well aware of the odds in favour of their success: on the other hand, it may indicate simply that the judges reserve their dissents for the more intricate and important appeals. In fact, both factors probably operate in conjunction. (The question of divided opinions is also considered above in Chapter V and below in Chapter XI.)

The Court of Appeal, like the Appeal Committee, seldom gives explicit reasons for granting or refusing leave to appeal, though reasons are given more frequently than in the Appeal Committee. The absence of reasoned decisions is because a complex combination of factors is usually involved: 'public importance' must be weighed against features of the particular litigation, costs, possible delays, triviality of subject matter, etc. Given a system which stipulates that leave is necessary, it is probably more desirable that the flexible criteria should be applied impressionistically from case to case rather than that rigid rules should be drawn up. The fetish of 'certainty' is not the ultimate virtue here.

We did come across one case in which the Court of Appeal gave full judgments on an application for leave. This was in *Jeffrey* v. *Jeffrey* (1962 Transcript No. 271A) in which the Court was divided (2:1) on the question of leave. This appeal however raised technical jurisdictional points relating to the granting of leave, analogous to those involved in the earlier House of Lords case of *B.* v. *B.* (*No. 2*) discussed elsewhere.

The following selection of factors taken into account by the court in considering applications for leave is derived from the numerous, but scattered, dicta recorded in the transcripts. Very often the reasons can be gleaned only by reading between the lines of the dialogue between court and counsel. The most important point to remember is that the process is impressionistic and not governed by hard and fast rules, except for the requirement of a point of 'general public importance'.

(*N.B.* The references after each case are to the Bar Library Transcript Numbers.)

(1) *Interlocutory Appeals*

'We do not as a rule give leave to appeal in interlocutory appeals', remarked Lord Denning, M.R., in *Beecham Group Ltd.* v. *Bristol Laboratories Ltd.* (1967 No. 110),[1] a statement borne out by our earlier analysis. The principle has been stated in numerous interlocutory applications: even in *Betty's Cafés* v. *Philips Furnishing Stores* (1956 No. 331), an important interlocutory case which had given rise to considerable judicial disagreement, the Court expressed considerable hesitation in granting leave. The appellant company failed in the Lords, [1959] A.C. 20. But this case fared better than *Lewis Altman & Co.* v. *Davison* (1962 No. 234) in which Harman L.J. rejected an application for leave with the words: 'I think these pleadings ought to go, not to the House of Lords, but to the waste-paper basket.' The important factor here is the need for a speedy end to litigation, and the same considerations apply in final appeals: *Cyprianou* v. *Cyprus Lentils Ltd* (1958 No. 201).

(2) *Points of Law*

Broadly speaking, the question must be one of law rather than fact; many applications are refused on this ground. On being asked for leave in *Broll* v.

---

[1] *Hill* v. *C. A. Parsons & Co. Ltd.* [1971] 3 W.L.R. 995, 1011; but see *J. T. Stratford & Son Ltd.* v. *Lindley* [1964] 2 W.L.R. 1002, 1036.

Westmore (1967 No. 69A), Harman L.J. remarked: 'That is a question of fact. Certainly not. You must go to their Lordships' House. They are always very ready to listen to appellants with no case.' Questions of pure construction of a particular document, such as a will or a contract, are usually designated a question of fact: *Fomento (Sterling Area) Ltd.* v. *Selsdon Fountain Pen Co.* (1956 No. 295); but leave may be granted if broad principles of construction are involved: *McLaren* v. *Aberconway* (1952 No. 194A). On occasions, the Court has granted leave in questions of mixed fact and law even where the case has been decided mainly on the facts, as in *Hayward* v. *Port of London Authority* (1955 No. 76). The attitude of the Court towards applications in cases involving concurrent findings of fact has been rather ambiguous, but there have been dicta indicating reluctance to grant leave in such cases. Recent examples include *Pickard* v. *N.C.B.* (1961 No. 165) and *Re Reynold Chain's Application* (Trade Mark) (1966 No. 66). Where statutory construction is involved, the Court may refuse leave if the statute is 'spent' at the time of the hearing: *L.C.C.* v. *Central Land Board* (1958 No. 271). Even in cases decided on their facts, other factors may outweigh this consideration. In *The 'Empire Jamaica'* (1955 No. 255), Lord Evershed M.R., remarked: 'Of course it is a question that we have decided solely on the ground that we thought the learned judge was justified in a matter of fact in reaching the conclusion; but there is a great deal involved and as it is a foreign company, on the whole we will give leave.'

(3) *Amount Involved*

Frequently the judges ask how much money is involved in the case, but this factor seems to play only a marginal and somewhat inconsistent part in the question of granting leave. In *'The Arabot'* (1959 No. 38), leave was refused after the Court had been told that £100,000 was at stake. In the same year in *'The Marinegra'* (1959 No. 38) (which, like *'The Arabot'*, involved a question of liability for a shipping collision) leave was granted, the sum at stake being £125,000. (However, a dissenting judgment was probably the decisive factor in the second example.) More recently, leave was refused in *Murray (Inspector of Taxes)* v. *I.C.I. Ltd.* (1967 No. 93) which involved a sum of £1,000,000. The most that can be said is that the amount at stake may prove decisive in marginal cases.

(4) *Triviality of Subject Matter*

It is sometimes apparent that the Court of Appeal is aware of the importance of the legal principle at stake, but is reluctant to give leave because the facts and subject-matter are trivial. This is illustrated by the refusal of leave in *Sanderson* v. *N.C.B.* (1961 No. 193), described as an important but 'very small' case, and in *Griffiths* v. *Liverpool Corporation* (1966 No. 162). Similarly, in *Sparrow* v. *Fairey Aviation Co. Ltd.* (1961 No. 288) Sellers L.J. said:

'Although I wish it were on better facts, we grant you leave.' (This factor is of great importance in considering the role of the individual litigant *vis-à-vis* the House of Lords acting as a court of cassation. Why should an important point of law remain unsettled, and an appellant be deprived of a judgment, simply because the Court of Appeal believe that a case with 'better' facts may someday arise on the same question?)

(5) *Hypothetical Point*

It was clearly established in *Sun Life Assurance Company of Canada* v. *Jervis* [1944] A.C. 111 that the House of Lords cannot deal with academic questions, in which one or both of the parties has no interest in the outcome of the appeal. This factor has weighed in several refusals of leave by the Court of Appeal, notably in *Warwick R.D.C.* v. *Miller-Mead* (1961 No. 435).

(6) *Hardship to Prospective Respondent*

Under the old *in formâ pauperis* regulations, the Court of Appeal were usually reluctant to give leave where hardship would be imposed on an unassisted person: in *Green* v. *Borough of Chelsea* (1952 No. 137) leave to appeal was refused on this ground, notwithstanding the fact that the Court judged it to be otherwise suitable for hearing by the House of Lords.

The other aspect of this question—reluctance to grant leave in a case where a successful non-legally aided party may not recover his costs—is to be found in *Chapman* v. *Honig* (1963 No. 121) in which Lord Denning said: 'This is a case in which we would certainly in the ordinary way, on account of its general importance, have given leave to appeal to the House of Lords, but in view of the small amount of money involved, and, of much more importance, in view of the present position of the law whereby an unassisted person may find himself saddled with a great amount of costs which would not be paid by the legally-aided person, we do not give leave to appeal. If the law should be altered in future, the position would be different;[1] we do not think, save in exceptional circumstances, that an unassisted person should be taken to the House of Lords and have to find a large sum of money out of his own pocket.'

(7) *Dissenting Judgment*

A division of opinion in the Court of Appeal may be a decisive factor in considering whether to grant leave (see above, pp. 144–5): *George H. Nolan (1956) (Pvt.) Ltd.* v. *H. A. Watson & Company Ltd.* (1965 No. 98) in which leave was granted 'in view of the difference of opinion'.

(8) *Revenue Cases*

Tax cases are a class apart. In *Barclay's Bank Ltd.* v. *C.I.R.* (1959 No. 186) Lord Evershed M.R. remarked exaggeratedly: 'The result of these modern

---

[1] See now Legal Aid Act 1964 and *Gallie* v. *Lee* (*No.* 2) [1971] A.C. 1039.

taxing statutes, complex as they are, is that every case goes to the House of Lords.' On the other hand, in *C.I.R.* v. *Bernstein* (1960 No. 366A) the Court expressed strong opposition to the idea of the taxpayer being used as a 'vehicle' for settling principles of revenue law in the House of Lords.

LEAPFROGGING

To some extent, the force of the argument in favour of abolishing the appellate hierarchy has been diluted by the provisions of the Administration of Justice Act 1969. Belatedly this Act permits certain categories of appeal to 'leapfrog' from the trial judge, over the backs of the Lords Justices, directly to the House of Lords. This idea is not new. It was proposed by Lord Greene M.R. during the 1940s, and adopted by Lord Evershed's Committee on Supreme Court Practice and Procedure which reported in 1953.[1]

The Committee's view on House of Lords reform were set out in a section entitled 'The Problem of the Double Appeal', which reads as follows:

(a) The risk of a double appeal has been much reduced since 1934, when effect was given to the recommendations of the Hanworth Committee[2] that appeals to the House of Lords should require the leave of the Court of Appeal or the House; and in revenue cases where (a matter of principle being involved) the Crown desired to appeal to the House of Lords, it is not uncommon for the Crown to offer to pay in any event the subjects' costs. But the problem still remains and several suggestions have been made in order to meet it. The only objection made, which has not raised insuperable objections, and which we have therefore very fully considered, is a suggestion associated with the late Master of the Rolls, Lord Greene. This is known as the 'leapfrog' scheme. The suggestion is to the effect that a case destined from its character to find its way eventually to the House of Lords should be enabled to go direct to the House from the court of first instance omitting in its progress (or 'leapfrogging') the Court of Appeal.

(b) One difficulty in the way of the scheme undoubtedly lies in the fact that in practice it is not by any means easy to identify at first instance the case so destined for the highest tribunal or the point which requires to be argued there, whatever wisdom may say after the event. We had upon this occasion the advantage of a discussion with all the Lords of Appeal in Ordinary who were, however, generally not favourable to the scheme.

(c) In the circumstances we have confined our recommendation for the adoption of the 'leapfrog' scheme to a limited class of case, viz. where the question at issue is an important point essential to the determination of the cause and is either (i) a question in regard to the construction of a statute which has been fully argued in the High Court, or (ii) is covered by a previous decision of the Court of Appeal, the validity of which it is desired to test.

(d) We confess that we would have liked somewhat to extend the scope of this recommendation. But it is wholly beyond our competence to consider procedure in the House of Lords. The limited recommendation which we have made appeared acceptable to the learned Law Lords, and we think it better and more prudent to give some start to the 'leapfrog' scheme in the hope that, should it be successful, its scope might be extended.

[1] Cmd. 8878. [2] Cmd. 4471, discussed above.

It seems almost a general rule nowadays that official reports must collect cobwebs for many years before being implemented, and this one was no exception.[1] But eventually the Administration of Justice Act 1969 (which took effect on 1 January 1970) gave effect to the leapfrogging proposals, albeit with modifications in points of detail. In particular, at the request of Lord Reid, the consent of all the parties was made a necessary prerequisite for leapfrogging.

The Administration of Justice Bill was introduced in the Lords in November 1968. The leapfrogging provisions proved acceptable in principle, but there were judicial misgivings on points of detail. As Viscount Dilhorne said:

> In my view, when a case comes before the House of Lords, it is of the greatest value to have the views of the Court of Appeal set out in their judgment. And one finds, oddly enough, that as a case progresses the points become crystallised and the point that finally emerges is one that may be thought to have had minor importance at the actual moment of the trial.[2]

Lord Reid too was apprehensive about the 'serious loss' of not having the Court of Appeal's judgments, and predicted that hearings in the House of Lords might take longer than before. However, his Lordship saw this as an experimental measure which could be modified or abolished if necessary.[3] Lord Denning said that he was not worried about cases 'leapfrogging' where the Court of Appeal was bound by the precedent, but felt it would be dangerous to bypass the usual 'sieve' in other cases. He favoured (and added that the Lord Chief Justice supported him on this) proposals to amend the Bill as drafted, so that the issue of leave to leapfrog would ultimately lie with the Appeal Committee rather than with the trial judge. Lord Morris of Borth-y-Gest felt, however, that, on balance, the trial judge should decide, so as to avoid the additional cost and delay of further proceedings before the Appeal Committee.[4]

By the time the Bill reached its committee stage[5] the Lord Chancellor had

---

[1] In the second reading debate on the Administration of Justice Bill, the Lord Chancellor said that the recommendations had not been carried out at the time because, 'although all the Lords Justices supported the Evershed Committee, the then noble and learned Lords of Appeal did not agree to it. The position today, I believe, is that the noble and learned Lords of Appeal agree but I think the Lords Justices, or the majority of them, do not. It is one of the facts of life which every Lord Chancellor has to consider, that seventy or eighty highly independent minds do not always agree . . . .' H.L. Debs., vol. 297, col. 441, 12 November 1968.

[2] Ibid., col. 462.   [3] Ibid., cols. 466–7.   [4] Ibid., cols. 480–2.

[5] H.L. Debs. 3 December 1968, col. 51 ff. See Practice Direction (House of Lords (Leapfrog) Procedure [1970] 1 W.L.R. 97. The first leapfrogging appeal, *American Cynamid* v. *Upjohn Co.* [1970] 1 W.L.R. 1507 was heard on 23/27/28/29 July 1970 on appeal from the judgment of Graham J. dated 3 February 1970, and judgment delivered on 27 October 1970. The new procedure clearly resulted in an expeditious and practical way of disposing of what might otherwise have been prolonged and expensive litigation. (Lord Wilberforce, at p. 1521G.) No Law Lord adverted to the absence of judgments from the Court of Appeal. A certificate to allow a leapfrog was granted to both appellant and respondent in *Ealing London Borough Council* v. *Race Relations Board* [1971] 1 Q.B. 309 and [1972] 2 W.L.R. 71. The second leapfrog case was *Todd* v. *Davison* [1971] 2 W.L.R. 898.

had further consultations with the Lords of Appeal. A compromise amendment was carried dealing with the question of who should grant leave: the final decision was placed in the hands of the Appeal Committee, which would decide the matter on the papers without a hearing. The Bill was further amended, at the suggestion of Lord Wilberforce, to allow the categories of case to which leapfrogging applied to be varied by Order in Council.

Part II of the Act is set out as part of Appendix 1, but basically the preconditions for a case to leapfrog are as follows:

(1) The parties must agree to leapfrog (s.12 (1) (c)).
(2) The judge must be satisfied that a sufficient case has been made to justify a leapfrogging application to be made (s. 12 (1) (b)).
(3) The case must either relate wholly or mainly to the construction of a statute or a statutory instrument, or be a case in which both the trial court and the Court of Appeal (though not the House of Lords, since it can now overrule its own previous decisions) are bound by a previous decision of the House of Lords or of the Court of Appeal (s. 12 (3) (a) (b)).

Having satisfied himself that these conditions are fulfilled, the trial judge[1] may issue a certificate which entitles the parties to apply for leave to leapfrog to an Appeal Committee of the House of Lords, which will determine the question without a hearing (s. 13 (3)).

At the time of writing, it is not possible to say how extensively the Act will be used, but its constitutional and procedural importance should not be underrated. No longer is the appellate hierarchy a straightforward ascent of three judicial tiers: in a limited category of cases the House of Lords will be called upon to act as the first, and only, appellate tribunal. (Though, by the terms of the Act, it will never act as a tribunal of fact, as the Court of Appeal so often does.) The Act emphasizes the supervisory role of the House of Lords by subordinating the importance of the review of a particular case to the public desirability of having important legal issues settled promptly and authoritatively.

So, far from the work of the Appeal Committee being lightened, it has been saddled with yet another administrative burden, albeit a small one; but at least their Lordships have been spared face-to-face confrontations with aspiring leapfroggers. In any event, the cases that are likely to encounter the leapfrogging provisions would be those where the parties are legally represented. The new procedure will doubtless be used with caution in its early days and its significance is circumscribed by the number of hurdles placed in the path of litigants who want to leapfrog. But if its practical importance will be minimal, leapfrogging has entrenched, rather than helped to dislodge, the House of Lords from the pinnacle of the judicial hierarchy.

[1] Or a judge in chambers hearing an interlocutory appeal from a Master, or a Divisional Court.

VIII

LAW LORDS AS JUDGES

LEGAL realists have always acknowledged that mechanistic 'law-finding' by judges is a myth. There is no such thing as depersonalized adjudication, particularly in the Anglo-Saxon legal system which gives so much scope to its judges to indulge in individual pyrotechnics. And it really does matter which judges are detailed to hear particular cases. At first instance, in the Queen's Bench Division of the High Court a case may come before any one of the forty or so puisne judges of that Division. An appeal to the Court of Appeal can be heard by any permutation of (usually) three judges selected from the ranks of thirteen Lords Justices, plus the Master of the Rolls[1]. Occasionally, moreover, osmosis may take place across the semi-permeable boundary separating these tiers of the hierarchy: a Lord Justice may act as supernumerary trial judge, a valuable and refreshing experience for an appeal judge normally isolated from grass-roots forensic jousting. Conversely, a puisne judge may be king for a day when asked to sit as temporary judge in the Court of Appeal. The latter court may also be reinforced by the occasional descent from Olympus of a Lord of Appeal in Ordinary: indeed it is not unheard-of for a Law Lord to sit at first instance.[2] Thus the expectant litigant can find himself confronting almost any one of an infinite range of judicial permutations and, unlike the juryman, a particular judge cannot be excluded by peremptory or any other sort of challenge, save recusal[3] as the result of the disclosure of a personal interest in the subject-matter of an appeal or an acquaintance with the parties.

In the lower courts (other than in the Inner House of the Court of Session which sits in two stereotyped divisions) neither the litigant nor his legal adviser can be absolutely certain—particularly in a finely balanced case—what the judicial reaction is going to be. The House of Lords is a different matter. Ten Lords of Appeal (plus the occasional *ex officio* member) and a large Appellate Committee (normally five judges) still leaves room for a large number of possible permutations, but a very much smaller range than is possible in

---

[1] Prior to the last war the Court of Appeal sat in a formal 'Chancery Division' and a 'Queen's Bench Division'. The distinction has since been relaxed. But it is still common for the Court to include two Lords Justices with Chancery experience when hearing Chancery appeals, and two Queen's Bench Lords Justices in hearing Queen's Bench appeals.

[2] See p. 182 *infra*.

[3] The method of objecting formally to a judge hearing a case.

the Court of Appeal. No outsider knows how the five judges are selected, but there have been instances where the five selected seemed to an outside commentator to be the least suitable. And there have been occasions when the selection of the court has appeared to present particular bias.[1] We shall consider in our final chapter whether it would be desirable to adopt the U.S. Supreme Court practice of providing that every Law Lord should be entitled to sit on every case.

Being a small and élite body of judges whose members are appointed until they retire from judicial life, or are carried prostrate from the forensic arena, the composition of the Court changes very slowly. At the beginning of 1969, only two of the ten Lords of Appeal had been appointed later than 1964 as compared with six of the twelve Lords Justices of Appeal. Table 12 shows the respective number of years (rounded to the number above) which the thirteen English Lords of Appeal who ended their terms of office as Lords of Appeal during the period 1952–68 served in the High Court, the Court of Appeal and the House of Lords respectively.

TABLE 12

Length of Service in Certain Courts of Lords of Appeal

Lord	High Court	C.A.	H.L.
Asquith	8	5	3 (d)
Cohen	3	5	9
Denning	4	9[b]	5
Devlin	12[a]	1	3
Evershed	3	15[c]	3
Jenkins	2	10	4
Morton	8	3	12
Oaksey	12	3	10
Pearce	9	5	7
Porter	4	—	6
Radcliffe	—	—	15
Somervell	—	8	6
Tucker	8	5	11
Total	73	69	94
Average	5·6 years	5·3 years	7·2 years

(d) died in office.

[a] Includes period of presidency of Restrictive Practices Court 1956–60.
[b] Excludes period as Master of the Rolls, 1962 to date.
[c] Includes period as Master of the Rolls, 1949–62.

[1] *Hedley Byrne & Co. Ltd.* v. *Heller & Partners Ltd.* [1964] A.C. 465 provides an illustration of this point. The eventual decision—which significantly extended the law of negligence—was reached by a Court consisting of Lords Reid, Morris of Borth-y-Gest, Hodson, Devlin, and Pearce. But in fact the case had originally come before Lords Radcliffe, Cohen, MacDermott, Jenkins, and Guest, and had been abandoned after one day to permit Lord Radcliff to preside over the Vassall Tribunal. This very 'Chancery' court might well have arrived at a different conclusion. (See R. B. Stevens's article on the case in 27 M.L.R. 121, and particularly n. 34 at p. 130.)

This table shows that those judges who ultimately become Law Lords spend on average to spend 40 per cent of their judicial lives in the House of Lords as compared with 29 per cent in the Courts of Appeal and 31 per cent as puisne judges. (It should be noted that these figures are distorted by one or two exceptional cases, notably Lord Radcliffe who was appointed a Lord of Appeal directly from the Bar, and Lord Devlin whose career as an appellate judge was short-lived owing to early retirement.) Of course, these figures cannot be regarded as indicating much about the career pattern of the judiciary as a whole, since they show only those judges whose exceptional jurisprudential agility ultimately enables them to reach the top of the tree; at the beginning of 1969, the fifty-eight puisne judges had already served for an average of 6·9 years, and the Lords Justices of Appeal for 5·2 years, in that office.[1]

But the fact remains that, whereas the lower courts are founded upon a mass of different combinations of individuals, the House of Lords has a continuity of personnel and a monolithic character all of its own: not perhaps the same degree of continuity which makes the U.S. Supreme Court a sitting target for the sophisticated statistical methodology employed in some modern jurimetric studies, but a quality which is essential to its role as a tribunal of supervision.

The term 'Appellate Committee' is one which is justified by the constitutional position of the House of Lords in its judicial capacity, though in the present context it is a misnomer. Although the Law Lords may represent or resist their *zeitgeist*—those symbolized forces which operate outside their own individualities—they are essentially autonomous individuals contributing to a composite result. The quite astonishing freedom given to the English judge in the style and substance[2] of his reasoned judgment is never more apparent than how the Law Lord tackles his appointed task.

To understand what manner of man sits in the Appellate Committee would be to begin to understand the nature of that court; but by what means are we to penetrate behind the inscrutable faces of these judges? How can we hope to evaluate the amalgam of psychological and social forces which shape the individual judicial ratiocination which, in turn, moulds the role and the character of the House of Lords? Unlike the Associate Justices of the Supreme Court of the United States, the Law Lords have not attracted the attentions of biographers. Nor have they themselves proved fertile in the production of autobiographies.[3] Sixteen of the thirty-four judges who sat in the Appellate Committee during the period 1952–68 are still alive at

---

[1] It is interesting to note that only two of the judges (Lords Evershed and Oaksey) had completed the fifteen years of service necessary to qualify for a full pension. Only Lords Porter and Somervell retired before they had completed fifteen years service, while Lords Devlin, Jenkins and Radcliffe retired shortly after completing this period of service.

[2] See J. G. Wetter, *Styles of Appellate Judicial Opinions.*

[3] Lord Macmillan's *Man of Law's Tale* being a refreshing exception.

the time of writing; the entries in the Dictionary of National Biography and obituary notices in *The Times* of those who have died are a poor substitute indeed for comprehensive biography. This dearth of biography may be applauded by those legalists who see justice as an impersonal process administered faithfully by faceless men, but it presents a considerable handicap to those concerned with discovering what judges do, and why.

Even those biographers who do focus their attention on the judges are likely to face some special difficulties. While judgments, considered as solo performances, may reveal something of their author's personalities, they do little to pierce the veil of judicial secrecy surrounding the interaction of judicial minds which does much to synthesize the judgment of a multi-judge court. What, for example, makes one judge decide to do no more than formally concur, while another is impelled to write at inordinate length his own reasoning for a unanimous decision, even though he proclaims unqualified support for the leading judgment?

Cardozo's remark that 'deep below consciousness are other forces, the likes and dislikes, the predelictions and the prejudices, the complex of instincts and emotions and habits and convictions, which make the man, whether he be litigant or judge'[1] is a truism. But even if we had infinite insight into the these subconscious forces, even if we could evaluate the nature and effect of social pressures and experiences infringing upon every judge, we would still face the daunting task of relating these factors to the end-product of the judicial process in the House of Lords, the individual reasoned opinion. That we lack such insight, and that our models of explanation are crude and unsophisticated, makes the task hopeless.

English judges are an inbred species, concealing much biographical information from the gaze of outsiders. By contrast in America a 'realist' approach to legal theory has flourished, largely because its prophets, men like Holmes, Brandeis, and Cardozo, were themselves judges. In this country we are still wallowing in the slough of Austinian positivism: there is nothing[2] to compare with, for example, the classic work written by Mr. Justice Cardozo, *The Nature of the Judicial Process*, published before that great judge went from the Court of Appeals of New York to Washington to grace the U.S. Supreme Court Bench.

If judges do not expatiate on their work, it is left to legal commentators to fill the gap, with their inherent handicap that any assessment is viewed ex-

---

[1] Cardozo, *The Nature of the Judicial Process*, p. 167.

[2] Unless one includes three essays by members of the Court of Appeal: Lord Evershed, *The Court of Appeal in England* (Athlone Press, 1950); Lord Asquith, 'Some Aspects of the Work of the Court of Appeal', 1 J.S.P.T.L. (this includes the delightful, if unfair, quip that 'a trial judge should be quick, courteous and right; that is not to say that the Court of Appeal should be slow, rude and wrong, for that would be to usurp the function of the House of Lords'); Lord Cohen, 'Jurisdiction, Practice and Procedure of the Court of Appeal', 11 C.L.J. (1951).

ternally and often misses the key internal factor. But, as Mr. Justice Frankfurter once wrote, the writings of those who are not judges are 'too often a
confident caricature rather than a seer's vision of the judicial process'. To
avoid being similarly dubbed we resisted the temptation to write detailed, but
necessarily highly subjective, pen-portraits of the three dozen judges who have
taken part in judicial business in the House of Lords during our period of
study. Apart from a section on the social background of the Law Lords, we
will concentrate more upon *what* the judges do, rather than engage at much
length in the vitally interesting, if somewhat futile speculation as to *why*
they do it. But before proceeding further we feel obliged to recant our statement of purpose to the extent of a short subjective essay on a triumvirate of
legal giants whose shadow has loomed so large as to dominate the course of
judicial business in the House of Lords during the past two decades, Lord
Reid, Viscount Simonds, and Viscount Radcliffe; between them they have
been responsible for nearly 30 per cent of the full opinions delivered in the
House of Lords during the seventeen years of our study, quite apart from their
collective and individual impact on the law of post-war Britain.

Lord Reid has been (and still is at the time of writing) so clearly and decisively the dominant judicial figure, both in length of stay (he was appointed
in 1948) and in his sustained judicial vigour, that it would be almost churlish
in a book on the judicial House of Lords of this period not to single him out
for special mention. A prominent practitioner at the Scots Bar and a politico-
legal figure for a short period as the war-time Lord Advocate, he attained
the highest judicial office direct from advocacy. (This has been quite a common factor among Scottish Law Lords.) Indeed, his judicial 'style' is not
infrequently redolent of his professional career. His questioning (or is it
cross-examining?) of counsel has always been laced with a tincture of advocacy. This is not altogether unwelcome to counsel at the Bar since an
adversary point put forcibly from the Bench is often easier to grapple with
than the more common, neutral observation which gives the speaker little
foothold in scaling the heights of judicial impassivity.

As a later table will show, Lord Reid sat on no fewer than 359 appeals
during the period 1952-68. In that time he dissented only on fifteen occasions,
and most of these judgments were given since he became senior Law Lord.[1]
In about four-fifths of the cases in which he appeared he delivered a fully-
fledged, reasoned opinion as opposed to a formal concurrence, a remarkably
large fraction though attributable to his seniority in the Court. All this is
testimony to a prodigious output of judicial writing: no branch of law has
escaped his imprint.

We would observe, with diffidence, that Lord Reid's vast output of judgments
never quite matched the brilliance of his performance during the hearing of

---

[1] Eight dissents during the period 1963-8.

an appeal. For this judge, the judicial process is a means of worrying out a legal problem to its logical result, and is exhausted within the forensic context. The legal solution is clearly and quickly perceived through the fog of case-law and often prolix advocacy, but the task of setting down on paper the reasoning process seems to have less intellectual attraction for Lord Reid. Usually short; invariably workmanlike and symmetrically unfussy, though spiced here and there with pithy aphorisms; never over-burdened with lengthy quotes from previous decisions; Lord Reid's judgments seldom aspire either to the highest levels of legal scholarship or to memorable literary attainments. Indeed, *triste dictu*, his judgments lack that enduring quality which ensures that a judge lives on after his departure from the Bench. Lord Reid's influence is very much that of today, and it is his peers who relish the true greatness of this wise judge.

The second member of the triumvirate, the late Viscount Simonds, had an unusual career-history. Appointed a Chancery judge in 1937 (he also served as Chairman of the National Arbitration Tribunal from 1940 till 1944) he was appointed a Lord of Appeal directly from the High Court Bench in 1944. In 1951 he was appointed Lord Chancellor in the Churchill government, and eventually gave way to Lord Kilmuir in October 1954. Instead of retreating into the limbo which his age might have demanded (he was then 73) Lord Simonds returned to the bench as senior Law Lord, until his retirement in 1962.

During the seven years of his final stint as Lord of Appeal, Lord Simonds left an indelible impression on the work of the Appellate Committee. Endowed with a powerful intellect, he ranks, by any standards, as a legal giant; but socially he was a reactionary. He epitomized the classical legalistic conservative lawyer, a breed which seems particularly common on the Chancery side of the legal profession. During the latter part of Lord Simond's term of office he was often joined on the bench with, among others, Lord Denning, to whom, ideologically, he was diametrically opposed. The open division between these two intellectually powerful, but irreconcilably different, judicial personalities is now part of legal folklore:[1] but it is perhaps a tribute to Lord Simonds (or, some might say, to the force of orthodox judicial caution) that he almost invariably found himself in the majority. At any event, one could not have contemplated the 1966 statement, changing the rule regarding precedent in the House of Lords, had Lord Simonds still been in harness.

But the fact remains that here was the epitome of the 'professional' judge. Strictly conventional, he produced always workmanlike and often scholarly

---

[1] See the remarks of Lord Simonds on statutory interpretation in an appeal heard during his first term as Lord of Appeal—*Magor and St. Mellons R.D.C.* v. *Newport Corporation* [1952] A.C. 189. See also *Rahimtoola* v. *Nizam of Hyderabad* [1958] A.C. 379 and *Scruttons Ltd.* v. *Midland Silicones Ltd.* [1962] A.C. 446. See also the clash between Viscount Simonds and Lord Denning during a debate on the Charities Bill in 1960. H.L. Debs., vol. 222, cols. 530 and 533.

judgments: not landmarks of legal literature, but a wealth of logically immaculate precedents for future generations of lawyers.

Viscount Radcliffe is the youngest of this trio[1] of judicial colossi. Like Lord Simonds he was a chancery lawyer, but one with far broader (and perhaps more liberal) horizons. A brilliant intellect (he was a Fellow of All Souls from 1922 to 1937) he served as Director of the Ministry of Information throughout the war, and was appointed a Lord of Appeal direct from the Bar in 1949. (It is interesting to note that none of these three great judges ever served in first-tier appeal courts.) During his legal career he was adviser to the Gulbenkian Trustees, and served on numerous public bodies including the Vassall Tribunal.

Sometimes he revealed almost a note of anarchy in his extra-judicial pronouncements (particularly those uttered after retirement), but his fastidious judgments were always notable for their eloquence and symmetry; his prose style was economical to the point of academic astringency, though he occasionally rose to heights of stylistic excellence which far surpassed his two great colleagues. His imprint on revenue law (he was the notable chairman of the Royal Commission) is indelible; in this branch of law there was a depth and sweep about his judgments that marked him out from among his colleagues. After serving his pensionable fifteen years he quietly departed, leaving the stage clear for his erstwhile colleague, Lord Reid.

The English legal profession, centred around its Inns of Courts, its rigid hierarchies and conventions, and a system of exclusive judicial recruitment from those with long service at the Bar, has been accused, not without justification, of obsessive clannishness, sometimes even (much less justly in modern times) of nepotism. A tendency for law to be a family profession, coupled with the special financial burdens which must be borne by a young man making his way at the Bar, have tended to make the profession the preserve of the rich, and of the exceptionally gifted. Gradually this picture is changing: the financial hazards of early practice have been mitigated by the advent of legal aid, and legal education is becoming available (if more slowly than in other subjects) to all classes in society.

But the House of Lords has never been a place for tyros. Even its present members, for the most part, were called to the Bar before the last war and underwent their legal apprenticeship at that time. Their values, largely the products of youthful socialization, are likely to be those of at least three decades past, before the educational reforms of the 1940s, before legal aid, before the advent of a comprehensive welfare state. In the Appellate Committee we would expect to find the last refuge of the lawyer cast in the mould of the nineteenth century Bar.

Who then are these lordly guardians of legal rationality? This question

---

[1] Lord Simonds was born in 1881, Lord Reid in 1890 and Lord Radcliffe in 1899.

prompts a wide variety of answers, ranging from an unadorned list of names, to a multi-volume series of judicial biography. The former would hardly serve any useful purpose; the latter, as well as demanding more than a lifetime's study, would choke the real flora and fauna with an impenetrable undergrowth of useless data.

A balance must be struck between these two extremes. Bearing in mind the terms of reference of the present study, we have selected certain categories of information which, besides being of general biographical interest, help to define the role of the House of Lords in terms of the personalities who constitute it, and enable us to draw some broad conclusions about the structure of the most exclusive sector of the higher judiciary. Fortunately the task of tabulating this data has been greatly facilitated by the fact that only sixty-three Lords of Appeal have been appointed since Lords Blackburn and Gordon became the first holders of the office in 1876, up to the time of Lord Dilhorne's appointment in 1969.[1]

Table 13 is largely self-explanatory: it lists the sixty-three Lords of Appeal in Ordinary who have held office since the passing of the Appellate Jurisdiction Act 1876, in order of the year of first appointment. Against each name is recorded information (where this is available) relating to the period of holding office as Lord of Appeal: age both on first appointment to the higher judiciary and on appointment to the House of Lords; father's occupation; political activity (including any government office); school and university; class of degree (if any), and whether or not the subject of the degree was law. This long and exhausting, but by no means exhaustive tabulation provides an interesting profile of the contemporary Law Lord and of his earlier counterparts.

Clearly it would not be rational to postulate a typical Law Lord. But statistics can be helpful, and for the purpose of statistical analysis we have divided our list of judges into three almost equal but arbitrary sections. The first (Group A) contains the twenty judges appointed in the thirty-eight years up to the beginning of the First World War; the second (Group B) includes the twenty-one Law Lords appointed between 1918 and 1948 (when Lord Reid, the present Senior Law Lord, was appointed); and the third (Group C) includes the twenty-two judges appointed between 1948 and 1969.

In Group A the mean age of the judge on appointment was 60·9 years ($\sigma=4·96$); in Group B 63·0 years ($\sigma=4·7$), and in Group C 61·4 ($\sigma=4·07$). Of course (as the high values for the standard deviations indicate) these average figures conceal a wide variation in individual figures, though only five of the sixty-two judges were aged less than 55 on appointment (Lord Radcliffe was only 50) and twelve were over 65 (Lord Hannen was 70, and Lord Romer 72).

[1] Lord Macmillan wrote a very useful article (97 *Law Journal* 541, 10 October 1947) which includes a list of Law Lords, but some of the dates which he gives appear to be wrong.

TABLE 13

Lords of Appeal in Ordinary since 1876

Name	Period as Lord of Appeal	Age when appointed	Age at 1st higher judicial appointment	Father's occupation and/or rank	Politics	School	University	Degree
A.								
Blackburn (Q.B.)	1876–87 (d. 1896)	63	46	Army		Eton	Cambridge	1 Maths
Gordon (Scot)	1876–9 (d.)	62	55—c.s.		Cons. M.P. Ld. Adv.	Royal Acad. Inverness	Edinburgh	LL.B.
Watson (Scot.)	1880–99 (d.)	53	direct	Cleric	Ld. Adv.	Private	Glasgow	LL.D. (Edin.)
Fitzgerald (Ir. Q.B.)	1882–9 (d.)	66	44	Merchant	Lib. M.P. A.G. (Ir.)			
Macnaghten	1887–1913 (d.)	57	direct	Lawyer (India) M.P. Bt. J.P.	Cons. M.P.	Dr. Cowan's	Cambridge	1 Maths & Classics
Morris (Ir. C.P.)	1889–99 (d. 1901)	63	41		Cons. M.P. A.G. (Ir.)	Gasmus Smith School Galway	Trinity (Dublin)	1
Hannen (Q.B./Pres., P.D.A.)	1891–3 (d. 1894)	70	47	Wine merchant	Lib. cand.	St. Paul's	Heidelberg	
Bowen (Q.B.)	1893–4 (d.)	58	44	Cleric		Rugby	Oxford	1 Classics
Killowen (Russell of)	1894 (few months) (P.-L.C.J.) (d. 1900)	62	direct	Merchant	Lib. M.P. & A.G.	St. Vincents C. Castlekn'	Trinity (Dublin)	No
Davey	1894–1907 (d.)	61	60—L.J.		Lib. M.P. & S.G.	Rugby	Oxford	1 Maths & Classics
Lindley (C.P.–L.J.) M.R.	1899–1905 (d. 1921)	62	47	Academic Botanist		U.C. School	U.C. (London)	No
Robertson (Scot.)	1899–1909 (d.)	54	46—L.P.	Cleric	Cons. M.P. Ld. Adv.	Rona High, Edinburgh	Edinburgh	M.A.
Atkinson (Ir.)	1905–28 (d. 1932)	61	direct	Doctor	Cons. M.P. A.G. (Ir.)	Belfast	Queen's Coll. (Galway)	1 Law
Collins (Q.B. M.R.)	1907–10 (d. 1911)	65	49	Irish Q.C.	Cons. cand.	Dungannon	Trinity (Dublin) & Cambridge	1 Classics

Name	Dates	Age		Father		School	University	Yes
Shaw (Scot.)	1909–29 (d. 1937)	59	direct	Baker	Lib. M.P. Lib. Adv.	Dunfermline	Edinburgh	
Robson	1910–2 (d. 1918)	58	direct, political	Merchant & J.P.	Lib. M.P. & A.G.	Privately	Cambridge	2 Moral Sciences
Moulton	1912–21 (d.)	68	62—L.J.	Cleric & Headmaster	Lib. M.P.	Kingswood	Cambridge & London	1 Maths
Parker (Ch.—not Q.C.)	1913–8 (d.)	56	49	Cleric		Westminster & Eton	Cambridge	1 Classics
Dunedin (Murray) (Scot.)	1913–32 (d. 1942)	64	56—L.P.	Writer to the Signet	Cons. M.P. Lib. Adv.	Harrow	Cambridge & Edinburgh	2
Sumner (Hamilton) (L.J.)	1913–30 (d. 1934)	54	50	Merchant	Cons.	Manchester Grammar	Oxford	1 Classics
B. Cave	1918–22 (P.) (d. 1928)	62	non-political	Business, Lib. M.P.	S.G., Home Secretary, L.C.	Merchant Taylors'	Edinburgh, Oxford	1 Classics
Carson (Ir.)	1921–9 (d. 1935)	67	direct	Architect	M.P. (U), A.G. (I), etc.	Portarlington	Trinity (Dublin)	Law
Blanesburgh (Younger) (Ch.)	1923–37 (d. 1946)	62	54	Brewer		Edin. Acad.	Oxford	2 Juris.
Atkin (K.B.)	1928–44 (d.)	61	46	Queensland Politician & Journalist		Christ's (Brecon)	Oxford	2 Classics
Tomlin (Ch.)	1929–35 (d.)	62	56	Barrister		Harrow	Oxford	1 Juris.
Thankerton (Watson) (Scot.)	1929–48 (d.)	56	direct	Law Lord	Cons. M.P. Ld. Adv.	Winchester	Cambridge	3 Law
Russell of Killowen (Ch.)	1929–46 (d. 1946)	62	52	Hereditary Peer, Law Lord	Ld. Adv.	Beaumont	Oxford	1 Juris.
Macmillan (Scot.)	1930–9 and 1941–7 (d. 1952)	57	direct	Cleric	U./non. pol. Ld. Adv.	Edinburgh	Edinburgh	1
Wright (K.B./M.R.)	1932–5 and 1937–47 (d. 1962)	63	56		Min. of Information	Privately	Cambridge	1 Classics & Moral Science

Name	Period as Lord of Appeal	Age when appointed	Age at 1st higher judicial appointment	Father's occupation and/or rank	Politics	School	University	Degree
Maugham (Ch.)	1935–8 and 1939–41 (d. 1958)	69	62	Solicitor	Cons. L.C.	Dover Coll.	Cambridge	1 Maths
Roche (K.B.)	1935–8 (d. 1956)	64	46	Doctor		Rugby	Oxford	1 Classics
Romer (Ch.)	1938–44 (d. 1944)	72	56	L.J.		Perse	Cambridge	2 Maths
Porter (K.B.)	1938–54 (d. 1956)	61	57				Cambridge	2 Law
Simonds (Ch.)	1944–51 and 1954–62 (d. 1971)	63	56	Brewer	Cons. L.C.	Winchester	Oxford	1 Classics
Goddard (K.B./L.C.J.)	1944–6 (d. 1971)	67	55	Solicitor	'Ind.' cand. (Tory)	Marlborough	Oxford	2 Juris.
Uthwatt (Ch.)	1946–9 (d.)	67	62	Landowner		Ballarat Coll.	Melbourne, Oxford	1
du Parcq. (K.B.)	1946–9 (d.)	66	52	Printer	Lib.	Victoria Coll. (Jersey)	Oxford	2 Classics
Normand (Scot.)	1947–53 (d. 1962)	63	51—L.P.		M.P. (U.) Lib. Adv.	Fettes	Edinburgh, Oxford, & Paris	
Oaksey (Lawrence) (K.B.)	1947–57 (d. 1971)	67	52	Hereditary Peer Judge		Haileybury	Oxford	3 Classics
Morton (Ch.)	1947–59	60	51	Stockbroker		Kelvinside	Cambridge	1 Law
MacDermott (Q.B. N. Ir.)	1947–51 P.-L.C.J. (N.I.) 1951–1971	51	48	Cleric	M.P. (U.) A.G. etc.	Campbell Coll. Belfast	Queen's (Belfast)	1 Law
C. Reid (Scot.)	1948–	58	direct	Farmer	M.P. (U.) Ld. Adv.	Edinburgh Academy	Cambridge	1 Law
Greene (M.R.)	1949–50 (d. 1952)	66	52—L.J.			Westminster	Oxford	1 Classics
Radcliffe (Ch.)	1949–64	50	direct		Min. of Inf. (Director)	Haileybury	Oxford	1 Classics
Tucker (K.B.)	1950–61	62	49			Winchester	Oxford	2 Juris.
Asquith (K.B.)	1951–4 (d.)	61	48	Prime Min.		Winchester	Oxford	1 Classics

Name (Division)	Period as Lord of Appeal	Age on appointment	Age & type of first higher judicial appointment	Occupation	Politics	School	University	Degree
Keith (Scot.)	1953–61 (d. 1964)	67	51—Sen. Coll. J.	business		Hamilton	Glasgow	Mod. Hist.
Somervell (Q.B.)	1954–60 (d. 1960)	65	57—L.J.	Knight Harrow Bursar	Cons. M.P. A.G., Home Sec.	Harrow	Oxford	1 History 1 Chem.
Denning (P.D.A./Q.B./M.R.)	1957–62 (P.-M.R.)	58	45	'Gentleman'		Andover G.S.	Oxford	1 Juris. Maths
Jenkins (Ch.)	1959–63 (d. 1969)	60	48	Indian C.S.		Charter-house	Oxford	2 Classics
Morris of Borth-y-Gest (Q.B.)	1960–	64	49	Bank manager	Lib. cand.	Liverpool Institute	Cambridge & Harvard	2 Law
Hodson (P.D.A.)	1960–71[1]	65	42	Cleric		Cheltenham	Oxford	Distinction wartime short course—Juris.
Devlin (Q.B.)	1961–4	56	43	Architect		Stoneyhurst	Cambridge	2(2) Law
Evershed (Ch./M.R.)	1962–5 (d. 1966)	63	45	Solicitor J.P.		Clifton	Oxford	2 Classics
Guest (Scot.)	1961–1971[2]	60	56—Sen. Coll. J.		Cons. cand.	Merchiston	Cambridge & Edinburgh	2 Law
Pearce (P.D.A./Q.B.)	1962–9	61	47	Teacher		Charter-house	Oxford	3 Classics
Donovan (Q.B.)	1963–71 (d.)[4]	65	52	Teacher K.C.	Lab. M.P.	Brockley G.S. & privately	Cambridge	1 Law/Engineering
Upjohn (Ch.)	1963–71 (d.)[3]	60	48			Eton		
Wilberforce (Ch.)	1964–	57	54		Cons. cand.	Winchester	Oxford	1 Classics
Pearson (Q.B.)	1965–	66	52	Indian judge		St. Paul's	Oxford	2 Classics
Diplock (Q.B.)	1968–	61	49	Barrister		Whitgift	Oxford	2 Chem.
Dilhorne (Manningham-Buller) (—)	1969–	64	direct	Solicitor	Cons. M.P. S.G., A.G., L.C.	Eton	Oxford	3 Juris.

KEY: Ir.—Irish; Scot.—Scottish; Q.B.—Judge of the Queen's Bench Division; C.P.—Judge of Common Pleas Division; Ch.—Judge of Chancery Division; P.D.A.—Judge of the Probate, Divorce & Admiralty Division; L.C.J.—Lord Chief Justice; L.C.—Lord Chancellor; M.R.—Master of the Rolls; L.P.—Lord President Court, of Session; L.J.—Lord Justice of Appeal; U.—Unionist; A.G. (Ir.)—Attorney-General (Ireland); S.G.—Solicitor General; Ld. Adv.—Lord Advocate. A.G.—Attorney-General; (d.)—died in office; P.—relinquished office as Lord of Appeal upon appointment to another judicial office. Except where otherwise indicated the 'first higher judicial appointment' is a puisne judgeship.

[1] Succeeded in April 1971 by Lord Simon of Glaisdale (formerly Sir Jocelyn Simon, President of the Probate, Divorce and Admiralty Division 1962–1971).

[2] Succeeded on 30 September 1971 by Lord Kilbrandon, Senator of College of Justice, and Chairman of Scottish Law Commission 1965–1971.

[3] Succeeded in February 1971 by Lord Cross of Chelsea, a Chancery Lord Justice of Appeal.

[4] Succeeded in January 1972 by Lord Salmon, a Common Law Lord Justice of Appeal.

There are interesting variations in the length of service of the judges shown in Table 14.

TABLE 14

Length of Service of Lords of Appeal in Ordinary by Nationality

Group	Nationality	No. in Group	Average period as Lord of Appeal (years)
A	English	12	8·0
	Scottish	5	14·2
	Irish	3	13·4
B	English	16	9·1
	Scottish	3	13·3
	Irish	2	6·0
C	English	19 (11)	6·3[a]
	Scottish	3 (1)	—
	Irish	0	—

[a] Average calculated only for those judges who had completed their careers in the House of Lords on 31 December 1968 (number shown in brackets).

To some extent the longer periods of service of the Scots Law Lords is explained by a slightly lower than average age on appointment, 59·8 years. The decline in the number of Irish judges is explained by the reduction in the geographical extent of the appellate jurisdiction of the House of Lords in Ireland since partition: and perhaps the absence of an Irish judge among the contemporary Lords of Appeal is explained by the strengthening of the Northern Ireland judiciary by the appointment of Lord MacDermott as Lord Chief Justice of Northern Ireland in 1951 (and by the fact that Lord MacDermott has also been one of the most consistently active *ex officio* Law Lords since 1951)[1] though he has never sat in that capacity in an appeal from Northern Ireland.

It is interesting to compare the previous judicial experience of the judges in the three groups. In Group A, six Law Lords (including two Scots and one Irish) were appointed to the House of Lords without having had previous higher judicial experience. Of the fourteen with previous judicial experience, two had been appointed directly as Lords Justices of Appeal, and two as Lord Presidents of the Court of Session: the average length of the period served by these fourteen judges in the lower courts was 12·9 years. In Group B only four Law Lords lacked previous experience. Of the seventeen appointees with judicial experience one had been Lord President; the average length of previous judicial experience was nine years. Finally, moving on to the present day judges in Group C we find only three direct appointments to the House of

[1] See below.

Lords, and one of these, Viscount Dilhorne, had had considerable previous experience as an *ex officio* member of the Appellate Committee by virtue of his former office as Lord Chancellor. Of the nineteen Law Lords remaining, two had been appointed directly as Lords Justices of Appeal and two as judges of the Inner House of the Court of Session: the average length of their experience was 12·0 years. Thus the House of Lords seems to be assuming a more clearly defined role as the top rung of a judicial promotion ladder, in restricting its membership very largely to lawyers with long records of service in the lower courts. (It must be remembered that even those appointed directly from the Bar have usually—if they were Queen's Bench lawyers—had some judicial experience, as recorders, as chairmen of quarter sessions, or as commissioners of assize.)

So far we have dealt only with the route by which the Law Lords reach the House of Lords and how long they stay, but by what route do they leave the House? Here the figures seem to indicate either that nowadays we are firmer and fairer in our provision for the retirement of our senior judges, or that we appoint judges who are physically more resilient than those of two generations past.

Of the twenty judges in Group A, nine died in office, one (Lord Russell of Killowen) was appointed Lord Chief Justice, and ten retired. The average age at death of those who died in office was 67·0 years: the others retired at an average of 73·1 years and lived for an average of 6·1 years after retiring. The longest-lived judges of the period were: the Scottish judge, Lord Dunedin, who retired at 83 and died ten years later; Lord Macnaghten, who died at 83 after twenty-six years in the House of Lords; Lord Atkinson who retired at 84 having served for twenty-three years (he died four years later); and another Scottish judge, Lord Shaw, who served for twenty years, retired at 79 and died at 87.

In Group B there is a significant drop in the number of Law Lords dying in office to a mere five. Fourteen of the remaining judges retired from office; Lord Cave left to become Lord Chancellor, and Lord MacDermott to become Lord Chief Justice of Northern Ireland. It is interesting that no fewer than four of the Law Lords in this group sandwiched a period of other office between two stints as Lord of Appeal: Lord Macmillan served for two years as Minister of Information, Lord Wright was Master of the Rolls, and Lords Maugham and Simonds held office as Lord Chancellor. The Law Lords who died in office did so at an average age of 75·8 years. The others who retired did so at an average of 75·0 years: four of them were still alive at the time of writing, but three of them died in 1971 aged respectively 84, 94 and 91 (Simonds, Goddard and Oaksey). The other ten lived for an average of 7·8 years after retirement. The group bears strong testimony to judicial longevity; Lord Wright who retired aged 78 after fifteen years as Lord of Appeal (broken by a two year interlude as Master of the Rolls) lived to be 93.

Viscount Maugham died, aged 92, after seventeen years of retirement. All the three who died in 1971 were significant additions to the number of lawyers among the population of nonagenarians.

Group C includes eleven Law Lords who have ended their judicial careers, one judge (Lord Denning) who left the House of Lords to become Master of the Rolls, and ten Lords of Appeal still holding office at the end of the period covered by this table. There has been a marked drop in the mean age of retirement to 68·0 years; only one of the judges, Lord Keith, stayed until the age of 75, and Lord Devlin retired at 59 after a mere three years in the House of Lords. (Of course, there is distortion in this figure because 'late retirers' are still serving.) Perhaps the judges are becoming increasingly aware of the opportunities to carve out new careers in non-judicial public service, viz. Lord Pearce who became chairman of the Press Council. Or perhaps the general tendency for earlier retirement (coupled with a favourable pension scheme) has impressed upon judges the advantages of leaving the Bench while still active, instead of being carried out feet first like so many of their predecessors.

One of the most interesting pieces of information in analysing the characteristics of an élite group is father's occupation—which not only tells us something about the social mobility of the judges but also throws light upon the question of whether the myth of legal 'dynasties' has any substance in fact. Analysis of published information (including Inns of Court records) has supplied information about the fathers of fifty-three of the sixty-three Lords.

Of the fifty-three judges, eighteen had fathers with some legal background. The Lord Russell appointed to the House of Lords in 1929 was the son of Lord Russell of Killowen, who had served as a Lord of Appeal for a few months in 1894, and then became Lord Chief Justice.[1] On the Scottish side, Lord Thankerton (also appointed in 1929) was the son of Lord Watson, who had been a Law Lord from 1880–99. Lord Oaksey was the son of the former Lord Chief Justice, Lord Trevethin (formerly A. T. Lawrence J.), and Lord Romer's father had been a Lord Justice of Appeal. Four more Law Lords were sons of barristers (two had taken Silk, one in Ireland). Four were the sons of solicitors, and one had a father who had been a Writer to the Signet. Lord Macnaghten's father had practised law in India, and the father of Lord Wilberforce had been a judge in that country. The fathers of three of the Law Lords had been Justices of the Peace, though this is more indicative of social standing than of a hereditary legal bent.

Most of the remaining Law Lords clearly come from solid middle-class professional backgrounds; eight fathers were in holy orders, eleven were in various categories of business (including two brewers), of whom only one could be described unequivocally as working class. One was a stockbroker, one had a military background. Three were farmers or landowners. Two more

[1] And the second Lord Russell of Killowen was the father of the present Lord Justice Russell.

were doctors, two were schoolmasters, two were architects, and one was a university teacher. Political careers appear to have been remarkably few and far between, though of course Lord Asquith's father was the Liberal Prime Minister.

All in all, the picture is one of unexciting but worthy professionalism; only a handful of the Law Lords seem to have burst through the class barrier and achieved judicial success after a humble upbringing. This is borne out by the pattern of their educational backgrounds: the list of schools which the Law Lords attended presents an almost unbroken sequence of Clarendon Public Schools and private tuition. Of the fifty-six judges whose schools are known, nearly a third attended either Winchester (6), Eton (5), Harrow (3), or Rugby (3): Lord Denning's attendance at Andover Grammar School, Lord Donovan's at Brockley Grammar School, and Lord Morris of Borth-y-Gest's at Liverpool Institute are lone palm trees in a desert of educational class privilege, matched only by Lord Sumner who was at Manchester Grammar School.

If exclusiveness is the order of the day as regards schools, the list of universities attended underlines this still further. Of sixty-one Law Lords whose universities are known, thirty attended Oxford (including Lord Normand, who also attended the Universities of Edinburgh and Paris). Sixteen went to Cambridge (including Lords Collins, Moulton, and Morris of Borth-y-Gest who also attended other universities). The Scottish Universities, Edinburgh and Glasgow, account for seven (all Scots) Law Lords (two of whom also attended other universities). Trinity College, Dublin was attended by four (including Lord Collins who then proceeded to Cambridge). Only Lords Lindley and Moulton attended the University of London: the former did not take a degree, and the latter had first attended Cambridge. Three judges attended overseas universities (two having taken degrees in England). Lord Atkinson attended Queen's College, Galway (which was part of the old Royal University of Ireland). The nearest approach to 'redbrick' was made by Lord MacDermott, who attended the Queen's University, Belfast. We have records of only three judges who took no degrees: Lord Lindley (already mentioned), Lord Russell of Killowen who attended Trinity College, Dublin, and Lord Donovan who attended no university.

The class of degree obtained is known in fifty cases. Thirty Law Lords obtained a first (or, in a few cases, a double first) in their final examination, a remarkably high proportion; sixteen obtained seconds, four obtained lower seconds or thirds (some of these had achieved a higher class in moderations). Only eighteen of the judges have degrees in Law or in Jurisprudence, an eloquent testimony to the robust tradition of 'on the job' training for members of the Bar. Most of the Law Lords had degrees in the classics or in Literary Humanities, though the list does include six mathematicians and a sprinkling of scientists.

Perhaps the most important information about the judges' backgrounds is their degree of party political affiliation. Political patronage would be unthinkable in the context of appointment to the contemporary higher judiciary. But, although the House of Lords acquired its present judicial role as recently as 1876, the elimination of political appointments has only taken place during the past few decades. Though if (particularly during the era of Lord Halsbury) some appointments to the bench have in the past involved a strong party political factor, this is by no means necessarily the same as saying that judicial quality has been sacrificed on the altar of political jobbery.

The twenty judges in Group A included no fewer than eleven former M.P.s (five Conservatives and six Liberals), ten Law Officers (several Lords Advocate) some of whom were also M.P.s, and three former Parliamentary candidates (two Conservative and one Liberal). Lord Sumner is also listed as a Tory supporter.

Group B shows a slight drop in overt political activity, five Conservative or Unionist M.P.s (including one Lord Chancellor), five Law Officers (only one of whom was 'non-political': Lord Macmillan, a Unionist supporter, became a 'non-political' Lord Advocate in the first Labour Government, all other law officers were M.P.s), and one Liberal (Lord du Parcq).

By comparison with their predecessors the political activism of the more recent Law Lords in Group C appears almost non-existent. Four M.P.s (two Conservative, one Unionist, and one Labour), one of whom was a Lord Chancellor; and one Conservative and one Liberal candidate. The M.P.s include two former Law Officers.

In earlier days it was by no means unheard-of for a Law Lord to retain government office while still on the bench. For example, from 13 November 1918 to 14 January 1919 Lord Cave was both a Lord of Appeal and Home Secretary.[1] Similarly, Lord Haldane remained at the War Office while sitting as a Law Lord; Lord James of Hereford was appointed to the Judicial Committee of the Privy Council in 1902 while Chancellor of the Duchy of Lancaster.

The era of political appointments probably passed away with the advent of Lord Sankey as Lord Chancellor in 1929;[2] eminently professional judges such as Lords Atkin, Tomlin, Russell, Thankerton, Macmillan, and Wright set the tone of the court during the 1930s. It is probable, however, that, even in its heyday, the extent of patronage, and the perniciousness of its effects on legal impartiality, has been greatly exaggerated. Professor Heuston quotes several dicta[3] of legal and political figures at the beginning of this century supporting the notion that political expertise is no bad thing for an appellate judge. But his careful analysis of the judicial appointments of Lord Hals-

[1] Heuston, *Lives of the Lord Chancellors*, p. 420.
[2] Abel-Smith and Stevens, *Lawyers and the Courts*, p. 118.
[3] Heuston, op. cit., p. 39, quoting Haldane.

bury[1] does much to undermine the myth that even Halsbury sacrificed quality to gain party political advantage. In any event there is little evidence to suggest that a judge with a political background must *ipso facto* be less legally competent, or that his ideology will adversely affect his judgments. It is far more likely that the uniformly middle-class backgrounds of the judges, coupled with a long spell of legal training (in itself, a powerful instrument of socialization) does much to shift the ideological complexion of the judiciary well to the right of centre, whatever the extent of overt party political affiliation in individual judges. But the problem here is one of impartial justice being seen to be done—particularly in areas of public law—and one has considerable sympathy for the Liberal Attorney-General, Robson, who wrote to Asquith in 1910 requesting the appointment of more Liberal Law Lords. The House of Lords, he argued, 'would have to play a great part in disputes that are legal in form but political in fact, and it would be idle to deny the resolute bias of many of the judges—there and elsewhere. That bias would probably operate more than ever in cases that touch on labour, educational, constitutional and, for the future I might perhaps add,[2] revenue questions.'[3]

It is easy to overestimate the importance of this single and rather crude factor, party politics, as a part of the inarticulate major premise which shapes the final product of a judge's reasoning. It is more relevant to look at the legal background and experience of Law Lords rather than to speculate on political bias which may or may not infect or shape judicial attitudes.

Perhaps the most graphic way of illustrating the changing legal and national composition of the House of Lords since 1876 is to look at the holders of the office of Lord of Appeal at regular intervals, and for this purpose we have calculated the composition of the House at the beginning of each decade from 1880 onward.

This table reflects the effects of a variety of statutes which have prescribed the maximum number of Lords of Appeal over the years:[4] no statute, however, has ever attempted to lay down the number of Law Lords to be appointed from the various branches of the profession, or the number of Scots and Irish judges who should sit in the House. This has resulted in a wide fluctuation, particularly in the ratio of common law judges to Chancery judges. As regards Irish judges, Lord Atkinson sat in the House for twenty-three years up to 1928 (and from 1921–8 two Irishmen were on the bench); then there was a gap of nineteen years before Lord MacDermott's brief term of office in the Lords. (The very small size of the Northern Ireland Supreme Court means that

---

[1] Ibid., Chapter 5.
[2] This remark displays considerable prescience if viewed from the era (now passing away) of S.E.T.
[3] Quoted by Heuston, op. cit., p. 151. The impact of the shifting complexion of the House of Lords is examined by R. B. Stevens in his article 'The Role of a Final Appeal Court in a Democracy: the House of Lords Today', 28 M.L.R. 509 (1965).
[4] See Chapter VI.

TABLE 15

Composition of the House of Lords, 1880–1970

Year	Law Lords				Total
	English C.L.	English Ch.	Scottish	Irish	
1880	1	—	1	—	2
1890	—	1	1	1	3
1900	1	2	1	1	5
1910	1	1	1	1	4
1920	1	2	2	1	6
1930	2	3	2	—	7
1940	3	3	1	—	7
1950	2	4	2	1	9
1960	3	4	2	—	9
1970	6	2	2	—	10

judicial talent of the calibre of Lord MacDermott is hard to find.) On the Scots side the number has been fairly stable at two since 1913, though with brief spells with only one Scot sitting, and a period 1930–2 when three Scots Law Lords sat.[1] As about one-fifth of all appeals heard are Scottish, a ratio of two Scots Law Lords out of ten seems quite reasonable: but what this does mean, on the other hand, is that even in a Scottish appeal (except in 'freak' circumstances) the Scots can never assume an overall majority in a court of five judges.[2]

We have already seen evidence of the fluctuations in the proportion of Chancery judges in the House of Lords, and the above table emphasizes this very strongly. In 1950 no fewer than four of the nine judges came from the Chancery Division,[3] by 1970 it was two out of ten: perhaps the Chancery side is now somewhat under-represented, particularly in view of the high percentage of revenue appeals. (Though since this is not exclusively a Chan-

[1] Lord Macmillan records (*Man of Law's Tale*, p. 149) that, of the Lords of Appeal who held office when he was appointed to the Lords in 1930, three (Lords Dunedin, Thankerton, and Macmillan) were Scots, Lord Atkin was born in Australia and Lord Russell of Killowen was an Irishman, 'so that Lord Tomlin alone could claim an unalloyed English origin'. (We are reminded of the quip that all the great English judges have been Scots, Irish, Welsh, Jewish or Catholic.)

[2] On 17 January 1968 Mrs. Ewing (Scottish Nationalist) asked the Secretary of State for Scotland 'if he will introduce legislation to set up a Scottish division of the Judicial Committee [*sic*] of the House of Lords and to provide that only judges trained in Scots law should act as the final appeal judges in Scottish civil cases'. The Minister (Mr. Ross) replied: 'It is established practice that two of the nine [as the establishment then was] Lords of Appeal in Ordinary are appointed from the Scottish Bench or Bar. It would not be practicable to maintain a separate Scottish division to deal with the small number of Scottish appeals presented to the House of Lords—12 and 5 in 1966 and 1967, respectively.' H.C. Debs., vol. 756, col. 579. See also col. 629, ibid.

[3] Lords Simonds, Morton of Henryton, Greene and Radcliffe.

cery subject—until recently, revenue cases were in Queens Bench list—there is little significance in this.)[1]

There is a tendency to think of the House of Lords as a monolithic institution trading in a commodity loosely described as 'English law'. This, of course, is only half the truth: the House is the final court of appeal for the whole of the United Kingdom, and this jurisdiction is wide indeed. One day the Law Lords may be dealing with a technical infringement of a gaming statute, the next day with a recondite Scottish land law case: family law, patents, shipping collisions, and (most frequent of all) revenue problems are all grist to the lordly mill. Yet in the lower courts there is considerable specialization of function: indeed it is interesting to consider the increasing generalization which takes place as one ascends the judicial pyramid. This is illustrated most clearly in the field of English tax law discussed in more detail in Chapter xv: a case proceeds from the Income Tax Special Commissioners—an august, but non-political body of experts in the field of revenue law—to a Chancery judge for whom tax is but one part (if an important one) of his wide jurisdiction, which includes such unlikely bedfellows as trusts, wards (until the Administration of Justice Act 1970), and partnerships. In the Court of Appeal, the appeal will be heard by three judges—usually including one or two, rarely all three, with Chancery backgrounds—whose day-to-day work is 'specialized' only to the extent that they deal exclusively with English appeals in civil and, since 1966, criminal causes. In the House of Lords, even this limited degree of specialization is lacking: and it is this omnivorous nature of the House of Lords which is part of the key to its utility as a unifying and supervising force (as well as its downfall by denying it sufficient material in any one area of lawmaking).

This catholicity inevitably has its impact on the structure of the court and upon the procedure for selecting those who are to man it. In law, as in so many professional fields, the cult of the generalist has passed. Thus the House of Lords at any given time will include judges whose training and background equips them to deal with highly specialized problems. The modern practice has been to include among the Law Lords two Scots judges, at least two English Chancery judges, and one judge from the Probate, Divorce and Admiralty Division of the High Court: there has also emerged the tendency for individual judges to specialize in particular fields, as exemplified by the late Lord Upjohn's activities in the field of patent law.

There really seems to be no hard and fast rule as regards the proportions of various categories of judge, though the House has always included at least one Scots judge, and in recent years, two. The number of Chancery judges has, as we have seen, varied considerably, and this is reflected in the proportion of judgments delivered. Table 16 expresses the ratio of attendances by English Chancery judges in civil appeals, to the attendances of English common law

1 See also Table 16, below and p. 317.

judges, for each of the years 1952–68. (We have omitted the Scots on the assumption that their presence is a neutral feature in this context).

TABLE 16

Ratio of Chancery Judges to Common Lawyers, 1952–1968
(civil appeals only)

Year	Chancery attendance	C.L. attendances	Ratio	'Chancery' cases[a] (%)
1952	23	56	0·41	42
1953	20	32	0·63	56
1954	27	37	0·73	33
1955	55	70	0·79	37
1956	71	58	1·2	12
1957	60	33	1·8	36
1958	37	36	1·03	33
1959	58	45	1·3	36
1960	71	44	1·6	25
1961	44	77	0·77	25
1962	37	78	0·47	32
1963	39	77	0·51	28
1964	44	49	0·90	29
1965	36	58	0·62	38
1966	37	58	0·64	34
1967	34	73	0·47	20
1968	29	54	0·54	41

[a] Revenue cases, patent, trade mark, and copyright cases and cases involving wills, settlements, and trusts. (*N.B.* percentages are based on relatively small totals.)

There was a time—from 1956–60—when the House was dominated by Chancery lawyers: this was, as we saw at the beginning of the chapter, the heyday of Lord Simonds, Lord Radcliffe, Lord Morton of Henryton and Lord Cohen. There was even a unique occasion when an appeal (a town and country planning case)[1] was decided by five Chancery lawyers (the four Chancery Law Lords, plus the then Master of the Rolls, Lord Evershed). It should be noted that, using as a rather crude index the total percentages of revenue cases, patent trade marks, and copyright cases, and those appeals involving wills, settlements and trusts, the percentage of 'Chancery-type' cases in each year seems to have little bearing on the structure of the court. This is only to be expected, since the composition of the court tends to be fairly static over the years—and (apart from bringing in suitably qualified outsiders to act as *ex officio* judges) there would be great difficulty in adapting it quickly to meet a changing case-load.

For the most part the composition of the court (in terms of the legal back-

[1] *East Riding County Council* v. *Park Estate (Bridlington) Ltd.* [1957] A.C. 223.

ground of the judges) tends to fall into a number of conventional patterns. The five most common types of composition in civil appeals during the period 1952–68 were as set out in Table 17.

TABLE 17

Composition of the House of Lords in Civil Appeals, 1952–1968

Number of Judges in each category			Nationality of Appeal	
Common Law	Non-Common Law	Scottish	English and Northern Irish	Scottish
1	2	2	57	27
2	2	1	70	6
2	1	2	38	29
3	1	1	64	8
1	3	1	29	5
			258	75

Thus 71 per cent of English and 74 per cent of Scottish appeals were heard by one of these combinations of judges. Scottish judges play a large role in Scottish appeals: 77 per cent of Scottish appeals were heard by a House containing two or more Scottish Law Lords, as compared with only 34 per cent of English and Northern Irish appeals.

In the majority of appeals (78 per cent) balance was maintained by the presence of at least one judge from each category; but in 103 civil appeals at least one category of judge was not represented. This total is made up as set out in Table 18.

TABLE 18

Civil Appeals in which One Category of Judge was not present, 1952–1968

Category of Judge not present	Nationality of Appeal[a]	
	English/Irish	Scottish
Common Law	13	3
Non-Common Law	38	14
Scottish	39	0

[a] The figures add up to 107 because of four cases in which two categories were not represented.

Occasionally a 'freak' of judicial selection resulted in the court containing only a single species of judge: one case[1] was heard by four English common

[1] *Verdin* v. *Coughtrie* [1961] A.C. 880.

lawyers only, two[1] were heard by five English common lawyers, and another (already mentioned) was heard by five Chancery judges. One remarkable appeal[2] resulted in only four judgments, delivered by three Scots judges and by Lord MacDermott, the Lord Chief Justice of Northern Ireland.

So far we have confined our discussion of the composition of the court to civil appeals. When we come to criminal appeals we find a markedly different pattern. The most marked characteristic of these cases is the dominance of English common law judges. Of the forty-six criminal appeals decided over the period 1952–68, only five were decided by a court containing as many as two Scots judges and nine contained no Scots. As regards English non-common law judges[3]—none were present in twelve criminal appeals, in three cases two judges in this category were present, but in three cases the three Chancery judges were actually in the majority. In sixteen of the cases four common lawyers were present and in two more five were present. (By comparison, in about ten times the number of English civil appeals only twenty-one were decided by a court containing four common lawyers, and two by five common lawyers; this did not occur in any Scottish or Irish appeals.)

So far we have only set out some of the bare facts relating to the composition of the House of Lords, but what is their importance? How do differently composed courts react to different types of legal problem? Alas, having brought the reader to the brink of this particular problem, we have to confess that a full treatment of this intriguing question lies outside the scope of an already very long chapter. The variables which would have to be considered in a full analysis include: the composition of the House of Lords itself; the division of opinion within the House; the outcome of the appeal in terms both of the result below and the degree of acceptance of the arguments adopted by the courts *a quo* (essentially an unquantifiable factor); the composition of the courts *a quo*; and the division of opinion among the appeal judges, and so forth.

The problem is that the data we are handling is relatively crude, whereas the sociology and psychology of the judicial process is highly complex. As mentioned in our introduction, we could attempt to explore hypotheses such as the 'Anglicization' of Scottish judges, or the degree of consensus among Chancery judges, but this would be to indulge a statistical whim and to unbalance the central purpose of this study. We confine ourselves, therefore, to an informed guess. Too much can be made of the Common

---

[1] *Earl Fitzwilliam's Wentworth Estates Co.* v. *Minister of Housing and Local Government* [1952] A.C. 362; and *Wheat* v. *E. Lacon & Co. Ltd.* [1966] A.C. 552.

[2] *C.I.R.* v. *Wilson's (Dunblane) Ltd.* [1954] 1 W.L.R. 282. The 'freak' composition of the court in this case resulted from the fact that Lord Simon, who had heard argument, died before judgment was delivered.

[3] This may well be the result of a deliberate policy on the part of the Lord Chancellor and his Permanent Secretary to ensure that only those with some experience of criminal trials should sit on criminal appeals.

Law versus Chancery versus Divorce factor. Anyone who reaches the House of Lords will have a sufficiently broad-based background to tackle most of the problems arising, and further expertise can be acquired on the job. In Part C, however, we analyse (impressionistically) the output of this élite body of judges in various areas of law in an attempt to add another dimension to this statistical picture.

In Chapter x we shall discuss the work of the Law Lords in their secondary capacity as fully paid-up members of the legislature. It remains for us to consider the amount of work they do in their principal role as judges. Just as one cannot hope to evaluate legislative activity simply in terms of bare attendance in the Chamber of the House of Lords, so judicial activity cannot be measured simply by counting the number of appearances on the Appellate Committee. The main reason for this is that in only a minority of cases does every one of the Law Lords hearing argument elect to write a full assenting or dissenting judgment: in most cases one or more of the judges formally concurs in the reasoning adopted in the leading speech; in a few cases only a single fully reasoned judgment is delivered. But one must be cautious in attributing judicial inactivism. A Law Lord, particularly a junior one, may write a judgment only to find that he is repeating what his senior colleagues have already written. He then withholds his own words and formally concurs. Table 19 shows that 27 per cent of the individual speeches delivered in English and Northern Irish civil appeals were formal concurrences in the result, as were 30 per cent of the judgments in Scottish appeals and 44 per cent of the judgments in criminal appeals.

The table as a whole consists of a comprehensive breakdown of the types of judgment delivered by each judge in every category of appeal during the period 1952–68: it is arranged in the form of a 'league table'[1] of judicial attendances in the Appellate Committee.

Perhaps the point which first strikes the reader of this table is the remarkable record of Lord Reid, alluded to earlier in this chapter. As the only judge whose judicial career has spanned the entire seventeen-year period of the present study, it is hardly surprising that he has dominated the work of the court: but the extent to which his work-load has eclipsed that of his brother judges is quite remarkable. Lord Reid has been present at about 70 per cent of all the appeals (and over 80 per cent of Scottish appeals) heard by the House of Lords during the period: he has delivered 14·4 per cent of all the *full* judgments in English and Northern Irish civil and criminal appeals, and 22 per cent of the full judgments in Scottish appeals, a phenomenal record for a single member of a court normally composed of five judges.

---

[1] It is only fair to point out that the 'league table' is an artificial device based upon judicial performance over an arbitrary range of years. Many of the judges listed will continue to make further contributions and the figures shown in the table are of value only to the extent that they throw light on the work of the Court during our period of study.

TABLE 19. *Judgments in House of Lords Appeals, 1952–1968*

Lords (in order of attendances)	Years of sitting[a]	Total full judgments			Total formal concurrences			Concur-rences as % of at-tendances	Full dissents		
		Eng.[a]	Cr.[b]	Sc.[c]	Eng.	Cr.	Sc.		Eng.	Cr.	Sc.
Reid (359)[e]	1952–68	190	18	76	55	10	10	21 (12)[f]	9	2	4
Simonds (174)	1954–66	117	7	25	19	1	5	14	6	1	1
Hodson (148)	1960–8	65	15	12	38	10	8	38	6	—	2
Guest (145)	1961–8	57	5	34	36	7	6	34 (15)	7	—	6
Morris of Borth-y-Gest (141)	1960–8	75	19	9	19	9	10	27	8	—	2
Morton (140)	1952–66	95	3	18	20	1	3	17	10	—	2
Tucker (140)	1952–63	57	5	13	47	4	14	46	3	—	—
Keith (136)	1954–63	64	—	37	31	1	3	25 (8)	18	—	4
Cohen (123)	1952–66 (excl. '64)	56	—	13	37	—	17	46	3	—	—
Radcliffe (115)	1952–64 (excl. '58)	79	5	6	16	2	7	22	7	2	1
Pearce (104)	1962–8	43	8	10	22	11	10	41	2	1	—
Upjohn (90)	1964–8	47	3	12	11	5	10	29	2	—	—
Denning (80)	1957–66 (excl. '64–5)	58	7	11	1	1	2	5	10	1	1
Somervell (73)	1954–9	37	1	1	24	1	9	47	4	—	—
Wilberforce (61)	1965–8	35	1	7	9	5	4	30	4	—	1
Oaksey (58)	1952–9 (excl. '58)	30	1	2	20	1	4	42	6	1	1
Pearson (53)	1965–8	23	3	4	11	4	8	43	3	—	1
Evershed (40)	1956–65 (excl. '60–2)	23	4	5	4	3	1	20	1	—	—
Jenkins (38)	1959–63	18	—	4	11	2	3	42	2	—	—
Devlin (36)*	1962–8 (excl. '65)	19	3	3	7	4	—	31	3	—	—
Dilhorne (35)	1952–67	17	7	5	4	1	1	17	2	—	1
Porter (34)	1952–6	20	—	1	9	3	1	38	4	—	—
Donovan (30)	1964–8 (excl. '67)	16	5	2	1	5	1	23	2	1	1
Normand (29)	1952–6	12	—	13	2	—	2	14 (13)	—	—	—
Asquith (27)	1952–4	14	—	2	4	2	5	41	1	—	—
Goddard (27)	1952 and 1955–61	12	3	1	7	2	2	41	—	—	—
MacDermott (25)	1952–67 (excl. '53, '57, and '64)	14	1	4	2	3	1	24	3	—	—
Kilmuir (24)	1955–62	14	2	8	—	—	—	—	—	—	—
Jowitt (17)	1952–7 (excl. '54)	8	—	2	7	—	—	41	—	—	—
Birkett (7)	1958, '59, and '61	1	—	1	5	—	—	70	—	—	—
Merriman (6)	1952, '56–7, '61	2	—	3	1	—	—		—	—	—
Simon (3)	1952–3	2	1	—	—	—	—		—	—	—
Gardiner (1)	1965	—	1	—	—	—	—		—	—	—
Parker of Waddington (1)	1961	—	—	—	—	1	—		—	—	—
Totals		1320	127	345	480	99	147	Av. 29%	132	7	28

For footnotes to this Table, see page 177.

It is interesting to note that, as we might have predicted, the Scottish judges as a group harness a high proportion of their energies to the hearing of Scottish appeals. Although English and Northern Irish (civil and criminal) appeals outnumber Scottish appeals in a ratio of about 4 : 1 the ratio of full judgments delivered by Scottish Law Lords in the two groups of appeals is about 2·2 : 1.

Lord Reid, of course, has been senior Law Lord since the retirement of Viscount Simonds in 1962, and this is another factor which must be taken into account. One would expect the presiding judge in each case, particularly in the House of Lords of recent years which has had such strong and able judges as Lord Reid and Lord Simonds as its senior members, should play a disproportionate part in the decision-making process. We would expect that an analysis of the judgments delivered by the senior judges in every appeal would reveal relatively few formal concurrences in the result, and even fewer dissenting judgments.

TABLE 20

The Role of the Presiding Judge, 1952–1968

Appeal	English Presiding Judge			Scottish Presiding Judge		
	Full assent	Dissent[a]	Formal Concurrence	Full assent	Dissent[a]	Formal concurrence
English/N. Irish (civil)	197	21	30	80	8	28
Scottish (civil)	40	1	6	42	3	10
Criminal	17	3	3	14	1	8
	254	25	39	136	12	46

[a] Includes partial dissents.

Table 20 (which should be read in conjunction with the previous table, Table 19), shows that a Scottish judge (almost invariably Lord Reid, but sometimes Lord Normand) presided in 37·9 per cent of all appeals and in

Footnotes to Table 19, p. 176.
   [a] English and Northern Irish civil appeals.
   [b] Criminal appeals.
   [c] Scottish appeals.
   [d] Includes any year during the period 1952–68, in which the judge sat at least once on the Appellate Committee, either as a Lord of Appeal, or as an *ex officio* member of the Court.
   [e] First figure in brackets indicates total number of times that the Law Lord sat.
   [f] Figure in brackets is percentage of concurrences by Scottish judges in *Scottish* appeals.

53·9 per cent of Scottish appeals. The English presiding judges formally concurred in 12·3 per cent of the appeals in which they presided, and Scottish presiding judges in 23·7 per cent of appeals; the combined figures are appreciably lower than the overall rate of formal concurrence of 20 per cent shown in Table 19. (There is evidence to suggest that Lord Reid has tended to deliver a somewhat lower percentage of full judgments in the latter part of the period, i.e., he was at his most 'active' before, and for a short time after, becoming senior Law Lord.) The dissent-ratio of presiding judges is also slightly lower than the overall average. Table 19 shows the overall proportion of dissents to full judgments as 10 per cent in English appeals, 8·1 per cent in Scottish appeals and 5·5 per cent in criminal appeals: the corresponding figures (inflated by a small number of part-dissents not shown in Table 19) for presiding judges are 8·0 per cent, 3·9 per cent and 8·5 per cent respectively (though the last two percentages are based on very small numbers). Scottish presiding judges are markedly less ready to dissent in English appeals and more prepared to dissent in Scottish appeals than are their English counterparts. But this may simply reflect the fact that a Scottish judge is more likely to preside in a Scottish appeal which *prima facie* raises difficult problems of Scottish law, and similarly that English judges may almost automatically be called upon to preside in difficult English appeals.

Although Lord Reid is the dominant individual figure in the House, it is clear that, out of a list of thirty-four judges who have made at least one contribution to the work of the Appellate Committee during the period, the real work-load has fallen upon the broad shoulders of a relatively small percentage of Law Lords. This is illustrated clearly by the fact that of 2,519 judge-attendances shown in Table 19, no fewer than 2,139 or 85 per cent are attributable to the top seventeen judges in the list.

One of the most important parts of the table is the column which expresses the number of times that a judge contents himself with a formal concurrence in the result, as a percentage of his total attendances (we have already seen that formal concurrence is most common in criminal appeals, and is slightly more common in Scottish civil appeals than in English civil appeals). Here we find a wide deviation from the mean of 29 per cent. Nearly half of Lord Somervell's judgments were formal concurrences, while Lord Denning is the outstanding figure at the other end of the scale with the remarkable record of only four formal concurrences in eighty attendances. The triumvirate of judicial giants whom we discussed earlier are all low on this particular index, as befits both their seniority of status and their intellectual dominance as judges.

There seems to be a tendency for a higher rate of formal concurrence among judges appointed since 1960: this stems probably from the growing proportion of criminal appeals in the work-load of the House, and hence a higher *overall* proportion of formal concurrences, though there has also been a slight increase in the incidence of single judgments in civil appeals.

As the figures in brackets in this column show, Scottish judges deliver full judgments markedly more frequently in Scottish appeals than they do in other categories of case.

Finally, the last three columns of the table show the number of dissenting judgments (these are included also in the totals in the 'full judgments' column) produced by each Law Lord in every category of appeal. This reveals Lord Keith as the leading dissenter: no fewer than 22 per cent of the full judgments delivered by him were full dissents. In second place, but quite a long way behind Lord Keith, is Lord Denning with 16 per cent of full judgments being dissents. Among the more recent Lords of Appeal, Lord Guest leads the field with nearly 14 per cent.

We have already seen that much of the work of the Appellate Committee is performed by a relatively small number of judges: indeed, as we have argued elsewhere, part of the virtue of the House of Lords as a court of last resort stems from the relative stability of its composition. But the fact remains that not all the work is done by the Lords of Appeal in Ordinary: Lord Chancellors, former Lord Chancellors, past and present holders of high judicial office (including retired Lords of Appeal) are qualified to take part in the work of the Appellate Committee and of the Judicial Committee of the Privy Council.

The presiding judge (even in a judicial system founded upon separate judgments) can exercise considerable influence over the course of argument presented to the court, and may even play a disproportionate part in drafting the final decision. Until recently, both the Lord Chancellor and ex-Lord Chancellors who sat on the Appellate Committee or the Judicial Committee automatically took precedence over the senior Lord of Appeal. In 1969 the rule was changed[1] to take account of the fact that, in modern times, Lord Chancellors have little opportunity by virtue of their executive and legislative duties to acquire that high degree of judicial expertise and experience required in the presiding judge of the ultimate tribunal: under the new rule the senior Lord of Appeal will always preside (regardless of his rank in the peerage) thus taking precedence over ex-Lord Chancellors. Thus Viscount Dilhorne, a former Lord Chancellor, who was appointed a Lord of Appeal in 1969, having been made a peer in 1962, takes precedence over Law Lords appointed after 1962, but would preside only when the other Law Lords had been appointed after 1969.[2] But somewhat incongruously, the Lord Chancellor of the day will continue to preside on the rare occasions that he can wriggle free from his Parliamentary duties on the Woolsack as well as from the seamless web of his Cabinet responsibilities. Lord Hailsham has shown much

---

[1] See the statement by Lord Gardiner, H.L. Debs., vol. 302, col. 469–70, 22 May 1969.

[2] See p. 181, n.1. And see, e.g., *National Westminster Bank Ltd.* v. *Halesowen Presswork & Assemblies Ltd.*, [1972] 2 W.L.R. 455.

greater enthusiasm for Judicial activity than did his predecessor Lord Gardiner.

How much work is done by the 'supernumerary' judges, like ex-Lord Chancellors: and how many retired Lords of Appeal return, like Caesar's ghost at Philippi, to relieve the memories of past forensic battles in the Appellate Committee?

Table 7 shows that a total of 1,790 full judgments were delivered in all the appeals heard by the Appellate Committee during the period 1952–68, and 726 formal concurrences in the majority speeches. The sum total of the contributions made by judges other than serving Lords of Appeal was 165 full judgments and 70 formal concurrences: in other words, more than nine-tenths of the work of the Appellate Committee fell upon the shoulders of the Lords of Appeal.

During the period, five former Lord Chancellors took part in hearing appeals: of these, Lord Simonds falls into a special category, since he returned to the judicial fold as a Lord of Appeal upon relinquishing the Lord Chancellorship in 1954. Thus his only *ex officio* attendances are the five hearings which he has attended since his retirement in 1962 and the six cases he sat in during his period as Lord Chancellor.

Viscount Simon died in 1953, having delivered only three judgments in the Appellate Committee during the first years of our period of study, 1952 and 1953. Earl Jowitt sat on seventeen occasions from 1952 until his death in 1957. He was particularly active in 1955, sitting six times, but he never sat on a criminal appeal. Viscount Kilmuir sat twenty-four times during his eight-year term as Lord Chancellor: after falling victim to the Macmillan hatchet in July 1962, he took up an industrial appointment (in itself the subject of fierce criticism) and never sat judicially again. (It was Viscount Kilmuir who delivered the notorious solitary judgment in *D.P.P.* v. *Smith*, discussed in Chapter XIII.)

The case of Viscount Dilhorne resembles that of Viscount Simonds, inasmuch as both men became Lords of Appeal in Ordinary after a spell in office as Conservative Lord Chancellor. But unlike Viscount Dilhorne, Viscount Simonds had also been a Lord of Appeal immediately prior to his appointment as Lord Chancellor, and resumed the judicial mantle immediately after being succeeded in office by Viscount Kilmuir. If his case resembled an inedible sandwich of Woolsack between two thick slices of ermine, Viscount Dilhorne's is more like an open sandwich: a period as Chancellor, followed by five judicially and politically active years out of office, and then appointment as Lord of Appeal. During his twenty-seven months as Lord Chancellor, Viscount Dilhorne sat in the Appellate Committee seven times: and during the period 1964–8 (when he was out of office) he sat on no fewer than twenty-six occasions (including four criminal appeals), a phenomenal record, particularly in view of his considerable contribution to the work of the Judicial Committee of the Privy Council[1] and his regular attendance as a Conservative spokesman in the Chamber of the Lords.

What of the other *ex officio* members of the Appellate Committee? By and large, holders of 'high judicial office' seldom find time to attend the House. Lord Chancellors, as they themselves constantly complain, have become a race apart. This is partly due to the expansion of their governmental responsibilities: the other culprit is the change in the timetable of the House of Lords since the last war. In the old days—some say the 'good' old days—the legislative business of the House began at 4.30 p.m. following the sitting, in the chamber, of the House in its judicial capacity. When the blackout moved back the legislative clock to 2.30 p.m., and then building operations necessitated the establishment of an Appellate Committee, the fate of Lord Chancellors, as active members of the judiciary, was finally sealed. Lord Gardiner himself sat only once during our period of study: and he delivered the solitary judgment in *Button and Swain* v. *D.P.P.* in 1965.[2]

As for Masters of the Rolls, Lord Denning sat only three times since resigning as Lord of Appeal in 1962 to take on his present office. Lord Evershed (before changing places with Lord Denning) sat in the Appellate Committee only seven times from 1952–62.

Lord Goddard C.J. sat thirteen times in the Lords between 1952 and his retirement as Lord Chief Justice in 1958; and fourteen times between 1959 and 1961, after which he never sat again. (Five of his twenty-seven appearances were in criminal appeals.) Lord Parker sat only once in the Appellate Committee since he was first appointed, and that was to concur formally in Viscount Kilmuir's lone judgment in *D.P.P.* v. *Smith.* (He has sat in the Judicial Committee of the Privy Council since his retirement as Lord Chief Justice in April 1971: see e.g., *Skeet* v. *John*, Privy Council Appeal No. 50 of 1970, and *Barker* v. *General Medical Council*, Privy Council Appeal No. 6 of 1971. Lord MacDermott, a Lord of Appeal until his appointment as Lord Chief Justice of Northern Ireland in 1951, has sat twenty-five times, fairly evenly spread over the period 1952–67 though never in an appeal from Northern

---

[1] On 26 July 1968 (see H.L. Debs., vol. 295, cols 224–5), Sir Peter Rawlinson asked the Attorney-General how many times judges other than Lords of Appeal had sat on the Appellate Committee or the Judicial Committee. It is believed that the question was asked in order to press the claims of Lord Dilhorne (the most active *ex officio* judge) to be appointed a Lord of Appeal when a vacancy arose.

The announcement of the change of practice, ending the right of ex-Lord Chancellors to preside (see p. 179, n. 1) was made very shortly before the announcement of Lord Dilhorne's appointment as Lord of Appeal. The change was probably precipitated in order to avoid any possible disruption of the existing order of judicial seniority.

[2] [1966] A.C. 591. He since sat once more: he formally concurred in the judgment delivered in *Commissioner of Valuation for Northern Ireland* v. *Fermanagh Protestant Board of Education* on 23 July 1969, [1969] 1 W.L.R. 1708, 1720. Soon after leaving the office of Lord Chancellor he sat as a supernumerary judge in *Johnson* v. *F. E. Callow (Engineers) Ltd.* [1971] A.C. 335, in which his successor, Lord Chancellor Hailsham, presided.

Ireland. (Mainly because, almost inevitably, he would have been party to the decision appealed from.)

Retired Lords of Appeal seem for the most part to stick to their original intentions in giving up active judicial life. Lords Evershed, Jenkins, Porter, and Radcliffe never sat after retiring. Lord Oaksey was lured back for a single appeal after retiring in 1959. Lord Devlin has sat only three times since his retirement in 1964 (although he has made some notable appearances in the Privy Council),[1] and Lord Tucker and Viscount Simonds have sat five times apiece. Only Lords Cohen, Morton of Henryton, and Normand among Law Lords in recent times have chalked up double figures in their post-retirement appearances.

As one would expect in a final court of appeal which takes its responsibilities seriously, the House of Lords is run largely by professionals. But in a court which normally sits with five judges, an element of variety, injected by the presence of a 'retired' judge or of one of the eminent presiding judges in the courts *a quo*, may stimulate judicial minds without unduly disrupting the continuity of the work of the courts.

It would be wrong not to mention the work of Law Lords in other courts, though as this is essentially a study of the House of Lords, we have not strayed far outside our terms of reference in collecting data about the work of other tribunals. The work of the Law Lords in staffing the Judicial Committee of the Privy Council is probably almost as extensive as their service on the Appellate Committee, though the Board frequently sits with only three members, and some of the work-load is borne by Commonwealth judges who are invited to sit. Somewhat less widely known is the extent of the occasional labour of Lords of Appeal in the Court of Appeal. We have analysed the transcripts of the Court of Appeal lodged in the Bar Library and examined the composition of the Court in each case decided in the single (and possibly atypical) year, 1967. This confirms our expectation that the descent of these judicial giants from Westminster to the Strand is a comparatively rare phenomenon. Of 428 appeals decided by the Civil Division of the Court of Appeal in 1967, eleven were heard by a Court containing one Law Lord, and two by a Court containing two Law Lords. Lord Pearson heads the 'league' with five attendances, Lord Upjohn heard four appeals, Lord Pearce heard four, and Lord Wilberforce two. Recently Lord Diplock stepped down two rungs of the ladder to try a patent case in the Chancery Division (of which he was never a member). Clearly a measure of interchange is mutually beneficial: the Law Lords are reminded of the tribulations of life as a Lord Justice, while the work of the Court of Appeal is enhanced by the presence of those eminent judges. Perhaps it is a pity that the Scots Law Lords do not take part in the work

---

[1] See *United Engineering Workers Union* v. *Devanayagam* [1968] A.C. 356, in which he dissented jointly with Lord Guest; *Jayasena* v. *The Queen* [1970] A.C. 618; and *Kum* v. *Wah Tat Bank Ltd.* [1971] 1 Ll.R. 439.

of the Court of Session: it might fortify them against charges of Anglicization, or (and perhaps this is what the Scots are afraid of) infect the Scottish judges with the same germ. In this survey of the judges who have shaped the role and character of the House of Lords during the years of our study we have inevitably left much unsaid. Law Lords, we have at least observed, are noble, learned, and extraordinary—noble by virtue of letters patent; learned by training and experience; and who can deny that, as members of an élite, unified by their legalistic ideology, yet contriving to be individualists within their narrow frames of reference, they are anything but 'Ordinary' as their full title misleadingly suggests?

But even if we have failed to penetrate beneath the façade of judicial characters, we have made greater efforts to analyse what the Law Lords have done in their judicial role. What does an analysis of the judgments delivered disclose? The answer to this question is prompted, if inadequately provided in our next chapter.

IX

THE NATURE OF JUDGMENT

In general the House of Lords (which has bequeathed the separate reasoned judgment to the Anglo-Saxon world) remains loyal to the practice of separate judgments, though, as we have seen, the formal concurrence in the result is quite commonplace. Table 21 shows that in 35 per cent of all appeals, every member of the court delivered a full judgment: in addition to this, in 22·7 per cent (116 appeals) only one judge declined to deliver a full judgment and in 16·6 per cent (85 appeals) two judges formally concurred. In other words in 74·3 per cent of cases (assuming the normal five-judge Court),[1] a majority of judges delivered a separate opinion. (This accords with our finding that 28·4 per cent of all judgments delivered are formal concurrences in the result.)

At the other end of the scale, Table 21 shows the infrequency with which the House of Lords indulges in the alien exercise of delivering the equivalent of a 'judgment of the court'. The average proportion of single judgment cases where the other Law Lords formally concur (the nearest thing to a judgment of the whole court) was only 11·3 per cent, markedly more frequent in Scottish than in English appeals, and very much more so in criminal appeals. But even in criminal appeals the House has never adopted a uniform practice. The disastrous decision in *D.P.P.* v. *Smith*[2] was founded upon a single judgment, while in the case of *Warner* v. *Commissioner of Police for the Metropolis*[3] every judge delivered a separate opinion, and Lords Reid and Pearce both dissented.

Dissenting judgments from a theoretical viewpoint have been considered elsewhere. It remains for us to consider how many dissenting judgments have in fact occurred in the House of Lords in recent years. This question is answered by Table 22 which shows the annual number of cases involving one or two dissenting judgments, sub-divided into civil and criminal appeals, and according to the nationality of the court *a quo*. For the purpose of this analy-

---

[1] Ninety-one per cent of civil appeals during the period 1952–67 were heard by a House of Lords composed of five judges.

[2] [1961] A.C. 290; so legally disastrous was the single judgment delivered by Viscount Kilmuir L.C. that their Lordships, for some time thereafter, abandoned the practice. In more recent times there has been a partial reversion to former practice, especially noticeable in gaming appeals: *Kursaal Casino Ltd.* v. *Crickitt (No. 2)* [1968] 1 W.L.R. 53; in *Cronin* v. *Grierson* [1968] A.C. 895, and in *D.P.P.* v. *Ottewell* [1970] A.C. 642 (only two out of five Law Lords in each case gave judgments).

[3] [1969] 2 A.C. 256.

TABLE 21

Single Judgments and Judgments by all Members of the Court, 1952–1968

Year	Single Judgments			Judgments by all Members of the Court		
	English/Irish Civil	Scottish	English/Irish Criminal	English/ Irish Civil	Scottish	English/ Irish Criminal
1952	— (16)*	— (8)	— (1)	5	3	—
1953	5 (14)	2 (3)	— (—)	3	1	—
1954	— (13)	— (5)	2 (2)	4	2	—
1955	— (30)	— (5)	— (—)	8	3	—
1956	1 (26)	— (7)	— (—)	10	1	—
1957	1 (21)	— (4)	1 (1)	4	1	—
1958	1 (17)	— (4)	— (1)	7	1	—
1959	1 (30)	— (7)	— (—)	6	3	—
1960	1 (23)	— (9)	1 (2)	11	4	—
1961	2 (23)	3 (8)	— (5)	13	2	4
1962	3 (24)	— (4)	— (6)	8	1	4
1963	2 (25)	1 (7)	1 (2)	7	3	—
1964	3 (18)	1 (10)	— (6)	8	7	4
1965	— (22)	— (4)	4 (6)	7	1	—
1966	6 (23)	1 (4)	— (3)	12	1	—
1967	1 (19)	4 (11)	3 (3)	10	4	—
1968	4 (20)	— (2)	3 (8)	5	—	2
Totals	31 (364)	12 (102)	15 (46)	128	37	14
% Appeals in each category	8·5%	11·8%	32·6%	35·2%	36·3%	30·4%

* *Note:* Total number of appeals in each category shown in brackets.

sis, we have defined a full dissent as a judgment which, had it constituted the majority view, would have produced a substantially different result from that which occurred in fact. A partial dissent (shown in brackets in Table 22) is one which would have produced a different result only on a subsidiary matter: for example, it may reflect a difference of opinion as to the quantum of damages to be awarded, or upon the apportionment of contributory negligence or, for example in a patent case involving several parts to a specification, there may be disagreement on subsidiary aspects of the patent. Sometimes a 'partial dissent' is hard to distinguish from an assent in the result reached by different argument.

The table shows the high proportion of cases which are not unanimous: 22·5 per cent of all appeals involved one or two full dissents. The proportion for English civil appeals was 24·6 per cent, for Scottish appeals 20·6 per cent and the considerably lower proportion for criminal appeals of 15·2 per cent.

There was an equal number of cases involving a 4:1 division of opinion compared with 3:2 decisions.

TABLE 22

Dissenting Judgments in the House of Lords, 1952–1968

Year	English/Northern Irish			Scottish			Criminal		
	Total Appeals	One Dissent	Two Dissents	Total Appeals	One Dissent	Two Dissents	Total Appeals	One Dissent	Two Dissents
1952	16	— (1)	1	8	—	—	1	—	—
1953	14	—	1	3	1	—	—	1	—
1954	13	—	3 (1)	5	1	—	2	—	—
1955	30	6 (1)	2	5	1	—	—	—	—
1956	26	3	3	7	—	—	—	—	—
1957	21	3 (2)	3 (1)	4	2	—	1	—	—
1958	17	3	3	4	—	—	1	1	—
1959	30	4	5 (1)	7	1	— (1)	—	—	—
1960	23	5 (1)	3	9	—	2	2	—	—
1961	23	3	1	8	1	1	5	— (1)	1
1962	24	4	2 (1)	4	1	—	6	2	—
1963	25	3 (1)	4	7	2	1	2	—	—
1964	18	— (1)	—	10	—	3	6	—	1ᵃ
1965	22	4	4	4	1	1	6	— (1)	—
1966	23	3	6	4	—	—	3	—	—
1967	19	1	— (1)	11	—	2	3	—	—
1968	20	2 (1)	2 (1)	2	—	—	8	—	1ᵃ
Total	364	44 (8)	43 (6)	102	11 (—)	10 (1)	46	4 (2)	3 (—)

Note: Partial dissents shown in brackets
ᵃ Proviso applied by the dissenters.

In Table 23 we turn to the all-important question of the *nature* of dissenting judgments. It must be confessed that it is sometimes only with the benefit of hindsight that a particular dissenting judgment becomes 'fundamental' and that it is not easy to consign judgments to pre-coded categories particularly when (for reasons discussed in Chapter v) judges are usually anxious to minimize the overt signs of disagreement.

This table tends to confirm our subjective impression, gained from a reading of all the dissenting judgments, that most dissents involve issues relating only to the particular case, rather than to fundamental policy clashes. We should argue that such dissents could, profitably for the most part, have been left unspoken. The 'great dissent' like the 'great dissenter', is a myth in English legal folklore.

Is there any particular type of case which attracts a disproportionately large element of dissent? For the purpose of this analysis, we have divided the subject-matter of appeals heard by the House of Lords into sixteen main categories: Table 24 shows the number and the percentage of dissenting judgments in each of these.

TABLE 23

Full Dissents (Civil Appeals Only, 1952–1968)

	English/Irish Appeals	Scottish Appeals
Straightforward differences of opinion regarding the interpretation of legislation or the terms of a contract, etc.	44	12
Different inference from the primary facts	15	5
Fundamental conflict on legal issues	18	2
Support for a legally 'unorthodox' approach in order to avoid injustice or anomaly	4	—
Defence of 'orthodoxy' against the revisionism of the majority	3	1
Two dissents on different grounds	1	—
Other	2	1
Totals	87	21

TABLE 24

Relationship of Subject-Matter to Full Dissents in Civil Appeals, 1952–1968

Case Category	Unanimous	One Dissent	Two Dissents	% of Non-Unanimous Decisions
Revenue	92	21	14	27·6
Fault liability	77	5	8	14·5
Contract	38	6	8	26·9
Trade Union and Restrictive Practices	8	—	—	—
Master and Servant	2	1	2	a
Law of property	56	11	7	24·3
Company law	5	—	—	—
Defamation	4	—	—	a
Patent, copyright, and trade mark	25	1	2	10·7
Practice and procedure	15	1	2	16·7
Administrative law	4	5	2	63·7
Family law	6	1	5	50·0
International law	7	1	1	a
Constitutional law	7	—	1	a
Transport law	2	—	—	a
Miscellany	10	2	1	23·1
Totals	358	55	53	Overall percentage 23·2

a Figures too small to justify percentages.

This table shows that there are few major deviations from the average percentage, noticeable exceptions being family law with at least one dissent in six of the twelve cases, and with five of the non-unanimous cases involving two dissents: and both patent and procedural cases giving rise to a much higher level of unanimity than the norm.

Having emphasized the importance of the function of dissenting judgments in a study of this nature, we confess that we are largely avoiding the central question of *why* judges dissent. This question requires sophisticated and lengthy exercises in attitude measurement which lie outside the scope of the present work. In the special context of the House of Lords, however, there is one aspect of the problem which must not be ignored. Unlike the Privy Council, the House of Lords is not an international court, but it does perform the vital function of co-ordinating the two disparate systems of law which operate in the United Kingdom, the common law of England and the civilian law of Scotland. For this reason, its composition is not homogeneous. Included in the ranks of the ten Lords of Appeal are two judges who have practised within the Scottish legal system.

The bi-national House of Lords has attracted criticism, particularly from those north of the Border who grimly recall instances of supposed adulterations of long-cherished Scottish legal traditions by ignorant judicial Sassenachs. Even the Scottish Law Lords have on occasion been accused of going over to the enemy camp: of permitting themselves to be brainwashed free of their Scottish law.

In dissenting judgments we have a blunt statistical tool for investigating the 'Anglicization' hypothesis: are these lordly apostles of Scottish jurisprudence prepared to stand up against their English brethren by dissenting in Scottish appeals? In cases involving two dissents, do the Scots judges tend to stick together? Table 25 relates the category of the judge or judges dissenting to the nationality of the court *a quo*. (It must, of course, be remembered that only four Scots judges sat during our period of study, a fact which means that the figures must be treated with caution.)

Prima facie, these figures tend to support the expectation that Scottish Law Lords tend to reserve their dissents for Scottish appeals. Of 150 dissenting judgments delivered in 101 non-unanimous English appeals, 40 (26·7 per cent) were delivered by Scottish judges. But of 33 dissents in 22 Scottish appeals, 16 (48·5 per cent) were delivered by the Scots Law Lords. Putting this another way, there were 39 English appeals (39 per cent) in which at least one Scottish judge dissented, as compared with 14 Scottish appeals (64 per cent). Scottish dissenters actually outnumbered English dissenters in Scottish appeals, even though Scottish Law Lords are very much in a minority.

But these figures tell only half the story: we have calculated from Table 19 in the previous chapter the attendance figures for Scottish and for English

TABLE 25

House of Lords Dissents and Part Dissents (Civil Appeals, 1952–1968)

	Court *a quo*	
Category of Judge(s) dissenting	English/Irish	Scottish
One C.L.[a]	22	2
One N.C.L.[b]	13	2
One Scot[c]	17	7
Two C.L.	8	1
Two N.C.L.	4	—
Two Scot	1	2
One C.L./One N.C.L.	15	3
One C.L./One Scot	13	3
One N.C.L./One Scot	8	2
	101	22

[a] English common law judge (including Divorce)
[b] English non-common law judge
[c] Scottish judge

judges in all civil appeals over the period 1952–68 and arrived at the following result:

English appeals
    Attendances by English judges   1,344 } ratio 3·02:1
    Attendances by Scottish judges   445 }

Scottish appeals:
    Attendances by English judges   318 } ratio 1·74:1
    Attendances by Scottish judges   183 }

Combining these figures with Table 25 we can obtain a matrix of dissents expressed as a percentage of attendances, thus:

	English dissenters	Scottish dissenters
English appeals	8·2	9·0
Scottish appeals	5·3	8·8

This demonstrates quite clearly that Scottish judges dissent as frequently as English judges do in English appeals, and that they dissent no more frequently in Scottish appeals than they do in English ones. But the figure also shows that the *overall* rate of dissent is considerably lower in Scottish appeals, and that what dissents there are tend, for the most part, to be left to the Scottish Law Lords.

Returning to Table 25, there seems to be little evidence of Scots judges 'sticking together' in cases involving two dissents. Of forty-nine English appeals in which two judges dissented only one involved two Scots dissenters, while twenty-one involved one Scot and one Englishman: there may be slight evidence that Scots dissenters find a greater affinity with English common lawyers than with Chancery judges, but small figures coupled with the fact that common law Law Lords have tended to outnumber non-common law lawyers, makes it difficult to draw any meaningful conclusions. In the ten Scottish appeals with two dissenters, two involved two rebellious Scots, and five involved one Scot and one Englishman, which is not unexpected given the preponderance of English Law Lords.

Dissent contravenes the primary rules of judicial uniformity, and dispels the myth of law-finding; it may also imply a fundamental schism in legal opinion on certain issues. One would expect therefore that dissenting judgments in the House of Lords would be more prevalent in cases where the lower court is being overruled; that, paradoxically, dissent is employed as a weapon in the cause of unanimity. Table 26 relates dissenting judgments to the effect of the judgment on the decision of the court below.

TABLE 26

Non-Unanimous House of Lords Decisions, Related to Outcome of Appeal, 1952–1968

H.L. Outcome	English/Irish		Scottish		Criminal	
	One Dissent[a]	Two Dissents	One Dissent	Two Dissents	One Dissent	Two Dissents
Allowed	20	21	7	7	1	1
Allowed in part	—	2	—	—	—	—
Dismissed	24	19	5	2	3	2

[a] Full dissents

Thus 50 per cent of non-unanimous English appeals were allowed wholly or in part as compared with 36 per cent of all English appeals. Similarly 67 per cent of non-unanimous Scottish appeals were successful as compared with 47 per cent of all Scottish appeals. These striking figures tend to support our hypothesis of judicial reluctance to overrule the considered opinion of the lower court. Further light is thrown on this question by Table 27 which analyses dissents in the House of Lords and the unanimity of the court *a quo*.

Where the Court of Appeal was unanimous (262 cases) its decision was reversed by the House of Lords 92 times, i.e. 35 per cent. Where it was divided (84 cases) it was reversed 40 times, 47·6 per cent. The corresponding percentages for Scottish appeals (bearing in mind that the sample is smaller) are 45·5 per cent reversal rate for a unanimous Court of Session and 50 per cent for a divided court. These figures may reflect a greater willingness on the part of the Law Lords to reverse a decision when they have the support of a dissenting judgment below, or merely that some cases are inherently more 'difficult' than others.

TABLE 27

Unanimity in House of Lords, by Outcome and Unanimity in the Court a quo, 1952–1968

	English/Irish			Scottish			Criminal		
	Unanimity in House of Lords			Unanimity in House of Lords			Unanimity in House of Lords		
Unanimity *a quo*	Unani- mous	One Dis- sent	Two Dis- sents	Unani- mous	One Dis- sent	Two Dis- sents	Unani- mous	One Dis- sent	Two Dis- sents
Court *a quo* reversed Unanimous	60	15	17	23	6	7	8	1	1
One dissent	28	5	7	11	1	—	—	—	—
Court *a quo* upheld Unanimous	139	17	14	38	4	1	22	3	2
One dissent	32	7	5	10	1	1	2	—	—

Of 132 reversals of the Court of Appeal, 12 (9·1 per cent) involved dissent at both appellate stages: of 214 cases where the Court of Appeal was upheld, 12 (5·6 per cent) involved two divided courts. A division of opinion in the lower court may give rise to psychological cross-pressures among the Law Lords, with a greater propensity to sway between two conflicting viewpoints.

In English appeals generally, the House of Lords was not unanimous in 24 per cent of cases. In 28·6 per cent of cases where there was one dissent below, the House was divided, as it was in 30 per cent of cases which involved *reversal* of a divided court *a quo*. These can hardly be described as significant differences.

Over-indulgence in the heady liquor of dissent can be attacked on various grounds, already discussed in Chapter v; it also produces an alarming (but statistically interesting) 'hangover' which throws light on the workings of a multi-tier judicial system. Given the present system, whereby a division of judicial opinion is publicly expressed, a respondent in the House of Lords may be unsuccessful in holding the judgment he had in his favour, and yet be able to claim that on a counting of heads of the judges who have decided the case in the various courts he ought to be declared the victor. This bizarre phenomenon is the inevitable concomitant of a three-tiered judicial process in which appellate judges have the right to dissent. But the litigant, if he is not actually disgruntled by such a process, may be forgiven bewilderment and disbelief in the justice of such a result. He might echo the sentiment of H. L. Mencken, that injustice is bearable; it is justice that really hurts.

Should the lawyer countenance this arithmetical quirk of the appellate process, or should the anomaly be eliminated in the interests of litigant-satisfaction?

TABLE 28

Minority Decisions

Court a quo			
Court of Appeal		Court of Session	
Minority of one	Minority greater than one	Minority of one	Minority greater than one
19[a]	3	3	9

[a] includes one appeal from the C.A. (N.I.)

During the period 1952–68 the House of Lords disposed of 466 civil appeals. Table 28 shows that in no fewer than 34 of these cases (7·3 per cent) a minority of judges, but a majority of Law Lords decided in favour of the appellant in the House of Lords. (Henry Cecil in his Hamlyn lectures, *The English Judge*, 1970, p. 169, says that minority decisions are 'fortunately extremely rare'—an example of legal opinion based on ignorance of data.) The arithmetic of minority decisions varies to some extent according to the hierarchy of courts through which the litigation has passed. Table 28 illustrates this point quite clearly: comparing English and Scottish minority decisions, 86 per cent of the former were by a minority of only one, as compared with 25 per cent of the latter. This difference is explained in part by the fact that in three of the Scots cases decided by a minority of 4:6, the unanimous Court of Session consisted of four judges (the usual composition of that Court). Had the Court comprised three judges, the eventual margin would have been reduced to one, but in no case would such a change have turned the minority into a majority, or even parity. The fact remains, however, that Scottish cases result in a noticeably larger proportion of minority decisions: this may rest only on the fact that the 'minority syndrome' can occur only in appeals successful in the House of Lords, and a much higher percentage of Scots appeals succeed.

In two of the Scottish cases, *Public Trustee* v. *C.I.R.* [1960] A.C. 398 and *Islip Pedigree Breeding Centre* v. *Abercromby* 1959 S.L.T. 161, the House of

Lords was composed of only four judges. The former case produced a 3:5 minority, while the latter—in which the four-judge House of Lords by a majority of 3:1 overruled a unanimous four-judge Court of Session—resulted in a minority decision by 3:6.

Two more of the cases, *Income Tax Special Commissioners* v. *Linsleys (Est. 1894) Ltd.* [1958] A.C. 569 and *James* v. *Secretary of State for Wales* [1967] 1 W.L.R. 171, proceeded from a three-judge Queen's Bench Divisional Court to the Court of Appeal, ultimately resulting in 5:6 minorities. In *Linsley's case* this result was achieved in spite of a unanimous House of Lords: neither case would have been minority decisions had they passed through the more usual '1:3:5' hierarchy of courts. In theory, any case passing through a '3:3:5' hierarchy could result in a 3:8 minority, though this has never been approached during our period of study.

Minority decisions are not uncommon; nor are they confined to appeals of trivial importance. Besides those cases already mentioned, the list includes *Ridge* v. *Baldwin* [1964] A.C. 40 (4:5 decision); *Williams* v. *Williams* [1964] A.C. 698 (4:5 decision); *Burmah Oil Co.* v. *Lord Advocate* [1965] A.C. 75 (4:6 decision); *Blythe* v. *Blythe* [1966] A.C. 643 (3:6 decision); and *Anisminic* v. *Foreign Compensation Commission* [1969] 2 A.C. 147 (4:5 decision).

Prima facie, the occurrence of minority judgments seems to undermine the arguments for a two-tier appeal system: indeed from the litigant's viewpoint, it must make a hollow mockery of the judicial process itself. So long as a litigant has available only one appeal from the decision of a single judge, a respondent in the appeal court—where the latter is composed of an uneven number of appeal judges—can never be deprived of his judgment by a minority of judges. If there is a dissentient voice, the most that a respondent can claim is a judicial tie. It is the existence of a second appellate tribunal that potentially creates the situation described above. And it matters not what the number of judges in the second appeal court may be, it is the mere existence of dissent at the ultimate stage of the judicial process. Further appeals would tend only to exacerbate the situation. Indeed, there is already evidence of this happening in those cases—revenue appeals and appeals which originate in awards by arbitrators—where litigation began in administrative tribunals. In *Evans Medical Supplies Ltd.* v. *Moriarty* [1958] 1 W.L.R. 66 the company tax-payer, cross-appealing in the House of Lords, won, although a majority of judges (5:4) held in favour of the Crown. To this majority of judicial heads must be added the composite wisdom on revenue matters of the Income Tax Commissioners who had also favoured the Crown's contentions. Abolition of the House of Lords would not entirely remove the grievance in these cases; if reform were contemplated, it might be simpler to provide appeals from arbitrators and Tax Commissioners direct to the Court of Appeal, as in cases from the Lands Tribunal.

Yet if this state of affairs argues in favour of a two-tiered system of appeals, countervailing observations must be made:

(1) The concept of the appellate process depends upon the existence of a hierarchy of courts with greater weight (in a purely mathematical sense) given to the vote of a judge in the higher court. Although the layman may regard one judge as having an equal voice with another, the truth is that judges who are members of an appellate court have not only enhanced status but also possess a greater voice in the judicial process, both individually and collectively by the influence of their persuasive powers on their appellate brethren. The very nature of an appeal—a review of the trial judge's decision on fact and law—involves a total substitution of the appellate decision for the judgment of first instance, a process which either absorbs and complements the first judgment or, if the judgment is reversed, obliterates it. Although the Law Lords, in reversing the Court of Appeal which itself reverses the trial judge, often talk of 'restoring' the trial judge's decision, they likewise are in reality substituting their judgment for that of the Court of Appeal.

If there were no declared dissenting view, as is the almost invariable practice of the criminal appeal court, the problem of minority decisions would not manifest itself publicly. But we do not think, for reasons adduced elsewhere, that dissenting judgments should be abolished; they should be deployed more sparingly.

(2) The process of counting judicial heads involves invalid comparisons. The function of the House of Lords cannot be equated with that of the Court of Appeal, just as the Court of Appeal has a function quite distinct from the trial court. The case of *Williams* v. *Williams* [1964] A.C. 698 was decided by a 4:5 'minority', but the three Law Lords in favour of allowing an appeal reviewed the whole law of cruelty much more thoroughly than could be expected of the Lords Justices whose decision was reversed. This point goes to the heart of the true function of the second appellate tribunal, and is the crux of the present study.

If this study should lend support (as we think it does) to the present structure of the courts, there will still need to be put in the balance the complaints of more than a handful of aggrieved respondents who will continue to lose their appeals in the House of Lords by a minority. Any feature of a legal system which, for no reason other than the existence of a peculiar hierarchy of courts, increases the number of disgruntled litigants must be the object of criticism. And if a few groans must be stoically suppressed for the benefit of the community, there is no reason why the burden on the aggrieved individual should not be lightened. One suggestion would be that an unsuccessful respondent in the Lords (particularly if both the lower courts sided with him) should not be called upon to pay his opponents' costs there. (In some instances, particularly in revenue appeals, the courts already impose on those seeking leave to appeal a condition that whatever the outcome of the appeal they will pay the other party's costs.) But in cases where no such condition is imposed, an appellant might feel that the fruits of his judgment should not be dissipated by failure to recover his costs, even if he was successful only at the final hurdle. A partial remedy, discussed elsewhere, would be greatly to extend the availablility of legal aid in House of Lords cases. In all non-legally aided appeals an unsuccessful respondent should not be asked to bear the costs of the hearing in the House of Lords. A respondent should not be obliged to pay substantial costs for the doubtful privilege of being not only defeated but defeated in an arithmetically anomalous manner. And a successful appellant should be awarded his just judgment without adding insult to his opponent's injury by a weighty bill of costs. If society demands a second appellate court because it performs a socially useful function beyond that of doing justice as between the parties, then society must foot the bill; and only the costs of litigating in the two lower courts should be visited on the losing party.

X

LAW LORDS AS LEGISLATORS[1]

THE shadow of Montesquieu still hangs over modern constitutional theory. Despite the many yawning gaps in the classical doctrine of separation of powers, students of the British constitution often find it convenient to classify institutions according to the otiose labels of the legislative, administrative and judicial functions.[2] It would hardly be surprising therefore to find the notion of judges participating in the legislative process denounced in some quarters as a constitutional heresy.

Yet the House of Lords, even in its judicial capacity, is regarded by its members as very much a part of Parliament;[3] not only are its proceedings conducted in the Palace of Westminster (sometimes in the Chamber of the House of Lords itself) but the form of the procedure and its vocabulary— 'petitions', 'speeches', and 'votes' (on the outcome of an appeal)—are essentially parliamentary in character. Moreover the Law Lords are not only judges, but are as entitled as any other peers to participate in legislative debate in the House of Lords.

Indeed, their presence in the House was recently given governmental blessing in the White Paper on Reform of the House of Lords,[4] the proposals in which came before Parliament in the shape of the ill-starred Parliament (No. 2) Bill in the Session 1968–9. The White Paper recommended that the Law Lords be exempted from the attendance qualifications and from the provisions for a compulsory retirement age prescribed for every other category of 'voting peer'. When a proposed amendment to this part of the Bill was debated in the House of Commons the general consensus was that the judges had an important role to play in the contemporary legislative and deliberative process.[5]

---

[1] This chapter is adapted from an article by Gavin Drewry and Jenny Morgan published in *Parliamentary Affairs*, vol. xxiii, pp. 226 ff. (July 1969). See also 'Judges in Parliament', by Gavin Drewry, vol. 119 *New Law Journal*, p. 431 (8 May 1969). The legislative role of Law Lords is compared with that of Bishops in an article by Gavin Drewry and Jenny Brock, "Prelates in Parliament", *Parliamentary Affairs*, vol. xxiv, pp. 222 ff (Summer 1971).

[2] See *Liyanage* v. *The Queen* [1967] 1 A.C. 259.

[3] A fact which was repeatedly asserted during the debates in 1948 (and subsequently) on the setting up of an Appellate Committee. See in particular H.L. Debs., vol. 155, cols. 737–47, 11 May 1948; H.L. Debs., vol. 169 cols. 20–2, 1 Nov. 1950; H.L. Debs., vol. 174, cols. 21–5, 13 Nov. 1951, etc. (Discussed above at pp. 111 ff.)

[4] Cmnd. 3799 of 1968, particularly paras. 59–62.

[5] H.C. Debs., vol. 781, cols. 432–54 and 504–36, 2 April 1969.

Is there not an element of irony in our alarm at the idea of judges 'legislating'? Modern jurisprudence has come to accept, almost as a truism, the notion that judges make law: unless they did so, any legal system, whether based upon common law modified by statute, or upon a civil code, would soon become wholly out of touch with contemporary social needs. And if Law Lords, *qua* judges, did not 'make law' then the theoretical underpinnings of the present study would be shattered.

Much of the consternation provoked by any supposed violation of 'separation of powers' stems largely from the manifest unreality of attempting to draw a hard and fast distinction between 'legislation' and 'adjudication'. These are not separate roles performed in watertight compartments by different groups of actors, though this is not to say that convenience does not make it necessary to entrust certain *aspects* of these functions to particular institutions. Constitutional myth has tended to obscure some of the bridges between the various parts of the system. The notion of parliamentary sovereignty jealously guarded by parliamentarians, and dutifully acknowledged by the courts, is a survivor from the era of the Stuarts. On the obverse of the constitutional coin we have, for example, the *sub judice* rule which precludes parliamentary debate on issues contemporaneously being considered by the courts: and the strong tradition that the Executive will not usurp the judicial function by liberally exercising the Royal Prerogative of Mercy.

But all this is merely part of a façade concealing a far more diffuse and complex governmental process. Parliamentary sovereignty is limited in practice by the creativity of judges called upon to interpret and apply often imperfectly drafted statutes to specific problems which arise in a rapidly changing society and to do so without the aid of such extraneous evidence of Parliament's intentions as *Hansard* and official White Papers. Parliament and the Executive do usurp the judicial function to some extent: the Royal Prerogative—though rarely used—is available as an appeal beyond the judicial last resort. Matters of administrative or political expediency lie ultimately within executive discretion: *Liversidge* v. *Anderson*[1] involved protracted litigation up to the House of Lords, which found for the executive, but the latter thereupon made the essentially political decision to release the internee. More recently, extradition proceedings in *Zacharia* v. *Republic of Cyprus*[2] proceeded to the House of Lords which rejected the appeal, but the crucial social question— one which was too broad for the operation of purely legalistic principles— was answered by the Home Secretary who refused to return the appellant to Cyprus, and to certain death. And more recently still, the Greek emigré Kotronis[3] was condemned by the House of Lords to be extradited, only to be rescued at the eleventh hour by a unique exercise of the Home Secretary's

---

[1] [1942] A.C. 206.   [2] [1963] A.C. 634.
[3] *Government of Greece* v. *Governor of Brixton Prison* [1971] A.C. 250.

discretion. (Small wonder that 'administrative law' has remained such a nebulous and incongruous part of English jurisprudence.) Finally Parliament has shown in recent years an increasing willingness to act as a third court by legislating the reversal of specific judicial decisions: cases like *Rookes* v. *Barnard*,[1] *Burmah Oil* v. *The Lord Advocate*[2] (retrospective reversal so as to deprive the private litigant of the fruits of judgment) and *Anisminic* v. *Foreign Compensation Commission*[3] spring readily to mind in this context. The issue of legislative reversal of judicial decisions is discussed in Chapter XVI.

The earliest phase in the development of medieval governmental institutions was marked by a total lack of any discernible distinction between 'legislation' and 'adjudication', and the loose-knit structure of the components of the King's Council was certainly not geared to any such distinction. Even now, in an age of complex delegation of functions and diffusion of powers the functional distinctions between the various components of government are still largely arbitrary. To maintain an equilibrium between the interacting components of this vastly complex machine it is vital that efficient channels of communication be maintained between the various parts of the system: it is here that the Law Lords play a major role.

Under the provisions of the Appellate Jurisdiction Act 1876, as subsequently amended, a Lord of Appeal in Ordinary receives a life barony upon appointment, unless he is already qualified to sit in the House of Lords. Since 1844 no lay peer has been permitted to vote in the judicial business of the House, but there is no converse convention that prevents a Law Lord from taking a full part in legislative business. The only constraint is the comparatively recent tradition (noted for example by Professor Bromhead)[4] that Law Lords should confine their contribution to debates which lie outside the arena of party political controversy, a self-denying ordinance in an age when almost every issue comes under the rubric of politics.

This is the constitutional theory behind the phenomenon of judges in Parliament, but how does it apply in practice? Are our judicial legislators really meek political eunuchs speaking in debate only in matters of highly technical legislation or where an issue arises directly affecting the administration of justice or the work of the judiciary? To answer these questions we have examined, via the relevant volumes of *Hansard*, the full extent of the participation of Law Lords in House of Lords debates in recent years, with figures for two earlier years juxtaposed for the purpose of comparison.

The term 'Law Lord' is usually employed to describe every category of peer entitled to participate in the judicial business of the House of Lords under the Appellate Jurisdiction Act 1876, including 'such peers of Parliament as are for the time being holding or have held ... high judicial office' (see Appendix

[1] [1964] A.C. 1129.   [2] [1965] A.C. 75.   [3] [1969] 2 A.C. 147.
[4] P. A. Bromhead, *The House of Lords and Contemporary Politics, 1911–57* (Routledge & Kegan Paul, 1958), p. 67 ff.

1). For the purposes of the present analysis we felt that an all-inclusive definition of this kind was too wide, and that retired Lords of Appeal and former holders of high judicial office should be excluded from the sample, even though they may continue to play an active role in parliamentary debate. In the first place, many Lords of Appeal are obliged to retire because of ill-health or old age, and take no further part either in judicial or in legislative business after retirement; their inclusion in the sample would distort our findings. In the second place, our primary concern in this section is with the extent to which *active* judges combine legislative activity with judicial work during the same period: thus the inclusion of retired judges would be superfluous. Lord Chancellors and former holders of 'high judicial office' (usually ex-Lord Chancellors) are excluded for a different reason: their position *vis-à-vis* the judicial and legislative functions of the House of Lords is *sui generis* and highly political in character. Their very considerable contribution to the work of the House merits a separate study.[1]

This leaves us with a sample containing all the twenty-six judges who have held the office of Lord of Appeal in Ordinary during the period 1952–68, plus two Lord Chief Justices, two Masters of the Rolls (both of whom were also Lords of Appeal for part of the period), and one President of the Probate, Divorce and Admiralty Division. Similarly constructed samples (though containing fewer judges) are involved in our calculations for the two earlier years 1880 and 1920. The names of all the judges in the 1920 and 1952–68 samples will be found in Tables 35A and B below.

In order to assess the proportionate contribution made by the Law Lords to the overall distribution of House of Lords business, we have, in Table 29, broken down the 1967 timetable of the House into six main categories. While acknowledging that no single year could be wholly representative, we felt that this would give at least some indication of the distribution of business over our main seventeen-year period of study.

TABLE 29

Overall Distribution of House of Lords Business, 1967

Types of Business	No. of Items
House of Lords Bills	70
House of Commons Bills	102
General Debates[a]	52
Ministerial Statements	115
Motions for Orders, Schemes, and Regulations	76
Questions	520 (approx.)

[a] We have defined General Debates as all debates other than on Bills or on motions and questions.

[1] See Chapter IX.

In enumerating the contributions of the Law Lords we have employed two indices which may at first sight appear somewhat confusing. We have found it necessary to make a distinction between 'Law Lord *Items*' which are defined as all the debates either on a Bill (all the stages being counted as a single item) or on a motion, in which at least one of the active Law Lords took part; and 'Law Lord *Debates*' which count the stages of such Bills as separate items. 'Items' enable us more readily to relate the business in which Law Lords take part to the overall distribution of business in the House, while 'Debates' give a clearer impression of the extent of Law Lord participation. We hope that the reader will bear with our clumsy attempts to enjoy the best of both worlds by intermingling the two concepts.

Table 30 relates the type of Law Lord Item debated in 1967 to the overall pattern of House of Lords business in the same year. Table 31 shows the respective individual contributions made by Law Lords and by non-Law Lords (i.e. those peers—the vast majority—who are *not* qualified to participate in appellate business under the 1876 Act) to Law Lord Debates.

TABLE 30

Law Lord Participation in House of Lords Business, 1967

	H.L. Bills[a]	H.C. Bills	General Debs.	Total
Total 1967 business	70	102	52	224
No. of Law Lord Items	5	5	—	10

[a] The distinction between Bills originating in the House of Lords and those originating in the Commons is significant only inasmuch as money Bills are invariably introduced in the Commons, while all consolidation Bills, and many (but not all) Bills dealing with technical matters of law reform, begin life in the Lords.

TABLE 31

Participation in Law Lords Debates, 1967

	H.L. Bills	H.C. Bills	General Debs.	Total
No. of Law Lord Debates	7	10	—	17
Law Lords' Contribution to Law Lord Debates	8	19	—	27
Non-Law Lords' Contribution to Law Lord Debates	26	174	—	200

The activities of the Law Lords in 1967 were confined to Bills; throughout the main period of the study, as well as in the two earlier years, they took part only in debates on Bills and in general debates. We found only one instance of a Law Lord asking a question in the House during the years studied; this could either be evidence of conscious political neutrality, or merely of the fact that Question Time happens to coincide with the sittings of the courts and the Appellate Committee.[1]

In view of the fact that our selected year, 1967, proved to be slightly atypical, in the sense that there were no general debates in which Law Lords took part, we have calculated the average annual extent of Law Lord participation over the whole period 1952–68 (Table 32).

TABLE 32

Average Extent of Law Lord Participation, 1952–1968

	H.L. Bills	H.C. Bills	General Debates	Total
Average no. Law Lord Debates (p.a.)	4·3	5·1	2·5	11·9
Average no. contributions by Law Lords to L.L. Debates (p.a.)	6·8	9·1	3·9	19.8
Average no. Contributions by non-Law Lords to L.L. Debates (p.a.)	32·3	53·0	21·6	106·9

This table shows that in Law Lord Debates (which are, by definition, the only business in which Law Lords have taken part) judicial contributors are outnumbered by six to one on the crude index of the number of contributions made. Table 30 indicated that Law Lords' business constitutes only a small proportion of the total work of the House, though this of course takes no account of the proportionate time devoted to the various categories of business. It seems clear, therefore, that in absolute terms the degree of participation of Law Lords in debate is not large. On the other hand, we should remember that they are a small group, prevented by judicial duties from attending most afternoon (at least early afternoon) sessions of the House: for this reason their degree of participation can be regarded as being quite substantial. It must be emphasized, moreover, that their role in making speeches on the floor of the House is only a small part of their contribution to the work of the legislature. They constitute a readily accessible body of highly expert opinion on technical points of legislation: their failure to speak on a particular measure may only mean that their views have been fully canvassed beforehand. This consultative role is more formalized in the Joint Committee on Consolidation Bills, always chaired by a Law Lord.

The next table (Table 33) shows the respective number of Law Lord Items

[1] The character of 'Questions' in the House of Lords is explained in Chester and Bowring, *Questions in Parliament*, (1962) pp. 313 ff.

and Debates for the period 1952–68 and for the years 1880 and 1920. This shows the distinct increase which has taken place in the annual totals of Law Lord contributions in recent years, possibly due to an increasing proportion of legislation which impinges upon the work of the courts and to the larger number of Law Lords; this process is likely to accelerate as the work of the Law Commission gains momentum.[1] Indeed this growth in participation is largely a reflection of the general expansion in the volume of legislation. The 1920 Law Lords (considering how few they were) were at least as legislatively active as their modern counterparts, and markedly more so in debates on House of Commons Bills; it is worth noting that, with one exception, these judges all had active party political backgrounds.[2]

It should also be noted that Law Lords are not infrequently called upon to preside over Government committees of inquiry which absorbs time which might have been spent on judicial or legislative business. This can be seen

TABLE 33

Law Lord Items and Debates, 1952–1968

Year	H.L. Bills		H.C. Bills		General Debs.	Total		Total L.L.
	Items	Debs.	Items	Debs.	(Items = Debs.)	Items	Debs.	Contrib. (Debs.)
1952	—	—	3	5	5	8	11	17
1953	—	—	1	1	2	3	3	6
1954	—	—	1	1	1	2	2	3
1955	2	4	—	—	1	3	5	6
1956	—	—	1	1	2	3	3	8
1957	3	6	3	4	1	7	11	13
1958	1	1	8	14	4	13	19	28
1959	3	6	5	8	5	13	19	36
1960	4	5	3	3	7	14	15	23
1961	5	9	7	9	2	14	20	24
1962	2	3	2	2	1	5	6	7
1963	1	1	5	8	3	9	12	18
1964	3	5	2	3	2	7	10	17
1965	4	7	5	13	1	10	21	32
1966	7	12	—	—	4	11	16	32
1967	5	7	5	10	—	10	17	26
1968	4	9	3	5	1	8	15	39
Totals	44	75	54	87	42	140	204	333
Average p.a.	2·6	4·4	3·2	5·1	2·5	8·2	12·0	19·6
1920	2	3	12	16	3	17	22	28
1880	—	—	3	4	1	4	5	5

[1] By October 1970 final reports had been submitted on eighteen topics, eleven of which had been implemented in full by Parliament, and two more in part.

[2] See Chapter VIII, particularly pp. 168–9.

from the following (not necessarily comprehensive) list of the extra-judicial appointments of the ten Lords of Appeal holding office at the end of 1969, gleaned mainly from the 1970 edition of *Who's Who*:

Reid (1948)—Chmn. Malaya Constitutional Commission, 1956–7.

Morris of Borth-y-Gest (1960) (1945 Q.B.)—Dept. Chmn. H.O. Advisory Cttee. under Def. Regs., 1940–4; Prepared report for Treasury on Requisitioning, 1941; Chmn. H.O. Cttee. on War Damaged Licensed Houses, 1942–3; Chmn. Cttee. on Selling Price of Houses, 1945; Chmn. Cts. of Inquiry into Engineering and Shipbuildings Wages Disputes, 1954; Referee to decide wage questions upon Settlement of Railway Strike, 1955; Chmn. Nat. Reference Tribunal under Coal-Mining Industry Conciliation Scheme, 1955–65; Chmn. H.O. Cttee. on Jury Service, 1963–4.

Hodson (1960) (1937 P.D.A.)—Mem. Permanent Court of Arbitration at Hague since 1949.

Guest (1961)—Chmn. Building Legislation Cttee., 1954–7; Chmn. Scottish Agricultural Wages Bd., 1955–61; Chmn. Scottish Licensing Law Cttee., 1959–63.

Pearce (1962) (1948 P.D.A.)—Chmn. Cttee. on Shipbuilding Costs, 1947–9; Mem. Royal Comm. on Marriage and Divorce, 1951.

Upjohn (1963) (1951 Ch.)—Mem. Statute Law Cttee., 1966.

Donovan (1963) (1950 K.B.)—Chmn. Br. Govt. Legal Mission to Greece, 1945; Mem. Denning Cttee. on Divorce Procedure, 1946; Mem. Lewis Cttee. on Ct. Martial Procedure, 1946–8; Chmn. Crim. Appeal Cttee., 1964; Chmn. Royal Comm. on T.U.s and Employers' Ass., 1965–8.

Wilberforce (1964) (1961 Ch.)—Senior U.K. Representative on Legal Cttee. of International Civil Aviation Organization, 1947—; Mem. Permanent Court of Arbitration.

Pearson (1965) (1951 Q.B.)—Mem. Legal Cttee. on Medical Partnerships, 1948; Supreme Ct. Rules Cttee., 1957–65; Chmn. Cttee. on Funds in Court 1958; Law Reform Cttee. 1963; Chmn. Cts. of Inquiry into: Dispute in Electricity Supply Ind., 1964, Dispute in Shipping Ind., 1966–7, Dispute in Civil Av. Transport Ind. 1967–8, Dispute in Steel Ind., 1968.

Diplock (1968)—Secy. Dept. Cttee. on the Law of Defamation, 1948; Mem. L.C.'s Law Reform Cttee from, 1952; Dep. Chmn. Boundary Commission for England, 1958–61; Pres. Nat. Assn. of Parish Councils, 1962–6; Chmn. Law Advisory Cttee., British Council, 1966.

(*N.B.* The first date shown in brackets is the year of appointment to the House of Lords. The second is the year of first appointment to the higher judiciary.)

In order to gain a clear impression of the nature of the Law Lords' contribution to the work of the legislature it is not enough merely to count the number of times they intervene in debate. Table 34 lists the subject-matter of Law Lord Items debated during the period 1952–68.

Few of the debates involved major political clashes, and certainly not along party lines. Indeed, our study reveals very little in the way of political activism on the part of the Law Lords, though, as we shall see, several items gave rise to dissension within the judicial camp. The range of Law Lord Items tends to confirm the hypothesis that the Law Lords confine themselves largely to acting as resident technical consultants to the legislature on legal points arising out of proposed legislation. Sometimes, however, they assume a more

TABLE 34
Subjects of Law Lord Items, 1952–1968

Subject of Debate	Number of L.L. Items
The legal system/procedural law	31
Crime/penal reform/law enforcement	24
Family law	20
Civil law reform/law commission	17
Foreign affairs (mostly constitutions)	8
Charity law	6
Transport law	5
Tribunals and inquiries	5
Licensing laws	5
House of Lords (membership and procedure)	3
Mass media	3
Miscellaneous	13
Total	140

controversial role, as self-appointed guardians of the nation's conscience in issues such as abolition of the death penalty, and relaxation of the law of abortion, where legal and ethical issues are woven closely together. They are also quick to defend the prerogatives of the courts, where, for example, a judicial decision is being reversed by statute (see Chapter XVI), and sometimes react strongly against proposals to reform the machinery of justice. In 1968, for example, a clause in the Justices of the Peace Bill abolishing the ancient magisterial jurisdiction of Aldermen of the City of London provoked a storm of judicial protest at the Committee Stage from nine serving Law Lords who were supported by the long-retired Lords Goddard, Cohen, and Simonds. The Government was eventually defeated on a compromise amendment moved by Viscount Dilhorne.[1]

So far we have said nothing about the contribution of individual Law Lords to House of Lords debates. Clearly the extent of each judge's participation will largely be a matter of temperament: the more controversially-minded might be expected to take part more frequently than their orthodox colleagues. Participation might also depend upon such factors as seniority and status: the senior Law Lord might act as unofficial spokesman for his brethren, the Lord Chief Justice might similarly act as spokesman for the Queen's Bench judges, particularly in matters of criminal law, and the Master of the Rolls, as presiding judge in the Court of Appeal, might be called upon to speak on behalf of the Lords Justices of Appeal.

Table 35A was compiled by dividing the number of times each Law Lord spoke or voted in debate by the length of the period (taken to the nearest month) during which he fulfilled the criteria for inclusion in our sample, and listing the judges in order of average participation per annum. The Table

[1] See Gavin Drewry, 'Justice in the City', vol. 119 *New Law Journal*, p. 931 (9 October 1969).

TABLE 35

'League Table' of Law Lord Participants in House of Lords Debates

A.   1953–1968

Law Lord (Ch.—denotes Chancery judge) (Scot.—denotes Scottish judge)	Length of period involved Years/Months	Total contribution	Average contribution p.a. (debates)
Lord Denning	11/7	79	6·83
Lord Wilberforce (Ch.)	4/2	21	5·04
Lord Parker of Waddington	10/2	39	3·84
Lord Morris of Borth-y-Gest	8/11	22	2·47
Lord Guest (Scot.)	7/11	17	2·14
Lord Reid (Scot.)	17/0	33	1·94
Lord Simonds (Ch.)[a]	7/4	12	1·64
Lord Cohen	8/7	14	1·63
Lord Merriman[a]	10/0	16	1·60
Lord Goddard[a]	6/7	9	1·37
Lord Pearson	3/9	5	0·77
Lord Hodson	8/2	11	1·32
Lord Morton of Henryton (Ch.)	6/2	7	1·13
Lord Porter[a]	2/9	3	1·09
Lord Oaksey[a]	5/3	5	0·95
Lord Keith of Avonholm (Scot.)[a]	7/0	6	0·86
Lord Evershed (Ch.)[a]	13/0	10	0·77
Lord Asquith of Bishopstone[a]	2/7	2	0·77
Lord Tucker	9/8	6	0·62
Lord Donovan[a]	4/11	2	0·41
Lord Upjohn[a]	5/0	2	0·40
Lord Radcliffe (Ch.)	12/6	4	0·32
Lord Pearce	6/7	2	0·30

Lords Devlin, Jenkins (Ch)[a] and Somervell of Harrow[a] made no contribution to debate during our period of study.

Average number of contributions per Law Lord p.a.: 1·37

[a] Now dead.

B.   1920

Law Lord	Nature of Office	No. of Contributions
Lord Sumner	Law Lord	9
Lord Reading	Lord Chief Justice	8
Lord Cave	Law Lord	7
Lord Atkinson	Law Lord	1
Lord Coleridge	K.B.D. Judge	1
Lord Moulton	Law Lord	1
Lord Shaw	Scottish Law Lord	1
Lord Dunedin	Scottish Law Lord	—
Lord Sterndale	Master of the Rolls	—

Average number of contributions per Law Lord: 3·11

shows Lord Denning as far and away the most prolific contributor to House of Lords debate: this probably reflects his unorthodox viewpoint on a wide range of legal issues, combined with his special position (since 1962) as Master of the Rolls. On the other hand, Lord Denning's predecessor in office, Lord Evershed, is low on the list, as is Lord Keith who produced even more dissenting judgments in the Appellate Committee than did Lord Denning. Lord Wilberforce's contribution for the short period of his peerage is significantly high. Tests reveal no correlations between the Law Lords' contributions and either their relative seniority at any given time (although the present senior Law Lord, Lord Reid, is very high on the list, together with Lord Morris who is second in seniority) or the divisions of the High Court in which they originally sat. Nor do Law Lords with records of overt political affiliation (see our earlier analysis, in Chapter VIII) speak more than others.[1] (It should be remembered that this 'league table' is an artificial device covering an arbitrary period: many of the Law Lords low on the list have only served for a short period and an average figure has little significance.)

TABLE 36

No. of Law Lords who Spoke or Voted on each Law Lord Item

	No. of Items			
Year	One Law Lord	Two Law Lords	Three Law Lords	Four or more Law Lords
1952	5	1	—	2
1953	2	—	—	1
1954	1	1	—	—
1955	1	2	—	—
1956	1	1	—	1
1957	5	1	1	—
1958	8	2	3	—
1959	5	6	1	1
1960	9	3	1	1
1961	10	2	1	1
1962	5	—	—	—
1963	5	1	3	—
1964	3	3	—	1
1965	3	4	2	1
1966	3	3	1	4
1967	7	1	—	2
1968	2	—	3	3
	—	—	—	—
Totals	75	31	16	18
	(53·5%)	(22·2%)	(11·4%)	(12·9%)
1920	10	4	1	3
	(55·0%)	(22·2%)	(5·6%)	(16·7%)
1880	4	—	—	—

[1] It should be remembered that this table takes no account of the degree of specialization of individual Law Lords. Thus although Lords Goddard and Hodson do not rank very high in our league they have both been active in debates on their respective specialities, criminal law and family law.

Turning now to the 1920 judges, whose 'league table' is shown in Table 35B, all but one of the Law Lords in this list (the exception being Lord Sterndale) were politically active before becoming judges, and this is reflected in their relatively high rate of participation, all the more significant in view of the fact that the 1920 House of Lords was involved with far fewer issues of pure law reform than its modern counterpart.

TABLE 37

Degree of Consensus in Law Lord Items

	(Two or more Law Lords participating)	
Year	Agreed	Disagreed
1952	3	—
1953	1	—
1954	1	—
1955	2	—
1956	1	1
1957	2	—
1958	2	3
1959	4	4
1960	4	1
1961	2	2
1962	—	—
1963	1	3
1964	3	1
1965	5	2
1966	5	3
1967	1	2
1968	4	2
Totals	41	24[a]
1920	1	7

In each of the four 1880 items only a single judge spoke.

[a] Percentage of cases in which there was disagreement: 37%.

Even if party political ties can be disregarded, is there any evidence of a Law Lord caucus in debate? A definitive index of this would be the frequency with which Law Lords disagreed among themselves in debates and divisions on Law Lords Items. Table 36 shows that in the majority of Items only one Law Lord spoke or voted (though multiple contributions are more common in recent years) and it is therefore the 46·5 per cent of Items involving two or more Law Lords, analysed in Table 37 showing the degree of consensus.

Predictably, Table 37 shows the Law Lords agree among themselves more often than they disagree, and the high proportion of items in which only one Law Lord participated (Table 36) may point to tacit agreement, or even the appointment of official spokesmen. Table 37 gives no indication of the degree of disagreement in each Item: in fact in eleven of the twenty-four instances of disagreement, the contentious points were minor ones; for example, on the form of the measure rather than its content.[1] The overall impression is of overwhelming judicial solidarity.

Listed below are the thirteen Law Lord Items which gave rise to a substantial measure of disagreement.

Year	Item	Main point(s) of disagreement
1956	Death Penalty (Abolition) Bill	Fundamental clash on capital punishment
1958	Artificial Insemination of Married Women (Motion)	Artificial insemination and the law of adultery
1958	Peers' leave of absence	Constitutional propriety of provisions for leave of absence
1959	Legitimacy Bill	Legitimation of adulterine children and children of void marriages
1960	Charities Bill	Cy-près doctrine
1961	Criminal Justice Bill	Minimum age for inflicting death penalty: corporal punishment of young offenders
1961	Licensing (Scotland) Bill	Non-adoption of recommendations of Lord Guest's Committee on the licensing laws
1963	Matrimonial Causes (Reconciliation) Bill	Reconciliatory resumption of marital intercourse as a bar to divorce
1963	British Museum Bill	Transfer of records from B.M. to Public Records office
1965	Murder (Abolition of Death Penalty) Bill	Fundamental clash on capital punishment
1966	Misrepresentation Bill	Efficacy of measure as drafted
1966	Divorce Laws (Motion)	'Breakdown' principle (*Putting Asunder*)
1967	Criminal Justice Bill	Majority verdicts; suspended sentences, etc.; parole board; no publicity of committee proceedings

The 1920 Law Lords disagreed among themselves on seven occasions, and none of the clashes could be described as 'minor'. The items giving rise to disagreement were: the Matrimonial Causes Bill (giving legislative expression to the Gorell Commission Report); Law of Property Bill; Punjab Disturbances and General Dyer's Case (focusing on the political dynamite of the Amritsar Riots) (Motion); Defence of the Realm (Acquisition of Land) Bill; Dyestuffs (Import Regulation) Bill; Agriculture Bill; and the Government of Ireland Bill (Home Rule once again). Only the first two of these Items could strictly be referred to as 'law reform'; clearly these judges interpreted their role as legislators a good deal more liberally than their modern counterparts.

In marked contrast to the items giving rise to dissension in 1920, the 1952–1968 list reveals only two which were *not* concerned with law or with penal reform. Several of the Items—particularly those relating to family law—

---

[1] The ten items giving rise to minor disagreement were: Variation of Trusts Bill (1958); Matrimonial Proceedings (Magistrates' Courts) Bill (1959); Charitable Trusts, Motion (1959); Section 14 (2) of the Factories Act 1961, Motion (1963); Criminal Appeals Bill (1964); Law Commission Bill (1965); Matrimonial Homes Bill (1966); Abortion (No. 2) Bill (1967); Domestic and Appellate Proceedings (Restriction of Publicity) Bill (1968); Theft Bill (1968).

raised issues which had given rise to dissent among the Law Lords in their judicial capacity. An example is Lord Hodson's opposition to the Matrimonial Causes Bill, which had been foreshadowed by a series of dissenting judgments by him.

The fundamental advantage of having active judges in the House of Lords is that they provide a two-way channel of communication between the courts and the legislature. During 1952–68 a number of important items of legislation arose directly as a response to dicta of members of the Appellate Committee in particular cases, drawing the attention of the legislature to specific defects in existing statutes. A study of all the appeals heard by the House of Lords during this period reveals fourteen instances where the Law Lords, in their judicial capacity, called expressly for legislative reform. These were:

> *Hayward* v. *Port of London Authority* [1956] 2 Ll. R. 1 (docks safety regulations)
> * *C.I.R.* v. *Hinchy* [1960] A.C. 748 (income tax penalty provisions)
> * *Cartledge* v. *E. Jopling & Sons Ltd.* [1963] A.C. 758 (limitation of actions)
> * *National Provincial Bank Ltd.* v. *Ainsworth* [1965] A.C. 1175 (deserted wife's equity)
> * *Cory (Wm.) & Son Ltd.* v. *C.I.R.* [1964] A.C. 1088 (stamp duty)
> *Westminster Bank Ltd.* v. *Zang* [1966] A.C. 182 (Cheques Act 1957)
> *Bates* v. *C.I.R.* [1968] A.C. 483 (tax legislation in the field of trusts)
> *Cleary* v. *C.I.R.* [1968] A.C. 766 (income tax)
> *Donaghey* v. *Boulton & Paul Ltd.* [1968] A.C. 1 (building regulations)
> * *Pettitt* v. *Pettitt* [1970] A.C. 777 (matrimonial property)
> * *Metropolitan Police Commissioner* v. *Hammond* [1965] A.C. 810 (offender's return to Eire)
> * *Myers* v. *Director of Public Prosecutions* [1965] A.C. 1001 (evidence of records)
> *Beswick* v. *Beswick* [1968] A.C. 58 (contract for benefit of third party)
> *Suisse Atlantique Société d'Armament Maritime S.A.* v. *N. V. Rotterdamsche Kolen Centrale* [1967] 1 A.C. 361 (fundamental breach)

So far as we have been able to ascertain, in only seven of these cases (those marked with an asterisk) was there a direct response to the call for reform; we thought it instructive to examine the House of Lords debates on these seven items of legislation. In two of the debates (those on the Finance Acts[1] which reversed the *Hinchy* and *Cory* cases) no Law Lords participated. Of the other two, in the relatively non-controversial Limitations Bill[2] debates, Lord Morris of Borth-y-Gest (who had sat in the hearing of the *Cartledge* appeal) was the sole representative of the Law Lords. In the debate on the Matri-

---

[1] Finance Bill debates in the House of Lords are not connected with specific legislative proposals but provide a peg whereon to hang a debate on broad policy issues.

[2] A departmental committee had already made recommendations on this point, and legislation was envisaged before the *Cartledge* decision.

monial Homes Bill—a measure which gave rise to a good deal of controversy —Lords Hodson, Cohen, and Wilberforce (all of whom had been members of the Appellate Committee which decided *Ainsworth*) were joined by Lord Denning. The latter's long-held support for the doctrine of 'deserted wife's equity' had produced the Court of Appeal decision in Ainsworth which had subsequently been reversed by the Appellate Committee. In debate, however, the Lords of Appeal presented a united front with the Master of the Rolls in criticising the unsatisfactory state of the law in this field. Of the other three only in the Matrimonial Proceedings and Property Bill debate did a Law Lord (Lord Denning) participate.

Several examples may also be cited of legislation specifically reversing decisions of the Appellate Committee (as opposed to amending defective *legislation* upon which judicial decisions were based). This question of statutory reversal of judicial decisions is discussed at length in Chapter XVI.

We have so far based our assessment of Law Lord participation upon such overt activity as speech-making or voting in House of Lords debates. An assessment of how frequently their Lordships *attend* debates in the House (without necessarily taking an active part in the proceedings) would have provided a useful supplement to our data, though the benefit accruable from this information had to be weighed against the considerable effort needed to peruse all the daily entries in the Journals of the House of Lords.

Since conducting this part of our research, however, a new source of information has become available. In an attempt to assess some of the probable effects of the (now defunct) Parliament (No. 2) Bill 1969, the House of Lords ordered a search to be made in the Journals of the House for the five Parliamentary Sessions covering the period 1963–8, and the number of sitting days on which each peer attended the House to be recorded. The results of this exercise were published as a House of Lords Paper entitled *Lords Attendances*.[1] From this document we have extracted, and set out in Table 38, the attendance figures relating to those Law Lords included in our main sample (see Table 35A above) who were still attending the House during all or part of the period 1963–8. For comparison we have added figures for Lords Gardiner and Dilhorne, who exchanged the mantle of Lord Chancellor in 1964 and who so frequently confronted one another in debate during the Labour administration.

It must be remembered that this Table is not strictly comparable to those included earlier in the present chapter, since the attendance figures cover only a five-year period. Moreover, Table 38 is calculated on Parliamentary Sessions, while we have based our tables upon calendar years. Several Law Lords find a place in the attendance table on the grounds that they were included as judges who were active during part of the period covered by our main sample, although they retired from office before, or shortly after 1963; their attendance figures are shown in brackets.

[1] H.L. 66, March 1969.

TABLE 38

Parliamentary Attendance of Law Lords, 1963–1968

	Session					
	1963–4	1964–5	1965–6	1966–7	1967–8	% of days attended (complete sessions only)
Total sitting days in sessions	110	124	50	191	139	
Lord						
Cohen	(18)	(33)	(15)	(42)	(16)	20
Denning	3	11	4	30	9	9
Devlin	3	(—)	(—)	(2)	(1)	1
Donovan	13[a]	33	5	16	7	12
Evershed	14	2	(—)	1[b]	(—)	6
Goddard	(19)	(23)	(9)	(17)	(2)	11
Guest	47	46	11	50	44	32
Hodson	21	42	9	50	38	26
Morris of Borth-y-Gest	59	80	33	103	85	59
Morton of Henryton	(23)	(33)	(8)	(44)	(37)	24
Parker of Waddington	5	12	3	22	6	8
Pearce	14	13	2	19	21	11
Pearson	—	12[a]	5	15	12	8
Radcliffe	7	(2)	(—)	(2)	(1)	2
Reid	26	15	5	43	19	18
Simonds	(36)	(46)	(17)	(49)	(34)	30
Tucker	(—)	(6)	(1)	(7)	(—)	2
Upjohn	20[a]	18	4	51	27	20
Wilberforce	—	30[a]	16	52	50	31
(Dilhorne)	105	114	46	145	110	85
(Gardiner)	65[a]	119	46	180	138	98

[a] Introduced after beginning of Session.
[b] Died during the Session.

Note: Figures in brackets indicate that the Law Lord concerned had retired from high judicial office.

Of the present Law Lords, Lord Morris of Borth-y-Gest with an attendance rate of 59 per cent wins by several lengths from his nearest rival Lord Guest (32 per cent). Other leading contributors were Lord Wilberforce, who came second in our 'league table' of contributors, at 31 per cent (his is a comparatively recent appointment; he shares with Lord Diplock the distinction of being the youngest of the present Law Lords) and Lord Hodson with 26 per cent. Lord Reid, the senior Law Lord, is well up with the field at 18 per cent. Several retired Law Lords, notably Viscount Simonds, Lord Morton of Henryton and Lord Cohen (all in their eighties) were then still regular attenders. Lord Denning M.R. (at the top of our 'league table', Table 30) and Lord Parker C.J. were both comparatively infrequent attenders at 9 and 8 per cent respectively, though this is hardly surprising in view of the hectic nature of their judicial life at the Strand which kept them away from Westminster. Clearly they attended only when they wished to contribute to a debate or to vote in a division.

Finally we draw attention to the two 'political lawyers' (Lord Gardiner and Lord Dilhorne) who, as one would have expected, make even the most regularly attending Law Lords appear indolent by comparison.

In many respects, bare attendance figures are an unsatisfactory index of legislative activity; a fleeting appearance in the chamber is sufficient to earn an entry in the Journal, which is the more easily achievable by, for example, a bachelor living in a London club. These figures, however, provide useful support for our conclusion that the Law Lords are by no means passive spectators on the touch-line, though they could hardly be regarded as cheerleaders; attendance figures make it clear that Parliament and the courts maintain a useful dialogue on legislative activity not normally involving party politics.

One of the most frustrating aspects of an empirical exercise of this kind is that it yields few surprises (though we should perhaps be happy that our initial hypotheses have largely been proved to be accurate). In absolute terms, the Law Lords as a group do not emerge as outstandingly active legislators, though their proportionate contribution is not insubstantial, particularly in view of their heavy judicial commitments and their strong tradition of political neutrality. The burden of contribution falls more heavily on some Law Lords than on others. For the most part they confine themselves to discussing the legal/moral rather than social implications of law reform, and they go to great lengths to avoid political involvement. Sometimes, however, their interventions become quite heated, particularly where (as in the War Damage Bill debate, see pp. 368 ff. below) the executive appears to be encroaching upon the traditional prerogatives of the courts. Occasionally intervention may be more individualistic, as in Lord Hodson's last-ditch stand in support of the doctrine of the matrimonial offence. But, by and large, the contemporary Law Lords (unlike their 1920 forebears) live up to their image as politically neutral legal advisers.

Small though their contribution to debate may be, its significance should not be underestimated, particularly in view of the fact that much of their work as legislative consultants takes place outside the House of Lords. A chamber of revision must, by definition, tidy up the work of the elected chamber: to do this effectively requires not only time but also expertise. The House of Commons contains a number of practising lawyers, but the House of Lords can go one better with a dozen or so senior judges (not to mention several retired who are, if anything, less reticent in debate) who can acquaint the House with the views of those whose job it is to interpret and apply the products of the legislature. Such an arrangement is eminently worth preserving.

In practice only a few of the Law Lords take part in the non-judicial work of the House of Lords. The main reason is the severely practical one that a day in court is sufficiently exacting not to induce them to listen for further long hours to debate in the chamber—much of it frankly tedious. But clearly the increasing output of the Law Commission will make demands on the Law Lords in assisting the passage of law reform Bills through Parliament.[1]

The Law Lords engage infrequently in parliamentary activity: still less often do they court combat with the political peers in the House of Lords. But in May 1971, unprecedentedly, Viscount Dilhorne, Lord Diplock and Lord Donovan took up the cudgels of legal logic in the face of ardent feminist agitation for a piece of reform embodied in a single provision in a Private Member's Bill from the Commons.[2] Gone was any affected neutrality: the Law Lords stoutly resisted a piece of legal reform adjudged desirable by the country's elected representatives and, indeed, by many of their fellow peers.

The issue was a modern variant of the widow's mite: should a widow, claiming damages for the loss of her husband under the Fatal Accident Acts 1846 to 1959, have her remarriage prospects assessed by the court, the more accurately to calculate the actual financial loss resulting from the death? The practice—embodying a fundamental principle of the English law of damages—has long been that the court estimates in cold financial terms what amount is required to compensate the deceased's dependants for what they would have obtained had their breadwinner not been killed. And it makes a great difference if the widow has remarried or is very likely to remarry: the loss to her will be considerably mitigated, if not extinguished by her acquiring a new financial provider.

The task of eyeing a widow in the witness box and calculating her marriage prospects—is it physical attraction or personal qualities that the judiciary look for?—is distasteful to judges.[3] Clause 4 of the Law Reform (Miscellaneous Provisions) Bill, introduced under the ballot by Arthur Probert, Labour Member for Aberdare, and as passed by the House of Commons, sought to put an end to the practice. It provided that, in assessing damages payable to a widow, 'there shall not be taken into account the remarriage of the widow or her prospects of remarriage'. The army of feminist supporters cheered at this minor blow for 'women's lib.' The Law Lords were prompted, however, to resist the reform primarily because of the supposed inegalitarian potential in the proposed change which resulted in a departure from conventional judicial principle. Suppose, two widows came before the court:

[1] A request was made, exceptionally, that the Law Lords should be available to counsel their colleagues on the intricate provisions of the Industrial Relations Bill: see H.L. Debs., vol. 317, col. 199 (6 April 1971). Similarly, legal advice will doubtless be sought over legislation to effect British entry into the European Economic Community.

[2] These three Law Lords put their names jointly to an amendment which had the effect of opposing the reform projected in a clause in the Law Reform (Miscellaneous Provisions) Bill (now the Law Reform (Miscellaneous Provisions) Act 1971). Strictly speaking, there were two amendments on the Order Paper in the names of the three Law Lords and an alternative amendment in the name of Lord Pearson.

[3] *Buckley* v. *John Allen & Ford (Oxford) Ltd.* [1967] 2 Q.B. 637, 644–5: '... it is time judges were relieved of the need to enter into this particular guessing game'.

one a young woman in her early twenties with a long expectation of life; the other a woman in the autumn of her life. If remarriage prospects were ruled out of the court's calculation of financial loss the younger (and supposedly more nubile) widow would get twice as much in damages as the elder because she prospectively would need financial support for twice as long. Yet to-morrow the younger might be married and the elder live out her lonely life with only a modicum of financial support. How unjust could the law be? Hence the judicial revulsion for the proposed reform, while acknowledging the repugnancy to judges of the present rule.

The three Law Lords resiled from their initial outright rejection of clause 4. They proposed instead a compromise formula. Courts could in future award, instead of or in addition to any lump sum, 'periodical payments'. Thus a widow could receive a weekly amount (much as she probably did while her husband was alive) and on any material change in her economic circumstances, such as remarriage, the person liable to pay damages (usually an insurance company) could have the order varied so as to reflect the widow's changed financial position. This would at least stop the guesswork, though perhaps at the cost of insurance companies spying on her to see whether her financial position drastically improved.

The notion of periodical payments in personal injury awards generally might be sound enough. But it runs counter to the present law of damages which, on the basis that there should be an end to such litigation, fixes the damages once and for all at the time of trial. If the estimate of the court as to the future financial position of the claimant proves wrong, well then some plaintiffs receive a windfall, others a disadvantage because their injury unpredictably worsens. That is in the nature of the system of a once-and-for-all award of damages.

The Law Lords fielded a full side for the debate;[1] Lords Diplock, Pearson, Dilhorne, Donovan, and Simon of Glaisdale unequivocally supported the amendment; Lord Denning agreed in principle that the existing law was unsatisfactory but expressed doubt about how he would vote, while Lord Morris of Borth-y-Gest spoke against the amendment, being both in favour of the change in the law as proposed in clause 4 and suspicious of the concept of periodical payments. In the event the Law Lords' olive branch did not assuage the ire of the feminists. It produced a virulent attack from Lady Summerskill who, while attracted to the general principle of periodical payments, was quite unwilling to accept the legal view of widows simply as financial dependants deprived of their financial support. Premature widowhood was a disaster shattering a prospectively life-long partnership in which there would be social and economic interdependence. Scathingly she rounded

[1] The debate on the committee stage is recorded in H.L. Debs., vol. 318, cols. 521 ff. (6 May 1971) and vol. 318, cols. 1527 ff. (14 May 1971). All the Law Lords, with the exception of Lords Reid and Guest, attended the debate on 6 May 1971.

on Lord Diplock (the principal spokesman for their Lordships) for his coldly calculating logic devoid of human reality. The judiciary, she said, were not living in 1971, but in a legalistic world of 1871.

No acceptable compromise formula could be found.[1] In the face of almost certain defeat in the lobby the Law Lords, as decorously as they were able, withdrew their amendment and retired once more into their judicial shells. The House of Lords was left to reflect on the fact that, hitherto, perhaps the Law Lords had kept aloof from such debates purely because at least then they could avoid being publicly worsted in intellectual and political argument—to the lawyer, an inelegant spectacle marring the image of judicial independence. Lawyer's law, to which the Lords have traditionally and exclusively confined their deliberative activities, has rarely stimulated much political adrenalin. But the Law Lords' political antennae might have told them that a widow's mite was bound to provoke heated debate. And so it did.

It may be a long time before we see again the Law Lords escape their judicial cocoon and step into the cauldron of a contentious Lords' debate. But it would be a pity if the effect of this single encounter were to be that they henceforth confined their activities as legislators to those matters of lesser social consequence where the judicial voice finds itself in tune with, or at least not discordant to, the House.

---

[1] Lord Dilhorne's suggestion that the matter should be left to the Law Commissioners found some support, though it was widely felt that their reply would be too belated to meet a pressing problem.

XI

TIME AND MONEY

THE House of Lords in its judicial capacity is essentially a public institution, serving the needs of society as a whole: yet it performs this task through the medium of private litigation. And its cost-effectiveness—the cost not only to the individual litigant but also to society—is one factor which must be reckoned in any evaluation of the court of last resort.

The efficacy of any tribunal partly depends upon public willingness to make use of its services. Thus the deterrent effect of the costs and delays which confront such litigants may hamper the performance of the House of Lords in shaping the law by denying it the raw material from which it fashions legal principles. And clearly, having accepted that the House of Lords is predominantly a *public* tribunal, we must examine the argument that the State should minimize the financial disincentives to certain categories of appellants which may deny the court opportunities of pronouncing upon important points of law.

Expressed crudely, two of the principal arguments raised by opponents of a second appeal are that such appeals are prohibitively costly and that they unnecessarily postpone the final judicial settlement of disputes. Certainly it must be admitted that litigation inevitably takes longer to pass through three courts than through two. And under the rough justice of our 'loser-pays-all' system of awarding costs, a loser in the House of Lords, unless he is legally aided, is faced by the costs of a trial and two appeals (plus the relative pin-prick of a bill for appearing before the Appeal Committee if he was refused leave to appeal in the court *a quo*). Since it is the appellant who, by definition, has to bring the appeal to the Lords, the loser-pays-all system is something of an incentive to bring an appeal. A party who has lost below is already faced with at least two bills of costs: thus by hazarding a stake equivalent to one additional set of costs the appellant can play a game which, in terms of the percentage of appeals allowed, gives odds of more than 1:2 in his favour. The hapless respondent stands to gain nothing: if he succeeds in holding the decision then he has spent valuable time, plus any money disallowed on a taxation of his costs. If the appeal is allowed, the respondent must generally pay three sets of costs as well as losing his case: his mortification will doubtless be increased if he finds that, on a counting of judicial heads, his opponent has been successful in a minority decision (see Chapter IX).

The loser-pays-all doctrine is as strictly observed in the House of Lords as in any other English Court: in 78 per cent of civil appeals heard during our period of study, the successful party was granted the full costs of the litigation, and in a further 2 per cent he was given a proportion of his costs. In 3 per cent of cases the winner had been put on terms to pay his own costs in any event, as a condition of obtaining leave. In a further 5 per cent of cases the only order was for legal aid taxation, and in 6 per cent of appeals there was no order made, often because the losing party appeared *in formâ pauperis*. This leaves a miscellany of 7 per cent of cases in which different orders were made: for example, in probate cases it is not uncommon for both sets of costs to come out of the disputed estate.

What then are the costs of an appeal to the House of Lords, in terms of hard cash and of delaying the final settlement of litigation? By answering this question we can assess some of the problems of placing a public supervisory function in the hands of an eminently constituted, but conventionally accusatorial tribunal of review.

Table 39 is based upon an analysis of all bills of costs in appeals submitted for taxation during our period of study. This accounts for 60 per cent of all civil appeals; the remainder, for reasons best known to the parties, are not taxed. (The percentage of bills submitted for taxation has remained fairly constant during the period under review.) Table 39 indicates quite clearly the wide range of costs that are incurred in appealing to the Lords: it is interesting if unhelpful to point out that 83 per cent of bills are spread evenly within the range £500–£3,000. These figures show little evidence of a marked increase in recent years, though nearly all the outstandingly large bills (£3,000 or more) fall into the second half of our period. The disappearance of really small bills after 1960 merely marks the passing of the *in formâ pauperis* procedure which accounted for all six of the sub-£250 bills.

A more comprehensive picture is provided by Table 40, which shows the annual average level of costs in the House of Lords for English and Northern Irish cases[1] and for Scottish cases respectively. This highlights the trend already noted in Table 39, namely that there has been a steady (though by no means uniform) upward trend in costs. This is noticeable in the figures for both Scotland and England, though the annual totals of appeals from the Court of Session are small, and the averages consequently subject to erratic variations.

Simple arithmetical means have serious drawbacks as methods of illuminating widely fluctuating figures of this kind, as the wide divergence between maximum and minimum figures in the 'range' columns clearly shows. It

---

[1] To assuage the feelings of those who may feel that Northern Irish appeals deserve separate treatment we have calculated a separate average for the nine Northern Irish bills taxed. This comes to £1,653, a figure very close to that for English and Northern Irish appeals combined.

TABLE 39

Bills of Costs in Civil Appeals, 1952–1968

Magnitude of bills (before taxation)	Total (% of bills taxed in brackets)	1952	1953	1954	1955	1956	1957	1958	1959	1960	1961	1962	1963	1964	1965	1966	1967	1968
Less than £50	—																	
£50–£249	6 (2·2)	1			1	1	1	1	1	1								
£250–£499	15 (5·4)	7	2		3	2			2	1	1	3						
£500–£749	44 (15·9)	4	2	2	6	4	3	3	2	2	4	1	1	1	1	1	3	1
£750–£999	43 (15·5)		2	1	4	6	1	3	2	3	5	3		6	1	1	1	
£1,000–£1,249	44 (15·9)	3	1	4	3	2	3	1	5	3	4	2	4	2	4	4	2	
£1,250–£1,499	26 (9·4)		2		1		2	1	4	2	1	1	1	3	1	2	2	
£1,500–£1,999	37 (13·4)	1	1	2	3	1	4	2	2	1	3	2	5	1	1	3	4	2
£2,000–£2,999	36 (13·0)		1	2	1	1	3	1	2	2		1	7	3	4	3	3	1
£3,000–£4,999	12 (4·3)			1	1				4			1	3			1		1
£5,000 or more	14 (5·1)			1							1		2	3	1	2	1	3
Bills taxed	277	16	11	13	23	17	17	12	24	15	19	14	23	19	13	17	16	8
Bills not taxed	189																	

TABLE 40

Taxed Bills of Costs of Losing Parties in House of Lords Civil Appeals, 1952-1968, by Year and Nationality of Appeal (excluding appeals in formâ pauperis)

Year	English Appeals and Northern Irish Appeals							Scottish Appeals						
	No. of bills taxed	Average magnitude	Range	Average taxed off	Range	Leading counsel's average brief fee	Range	No. of bills taxed	Average magnitude	Range	Average taxed off	Range	Leading counsel's average brief fee	Range
1952	8	£1,073	£546-2,156	£236	£0·5-706	£266	£110-1,100	6	£813	£521-1,304	£228	£18-675	£174	£110-275
1953	9	£1,202	£470-2,475	£304	£7-1,036	£254	£107-550	2	£467	£425-509	£109	£48-£170	£189	£157-£220
1954	8	£2,661	£1,090-6,413	£1,213	£83-£4,584	£757	£110-1,100	5	£848	£571-1,146	£192	£152-237	£242	£165-275
1955	17	£1,444	£330-3,144	£364	nil-£2,182	£265	£82-826	5	£932	£642-1,083	£258	£140-368	£242	£165-275
1956	7	£971	£542-£1,870	£298	£52-£765	£228	£110-385	7	£1,085	£684-2,646	£377	£10-£1,725	£279	£192-£550
1957	11	£1,515	£571-2,658	£601	£18-820	£380	£164-826	4	£921	£535-£1,409	£159	£2-£408	£199	£165-220
1958	8	£1,126	£513-1,654	£387	£6-816	£308	£110-716	3	£1,353	£704-2,407	£487	£198-855	£275	£165-385
1959	19	£1,306	£210-4,119	£428	nil-£1,639	£309	£82-787	4	£2,156	£667-3,642	£662	£114-1,274	£403	£165-826
1960	13	£1,480	£441-2,865	£350	nil-£821	£342	£82-550	6	£858	£548-£1,144	£181	nil-£424	£281	£220-529
1961	12	£1,392	£329-6,108	£673	nil-£4,969	£408	£110-2,200	6	£986	£740-1,598	£200	£103-395	£273	£262-275
1962	21	£1,470	£294-3,925	£273	£1-1,150	£321	£110-1,760	2	£483	£338-627	£76	£8-£143	£248	£220-275
1963	11	£2,578	£464-5,817	£590	£7-3,536	£568	£165-2,200	3	£1,075	£1,023-1,162	£46	£42-48	£257	£220-275
1964	11	£1,916	£745-5,560	£319	£15-1,321	£381	£110-550	7	£2,416	£815-11,346	£480	£1-3,057	£647	£220-2,756
1965	12	£2,019	£689-6,405	£307	nil-£1,788	£394	£220-1,100	1	£1,229	£1,229	£57	£57	£275	£275
1966	15	£3,802	£847-28,705	£555	nil-£4,082	£588	£165-1,653	2	£903	£694-£1,182	£17	nil-£33	£305	£275-£334
1967	7	£2,908	£1,112-8,625	£664	£52-£2,458	£751	£220-2,205	9	£1,103	£698-1,776	£75	£4-155	£263	£110-330
1968	7	£3,550	£519-8,545	£800	£6-£3,241	£783	£82-£2,205	1	£1,776	£1,776	£603	£603	£441	£441

becomes almost meaningless to talk about an 'average' cost of English appeals in 1966 being £3,802, when one appeal alone produced a bill of £28,705.

Counsel's brief fees have tended to rise slightly over the years—though the trend is not very marked. Briefs marked at 1,000 guineas or more are slightly more common than was the case at the beginning of the 1950s, and there are still several cases every year where counsel come before the court of last resort with briefs marked at 100 or 150 guineas. Counsel from Scotland appear at first sight to do rather worse than their English brethren. But, on balance, the more complex and lengthy appeals tend to come from England: and a glance at the 'range' columns reveals that, at the *lower* end of the fee-scale, the Scots advocates command marginally higher fees than do English barristers.

Of course the fee marked on leading counsel's brief does not tell the whole financial story: additional consultation fees, plus refreshers for each day's attendance in court can, in a long case, exceed the brief by a substantial margin. Thus to take one outstanding instance in a 1966 appeal: leading counsel's brief was marked at 1,500 guineas, but numerous refreshers bolstered his total income from the case to some £8,000. As this was one of those rare instances where the parties had been permitted to brief three counsel[1] (and, according to long tradition, the leader's two deputies receive up to two-thirds of his fees) it is not surprising to find that the bill of costs presented reached the astronomical heights of £28,000. Table 41 shows the annual ratio between the average *total* fee ultimately payable to counsel and the average brief fee.

Quite clearly a substantial factor must be added to counsel's brief fee to reflect the earnings on refreshers in order to ascertain how much he is actually paid, though the exact figure depends upon such matters as the length of the hearing and the complexity of the issues which may necessitate frequent (and costly) consultations. Table 41 reflects the fact that in contrast to Scottish appeals there has been a distinct tendency in English ones for the *total* fees of counsel to rise, in proportion to their brief fees which (as Table 39 showed) have remained fairly constant. To some extent this reflects a recent trend towards slightly longer hearings, which has brought about an increase in the number of refreshers. This trend has not affected Scottish litigation to the same extent. Scottish appeals have always had a tendency to be disposed of more quickly than English ones, hence refreshers are a very much less significant element in Scottish bills of costs. Moreover one area of law which has

---

[1] An examination of the seventy-three Scottish bills reveals that in ten cases the successful party was represented by three counsel, and in only one case was this cost allowed on taxation. On the other hand, three Scottish litigants were represented only by one counsel. Of 194 taxed English and Northern Irish appeals, eighteen claims for three counsel (including seven appeals from Northern Ireland) were disallowed on taxation: eight claims were allowed while six English parties appeared by one counsel only.

tended to involve abnormally long hearings—patents, copyrights, and trade marks—has never been touched upon in an appeal from Scotland.

Time is an important ingredient in the total cost of an appeal: not only is counsel's fee usually increased by a refresher paid for each day in court, but the length of a case is often indicative of its complexity—and this in turn may increase the size of the brief fee, as well as calling for many expensive consultations between legal advisers. We have calculated that the average cost

TABLE 41

Ratio of Total Fee to Brief Fee (Leading Counsel)

Year	English	Scottish
1952	1·57	1·22
1953	1·74	1·00
1954	1·48	1·38
1955	1·48	1·15
1956	1·50	1·44
1957	1·43	1·58
1958	1·34	1·77
1959	1·39	2·06
1960	1·28	1·18
1961	1·30	1·32
1962	2·06	1·00
1963	1·71	1·49
1964	2·03	1·38
1965	1·67	1·89
1966	2·20	1·29
1967	1·45	1·18
1968	2·15	1·25

(before taxation) of an English civil appeal over the period 1952–68 was £1,928 while the corresponding figure for Scotland was £1,172. The average number of days (or part days) taken to hear each English appeal included in that calculation was 3·65 days, while the corresponding Scottish figure was 2·73. Relating these sets of figures we can calculate an average cost per appeal-day over the period. The figure for English appeals is £529, and that for Scotland £429. Thus the discrepancy between the two countries is not so marked as it might appear.

Even so, its existence is interesting. The largest factors in a bill of costs (except in exceptionally long cases) are the 'fixed' costs such as the brief fee, solicitor's disbursements, cost of producing the record and court fees. Thus any group of appeals which, on average, take less time in court, would be expected to cost *more* per appeal day, since the spread of costs is less: in this instance the reverse is true. Thus the discrepancy between English and Scottish costs is not simply a matter of time taken in court. One relevant factor is the size of the brief fee payable to leading counsel (as opposed to total fees payable to counsel, including refreshers). Here there is a marked difference between the average figures, £422 in English appeals and £299 in Scottish (70·8 per cent of the English figure). But the discrepancy still does not fully account for Scottish appeals being cheaper. If we take the difference between the figures and multiply the result by $1\frac{2}{3}$ (to take account of junior counsel's fees in those cases—the vast majority—where a leader and a junior are briefed), the average difference still amounts only to £205 per case.

What of other fixed costs? We have investigated the long-standing legends about astronomical printing bills, in the bad old days before their Lordships permitted bound cases to be typed. Certainly there are numerous instances where printing bills comfortably exceeded 10 per cent of the total bill. The most notable instances of outstandingly large claims for printing, binding, and sometimes photographs, are as follows:

Year	Amount (£)	Total Bill (£)
1953	340	1,396
1954	466	1,784
1954	385	2,883
1955	460	1,754
1955	325	1,083
1955	168 (24 taxed off)	930 (Scottish appeal)
1955	654	1,702
1955	137	698
1956	302	838
1956	336	1,119
1958	178	513
1958	308	933
1959	1,380	4,119
1959	667	2,108
1960	1,243	2,865
1963	453	2,011
1965	1,010	6,405
1966	1,756	28,705
1967	628	1,776 (Scottish appeal)

Thus large printing bills, in the days before the rule requiring printing was abolished, were by no means uncommon, though in some 90 per cent of appeals the amount did not exceed 10 per cent of the total. It is noticeable that in only one of the cases listed was part of the claim (a very small part) disallowed on taxation.

How does the subject-matter of appeals affect the bills of costs? The answer to this question may be found in Table 42 which sets out the range of bills of costs (prior to taxation) in relation to the broad subject-matter of the appeals. On looking at this table one is struck by the relatively even spread of different sizes of bill among the various subject categories, and the small number of cases in each category do not encourage us to draw rigid conclusions. The distribution of bills among the four main categories of appeal,

TABLE 42

Bills of Costs in Civil Appeals, 1952–1968, by Subject-Matter of Appeal

Case Categories[a]

Magnitude of bills (before taxation)	Total bills taxed	Revenue	Fault liability	Contract	Trade union	Master and servant	Property	Company law	Defamation	Patents, etc.	Practice and procedure	Admin. law	Family law	International law	Constitutional law	Miscellaneous
£50–£249	6	—	1	1	—	1	1	—	—	—	1	—	—	—	—	1
£250–£499	15	6	1	—	—	—	3	—	—	—	1	2	1	—	—	1
£500–£749	44	16	10	3	1	—	7	—	—	1	3	—	1	—	—	2
£750–£999	43	13	9	3	—	2	11	—	—	—	2	—	1	—	—	2
£1,000–£1,249	44	7	11	7	—	1	10	—	—	2	2	1	1	—	—	2
£1,250–£1,499	26	11	6	3	1	—	2	—	1	—	—	—	1	1	—	—
£1,500–£1,999	37	12	5	4	1	—	4	2	—	3	—	1	1	—	1	—
£2,000–£2,999	36	6	7	6	—	—	5	1	—	3	—	1	4	4	—	1
£3,000–£4,999	12	3	4	1	—	—	—	1	—	—	1	2	2	—	—	3
£5,000 or more	14	3	1	3	2	—	—	—	1	2	—	—	—	—	2	—
Total	277	77	52	31	5	4	43	4	2	11	10	7	11	5	3	12

[a] This is our standard case-classification: see pp. 244–5.

revenue, fault liability, contract, and property is close to the overall distribution, though among the more 'commercial' categories (contract, company law, and patents) there is a slight concentration at the upper end of the costs range.

TAXATION OF COSTS

As is the practice in all English courts, the House of Lords provides machinery for taxation for costs. This means that a losing party who is ordered to pay his opponent's costs is entitled to have these costs taxed by the Taxing Officer of the House of Lords. This procedure ensures that the loser will only have to pay costs reasonably incurred and will not have to bear the brunt of his opponent's extravagance or over-insurance. If one party decides unilaterally to brief two leading counsel, then, come what may, he will pay at least the costs of one of them.

A formidable list of items allowable on taxation is set out in a twenty-four page document called 'Forms of Bills of Costs (as between Party and Party)[1] applicable to Judicial Taxations in the House of Lords in Appeals'. This is divided into two parts dealing respectively with English and with Scottish appeals, and each section is further sub-divided into appellants' and respondents' costs. Woe betide the incautious solicitor who deviates from the holy writ set out in this gospel: such transgression will be heavily penalized by the Taxing Officer.

The document makes interesting reading: it includes such choice items as 'Attending at the Judicial Office Enquiring as to the State of the Cause List' —£1: 'Attending Lodging Appeal at Judicial Office'—£2·50 (£2 10s) Counsel were allowed the princely fee of £7·72½ (£7 14s 6d) for arguing a petition for leave before the Appeal Committee (until May 1970 when the amount went up to £11). (A comparison between the latest—1971—edition of the document and the edition dated 1952 reveals that fees have moved with the times: solicitors can for example now claim 50p (10s) for 'writing to the Clerk of the Parliament applying for leave to appear by counsel before the Appeal Committee' instead of 25p (5s).)

We have already seen in Table 39 that in almost 60 per cent of civil appeals bills of costs are taxed. Table 40 shows that between 15 and 45 per cent of the average total amount of bills submitted annually are taxed off. The most 'taxing' year for English appeals was 1954 (45·6 per cent taxed off) and for Scotland 1958 (34·7 per cent taxed off).

As one would expect, cases involving the heaviest costs suffer most on taxation, though there are several examples of relatively modest claims

---

[1] The most usual order for costs involves 'party and party costs'. Very rarely the court may invoke the far more generous 'solicitor and client', or even 'solicitor and own client', taxation as a penalty against a vexatious—or merely vexing—losing party. Taxation under the Legal Aid and Advice Acts also takes the form of 'solicitor and client' costs.

being cut by more than half. Several points emerge. First, that counsel's refresher fees are nowadays measured more realistically than in the early 1950s when nominal refreshers of 10 guineas a day were the rule. Second, the most substantial cuts are made when a third counsel is briefed. Third, the size of brief fees in the House of Lords has risen markedly during recent years, though very large fees are still very much the exception. Over the period 1952–68, 277 bills of losing parties in civil appeals were taxed, and in only 56 (20·2 per cent) was leading counsel's brief marked at 500 guineas or more. During the period 1952–62 only 28 briefs out of 169 were as large as this (two of them were 1,000 guineas and two were 2,000 guineas): only five of these were allowed on taxation, and the highest sum allowed was 550 guineas (on a brief marked at 2,200 guineas). But during 1963–68, 28 out of 96 briefs were 500 guineas or more: six of these were 1,000 guineas, two were 1,500 guineas, two were 2,000 guineas and one was 2,500 guineas. Eleven of the twenty-five were allowed in full on taxation, and seven briefs of 1,000 guineas or more were either allowed in full or reduced to a lower four-figure sum. The largest brief fee allowed was 1,750 guineas (on a brief marked at 2,500 guineas) and a 1,500 guineas brief was allowed in full.

Stories about the astronomical sums payable to counsel appearing in the Lords are a part of folklore. By what criteria, therefore, are counsel's fees adjudged to be 'reasonable'? The precise answer to this question is closely sealed within the breast of the Taxing Officer, but clearly some assessment must be made of the complexity and the importance of the appeal; the degree of eminence of the counsel involved is treated as irrelevant.

Clearly the efficiency of any court in an accusatorial system is dependent in part upon the quality of the advocates appearing before it: and it is to the benefit of the legal system as a whole that the fees paid should attract barristers of the highest standing to the court of last resort. But we would add that members of the Bar (while not entirely oblivious of the pecuniary aspects of their profession) regard it as a privilege—and often as an important milestone in their careers—to appear before this distinguished tribunal. And many a barrister has been only too willing to appear *gratis* in poor person's appeals where legal aid has not been available.

PETITIONS FOR LEAVE TO APPEAL

Where a successful application to the Appeal Committee for leave to appeal is followed by the lodging of the appeal, the costs of the application normally become costs in the cause. But when no appeal follows, or where leave is refused, the bill of costs for the hearing before the Appeal Committee will be taxed separately. Table 43 shows the average bills of costs in petitions for leave to appeal during the periods 1952–60 and 1961–8, the cases in the latter period being divided according to whether or not the successful parties were legally aided.

TABLE 43

Bills of Costs in Petitions for Leave to Appeal, 1952–1968

Period	Total bills taxed	Average size	Range of costs	Average taxed off	Average net
1952–60	42	£42·5	£15–£132	£19·6	£22·9
1961–8	79	£77·0	£10–£291	£37·8	£39·5
1961–8 (L.A.)	22	£172·6	£68–£324	£39·4	£133·2

Three things stand out from this table. First, the annual average bill of costs rose substantially during our period of study, from £42·5 (gross) in the first half of the period to £77·3. Second, the Taxing Officer was exceptionally severe in these cases; any bills greatly in excess of the norm were ruthlessly pruned. Thus one bill of £251 was taxed down to £45; another bill of £206 to £39, and, the most striking example, a bill of £313 to a mere £37. The largest amount allowed up to the end of 1968 on a bill (other than in a case involving legal aid) was £95. Petitioners who brief leading counsel on a petition, at a fee commensurate with his degree of eminence, are likely to find themselves allowed a nominal sum of £11 for junior counsel, and nothing at all for the leader. (We have already noted that silks are briefed on a high proportion of petitions, see Table 4, p. 127.) Third, we note the growing part played by legal aid in petitions for leave to appeal: the larger bills in these cases are explained by the less stringent taxing requirements of the Legal Aid and Advice Act.

We discuss elsewhere some of the drawbacks of the present system for granting leave: we would add to this that the respondent to a hopeless petition for leave to appeal often has little hope of recovering his costs. It appears that only about a quarter of successful respondents even bother to have their costs taxed.

LEGAL AID

The civil law is a social service which provides machinery for the rational and peaceable settlement of disputes. But using it costs money—often very large sums of money—and those concerned with reforming the machinery of justice have always regarded the provision of an adequate system of financial help for impecunious litigants as a matter of the highest priority.

In the House of Lords a further issue is involved. The court of last resort does not merely enable litigants to have their private litigious disputes resolved; it is concerned with laying down general principles of law. And legal aid is clearly a matter of fundamental importance in an exercise of this kind. A 'public' institution must operate at all levels of society: a workman's compensation case is socially as important as one involving surtax evasion or the fiscal liability of a huge industrial empire. If such a case is sufficiently intricate and jurisprudentially perplexing as to cause difficulties in the lower courts and to hinder the development of settled principles of law, then it is vital to the public interest that the difficulty be resolved by the court of last resort. If, in such a case, the litigant cannot afford to appeal then he should receive a subsidy from public funds.

The Evershed Committee on Supreme Court Practice and Procedure, which published its final report in 1953, suggested that the Attorney-General should be empowered to issue a certificate for the use of public funds in appeals to the House of Lords which are of outstanding public importance.[1] And more recently a sub-committee of Justice[2] advocated a wider scheme for a suitors' fund to indemnify respondents who, through no fault of their own, lose in the appeal courts and have to pay the costs of several proceedings. As we shall argue later, neither of these schemes goes far enough in meeting the special problems raised by appeals to the House of Lords.

The crucial question is, how many litigants, whose cases raise important questions of law, are at present denied access to the court of last resort solely on the grounds of poverty? We confess at once that we are unable, due to the lack of sufficient data, to answer this question with any degree of precision, but we propose to throw some light on it by examining the provisions relating to poor persons' appeals to the House of Lords during our period of study.

The period can be divided into two. Up to December 1960 poor persons' appeals from England and Scotland were covered by the rules governing appeals *in formâ pauperis*. This procedure (which may still survive in Northern Irish appeals) dates back to the Appellate Jurisdiction Act 1876 which was amended by the Appeal (Formâ Pauperis) Act 1893.[3] An appellant who obtained leave to appeal *in formâ pauperis* was exempt from court fees and from the stringent requirements for printing a case. He would normally have no difficulty in finding a counsel prepared to represent him *gratis* or for a nominal fee. And, perhaps the most important concession of all, he was exempt from lodging £700 (as it then was) as security for costs. The bills of costs in these cases never exceeded £350 during our period of study, and were invariably taxed down to a figure between £100 and £150. When petitioning the House under this procedure it was necessary for the appellant to swear an affidavit to the effect that he was extremely poor: this had to be supported by a further affidavit sworn by some person of standing in his local community (usually the parish clergyman). The petition was referred to the Appeal Committee who examined the degree of poverty of the petitioner, and also (under the 1893 Act, above) whether there was a prima facie case for success on appeal. It was the latter provision which proved the main stumbling block to petitioners whose cases fell within our period of study.

---

[1] Cmd. 8878, s. IX.   [2] 'Proposals for a Suitors' Fund', March 1969.
[3] See Appendix 1.

During the period 1952–68 there were forty petitions for leave to present an appeal *in formâ pauperis*. These are analysed in Table 44.

TABLE 44

Petitions to House of Lords for Leave to Appeal in formâ pauperis

Court *a quo*	Presented	Refused	Granted
Court of Appeal	22	1	21
Court of Session	13	7	6
Court of Appeal (N.I.)	5	3	2

The disparity between the success-rates of appeals from different courts of appeal stems from the different leave requirements: the Appeal Committee inevitably gave closer attention to the merits of appeals from Scotland and Northern Ireland, which lay as of right, than to English appeals which (in all but four cases, where the Appeal Committee itself gave leave to appeal) had already been granted leave by the Court of Appeal. All the unsuccessful petitioners from Scotland and Northern Ireland presented petitions of appeal to the House, but only one pursued the matter further (see below). Two of the successful English petitioners eventually abandoned their appeals.

Up to the end of 1960, when legal aid was introduced, there were twenty-three appeals *in formâ pauperis*. These are listed in Annex A. Table 45 analyses these appeals and their comparative rates of success in relation to the total case-load of the House of Lords.

During the period 1952–60, 9·4 per cent of all civil appeals in the House of Lords were presented *in formâ pauperis*. (And one case was defended *in formâ pauperis*, by a respondent in person.) Although the numbers involved were small it is clear that appellants appearing *in formâ pauperis* were not significantly more successful than other appellants. The requirement for leave to appeal *in formâ pauperis* proved no more stringent in practice than for ordinary petitions for leave to appeal.

A glance at the list of appeals in Annex A gives a clear impression of the categories of appeal which came before the House of Lords under this procedure. No fewer than ten of the twenty-three cases involved fault liability; four involved trade or employment, master and servant, or trade union membership; two involved family law and two involved administrative law. Many of the cases were of crucial importance, for example *Best* v. *Samuel Fox* (damages payable to wife for sexual impotence of husband); *Vine* v. *National Dock Labour Board* (delegation of disciplinary powers by a statutory tribunal); *Smith* v. *East Elloe R.D.C.* (the extent to which the exercise of statutory powers can be challenged for *mala fides*). And the House of Lords might have been a less colourful place had Colonel Wintle not availed himself of the procedure to appear in person before it (*Wintle* v. *Nye* [1959] 1 W.L.R. 284).

Consideration of applications for leave to appeal *in formâ pauperis* produced bizarre results in at least two instances. In the Northern Irish appeal, *Cavanagh* v. *The Ulster Weaving Co.* (1959), the Appeal Committee rejected

TABLE 45

A) *Appeals* in formâ pauperis, *1952–1960*

Court *a quo*	Total appeals	% successful	Total appeals *in formâ pauperis*	% successful
Court of Appeal	184	36·4	15	40
Court of Session	53	47·0	6	50
Court of Appeal (N.I.)	7	57·0	2	50

B) *Appeals involving legal aid, 1961–1968*

Court *a quo*	Total Appeals	% successful	Appellant legally aided	Respondent legally aided	Both parties legally aided	legally aided appellants successful
Court of Appeal	167	35·9	18	8	4	11 (50%)
Court of Session	50	48·0	11	2	1	7 (58%)
Court of Appeal (N. I.)	7	57·0	1	—	—	— (—)

an application to appeal *in formâ pauperis* because there was no prima facie case; but the persistent appellant eventually won his case before the Appellate Committee by the ordinary procedure. In the same year the Appeal Committee backed a loser by giving leave to appeal *in formâ pauperis* in another Irish case—*Smyth* v. *Cameron*—presumably on the strength of a dissenting judgment by Lord MacDermott in the Court of Appeal in Northern Ireland. But this appeal was dismissed without the respondent being called upon.

There may be something to be said for the courts assuming the responsibility for applying a poor person's procedure, but clearly the very stringent test of a prima facie case is too severe, though in practice this is a significant criterion in all applications for leave to appeal: and even if the results of these appeals show that the requirement was mitigated in practice, it militates against the function of the court of last resort as a public tribunal by over-emphasizing its role in reviewing particular litigation.

Some impecunious litigants could not bring themselves within the *in formâ pauperis* provisions, even though legally-aided below, and in one case this prompted judicial criticism of a system under which both appellant and respondent were liable to suffer hardship: see *Anderson* v. *Lambie*, part of which is set out as Annex C.

In December 1960 the first civil appeal came to the House of Lords under the provisions of the Legal Aid and Advice Act 1949 which was extended to cover proceedings in the court of last resort. This was *Chapman* v. *Rix* in which the appellant had originally been given leave to appeal *in formâ pauperis*. Annexed to this chapter is a list (Annex B) of the forty-six civil appeals during the period 1960–8 in which either or both of the parties were legally-aided. Table 45B summarizes the outcome of these appeals.

During this period there were 167 English appeals (17·9 per cent legally-aided), 50 Scottish (28·0 per cent legally-aided) and 7 Northern Irish (one legally-aided). At first sight it may appear that the proportion of persons legally aided dramatically exceeds the proportion of litigants who appeared *in formâ pauperis* during the 1950s (9·4 per cent). But this ignores one important distinction between legal aid and *in formâ pauperis*; the former procedure has assisted not only appellants but also a number of *respondents* in the House of Lords, while the latter procedure in practice applied almost exclusively to appellants. During the period 1961–8, 15·3 per cent of appellants were legally-aided, a significant, but by no means dramatic, increase over the *in formâ pauperis* percentage. And in practice the introduction of legal aid has made its greatest mark in Scottish appeals. During 1952–60, only 6 out of 53 Scottish appellants (11·3 per cent) appeared *in formâ pauperis*, as compared with 11 out of 50 post-1960 legally-aided Scottish appellants (22 per cent). Whereas 8·2 per cent of English appellants appeared *in formâ pauperis* before 1960, 13·2 per cent were legally-aided during 1961–8: an appreciable but hardly dramatic increase.

Table 45B makes it clear that assisted appellants are marginally more successful in the House of Lords than litigants who pay their own way, though the figures are too small to be statistically significant. One cannot go even so far as to say that the Legal Aid Area Committees are much better at picking winners than was the Appeal Committee in considering *in formâ pauperis* petitions.

During the debate on the second reading of the 1969 Administration of Justice Bill in the Lords, several Law Lords (notably Lord Denning and Lord Reid)[1] said that the advent of legal aid had made a significant impact on the character and the size of the case load of the House of Lords. Our findings appear to cast doubt upon that conclusion: little has changed since the disappearance of the *in formâ pauperis* procedure except perhaps that the financial burden of a small proportion of respondents (6·7 per cent) has been eased.

A glance at Annex B reveals that the distribution of case categories still

---

[1] H.L. Debs., vol. 297, col. 468 (Lord Reid) and col. 470 (Lord Denning), 12 November 1968.

gives pride of place to fault liability (twenty cases), family law (eight, all the post-1960 English family law appeals involved legal aid), and trade unions (three). Indeed the large proportion of these cases (both in the legally-aided list and in the list of appeals *in formâ pauperis*), prompts the conclusion that the availability of financial assistance to poor persons in the House of Lords has been a crucial factor in the development of these areas of law.

Almost every case in Annex B is of central importance: *Bridge v. Campbell Discount Co.*; *Gollins v. Gollins*; *Hughes v. Lord Advocate*; *Ridge v. Baldwin*; *Rookes v. Barnard*; *National Provincial Bank v. Ainsworth*; *Beswick v. Beswick*: all are leading cases in their respective fields. Yet had legal aid not been available, some or all of them might never have reached the court of last resort, and the law as a whole would have been the poorer.

Can it happen that an important case is excluded from the Lords simply because an impecunious appellant cannot get legal aid? The complete answer lies buried in the confidential files of the Law Society; but on one occasion at least the issue was argued openly in the courts. In 1967 the case of *Rondel v. Worsley* came before the Appeal Committee of the House of Lords on an application for leave to appeal: leave was granted, and the appellant thereupon applied for legal aid. This application was refused by the legal aid Area Committee on the ground that 'it appears unreasonable that you should receive legal aid in the particular circumstances of the case.' Subsequently, the Divisional Court rejected an application for *mandamus* against the Area Committee on the grounds that the Committee's wide discretion entitled it to consider, among other things, the merits of the action.[1]

In the result, the appeal was heard by the House of Lords through the respondent's generosity in waiving the requirement of security for costs, and with counsel appearing for the appellant without a fee. The case was a important one involving the liability of counsel for negligence in conducting a case in court:[2] it is, to say the least, unsatisfactory that once leave has been given, the Lords might be denied the opportunity of hearing an appeal which its own Appeal Committee has adjudged to be of general public importance. Such instances are rare. But the fact that they can happen underlines an important weakness in the present system.

The Law Lords themselves are conscious of their position as the custodians of a public tribunal. In November 1970, after the House had delivered its judgment in the appeal, *Saunders v. Anglia Building Society*,[3] counsel were heard on the question of costs, whether the successful respondent company was entitled to receive its costs of appealing out of the legal aid fund under the provisions of the Legal Aid Act 1964, and their Lordships took the unusual step of reserving judgment on this point. In reaching the decision

---

[1] *R. v. Legal Aid Committee No. 1 (London) Legal Aid Area, ex. p. Rondel* [1967] 2 Q.B. 482.

[2] *Rondel v. Worsley* [1969] 1 A.C. 191.   [3] Reported as *Gallie v. Lee* [1971] A.C. 1004.

that the respondent should receive costs only in respect of the appeal to the House of Lords and not in respect of the proceedings in the Court of Appeal, the Law Lords carefully distinguished between the respective roles of the two tribunals. To quote Lord Reid:

> I think we must consider separately costs in this House and costs in the Court of Appeal. Cases can only come before this House with leave, and leave is generally given because some general question of law is involved. In this case it enabled the whole vexed matter of *non est factum* to be re-examined. This seems to me a typical case where the costs of the successful respondent should come out of public funds.
>
> But different considerations apply to the respondents' costs in the Court of Appeal. When the use of public funds in affording legal aid has been the direct cause of the successful unassisted party having to incur additional costs, there appears to me to be a very strong case for holding that it is just and equitable that such additional costs should be made good to him out of public funds. But in the present case the respondents were not taken to the Court of Appeal by their legally aided opponent. They had to go to that Court because the decision at first instance was against them. They may say that the action would never have started if Mrs. Gallie had not had legal aid from the beginning. But that appears to me to be too remote. Although the respondents have ultimately succeeded they cannot recover their costs at first instance because they are not impecunious. I cannot see any sufficient reason why they should recover from public funds costs which they chose to incur in appealing against an adverse decision at first instance.[1]

Our suggestion for a remedy for defects in the present system is both simple and comprehensive, and could be accommodated within the present legal aid system. Where leave to appeal had been given, legal aid would automatically be available to both parties, excluding legal persons. If a party wished to avail himself of the State's financial assistance, *then* a means test would be applied, and a contribution exacted up to 100 per cent of the total costs. This would eliminate all considerations of 'merit', which should be only of marginal importance in the role of a court of last resort: such a scheme would not require the establishment of a separate fund.

The only drawback is that this scheme is tied to the present system for granting leave, which itself has serious flaws as we have seen. If the requirement of leave is abolished (also in present Scottish appeals which lie as of right) the need would be met by the grant of a certificate of public importance (as in criminal appeals since 1960) by the court *a quo*. Such a procedure would not necessitate a separate judicial hearing, and would enable the courts to determine the urgency of the case independently of 'merits'. The recipient of a certificate would then be entitled to legal aid on the basis of the last paragraph.

TIME

We come now to the problem of time. There are three elements in this: how long do cases take to reach the House of Lords; how long do proceedings

---

[1] *Gallie* v. *Lee* (No. 2) [1971] A.C. 1039, 1048.

last once they have got there; and how long do their Lordships take to reach a decision? All these are pure questions of fact and can be answered briefly.

First, how long does a case take to get to the House of Lords? The answer to this depends upon the point from which the time is measured. Taking the starting-point as the issue of the writ (or other originating procedure), we find that 85·5 per cent of cases took four years or less until judgment was delivered in the Lords; 7 per cent between four and five years, and 7 per cent more than five years. Two-thirds took between two and four years. Only 4 per cent (invariably by originating motion in the Divisional Court) took less than eighteen months. Inevitably the pre-trial process varies enormously in terms of such factors as the complexity of the issues or the elusiveness of witnesses. As an alternative starting-point, therefore, we have taken the date of the trial judgment: the results of a calculation on this basis are analysed in Table 46.

TABLE 46

Interval from Trial Judgment to House of Lords Judgment in Civil Appeals, 1952–1968

Period (months)	Total	Court *a quo*		
		Court of Appeal	Court of Session	Court of Appeal (N.I.)
Up to 12	11	6	5	—
12–17	131	95	32	4
18–23	206	158	42	6
24–9	81	58	19	2
30–5	25	22	2	1
36–47	10	8	1	1
48 or more	1	—	—	1
Unknown	3	1	2	—

This shows that 72·2 per cent of appeals take between one and two years to pass through two appellate stages, and only 3 per cent take more than three years. There is no appreciable difference between the times taken by appeals from the different courts *a quo*. Most of the cases in the longer time-range are concentrated in the second half of our period; twenty-eight of the thirty-six cases taking thirty months or more came in the period 1960–8. There is a fairly even distribution as between subject categories: revenue cases tend to take rather less time than the average, while patent and contract cases take more.

While it is important to consider the time spent in taking a case through the three-tier hierarchy it is perhaps even more so to examine the period which elapses between judgment in the court *a quo* and the hearing in the House of Lords, and then the time for which the House reserves judgment. The sum of these is the delay which must be entered on the liabilities side of the balance sheet when considering the value of the second appeal.

Table 47 shows the time which elapsed between judgment in the court *a quo* and the first day of hearing in the Lords: to see whether there is any evidence of a trend, one way or the other, we have divided our period into two nearly equal parts.

TABLE 47

Delay between Judgment in the Court of Appeal and First Day of Hearing in the House of Lords: Civil Appeals, 1952–1968

Period of delay (months)	English and Northern Irish appeals		Scottish appeals		Total
	1952–9	1960–8	1952–9	1960–8	
0–5	—	8	—	2	10 (2·1%)
6–8	14	50	3	15	82 (17·6%)
9–11	57	70	11	29	167 (35·8%)
12–14	65	36	16	11	128 (27·4%)
15–18	23	23	8	2	56 (12·0%)
18–21	3	8	5	—	16 (3·4%)
21–24	2	4	—	—	6 (1·3%)
More than 24	—	1	—	—	1 (0·2%)
Totals	164	200	43	59	466

The median figure is about eleven months, and over the whole period more than four-fifths of all appeals were heard in less than fifteen months from judgment in the court *a quo*. Scottish appeals were heard marginally sooner than English appeals. For both English and Scottish appeals there is evidence of a *decrease* in the delay in the second half of the period: in 1952–9 only 41 per cent of appeals were heard in less than twelve months, as compared with 67·5 per cent in 1960–8.

As one would expect, the delay is increased if the parties request further time for the submission of cases; but although appeals came on sooner during the second half of the period the number of petitions for further time increased appreciably and the proportion of cases in which no petitions for further time were submitted fell from 33·5 per cent to 26·0 per cent. During 1952–9 the cases heard in less than twelve months each involved an average of 0·68 petitions for further time, and those heard after twelve months or more involved an average of 1·46 petitions. Corresponding averages for 1960–8 were 0·95 and 2·10.

The largest number of petitions for further time was nine in *Glinski* v. *McIver* in 1962; in the case which involved the longest delay between judgment in the Court of Appeal and a hearing in the House of Lords (two years and one month), *Henry Kendall and Sons* v. *Suffolk Agricultural and Poultry Producers Association Ltd.* in 1968, the appellant submitted a mere six petitions for further time.

Delays involved in hearing criminal appeals are shorter. It has been rare for criminal appeals to be delayed more than six months, and even that is unusual. Normal delay has been four to six weeks, though since criminal appeals became more common after 1960 delays of three to six months are not uncommon. By far the longest was in *Adcock* v. *Wilson*, from judgment in the Divisional Court on 10 February 1967 to first day of hearing, 8 February 1968.

It must be stressed that there is a slight arithmetical unreality about all these figures in that we have not taken any account of vacations or of any additional delays involved in obtaining leave to appeal from the Appeal Committee. It is for this reason that the figures are presented purely as a factual statement about the impact of the House of Lords on the final settlement of litigious disputes, and not as carefully weighted averages heavily endowed with statistical significance.

The second factor contributing to 'delay' is the duration of the hearing in the Lords. Over the whole period, 79 per cent of appeals (96 per cent of Scottish appeals, 74 per cent of English civil appeals, and 81 per cent of criminal appeals) occupied four days or less in the House of Lords: 8 per cent took only one day (or part day), 19 per cent of Scottish appeals, 4 per cent of English civil appeals and 15 per cent of criminal appeals. Only 3 per cent of Scottish appeals occupied seven days or more, as compared with 9 per cent of English civil appeals and 11 per cent of criminal appeals. (The reasons for the difference between Scottish and English appeals is discussed elsewhere.) There is little variation between the duration of hearings in different subject categories, though nine of the twenty-eight patent cases took seven days or more, while fifteen of the eighteen cases involving procedure took only one or two days.

Finally, we come to the question of reserved judgments. Their Lordships reserved judgment in all but two civil appeals during our period: the exceptions were *Wintle* v. *Nye* [1959] 1 W.L.R. 284 and *McClelland, Pope and Langley* v. *Howard* (1966, originally unreported, but later noted at [1968] 1 All E.R. 569). In seven criminal appeals,[1] however, the House reserved judgment, having announced its decision at the conclusion of the hearing. The average period for which judgment was reserved in both civil and criminal appeals was about six weeks. Given that delays in many courts abroad are

---

[1] *Davies* v. *D.P.P.*; *Bedder* v. *D.P.P.*; *Bratty* v. *Attorney-General for Northern Ireland*; *Chandler* v. *D.P.P.*; *Rumping* v. *D.P.P.*; *Zacharia* v. *Republic of Cyprus*; *Churchill* v. *Walton*.

considerably longer, this is a remarkable feat of judicial athleticism and productivity. There were only sixteen civil appeals (3·6 per cent) and five criminal appeals (11 per cent) in which judgment was reserved for three weeks or less. Only in about 30 per cent of cases ultimately reaching the House of Lords had judgment been reserved by the court *a quo*, and then usually for only two or three weeks: this supports the view that the House of Lords gives exceptionally weighty consideration to important cases, which lower courts simply have not the time to give.

GENERAL CONCLUSIONS

The costs and delays involved in appealing to the Lords are of general importance only if they adversely affect the performance of the House of Lords by deterring litigants from bringing important cases. Our analysis shows that in terms of expense and delay, there is little cause for complaint. Indeed the House of Lords is remarkably cheap and quick, considering the high quality of service that it provides. One factor which we have not so far taken into account, largely because no precise estimate can be made, is the cost to the Exchequer of running the institution. Given a salary bill of £155,000 payable to the ten Law Lords, judicial pensions, administrators and secretaries' salaries amounting (at most) to £20,000, and such imponderables as printing costs, office equipment, and the use of scarce accommodation in the Palace of Westminster, the annual account cannot be more than £250,000, probably considerably less. This surely is a negligible price to pay for an institution exercising functions of such value to the community.

Our suggestions for reform, arising out of the findings in this chapter, are that the level of security for costs should be raised to £1,500 to take account of the actual size of bills taxed in recent years, and that considerations might be given to imposing security of £40 on all applicants for leave to appeal, always assuming that the system for granting leave continues in its present form. To mitigate the deterrent effect of such an increase—and to give due recognition to the unique public role of the House of Lords—we would greatly extend the system for granting legal aid in House of Lords appeals.

A distinguished member of the House of Lords once quipped: 'The function of a trial judge is to be quick, courteous and right. That is not to say the Court of Appeal should be slow, rude and wrong, for that would be to usurp the function of the House of Lords.' We can say emphatically that even if, like all human institutions, their Lordships are occasionally wrong (and anyhow the legislature can put them right) they are never rude and seldom slow in handing down their judgments.

ANNEX A

Civil Appeals *in formâ pauperis*

Name of Case	Year decided	Category	Court *a quo*	Outcome
Best *v.* Samuel Fox	1952	Personal injuries	C.A.	D
Edwards *v.* Railway Executive	1952	Occupiers' liability	C.A.	D
Jamieson *v.* Jamieson	1952	Divorce	C.S.	A
Martin *v.* Scottish T.G.W.U.	1952	Trade union	C.S.	D
Starkowski *v.* Attorney-General	1953	International	C.A.[1]	D
Marshall *v.* Gotham Co.	1954	Mining regulations	C.A.	D
Bonsor *v.* Musicians' Union	1955	Trade union	C.A.	A
Galloway *v.* Galloway	1955	Custody	C.A.	A (3:2)
Lister *v.* Romford Ice & Cold Storage Co.	1956	Master and Servant —insurance	C.A.	D (3:2)
Vine *v.* National Dock Labour Board, *et è contra*	1956	Statutory tribunal— delegation	C.A.	A
Smith *v.* East Elloe R.D.C.	1956	Exercise of statutory powers	C.A.[1]	A.i.p. (3:2)
Goodrich *v.* Paisner	1956	Landlord and tenant	C.A.	A (4:1)
Hayward *v.* Port of London Authority	1956	Docks regulations	C.A.	D
McClelland *v.* N. Ireland Gen. Health Services Board	1957	Contract of employment	C.A. (N.I.)	A (3:2)
Taylor *v.* Nat. Assistance Board	1957	Legal aid	C.A.[1]	D
Cade *v.* B.T.C.	1958	Railway accident	C.A.	D (4:1)
Wintle[2] *v.* Nye	1958	Will	C.A.	A
Miller *v.* South of Scotland Electricity Board	1958	Negligence	C.S.	A
T. Oertli A.G. *v.* E. J. Bowman	1958	Company	C.A.[1]	D
Junor *v.* McNicol	1959	Negligence	C.S.	D
Mortimer *v.* Samuel B. Allison Ltd.	1959	Building regulations	C.S.	D
Smyth *v.* Cameron	1959	Negligence	C.A. (N.I.)	D
Watson *v.* Winget	1960	Limitation of action	C.S.	A (3:2)
Braithwaite & Co. (Structural) Ltd. *v.* Caulfield[3]	1961	Negligence	C.A.	D

[1] Leave to appeal granted by the Appeal Committee.
[2] Appellant in person.
[3] Respondent appeared in person *in formâ pauperis*.

ANNEX B

Civil Appeals involving legal aid

Name of Case	Year decided	Category	Court a quo	Outcome
Chapman v. Rix (A.P.)†	1960	Negligence—doctor	C.A.	D (2:1)
Wainwright v. Symes (A.P.)	1961	Road accident	C.A.	A
Dingwall (A. P.) v. Wharton Ltd.	1961	Ship unloading accident	C.S.	A
Gardiner (A. P.) v. Motherwell Machinery	1961	Factory—industrial dermatitis	C.S.	A
Bridge (A. P.) v. Campbell Discount Co.	1962	H.P.—penalty	C.A.	A (3:2)
Glinski (A. P.) v. McIver	1962	Malicious prosecution	C.A.	D
Ross Smith v. Ross Smith (A.P.)	1962	Nullity—jurisdiction	C.A.	A (5:1)
McWilliams (A.P.) v. Sir Wm. Arrol & Co. Ltd.	1962	Factory—safety belts	C.A.	D
Thompson (A.P.) v. Glasgow Corporation	1962	Process—leave to amend	C.S.	D
Wigley (A.P.) v. British Vinegars	1962	Window cleaner— independent contractor	C.A.	D
Cartledge (A.P.) v. Jopling Ltd.	1963	Limitation of Action	C.A.	D
Faramus (A.P.) v. Film Artistes Association	1963	Trade union rules	C.A.	D
Gill (A.P.) v. Humberstone Ltd.	1963	Building regulations	C.A.	D
Gollins (A.P.) v. Gollins (A.P.)	1963	Divorce—cruelty	C.A.	D (3:2)
Hughes (A.P.) v. Lord Advocate	1963	Negligence—Foreseeability	C.S.	A
Official Solicitor v. Kitson (A.P.)	1963	Wardship—reports— disclosure	C.A.	A
Ridge (A.P.) v Baldwin	1963	Natural justice	C.A.	A (4:1)
West & Sons v. Shephard (A.P.)	1963	Damages—loss of amenities	C.A.	D (3:2)
Williams (A.P.) v. Williams (A.P.)	1963	Divorce—cruelty— insanity	C.A.	A (3:2)
Kelly (A.P.) v. Cornhill Insurance	1964	Insurance	C.S.	A (3:2)
McCutcheon (A.P.) v. Macbrayne Ltd.	1964	Shipping contract— previous experience	C.S.	A
Ross (A.P.) v. Associated Portland Cement Mnfrs.	1964	Safe system of work	C.A.	A
Waugh (A.P.) v. Allan Ltd.	1964	Negligence—awareness of illness	C.S.	D
Douglas (A.P.) v. Cunningham (A.P.)	1964	Process—jury reversal	C.S.	A
Haley (A.P.) v. L.E.B.	1964	Negligence—blind pedestrian	C.A.	A
Rookes (A.P.) v. Barnard	1964	Trade union—intimidation	C.A.	A
Stratford v. Lindley (A.P.)	1964	'Trade dispute'	C.A.	A
Godfrey (A.P.) v. Godfrey	1964	Divorce—connivance at adultery	C.A.	D

† A.P. denotes assisted person.

Name of Case	Year decided	Category	Court a quo	Outcome
N.P. Bank Ltd. v. Ainsworth (A.P.)	1965	Deserted wife's equity	C.A.	A
McGlone (A.P.) v. B.R.B.	1965	Railway transformer— duty of care	C.S.	D
Scottish Omnibuses v. Wyngrove (A.P.)	1966	Negligence—open door of bus	C.S.	A
Hemphill Ltd. v. Williams (A.P.)	1966	Vicarious liability	C.S.	D
Wheat (A.P.) v. Lacon Ltd.	1966	Occupiers' liability— public house	C.A.	D
O'Hagan (A.P.) v. N.I. Farmers' Bacon Co.	1966	Factory	C.A. (N.I.)	D
Blyth (A.P.) v. Blyth	1966	Adultery—condonation	C.A.	A (3:2)
Price (A.P.) v. Claudgen Ltd.	1967	Building regulations— neon sign	C.S.	D
Milne (A.P.) v. Gerard Ltd.	1967	Building regulations— fence	C.S.	A. i.p.
Indyka (A.P.) v. Indyka (A.P.)	1967	Divorce—foreign decree	C.A.	D
Donaghey (A.P.) v. Boulton Paul Ltd.	1967	Building regulations	C.A.	A
Beswick (A.P.) v. Beswick (A.P.)	1967	Privity of contract	C.A.	D
O'Donnell (A.P.) v. Murdock McKenzie & Co. Ltd.	1967	Building regulations	C.S.	A (3:2)
Conway (A.P.) v. Rimmer	1968	Crown privilege	C.A.	A
Bersel Manufacturing Co. Ltd. v. Berry (A.P.)	1968	Company	C.A.	A
Gloucestershire County Council v. Richardson (A.P.)	1968	Contract	C.A.	D (4:1)
Branwaite (A.P.) v. Worcester Works Finance Ltd.	1968	Hire purchase	C.A.	A
Avais (A.P.) v. Hartford, Shankhouse & District Workingmen's Social Club & Institute Ltd.	1968	Contract	C.A.	A

ANNEX C

Anderson v. *Lambie* H.L. (Scotland) [1954] 1 W.L.R. 303.

Lord Reid. On the question of costs your Lordships are confronted with a difficult situation. In the Inner House (though not in the Outer House) the Respondent was an assisted person. One must presume therefore that he is a person of such modest means that he could not properly be expected to bear the full expenses of litigating in the Court of Session. Under the legal aid scheme in its present form there is no provision for legal aid in this House, even for a Respondent who has been success-ful as an assisted person in the Court of Session or the Court of Appeal. In the pre-sent case we are deciding against such a respondent, and if the usual order as to costs were made he would be ordered to pay the whole costs of the Appellants in this House. Costs in this House may far exceed expenses in the Court of Session, yet the scheme operates to relieve such a litigant of the lesser liability in the Court of Session and does nothing to protect him against a greater liability in this House which he can in no way avoid. Even if he failed to appear and the appeal were heard *ex parte* he would normally be ordered to pay the costs of the successful appellant, and in this important and difficult case it would have deprived us of much assistance if the Respondent had failed to appear by counsel. I can quite understand that it may be good policy to refuse assistance to one who seeks to appeal to this House, but it may be that the position of a respondent who had been an assisted person was not specially considered when the present scheme was made. Of course a respondent who is sufficiently poor can be allowed to appear in the House *in formâ pauperis* but it would seem probable that this was not open to the present Respondent. So in a case like the present both the privilege and the protection of legal aid must be refused to a respondent in this House who has had protection in the Court below and has been brought here against his will. I realize that if we do not make the usual order in favour of the Appellant in this case we would be discriminating against him for no fault of his, but it seems to me that the facts which I have stated ought not to be entirely neglected, and I think that the situation might properly be met by ordering the Respondent to pay only a part[1] of the Appellant's costs in this House.

Lord Keith. In the matter of costs I agree with my noble and learned friends Lord Morton of Henryton and Lord Reid. The position is anomalous. There is no question that the Respondent, financially, is any better off than when he received legal aid in the Inner House. It may be that so long as legal aid is not available generally in connection with proceedings on appeal from the Court of Session to this House, the special position of a respondent who has received legal aid in the Court of Session and is brought here on appeal could be met by a regulation under section 12 (3) (c) of the Legal Aid & Advice Act of 1949, or some other provision of that Act. But that is for the appropriate authority to decide.

1 Three-quarters.

XII

STATISTICAL PICTURE

IN drawing our sketch of the Law Lords in action, we have already made considerable use of statistical data. While it is impossible to quantify many aspects of the work of a legal institution, statistics do provide a firm foundation for a more evaluative impression of the work of the final court of appeal. This short chapter is intended to round off the statistical part of our study and to fill in some of the gaps left by earlier chapters.

This should be regarded as a source of reference rather than as a self-contained essay with a coherent theme: for this reason we have not attempted to shape our commentary into a continuous narrative but have tried instead to provide a profile of the House of Lords at work which will valuably augment the analysis developed elsewhere. Inevitably there will be some duplication of material which appears in other chapters, though we have striven to avoid this.

Table 48 shows the case-load of the House of Lords from each court *a quo* for each of the years 1952–68, broken down by outcome: for comparison we have added corresponding figures for 1969 and 1970, though, except where otherwise stated, all calculations of averages, etc., relate to our main period, 1952–68.

A number of points emerge from this table—First, the uniformity in the total number of appeals heard each year, particularly since 1959, with very little deviation from the average case-load of thirty appeals a year. The year 1969, with no fewer than fifty-three appeals, must be accounted a phenomenon. The number of English civil appeals has remained virtually constant, particularly during the latter part of the period, but the annual totals of Scottish appeals have fluctuated widely between two (in 1968) and eleven (in 1967). Appeals from Northern Ireland are a rarity, and no fewer than seven of the fifteen civil appeals heard during the period are concentrated in the single year 1959.

The table shows clearly the dramatic effect of the Administration of Justice Act 1960 on the extent of the jurisdiction of the House. From 1952 to 1960 only 7 out of 249 appeals (2·8 per cent) were in criminal causes, but during the period 1961–8 the corresponding figure was 39 out of 263 (14·8 per cent). Seventeen of the post-1960 criminal appeals came from the Queen's Bench Divisional Court which, by the provisions of the Act, for the first time fell

TABLE 48

Annual Case-Load of the House of Lords, 1952–1968, by Outcome and Court a quo

Court a quo/Outcome

Year	Total Appeals	From English C.A. (Civil)			From Court of Session			From C.A. in N.I. (Civil)			From C.C.A. C-MAC and C.A. (Crim.)			From Q.B. Div. Court (Crim.)			From C.C.A. in N. Ireland			Total appeals A'd or A.i.p.	
		A'd	A.i.p.	D'd	A'd	A.i.p.	D'd	A'd	A.i.p.	D'd	A'd	A.i.p.	D'd	A'd	A.i.p.	D'd	A'd	A.i.p.	D'd	Civil	Criminal
1952	25	3	1	12	4	1	3	—	—	—	1	—	—	—	—	—	—	—	—	9	1
1953	17	4	1	9	1	—	2	—	—	—	—	—	—	—	—	—	—	—	—	6	—
1954	20	4	1	8	3	—	2	—	—	—	—	—	2	—	—	—	—	—	—	8	—
1955	35ᵃ	15	—	15	2	—	3	—	—	—	—	—	—	—	—	—	—	—	—	17	—
1956	33	7	1	18	3	—	4	—	—	—	—	—	—	—	—	—	—	—	—	11	—
1957	26	4	1	15	2	—	2	1	—	—	—	—	1	—	—	—	—	—	—	8	—
1958	22	5	—	12	2	—	2	—	—	—	—	—	1	—	—	—	—	—	—	7	—
1959	37	9	—	14	3	—	4	4	—	3	1	—	1	—	—	—	—	—	—	16	1
1960	34	9	1	13	2	—	7	—	—	—	1	—	1	—	—	—	—	—	—	12	1
1961	36	6	—	16	5	—	3	—	—	1	—	—	2	—	—	1	—	—	1	11	—
1962	34	6	—	17	1	—	3	1	—	—	—	—	4	—	—	2	1	—	—	8	1
1963	34ᵃ	7	1	16	5	—	2	1	—	—	—	—	1	—	—	—	—	—	—	14	—
1964	34	8	—	8	7	—	3	2	—	1	1ᵇ	—	1	1	—	1	—	—	—	17	2
1965	32	8	—	13	—	—	4	—	—	1	2	—	—	—	—	3	—	—	—	8	2
1966	30	7	—	15	2	—	2	—	—	—	—	—	2	—	—	3	—	—	—	9	—
1967	33	5	3	11	3	1	7	—	—	—	1	—	—	1	—	1	—	—	—	12	2
1968	30	9	—	11	1	—	1	—	—	—	1	—	3	1	—	3	—	—	—	10	2
Total	512	116	10	223	46	2	54	9	—	6	8	—	19	3	—	14	1	—	1	183	12
1969	53	17	—	14	3	—	7	—	1	3	—	—	1	5	1	1	—	—	—		
1970	35	11	—	14	2	—	3	1	—	—	—	—	3	1	—	1	—	—	1		

A'd=Allowed; A.i.p.=Allowed in part; D'd=Dismissed.

ᵃ Totals for 1955 and 1963 each exclude one civil appeal in which the House, after a hearing, dismissed the appeal for want of jurisdiction.

ᵇ Decision reversed, but proviso applied.

within the supervisory jurisdiction of the House of Lords. In Chapter XIII we shall discuss the recent improvement of the performance of the House of Lords in the field of criminal law, an improvement which is to some extent attributable to the enlargement of its case-load in this field.

Elsewhere we have alluded to the differential success-rates of appeals from different courts *a quo*: the precise figures can be calculated from Table 48. During the period 1952–68, 195 out of 512 appeals (38 per cent) were allowed wholly or in part. This total is made up as follows:

English civil appeals	126 successful out of 349	36·1%
Scottish civil appeals	48 ,, ,, ,, 102	47·0%
Northern Irish civil appeals	9 ,, ,, ,, 15	60·0%
English/N. Irish criminal appeals	12 ,, ,, ,, 46	25·1%

Total 195   512

If we divide the period into two nearly equal parts, we find remarkable consistency in the rates of success for both English and Scottish appeals. The rate for English (civil) and Scottish appeals during the period 1959–60 were 36·2 per cent and 44·3 per cent respectively, while the corresponding figures for 1961–8 were 35·9 and 49 per cent.

We have already noted in Chapter VII that there is no significant difference in the rates of success of appeals by leave of the Appeal Committee compared with those by leave of the Court of Appeal. The discrepancy between English and Scottish appeals will be discussed in Chapter XVI.

The lowest success-rate occurs in criminal appeals, though the numbers involved are quite small. There is some indication that their Lordships are better disposed towards appeals brought by the prosecution than towards appeals by the accused. Fourteen of the forty-six criminal appeals were by the prosecution, and six of these (42·8 per cent) succeeded: successes among accused appealing was six out of 32 (18·8 per cent).

It should be noted that for the totals in Table 48 and (except where otherwise stated) throughout this study, we count appeals and cross-appeals heard at the same time as *two* appeals: consolidated appeals involving a common hearing and a single set of judgments are counted as single items. During our period sixteen civil and one criminal appeals involved cross-appeals: thus the number of appeal *hearings* during the period was 495 (512 minus 17). Twenty-nine civil appeal-hearings involved consolidated appeals: in seventeen cases two appeals were consolidated; in five, three were consolidated; in four, four appeals were consolidated and in three cases five were consolidated.

A few specific points should be made about the proceedings in the courts below. Table 48 shows that 74·8 per cent of civil appeals came from the English Court of Appeal, 21·9 per cent from the Court of Session, and 3·3 per cent from the Court of Appeal in Northern Ireland. About two-thirds of the appeals from the Court of Session had been heard by the First Division of that Court (the Division which deals with most revenue appeals in Scotland).

One would expect a final appellate court dealing with cases of general public importance to encounter relatively few appeals either in interlocutory matters or in cases tried in county courts; the latter generally deal with cases involving limited monetary value. This is borne out by the statistics, though it must be remembered that some very important cases have come to the House of Lords in interlocutory matters where problems of great complexity and importance have arisen, for example, on the question of whether pleadings disclose any cause of action against a barrister for professional negligence,[1] or whether the Crown is entitled to claim privilege from the discovery of documents.[2] Moreover in Scottish litigation many appeals arise from a challenge by the defender of the relevancy of the pursuer's averments during the course of the lengthy interlocutory proceedings which take place before the record is closed and the case comes to trial. In the result only ten English civil appeals came via the route used in interlocutory matters, namely, an appeal from a Master of the Supreme Court to a judge in chambers and thence to the Court of Appeal. But twenty-two Scottish appeals stemmed from a challenge to the relevancy of averments.

County courts too, notwithstanding their relatively humble status, sometimes unearth important legal problems which eventually find their way to the House of Lords. Two subjects which spring to mind in this context are the troublesome questions relating to the renewal of business tenancies under the Landlord and Tenant Act 1954, and hire purchase contracts involving relatively small sums in particular cases but giving rise to difficulties which affect large numbers of individuals and finance companies. Altogether, however, only ten appeals came to the House of Lords from county courts and a further six from sheriff courts in Scotland.

Jury trial has become a rarity in civil proceedings and only rarely are jury verdicts open to challenge on appeal. During our period only seventeen civil appeals had originally been tried before a jury, and six of these cases were from Northern Ireland.

We turn now to the subject-matter of appeals, where we encounter a formidable problem of classification. Any subject-classification we construct is essentially arbitrary, and the assignment of marginal cases to particular categories is often extremely difficult. To take just one instance, *Pfizer Corporation* v. *Ministry of Health*[3] involved the construction of patent legislation: yet the central issue had little to do with patent law but belonged to the province of the administrative lawyer, since the case turned upon the problem of defining the status of the National Health Service in respect of the statutory phrase 'for the service of the Crown'.

It is with some diffidence, therefore, that we proffer our classification con-

[1] *Rondel* v. *Worsley* [1969] 1 A.C. 191, discussed at pp. 91–2 above.
[2] *Conway* v. *Rimmer* [1968] A.C. 910, discussed at pp. 264–5 below.   [3] [1965] A.C. 512.

sisting of the thirty-six 'extended categories' (plus a 'miscellaneous' category) set out in Table 49. It should be noted that because this number is rather unwieldy we have amalgamated some of them into a smaller list of sixteen 'Main categories' which we employ in several of the tables appearing elsewhere in this work. This tends to exacerbate the difficulties, alluded to earlier, which arise from the drawing of arbitrary divisions; it is arguable, for example, that rating appeals should be subsumed under 'revenue law' rather than under 'property law'. In mitigation we would plead that any classification is largely a matter of personal preference and that its validity depends also upon the use to be made of information so classified.

Table 49 itself is largely self-explanatory. Three points should be made, though all are alluded to elsewhere. First, the preponderance of revenue appeals (30·4 per cent of English civil appeals, 19·6 per cent of Scottish appeals): only in the fields of fault liability (19·3 per cent of all civil appeals), contract (11·2 per cent of all civil appeals) and the 'law of property' (15·9 per cent of all civil appeals) is the case-load of barely comparable size. And each of the last three categories is highly amorphous. This leads to the second point, one to which we have frequently alluded throughout this study; that, as Table 49 clearly shows, in no area of law, apart from revenue law, has the House of Lords encountered enough cases to enable it to fashion a coherent body of jurisprudence. It would be foolish to suggest that case-law is formulated within watertight compartments corresponding to our subject categories, but certainly many fields of law require peculiar expertise in that field.

The third point is that the distribution of cases from Scotland is slightly different from the distribution of English appeals, though the small number of cases in each category makes it impossible to draw firm conclusions. Revenue appeals are markedly less common from the Court of Session, and indeed are actually outnumbered by appeals in factory accident cases. No appeals in the field of patents, copyrights, and trade marks came from Scotland, and only two cases in family law.

An examination of the relationship between subject-matter and outcome on appeal reveals a fairly uniform rate of success, and again, the small sub-categories mean that any apparent deviations from the norm should be interpreted with caution. Overall, 39·2 per cent of civil appeals were successful; examples of success rates which deviate appreciably from this are revenue (32 per cent), factory (49 per cent), non-physical torts (25 per cent), wills, settlements, and trusts (50 per cent), family law (58 per cent).

One of the principal objects of this study is to discover whether the House of Lords produces 'better' results than the courts a quo. This, as we have already said, involves considerable difficulties, both philosophical and methodological; but as a tentative step towards this goal we have tried to ascertain in each case the relationship between the eventual decision reached by the House of Lords and the decision of the court a quo. In particular we were

TABLE 49

Subject-Matter of Civil Appeals, 1952–1968, by Court a quo

Main category	'Extended category'	Court of Appeal	Court of Session	Court of Appeal (N.I.)	Total
Revenue	Revenue	106	20	1	127
Fault liability	Factory (etc.) accident[a]	30	21	5	56
	Occupiers' liability	2	1	—	3
	'Physical' torts[b]	10	8	1	19
	Non-physical torts[c]	12	—	—	12
Contracts	Sale of goods	3	—	—	3
	Banking and insurance	5	1	—	6
	Shipping contracts	17	2	—	19
	General contracts	17	6	6	24
Trade union	Trade union	6	2	—	8
Master and servant	Master and servant	2	2	1	5
Law of property	Landlord and tenant	12	—	—	12
	Land Law	4	4	1	9
	Rating	19	3	1	23
	Town & country planning	13	1	—	14
	Wills, settlements, trusts	9	7	—	16
Company	Company	3	2	—	5
Defamation	Defamation	4	—	—	4
Patents, etc.	Patents, copyrights, trade marks	28	—	—	28
Practice and procedure	Practice	4	5	—	9
	Evidence	—	2	—	2
	Legal aid	1	—	—	1
	Jurisdiction	—	1	—	1
	Limitation of action	3	2	—	5
Administrative law	Crown prerogative	2	1	—	3
	Tribunals & inquiries	6	—	—	6
	Natural justice	2	—	—	2
Family law	Divorce	6	2	—	8
	Nullity	1	—	—	1
	Separation & maintenance	1	—	—	1
	Custody	2	—	—	2
International law	Public international law	1	—	—	1
	Private international law	7	—	—	7
	Naturalization	1	—	—	1
Constitutional law	Constitutional law	4	2	2	8
Transport	Transport law	1	1	—	2
Miscellaneous	Miscellaneous	5	6	2	13
	Total	349	102	15	466

[a] i.e. breach of statutory duty and/or common law negligence.
[b] i.e. common law negligence resulting in injury, assault, etc.
[c] e.g. *Rylands* v. *Fletcher* cases, trespass, etc.

anxious to discover the proportion of appeals in which the Law Lords merely 'rubber-stamped' the judgments delivered below.

Even this limited exercise raised difficult problems, the most important of which stemmed from the fact that limited time precluded us from reading more than a fraction of the judgments of the courts below. Moreover, the Law Lords themselves do not always make it clear whether they are consciously adopting a different line of reasoning from that of their brethren below, and indeed the frequent multiplicity of judgments both in the lower appeal court and in the House of Lords itself often makes it difficult to say with confidence precisely what line of reasoning constitutes the *ratio decidendi*. In the end, therefore, one often has to rely upon general impressions of the judgments and their effect, and for that reason Table 50 which sets out the results of this exercise should be interpreted with circumspection.

The conclusion which emerges from Table 50 broadly coincides with our subjective impression gained from looking at the appeals as a whole, that only in a minority of cases does the House of Lords deviate to any measurable extent from the approach adopted by the judges below. As one might expect, the incidence of deviation is higher among the 39·2 per cent of appeals that succeed, but even here in more than half the cases the difference of opinion concerned only a matter of construction or of interpreting and applying primary facts; differences of emphasis rather than of principle. Although the proportion of cases where the decision of the House of Lords effects major changes in the law is small, it should be noted that a substantially different approach was adopted in more than 100 appeals, and that in twelve cases the House of Lords expressly overruled a precedent[1] binding on the lower court. While 'different' does not mean 'better', a figure of this size supports our view that the House of Lords earns its keep by acting as substantially more than a 'rubber stamp'. And indeed even a rubber stamp can perform a valuable function by putting an imprimatur of authoritative approval upon judicial decision-making. While figures of this kind may provide helpful indicators, the acid test is to be found in the appeals themselves.

It will be noted that two appeals were allowed on the basis of an argument raised by the appellant for the first time in the House of Lords. It is an unwritten, but firm rule of the House not to consider arguments which have not been considered by the courts below. In only twelve cases during our period of study was this rule expressly waived.[2]

One measure of the legal importance of a case is its appearance, or non-

---

[1] This figure is certainly a gross underestimate of the total number of authorities overruled or destructively distinguished: it refers only to appeals expressly allowed on the grounds that a previous decision, binding upon the court *a quo*, was wrongly decided.

[2] A recent, but unsuccessful, attempt was made in *P. & M. Kaye Ltd.* v. *Hosier & Dickinson Ltd.* [1972] 1 W.L.R. 196 (Lord Diplock dissenting) to raise, at the eleventh hour, an entirely new argument on construction of a document.

TABLE 50

Relationship of the House of Lords' Decision to that of the Court a quo: *Civil Appeals, 1952–1968*

	Court of Appeal	Court of Session	Court of Appeal (N. Ireland)	Total
(A) *Appeal dismissed*				
No appreciable difference in approach by House of Lords	191	48	6	245
Substantial difference in approach by House of Lords	29	6	—	35
House of Lords supports lower court's departure from established law	3	—	—	3
(B) *Appeal allowed (wholly or in part)*				
Lower court's decision held to be wrong in law	37	9	2	48
Difference in statutory or documentary construction	46	22	3	71
Different view of, or application of law to, the primary facts	18	12	1	31
Lower court bound by precedent, overruled by House of Lords	10	1	1	12
Lower court held to have stated the law correctly but to have applied it wrongly	8	3	—	11
Lower court held to have exceeded its jurisdiction or to have proceeded beyond the proper function of an appellate court	5	1	2	8
Appeal decided on the basis of argument raised for the first time in the House of Lords	2	—	—	2
Total	349	102	15	466

appearance, in the *Law Reports*. Unlike newspaper reports of court proceedings the various series of law reports are concerned solely with recording precedents: thus as a case ascends the hierarchy of courts and becomes the subject of increasingly authoritative judicial pronouncements its chances of finding a place in law reports increases dramatically. Only a small proportion of trials before a single High Court Judge are reported, but the figure rises to about a quarter of the case-load in the Court of Appeal and in the House of Lords, where precedents are established by virtually every case, it is rare for an appeal not to be reported.

There is a distinct hierarchy of reports. The most authoritative series (at least in England) is the *Law Reports*, published by the semi-official Incorporated Council of Law Reporting for England and Wales. The most important decisions of the House of Lords and of the Judicial Committee of the Privy Council are published in the *Law Reports* series entitled Appeal Cases (A.C.) The Incorporated Council also publishes the *Weekly Law Reports* (W.L.R.) which appear in three volumes: volumes 2 and 3 contain cases which will later appear in the *Law Reports* themselves in which the judgment is augmented by a report of counsels' argument. Cases of slightly less importance are consigned to volume 1, and are not normally reported in the *Law Reports*. The only other 'general' series (one which includes cases of all kinds) is the *All England Law Reports* (All E.R.) covering approximately the same ground as the *Weekly Law Reports*.

Apart from this there are series dealing exclusively with Scottish cases, the most important of which are *Session Cases* (S.C.) and *Scots Law Times* (S.L.T.) and another which covers cases in Northern Ireland, the *Northern Ireland Reports* (N.I.). And there are numerous series covering special areas of law: for example *Tax Cases* (T.C.), *Reports of Patent, Design and Trade Mark Cases* (R.P.C.), and *Knights' Industrial Reports* (K.I.R.). All these series report House of Lords appeals in their appropriate fields.

An analysis of the extent to which House of Lords decisions are reported reveals that virtually every civil appeal is reported in one series or another. Appeal cases cover 71 per cent of English appeals, but only 28 per cent of Scottish appeals: this reflects the fact that Scottish appeals tend to include a high proportion of cases which are of importance only in the context of Scots law. A further 17 per cent of English appeals and 23 per cent of Scottish appeals are published in volume 1 of the *Weekly Law Reports* and two Scottish appeals, not appearing in *Weekly Law Reports*, were published in *All England Reports*. The two principal Scottish series publish a further 38 per cent of Scots appeals which do not appear in the English series. The specialist series account for a further 8 per cent of English appeals and for 4 per cent of Scottish appeals.

This leaves a hard core of twenty-five appeals, fifteen from England (4 per cent), six from Scotland (6 per cent), and no fewer than four from Northern Ireland which are, so far as we can ascertain, unreported, though ten are reported in condensed law reports published in *The Times* newspaper. Whether the figure of 5 per cent of unreported appeals means that these cases are unimportant and should not have been given leave (though this does not apply to the Scottish appeals) or whether the editors of the various series of law reports are too restrictive in selecting cases is difficult to judge, though most of these cases are of little general importance. The unreported cases are listed in an Annex to this chapter, and we leave it to the reader to form his own opinion about the reason why they were not reported.

We end this chapter by noting three procedural points not dealt with elsewhere.

(1) Use of *amicus curiae*. There were only three civil appeals during the

period in which an *amicus curiae* (other than the Queen's Proctor in matrimonial appeals) appeared. These were *Chapman* v. *Chapman*,[1] *C.I.R.* v. *Baddeley*,[2] and *Belfast Corporation* v. *O.D. Cars Ltd.*[3]

(2) In twenty-one appeals (including eight from Scotland and four from Northern Ireland) the respondent's counsel was not called upon to reply. Five further appeals were heard *ex parte*.

(3) Strength of the court *a quo*: in only five appeals did the Court of Appeal sit with two judges. In Scottish appeals the Court of Session sat with three judges in 59 per cent of appeals and with four judges in the remaining 41 per cent.

[1] [1954] A.C. 429.   [2] [1955] A.C. 572.   [3] [1960] A.C. 490.

ANNEX: UNREPORTED HOUSE OF LORDS APPEALS

Year	Case	Result	Subject-Matter
1954	Epsom Grandstand Ass'n v. Knight (L)	A	Private statute (Times 12 Mar. 1964)
1954	M'Grath v. N.C.B.[1]	D	Mining Accident
1955	Qualcast Ltd. v. Thorpe (L)	A	Safe system of work
1955	Stewarts and Lloyds Ltd. v. Zoes (L)	D	Commission contract (Times 5 July 1955)
1958	Koppelman v. Kopel (i.p.) (L)	A	Special examiner
1959	Junor v. McNicol[1]	D	Negligent doctor (Times 26 Mar. 1959)
1959	McKeown v. Thos. Burrell[2]	D	Road accident (jury)
1959	Rental Holdings Ltd. v. Hall[2]	D	Lease
1959	Smyth v. Cameron[2]	D	Negligence (jury)
1960	Bradford Property Trust v. Hunter[1]	D (3:2)	Contract
1960	Chapman (A.P.) v. Rix	D (3:2)	Negligent doctor (Times 22 Dec. 1960)
1960	London Clinic v. Hoare (i.p.) (L)	A	Contract (Times 25 Mar.1960)
1960	Law v. Lord Advocate[1]	D	Estate duty
1961	Wainwright v. Symes (A.P.) (L)	A	Road accident—procedure (Times 6 Feb. 1960)
1961	Wilts. and Dorset Motor Service v. Kitto (L)	A	Road accident—procedure
1961	Braithwaite & Co. v. Caulfield	D	Safe system of work (Times 5 May 1961)
1961	Warden (i.p.) v. Warden[1]	D	Divorce
1962	B.T.C. v. Compensation Appeals Tribunal	D	Compensation (Times 22 Feb. 1962)
1962	Moore (i.p.) v. Lea (L)	D	Landlord and tenant
1962	S.W. Gas Board v. Hickin	A	Compensation
1963	Vizor v. Multi Spring Ltd. (L)	D	Evidence
1965	A. E. Farr Ltd. v. M.O.T.	A (3:2)	Contract

1966	Smith *v.* Colvilles Ltd.[1]	A	Factory
1966	O'Hagan (A.P.) *v.* Northern Ireland Farmers' Bacon Co. Ltd.[2]	D	Factory (Jury)
1966	McClelland, Pope and Langley Ltd. *v.* Howard (L)[3]	D	B.O.T. inquiry (Times 31 Mar. 1966)

Note: (i.p.) denotes party appearing in person; (A.P.) denotes assisted person; (L) denotes that leave to appeal had been granted by the Appeal Committee

[1] Scottish appeal. The case of *Warden* v. *Warden* is referred to in later proceedings, 1962 S.L.T. 33.

[2] Northern Irish appeal.

[3] The case appears as a note to *Selangor United Rubber Estates Ltd.* v. *Cradock*, (*No. 2*) [1968] 1 All E.R. 567, 569.

PART C

APPEALS
1952–1968

XIII

THE HOUSE OF LORDS AND PUBLIC LAW

A) ADMINISTRATIVE AND CONSTITUTIONAL LAW

THE term 'public law' is tautologous: all law properly so called is 'public'. In one sense law comprises a body of ascertainable rules operating within the context of a particular socio-legal system. But lawyers have come to use the expression 'public law', as shorthand for the body of substantive and procedural jurisprudence governing the relationship between governors and governed. On this broad definition public law embraces criminal law,[1] though on the whole the strongly and peculiarly normative connotations of crime lead to its being treated by lawyers as *sui generis*. Public law, in its narrower sense, is an amalgam of those nebulous areas of civil law termed 'administrative law' and 'constitutional law'.

Just as all law is inherently public, the same applies both to legal institutions and to the legal processes with which they are concerned. In a system where *stare decisis* is king, at times uncrowned, the judicial process involves a perpetual synthesis of legal rules. On its face, each piece of litigation, each forensic foray, is a unique event, involving only the specific quarrels of individuals and corporate bodies. Indeed it is a long-established rule of English law that the courts will not determine an academic or hypothetical point of law, however important to the parties.[2] But in practice the obsession with accusatorial conventions is little more than a façade behind which the courts are moulding a coherent body of precedents. This process is not particularly marked in courts of first instance, but in appellate courts with their lighter case-loads, less hasty procedure and greater authority, the private litigant may become a pawn in an essentially public-oriented game of law-making. And in the House of Lords, dealing with a hand-picked case-load sieved through the fine mesh of 'general public importance', the public aspect of litigation is carried to its logical conclusion.

Among the cases which aspire to these rarified appellate heights are some which fit the orthodox definition of public law. A court, whose very *raison d'être* is judicial legislation, finds itself confronted with cases involving the executive as a litigating party. Here surely is a phenomenon of unique im-

---

1 Though, strictly speaking, such matters as extradition proceedings should be included.
2 See, for example, the remarks of Viscount Simon L.C. in *Sun Life Assurance Co. of Canada* v. *Jervis* [1944] A.C. 111. One exception to the rule is the Special Reference procedure provided by s. 4 of the Judicial Committee Act 1833.

portance in a study of the relationships between law and the State and between State and citizen: here we find a blurring of the always elusive dividing
line between 'law-giving' and 'law-finding'.

So nebulous is the concept of administrative law that precise definition is
impossible. Indeed it is founded upon an uneasy alliance between two disparate philosophies. At one end of the scale is the legalistic ideology[1]
founded upon a belief that a set of clear and consistent legal rules, applied
in a value-free way by skilled and objective judges, provides society with a
commodity free from the taint of 'dirty' politics. At the other end of the scale
is an archetypal bureaucratic-administrative attitude which holds that policy
is made by democratically elected government, and that its implementation
must not be hindered by lawyers' 'quibbles' about individual rights and
strict legal forms.

Both attitudes are caricatures. In the past few decades (certainly since Lord
Hewart's unjudicial, and injudicious outburst in *The New Despotism*) the
executive has made considerable concession to the pressures for judicially
acceptable procedures in public administration. The courts, for their part,
have always distinguished—artificially—the separate provinces of 'law' and
'policy', and have, for the most part, contented themselves with regulating
such matters as the extent of powers conferred by statute, and the observance
of such judge-made procedural rules as 'natural justice'. But the equilibrium
of institutions is not entirely stable. The judiciary seems to alternate between
zeal and inertia when it comes to develop coherent administrative remedies.

The nebulous character of 'public law' hardly eases the task of defining
what cases are 'administrative'. Are we to extend the definition to every
case in which a public authority is a litigating party? If so, we will have to
include such cases as *Gloucestershire County Council* v. *Richardson*[2] where the
litigation concerned a building contract between a local authority and a firm
of contractors, which raised no principles peculiar to public law. This
definition might, moreover, beg the central question raised on appeal, whether
one of the parties really is a 'public authority'.[3] And what about tax and rating
appeals which constitute 27 per cent and 5 per cent respectively of the total
civil case-load of the House of Lords? Certainly they involve 'public' issues,
but such cases represent a uniquely statute-orientated area of jurisprudence
which can hardly be discussed in the same breath as administrative law; we
have therefore consigned them to a separate chapter.

For the purpose of this analysis we have considered every civil case in
which judgment was delivered by the House of Lords between 1952 and
July 1969 in which: (a) a public authority (including a body purporting to have
this status) or a representative of such an authority (litigating in his official

---

[1] Discussed at length by Judith Shklar, *Legalism* (1964), *passim*.
[2] [1969] 1 A.C. 480.
[3] e.g. *Marshall* v. *Scottish Milk Marketing Board*, discussed below.

capacity) was a party to the litigation; *and* (b) the case involved some recognizable administrative or constitutional principle, such as the extent of statutory powers or the manner in which they are exercised. The twenty-five cases in this category are listed in an annex to this section.

In some instances the claims of a particular case for inclusion in the sample have been dubious. On the one hand the case may involve the traditional subject-matter of public law, planning, the jurisdiction of a tribunal, and so forth, while raising no issue of general principle. The fifteen cases rejected on this rather subjective basis are listed separately.

The growth of administrative law is a corollary of the vast increase in governmental activity which, in the past few decades, has spread its bureaucratic tentacles. At the turn of the century,[1] and for many years afterwards, the House of Lords remained firmly committed to the *laissez-faire* traditions of nineteenth-century politics. Most of the Law Lords themselves had been former Liberal or Conservative politicians.[2] Socialism, or even social democracy of the left, was something new, probably incomprehensible and possibly downright distasteful to judges of the old school: the working man had no place in the civil courts, even assuming he could afford to litigate, and the upsurge of social legislation following the First World War presented the judges with unfamiliar and difficult socio-political problems.

Certainly the decisions of the House of Lords during this era did little to stimulate the growth of administrative law. *Local Government Board* v. *Arlidge*[3] (decided by a House of Lords consisting of a Liberal Lord Chancellor and three Law Lords who were former Liberal politicians)[4] represented what Professor Wade calls 'a reaction against the judicialization of administrative procedure'.[5]

Roberts v. *Hopwood*,[6] on the other hand, was decided in a *laissez-faire* manner favourable to the cause of judicial control and to the private citizen (personified in the ratepayers of Poplar) which, as Laski observed in his largely unsubstantiated thesis that judges were antipathetic to left-wing

---

[1] A useful commentary on the activities of the House of Lords during the early part of this century is to be found in an article by Robert Stevens, 'The Role of a Final Appeal Court in a Democracy: the House of Lords Today', 28 M.L.R. 509 (1965). Another fruitful source is Heuston's *Lives of the Lord Chancellors, passim.*

[2] It is interesting to note that in 1910 the Liberal Attorney-General (Robson) wrote to Asquith asking for the appointment of more Liberal Law Lords. The House of Lords, he said, 'would have to play a great part in disputes which are legal in form but political in fact, and it would be idle to deny the resolute bias of many of the judges—there and elsewhere. That bias would probably operate more than ever in cases that touch on labour, educational, constitutional and, for the future I might perhaps add, revenue questions.' Heuston, op. cit., p. 151.

[3] [1915] A.C. 120.

[4] See Abel-Smith and Stevens, *Lawyers and the Courts* (1967), p. 115.

[5] *Administrative Law* (2nd ed.), p. 175.

[6] [1925] A.C. 578. The background to this fascinating case is discussed by B. Keith-Lucas, 'Poplarism' *Public Law* 52 (1962).

politics, did little to enhance the image of the judiciary as paragons of social enlightenment. Here the judges waxed indignant at a local authority's attempt to fix wages for its employees, under statutory powers bestowed by Parliament, at a rate higher than economic forces alone would dictate to a commercial man. The Labour councillors, who voted for a wage increase commensurate with a dignified minimum condition of living, were held to have been rightly surcharged by the auditor.

By 1930 the character of the House had begun to change, as professional judges took over from those who had dominated the Court for so many years. 'By 1932', Professor Robert Stevens says,[1] 'only Lord Russell of Killowen[2] was not an advocate of judicial restraint where social legislation was involved; and that brilliant trio of judges—Macmillan, Atkin, and Wright—steered the House away from the dangers of giving decisions in the field of public law which might appear to interfere with the policies of a democratically elected government.'[3] This posture of dedicated self-restraint continued throughout the 1930s and hardened still further under pressure of wartime stringency. The sweeping rule of Crown privilege with regard to the discovery of official documents laid down by Lord Simon in *Duncan* v. *Cammell Laird and Co.*[4] has only recently been obliterated,[5] and *Liversidge* v. *Anderson*,[6] notable for Lord Atkin's resounding dissentient warning against judges becoming 'more executive-minded than the executive', marked the peak of judicial subservience.

Even after the war, as if in response to Aneurin Bevan's grim warning to the judges against sabotaging the impending legislative programme, the House of Lords continued to tread warily. In the case of *Franklin* v. *Minister of Town and Country Planning*[7] the House went out of its way to postulate a narrow approach to the common law rule against 'bias' in administrative decisions. The House of Lords, soon to acquire a new Lord Chancellor in Lord Simonds, entered the 1950s with a record of extreme caution in matters of public law. What follows is an analysis of the ensuing period, which eventually saw the emergence of a more spirited attempt to accommodate administrative rules within a precise legalistic framework.

It is significant that in the case leading our list first blood was drawn by the executive. In *Earl Fitzwilliam's Wentworth Estates Co.* v. *Minister of Housing and Local Government* both the House of Lords and the majority of the Court of Appeal (Denning L.J. characteristically dissenting) held that the

---

[1] See Abel-Smith and Stevens, op. cit., pp. 118–19. Also Stevens, 28 M.L.R. (1965), at pp. 516–17 and *passim*.
[2] See, for example, his powerful lone dissent in favour of a narrow construction of statutes purporting to take away property, in *Minister of Health* v. *the King, ex p. Yaffe* [1931] A.C. 494.
[3] Stevens, 28 M.L.R. (1965) at p. 516.   [4] [1942] A.C. 624.
[5] See *Conway* v. *Rimmer*, below.   [6] [1942] A.C. 206.
[7] [1948] A.C. 87. Cf. *Nakkuda Ali* v. *Jayaratne* [1951] A.C. 66 (P.C.).

Central Land Board had acted *intra vires* in employing its statutory powers to make an example of a landowner, effectively for the purpose of enforcing its policy of price control. Thus 'ulterior motive' was ruled out as an effective ground for challenge.

Several other important appeals heard during this period involved issues of *vires*, or the extent of jurisdiction. In *Preston and Area Rent Tribunal* v. *Pickavance* their Lordships upheld a dissenting judgment by Jenkins L.J., the majority of the Court of Appeal having done its best to undermine the rent control legislation enacted during the late 1940s by adopting an over-literal approach to statutory interpretation.[1] A victory for common sense, and another chalked up for the Executive.

Two appeals in the list concerned the related problems of Crown immunity (*Bank Voor Handel en Scheepvart N.V.* v. *Administrator of Hungarian Property*) and the definition of a public authority (*Marshall* v. *Scottish Milk Marketing Board*). In the former case the majority of the House of Lords[2] held that the Crown could assert an immunity from the payment of tax: this ironically was a decision *against* the contention of the Crown since the case was brought to determine whether or not a sum of money held by the Administrator (who was held to be a Crown servant) should be repaid minus the tax which had been paid on it. The *Marshall* case involved the now repealed Public Authorities Protection Act of 1893:[3] reversing the Court of Session, the House of Lords unanimously decided that the Scottish Milk Marketing Board was not a public authority and that an action against the Board for negligence was not out of time. The issue of Crown servants cropped up again in *McClelland* v. *Northern Ireland General Health Services Board* where three of the Law Lords held (reversing the majority of the Court of Appeal in Northern Ireland) that a woman officer employed by a statutory board could not be dismissed at pleasure under regulations purporting to require the resignation of woman employees on marriage.

One of the most important Scottish appeals of this period was *Glasgow Corporation* v. *Central Land Board* in which the House of Lords refused to extend to Scotland the broad rules of Crown privilege laid down by Lord Simon fourteen years earlier in *Duncan* v. *Cammell Laird*. As well as opening the door to a subsequent reassertion of the power of the courts[4] when faced with claims for privilege, the case raises important issues relating to the extent of the doctrine of *stare decisis* in House of Lords decisions.[5]

[1] See note by Griffith, 16 M.L.R. 79 (1953).

[2] This is one of those cases where, on a counting of judicial heads at each stage of the litigation, the majority of the House of Lords found themselves in an overall minority. This situation seems particularly common in public law appeals. See pp. 191–4, *ante*.

[3] The Act was repealed by the Law Reform (Limitation of Actions etc.) Act 1954, following recommendations of the Tucker Committee, Cmd. 7740.

[4] See *Conway* v. *Rimmer*, below.

[5] See T. B. Smith, 'Public Interest and the Scope of House of Lords Precedents', 19 M.L.R. 427 (1956).

Looking at the cases discussed so far, we can discover no particularly startling principle. *Earl Fitzwilliam's* case might be considered as following the timid pattern of the 1940s, but the *Bank Voor Handel* and *Glasgow Corporation* appeals revealed a capacity to wriggle free of the shackles of executive-mindedness.

But so far no mention has been made of the most important decision during the period, one which appeared at the time to deny any real hope that the judges could eventually come to grips with the fundamentals of public law. *Smith v. East Elloe Rural District Council* was concerned with a provision in the Acquisition of Land (Authorization Procedure) Act 1946 that after a six-week period 'a compulsory purchase order shall not be questioned in any legal proceedings whatsoever.' An action was brought after the six weeks had expired alleging that the order was invalid on the ground of *mala fides*. The House of Lords held unanimously that an action lay against the clerk of the council but, by a majority of 3:2,[1] that the six-weeks' clause effectively barred the action against the local authority and the government department.

If this case marked the high-water mark of judicial timidity in matters of public law, it also marked the turn of the tide. Most of the important appeals decided subsequently adopted a rational and often imaginative approach to the issues of principle at stake. Thus in *Vine v. National Dock Labour Board* the House affirmed the rule against sub-delegation of statutory powers,[2] and also said some kind words about the use of declaratory judgments as a more flexible remedy than the traditional prerogative orders against administrative transgressions.

The declaratory judgment was very much to the forefront in the later case of *Pyx Granite Co. Ltd.* v. *Minister of Housing and Local Government* where it was held that a declaration could be granted notwithstanding the statutory provision for determination of the question by a local authority. This case, Professor S. A. de Smith declares, not only confirmed a trend for the extension of the declaratory remedy by the courts, but also disclosed an increasing tendency to 'lean heavily against methods of statutory interpretation that would lead to acquiescence in the exclusion of the courts' jurisdiction in questions of law'.[3] In *Fawcett Properties Ltd.* v. *Buckinghamshire County Council* the House held by a 4:1 majority that a local authority was acting *intra vires* in attaching planning conditions to the effect that dwellings were

---

[1] This is one of those House of Lords judgments—all too common in recent years—where it is difficult to determine by reading the speeches exactly what the case did decide. At least two Law Lords argued that fraud was no ground for challenge even *within* six weeks. See appendix to Wade, op. cit., pp. 323–4. See also subsequent criticism of the decision by Lord Denning M.R. in *Webb* v. *Minister of Housing and Local Government* [1965] 1 W.L.R. 755.

[2] This case thus affirmed the decision of the Court of Appeal in *Barnard* v. *National Dock Labour Board* [1953] 2 Q.B. 18.

[3] Note in 22 M.L.R. 664 (1959).

to be used only to house agricultural labourers. This decision, de Smith argues,[1] showed that the courts were still reluctant to look into the merits of administrative decisions or to lay down criteria of 'reasonableness'.

Before proceeding to the cases of the 1960s we should consider two important Northern Irish appeals. These cases are now of academic interest, since the section of the Government of Ireland Act 1920 under which they were brought has been repealed.[2] But they were important in bringing the House of Lords into unaccustomed confrontation with the need to determine the *validity* of legislation,[3] a role alien to the English judiciary.

Sections 49 and 50 of the Government of Ireland Act 1920 provided an appeal to the House of Lords from the courts of Northern Ireland, not only in matters which had lain within the jurisdiction of the House before 1920, but also in all matters arising in the course of litigation which concerned the validity of legislation enacted by the Northern Ireland Parliament.

Both *Belfast Corporation* v. *O.D. Cars Ltd.* and *McCann* v. *Attorney General for Northern Ireland* concerned s. 5 (1) of the 1920 Act which precluded 'the taking of property without compensation', the so-called doctrine of eminent domain. In *O.D. Cars* the House of Lords upheld the contention of the appellant Corporation that a refusal of planning permission was not a taking of property. It is not altogether clear, however, whether they held that the respondents' interest was no 'property' or whether there was no 'taking', or whether both arguments applied.[4] In *McCann*, their Lordships found no difficulty in concluding that the requirement of a bookmaker's licence under betting legislation was not avoided by s. 5 (1).

In *Essex County Council* v. *Essex Incorporated Congregational Church Union* the House returned to more familiar pastures and disclaimed the jurisdiction of the courts to determine a rating question. It confirmed the principle that consent cannot compensate for a tribunal's lack of jurisdiction.

If *Smith* v. *East Elloe* was a retrograde step in the history of public law, *Ridge* v. *Baldwin*, which was decided in 1963, was one step forward for the Law Lords, and a huge stride forward for public law. It was held by a majority[5] (Lord Evershed dissenting) that police disciplinary regulations should have been applied by a watch committee in hearing allegations of neglect of duty against a Chief Constable: and Lords Reid, Morris of Borth-y-Gest, and Hodson held that in any event the decision was contrary to the rules of natural justice, a duty to observe such rules arising by implication from the nature of the power conferred upon the committee and not just from a power to which was annexed a duty to act judicially. To quote S. A. de Smith:[6]

---

[1] Ibid.   [2] Northern Ireland Act 1962, s. 14.

[3] The early history of the legislation, and some of the cases arising under s. 5 (1) (below) are discussed in an article by Lord MacDermott in 22 J.S.P.T.L. (N.S.) 201 (1952).

[4] See note by Newark, 23 M.L.R. 302 (1960).

[5] Another overall 'minority'—see p. 259, n. 2, above.

[6] Note in 26 M.L.R. 543 (1963).

The general tenor of the judgments delivered by Lords Reid, Morris of Borth-y-Gest and Hodson shows an awareness that the courts have been straying from paths of righteousness, and a readiness to determine the proper scope of judicial review by reference to consideration of principle and rationality rather than formal analytical categories. They reflect a significant change in judicial attitudes, a belated *amende honorable* for the unimaginative years.

The cases of the past era, *Nakkuda Ali* (a Privy Council decision on appeal from Ceylon) and *Franklin* (discussed above) were effectively consigned to limbo. *Liversidge* v. *Anderson* was condemned by Lord Reid as 'a very peculiar decision of the House'.[1] This one decision went a long way to redeem the House of Lords from the odium engendered by its past vapidity.

Why did the mood change? The answer lies, we think, at least in part, in the changed composition of the House of Lords at this time. The following table, setting out the retirements from, and new appointments to the House during the period 1959 to 1962, makes clear the extent of the transformation.

TABLE 51

Retirements from and New Appointments to the House of Lords, 1959–1962

	Retirements	First appointed	New appointments
1959	Lord Morton of Henryton	(1947)	Lord Jenkins
1960	Lord Cohen	(1951)	Lord Morris of Borth-y-Gest
	Lord Somervell	(1954)	Lord Hodson
1961	Lord Tucker	(1950)	Lord Devlin
	Lord Keith of Avonholm	(1953)	Lord Guest
1962	Lord Simonds	(1944)[a]	Lord Evershed
	Lord Denning	(1957)	Lord Pearce

[a] Lord Chancellor from 1951–4.

Almost overnight the character of the court changed: the Chancery judges[2] were reduced from four to three but, most significantly, Viscount Simonds who had dominated the Court throughout the 1950s retired as senior Law Lord, to be replaced by the more flexibly-minded and judicially venturesome Lord Reid.[3] Of the old guard, only Lords Reid and Radcliffe remained, and neither could justly be called dyed-in-the-wool reactionaries, except in so far

[1] See also the remarks of Lord Parker C.J. in *Re H.K.* (*an infant*) [1967] 2 Q.B. 617.

[2] On balance, Chancery judges seem more dedicated to 'legalism' than their common law brethren.

[3] Of the nine public law appeals heard between 1955 and 1961, Lord Simonds both presided and gave a full opinion in five (including *Smith* v. *East Elloe*)—and also delivered a full speech in one case where the Lord Chancellor presided.

Of the thirteen appeals heard after 1962 Lord Reid presided in no fewer than twelve, including *Ridge* v. *Baldwin*, *Padfield* and *Conway* v. *Rimmer* (discussed below). He delivered a full opinion in all but two. The one case where he was not present was *McEldowney* v. *Forde*: it is hard to believe that that decision would have gone the same way had Lord Reid presided rather than Lord Hodson.

as most judges are discouraged from radicalism by the very nature of the judicial process.[1] The whole court seemed suddenly to be afflicted with something remarkably akin to renewed vigour and imagination—particularly in relation to public law. *Ridge* v. *Baldwin* was the first of a series of important, generally more adventurous, not always uncontroversial decisions in this area of jurisprudence.

In *Burmah Oil Co. Ltd.* v. *The Lord Advocate*[2] their Lordships by a majority held that compensation was payable by the Crown to the owners of property destroyed under the Royal Prerogative in the course of war. There was some doubt whether the relevant law to be applied was English or Scottish. And words like 'public policy' and 'justice' were bandied about. The House did little to clarify the general principle by which compensation was to be assessed. Lord Radcliffe, in a powerful dissenting judgment, came down in favour of the Crown on the grounds of necessity: the notion of prerogative, he said, was too vague to be of much use. In the event, this controversial legal decision was matched by the equally controversial War Damage Act 1965. (We allude to the fascinating constitutional struggle that ensued in Chapter XVI.)

Chertsey Urban District Council v. *Mixnam's Properties Ltd.* was another caravan licensing case involving the reasonableness of conditions imposed by a local authority. The conditions imposed related not to the physical use of the land but to rents charged and other conditions of tenancy, in effect treating the letting of the site as analogous to that of a rent-controlled house. The House held (Lord Radcliffe strongly *dubitante* and Lord Guest dissenting in part) that the Court of Appeal had been correct in holding that the conditions were invalid.

The case of *Pfizer Corporation* v. *Ministry of Health*[3] concerned the importation of the drug Tetracycline from Italy for use in National Health Service hospitals, to the consternation of British patent holders. The House held (Lords Pearce and Wilberforce dissenting) that the use of the drug by the National Health Service amounted to 'making using or exercising for the services of the Crown' within the meaning of s. 46 of the Patents Act 1949, thus preserving the Crown's immunity from patent law.

The case of *Ministry of Social Security* v. *A.E.U.* involved an important and intricate question relating to the jurisdiction of the Medical Appeal Tribunal. A deputy commissioner had made a determination to the effect that a workman's injuries had been caused by an industrial accident and awarded industrial injury benefit; but the Medical Appeal Tribunal on the same

---

[1] Lord Reid's radicalism has been especially marked in shaking off the octopus-like grip of the rapacious Executive. From *Ridge* v. *Baldwin* to *Attorney-General* v. *Nissan*, the Crown's solitary victory in some twenty appeals came in the *Pfizer* case.

[2] See A. L. Goodhart, 'The Burmah Oil Case and the War Damage Act 1965', 82 L.Q.R. 97 (1966); also, note by Paul Jackson, 27 M.L.R. 709 (1964).

[3] See note by Blanco White, 28 M.L.R. 355 (1965).

contested medical evidence denied the claim for disability benefit. The majority of the House of Lords held (upholding the majority of the Court of Appeal, who in turn had reversed the Divisional Court) that the tribunal's jurisdiction was confined to determining the loss of faculty resulting from the injury as established by the deputy commissioner.

James v. *Secretary of State for Wales* was an appeal against the Minister's refusal to allow an appeal against an enforcement notice. Four Law Lords set themselves resolutely against the combined might of a dissenting Lord Morris of Borth-y-Gest, three Lord Justices and three members of the Divisional Court (another 'minority decision'). The question concerned the validity of an 'existing site' application for a caravan site licence and the scope of the effect of a prior grant of planning permission. One of the central issues was the validity of the planning authority's decision given after the expiry of the statutory two-month period. It was held that the latter requirement was directory and mandatory, rendering it unnecessary for the House to decide the more general question of whether the decision was void rather than voidable.

All these cases—*Burmah Oil, Pfizer, A.E.U.*, and *James*—involved issues of some importance in public law, though on a somewhat narrow front. After 1966 (when *James* was decided) came a sequence of four major appeals which together amount to something like a frontal assault on the conventional boundaries of public law.

Perhaps the most exciting of all these cases is *Padfield* v. *Ministry of Agriculture*[1] which went to the very heart of the scope of statutory powers granted to the executive. Briefly, the facts were these. The Agricultural Marketing Act 1958 established a Milk Marketing Board Scheme under which differential payments would be made to producers in different areas. The south-eastern area producers claimed that the differential applying to them was insufficient and, when the Board refused to act on their complaint, they asked the Minister to refer the matter to the committee of investigation provided by s. 19 of the Act. The Minister claimed that the phrase used in the Act—'if the Minister in any case so directs'—gave him absolute discretion, and accordingly he refused to refer the complaint. The complainants then applied to the courts for an order of mandamus: in finding for the complainants the majority of the House of Lords (Lord Morris of Borth-y-Gest dissenting) held that the discretion should be exercised in accordance with the 'general purpose' of the Act, and that once the Minister was satisfied that the complaint was not frivolous or vexatious he must refer it to the committee, a far cry from the subjective approach to ministerial discretion adopted in *Liversidge* v. *Anderson*.

The doctrine of Crown privilege in relation to the discovery of official documents has a long and stormy history, and the unanimous decision of the

[1] See note by Garner, 31 M.L.R. 446 (1968).

House of Lords in *Conway* v. *Rimmer*[1] had the air of an inevitable *coup de grâce*. The broad doctrine laid down in *Duncan* v. *Cammell Laird* had met with increasing criticism, notably in the English Court of Appeal and in various Commonwealth courts. Already, as we have seen, the House had qualified the doctrine in a Scottish appeal,[2] and the Law Lords did not mince their words in demolishing the principle that the courts are bound to accept without question the Minister's blanket affidavit that a whole 'class' of documents must be withheld on the grounds of public interest. Taken together, *Padfield* and *Conway* v. *Rimmer* must rank as an unprecedented judicial rebuff for the unfettered discretion of the executive: at last 'judicial control of administrative action' transcended empty rhetoric.

The next case on the list, *Anisminic* v. *Foreign Compensation Commission*, was hardly less important, since it concerned the very essence of judicial control over the proceedings of inferior tribunals. The Foreign Compensation Act 1950 established a body called the Foreign Compensation Commission to distribute compensation among British citizens whose overseas property was seized by foreign powers. Section 4 (4) of the Act provided that 'the determination by the Commission of any application made to them under this Act shall not be called in question in any court of law.' The House of Lords decided that the section did not oust judicial review where it was alleged that the 'decision' was a nullity, since it was based upon irrelevant considerations. As Lord Reid said in summarizing the appellant's contentions, 'if one seeks to show that a determination is a nullity, one is not questioning the purported determination, one is maintaining that it does not exist as a determination.' By a 3:2 majority (and another overall 'minority') their Lordships granted a declaration that the decision was a nullity. The decision, a bold reassertion of the supervisory jurisdiction of the courts (*Smith* v. *East Elloe* was destructively distinguished by the majority) provoked the Government to draft legislation permitting the Commission to make unreviewable determinations even of the extent of its own jurisdiction. The proposal provoked a storm of protest,[3] and was eventually amended out of existence at the Bill's committee stage in the Lords. The Foreign Compensation Act 1969 now provides for an appeal to the Court of Appeal, but no further, on points of law.

Nissan v. *Attorney-General*[4] was a complex case involving the defence of Act of State in a case where a hotel in Cyprus owned by a naturalized British citizen was damaged while under requisition by British troops. The House of

---

1 See note by Wade, 84 L.Q.R. 171 (1968). This seems to be the first instance of the House refusing to be bound by one of its previous decisions under the change of practice announced in July 1966—though only Lord Morris and Lord Hodson unequivocally admit this.

2 See *Glasgow Corporation* v. *Central Land Board*, above.

3 See Drewry, 'A Sequal to Anisminic', 119 New L.J. 159 (1969).

4 See note by de Smith, 32 M.L.R. 427 (1969).

Lords, by a variety of logical (and illogical) routes, held that the defence did not avail the Crown since the acts in question did not come within the ambit of Act of State. It is disturbing to note however that (as de Smith points out) 'three of their Lordships gave the impression of thinking that Act of State might, in certain circumstances, be a good defence against a British subject's actions based on a direct interference with his private rights.'[1]

We are now nearing the end of this journey: but two important cases decided in 1969 remain to be discussed. *McEldowney* v. *Forde*, an appeal from Northern Ireland, strikes a particularly poignant note in view of current trouble in the six counties. The case concerned a 1957 regulation made under emergency legislation dating back to 1922: the regulation purported to prescribe 'Organizations . . . describing themselves as "republican" clubs or any like organizations howsoever described'. The majority decision of the House of Lords in declining to condemn the regulations appears, *triste dictu*, to be a regression to the Dark Ages. In a powerful dissent, in a tone redolent of Lord Atkin's judgment in *Liversidge*, Lord Pearce said that the Court

cannot take the easy course of 'passing by on the other side' when it seems clear to it that the Minister is using a power in a way in which Parliament, who gave him that power, did not intend. But if it seems clear on grounds of rationality and common sense that he was exceeding the power with which Parliament were intending to clothe him to further the purposes of the Act, the courts have a duty to interfere. The fact that this is not an easy line to draw is no reason why the courts should give up the task and abandon the duty to protect the citizen.

These words are surely the essence of the spirit which should underlie the exercise of the supervisory jurisdiction.

Finally we come to the case of *Wiseman* v. *Borneman* which concerned the applicability of rules of natural justice to the proceedings of a tribunal set up under s. 28 of the Finance Act 1960 to determine alleged cases of 'tax advantage'. The procedure is for the Commissioners of Inland Revenue to serve a notice on the respondent, whereupon it is open to him to make a statutory declaration: if the Commissioners are not satisfied they refer the matter to the tribunal, who decide the issue on the basis of the notice, the declaration and a counter-statement submitted by the Commissioners. If the tribunal determines that a prima facie case has been made out, then the Commissioners can take measures to make 'adjustments' in the taxpayer's tax position: against these adjustments there is provision for several appeals to the courts. The appellant taxpayer in this case complained that the Commissioners had refused to give him a copy of their counter-statement, contrary to the rule of natural justice. The courts below rejected the contention on the ground, *inter alia*, that where a tribunal is simply called upon to decide whether a prima facie case exists there is no initial presumption that the rules of natural justice must apply. The House of Lords rejected this approach and

---

[1] Ibid.

chose instead to look at the intentions underlying the statute. Unanimously, they dismissed the appeal: Lord Donovan said 'I do not believe that Parliament intended that the additional safeguard given to the taxpayer by this preliminary procedure should develop into a round by round contest conducted on paper.' In the result the decision made no particular inroads into the general applicability of the principles of natural justice, but neither did their Lordships feel inclined to extend the doctrine to a procedure closely circumscribed by statute.

It is dangerous to try to draw firm conclusions from a survey of twenty-five cases whose only common feature stems from an arbitrary definition. One or two juristic swallows hardly make a public law summer. Although, when the swallow flies at such an exalted height, it attracts attention beyond the intrinsic fact of flight, not only in the lower courts but also among those professionally concerned with public administration.

Value-judgments depend entirely upon one's ideological position along the legalistic/bureaucratic continuum. Some applaud judicial boldness against executive encroachment on the rule of law; others see the same case as a piece of unwarranted interference in legitimate administrative activity; yet others see judicial control being exercised only in those areas of social policy best left to administrators, and as conservative reaction to left-wing policies. Which view is right? Anyone who could give a satisfactory answer would possess the key to the central enigmas of administrative law.

It is difficult to discern any rational principle in the sequence of appeals discussed. If *Smith* v. *East Elloe R.D.C.* represents the nadir of judge-made administrative law, then cases like *Ridge* v. *Baldwin, Padfield* v. *Minister of Agriculture*, and *Conway* v. *Rimmer* approached the zenith. *McEldowney* v. *Forde* might be thought to represent a psychological reaction to the boldness displayed in these earlier cases; more probably it reflects the vagaries of an unusually constituted House of Lords.[1]

To predict which way the House will jump in subsequent appeals is no easy task. Paradoxically, a reactionary period might be no bad thing in stimulating the development of new institutions, perhaps even an 'administrative court'. The conflict inherent in 'administrative law' between policy-making and adjudication means that the courts can develop this area of jurisprudence only within prescribed limits. The pendulum swings only within a restricted arc. As long as the courts persist in drawing an artificial dichotomy between law and policy, development will be stunted.[2] Unless 'law' itself comes to mean something very unfamiliar, then remedies must continue to be confined within the narrow boundaries of legalism. As long as the courts make a credible

[1] Lords Hodson, Guest, Pearce, Pearson, and Diplock (significantly, it is one of the rare instances since 1962 of an important appeal not being presided over by Lord Reid).
[2] *Commisioner for Local Government Lands and Settlements* v. *Kaderbhai* [1931] A.C. 652; *Blackburn* v. *Attorney-General* [1971] 1 W.L.R. 1937.

attempt to approach as close to these boundaries as they dare, then a kind of Gresham's law may operate: the limited virtues of the situation of today will act as a restraint upon large-scale reform in the future. Given this self-imposed judicial restraint on the ambit of control over administrative action, there will undoubtedly be strong pressures for major change in the shape of an Administrative Division of the High Court exercising a wholly new and ample jurisdiction. In the absence of wholesale change, we think there are at least two threads running through the more recent House of Lords decisions which deserve legislative attention.

a) Legal anachronisms, however respectable their judicial lineage, which tend to perpetuate and even to extend the use of prerogative powers without payment of compensation to those individuals who suffer loss in consequence of such use, have received no quarter from their Lordships: *Nissan* v. *Attorney-General* (Act of State); *Burmah Oil* v. *Lord Advocate* (State necessity). Their Lordships, in the absence of any remedy of monetary compensation, have accepted the principle of communal responsibility in this sphere—to the possible detriment of State interests.

b) Judicial power to supervise the processes of central or local administration will not concede any erosion, even when the courts' jurisdiction, on the face of the provisions in a statute, has been ousted by Parliament itself: *Ridge* v. *Baldwin*; *Padfield* v. *Minister of Agriculture, Food & Fisheries* and *Anisminic* v. *Foreign Compensation Commission*. Could this be an echo of that fondly-held belief that the legislature can no longer understand the complexity, or cope with the weight, of proposed legislation (including subordinate legislation) put before it? We venture to think that, as in so much in this field, the House of Lords is, in the absence of any specific constitutional role, indirectly exerting a limited power of overruling Parliament. May not this be a foretaste of a desire, if not a positive need, for a Bill of Rights?

PUBLIC LAW APPEALS 1952–1969

(1) *Earl Fitzwilliam's Wentworth Estates Co.* v. *Minister of Housing and Local Government* [1952] A.C. 362—Appeal dismissed. Lords *Porter*, Goddard, Oaksey, MacDermott, and Tucker.

(2) *Preston and Area Rent Tribunal* v. *Pickavance* [1953] A.C. 562—Appeal allowed. Lords Porter, (Oaksey), Reid, Tucker, and (Asquith).

(3) *Bank Voor Handel en Scheepvart N.V.* v. *Administrator of Hungarian Property* [1954] A.C. 584—Appeal allowed. Lords *Reid*, Tucker, and Asquith; Lords Morton and Keith dissenting.

(4) *Glasgow Corporation* v. *Central Land Board* 1956 S.C. (H.L.) 1—Appeal dismissed. Lords *Simonds*, Normand, Radcliffe, Keith, and (Somervell).

(5) *Marshall* v. *Scottish Milk Marketing Board* 1956 S.C. (H.L.) 37—Appeal allowed. Lords Simonds, Reid, (Tucker), Keith, and (Somervell).

(6) *Smith* v. *East Elloe Rural District Council* [1956] A.C. 736—Appeal allowed in part. Lords Simonds, Morton, and Radcliffe; Lords Reid and Somervell dissenting.

(7) *Vine* v. *National Dock Labour Board* [1957] A.C. 488—Appeal allowed;

cross-appeal dismissed. Lords *Kilmuir L.C.*, Morton, Cohen, Keith, and Somervell.

(8) †*McClelland* v. *Northern Ireland General Health Services Board* [1957] 1 W.L.R. 594—Appeal allowed. Lords *Oaksey*, Goddard, and Evershed; Lords Tucker and Keith dissenting.

(9) †*Belfast Corporation* v. *O.D. Cars Ltd.* [1960] A.C. 490—Appeal allowed. Lords Simonds, Radcliffe, (Cohen), and (Keith).

(10) *Pyx Granite Co. Ltd.* v. *Ministry of Housing and Local Government* [1960] A.C. 260—Appeal allowed. Lords Simonds, Goddard, (Oaksey), Keith, and Jenkins.

(11) *Fawcett Properties Ltd.* v. *Buckinghamshire County Council* [1961] A.C. 636 —Appeal dismissed. Lords *Cohen*, Keith, Denning, and Jenkins; Lord Morton dissenting.

(12) †*McCann* v. *Attorney General for Northern Ireland* [1961] N.I. 102—Appeal dismissed. Lords Kilmuir L.C., Simonds, Radcliffe, Denning, and Hodson.

(13) *Essex County Council* v. *Essex Incorporated Congregational Church Union* [1963] A.C. 808—Accepted preliminary objection and declined jurisdiction. Lords Reid, (Jenkins), Morris, Hodson, and Devlin.

(14) *Ridge* v. *Baldwin* [1964] A.C. 40—Appeal allowed. Lords *Reid*, Morris, Hodson, and Devlin; Lord Evershed dissenting.

(15) *Chertsey Urban District Council* v. *Mixnam's Properties Ltd* [1965] A.C. 735 —Appeal dismissed. Lords *Reid*, Upjohn, and (Donovan); Lord Radcliffe, strongly *dubitante*; Lord Guest dissenting in part.

(16) **Burmah Oil Co. Ltd.* v. *Lord Advocate* [1965] A.C. 75—Appeals allowed; cross-appeals dismissed. Lords Reid, Pearce, and Upjohn; Lords Radcliffe and Hodson dissenting.

(17) *Pfizer Corporation* v. *Ministry of Health* [1965] A.C. 512—Appeal dismissed. Lords *Reid*, Evershed, and Upjohn; Lords Pearce and Wilberforce dissenting.

(18) *Minister of Social Security* v. *Amalgamated Engineering Union* [1967] 1 A.C. 725—Appeal dismissed. Lords (Reid), Morris, Hodson, and (Guest); Lord Wilberforce dissenting.

(19) *James* v. *Secretary of State for Wales* [1967] 1 W.L.R. 171—Appeal allowed. Lords *Reid*, Guest, Upjohn, and Wilberforce; Lord Morris dissenting.

(20) *Padfield* v. *Ministry of Agriculture* [1968] A.C. 997—Appeal allowed. Lords Reid, Hodson, Pearce, and Upjohn; Lord Morris dissenting.

(21) *Conway* v. *Rimmer* [1968] A.C. 910—Appeal allowed. Lords *Reid*, Morris, Hodson, Pearce, and Upjohn.

(22) *Anisminic Ltd.* v. *Foreign Compensation Commission* [1969] 2 A.C. 147— Appeal allowed. Lords Reid, Pearce, and Wilberforce; Lord Morris and Lord Pearson dissenting.

(23) *Attorney-General* v. *Nissan* [1970] A.C. 179—Appeal dismissed, cross-appeal allowed. Lords *Reid*, Morris, Pearce, Wilberforce, and Pearson.

(24) †*McEldowney* v. *Forde* [1971] A.C. 632—Appeal dismissed. Lords Hodson, Guest, and Pearson; Lords Pearce and Diplock dissenting.

(25) *Wiseman* v. *Borneman* [1971] A.C. 297—Appeal dismissed. Lords Reid, Morris, Guest, *Donovan*, and Wilberforce.

Note: Judges whose names are *italicized* delivered, what the authors regard as, the leading judgment, while those shown in parentheses (–) formally concurred in the result

    * Appeal from the Court of Session

    † Appeal from the Court of Appeal in Northern Ireland

APPEALS OF 'SECONDARY' IMPORTANCE IN PUBLIC LAW

L.C.C. v. *Marks and Spencer Ltd.* [1953] A.C. 535 (Planning)—Appeal dismissed.

Parke Davis & Co. v. *Comptroller General of Patents* [1954] A.C. 321 (Jurisdiction of the Comptroller)—Appeal dismissed.

Corporation of City of London v. *Cusack-Smith* [1955] A.C. 337 (Planning)—Appeal allowed (Lords Porter and Oaksey dissenting).

East Riding County Council v. *Park Estate (Bridlington) Ltd.* [1957] A.C. 223 (Planning)—Appeal dismissed.

*Walsh v. *Lord Advocate* [1956] 1 W.L.R. 1002 (National Service Exemption)—Appeal dismissed.

West Suffolk County Council v. *W. Rought Ltd.* [1957] A.C. 403 (Compensation)—Appeal allowed.

*Glasgow Corporation v. *Western Heritable Investment Co. Ltd.* [1956] A.C. 670 (Housing)—Appeal dismissed.

British Transport Commission v. *Westmorland County Council* [1958] A.C. 126 (Highways—Railway Acts)—Appeal dismissed.

Baldwin & Francis v. *Patent Appeal Tribunal* [1959] A.C. 663 (Error on the face)—Appeal dismissed.

Ching Garage Ltd. v. *Chingford Corporation* [1961] 1 W.L.R. 470 (Highways)—Appeal dismissed.

British Transport Commission v. *Compensation Appeals Tribunal*—reported only in *The Times* 22 February 1962 (Compensation)—Appeal dismissed.

Davy v. *Leeds Corporation* [1956] 1 W.L.R. 445 (Planning—Compensation)—Appeal dismissed.

Minister of Housing and Local Government v. *Hartnell* [1965] A.C. 1134 (Caravan Licensing—Compensation)—Appeal dismissed.

Coleshill and District Investment Co. v. *Ministry of Housing and Local Government* [1969] 2 All E.R. 525 (Planning—'Development')—Appeal dismissed.

Birmingham Corporation v. *West Midland Baptist (Trust) Association* [1970] A.C. 874 (Planning—Compensation)—Appeal dismissed.

* Appeal from the Court of Session

(B) CRIMINAL LAW

The criminal law has long been, and still is (though to a lesser extent) the jurisprudential Cinderella of the English legal system; although the part it plays within the system has not been so much despised as disdainfully ignored. With the notable exception of such unlikely Prince Charmings as Mr. Justice Stephen in the last century and Lord Devlin in this, English judges have appeared anything but eager to conduct a juristic courtship with either the administration of criminal justice or the substantive criminal law.

This is due as much as anything to the absence, until this century, of any formalized appellate process. And when the Court of Criminal Appeal was finally established in 1907, it was virtually the final Court of Appeal in criminal matters; the House of Lords remained hermetically sealed-off from the process of laying down the fundamental principles of the criminal law, save in the comparatively rare instances where the Attorney-General broke the vacuum by granting his fiat to either prosecution or defence for an appeal to the Lords; the measure of lordly inactivity in criminal appeals lies in the fact that only twenty-three appeals were heard over a period of fifty-three years.

Even this heavily qualified right of appeal was an afterthought. It was not until the report stage of the Criminal Appeal Bill that the Attorney-General of the day introduced an amendment by which the holder of his office could give a fiat for an appeal, both if the decision of the Court of Criminal Appeal involved a point of law of exceptional public importance and if it was desirable in the public interest that a further appeal be brought. Since the Court of Criminal Appeal was to be staffed solely by the Lord Chief Justice and the puisne judges of the King's Bench Division—a situation that prevailed until 1966—criminal work was, by implication, deemed unworthy of the attention of appellate judges of either the intermediate or the final court of appeal. The mild concession made by the introduction of the fiat procedure was to permit only those criminal cases of exceptional importance to percolate through to the Law Lords, and then only at the discretion of the Crown's official prosecutor.

The principal object of the Criminal Appeal Act 1907 was to mollify public disquiet over miscarriages of justice, so pitiably disclosed by the *Oscar Slater case*, by replacing the unsatisfactory method of judicial reference to the old Court for Crown Cases Reserved by a form of appellate procedure. There had, before 1907, already existed a concurrent remedy of an appeal by writ of error direct to the House of Lords: it was this limited procedure, available only upon the grant of a fiat by the Attorney-General, which provided the precedent for the amendment to the 1907 Bill.

The procedure by way of writ of error had been no less unsatisfactory than that provided under the Crown Cases Act 1848 which gave statutory effect to the age-old practice whereby the trial judge, could, after the accused's conviction, reserve a point of law for the opinion of all his brother judges. Since this procedure depended entirely on the trial judge's attitude to any legal issue in the trial, there was little professional (to say nothing of public) satisfaction with its operation. The writ of error procedure depended upon the error appearing on the face of the record; as Mr. Justice Stephen observed in his History of the Criminal Law,[1] 'on the record takes no notice either of the evidence or the direction by the judge to the jury', with the result that 'the grossest of errors of fact or law may occur without being in any way brought upon the record.'

The reform of 1907 was a modest start towards establishing a fully appellate process for the criminal law. But while it was a step in the right direction it was not surprising that the fiat procedure came under public attack, both because the grantor of the fiat might have appeared as counsel in the case for which his fiat was subsequently sought (and he would appear to be a judge in his own

---

[1] Vol. 1, p. 309, where the law and practice prior to 1907 is stated with characteristic lucidity.

advocate's pride, if not forensic cause), but also because political considerations obtruded into some of the criminal appeals.[1] Clearly, the fiat procedure represented a much greater procedural hurdle than ever existed for aspiring appellants in the civil jurisdiction, and this in itself excited unfavourable comparison. In an increasingly democratic and open society the fiat procedure was doomed.

Although our period of study starts with 1952, the criminal jurisprudence of the House of Lords can be seen to emanate from the fundamental change in procedure wrought by the Administration of Justice Act 1960.[2] By that Act the fiat procedure was superseded by a double-track judicial system whereby the aspiring appellant has first to obtain from the Court of Criminal Appeal or from the Queen's Bench Divisional Court a certificate that the case raised a point of law of general (as opposed to 'exceptional' in the fiat procedure) importance and, second to obtain leave to appeal either from the court *a quo* or from the Appeal Committee of the House of Lords. Failure to obtain a certificate from the court *a quo* precludes any possibility of an appeal.[3]

The 1960 change in the appellate procedure to the House of Lords left totally untouched the absence of access by the Scots to the House of Lords in criminal matters. Scots lawyers, many of whom regard the right of appeal in civil matters to Westminster as at best a mixed blessing and at worst an alien imposition, have shown little eagerness for the injection of a foreign criminal jurisprudence into their system. The jurisdiction in criminal appeals in Scotland dates back to the immediate post-union era when the House of Lords assumed, without any explicit parliamentary authority, the appellate jurisdiction of the defunct Scottish Parliament: as the latter jurisdiction had never extended to criminal causes, the House eventually refused to entertain Scottish criminal appeals.[4] To this day, the High Court of Justiciary, sitting in Edinburgh, is the final criminal appeal court for Scotland, comparable in status to the English Court of Appeal (Criminal Division). Criminal appeals may come from Northern Ireland, and there have been four such cases since 1960.[5]

In the half-century or so of the fiat procedure only twenty-three criminal cases went to the Lords. Nine involved questions on the construction of statutes; the remaining fourteen involved common law issues. As the well-

---

[1] *R.* v. *Casement* [1917] 1 K.B. 98 was a notable instance.

[2] ss. 1 and 2; now s. 33, Criminal Appeal Act 1968. See D. G. T. Williams, 'The Administration of Justice Act 1960', Crim. L.R. 87–104 (1961), and Karlen, *Appellate Courts in the United States and England*, Chapter 8. During the life of the fiat procedure there were six appeals by the Crown, seventeen by the defence. Eight appeals were allowed, two of them in favour of the Crown.

[3] *Gelberg* v. *Miller* [1961] 1 W.L.R. 459. In habeas corpus appeals from the Divisional Court only leave to appeal is necessary; see s. 15 of Administration of Justice Act 1960.

[4] See T. B. Smith, op. cit., p. 87; also Lord Mansfield's speech in *Bywater* (1781) 2 Paton 563. And see Chapter XVII.

[5] *Bratty* v. *Attorney-General for N.I.; Gallagher* v. *Attorney-General for N.I.; Arthurs* v. *Attorney-General for N.I.;* and *Kennedy* v. *Spratt.*

informed anonymous author of 'Appeals to the House of Lords' wrote in the *Criminal Law Review*,[1] 'it might be thought that the point of construction in *Milne* v. *Commissioner of Metropolitan Police*[2] was a little esoteric; that the point at issue in *Stirland* v. *D.P.P.*[3] was too fine to qualify as one of exceptional public importance, and that the argument of the appellant in *Wicks* v. *D.P.P.*[4] was not substantial enough to merit the consideration of the House of Lords', nevertheless the remainder[5] deserved the attention of the supreme appellate court. One at least of them, *Woolmington* v. *D.P.P.*,[6] made an indelible and distinctive mark on English law, that the burden of proof in a criminal trial is throughout on the prosecution to establish guilt beyond reasonable doubt.

The certificates granted by the Attorney-General in the thirteen cases involving common law issues raised questions of varying importance. Three of them concerned the defence of provocation to a charge of murder.[7] The cases all arose during the period when capital punishment was the mandatory penalty for all murders and on this account alone could justifiably be considered even if the point of law was of something less than exceptional public importance. Two of the three cases laid down important criteria for the common law defence of provocation. Of a fourth case,[8] Lord Sumner, expressing regret that the fiat had been issued, said: 'It raises no new principle of law; it elucidates no new aspect of familiar principles. It is a mere question of the application of the rules of evidence to this particular case': the same comment could apply to *R.* v. *Ball*,[9] the first case in which the fiat, rather rashly, was granted, and to *Crane* v. *D.P.P.*[10] The other eight cases[11] provide a cluster of decisions on disparate problems of criminal law, culminating in

---

[1] Crim. L.R. 566, 568 (1957). The admirable analysis of the law and practice of the fiat procedure is so well-informed and documented that the anonymity of the author is explicable by the fact that the article must have been 'an inside job' written by someone familiar with the Law Officers' Department.

[2] [1940] A.C. 1.   [3] [1944] A.C. 315.   [4] [1947] A.C. 363.

[5] *Leach* v. *R.* [1912] A.C. 305 (Criminal Evidence Act 1898 dealing with compellability of a wife-witness); *Felstead* v. *R.* [1914] A.C. 354 (Trial of Lunatics Act 1883; repealed by the Criminal Procedure (Insanity) Act 1964); *Maxwell* v. *D.P.P.* [1935] A.C. 309 (Criminal Evidence Act 1898 dealing with admissibility of previous charge); *Joyce* v. *D.P.P.* [1946] A.C. 347 (Treason Act 1351); *D.P.P.* v. *Head* [1959] A.C. 83 (s. 56, Mental Deficiency Act 1913); and *Welham* v. *D.P.P.* [1961] A.C. 103 (s. 4, Forgery Act 1913—meaning of 'intent to defraud').

[6] [1935] A.C. 462.

[7] *Mancini* v. *D.P.P.* [1942] A.C. 1; *Holmes* v. *D.P.P.* [1946] A.C. 588; *Bedder* v. *D.P.P.* [1954] 1 W.L.R. 1119.

[8] *Thompson* v. *R.* [1918] A.C. 211, 236.   [9] [1911] A.C. 47.   [10] [1921] 2 A.C. 299.

[11] *R.* v. *Christie* [1914] A.C. 545 (admissibility of evidence). *D.P.P.* v. *Beard* [1920] A.C. 479 (drunkenness as a defence to criminal responsibility). *Woolmington* v. *D.P.P.* [1935] A.C. 462 (burden of proof); *Andrews* v. *D.P.P.* [1937] A.C. 576 (motor manslaughter); *Harris* v. *D.P.P.* [1952] A.C. 694 (admissibility of similar offences); *Davies* v. *D.P.P.* [1954] A.C. 378 (corroborative value of accomplice evidence); *Board of Trade* v. *Owen* [1957] A.C. 602 (conspiracy in England to commit crime abroad); *D.P.P.* v. *Smith* [1961] A.C. 290 (intent to kill).

TABLE 52

Criminal Appeals in Relation to the Total Case-load of the House of Lords, 1952–1968

Type of Appeal	Year																	Total
	1952	'53	'54	'55	'56	'57	'58	'59	'60	'61	'62	'63	'64	'65	'66	'67	'68	
Civil																		
English & Northern Irish	16	14	13	30	26	21	17	30	23	23	24	25	18	22	23	19	20	364
Scottish	8	3	5	7	7	4	4	7	9	8	4	7	10	4	4	11	2	102
Criminal																		
From C.C.A. & C-M.A.C.[a]	1	—	2			1	1	—	2	4	4	2	2	3	2	1	4	29
From Q.B. Divisional Ct.				No appeals prior to 1960 Act						1	2	0	4	3	1	2	4	17
Total Appeals	25	17	20	35	37	26	22	37	34	36	34	34	34	32	30	33	30	512
Total Criminal Appeals	1	0	2	0	0	1	1	0	2	5	6	2	6	6	3	3	8	46
% Criminal Appeals	4	—	10	—	—	4	5	—	6	14	18	6	18	19	10	12	27	9% av.

[a] There were only two appeals from the Courts-Martial Appeal Court during this period: *Cox v. The Army Council* in 1962, and *Secretary of State for Defence v. Warn* in 1968.

the last, and quite the most controversial, of the fiat cases, *D.P.P.* v. *Smith*.[1]

The era of the Attorney-General's fiat produced an average of less than one case every two years. Only seven cases fall within our period of study and represent an average of less than one a year. In the years following the replacement of the fiat procedure the House of Lords heard in eight years thirty-nine criminal appeals, an average of five a year. The dramatic impact of the 1960 Act upon the criminal jurisdiction of the House is shown in Table 52 above which illustrates the annual totals of appeals to the House of Lords, civil and criminal, during the period 1952–68.

The table shows at a glance that the House of Lords has recently acquired a substantial criminal jurisdiction. In the period 1952–60, a mere 3 per cent of appeals were from the Court of Criminal Appeal or from the Courts-Martial Appeal Court. The total percentage of criminal appeals heard during the period 1961–8 was 15 per cent; about half of these (7 per cent of all appeals) came from the Divisional Court, which had not, until the 1960 Act, been subject to the supervision of the House of Lords. Thus the legal problems quite frequently thrown up in cases before magistrates' courts came, for the first time, within the supervisory ambit of the Law Lords, although most appeals (56 per cent) still come from the higher courts.

What are the implications of this increased jurisdiction? Historically the House of Lords has always been pre-eminently a civil court: indeed the very notion of permitting appeals from sacrosanct jury-based criminal verdicts is of comparatively recent origin. But a supreme tribunal should range over the whole field of the law: civil and criminal jurisprudence, while reasonably distinguishable on the basis of arbitrary criteria such as 'punishment' versus 'compensation', or 'State intervention' versus 'private remedies', should not be developed in watertight compartments. In many areas of the law, principles of civil and criminal law overlap, and there is much to be said for providing a single tribunal which can supervise both systems concurrently. The absorption (by the Criminal Appeal Act 1966) of the Court of Criminal Appeal into the newly created Criminal Division of the Court of Appeal was a logical step in this process of rationalization. But the House of Lords is still required as a long stop; what has long been sauce for the civil goose is now recognized as being sauce for the criminal gander.

Naturally, any newly acquired jurisdiction has its pitfalls; this one more than most. Just as Scots lawyers complain of the aberrations of English judges in the field of Scots law, so criminal lawyers might complain that the criminal expertise of Law Lords may have become atrophied down the years (if indeed they ever handled criminal cases) by their continuous preoccupation with the civil law. Even if this be true—and the Chancery members of the House of Lords will rarely have had more than nodding acquaintance with the criminal law—it can easily be overstated. The criminal law is a branch which

1 [1961] A.C. 290.

the first-class intellect can quickly grasp; it is, by and large, free from technicalities requiring any great measure of expertise. This is borne out by the fact
that some of the outstanding judgments in this area of the law have come from
those Law Lords who had previously least experience of the criminal law.

It must be regarded as a pity, however, that currency was given to the
charge that the House of Lords was ill-equipped to involve itself in the criminal
appeal jurisdiction by the first two decisions under the new procedure—*Shaw*
v. *D.P.P.*[1] and *Sykes* v. *D.P.P.*,[2] following hard on the heels of that much
maligned decision of *D.P.P.* v. *Smith*.[3] The criminal law since 1960 has been
dominated—some would say haunted—by the spectre of *D.P.P.* v. *Smith*,
although it was widely ignored by the courts[4] and was finally spurned by the
legislature.[5] Together with *Shaw* and *Sykes* this case formed an alliterative
trio that did not augur well for an enlarged criminal jurisdiction for the House
of Lords. But in eight years in thirty-nine criminal appeals, is there discernible
some pattern of legal development or jurisprudential symmetry emerging
from their Lordships' rulings?

A supreme tribunal, once to all intents and purposes a civil court, has at
last been given a chance (a numerically restricted one) to exercise a substantial
criminal jurisdiction: has it grasped the opportunities to evolve a rational and
coherent criminal jurisprudence geared both to social need and to legal
rationality?

D.P.P. v. *Smith* represented the apotheosis of the law's reasonable man.
A suspected thief driving a car was stopped by a police officer on traffic duty;
while the latter was challenging the accused, he drove off with the officer
hanging on to the bonnet. As the vehicle zig-zagged down the road, the oncoming traffic hit the prostrate body of the officer who was eventually thrown
off into the line of traffic. Was the accused guilty of murder? The House of
Lords, in a single judgment of an oddly composed court[6] held that the objective test, viz. the test of what a reasonable man (and not this particular
accused) would contemplate as the probable results of his act, and therefore
would be presumed to intend, was the right test of intention to kill. In so
doing the House of Lords upheld the trial judge and restored the verdict of
capital murder; but the accused had already been promised a reprieve in the
event of such a reversal of the Court of Criminal Appeal's decision.

The decision evoked immediate academic criticism,[7] professional hostility,
and judicial conflict within the Commonwealth; no less a judicial figure than
the Chief Justice of Australia, Sir Owen Dixon, said that in future the High

---

[1] [1962] A.C. 220.

[2] [1962] A.C. 528; the decision has been superseded by s. 5, Criminal Law Act 1967.

[3] [1961] A.C. 290.   [4] e.g. *R.* v. *Grimwood* [1962] 2 Q.B. 621.

[5] S. 8, Criminal Justice Act 1967.

[6] The only judgment was delivered by Lord Kilmuir L.C.; Lords Goddard, Tucker,
Denning, and Parker C.J. formally concurred.

[7] Glanville Williams, 'Constructive Malice Revisited', 23 M.L.R. 605 (1960).

Court of Australia would feel free to differ from decisions of the House of Lords.[1] *D.P.P.* v. *Smith* may now be seen as a judicial aberration (one slipshod sentence in Lord Kilmuir's judgment caused the professional furore). At the time the decision was handed down it represented a grave portent of worse setbacks to the healthy development of a modern criminal law. And both *Shaw* v. *D.P.P.* and *Sykes* v. *D.P.P.*, which followed hard on its heels, did nothing to quell the storm that had begun to break over the criminal law.

Shaw v. *D.P.P.* revived a lurking fear in the public mind that the judges might one day strike out in favour of creating new crimes. In that case the publisher of a booklet, *The Ladies' Directory*, filled his magazine with sexually suggestive advertisements together with the addresses or telephone numbers of prostitutes; he was prosecuted on an indictment containing three counts. The charges of obscene libel and living off immoral earnings excited little comment. The third raised a howl of liberal protest. Save for a resounding dissent from Lord Reid, the House of Lords declared itself the residual guardians of public morals, and where Parliament had not intervened to protect the morals of the community the Court, they declared, could fill the gap by resort to the use of the crime of conspiring to corrupt public morals.

The Law Lords had at least reverted to type in that the composition of the Court was no different from the ordinary; and the practice adopted in *D.P.P.* v. *Smith* of deploying only one judgment was noticeably dropped. In the event the dissent of Lord Reid was widely acclaimed; the offence-creating powers, proclaimed by the other Law Lords, are not likely to be revived.[2] Within a month, however, the dormant offence of misprision of felony—the non-disclosure of the commission of a felony—was revived in all its pristine glory, although the exact ambit of the liability to inform was left vague. In that case, *Sykes* v. *D.P.P.*, the accused had not actively concealed the purchase of fire-arms by certain members of the I.R.A. but had taken no steps to reveal his extensive knowledge of their dealings in weaponry. Again Lord Goddard was prised out of retirement along with Lord Morton of Henryton (a former Lord of Appeal) to sit—this time not in silence, since all five Law Lords delivered judgment. The worrying aspect of the case was the latitude of the crime as seen by Lord Goddard.[3] 'It is very easy to poke ridicule at the offence and say that it obliges people to inform against a boy stealing an apple. The law nowadays is administered with dignity and commonsense. And if it is said that it obliges a father to inform against his son, or vice-versa, I would answer that in the case of a really heinous crime be it so.' Fortunately with the aboli-tion of felonies and misdemeanours in the Criminal Law Act 1967, the crime of misprision of felony disappeared into a legal oblivion, to be superseded by a

1 *Parker* v. *R.* (1963) 111 C.L.R. 610, 632, and see 79 L.Q.R. 313.
2 See *D.P.P.* v. *Bhagwan* [1970] 3 W.L.R. 501.   3 [1962] A.C. 528, 569.

restricted substitute offence of concealing criminal conduct or of giving false information.[1]

The three cases had one other common feature that could hardly fail to attract adverse comment from liberal reformers. They reflected the innate public sense, which judges are not slow to echo, that in an era of supposed increasing criminality the appeal courts exist to buttress jury verdicts rather than to act as bastions of individual liberty. In none of the three cases was much judicial concern shown for the danger that the liberty of the subject was being perceptibly eroded. Law enforcement agents, on the other hand, could not fail to feel well content that their efforts at crime detection and at securing criminal conviction of the guilty were not being quietly subverted in the ivory-towers of judicial impartiality. Unlike the Supreme Court of the United States, which is being constantly upbraided for its supposed softness towards offenders in standing firm on the basic protective rules of the criminal law, the House of Lords avoided any breath of such criticism; indeed it positively sought the plaudits of the get-tough brigade.

But that is nearly a decade ago. The Smith–Shaw–Sykes judicial syndrome has been effectively halted in its tracks. A study of criminal jurisdiction since 1961 discloses two main strands in the judicial texture: a growing awareness of the preponderance of prosecution power in the criminal process, and a distaste for the over-technical rules (relics, perhaps, of the writ era) that have cosseted the accused and tend only to deflect the court from the attainment of an abstract idea of sensible criminal justice. In the last three years particularly, the former attitude has resulted in some judicial assertions of principles of individual liberty: *Commissioners of Customs & Exercise* v. *Harz and Power*;[2] *Sweet and Parsley*;[3] *R.* v. *Churchill*;[4] *Armah* v. *Government of Ghana*.[5] The hard line against criminals persists discernibly in cases like *Selvey* v. *D.P.P.*;[6] *Jones* v. *D.P.P.*;[7] *Connolly* v. *D.P.P.*;[8] and *Myers* v. *D.P.P.*[9]

The criminal jurisdiction of the House of Lords is quite new, and there are large areas of the criminal law that have remained untouched or only peripherally dealt with the House of Lords, so that any assessment of the influence of their Lordships must be premature. The law of homicide, for example, has barely been judicially pronounced upon, although it is productive of appeals due to the extreme penalty involved. Since the Homicide Act 1957 (when capital murder was limited to five categories of homicide), only five convictions (two from Northern Ireland) have found their way to the Lords. The two Northern Ireland cases, *Bratty* v. *A.-G. for Northern Ireland*[10] and *Gallagher* v. *A.-G. for Northern Ireland*[11] raised the issues of drunkenness and automatism as defences. Of the other three convictions for homicide

---

[1] s. 5, Criminal Law Act 1967.   [2] [1967] 1 A.C. 766.   [3] [1970] A.C. 132.
[4] [1967] 1 A.C. 224.   [5] [1968] A.C. 192.   [6] [1970] A.C. 304.
[7] [1962] A.C. 635.   [8] [1964] A.C. 1243.   [9] [1964] A.C. 1001.
[10] [1963] A.C. 386.   [11] [1963] A.C. 349.

offences, *Smith* v. *D.P.P.* did not directly involve a construction of the Act; of the other two cases, *Jones* v. *D.P.P.* dealt with the admissibility of evidence of similar facts by cross-examination of the accused, and *Rumping* v. *D.P.P.*[1] with the nature of privileged communications between spouses and as such belongs more to our section on family law.

The academic controversy[2] over the effect of section 3 of the Homicide Act 1957 on the common law defence of provocation remains only technically unresolved, since there is now the authoritative pronouncement of the Privy Council in *Glasford Phillips* v. *R.*[3] (contemporaneously, the Court of Appeal gave a certificate, but declined leave to appeal in *R.* v. *Walker*,[4] which reviewed the same questions). Similarly, it was the Privy Council in *Rose* v. *R.*[5] which endorsed the ruling of the Court of Criminal Appeal in *R.* v. *Byrne*,[6] finally explaining the defence of diminished responsibility, newly introduced into the law of homicide. While the House of Lords rejected the Australian-developed doctrine of issue estoppel (or *res judicata*) in criminal cases,[7] nothing has yet been said about a new species of manslaughter whereby, if excessive and lethal force is used in self-defence, the offender is guilty of manslaughter and not murder.[8] There are indications, however, that yet another Australian legal innovation, that an absence of negligence may be a defence to an offence of strict liability,[9] may be favourably received into English jurisprudence.[10] This receptiveness may be matched by fundamental re-thinking of the doctrine in *Woolmington* v. *D.P.P.* to the effect that the burden of proof in a criminal case is throughout on the prosecution to establish the accused's guilt beyond reasonable doubt; that much appears from some observations of Lords Reid and Pearce in *Sweet* v. *Parsley*. Here again the House of Lords' decision may be considered pre-empted by the Privy Council in *Public Prosecutor* v. *Yuvaraj*.[11]

English appeal courts have generally been little troubled with the substantive criminal law. With the exception of the crime of murder which, because it has until recently involved the death penalty, attracted particular judicial interest, other branches of the law do not raise legal issues. The House of Lords' activity accurately reflects the comparative insignificance of substantive law. Misprision of felony,[12] conspiracy to corrupt public morals,[13] and

---

1 [1964] A.C. 814.   2 [1970] Crim. L.R. 249 and 446.
3 [1969] 2 A.C. 130. During the period of the fiat there were no fewer than three cases—*Mancini, Holmes,* and *Bedder*—dealing with aspects of the law of provocation.
4 [1969] 1 W.L.R. 311.   5 [1961] A.C. 496.   6 [1960] 2 Q.B. 396
7 *Connolly* v. *D.P.P.* [1964] A.C. 1254; *Mraz (No. 2)* v. *The Queen* (1956) 96 C.L.R. 62.
8 *R.* v. *Howe* (1958) 100 C.L.R. 448. But a Privy Council decision, *Palmer* v. *The Queen* [1971] A.C. 814 would appear to settle the issue adverse to any new form of manslaughter. See also *R.* v. *McInnes* [1971] 1 W.L.R. 1600.
9 *Proudman* v. *Dayman* (1941) 67 C.L.R. 536.
10 *Sweet* v. *Parsley* [1970] A.C. 132, per Lord Reid at p. 148 and Lord Pearce at p. 156.
11 [1970] A.C. 913.   12 *Shaw* v. *D.P.P.* [1962] A.C. 220.
13 *Sykes* v. *D.P.P.* [1962] A.C. 528.

intent to defraud in forgery;[1] road traffic offences by soldiers abroad;[2] obtaining credit by false pretences,[3] and variations on the theme of gaming offences under the gaming legislation of 1960 and 1963,[4] contained in a constant stream of cases, represent the sum total of judicial involvement in shaping a criminal code.

In recent House of Lords cases, there emerges a welcome departure from pure logic towards the adaptation of the criminal law to modern criminogenic factors. Society is in constant flux; nowhere more so than in post-war Britain. The need to combat delinquent behaviour emerges, first vaguely felt and unexpressed, then developing into a force to be reckoned with by the agencies of social control. Law as an agent of social control is not then simply a manifestation of logical deduction, since it also presupposes sociological inquiry. It is the nature of this interplay that will bring strength and purpose to the principles of criminal law as expounded by the courts, and the court of last resort must play its due part in the process.

Toohey v. *Metropolitan Police Commissioner*,[5] an unheralded decision touching the nature of testimony, may prove to have been, sociologically, the most decisive step forward, if not the nearest approach to a revolution in criminal jurisprudence yet achieved. Medical evidence was held admissible to cast doubt on the reliability of a prosecution witness who was the victim of an assault. Lord Pearce, delivering a remarkable judgment in which the other Law Lords formally concurred, said:

Human evidence shares the frailty of those who give it. It is subject to many crosscurrents such as partiality, prejudice, self-interest and, above all, imagination and inaccuracy . . . . If a witness purported to give evidence of something which he believed that he had seen at a distance of fifty yards, it must surely be possible to call the evidence of an oculist to the effect that the witness could not possibly see anything at a greater distance than twenty yards.

(The witness's fall to the ground in that case was shown by medical evidence to have been induced by an hysterical attack and not by the accused's fist.) Here was the first judicial refutation of the notion, still remarkably prevalent, that the faithfully sworn testimony of a mentally competent witness is in general to be regarded as an exact presentation of reality. Account was taken for the first time of the fallibility of human testimony due to the witness's selectivity in perception and recall.

The accuracy of testimony in court, even by persons who fully intend to tell the truth, is often seriously affected by the working of psychological selectivity. Human beings are equipped with eyes and ears which function in very much the same way from person to person. Yet accounts of an incident such as a crime are often given in contradictory ways by different observers.

---

[1] *Welham* v. *D.P.P.* [1961] A.C. 103.   [2] *Cox* v. *Army Council* [1963] A.C. 48.
[3] *Raven* v. *Fisher* [1964] A.C. 210.   [4] *Payne* v. *Bradley* [1962] A.C. 343.
[5] [1965] A.C. 595 reversing *R.* v. *Gunewardene* [1951] 2 K.B. 600.

Such distorted accounts demonstrate that 'we don't see with our eyes alone' or 'hear with ears alone'. We see and hear with our whole person; and under certain conditions our eyes and ears become mere instruments serving our desires, partisanships and prejudices. They ultimately may deceive us in the relating of our observations.[1] Awareness by the courts of the fallibility of testimony—accepting the credibility of the witness—may prove to be the one major revolution in the modern criminal trial process. Wittingly or un-wittingly, the House of Lords has shown that the machinery for testing evidence by expert medical (including psychological) testimony exist; the question is, will the advocates and the courts use it? Identification parades could well be the first casualties of this legal development.

Lord Pearce's forward-looking judgment responds to the plea made eloquently by Mr. Justice Barry, the outstanding Australian judge, who wrote:

Judges require also the fabric of knowledge of the mainspring of human conduct. The history of science is a continuous record of the detection and discarding of false assumptions and wrong theories.... The function of the criminal law is by its nature only an approximation, often rough and crude, to ideal justice, for the courts are ill-equipped to walk the secret ways of the human spirit.[2]

Toohey's case is a refreshing rejection of an outworn notion of human testimony; the English criminal law will as a result be less rigid and crude in its approximation to the ideal of abstract justice.

A similarly growing awareness of the springs of human conduct prompting anti-social (hence criminal) behaviour is perceptible in the actions of the courts. English judges are slowly becoming receptive to criminological theory, and as a consequence are beginning to sense the sociologically essential synonymity of criminal justice and penal sanctions. Mr. Justice Stephen's aphorism that 'the sentence of the court is the pith and substance of the whole criminal process' is fast gaining general acceptance in the courts. Matters of policy are no longer divorced from the policy of criminal justice, though the House of Lords itself has yet to make a major contribution to penological jurisprudence. But two problems of sentencing have arisen in recent appeals, both at the instance of the Court of Criminal Appeal which gave leave to appeal.

In *Verrier* v. *D.P.P.*[3] it was held that while normally it would be wrong to pass a severer sentence for an attempt to commit a crime than was statutorily the maximum for the substantive offence, there was nothing to bar a court, in

1 See 'Psychological selectivity in the courtroom', Blom-Cooper and Wegner, *Medicine, Science and Law* (1968), p. 31.
2 'Introduction to Studies in Criminal Law' by N. Morris and C. Howard (Clarendon Press, Oxford, 1964).
3 [1967] 2 A.C. 195. Only a year earlier the Appeal Committee had declined to give leave to some of the train robbers who raised precisely the same point; *Field, Field & Wheater* v. *D.P.P.* (unreported).

a proper case, from passing a longer sentence for conspiracy than could be given for the substantive offence. By its decision in *D.P.P.* v. *Ottewell*,[1] that courts could, under section 37 of the Criminal Justice Act 1967, impose an extended sentence of imprisonment although the term of imprisonment so extended must not exceed the maximum term for the particular offence, the House of Lords saved a statutory penal provision from having misfired. But the wariness of the Lords in concerning itself with penal problems is still unhappily prevalent. In *Savundranayagam* v. *D.P.P.*[2] the Appeal Committee declined to entertain an appeal testing the question whether a court may pass a prison sentence as an alternative to a fine, consecutive to a prison sentence on another count, where the fine is illusory on the grounds that the offender is bankrupt. It cannot be long now before the penal policy of the courts will be defined more often and resoundingly by the House of Lords. But it has yet to assert its judicial dominance in penal matters by granting leave to appeal in such cases.

How far will the House of Lords develop the equivalent English rules to what Americans call 'due process'—the technical rules which ensure a fair trial both by control of prosecution methods and by the rules of evidence and proof? By its assault on the doctrine of strict liability, the House of Lords in *Sweet* v. *Parsley* has pronounced its faith in its protective role, although this represented a conversion from the earlier 'dangerous drugs' decision, *Warner* v. *Metropolitan Police Commissioner*.[3] The question is where the House of Lords will strike the balance between the public's right to have the guilty convicted and the accused's expectation to be protected against unfair police practices. There is discernible the philosophy of Mr. Justice Holmes that it is 'a less evil that some criminals should escape than that the government should play an ignoble part'.[4] The balance at present is being struck only after a considerable swing of the pendulum towards public protection against criminals.

(C) INTERNATIONAL LAW

National courts do not ordinarily attract international attention. But, in a world which shrinks progressively in size and hence facilitates a higher degree of mobility and of social and commercial contact among its dwellers,

[1] [1970] A.C. 642, reversing the Court of Appeal, [1969] 1 Q.B. 27 which gave leave to appeal.
[2] [1969] 1 W.L.R. 339. The decision of the Court of Appeal on this point directly conflicted with a later decision of another division of the Court of Appeal in *R.* v. *Dennis Clarke* (1968). Their Lordships recently had to consider the constitutional status of the suspended sentence during the period of emergency in Northern Ireland: *Kennedy* v. *Spratt* [1971] 2 W.L.R. 667.
[3] [1969] 2 A.C. 256.
[4] *Olmstead* v. *U.S.* 277 U.S. 438,469(1928) quoted by Mr. Justice Frankfurter in *On Lee* v. *U.S.* 343 U.S. 747,758(1952).

foreigners do, however, occasionally invoke the assistance of courts abroad. Thus national courts are, from time to time, driven to recognize the existence of foreign laws, to take account of foreign decisions, and, less frequently, even to apply foreign laws and enforce judgments of foreign courts. To a limited extent, all national courts are thrust, willy-nilly, onto the international legal stage. The domestic prestige of a hierarchy of courts in any national legal system will, however, dictate the frequency with which non-nationals outside the jurisdiction are willing either to resort to the courts or to submit to the courts' jurisdiction when pursued by a national of those courts or by a fellow non-national.

There are two aspects of the problem. The first is to determine how far the legal system of a country is willing to forego the application of its own law in favour of an alien law. The extent to which the courts are willing to apply a foreign jurisprudence in cases involving an international element is a measure of the internationalism or insularity of that legal system. The second issue is to ascertain how far the foreign litigant submitting his dispute to be determined in an alien court by an alien law is nevertheless accommodated in the native litigious process. Is he discriminated against? Are the rules weighted against him? Perhaps only those alien litigants who have tasted the English forensic process can provide an answer. In any event, the second issue is more readily susceptible of discussion in terms of the trial process rather than of appellate functions: hence it is a problem which lies outside the purview of the present study.

The first issue focuses on the specialist subject, the conflict of laws (*alias* private international law); and here the appellate courts have developed rules which, unlike almost any other branch of jurisprudence, are still largely unfettered by statutory provisions. This is an area, therefore, where judicial creativity is theoretically most marked. To show how creative the Law Lords have been in practice is, in part, the aim of this chapter: indeed it is the central objective of our entire study. And whatever degree of creativity has been exhibited in this area, we must not in this study ignore the House of Lords' international prestige by perceiving it in a purely domestic setting.

Well away from the political scene, the House of Lords has been adept at constructing internationally workable and acceptable rules in the law of obligations. From *Kahler* v. *Midland Bank* and *Zivnostenska Banka National Corporation* v. *Frankman*,[1] which were decided just prior to the period of our study, until the twin decisions of *National Bank of Greece and Athens S.A.* v. *Metliss*[2] and *Adams* v. *National Bank of Greece S.A.*,[3] the House of Lords wrestled with the problem of the effect of foreign legislation. The ultimate objective was to safeguard contractual rights against foreign legislation seeking to affect adversely the alien's vested legal obligations.

---

[1] [1950] A.C. 24 and 57.   [2] [1958] A.C. 509.   [3] [1961] A.C. 255.

There are numerous reported cases on international contractual rights but few dealing with other obligations. Until the decision in *Boys* v. *Chaplin*[1] no one could say how English courts would deal with the following, increasingly familiar, problems. Two English motorists holidaying in a foreign country are in collision. The law of the country where the accident happens awards no damages for pain and suffering. English law compensates the victim for his pain and suffering. Which law applies? If the Law Lords, in five separate assenting judgments, displayed remarkable inconsistency as between themselves (an unfortunate result as we have argued elsewhere), at least a major innovation was made in this area of the law.

The old rule was that the law of the place of the accident governed. All five Law Lords gave different reasons for rejecting it; and none agreed entirely what was to replace it. The presiding Law Lord, Lord Hodson, found the old rule attractive and worth following, but not invariably: it remained a general rule, admitting of exceptions. Lord Guest, true to Scottish tradition felt that a distinction should be made between pain and suffering (*solatium* in Scottish legal terminology) as a right of action and as an ingredient of general damages: the former to be governed by the old rule, the latter by the law of the place where the suit is brought. Lord Wilberforce adopted an elaborate argument showing that ordinarily the law of the place where the accident happened prevailed, subject to the question whether the relevant foreign rule (in this case no damages for pain and suffering) ought, as a matter of social policy, to be applied. Lord Pearson completed the circle by concluding that the English rule, giving a predominant role to the law of the place where the action is fought, was well established. These diverse approaches had one thing in common: the Law Lords were attempting to discourage blatant 'forum shopping', namely, preventing victims of accidents choosing the court whose law would be most favourable to their claims for damages. In so doing, the Law Lords freed the law from its former rigidity, only to impose a flexibility unhappily productive of uncertainty.

A more compendious result was achieved by the Law Lords in the development of the new law relating to the recognition of foreign decrees of divorce in *Indyka* v. *Indyka*[2] to which we have alluded elsewhere. As an example of judicial creativity in the field of family law, it has no modern equivalent. It characterized the spirit of judicial law-making at its best. The decision was motivated by the laudable desire to prevent the proliferation of limping marriages, i.e. those instances where spouses find themselves married in one country but divorced in another.

Foreign governments, other than nationalized corporations (which are

[1] [1971] A.C. 356. See the penetrating article by Harvey McGregor, 'The International Accident Problem', 33 M.L.R. 1 (1970).

[2] [1969] 1 A.C. 33; now superseded by the Recognition of Divorces and Legal Separations Act 1971.

nothing more than emanations of the State) are not infrequent litigants before our civil courts.[1] The English courts' unwillingness to become embroiled, even peripherally, with affairs of state has, however, been most marked. It is underlined by a long-standing rule of law, evolved by the courts without any statutory prompting, that whenever an issue is raised as to the status of a foreign government the parties must seek a certificate from the Foreign Secretary, the terms of which bind the courts. Judges have repeatedly declined to go behind the certificate, on the ground that the sovereign and her courts cannot speak with different voices on the international status of a foreign power.

The American courts have long appreciated the absurdity of bowing dutifully to the executive for political reasons, refusing to accord *de jure* or *de facto* recognition to a government which in all other respects is treated as effective. This, say the American judges, would be to treat the officers of that government as nothing more than a band of robbers. In the event the American courts evolved a doctrine of judicial recognition of the commercial and non-governmental acts of the citizens of a foreign state, even though it meant giving effect to the laws of a state which had not been recognized *de facto* by the U.S. Government.

When the House of Lords came face to face with the identical problem in *Carl-Zeiss Stiftung* v. *Rayner & Keeler Ltd.* (*No. 2.*)[2] the same result was achieved in relation to an East German foundation, but by a devious and jurisprudentially unsatisfactory route. Only Lord Wilberforce seemed prepared to contemplate an adoption of the American technique of giving legal recognition to commercial and non-political laws of an established government even though unrecognized by the U.S. Government. The Foreign Office had stated that East Germany was not recognized by H.M.G. other than as an agent of the Soviet Union which had been recognized since 1919. Their Lordships held that an emanation of a recognized sovereign government was itself to be recognized. Thus a challenge to the *ipse dixit* of the Foreign Office was sidestepped, and the American compromise formula was not adopted but quietly put on one side to be re-examined if and when the occasion demanded.

Encapsulated by political considerations, appeals before the House of Lords receive the predictable treatment of judicial disengagement. On the other hand, if the litigation presents no direct political consequences, the House of Lords asserts a freedom as refreshing as their politico-legal inhibitions are depressing. The *Carl-Zeiss* case is an exemplar of this schizoid behaviour. Once they had found a formula which obviated the need to go against the Foreign Office and recognize East Germany, their Lordships displayed the judicial boldness becoming to a judiciary priding itself on independence and international-mindedness. The East German foundation had

---

[1] *Rahimtoola* v. *Nizam of Hyderabad* [1958] A.C. 379; *United States of America* v. *Dolfuss Mieg et Cie S.A.* [1952] A.C. 582; *Government of India* v. *Taylor* [1955] A.C. 491.
[2] [1967] 1 A.C. 853.

proceeded to press its claims to protect its rights in the famous optical instruments in courts all over the world. Most noticeably of all the national
courts, the West Germans had disdainfully, and with faintly concealed political bias, declined to accord any recognition to the decree of the East German
courts in favour of the plaintiffs. The House of Lords could see no obstacle to
giving full faith and credit to the eminently respectable judgments of the East
German courts; a nice instance of the a-political approach of English judges
when faced with legal problems. (Or just manifestation of an almost religious
belief that law and politics are divisible?)

In other cases where political factors operate, just below the surface of the
legal issues, the House of Lords has shown its ability to be creative. In
Regazzoni v. *Sethia*[1] a device by international merchants trading in jute bags
to avoid the Indian law prohibiting export to South Africa for political
reasons was held to make the transaction between a Swiss merchant and an
Indian (trading from London and selling jute bags c.i.f. Hamburg) illegal and
unenforceable. Laws were to be enforced even if the sellers' motivations were
politically colourable.

Further proof of the courts' disinclination to become entrapped in politico-
legal issues is the rule that an English court has no jurisdiction to entertain an
action for the enforcement, directly or indirectly, of a penal, revenue, or other
public law of a foreign state. The full extent of this rule of unenforceability
was adopted in *Government of India* v. *Taylor*[2] where the Indian government
sought to prove in the voluntary liquidation of an English company for a
sum in respect of Indian income tax, including capital gains tax, then unheard-
of in England. Their Lordships thought it elementary that a foreign government cannot come to these shores and sue a person for taxes levied. One
sovereign will not act as tax collector for another, even though nowadays the
two are willing to enter into double taxation agreements whereby the taxpayers of each country will not be taxed twice on the same income or capital.
History conclusively favours the approach adopted by their Lordships,
although there is little to be said nowadays for regarding the fact of taxation
as penal and unenforceable, whatever may be the view about the swingeing
rate of such taxation. *Regazzoni*'s case seems inconsistent with this rigid
rule. The Law Lords in that case were prepared to enforce an Indian law
prohibiting jute exports to South Africa, though on the face of it penal,
because to ignore the law would be to countenance the right to smuggle.
And, in any event, the English courts would not enforce a contract which
violated a law of a friendly state.

Invariably foreign governments are parties to extradition proceedings: they
are the applicants for the return of fugitive criminals to face trial or serve
prison sentences abroad. It is in this much publicized politico-legal area that
the status of our courts is most readily assessed internationally, if only on the

[1] [1958] A.C. 301.   [2] [1955] A.C. 491.

level of emotional public sympathy for the refugee from a foreign judgment. And the House of Lords, during the period of our study, has played a crucial part in determining the way in which extradition laws have evolved in a world which, in the aftermath of war, has yielded to public demands for the return of fugitive offenders. Indeed, prior to 1960—ninety years after the Extradition Act 1870, in which the jurisdiction of the courts was invoked as an aid to the Executive's often delicate decision whether to return fugitive offenders—the House of Lords had not been troubled by this sensitive branch of law. The reasons for such judicial inactivity were (a) the relative infrequency of governmental requisitions for extradition, stemming from the comparative immobility of offenders: and (b) the minor criminal appellate role of the House of Lords, until the Administration of Justice Act 1960 extended its role.

Apart from consigning to the courts the task of ascertaining that the crime for which extradition is sought is extraditable (i.e. in the list of crimes in the relevant extradition treaty) and of ensuring that the apprehended fugitive is identical to the offender sought to be surrendered, the Extradition Act 1870 enshrined statutorily the English tradition of political asylum. The courts were assigned the vital duty of ensuring the protection of political refugees.

The Select Committee of the House of Commons on Extradition published its report in 1868.[1] Paragraph 9 of the report put its political point pithily: 'That upon the hearing of the case, on habeas corpus, it shall be open to the accused to question the bona fides of the demand for extradition, upon the ground that his surrender has in fact been sought for political reasons'. No more preise language could have been used to reflect the Committee's insistence that the courts (and not Ministers of the Crown) should safeguard the political refugee against surrender to a foreign power which is his political opponent.

Section 3 (1) of the Act for all the world appears to reflect accurately the Committee's declared will. It provides that 'a fugitive criminal shall not be surrendered if the offence, in respect of which his surrender is demanded, is one of a political character, or if he prove to the satisfaction of the police magistrate or the court before whom he is brought on habeas corpus, or to the Secretary of State, that the requisition has in fact been made with a view to try or punish him for an offence of a political character.' But in *Schtraks* v. *Government of Israel*[2] the House of Lords, in a case which on its facts was doomed to failure for the fugitive offender (since it was sought to argue that the kidnapping of a Jewish child, because the child's parents did not obey orthodox religious teaching, was an offence of a political character) put a strange, if not strained construction on the words of the section. Without dilating on the reasoning advanced by their Lordships, we would say that the decision was both regrettable and wrong. It was held that the second limb of the section did not, as the words appeared to indicate, permit a fugitive

[1] Cmd. 393.   [2] [1964] A.C. 556.

offender to question in the courts the good faith of the requisitioning state or to demonstrate to the judges that extradition was being sought by the foreign government not to punish him for a crime but *actually* to get him back and punish him for a political reason unconnected with the crime for which extradition was granted. The Law Lords declared that the section was only evidential; that it was an alternative method of showing that in fact the otherwise extraditable crime had a political flavour, in the sense that it was committed in the context of political activity, such as murdering a politician to effect a revolution.

This point in the *Schtraks* case was faintly re-argued, without much hope that their Lordships would have a change of heart within five years, in *Government of Greece* v. *Governor of Brixton Prison and others*.[1] Their Lordships stuck to their line of severely limiting the political involvement of the Court. Thus with a stroke of a judicial pen the House of Lords had negatived a Parliamentary intention of providing a judicial safeguard for political refugees. If the 1868 Committee report did not bear out this contention to the full, post-1870 events put the matter beyond doubt.

Negotiations between the U.S. and British governments between 1871 and 1876 showed that the American authorities wanted to delete the latter part of section 3 (1) from any Anglo-American Treaty;[2] the U.S. Government pressed for issues of political offences to be dealt with exclusively by the Secretary of State, but the United Kingdom Government replied that 'it would be vain to ask the House of Commons to dispense with any of the safeguards which after much discussion were introduced into that clause.' In the event, negotiations for a new treaty foundered on that point alone, and were abandoned until 1935.

Further, in 1878, the Royal Commission on Extradition was set up to review the working of the 1870 Act. One of its members, W. M. Torrens, had been a member of the 1868 Select Committee, and it was his version of section 3 (1) which had been accepted by the Attorney-General during the passage of the 1870 Act through Parliament.[3] Mr. Torrens attached a separate opinion to one aspect of the 1878 Royal Commission's report. He alluded to the attempts by foreign governments to obtain the return of fugitives on ostensibly political grounds long since abandoned; this aspect of the problem was 'obsolete', but Mr. Torrens concluded: 'The statute of 1870 was designed to guard against the different and more insidious danger, namely that of our authorities being made use of to deliver up fugitives who have become the object of suspicions, espionage or persecution by arbitrary power, upon the alleged breach of some ordinary law for the protection of property or life.'

It is blindingly clear that Parliament, the government of the day, and its legal advisers were insistent that section 3 (1) should afford the political

---

[1] [1971] A.C. 250.   [2] *British Digest of International Law*, vol. 6, pp. 665–8.
[3] H.C. Debs., 3rd Ser., vol. 202, col. 1425, 4 July 1870.

refugee every opportunity to raise, both in the courts and before the Secretary of State, the matters which the 1870 Act said he might raise. Parliament was well aware of the deviousness of foreign despotic governments, and was accordingly building into the extradition process a double, judicial and executive, safeguard. It is incontestable, moreover, that section 3 (1) was intended to cover not only foreign governments' attempts to extradite for political offences but also for 'colourable' extraditions, namely extraditions for nominally common crimes but with the ulterior motive of dealing with the fugitive for political obnoxiousness, and not necessarily by the process of criminal prosecution.

The House of Lords has thus abdicated its role as the judicial guardian of fugitive offenders in favour of executive action to shield the refugee seeking political asylum. Without the compelling political involvement inherent in a court interpreting the fundamental norms of a written constitution, English judges in the international field have taken cover beneath the umbrella of executive discretion.

If evidence were needed to buttress such an assertion, the House of Lords has provided ample testimony. In *Atkinson* v. *Government of United States* and the twin decision of *Government of Greece* v. *Governor of Brixton Prison and others* the House of Lords, which in other fields has shown itself as a fierce proponent of the precepts of natural justice,[1] was quite content to leave claims to breaches of natural justice by foreign tribunals to the Secretary of State in the exercise of his statutory functions in extradition, even though the ministerial decision to return a fugitve offender might involve relegating fundamental rights to a lower priority than diplomatic considerations. The fact, moreover, that no Home Secretary had ever denied a requisition to a foreign government after an application to the courts had resulted in a committal to await surrender did not make their Lordships hesitate before abdicating their judicial role.[2] Executive discretion was intended as a long-stop behind the judicial wicket-keeper; the courts have, however, promoted the Minister to act immediately behind the stumps.

Even when faced with the return of offenders within the Commonwealth, the House of Lords has been noticeably reticent to don the mantle of protective agent for fugitive offenders. This is so even though the legislation, in contradistinction to the Extradition Act, provides an apparently unfettered judicial discretion. Section 10 of the Fugitive Offenders Act 1881 (now section 8 of the Fugitive Offenders Act 1967 in a more limited but explicit form) permitted refusal to return the offender if the return would be unjust or oppressive. When two Cypriots showed that their return to Cyprus would mean their instant murder by their compatriots for having assisted the British auth-

[1] *Rookes* v. *Barnard* [1964] A.C. 1129; *Wiseman* v. *Borneman* [1971] A.C. 297.
[2] Unprecedently, the Home Secretary did refuse, on 8 December 1969, to return Christos Kotronis to Greece.

orities during the rebellion, the Law Lords declined to intervene.[1] Only Lord Radcliffe, in a wholly persuasive dissent, was sufficiently alive to the Cypriot political situation (he had been earlier the draftsman of an independent constitution for the island) to appreciate the validity of the two fugitives' claim that their lives would be in danger. (Paradoxically it was Lord Radcliffe's speech in *Schtraks* which took the most restrictive view of the courts' function in testing political motive in the context of the Extradition Act.) The Home Secretary, however, came to the rescue and declined to hand over the two Cypriots. That a long-stop was needed says little for the quality of the wicket-keeper, particularly where both fieldsmen had precisely the same statutory part to play.

In the *Kwesi Armah* case,[2] which involved a former Ghanaian Minister, the appellant escaped surrender to his political opponents who had seized power in a coup d'état only on the technical ground that the committing magistrate had applied the wrong test under the 1881 Act for the burden of proof in committing him to prison to await extradition. An alternative ground of appeal that the Ghana Government could and would, under the new law, punish the ex-Minister for his political crimes was deftly avoided, although two Law Lords did indicate that the courts would not entertain undertakings made *ad hoc* by applicant governments that they would not deal with an offender other than for the crime for which extradition was being sought.[3] The Fugitive Offenders Act 1967, in this respect replicating the Extradition Act 1870 for Commonwealth countries, has obviated the need for any future undertakings.

If and when either the House of Lords itself is more willing to shoulder politico-legal problems, or Parliament decides to thrust such problems more unequivocally on to the judges—which it has done in the case of the return of offenders within the Commonwealth[4]—an exciting future opens up. The reputation of the House of Lords internationally is high in terms of sheer judicial quality. It would be immeasurably higher were the Law Lords to face up squarely to the dictates of contemporary society calling, even more stridently, for judicial intervention to safeguard the citizen against executive action. In recent years this role has been performed fairly consistently in domestic administrative law, even if the judges have been somewhat inclined to decide against the necessary trappings of the welfare state.[5] But no such activity is discernible in the international field. A prime role of the final appellate court is to fulfil every role in the judicial process, and not merely to decline to enter into areas where politicans (anything but angels) display little or no fear when treading upon individual human rights.

---

[1] *Arestidou and Zacharia* v. *Government of Cyprus* [1963] A.C. 634.   [2] [1968] A.C. 192.
[3] This view has been substantially retracted in *Keane* v. *Governor of Brixton Prison* [1971] 2 W.L.R. 1243 in the context of the Backing of Warrants (Republic of Ireland) Act 1965; but not in the interpretation of the reciprocal legislation in the Republic of Ireland: *Bourke* v. *Attorney-General & Wymes* (1970) 31st. July, unreported.
[4] See s. 4 (1), Fugitive Offenders Act 1967.   [5] See section (A), *ante*.

XIV

THE HOUSE OF LORDS AND PRIVATE LAW

(a) THE LAW OF 'OBLIGATIONS'

THERE is a time-honoured division in English law between the law of contract and of tort. But both are in essence a species of the law of obligations, and historically both grew out of the concept of individual indebtedness. An obligation in law signifies a legal bond between two persons, whereby one is bound either to pay the other a sum of money or to do, or to refrain from doing, some act for the benefit of that other. Since the legal rights and duties arising from contract and tort are species of the same genus and in practice increasingly overlap within a single disputatious situation, there is little purpose in perpetuating a division, justified in terms of legal history, that seems only to impede a sound and logical development of a law of obligations. For that reason alone we have subsumed the decisions in contract and in tort under a single rubric.

The abiding impression of House of Lords' decisions over the period of our study is how infrequently major issues in this field have come up for decision. (Throughout our study we have been conscious that in all areas (save revenue law) too few appeals come to the House of Lords.) In this area the Law Lords have been starved of work that might have produced clarification of the law. The smallness of the case-load has meant that no consistent or current contribution has been made to the body of jurisprudence in this field.

The result has been, to say the least, unfortunate, if not in one or two instances downright disastrous. In *Boys* v. *Chaplin*,[1] as we have discussed elsewhere, the quintuplicate judgments deepened rather than dispersed the fog surrounding the problems of torts committed abroad. The House of Lords had never been confronted with the problem; and the leading cases, *Phillips* v. *Eyre*[2] and *The Halley*[3] were a hundred years old; *Machado* v. *Fontes*[4] was seventy. All that can be said for their Lordships' attempt to write a *vade mecum* on the subject of international torts is that the speeches disclosed an example of the urge to indulge in generalizations all too apparent whenever the Law Lords are acutely aware that the issue will come up only once in a judicial generation. The result is often to promote confusion by the chasing of too many hares. The inbred judicial approach of never deciding

---

1 [1971] A.C. 250. See p. 284, *ante*.   2 (1870) L.R. 6 Q.B. 1.
3 (1868) L.R. 2 P.C. 193.   4 [1897] 2 Q.B. 231.

more than is necessary to the particular decision is justifiably modified in the light of the uniquely supervisory role of the House of Lords; but sadly it deserts altogether the final appellate judge who realizes that he can never hope to build a clear cut jurisprudential policy from case to case, and has to indulge himself at one fell swoop. All the relevant jurisprudence must be fashioned on a single case, which too often cannot bear the weight of such treatment.

The decision in *Suisse Atlantique Société d'Armament Maritime S.A.* v. *Rotterdamsche Kolen Centrale*[1] must be regarded as a singularly disastrous decision of their Lordships. Until the decision it was generally believed that there was a rule of law according to which no exemption or limitation clause could protect a party in breach of his contract if such breach went to the root of the contract. The difficulty was that there was no authoritative ruling on the question, and the decisions of the Court of Appeal were not easily re- concilable.

If ever a case called for the full sweep of the Lords' supervisory role this was it: in the result it was held that there was no such rule of law, and each case had to be decided on the true construction of the contract. If that alone did not leave the law in confusion, the case is further obfuscated by the finding that the specific exemption clause, which the appellants claimed had been de- stroyed by the respondents' fundamental breach, was not an exemption clause at all, but one included for the benefit of both parties.

Driven to that conclusion, their Lordships might have refrained from in- dulging in will-o'-the-wisp propositions about the concept of fundamental breach which on any view have seriously whittled away its potential applic- ability. But the temptation proved too strong and five separate judgments have served only to leave confusion worse confounded.

Lord Reid clearly denied the existence of any such rule of law:[2] . . . in the earlier cases I do not find any reliance on any rule of law that a party guilty of a breach going to the root of the contract can never rely on clauses excluding his liability', and again disapproving of the observations of Parker L.J. in *Karsales (Harrow) Ltd.* v. *Wallis*:[3]

. . . this is a clear statement of a rule of law. If it is right, it would be irrelevant that on its true construction an exempting clause must be held to apply to the breach in question, and that it is not so wide in its terms that as a matter of construction in its context its applicability must be limited. It must mean that the law does not permit contracting out of common law liability for a fundamental breach.[4]

Lords Hodson and Wilberforce quoted with approval[5] an observation of Atkin L.J. in *The Cap Palos*:[6] 'I am far from saying that a contractor may not make a valid contract that he is not to be liable for any failure to perform his

[1] [1967] 1 A.C. 361: and see note by Kemball F. A. Johnston in 67 *Law Society's Gazette* 721 (November 1970); matched possibly by *Jones* v. *Secretary of State for Social Services* [1972] 1 All E. R. 145.
[2] [1967] 1 A.C. 361, 400B.   [3] [1956] 1 W.L.R. 936.   [4] [1967] 1 A.C. 361, 401D.
[5] Ibid., 410E and 432D.   [6] [1921] P. 458, 471–2.

contract, including even wilful default; but he must use very clear words to express that purpose. . . .'

These observations lead one to conclude that what would otherwise be a fundamental breach may be limited in its effect, or even excluded altogether, by a clause which exactly covers the breach. But there are other observations which make one hesitate in arriving at such a conclusion. Lord Reid himself said in an earlier passage '. . . when the innocent party has elected to treat the breach as a repudiation . . . the whole contract has ceased to exist, including the exclusion clause, and I do not see how that clause can then be used to exclude an action for loss which will be suffered by the innocent party after it has ceased to exist, such as loss of the profit which would have accrued if the contract had run its full term.'[1] Lord Upjohn, to similar effect: '. . . the principle upon which one party to a contract cannot rely on the clauses of exception or limitation of liability inserted for his sole protection is . . . that if there is a fundamental breach accepted by the innocent party the contract is at an end; the guilty party cannot rely on any special terms in the contract.'[2]

These observations are not irreconcilable with Lord Wilberforce's view that 'an act which, apart from the exceptions clause, might be a breach sufficiently serious to justify refusal of further performance, may be reduced in effect, or made not a breach at all, by the terms of the clause.'[3] This would accord with the general trend suggesting that what would otherwise be a fundamental breach may be excluded by an exactly drawn exemption clause. Thus a contract containing such a clause might be broken fundamentally by some breach which the exemption clause was not designed to cover at all. In that case, the exemption clause would cease to exist, along with the rest of the contract. One kind of fundamental breach that is not covered by any kind of exemption clause is the breach of an implied term necessary to 'give the contract that business efficacy which the parties as reasonable men must have intended it to have' and without which it does not have that efficacy.

Explicable and reconcilable as these observations may be, they are hardly the language of legal clarity and certainty. There can be no gainsaying the charge that here the House of Lords failed to perform its vital supervisory function when it had every incentive and opportunity to do so. No court faced to-day with the problem of exemption clauses can find much guidance or comfort in the *Suisse Atlantique* decision.[4]

That much said, it must be readily conceded that there have been one or two seminal decisions on the law of obligations during the period of our study. The decision in *Hedley Byrne & Co. Ltd.* v. *Heller & Partners Ltd.*[5] extended the law of negligence to encompass both liability for negligent misstatements by those holding themselves out as offering an advisory service,

---

[1] Ibid., p. 398.   [2] Ibid., p. 425.   [3] Ibid., p. 431 F.
[4] e.g. *Harbutt's Plasticine Ltd.* v. *Wayne Tank and Pump Co. Ltd.* [1970] 1 Q.B. 447.
[5] [1964] A.C. 465.

and damages for economic loss. The implications of this decision for the commercial and banking community, not to mention professional advisers, have been immense.

If *Hedley Byrne* had left any doubts as to the ambit of the liability for professional negligence, *Rondel* v. *Worsley*[1] confirmed the breadth of the professional duty to take care, even though the decision retrogressively reaffirmed the peculiar immunity of barristers and solicitor-advocates for anything done in the course of advocacy: here surely was a missed opportunity to bring a part of the machinery of justice to terms with twentieth-century reality.

In the same category of importance must come the decision in *Home Office* v. *Dorset Yacht Co.*[2] where the Borstal authorities were held potentially liable for negligence, to the inhabitants living in the neighbourhood of a Borstal, for damage caused by absconding Borstal trainees. The refusal to apply any kind of exemption to government departments or to civil servants from liability for negligent acts has profound implications for the penal system, and by its more general implications is perhaps the most significant development in the English law of obligations in recent times. On a slightly less exalted plane are the decisions in *British Transport Commission* v. *Gourley*[3] (the tax factor in measuring damages), *Hughes* v. *Lord Advocate*[4] (the apotheosis of the foreseeability test in tort liability), *Bridge* v. *Campbell Discount Company*[5] (the death-knell of penalty clauses in hire-purchase contracts), and *Davis Contractors* v. *Fareham U.D.C.*[6] (the last word on the doctrine of frustration of contract). Apart from two areas—the law relating to trade unions and the measure of damages in tort and contract—the rest of the field are stragglers in the jurisprudential stakes. Some fifty appeals from English courts over the seventeen-year period represent an almost derisory proportion of the cases in this area which came before the lower courts, and only a handful of these appeals gave rise to decisions of first-class importance.

Although it is widely propagated that trade unions are above the law, the courts have played a not insignificant part in shaping the role of the unions in the run-up to the Industrial Relations Act. A half-dozen cases involving trade unions occurred in our period.[7] The lack of understanding, if not ill-concealed dislike, of trade unions, which Professor Laski detected[8] in the Lords' decisions in the first third of the century, has been perpetuated in the second. An apparent antipathy towards organized labour is perhaps the last remnant of that economic interpretation of the law, most prevalent during the last century, which sought to protect private property. But this attitude has never been peculiar to the judiciary; nor have all judges been afflicted by it. Just

[1] [1969] 1 A.C. 191.   [2] [1970] A.C. 1004.   [3] [1956] A.C. 185.
[4] [1963] A.C. 837.   [5] [1962] A.C. 600.   [6] [1956] A.C. 696.
[7] *Bonsor* v. *Musicians' Union* [1956] A.C. 104; *Faramus* v. *Film Artistes' Association* [1964] A.C. 925; *Rookes* v. *Barnard* [1964] A.C. 1129; *Stratford & Son* v. *Lindley* [1965] A.C. 269; and *Martin* v. *Scottish T.G.W.U.* [1952] S.C. (H.L.) 1.
[8] 'Justice and the Law', from *Studies in Law and Politics* (1932).

as in the early part of the century, so now the House of Lords seems almost invariably to reverse any Court of Appeal decisions in favour of the trade unions. In one such instance, *Rookes* v. *Barnard*,[1] the decision gave rise to so much disquiet, undermining as it did the spirit of the Trade Disputes Act 1906, that partial statutory repeal was deemed necessary. It is little wonder that the modern trade unionist asks only of the law that he should be left to work out his industrial salvation with his employers without legal interference or intervention—unavailing in the light of the Industrial Relations Act 1971. This is an area in which the House of Lords has singularly failed to distinguish itself, although the well-thought-out pronouncements of Lord Devlin in *Rookes* v. *Barnard* on the principles relevant to the law of damages partially redeem the dismal record.

The law of damages has come up with sufficient frequency for some jurisprudential thread to be woven into the fabric of the law of remedies. In the event, however, the exercise has not been entirely successful. The product of five separate judgments in *Koufos* v. *Czarnikow*,[2] concerned with calculating loss of profit to a charterer, has left confusion in determining the right test for measuring damages. *West and Son* v. *Shephard*[3] definitively established that not too substantial damages should be awarded for loss of amenities of life to 'lame brain' accident victims, technically living but perpetually unconscious: the parsimony of the Law Lords was not replicated by the Australian courts.[4]

Gourley's case,[5] one of only two appeals during our period of study to come before a court of seven,[6] raised more problems than it solved in importing the tax factor into the mathematical calculation of damages. The instant case decided that income tax on the lost earnings of the injured claimant should be taken into account, thus substantially reducing the amount recoverable from the tortfeasor. The House of Lords seemed to have erred in principle in seeking to hold the scales evenly between the unfortunate victim of physical injury and the culprit (often insured) who finds that his victim was a highly skilled or professional man. Income tax is not an element of cost in earning income; it is a disposition, required by law, of a portion of the earned income. A logical extension of the *Gourley* decision is that *all* prospective liabilities should be taken into account, which would involve the courts in impossible actuarial calculations. *Gourley* was an aberration: perhaps someone, possibly even the Law Lords themselves, now freed from the shackles of their own past mistakes, will challenge its correctness in the near future. (It must be remembered —and will be by proponents of abolition of the House of Lords—that until *Gourley* the contrary rule, that tax was irrelevant to the calculation of damages, had been established by the Court of Appeal.)[7]

---

[1] [1964] A.C. 1129.   [2] [1969] 1 A.C. 350.   [3] [1964] A.C. 326.
[4] *Skelton* v. *Collins* (1966) 39 A.L.J.R. 480.   [5] [1956] A.C. 185.
[6] The other was *Ross Smith* v. *Ross Smith* [1963] A.C. 280: see Appendix 6.
[7] *Billingham* v. *Hughes* [1949] 1 K.B. 643.

Personal injury actions bulk large in the total volume of tort litigation: about 80 per cent of all writs issued in the High Court are claims for damages by persons injured on the roads or in factories. The victim of a factory accident has two strings to his bow, an action for common law negligence, or failing that, an action based upon a breach by the employer of a statutory duty imposed either by the Factories Act 1961 (or its forerunner, the Act 1937) or by regulations made for specific industries under the Factories Acts.

The civil liability of the employer who is in breach of a statutory duty (which itself is a criminal offence) has been engrafted on to the statutes solely by judge-made law; the principles enunciated by the courts have built on the statute, but have developed separate from it. Parliament has remained totally silent about any civil remedy co-existing with the employer's criminal responsibility; thus, the courts have been left to their own devices in establishing a new branch of civil wrongs.

This modern creative role for the judges, in which the House of Lords has played a dominant part (12 per cent of all House of Lords civil appeals involve civil claims arising out of breaches of statutory duties) posed an initial question: is an employer his workmen's insurer? Not surprisingly the courts have declined to adopt so radical and absolute a solution. But how and to what extent have the courts modified the apparent absolute liability of employers in breach of statutory duties?

The employer performs his duty through his servants and agents. But by doing so he does not rid himself of his duty. He remains vicariously responsible for any failure by any one of them to carry out the terms of the regulations. Thus every act of an employee may involve the employer in a breach of a statutory duty. If another employee is injured, the clear breach of duty by the employer involves him in civil liability; he has no defence to the action. But what if, as is more common, the injured employee is the sole author of his own misfortune, brought about by his own breach of a statutory duty? Here, the judges have imported morality into the law. As Lord Diplock put it in *Boyle* v. *Kodak Ltd.*,[1] an exegesis on the civil remedies under factory legislation: 'To say "You are liable to me for my own wrongdoing" is neither good morals nor good law.' If, in other words, the employer can show that the only act or default of anyone which causes the accident was the injured workman's own unaided behaviour, then the employer has a good defence. If the workman was only partly to blame, then that may reduce the amount of damages recoverable. This reflects a long-standing view of the judiciary. Lord Atkin put it crisply in 1939 in *Harris* v. *Associated Portland Cement Manufacturers*[2] (a case under the Workmen's Compensation Act 1925): 'The peril which a workman encounters in the course of doing his work by doing it negligently is *not* a peril which he is obliged to encounter; in fact by his contract of service

1 [1969] 1 W.L.R. 661.   2 [1939] A.C. 71, 79.

he is obliged not to encounter it; for it is an implied term that he should work with reasonable care.'

The high-water mark of judicial exoneration of employer-liability came in *McWilliam* v. *Sir William Arrol & Co. Ltd.*[1] In 1962 the House of Lords held that the workman, a steel erector who had fallen to his death as a result of not being strapped to scaffolding by a safety belt, had to establish (or rather his widow did) not only a breach of duty by his employer in not supplying a belt, but also the causal connection between the breach of duty and the workman's death. And if, as was shown in that case, the workman would not have used a safety belt even if his employer had supplied him with it, there was no liability when injury followed on the failure to wear a belt. Moreover, the employer was held not even to be under a duty to exhort a workman (even though known to be a highly experienced one) to wear a belt. An employer discharges his duty by instructing his employees how to avoid obvious dangers and how to apply the regulations in situations where there is no apparent danger.

Thus the notion of fault has been imported judicially into the civil action for breach of statutory duty. If the workman is the sole author of his own wrong, he becomes disentitled to recover damages. No account is taken by the courts of the fact that the workman, whatever folly he may exhibit, is not the owner of the machinery that does the damage; nor that the workman may in fact be obliged to encounter a risk to his life and limb, whatever his contract of service may implicitly say. The morality of negating the employer's absolute liability, whenever the employee is the sole cause of his particular injury, is not at all as clear as Lord Diplock would have us believe. It follows from Lord Diplock's logic that to protect an employee from his own foolish action would also not be good morals; yet it is the essence of welfare legislation that factory employers should do just that.

Factory legislation is designed to cut the accident rate to an absolute minimum. Anything that can help to persuade management into recognizing its social responsibility towards those employed is desirable. Payment of damages to workmen injured through factory conditions that do not comply with the statutory requirements is one method used to induce safety control. Workmen very often need to be protected against their own folly. To relieve employers of liability when workmen are the sole authors of their own wrongful act leading to injury is, in some small measure, to let employers worry less about their workmen. Thus the House of Lords has failed to make the contribution it might in constructing a new civil wrong which statutorily imports no notions of fault liability, but simply establishes an insurance for workmen against breaches of statutory duties, whoever be the authors of those breaches.

For the rest, the House of Lords has been engaged in a variety of problems

[1] [1962] 1 W.L.R. 295; applied by the House of Lords in *Wigley* v. *British Vinegars Ltd.* [1964] A.C. 307.

arising from interpreting the specific provisions in the Factory Acts and the regulations made thereunder. One of the most unreal decisions was *Sparrow* v. *Fairey Aviation Co. Ltd.*[1] where, bound by its own previous decisions, the House of Lords held that the duty to fence dangerous machinery was a duty to fence against contact between the human operator and his machine. The duty, the Law Lords felt bound to declare, did not comprehend fencing against an extension of the workman in the shape of a tool in his hand. They were not even certain whether the operator's clothes were so much a part of their wearer that there is a duty to fence against clothing. Lord MacDermott's trenchant dissent will survive long after the majority's decision is reversed by statute.

Apart from the one or two shining examples we have alluded to, the House of Lords' record in the field of obligations has been, to say the least, undistinguished. The fault has lain partly in the quality and quantity of the case-load: this is not an area where litigiousness, at least at the appellate stage, is rife. Only the personal injury cases, supported by the comparatively long purse of the victim's trade union, are persisted in to the top of the judicial ladder. Commercial men have, in recent times, taken their problems away from the courts to trade association tribunals deciding in private the various commercial issues. So long as arbitrators settle the businessmen's disputes, the law will lie fallow, and development and change (if any) will be left to the legislature rather than to judicial creativity.

Given a biased case-load, it is unlikely that the courts, and in particular the House of Lords with its distilled appellate work, will bring either clarity or certainty to the law of obligations. Instead, a few judicial nibbles will be taken sporadically at the law which will bear only marginally on the commercial community. It must be said that the Court of Appeal has not been noticeably more successful in either of these fields, for much the same reasons. It can claim only to provide a cheaper solution to the litigant, but one which is still not able to compete with the rival (and, incidentally, more costly) attraction of arbitration.

(b) PATENT, TRADE MARK, AND COPYRIGHT APPEALS

Of all the numerous categories of litigation which come before the court of last resort, appeals involving patents, trade marks and copyrights are the most incongruous. They produce the unusual and sometimes bizarre spectacle of five senior judges, well accustomed to the intricacies of legal argument, trying manfully to wrestle with abstruse problems involving questions of mechanical detail, or chemistry, or electrical circuitry, problems which might tax even a trained technologist. Here we find the House of Lords acting largely, if not exclusively, as a tribunal of mixed fact and law, far removed

[1] [1964] A.C. 1019.

from its accustomed task of statutory interpretation or the enunciation of principles of the common law.

Here too we frequently find that the ordinary criterion of 'public import-ance' employed in considering applications for leave to appeal is interpreted in terms of *commercial* importance and pecuniary magnitude. Perhaps in an age dominated by an obsession both with technological progress and with in-ternational commerce, this shift of emphasis is inevitable: who is to say that public importance does not embrace the economic well-being of a mighty industrial enterprise whose commercial eggs are contained within the basket of a single patent or group of patents? And sometimes the astronomical sum of money involved in these cases might make a real impact on the country's trading balance.

The immensity of the sums at stake is reflected in the size of the bills of costs in these actions: as we have seen in Chapter XI on Time and Money, patent cases are the most expensive category of appeal heard by the Lords. Apart from the fact that complex technical arguments take up many days in court, the cost of preparing these cases, in a form which is digestible by the judges, is often astronomical. Furthermore, a company which becomes involved in a full-scale patent action often has to redeploy senior research scientists to help with the technicalities of the case: this item is not included in bills submitted for taxation.

The law does not easily move with the times: most of the work of lawyers is concerned with matters which, in form at least, have changed little over the centuries: technical advance, however, waits for no man, least of all for lawyers. And the law relating to patents, copyrights, and trade marks, founded upon an amorphous concatenation of statute, commercial conven-tion, and technological principle, has had to adapt itself to these changes. Most lawyers regard this area of law with a suspicion borne of a fear of the unknown and perhaps even with an element of contempt for a field which they suspect contains precious little law and a great deal of fact.[1] This situation breeds experts and specialists in the field of patent law; the 'patent bar' and the 'patent judge'[2] are a breed apart from the mainstream of the legal profession,

---

[1] It is true that patent law does involve a great deal of fact; it is not true that few appeals raise issues of legal principle. On the contrary, there is perhaps as much 'lawyers' law' in patent law as in other branches of the law, but this is considerably obscured by the overlay of difficult facts. Few patent cases are reported outside the specialist Reports of Patent Cases probably because the legal principles contained in the cases are generally not of wider application. Of the ten patent appeals during our period of study, eight were reported only in the Patents reports. *Benmax* earned a place in Appeal Cases presumably because it raised important issues as to the role of appellate courts. The only purely patent case to be generally reported—*Amp*—was consigned to vol. 1 of the Weekly Law Reports.

[2] Given that a mastery of patent law is assisted by a measure of technical expertise outside the field of law, it is interesting to reflect on the educational backgrounds of the Lords of Appeal in Ordinary. Of the fifty-eight Law Lords (1876–1969) whose degree subjects are known, forty-eight read subjects exclusively in the Arts, the Humanities, or in Law or Jurisprudence. Four have been mathematicians, and three more read mathematics as part

even in an era where a high degree of specialization has become evident in most other areas of jurisprudence.

The work of the House of Lords in this field has not been large, though it could hardly be termed negligible. Between 1952 and 1968 the House heard ten appeals involving patents and a further eight where a patent element was incidental to the main issues raised. There were four trade mark appeals, another appeal involving copyright (this being an area in which contested litigation is very rare) and one involving passing-off. Thus, and counting four cross-appeals, there were twenty-eight appeals in this area of law, amounting to 8 per cent of the total number of English civil appeals heard by the House during the period.

There has in recent years been a slight increase in the number of these cases coming before the House of Lords, though this may simply reflect a general upward trend in litigation in this field.

The ten fully-fledged patent appeals involved a wide variety of subject-matter ranging from ball-point pens to hay-rakes. In only two of these cases was leave given by the Appeal Committee: one of these is the first case on our list, *Benmax* v. *The Austin Motor Company*.[1]

Apart from the substantive question of 'prior use' and 'obviousness', on which their Lordships merely echoed the arguments in the Court of Appeal, the important issue raised was whether the trial judge's finding of 'obviousness' was one of fact which could not be the subject of interference by appellate courts. Their Lordships (led by Lord Simonds) rejected this contention, holding that the question was a matter of the inference to be drawn from primary facts. Certainly the case did not make any impact in the field of patent law, though it is cited whenever the extent of an appellate court's power of reviewing findings of fact is called into question.

The next case, *Martin & Biro Swan* v. *H. Millwood Ltd.*[2] was a different matter, raising complex issues relating to claims that an invention embodies original combinations of previously patented features. Although the judgment of Lord Simonds gives useful general guidance on the approach to combination claims, the House did not carry the case much further than did the judgment of the Court of Appeal.

Multiform Display v. *Whitmorley Display*[3] is more remarkable for its curious history than for any unusual issues of patent law. It originally took the form of an attempt to have the defendants committed for contempt of court, they having started to market a modified version of their product after

---

of their degree. Only three Law Lords, all post-war, have serious claims to a scientific background. Lord Somervell read Maths (Moderations) and Chemistry (Finals) and was a double first; Lord Diplock took a degree—a second class—in Chemistry; and the late Lord Upjohn (the 'patent king' in the Lords in recent years) gained a double first, in Part I of the Mechanical Sciences Tripos and in Part II of the Law Tripos and also 'pupilled' in patent chambers. See Chapter VIII.

[1] [1955] A.C. 370.   [2] [1956] R.P.C. 125.   [3] [1957] R.P.C. 260.

submitting to judgment (on an amended specification) in an earlier action for infringement. In the result the House of Lords reversed the Court of Appeal purely on the issue of construction, but their Lordships sidestepped the question of the proper approach to be adopted in construing an amended specification and the extent to which the unamended version should be taken into account.

Amp Incorporated v. *Hellerman*[1] raised the important issue whether the addition of a further integer into a claim could be disclaimer within the meaning of s. 31 (1) of the Patents Act 1949, and whether such an amendment added matter not in substance disclosed in the original specification, so that the courts were empowered to allow an amendment. In this case the House held (Lords Simonds and Devlin dissenting) that the Court of Appeal had wrongly rejected the contentions of the patentee, because the test they had applied (as to the substance of the invention), was the wrong one under the 1949 Act. The decision widened the scope of allowable amendments under the Patents Act—arguably, it even went too far in this respect.

C. Van Der Lely v. *Bamfords Ltd.*[2] is one of the longest cases heard by the House of Lords during our period[3] it lasted nineteen days (nearly five full weeks of hearing). It raised the important issues of anticipation by photograph and of the doctrine of 'pith and marrow'. Their Lordships greatly confined the effect of the latter doctrine (though Lord Reid would have applied it) placing much more emphasis upon a strict interpretation of the wording of claims. A much greater onus is now placed upon patentees to draft their claims sufficiently widely to anticipate all eventualities: the courts will no longer rescue them from their own lack of prescience or of precision. On the anticipation point, the courts were unanimous in holding that photographs could not be the subject of documentary construction by the court: they must be interpreted in terms of the perceptions and probable inferences of a man skilled in the subject concerned.

Henriksen v. *Tallon Ltd.*[4] was another long case (eight days) arising this time out of an action for infringement of a patent for ball-point pens. The central issue was the interpretation of a patent which was 'absurd', in the sense that one of the alternative devices described would not work if applied to one of the two types of pen covered by the patent. The House of Lords (Lord Guest dissenting) reversed the Court of Appeal, holding (in effect) that the patent required the skilled addressee to interpret the patent so as to employ the alternative device which *would* work. This functional approach

---

[1] [1962] 1 W.L.R. 241.   [2] [1963] R.P.C. 61.

[3] Even more remarkable for its length was *Carl-Zeiss Stiftung* v. *Rayner & Keeler Ltd.* (*et è contra*) [1967] A.C. 853, an extraordinary interlocutory appeal in a passing-off action on the question of issue estoppel in private international law, which involved a twenty-six-day hearing before the House. This case is discussed in the section on international law. (See Chapter XIII above.)

[4] [1965] R.P.C. 434.

appeals to one's common sense, though it does not simplify the task of a practitioner advising a patentee as to the validity of his claim. It marks a distinct change of attitude to construction of patent claims from the more rigid 'literal interpretation' outlook prevailing in the pre-war and immediate post-war years.

The next case, *Deere & Co.* v. *Harrison McGregor & Guest*,[1] raised nothing more than a pure issue of patent construction; it is difficult to believe that the Court of Appeal would have granted leave had not one of its members dissented. The House of Lords unanimously upheld the rejection of an action for infringement holding that the patentees could have drafted their claim to cover the alleged infringement but had not done so.

Ransburg & Co. v. *Aerostyle Ltd.*[2] was also largely a matter of patent construction, though on this occasion their Lordships unanimously reversed the Court of Appeal and adopted a markedly pro-patentee approach in holding that a patent (for the coating of materials with liquid by an electrostatic process) was both valid and infringed.

In many respects the next case, *Rodi & Weinenberger* v. *Henry Showell*[3] provides the most interesting insight into the legal philosophy underlying patent cases. The case concerned the alleged infringement of a patent, the subject of which was an expanding watch bracelet. The law relating to 'mechanical equivalents' came under review and the old doctrine of 'pith and marrow' (already confined by the House of Lords in *Van Der Lely*) reared its head yet again. In the result the House of Lords upheld the Court of Appeal in rejecting the claim for infringement, but there was a division of opinion. The majority, led by Lord Upjohn, adopted a strictly constructional approach, upholding the tradition (particularly marked before the last war) that the public must be protected from monopoly and the patentee held to the strict terms of his claim so that everyone knows where he stands. Lords Reid and Pearce held to the pro-patentee spirit which had been so much in evidence in *Van Der Lely*: the essence of this philosophy is a desire to see that inadequate foresight by the draftsman of the claims does not prevent an inventor from reaping the just fruits of his invention. Would a differently constituted House of Lords have produced a different result? This is always difficult to prove. It is interesting to note that both the judges who supported Lord Upjohn, Lord Morris of Borth-y-Gest and Hodson, are common lawyers, as is Lord Pearce who supported Lord Reid.

The final case in this list, *Rado* v. *John Tye & Co.*,[4] involved only a narrow issue of obviousness, though technically the case was quite involved. The only judgment was delivered by Lord Upjohn who agreed with the Court of Appeal in upholding the defendants' plea of obviousness.

What can we learn from these cases? In all but two of the appeals the

1 [1965] R.P.C. 217.   2 [1968] R.P.C. 287.
3 [1969] R.P.C. 367.   4 [1968] F.S.R. 563.

House of Lords followed a legal course similar to that adopted by the Court of Appeal: perhaps in *Amp* v. *Hellerman* the pro-patentee approach of the House contrasts favourably with the more rigid interpretation of the Court of Appeal, while in *Henriksen* v. *Tallon* their interpretation was more sensible than that of the court *a quo*. Certainly six of the cases, *Benmax, Martin, Amp, Van Der Lely, Henriksen*, and *Rodi*, raised issues of law which justified a hearing by the final tribunal. It is interesting to reflect that these cases occupied an average of eight hearing days apiece, as compared with the overall average of about four days for English civil appeals. This reflects the sheer technical complexity of the cases, which often submerges their Lordships in a mass of paper and a welter of unfamiliar jargon.

It will be noted, however, that of the ten patent cases heard by the Lords nine involved comparatively simple mechanical issues: *Ransburg* is the solitary exception. This reflects the distribution of cases arising at first instance. The electronics, computer, and chemical industries whose work is usually of a very high order of technical complexity have steered clear of litigation, though they are not averse to disputing issues at the level of the Patents Office. Very recently, however, there has been a certain amount of litigation in the chemical and in the electronics fields, so perhaps their Lordships will soon be confronted by some really baffling problems.

The judicial philosophy of the House, the conflict between the desire to confine a monopoly and the desire to give the patentee the fruits of his endeavour, has already been discussed in the context of *Rodi*. By and large, Lord Reid (as he demonstrated in his leading judgments in *Martin* and *Van Der Lely* and by his dissent in *Rodi*) has led the pro-patentee faction. While Lord Simonds, and, more recently, Lord Upjohn (in *Rodi*) has followed the more orthodox approach of strict construction. Certainly, in recent years, Lord Upjohn was distinctively the 'patent judge', but his recent death will leave matters in the hands of Lord Diplock (himself a graduate in chemistry) who, when in the Court of Appeal, displayed a marked tendency to find *against* the patentee.

Mention has already been made of the eight appeals where the patent element was a secondary feature of the litigation: in other words, the action did not take the conventional form of an action for infringement (i.e. in tort) met by the defence of invalidity. Rather than discuss these cases in detail, we list them in tabular form, mentioning the principal points of interest.

These cases are more in character with the 'conventional' work of the courts, involving statutory or documentary construction; hence all but two of the eight have been reported in Appeal Cases or in vol. 1 of the Weekly Law Reports. (See table on pp. 304–5.)

There were four[1] trade mark appeals during our period of study, one of

---

[1] Excluding *Carl Zeiss*, p. 301, n. 3 above.

Case	Reported	Subject-Matter	Leading Speech	Dissents	Effect on C.A.	Remarks
Parke Davis & Co. v. Comptroller General of Patents	[1954] A.C. 321	Grant of licence within the years of grant of patent—whether subject to international convention prohibiting licence within three years. Compulsory licence—action for prohibition	Lord Cohen	None	Unanimously affirmed	Fairly small case—slight general importance
Sterling Engineering Co. v. Patchett	(1955) 72 R.P.C. 50	Apportionment of royalties as between employer and employee—inventor—s. 5. 56(2) of Patents Act 1949	Lord Simonds	None	Unanimously reversed	Important case—very narrow, legalistic construction by the H.L.
Tool Metal Manufacturing Co. v. Tungsten Electric Co.	[1955] 1 W.L.R. 761	Compensation clause — whether (a) A penalty; (b) in restraint of trade or (c) contrary to s. 38 of Patents & Designs Act 1907—equitable estoppel	Lord Reid	None	Unanimously reversed	Important, curb on *High Trees* doctrine narrowed the effect of s. 38, Patents & Designs Act 1907
Fomento (Sterling Area) Ltd. v. Selsdon Fountain Pen Co.	[1958] 1 W.L.R. 45	Construction of Patent Licence—duty of licencees to inform patentees about sales apart from sales of admittedly patented goods—third party agreement	Lords Simonds and Morton	See next column	Reversed on 'information' issue, Lords Simonds and Tucker dissenting	Little general importance—H.L. decision a deterrent to dishonest licensees

Case	Reported	Subject-Matter	Leading Speech	Dissents	Effect on C.A.	Remarks
Baldwin & Francis v. Patents Appeal Tribunal	[1959] A.C. 663	Certiorari—jurisdiction of courts to reverse decision of P.A.T. for error on the face where the decisions were based upon technical constructions—evidence admissible by courts	None (Lord Morton presided)	None, though Lord Denning's reasoning quite different	Affirmed on different grounds	Great importance in administrative law generally—H.L. decision a great improvement on C.A.—Lord Denning's approach has proved more durable
Pfizer Corporation v. Ministry of Health	[1965] A.C. 512	Patents Act 1949, s. 46—'for the services of the crown' — Drugs supplied to N.H.S. — 'sale' to out-patients in N.H.S. hospitals	None (Lord Reid presided)	Lords Wilberforce and Pearce	Affirmed on substantially same grounds	Considerable importance in administrative law in defining crown status
Churchill Gear Machines v. Broach & Machine Co.	[1967] 1 W.L.R. 384	Construction of licensing agreement — obligation to disclose 'improvements', — principles of interpretation —position after expiry of agreement	Lord Upjohn (only speech)	None	Affirmed. Different grounds on 'improvement' point	Slight general importance though other agreements might be affected
Fluflon Ltd. v. William Frost & Sons Ltd.	[1968] R.P.C. 508	Construction of licence agreement — 'the invention' —whether includes the subject of three as yet undisclosed patent applications	Lord Pearson	None	Unanimously affirmed	Very slight importance —though other agreements involved

which took the form of a passing off action. In addition, there was one passing-off appeal and one copyright case.

In *Yorkshire Copper Works Ltd.* v. *Registrar of Trade Marks*[1] the issue at stake was the meaning of the phrase, 'inherently adapted to distinguish', in the 1938 Trade Marks Act. Two cases (one from the Court of Appeal, one from the House of Lords) both decided before the passing of the Act, were under review. The House of Lords unanimously upheld the Registrar's refusal to accept the registration and the case reflects the marked deference which judges, inexperienced in this field, accord to the rulings of the Registrar.

Hovis Ltd. v. *Spillers Ltd.*[2] was decided in the same year as the *Yorkshire Copper Works* appeal. The issue was whether the registration of a trade-mark for one type of commodity (flour) extended to a related commodity (bread). In the result the House unanimously endorsed the judgments of the Court of Appeal in holding that trade marks rights extend only to the goods in respect of which the mark is registered: a commercially sensible decision.

The importance of the next appeal, *Electrix Ltd.* v. *Electrolux Ltd.*,[3] depended, as was the case with *Hovis* v. *Spillers*, on whether the House of Lords was going to reverse the law established by the lower courts: in the result it did not, although the appeal was dismissed by only 3:2. The issue was the inherent registrability of the word 'Electrix', bearing in mind its phonetic resemblance to the word 'Electrics'. The majority of their Lordships (led by Lord Simonds) contented themselves with endorsing the decisions of the Court of Appeal, which held (sensibly enough) that the phonetic equivalent of an unregistrable word is itself not registrable.

Parker Knoll v. *Knoll International*[4] raised the important issue of whether it is a valid defence to a claim for passing-off that you merely use your own name honestly and with no intention to deceive. The House of Lords on the whole did not answer the question to anyone's satisfaction: indeed the ratio is very difficult to extract from the five separate judgments. The Court of Appeal judgments, which found majority support in the House of Lords on all the issues raised, are much clearer than those of the Law Lords. (Indeed, the uncertainty ultimately resulted in contempt actions for breaches of the injunctions granted by the Court of Appeal: and the defendants lost, after a great deal of further argument.) We come now to the solitary passing-off action, *T. Oertli* v. *E. J. Bowman*.[5]

This case involved the question of the extent to which a defendant's conduct in continuing to sell branded goods after the expiry of a licence is valid in passing-off actions. Since the plaintiff (a foreign company) did not make a registered users' agreement with the defendant to protect its trade mark, it had to prove its reputation in this country. This it failed to do, and the House of Lords unequivocally affirmed the Court of Appeal in rejecting the action: in

[1] (1954) 71 R.P.C. 150.   [2] (1954) 71 R.P.C. 234.   [3] [1959] R.P.C. 283.
[4] [1962] R.P.C. 265.   [5] [1959] R.P.C. 1.

doing so the Law Lords reaffirmed the existing law of passing-off and refused to widen it by introducing notions of equity: a salutary warning to foreign traders, but there is little legal novelty in the decision itself.

So we come finally to the one and only copyright appeal in the House of Lords, *Ladbroke Ltd.* v. *William Hill Ltd.*[1] Judges are not notably enamoured of the laws of chance,[2] but here their Lordships were confronted with an issue of copyright in fixed odds football coupons. The House of Lords supported the majority of the Court of Appeal in sustaining the plaintiffs' contention that a copyright did exist, and that the coupon should be examined as a whole, and not merely as a collection of separate items. The case was important since it clarified the test to be applied to original compilations of material: certainly it gave a unique insight into an area of law into which their Lordships are seldom asked to venture.

The cases in this field of law occupy a considerable proportion of the sitting days of the House of Lords. Altogether the twenty-four appeals (and four cross-appeals) on our list occupied 127 sitting days: by comparison, during 1968 the House sat only for a total of 125 days to dispose of a whole year's business. It seems rather odd that their Lordships should be called upon to deal with matters of this kind; it is not as if they were of a particularly high order of legal intricacy, or that their Lordships are particularly well-equipped to solve technological conundra. Usually there has been very little difference between the reasoning of their Lordships and that of the Lords Justices, and honours seem to be fairly even when we come to compare the relative merits of the performances of the two courts.

We feel certainly that issues of pure technical construction, such as *Deere*, are not fit subjects for the final tribunal. If blame is attributable for sending cases to the Lords, it is the Court of Appeal which has granted leave in most of these cases. On the whole the trade-mark cases, besides being fewer in number and shorter in duration, have involved their Lordships in the more familiar exercise of construing statutes and non-technological legal documents.

(c) FAMILY LAW

No branch of law has in recent years asked so much of the law reformer than that relating to the family. In an age when the basic social unit has been both cosseted by a myriad of social security provisions and socially buffeted by the impact of a modern industrial state, the demands on the law have been correspondingly great. Parliament has been the prime responsive agent to this demand; but the courts are beginning both to interpret the growing statutory law and to develop the hitherto undeclared common law rules.

[1] [1964] 1 W.L.R. 273.
[2] Though their experience of the punter's art has no doubt been widened by the recent spate of betting and gaming appeals from the Divisional Court.

Much of the law's hesitancy about intruding into the Englishman's castle has sprung from the over-simplified but deeply entrenched view that family responsibilities are not intended to create legal obligations: that family relations are generally none of the law's business. If the law felt obliged to express itself only where family quarrels were irresoluble at the domestic hearth, the increasing resort to the courts by fractious families over a range of problems, both personal and proprietorial, has forced the judges into grasping the nettle of domestic disputes. Few family problems now lie totally outside the purview of the law.

English law had never formally accorded family relationships the dignity of a separate rubric within the legal system; it is indeed only in the most recent of statutory changes that the word 'family' has appeared in the title to an Act of Parliament;[1] and textbooks on 'Family Law' are of very recent origin. Not surprisingly, in those areas where the law was forced into principles governing the personal and proprietorial rights of individuals as members of a family, rules have developed higgledy-piggledy: such principles have originated from disparate sources of the law, mainly the law of property, and the decisions of the courts bear eloquent testimony to the incoherent nature of these principles when applied to unaccustomed fields. Gradually, however, order is being produced out of chaos, thanks mainly to the House of Lords.

Apart from an early post-war aberration when, irrationally, a wife was held not entitled to sue for the impairment of the matrimonial consortium as a result of a serious factory accident to her husband,[2] their Lordships have both tidied up family law and pointed it in the direction of modern rationality. The outstanding decision, *National Provincial Bank Ltd.* v. *Hastings Car Mart Ltd.*,[3] may not be readily appreciated in that light; but if its immediate effect was to negative a valuable right acquired by potentially homeless wives and their dependent children, its devastating impact on the plight of deserted wives prompted, if not actually forced, legislation[4] providing a remedy of a kind which the courts over two decades had proved powerless to grant.

Ever since the decision in 1952 in *Bendall* v. *McWhirter*,[5] the Court of Appeal, under the forceful leadership of Lord Denning, had been hammering out the doctrine of the deserted wife's equity, a right to occupy the matrimonial home so long as she remained the houseowner's wife. As against her husband, who might wish to gain the sole occupancy of the family home, the wife found a ready proponent of her cause in the courts. But what of the case where the husband parted with his property to a mortgagee, how did the wife fare when the new owner sought vacant possession?

The situation which gave rise to the *Hastings Car Mart* case was a common

[1] Family Law Reform Act 1969. There is now a 'Family Division' of the High Court.
[2] *Best* v. *Samuel Fox & Co. Ltd.* [1952] A.C. 716; see (1961) 24 M.L.R. 103 ff, and *Spaight* v. *Dundan* (1962) 96 I.L.T.R. 69, where the Supreme Court of Ireland followed the House of Lords; cf. *Tookey* v. *Hollier* (1955) 92 C.L.R. 618 in the High Court of Australia.
[3] [1965] A.C. 1175.   [4] Matrimonial Homes Act 1967.   [5] [1952] 2 Q.B. 466.

example. A husband deserted his wife, leaving her and their children in the matrimonial home. He then conveyed the house to a company in which he had a controlling interest and which in turn charged the property to the National Provincial Bank to secure a loan. The loan was not repaid, and the bank as mortgagee claimed possession of the house. The Law Lords, in reversing the decision of the Court of Appeal, unanimously rejected the wife's claim to remain in the house; they rejected the suggestion that, unless the purchaser from the husband made inquiries about the marital status of the husband and his wife's occupancy of the house, the wife had a right to stay on. It would be intolerable if a prospective purchaser of land had to discover precisely those rights existing in the land which were of such a highly personal nature, and which were under the existing law not registrable with the Land Registry.

If, by the Lords' decision, equity had now deserted the wives,[1] the legislature was pressed into providing what the courts could not do, namely, establishing a system of registration whereby a purchaser would be bound by the wife's occupancy only if her claim was to be found in the Land Registry. The Matrimonial Homes Act 1967 was the result of the work of the Law Commission, which could not delay in recommending reform to remedy the precarious plight of deserted wives. Thus an aspect of family law was speedily rectified after fifteen years of a confused and confusing crop of case law from the Court of Appeal, which gave, at best, only partial and uncertain relief to deserted wives.

Having dealt with the spouses' rights over the matrimonial home against third parties, the Law Lords were soon pitchforked into resolving the problem of house ownership as between husband and wife. Section 17, Married Woman's Property Act 1882 provides that 'in any question between husband and wife as to the title to or possession of property, either party . . . may apply by summons or otherwise in a summary way to any judge . . . and the judge . . . may make such order with respect to the property in dispute . . . as he thinks fit.' Did this provision mean that the matrimonial home bought by a husband and conveyed into his name could be adjudicated as jointly owned by himself and his wife; or did the section merely provide a procedure for determining the strict legal rights of the spouses? If one spouse contributed directly to the purchase of the matrimonial home, then to the extent of that contribution that spouse is entitled to a share in the house and to an equal proportion in the proceeds of sale, if and when the marriage breaks up. But what if, as is more common, one spouse's contribution is not a directly financial one? In *Appleton* v. *Appleton*[2] the husband, a wood carver, had con-

---

1 It is interesting to observe that, exceptionally, the House of Lords was in this case composed of three Chancery lawyers, Lords Cohen, Upjohn and Wilberforce. Two of these three Law Lords referred pointedly to the recommendations of the Royal Commission on Marriage and Divorce (1956) Cmd. 9678 in this regard.

2 [1965] 1 W.L.R. 25; see similarly *Jansen* v. *Jansen* [1965] P. 478.

siderably enhanced the value of a cottage belonging to his wife by effecting extensive renovations; the Court of Appeal, once again propelled by Lord Denning into making new law, held that on a sale of the cottage the husband was entitled to a share in the proceeds proportionate to the amount of the increased value due to the work and materials he supplied. Subsequently, on consecutive days, two divisions of the Court of Appeal—Lord Justice Danckwerts was the only member common to both courts—found themselves saddled with the binding precedent of *Appleton*'s case. In *Pettitt* v. *Pettitt*[1] the husband put his hand to making considerable improvements to a cottage which was sold for a handsome profit with which a new cottage was bought; reluctantly, the Court held he was entitled to participate in the proceeds of sale of the second cottage, even though it was owned solely by his wife. In *Button* v. *Button*,[2] however, *Appleton* was deftly side-stepped, since in that case the work done by the wife was found to have been performed in the ordinary course of wifely duties—decorating, painting and gardening—and was not the sort of work for which even undomesticated spouses would have employed outside contractors.

The real test of whether a spouse can claim a financial stake in the matrimonial home, which has been bought exclusively with the other spouse's money, simply on the ground that work has been done to sustain the roof over the family, had come before the Court of Appeal in *Gissing* v. *Gissing*.[3] There, the wife who had worked most of her married life paid for her own and her son's clothing and for some of the furniture and equipment, and, of course, she did all the housekeeping. She made no contribution directly to the purchase of a house conveyed to her husband neither did she contribute to any of the mortgage repayments. The Court of Appeal, by a majority, held that the wife was entitled to half the proceeds of its sale. Lord Justice Edmund Davies's trenchant dissent sounded the death knell of yet another equitable doctrine, invented (rather than discovered) by Lord Denning, and the appeal was unanimously allowed by the House of Lords.[4] Indeed an observation that fell from Lord Upjohn in *National Provincial Bank Ltd.* v. *Hastings Car Mart Ltd.*[5] that *Appleton* was wrongly decided was a clear warning that the House of Lords would once again sweep away a line of decisions which, while well-motivated, tried to pour a drop of justice into a rigid legal rule that only ownership or contractual rights (express or implied by specific conduct) could give proprietorial rights in the matrimonial home. In *Pettitt* v. *Pettitt*,[6] when it came to the House of Lords in 1969, their Lordships duly and predictably swept away another wives' equity, by saying that s. 17 of the Married Woman's Property Act 1882 gave the courts no power to vary agreed or established titles to property. Once ownership is established by the evidence, and there is no agreement between the spouses to vary the original rights of the spouses, the

[1] [1968] 1 W.L.R. 443.   [2] [1968] 1 W.L.R. 457.   [3] [1969] 1 W.L.R. 525 and 1208.
[4] [1971] A.C. 886.   [5] [1965] A.C. 1175, 1236.   [6] [1970] A.C. 777.

Court cannot give the spouse without rights in the property an interest in the proceeds of sale, merely because it thinks that in the light of subsequent events the original agreement was unfair.

Here again only the legislature could intervene to lay down specific rules about the entitlement of marriage partners to sharing their matrimonial property. The House of Lords' decision was almost anticipated by the Law Commission, which produced its proposals for a reform of matrimonial property. The Matrimonial Proceedings and Property Act 1970 was the result. Section 37 provides that where one spouse's contribution is substantial it shall, subject to any agreement to the contrary, confer a beneficial interest on that spouse. It the Lords' decision in *Pettitt* was less momentous, and hence less disastrous, to married women than the *Hastings Car Mart* decision, it did at least produce a valuable catalyst in a significant piece of statutory family law reform.

The House of Lords' intrusion into the law relating to the ownership and occupation of the matrimonial home has been both jurisprudentially and socially significant. By contrast, its excursion into the field of divorce law may have set the jurists by the ears; but it has made little or no social impact on the ability of spouses to obtain their matrimonial relief. The twin cases of *Gollins* v. *Gollins*[1] and *Williams* v. *Williams*[2] consigned a morass of case law on what is cruelty to the legal history museum. In *Gollins* the majority opinions[3] disposed of the idea that cruelty could exist at law only if the errant spouse aimed his cruel behaviour at his or her spouse: so long as it was proved that a normally healthy spouse had been reduced to a state of ill-health by the inexcusable conduct of the other spouse, that was cruelty, even though, while he knew the damage he was causing, he neither wished nor intended to injure his wife, but was oblivious to the consequences.

Gollins will be memorable to divorce law practitioners; its significance to a wider audience will lie in its being the first salvo at the unreasoning doctrine of the reasonable man, who is said always to be presumed to intend the natural consequences of his acts (cf. *D.P.P.* v. *Smith*, discussed in Chapter XIII, *ante*). 'If I say I intend to reach the green, people will believe me, although we all know that the odds are ten to one against my succeeding; and no one but a lawyer would say that I must be presumed to have intended to put my ball in the bunker because that was the natural and probable result of my shot.' That graphic and charming golfing analogy from Lord Reid may eventually force lawyers to emulate the economist who abandoned, on the ground of its doubtful utility, the concept of 'economic man'. Half a century of Freud and the work of social and clinical psychologists over the last quarter of a century

---

1 [1969] A.C. 644.
2 [1964] A.C. 698. In both these cases each party was legally-aided, a comparatively rare phenomenon in the House of Lords.
3 Lord Morris of Borth-y-Gest and Lord Hodson dissented.

have cast serious doubts on the reality of the eminently rational man who travels daily on the Clapham omnibus, blissfully oblivious to the exalted status accorded to him by lawyers. Lord Reid's pronouncement in *Gollins* has effectively destroyed one of the myths that supported the continued use of the reasonable man as a viable concept for judging human behaviour.

Williams v. *Williams* carried the objective test of cruelty in *Gollins* to its logical conclusion. Proof of a spouse's insanity, and hence an inability to form an intention to harm, was held to be no answer to a charge of cruelty. The sole question is: has the spouse treated the other with cruelty? Cruelty connotes acts painful to the recipient of such behaviour; it does not imply that the doer is conscious of the moral wrong of his acts (otherwise such phrases as the 'cruel sea' or a 'cruel fate' would be meaningless).[1] Objectivity in divorce law was thus triumphantly proclaimed. The concept of cruelty has now been swallowed up in the provisions of the Divorce Reform Act 1969.

Gollins and *Williams* had presented the House of Lords with a golden opportunity for a jurisprudential tidying-up operation which was avidly seized. Other divorce cases before their Lordships, however, served up rather mundane problems. In *Godfrey* v. *Godfrey*[2] the old legal jingle 'once connivance always connivance' was given the supreme judicial coup de grâce. (How does a jealous man behave but by issuing a challenge to his wife?) Their Lordships decided that, if the spouses had become truly reconciled, a previous connivance to a matrimonial offence became spent, and the previously connived adultery could not be revived to found a divorce petition. Equally, a lapse of time or a lack of causal connection between the connivance and the adultery could terminate connivance. Connivance gave way to condonation in *Blyth* v. *Blyth*,[3] where the point at issue was purely evidential; it was held to be unnecessary for a party to show an absence of any condoning of adultery according to the standard of proof in a criminal case, i.e. beyond reasonable doubt. The fact that two Law Lords dissented hardly elevated the legal dispute above the mundane.

The other three domestic divorce cases to come before their Lordships all came from Scotland. None was jurisprudentially earth-shattering. Two of them, *Jamieson* v. *Jamieson*[4] and *King* v. *King*,[5] concerned aspects of the law of cruelty; both came to the House of Lords as of right, because in each, one judge had dissented in the Court of Session. Both cases stated the obvious, that the conduct to be cruel must be grave and weighty. Nagging in *King*, if persistent enough and damaging to health, could suffice, and the question is whether this particular conduct by this man to this woman, or vice versa, was cruel. *Duchess of Argyll* v. *Duke of Argyll*,[6] a third Scottish appeal, calls for no comment save that the mere notoriety of the parties, it appears, sufficed to

---

[1] See Donovan L.J. in the Court of Appeal [1962] 3 W.L.R. 977, 993.
[2] [1965] A.C. 444.   [3] [1966] A.C. 643.   [4] [1952] A.C. 525.
[5] [1953] A.C. 124.   [6] 1962 S.C. (H.L.) 88.

carry their matrimonial bickering through the gamut of courts to the final appeal tribunal. (The appeal lay as of right; hence there was no procedural impediment to bringing it.)

Family law is one of the notable areas where the legislature had until recently injected few, if any, rules relating to international problems. The conflict of laws is almost the last remaining branch of law where the common law functions unhampered or unaided by statute; the judges are thus free to hammer out rules which reflect unadulterated judicial law-making. *Indyka* v. *Indyka*[1] would have brought about ample recognition in English courts of divorce decrees granted abroad had the legislature not promptly stepped in. Section 3, Recognition of Divorces and Legal Separations Act 1971 provides for wide grounds of recognition such as to disperse with the need for the rule in *Indyka*. In laying down a liberal rule for the recognition of foreign decrees, their Lordships did not shrink from their law-making role. Lord Reid put it boldly: 'obviously we cannot revise an Act of Parliament: the most we can do is to suggest matters which might be borne in mind when an amending Bill is being drafted and passed. But Parliament has rarely intervened in the matter of recognition of foreign matrimonial decrees. The existing law is judge-made [referring to *Travers* v. *Holley*[2] and cases exemplifying that decision] and I see no reason why that process should stop.'

Travers v. *Holley* had said that where the English legislature had provided, as a jurisdictional basis for granting decrees of divorce, that a wife's residence for three years in England immediately prior to her divorce sufficed as a ground for jurisdiction, a divorce decree based on a similar jurisdictional rule of a foreign court would be recognized. *Indyka* v. *Indyka* went much further by laying down that a real and substantial connection between the petitioner in the foreign divorce and the country or territory whose courts had granted a divorce was enough to afford recognition of that divorce in England.

Ever since *Travers* v. *Holley* fifteen years earlier, the divorce judges had struggled to apply a sufficiently flexible rule so as to avoid the continuous injustice of limping marriages, marriages dissolved in one country and yet subsisting in another, particularly where one or both of the parties to the divorce had married again. It is significant that leave to appeal to the House of Lords in *Travers* v. *Holley* was refused by the Court of Appeal and by the Appeal Committee of the House of Lords. Would an unfettered right of appeal in 1952 have meant that the rule in *Travers* v. *Holley* would have been extended in the manner of *Indyka* in 1967? It may be that in the judicial process the adage 'horses for courses' applies, and that the Law Lords of a former era would have been less venturesome than their judicial successors, but this is a matter for speculation rather than scientific prediction.

An earlier international family law problem led to a less bold decision in

1 [1969] A.C. 35.
2 [1953] P. 246.

Ross Smith v. *Ross Smith.*[1] The question there was: did the fact alone that the marriage ceremony was performed in England give the English courts jurisdiction to annul a marriage on the ground of the husband's incapacity or wilful refusal to consummate the marriage? Seven Law Lords[2] debated whether a case *Simonin* v. *Mallac*,[3] decided in 1860, had stood the test of time. In the result, the majority held that for a *voidable* marriage the place of the ceremony of marriage was insufficient to confer jurisdiction on the English courts. But, while seriously doubting that there was, for the purpose of jurisdiction, any distinction to be drawn between *void* and *voidable* marriages, the Lords left *Simonin* v. *Mallac* intact, but precariously so. It took the judicial ingenuity and legal scholarship of Sir Jocelyn Simon P. (as he then was) in *Padolecchia* v. *Padolecchia*[4] to demonstrate that in void marriages jurisdiction could properly be founded on the simple and naked fact that the marriage had been solemnized in England.[5]

A third and earlier conflict of laws case, which involved the retrospective validation of an invalid wartime marriage in Austria, was the only one of the many family problems that found its way to the apex of the English judicial hierarchy.[6]

The parent–child relationship brought no problems to the House of Lords until very recently. The status of confidential reports by social welfare agencies in custody proceedings was authoritatively and unequivocally stated in *Re. K.* (*infants*).[7] Their Lordships laid down that custody proceedings were not to be treated like ordinary litigation, but were in the nature of an administrative inquiry in which the best interests of the child were paramount; a parent contesting custody had no right to see a confidential report made to the court, but the trial judge in his discretion could, and usually would, let the parent see the report unless disclosure would be harmful to the child. In so ruling, the Law Lords reversed the Court of Appeal and set the pattern for much welfare work in the courts.

The paramountcy of the child's welfare came up for decision in an acute form in *J.* v. *C.*[8] Ever since the Guardianship of Infants Act 1925 there had been doubts whether the paramount consideration of the child's welfare

---

[1] [1963] A.C. 280.

[2] Lord Reid (with whom Lord Morton of Henryton concurred), Lord Cohen, Lord Morris of Borth-y-Gest, and Lord Guest all gave judgments: the seventh member, Lord Merriman, died on the morning that judgment was due to be given. His speech, a dissenting one, was adopted by Lord Hodson and added to the end of his speech. (See p. 102, no. 2.)

[3] (1860) 2 Sw. & Tr. 67.   [4] [1968] P. 314.

[5] In that case an Italian, who in his wanderings to Belgium, Luxembourg, and Mexico (where he obtained a divorce from his Italian wife) had never lost his domicile in Italy, met a Danish girl in Copenhagen. They came for a week to London, where they married and left for Europe, never to return, except for the husband metaphysically to seek from the English Court an annulment of his English marriage, on the ground that his Mexican divorce could not have validly dissolved his indissoluble Italian marriage.

[6] *Starkowski* v. *Attorney-General* [1954] A.C. 155.   [7] [1965] A.C. 201.

[8] [1970] A.C. 668. Twice, recently, their Lordships heard appeals in adoption cases—the first since legal adoption was introduced into English law in 1926: *Re W* [1971] A.C. 682 and *O'Connor* v. *A & B* [1971] 1 W.L.R. 1227.

applied only in a dispute between the child's parents or relatives; or whether, in cases where a natural parent was seeking the return of his or her child from foster-parents (strangers in blood to the child), the parental right to his or her child took priority over considerations of the child's welfare.

The House of Lords, basing itself on a questionable view of the history of the common law and of the parliamentary intention reflected in the 1925 Act, held that in every custody proceeding the child's welfare was the paramount consideration; they affirmed the lower courts' decision to leave a Spanish child with English foster-parents who had looked after him for most of his ten years of life, as opposed to sending him to Spain, a country totally alien to him except for the fact of his Spanish birth.

Much less momentous decisions in the field of custody were resolved by the House of Lords in *Galloway* v. *Galloway*[1] and *S.* v. *S.*[2] In the former, English courts granting matrimonial relief were held to have exactly the same power to make orders relating to custody, access, and education of illegitimate children as they had in the case of legitimate children, a problem made complex only as a result of obscure draftsmanship in the Matrimonial Causes Act 1950. In the latter case, a tricky jurisdictional point of Scots law over a grandparent's right of access to the child was resolved.

Murder is essentially a domestic crime; but it must nevertheless be rare for a point of family law to arise as the crucial issue in a murder trial. In *Rumping* v. *D.P.P.*[3] the House, against the powerful dissent of Viscount Radcliffe, held that, apart from certain statutory provisions, there was no rule of law which precluded the reception in evidence of communications between husband and wife; and an intercepted letter in which the husband confessed his killing to his wife was clearly admissible in evidence.

If the House of Lords has not been as active as it might in resolving family law problems, it is due, in fact, to a curious rule of adjectival law limiting the scope of the Lords' jurisdiction. Section 27 (2), Supreme Court of Judicature (Consolidation) Act 1925 provides that 'the decision of the Court of Appeal on any question arising under the provisions of this Act relating to matrimonial causes or matters and to declarations of legitimacy, and the validity of marriage shall be final, except where the decision is either on the grant or refusal of a decree on a petition for dissolution or nullity of marriage or for such a declaration as aforesaid, or on a question of law on which the Court of Appeal gives leave to appeal'. In *B.* v. *B.* (*No. 2*)[4] a custody appeal that arose in a divorce case was held incompetent to be heard because the Court of Appeal had declined to grant leave. There seems little point in thus circumscribing the Lords' jurisdiction where a custody issue between parents which started by way of ward of court proceedings in the Chancery Division[5] could

---

[1] [1956] A.C. 299.   [2] 1967 S.C. (H.L.) 46.
[3] [1964] A.C. 814.   [4] [1955] 1 W.L.R. 557.
[5] Now transferred to the Family Division of the High Court by section 1 and schedule 1 to the Administration of Justice Act 1970.

not be barred from their Lordships' consideration if they thought it raised important issues of principle.

If there are large areas of family law either unresolved or in a state of flux which have not yet troubled the House of Lords, the indications are that more cases will go to the final court of appeal. So far, the Lords have made only a peripheral impact on this branch of law, save to prompt remedial legislation as a direct result of socially unacceptable legal solutions in two distinct problem areas. But in both instances, the prompting of legislation served the much needed purpose of obliterating a hugger-mugger of Court of Appeal decisions. Elsewhere the Lords have brought both certainty and clarity to the law. *Indyka* and *J.* v. *C.* qualify as sensible and rational solutions to current major social problems. And that says much for a body that has too often shyly eschewed judicial law-making, particularly in an area of human conduct traditionally considered not to be the law's business. But unconsciously the House of Lords has shaken off the inhibition of non-intrusion into domestic relations. It is a far cry from the day when a distinguished Lord Justice could say, with general judicial approval, that sociological knowledge is better left out of discussion of legal questions.[1] The reception of such knowledge by the judiciary is the beginning of the development of a sound family law.

[1] *Place* v. *Searle* (1932) 48 T.L.R. 428 *per* Scrutton L.J. at p. 430.

XV

REVENUE AND RATING APPEALS

APPEALS in the field of revenue and of rating law bulk large in the case-load of the House of Lords: so large in fact that the House might on occasions be mistaken for an ennobled extension of the Income Tax Special Commissioners, with appeals in less prolific areas of litigation being no more than incidental diversions. During our period of study, revenue appeals accounted for 30 per cent of English civil appeals and for 20 per cent of Scottish appeals, while rating appeals accounted for another 5 per cent and 3 per cent respectively. Out of 466 civil appeals during 1952–68 no fewer than 150, almost one-third, fell into one of these two categories. Such a marked predominance of appeals in a single area clearly has important implications for the work of the final court of appeal and, *ipso facto*, for our present study.

One might be tempted to draw a comparison between the work of the House of Lords in revenue and rating law and its performance, say, in the field of patents, trade marks and copyright, discussed elsewhere. Both involve litigation on technical issues, decided at first instance by an expert tribunal or assessor, and both involve the judge in the exercise of interpretative skills; but at this point all resemblance ends. The construction of a patent specification subordinates the utility of legal expertise to that of technological skill in which, as we have seen, the generalist-lawyer who has had little or no opportunity to acquire expertise, is often a long way out of his depth. Revenue law, however, finds the lawyer, on both the common law and the chancery side of the profession,[1] in his element, interpreting and applying statutes, an activity which, after all, is meat and drink to the lawyer. While any good lawyer can cope with the maze of tax legislation, it is fair to point out that there is a specialist Tax Bar.

Thus, in quantitative terms, revenue litigation has come to occupy a familiar part of the appellate scene. By contrast, patent cases tend to be sent to expert arbitrators, by-passing the courts altogether, largely because industrialists do not trust judges to cope with technical issues upon which industrial fortunes can be made or lost, and for which legal training is, by itself, poor equipment.

---

[1] It is only comparatively recently that revenue matters were transferred from the Queen's Bench list to the chancery side of the High Court; certainly there is nothing inherent in this area of law which makes chancery or common law practitioners respectively either more or less capable of handling it. Indeed the transfer was formal only and has no legal significance.

Revenue and rating matters are recognized, both by statute and by popular demand, as resting squarely within the legitimate domain of lawyers. It has been sculptured by the hands of lawyers out of the granite stone hewn by legislators. In no other area is the legislature more conscious of the brooding shadow of the courts waiting to interpret and criticise its handiwork, and in no other area of law is the legislature more constantly poised to retaliate than in the litigation over assessments to tax.

For most people, Finance Acts are both recondite and a profound bore, whose interpretation is an unfathomable art best left to the initiate. For the happy few, they are stimulating challenges to the intellect: for the dispassionate, what are they but ponderous moves in a long-drawn-out game of chess between the taxpayer and the legislature? Behind the taxpayer stand, or perhaps crouch, the best brains of the Tax Bar and the Accountancy profession. Indeed, to take the game analogy further, this form of litigation is one of the most 'kibbitzed' in existence—in the wings there are countless lobbyists and politico-economic experts bombarding both sides with advice. In the short run the odds are slightly in favour of the taxpayer. For many years the judges have been on his side. As one of the Scots judges put it in 1929:

No man in this country is under the smallest obligation, moral or other, so to arrange his legal relations . . . so as to enable the Inland Revenue to put the largest possible shovel into his stores. The Inland Revenue is not slow . . . to take every advantage which is open to it . . . for the purpose of depleting the taxpayer's pocket. And the taxpayer is, in like manner, entitled to be astute to prevent, so far as he honestly can, the depletion of his means by the Inland Revenue.[1]

The classic example of such astuteness is the device of 'dividend-stripping' which flourished like a green bay-tree (of rather a nasty shade of green?) in a variety of forms, until the rules of the game were altered in 1955, 1958, and 1960, although its litigious after-effects have rumbled on for many years.[2]

As if all this were not enough, for years judges have been fond of remarking that taxing statutes are subject to the rule of strict construction: their language must be 'clear and free from doubt'.[3] As one judge put it, if the construction of such a statute 'is open to two views, the one more favourable to the Crown and the other to the subject, then the latter construction *should be adopted*'.[4]

There is, indeed, one case—decided as late as 1946, and by the House of Lords—where a statute, obviously designed to make taxable the profits of mutual insurance societies, was held to have failed through a simple drafting

[1] Lord Clyde in *Ayrshire Pullman Motor Services and Ritchie* v. *I.R.C.* (1929) 14 T.C. 754, 763.

[2] *Lupton* v. *F.A. and A.B. Ltd.* [1969] 1 W.L.R. 1627; *Thomson* v. *Gurneville Securities Ltd.* [1970] 1 W.L.R. 477.; *Greenberg* v. *I.R.C.*, *Tunnicliffe* v. *I.R.C.* [1971] 3 W.L.R. 386.

[3] *Russell* v. *Scott* [1948] A.C. 422, 433; *Cape Brandy Syndicate* v. *I.R.C.* [1921] 1 K.B. 64, 71; *Canadian Eagle Oil Co.* v. *R.* [1946] A.C. 119, 140.

[4] *Clifford* v. *I.R.C.* [1896] 2 Q.B. 187,193 per Pollock B. cf. *I.R.C.* v. *Bladnoch Distillery Co. Ltd.* [1948] 1 All E.R. 616 per Lord Thankerton at 625H.

mistake so that the words used, which were re-enacted in the consolidation of
1952,[1] meant nothing, and led nowhere. Lord Macmillan observed how the
legislature had misfired: 'The Attorney-General'—Sir Hartley Shawcross (as
he then was)—'with engaging candour submitted that he ought to succeed
because, though the subsection might not in terms fit the case, it was nevertheless manifest that Parliament must have intended to cover it; if it did not cover
it, he could not figure any case which it could cover and Parliament must be
presumed to have intended to effect something':[2] his Lordship concluded
that the legislature had 'plainly missed fire'.[3]

From time to time, however, other voices can be heard from the Bench,
sounding a rather different note, a sour one in the ears of taxpayers. For
example: (1899) 'I know of no authority for saying that a taxing Act is to be
construed differently from any other Act. The duty of the court is . . . in all
cases the same . . . namely, to give effect to the intention of the legislature as
. . . gathered from the language employed, having regard to the context....';[4]
(1926) 'A statute is designed to be workable, and the interpretation thereof by
a court should be to secure that object, unless crucial omission or clear direction makes that end unattainable';[5] (1940), in the context of company law,
'. . . If the choice is between two interpretations, the narrower of which would
fail to achieve the manifest purpose of the legislation, we should avoid a construction which would reduce the legislation to futility and should rather
accept the bolder construction based on the view that Parliament would
legislate only for the purpose of bringing about an effective result';[6] (1942)
'For years a battle of manœuvre has been waged between the legislature and
those who are minded to throw the burden of taxation off their own shoulders
onto those of their fellow subjects. In that battle the legislature has often been
worsted by the skill, determination and resourcefulness of its opponents. . . .
It would not shock us in the least to find that the legislature had determined
to put an end to the struggle by imposing the severest of penalties. *It scarcely
lies in the mouth of the taxpayer who plays with fire to complain of burnt
fingers.*'[7]

Now, look at the other side of the chess-board: and note the seemingly
unbroken rule that in the long run every device of *tax avoidance*, i.e. the lawful
arranging of one's legal relations so as most effectively to parry the Inland
Revenue shovel—as distinct from *tax evasion*, which is illegal from the start—

[1] s. 444 (1), I.T.A. 1952.
[2] *I.R.C.* v. *Ayrshire Employers Mutual Insurance Association Ltd.* [1946] 1 All E.R. 637,
640 E–F; cited by Megarry J. in *Bromilow & Edwards Ltd.* v. *I.R.C.* [1969] 1 W.L.R. 1180,
1188, and by the Court of Appeal, [1970] 1 W.L.R. 128, 130.
[3] Ibid., at p. 641A.
[4] *Attorney-General* v. *Carlton Bank* [1899] 2 Q.B. 158, 164 per Lord Russell C.J.
[5] *Martin* v. *I.R.C.* [1926] 1 K.B. 550, 561 *per* Atkin L.J.
[6] *Nokes* v. *Doncaster Amalgamated Collieries Ltd.* [1940] A.C. 1014, 1022 per Viscount
Simon L.C.
[7] *Howard de Walden* v. *I.R.C.* [1942] 1 K.B. 389, 397, per Lord Greene M.R.

must come to light, and must (unless minimal) in due course be subjected to remedial surgery by Parliamentary draftsmen. Every tax appeal destined for the ultimate court of appeal is thus shadowed by a watchful legislature ready to pounce upon any decision unfavourable to the nation's Exchequer. In no other branch of law does Parliament so zealously apply its corrective law-making power. The annual Finance Act, to enact the Chancellor's Budget proposals, provides a regular and frequent opportunity for the Revenue to slip in provisions of fiscal reform. Hence the 'finality' of a final appeal becomes considerably diminished.

But even though there is a constant weapon of retaliation in the hands of the legislature, the initiative still lies very much with the taxpayer. It often takes a long time for any new tax-avoidance device to come to light and for the courts to rule on its effectiveness. While the process of detection and judicial testing is undertaken there are usually pretty pickings to be had for years on end before Parliament (a) *can* do anything about it; (b) actually does it; and (c) does it *effectively* (it took the legislature three bites at the dividend-stripping cherry before the practice was finally checked).

All these factors are of fundamental importance when we consider the role of the House of Lords as a final appellate court. It is a product of the judicial hierarchy that, as one ascends it, the case-loads of the courts become progressively smaller. The House of Lords deals with an average of about thirty-five appeals each year, as compared with the figure of nearly 1,000 appeals heard annually by the Court of Appeal and the Divisional Courts: this is both a strength and a weakness. On the one hand, the House can give weighty consideration to every question that comes before it, but on the other hand it has virtually no opportunity to build up a specialist expertise in any one particular area of jurisprudence. True, the members of the House do not, immediately upon appointment, forget everything that they have learned while serving in the courts below; nor are their Lordships wholly cut off from all that is happening in the lower courts. Nevertheless, a glance at Table 49, p. 246, above, reveals a very real problem; in seventeen years the House has dealt with twenty-eight patent, trade mark and copyright cases, with twelve cases in the field of family law, with twenty-five cases on administrative law and planning, and in many areas even fewer cases came before the court. Even with an average of (say) two cases a year on any one subject it would still be difficult for any court to develop a coherent pattern of jurisprudence, and in the House of Lords many subject-areas fall well below even this modest average. Only in revenue appeals and, to a lesser extent, fault liability (which is an area which tends to be less technical jurisprudentially, dealing principally in inferences to be drawn from established primary facts) has the House been fed sufficient fuel for recognized patterns of legal development to become established.

Why should revenue and rating appeals constitute so substantial a part of the case-load of the House of Lords? We have already noted elsewhere that the criterion of 'general public importance' tends to assume a rather elastic meaning when the Court of Appeal or the Appeal Committee is considering applications for leave to appeal. Sometimes (though by no means always) a large sum of money involved in litigation can by itself amount to a passport to the House of Lords. We have already seen[1] that in the Court of Appeal applicants for leave to appeal in revenue cases are nearly two and a half times as likely to obtain leave than other kinds of applicant, though in about half the cases where the Crown obtained leave it was put on terms as to costs. It is quite clear that the subject-matter of revenue litigation, involving, as it always does by the time it reaches the Court of Appeal, the eminently justiciable element of complex statutory interpretation, combined with public importance in the sense that tax liability is one of those 'certainties' in the lives of almost every citizen, makes the granting of leave something of a formality. As Lord Evershed once remarked with a degree of hyperbole: 'The result of these modern taxing statutes, complex as they are, is that every case goes to the House of Lords.'[2]

So far we have confined most of our remarks to revenue cases, though because of the obvious similarities in subject-matter (direct taxation in one form or another) this chapter is concerned also with rating appeals which, in numerical terms, form a very much smaller, though by no means insignificant, fraction of the total case-load of the court of last resort. It is important, however, from the outset, to appreciate some of the important differences which distinguish these two areas of litigation.

In the one, the Commissioners of Inland Revenue try to wield 'the largest possible shovel', although, as we have mentioned, it is possible to detect periods during the last fifty years when the appellate courts have been broadly 'anti-shovel'. In rating appeals, the position of the courts is aptly described, paraphrasing language used by Lord Radcliffe,[3] as that of 'neutral officials charged with the duty of maintaining valuation lists in correct and legal form'; in other words, they try to hold the scales fairly between ratepayers and rating authorities. Both, however, have one important feature in common: one side is trying to get out of paying what the other side considers to be due for payment. There is a dispute either as to the method of computation used, or as to the status or circumstances (in law and/or in fact) of the taxpayer or ratepayer involved in the dispute before the court.

There are significant differences too in the hierarchies of tribunals through which disputes in these fields must pass *en route* for the House of Lords. The common course of an English rating appeal is as follows: a proposal is made

---

1 See Chapter VIII, pp. 141–3.
2 Ibid., at pp. 148–9. Two out of every three revenue cases which get as far as the Court of Appeal go on to the House of Lords.
3 *Society of Medical Officers* v. *Hope* [1960] A.C. 551, 565. Annex B, Case 23.

to alter the valuation list; there is an objection, against which the proposer appeals to a local valuation court; there is then an appeal, by way of complete re-hearing, to the Lands Tribunal, from which appeals lie (on a question of law only) to the Court of Appeal, and thence by leave to the House of Lords. Tax appeals too begin life before fact-finding tribunals, but there is one additional step in their progression through the courts. First, the taxpayer appeals against a Revenue assessment, direction or notice, etc., to Appeal Commissioners, who reach a decision after a hearing in private. The decision includes a finding as to the primary facts against which there is no appeal, but either party may instantly 'express dissatisfaction with the determination as being erroneous in point of law' and may thereupon appeal to the courts by way of case stated. The appeal is heard at first instance by a single judge of the Chancery Division, whence further appeals lie to the Court of Appeal and the House of Lords. In drawing inferences from primary facts, the Commissioners (General or Special) have a certain amount of elbow-room unless the primary facts are such that 'the true and only reasonable conclusion' points one way or the other.[1] Where the facts do fall in this elbow-room area, the courts are not entitled to substitute their own inferences for those of the Commissioners.

It is against this background that any survey of revenue and rating appeals must be seen. Our examination of the cases from 1952–70, which follows, calls for interpretation and analysis peculiar to this area of litigation. For this reason (and because of the sheer volume of case law) we have reduced the examination to tabular form which appears in two annexes to this chapter. But some general observations are pertinent.

During 1952–70 there were heard 133 revenue appeals and 23 rating appeals. Over half of the revenue appeals dealt with income tax (54 per cent); the remainder involved estate duty (16 per cent), surtax (10 per cent), stamp duty (8 per cent), profits and excess profits tax (8 per cent) and excess profits levy, S.E.T., etc. (4 per cent). Where the Crown appealed, the success rate of appellants was marginally higher (37·3 per cent to 33·3 per cent).

There were on average three speeches per appeal, 365 majority judgments and 56 dissents. Lord Reid was the most prolific writer of judgments. He delivered speeches in over half the cases; 66 majority and 8 dissents. Lord Simonds provided half that number (37 and 1). Lord Radcliffe was more sparing (25 and 6) but wrote to more telling effect.

More than half of the appeals involved, by our criteria, issues of general public importance: only about 10 per cent of the appeals (most of them where the taxpayer appealed) did not appear to merit the consideration of a second appeal court. In two-thirds of the cases the degree of doubt about the law on the particular topic was either moderate or great, and in a high percentage of the total number of appeals the House of Lords' decision resolved the doubts and confusion which had persisted in the law.

[1] *Edwards* v. *Bairstow* [1956] A.C. 14.

However often the law was clarified and improved by the decisions of the House of Lords, the legislature was not slow to wield its statutory pen, and it did so more frequently to reverse a loss to the Revenue in the litigation. Table 53 shows the statutory reversals.

TABLE 53

Statutory Variation of House of Lords Decisions in Revenue Appeals

Where the Crown ultimately lost

(a) taxpayer-appellants succeeding
   (Case nos. 1, 34–36, 48, 96, 105, 108, 114)   9
                                                          } = 18
(b) taxpayer-respondent succeeding
   (Case nos. 26, 57, 58, 61, 62, 66, 74, 103, 111)   9

Where the Crown ultimately won

(a) taxpayer-appellant losing   5
   (Case nos. 16, 33, 37, 115, 129)   } = 9
(b) taxpayer-respondent losing   4
   (Case nos. 4, 29, 56, 63)

Note: See annexes below for the numbered cases.

In 27 out of 133 revenue appeals the legislature reversed the decision of the House of Lords. In three-quarters of the instances of statutory intervention Parliament came to the aid of the Crown who had lost the judicial stakes. In half of these cases the legislature would presumably have acted to reverse the Court of Appeal's decision had the taxpayer not tried his luck at the last judicial hurdle.

Where the Crown won, Parliament intervened in only nine instances, of which only four involved income tax: (a) *Brown* (16) the question whether a solicitor is entitled to earned income relief on interest from clients' deposits; (b) *Hinchy* (63), the question being whether the penalty for back duty should be three times the total tax due in addition to the amount of understated income; (c) *Phoenix Assurance* (115) which was repealed only temporarily: the phrase 'expenses of management' recurs in Finance Act 1965; and (d) *Whitworth Coal* (129)—as to one *ratio* only. The three other cases included two stamp duty cases and one estate duty (where taxpayers are in any event more frequently successful). One of the stamp duty cases was in essence the old quarrel over what qualifies for charitable status, which was resolved by the Recreational Charities Act 1958.

The final questions we asked ourselves were: to what extent (a) did the House of Lords provide a 'right' answer, and (b) did the answer prove more satisfactory than that given by the Court of Appeal?

If any man has such a good opinion of his legal acumen as to feel entitled to pronounce, headmaster-like and with authority, on the performances of their Lordships in these particular 156 appeals, he is either mistaken or should instantly be promoted to the House of Lords. We do not wish to pretend that we are made of such stuff; and all that follows is diffidently tendered as a basis for informed discussion. Reiterated expressions of profound humility should, therefore, be deemed to have been inserted in every sentence, and are in fact omitted solely in the interests of brevity and coherence.

Subject to the above, we would give the House of Lords very substantially higher marks than the Court of Appeal in these two fields: in short, the results definitely strengthen its claim to be retained as a supreme appellate court. And such claim is based, in part at least, on the fact that the volume of revenue work has provided the opportunity for concerted and systematic law-making. There are not many decisions in the batch that one could condemn, with any confidence, as 'wrong'. In what senses, though, can a Lords' decision be said to be 'wrong'? There is one acid test. A decision may contain within itself essential strands of reasoning which the critic may *know* to be false: putting it another way, he may at least be sure that an ideal Court Above would expose their falsity and reverse judgment accordingly.

Cricketers sometimes amuse themselves by selecting an Elysian XI: Hobbs and W. G. Grace open the batting, with Bradman in next, and so forth. Whom one selects for one's Elysian Court will depend on individual taste: as a draft, try Holmes (U.S.A.) in the chair, Atkin, Blackburn, Palles (Ireland). Batting at no. 5, one of these: Bowen, Mansfield, Davey, Eldon, Macnaghten, Shaw, Sumner, Watson. From an Elysian Court, one expects ideal judgments: which will not merely express a convincing *ratio* but will somehow illumine the inner *ratio*, of which the case *ratio* is but a branch. They must so harmonize statute law with common law, with equity, and with common sense so as to be ultimately satisfying. How many of the 156 decisions of the House of Lords in revenue and rating cases would the Elysian Court reverse? Brief comments are tendered on just four revenue and two rating candidates.

Revenue case (60): Griffiths v. *J. P. Harrison (Watford) Ltd.*[1] where a 3:2 majority upheld a simple dividend-strip. Of the majority, Lord Guest's view, that 'one has to look at the transaction by itself, *irrespective of the object, irrespective of the fiscal consequences*' has effectively been overtaken by case 51,[2] and by two decisions, delivered 21 October 1971, in cases where two differently-constituted Courts of Appeal had come to opposite conclusions.[3] The upshot is that *Griffiths* v. *J. P. Harrison (Watford) Ltd* survives as 'a very narrow decision indeed . . . a share-dealing which is palpably part of the trade of dealing in shares will not cease to be so merely because there is inherent in it an intention to obtain a fiscal advantage . . .; [but] if the

---

[1] [1963] A.C. 1.   [2] *Finsbury Securities Ltd.* v. *C.I.R.* [1966] 1 W.L.R. 1402.
[3] *Lupton* v. *F.A. and A.B. Ltd.* [1969] 1 W.L.R. 1627, and *Thomson* v. *Gurneville Securities Ltd.* [1970] 1 W.L.R. 477. And see, [1971] 3 W.L.R. 670 and 692.

appearance of the transaction leaves the matter in doubt, an examination of its paramount object will always be relevant, and will generally be decisive.'[1]

Revenue case (12): I.R.C. v. *Brebner:*[2] certain shareholders fearing a take-over bid, wanted to secure control of a company to preserve it in being. This was a bona fide commercial reason. To acquire control, they needed to buy shares. To buy shares, they needed money. The company had taxed reserves: if these had been distributed by way of dividend, surtax would have left them too little. So, with the avowed immediate object of a surtax-free milking of the reserves, they adopted the device of (a) increasing capital (by capitalizing reserves) (b) reducing capital to what it was before (by distributing the reserves, as a return of capital, to the shareholders). Control was then acquired as planned. The Finance Act 1960, s. 28 countered this avoidance of surtax unless the shareholders could show that '*none* of the transactions had as . . . one of their main objects to enable tax advantages to be obtained'.

The House upheld a finding in the shareholders' favour. It is suggested that the *only* object of the manœuvre of increase/reduction was to avoid surtax on the reserves. The effect of the decision seems to be that a plea of poverty can avail the would-be surtax-avoider. 'True, I deliberately avoided surtax by these transactions,' he says, 'but I was so poor that, if I hadn't, my ultimate commercial object would have foundered. . . .' Can this be the true construction of s. 28?

Revenue case (31); Cleary v. *I.R.C.;*[3] another case on the Finance Act 1960, s. 28. Pennycuick J.'s judgment is suggested to be right. Mrs. Cleary sold her shares in one company (which she and her sister controlled) to another (which they also controlled). The Crown case, using the exposition of the meaning of 'tax advantage' by Lord Wilberforce in case 95, was that she received money, from the reserves of the purchasing company, so that she did not pay tax on it. She could have received that money in another, taxable, way: viz., by way of dividend. Pennycuick J. objected that this was not comparing like with like. What she received was not just 'money' but 'a fair price for shares'. There is no alternative taxable way of getting a price for something you sell. The Court of Appeal and the Lords, however, adopted the Crown view.

Revenue case (117); Morgan v. *Tate & Lyle;*[4] the 'Mr. Cube' case. Their Lordships held that propaganda costs of opposing sugar nationalization were 'wholly and exclusively laid out for the purposes of the company's trade' and were an admissible deduction from its profits. Was political resistance to threatened legislation really 'wholly and exclusively . . . for the purpose of the company's trade . . .'?

---

[1] *F.A. & A.B. Ltd.* v. *Lupton* [1971] 3 W.L.R. 670, 690–1 *per* Lord Simon of Glaisdale. Of the other judges, Lords Morris & Guest spoke to the same effect: Lord Donovan & Viscount Dilhorne flatly said *Harrison* was wrong.

[2] [1967] 2 A.C. 18.   [3] [1968] A.C. 766.   [4] [1955] A.C. 21.

Rating case (10): Imperial Tobacco Ltd. v. *Pierson:*[1] this is the one decision which we think is demonstrably wrong. Lord Denning's dissent is good law. Both (a) the concept of a hereditament varying in rateable value according to the money actually spent on its provision, in the real world by the real tenant, and (b) the notion of an advertising right becoming rateable, though unexercised and (because the advertising structure has yet to be built and erected) unexercisable, at the moment 'the ink is dry on the document' (as counsel for the appellants contended) are utterly foreign to rating law.

Rating case (2): Dawkins (V.O.) v. *Ash Bros. & Heaton Ltd.;*[2] Lords Guest and Donovan, dissenting, express the traditional view of the hypothetical tenancy, and the majority do not seem to have grasped the distinction between a real and present disability in the real hereditament—e.g. crumbling and damp walls, and intimidatory notices—and the non-physical effect of the precise length of tenure of the tenancy on the minds of the parties. The former affect value, because they are part of the actual condition of the actual hereditament, and so will be considered both by the *hypothetical* landlord and the *hypothetical* tenant in negotiating the *hypothetical* rent. The latter cannot affect value, for the terms of the statutory and hypothetical tenancy are sacrosanct. Lord Wilberforce imagined a board on the hereditament reading 'Due for demolition in 1965'. Suppose some vandal substituted the words 'no tenancy from year to year with a reasonable prospect of continuance!' just before the visit of the hypothetical tenant to the property to discuss the hypothetical rent, what then? It is submitted that the hypothetical landlord would only need to draw his visitor's attention to Ryde on Rating for the notice to be wholly discounted as the work of a lunatic.

In five of these six cases, the House of Lords agreed with the Court of Appeal: hence the members of the final tribunal did no worse than their judicial brethren in the lower court. No advantage would have been involved in decapitating the final appellate process. Only in Rating Case (10), where the legislature intervened to restore the view of the Court of Appeal, would the absence of a second-tier appeal have been beneficial. There are, however, many cases where the House of Lords in allowing the appeal—one in three—produced a more satisfying solution. For most of the remaining two-thirds there was no loss in another appeal and indeed a marginal gain in clarification of the law. What more can one ask?

[1] [1961] A.C. 463.   [2] [1969] 2 A.C. 366.

ANNEX A—REVENUE APPEALS (133)

Cases are listed alphabetically according to the names of taxpayers (or ratepayers in Annex B) involved. C.A. = Court of Appeal (England): C.S. (I) and (II) = Court of Session, 1st and 2nd Division: C.A. (N.I.) = Court of Appeal (Northern Ireland): C.I.R. = Commissioners of Inland Revenue: Div. Ct. = Divisional Court: G.C. and S.C. = General Commissioners and Special Commissioners: L.T. = Lands Tribunal: F.A. = Finance Act: I.T.A. = Income Tax Act 1952: I.C.T. = Income and Corporation Taxes Act 1970: U = unanimous decision: affg. & rvsg. = affirming and reversing: S.G. = Sui Generis: P.P. = Part of a Pattern: V.O. = Valuation Officer.

CASE	Subject and Degree of General Public Importance	Decisions Below	Report, Result, Speeches	Subsequent Reversal	Sui Generis, or Part of a Pattern	Epitome
1. ABBOTT v. Philbin	Income Tax— Moderate	C.A. (U.) rvsg. ROXBURGH	Allowed (DENNING & KEITH diss.) SIMONDS, REID, RADCLIFFE [1961] A.C. 352	F.A. 1966, s. 25 and Sch. 4	P.P.	A. paid £20 for option to buy shares in employer co. at then market price and 18 months later, when price higher, exercised option. *Held*, option itself was perquisite when granted: rise in value not taxable.
2. AUSTRALIAN PROVIDENT SOCIETY Ostime v.	Income Tax— Small	C.A. (U.) affg. UPJOHN	Dismissed (DENNING diss.) RADCLIFFE [1960] A.C. 459		P.P.	Life fund interest of appellant *held* assessable only under the Double Taxation ... (Australia) Order 1947.
3. BAIRSTOW & HARRISON Edwards v.	Income Tax— Great	C.A. (U.) affg. WYNN-PARRY	Allowed (U.) SIMONDS, RADCLIFFE [1956] A.C. 14		P.P.	Finding by General Commissioners, that purchase and sale (in lots) of a spinning plant was not 'an adventure in the nature of trade', reversed because 'the true and only reasonable conclusion' contradicted them.
4. BADDELEY C.I.R. v.	Stamp Duty— Great	C.A. (U.) rvsg. HARMAN	Dismissed (REID diss.) SIMONDS, TUCKER, SOMERVELL [1955] A.C. 572	Recreational Charities Act 1958	P.P.	Trusts for the promotion of 'the religious social and physical well-being' or 'the moral, social and physical well-being' of specified persons, *held*, not charitable.

[327]

CASE	Subject and Degree of General Public Importance	Decisions Below	Report, Result, Speeches	Subsequent Reversal	*Sui Generis*, or Part of a Pattern	Epitome
5. BAMBRIDGE *v.* C.I.R.	Income Tax— Small	C.A. (U.) rvsg. in part HARMAN	Dismissed (U.) COHEN [1955] 1 W.L.R. 1329		P.P.	B. acquired right to income of Canadian company by means of a 'transfer' and 'associated operations' within predecessor of s. 412, I.T.A.
6. BARCLAY, CURLE & CO. LTD. *v.* C.I.R.	Income Tax— Great	C.S. (I.) (U.) rvsg. SP. COMRS.	Dismissed (HODSON & UPJOHN diss.) REID, GUEST, DONOVAN [1969] 1 All E.R. 679		P.P.	Expenditure on excavating and concreting a dry dock qualified as 'on the provision of machinery and plant' so as to qualify for an initial allowance under I.T.A., s. 279 (1).
7. BARCLAYS BANK LIMITED *v.* C.I.R.	Estate Duty— Moderate	C.A. (U.) rvsg. DANCKWERTS	Dismissed (REID diss.) SIMONDS, COHEN, KEITH, DENNING [1961] A.C. 509		P.P.	Settlor retained control of company hence, on his death, assets valuation under F.A. 1940, s. 55 because (1) first-named trustee in its register his vote prevailed under the Articles (Simonds & Cohen); or (2) because of s. 58 (4) (Denning & Keith).
8. BARR C.I.R. *v.*	Income Tax— Moderate	C.S. (1) (U.) rvsg. SP. COMRS.	Allowed (U.) MORTON, REID [1954] 1 W.L.R. 792		P.P.	B. sold his business as a going concern, £4,000 of the price being for plant. *Held*, he was liable to balancing charge, because the sale took place before the trade was permanently discontinued.
9. BATES *v.* C.I.R.	Surtax— Great	C.A. (U.) rvsg. PLOWMAN	Dismissed (U.) REID, MORRIS, GUEST, UPJOHN WILBERFORCE [1968] A.C. 483		P.P.	B. settled shares in his private company on his daughters. In two of the years in which their trustees received dividends the company paid him sums by way of temporary loan. An assessment on the second sum was *upheld* as a capital sum (within I.T.A. s. 408) paid him by 'a body corporate connected with the settlement' (within s. 411 (4)). *Obiter*: strong criticisms of the state of the law since 1951, of the draftsman, and of 'extra-statutory concessions'.

No. & Case	Subject	Court	Decision	Holding	
10. BELL Heaton v.	Income Tax— Great	C.A. (U.) rvsg. UNGOED-THOMAS	Allowed. REID, MORRIS, HODSON, UPJOHN, DIPLOCK [1970] A.C. 728	Employee, on agreeing decrease in wages of £x, was lent a company car. *Held* £x formed part of his emoluments because (1) his wage had not really decreased (REID diss.); (2) use of the car was a taxable perquisite worth £x (HODSON & UPJOHN diss.).	P.P.
11. BENNETT v. Rowse	Income Tax— Small	C.A. (U.) affg. UPJOHN	Dismissed (U.) SIMONDS (1959) 38 T.C. 476	Appellant hired two aircraft to F. Ltd. Immediately on hearing that one had crashed, he cancelled both hirings and discontinued his hiring business. *Held*, the aircraft was destroyed *before* the trade was permanently discontinued: So a balancing charge under s. 17, I.T.A. 1945 (now s. 33, Capital Allowances Act 1968) was exigible.	S.G.
12. BOWATER PAPER CORP. v. Murgatroyd v. C.I.R	Income Tax, Profits Tax— Moderate	C.A. (U.) rvsg. CROSS	Dismissed (U.) DONOVAN, WILBERFORCE [1970] A.C. 266	Appellant got dividends from a Canadian subsidiary; because of Canada's different treatment of depreciation, 'distributable profits as shown in the accounts' (*A*) exceeded 'profits on which foreign tax had been assessed' (=*I*). *Held* (1) that 'relevant profits' in I.T.A., Sch. 16, para. 9 (1) were *A*. not *T*.: (2) the dividends should not be deemed paid primarily out of taxed profits.	S.G.
13. BREBNER C.I.R. v.	Surtax— Great	C.S. (I) (U.) affg. SP. COMRS.	Dismissed (U.) PEARCE, UPJOHN [1967] 2 A.C. 18	In F.A. 1960, s. 28, 'main object' must be construed subjectively and in the context of the whole scheme: so *held*, Sp. Comrs. were entitled to find that the deliberate extraction of £58,500 surtax-free, by shareholders from the company, in order to enable them to buy enough shares to prevent a take-over bid, was *not* one of their 'main objects'.	P.P.
14. BRITISH COMMONWEALTH INTERNATIONAL NEWSFILM AGENCY v. Mahany	Income Tax— Moderate	C.A. (U.) affg. PLOWMAN	Dismissed (U.) MACDERMOTT, COHEN [1963] 1 W.L.R. 69	Payment to the appellants by Rank under covenant *held* to be a trade receipt, so that tax was not recoverable by them.	P.P.

ANNEX A—REVENUE APPEALS (133)

CASE	Subject and Degree of General Public Importance	Decisions Below	Report, Result, Speeches	Subsequent Reversal	*Sui Generis*, or Part of a Pattern	Epitome
15. BRITISH SOUTH AFRICA v. Varty	Income Tax— Moderate	C.A. (DANCKWERTS diss.) rvsg. WILBERFORCE	Allowed (diss. GUEST) MORRIS, HODSON, DONOVAN [1966] A.C. 381		P.P.	When investment company exercises an option to acquire shares it does not dispose of an asset (= the option) so as to give rise to an assessable profit.
16. BROWN v. C.I.R.	Income Tax— Moderate	C.S. (I) U. affg. Gen. Comrs.	Dismissed (U.) REID, EVERSHED, GUEST, UPJOHN, DONOVAN [1965] A.C. 244	Solicitors (Scotland) Act 1965	S.G.	Solicitor received interest on client's money deposited with him (a) from the bank (b) on lending it to other clients. *Held*, he was *not* entitled to earned income relief, as the interest belonged to his clients anyway.
17. BUCCLEUCH v. C.I.R.	Estate Duty— Great	C.A. (WINN diss.) affg. L.T.	Dismissed (U.) REID, MORRIS, HODSON, GUEST, WILBERFORCE [1967] 1 A.C. 506		P.P.	Large estate valued as if divided into 486 convenient units, all sold in open market at date of death.
18. BUTTERLEY Co. LTD. C.I.R. v.	Profits Tax— Moderate	C.A. (U.) rvsg. ROXBURGH	Dismissed (U.) SIMONDS, MORTON, RADCLIFFE, SOMERVELL [1957] A.C. 32		S.G.	*Held*. 'Interim income', revenue, and further revenue payments to expropriated colliery by NCB were not part of its profits for profits tax purposes because (1) not arising from a trade or business carried on by it and (2) not income of 'investment or other property' and (3) even if (1) was wrong, trade or business was not carried on when payments were made.
19. CAMILLE & HENRY DREYFUS FOUNDATION v. C.I.R.	Income Tax— Moderate	C.A. (U.) affg. WYNN-PARRY	Dismissed (U.) MORTON, NORMAND [1956] A.C. 39		P.P.	*Held*, appellants because incorporated in U.S.A., were not a 'body of persons . . . established for charitable purposes only' so as to be exempt from income tax.

[330]

Case	Subject	Court below	Decision / Citation		Note
20. CAMPBELL v. C.I.R.	Income Tax—Great	C.A. (U.) affg. BUCKLEY	Dismissed (U.) DILHORNE, HODSON, GUEST, UPJOHN, DONOVAN [1969] 1 A.C. 77	P.P.	Covenant payments received by trustees of a charitable trust were 'applied to charitable purposes only' but, as the scheme was that they be used to buy assets from the covenantors, they never became 'income' of the trustees.
21. CARRON C.I.R. v.	Income Tax—Small	C.S. (I) U. affg. Sp. COMRS.	Dismissed (U.) REID, GUEST, WILBERFORCE 1968 S.C. 47 (H.L.): 45 T.C. 18	P.P.	Expense in obtaining a supplementary charter, designed to improve management and conduct of business, *held*, allowable revenue expenditure.
22. CENLON FINANCE v. Ellwood	Income Tax—Great	C.A. (U.) rvsg. CROSS	Dismissed (U.) SIMONDS, REID, DENNING [1962] A.C. 782	P.P.	(1) Capital dividend is taxable in share-dealer's hands under Case I. (2) Inspector makes a 'discovery', though learning no new facts, when he alters his view of the law. (*Obiter dicta* by SIMONDS & DENNING *held* 'per incuriam' in F.S. SECURITIES below.)
23. CENTRAL & DISTRICT PROPERTIES v. C.I.R.	Stamp Duty—Small	C.A. (U.) rvsg. UNGOED-THOMAS	Dismissed (U.) REID, MACDERMOTT, HODSON, PEARSON [1966] 2 All E.R. 433	S.G.	Device to save £109,098 stamp duty ineffective.
24. CHANCERY LANE SAFE DEPOSIT v. C.I.R.	Income Tax—Great	C.A. (U.) rvsg. PLOWMAN	Dismissed. (REID and UPJOHN diss.) MORRIS, WILBERFORCE, PEARSON [1966] A.C. 85	P.P.	If a company deliberately charges expenditure against capital in its accounts, it cannot charge it against income tax for tax purposes.
25. NOBES v. C.I.R.	Income Tax—Great	C.A. (U.) rvsg. PLOWMAN	Dismissed (U.) MORRIS, WILBERFORCE [1966] 1 All E.R. 30	P.P.	Virtually concluded by Chancery Lane decision; similar facts.

[331]

ANNEX A—REVENUE APPEALS (133)

CASE	Subject and Degree of General Public Importance	Decisions Below	Report, Result, Speeches	Subsequent Reversal	Sui Generis, or Part of a Pattern	Epitome
26. CHEYNEY'S EXECUTOR Carson v.	Income Tax— Moderate	C.A. (U.) affg. HARMAN	Dismissed (U.) SIMONDS, MORTON, REID, KEITH [1959] A.C. 412	F.A. 1960, ss. 32, 33 F.A. 1968, s. 18 (1)	P.P.	Post-mortem royalties of author's professional activities (which cease with his death) are not assessable on his executors. *Stainer's Executors v. Purchase* [1952] A.C. 280 applied.
27. CHLORIDE BATTERIES v. Gahan	Profits Tax— Moderate	C.A. (U.) rvsg. UPJOHN	Dismissed (U.) SIMONDS, RADCLIFFE. [1956] 1 W.L.R. 391		S.G.	By virtue of a 'grouping notice', parent of appellant paid £209,400 instead of £131,700. Held, most the appellant could claim was 'profits tax which by virtue of the notice is payable' by the parent, i.e. £77,700.
28. C.H.W (HUDDERSFIELD) v. C.I.R.	Surtax— Great	C.A. (U.) affg. PLOWMAN	Allowed. (GUEST diss.) REID, HODSON, PEARCE [1963] 1 W.L.R. 767		P.P.	Shareholders, who sold their shares three days before end of accounting period, could not have surtax direction made on them on basis of actual income accruing throughout that period.
29. CITY OF GLASGOW POLICE ATHLETIC ASSOCN. C.I.R. v.	Income Tax— Great	C.S. (I) (U.) affg. Sp. COMRS.	Allowed. (OAKSEY diss.) NORMAND, MORTON, REID, COHEN [1953] A.C. 380	Recreational Charities Act 1958	P.P. (cf BADDELEY)	Providing recreation to the police members of the association was a non-charitable purpose.
30. CITY OF LONDON (As Conservators of Epping Forest) C.I.R. v.	Income Tax— Moderate	C.A. (U.) rvsg. DONOVAN	Dismissed (U.) NORMAND, REID [1953] 1 W.L.R. 652		P.P.	Contributions by the City, to the Epping Forest Conservatory (established for charitable purposes only) under statute, held 'pure income profit' so conservators recovered tax deducted therefrom by the City.

[332]

Case	Subject—Severity	Court below	Decision	Statute / Note	Holding
31. CLEARY v. C.I.R.	Surtax— Great	C.A. (U.) rvsg. PENNYCUICK	Dismissed (U.) DILHORNE, MORRIS, UPJOHN [1968] A.C. 766	P.P. (cf. PARKER)	Shareholders controlling companies G. and M. obtained tax advantages within s. 28 F.A. 1960 on selling their shares in M. to G. for £121,000.
32. COATHEW INVESTMENTS v. C.I.R.	Surtax— Moderate	C.A. (U.) affg. UNGOED-THOMAS	Dismissed. (diss. GUEST) DILHORNE, HODSON, UPJOHN [1966] 1 All E.R. 1032; 43 T.C. 301.	S.G.	'Actual income' of investment company *not* reduced by covenanted payments to a charity.
33. COATS' TRUSTEES v. Lord Advocate	Estate Duty— Moderate	C.S. (II) (WHEATLEY diss.)	Dismissed. (diss. DILHORNE and DONOVAN) SIMONDS, MORRIS, GUEST 1965 S.C. 45 (H.L.)	Succession (Scotland) Act 1964 P.P.	Fiction of death of guilty spouse on divorce does not enure to advantage of issue.
34. COLEN-BRANDER Bray v.	Income Tax— Moderate	C.A. (U.) affg. DANKWERTS	Dismissed (U.) NORMAND, MORTON [1953] A.C. 503.	P.P. (F.A. 1966, s. 10 rationalizes this field)	Taxpayers, foreign nationals employed under foreign contracts to work in U.K., *held* assessable only on so much of their remuneration as they received in the U.K.
35. COLLCO DEALINGS LTD. v. C.I.R.	Income Tax— Moderate	C.A. (U.) affg. VAISEY	Dismissed (U.) SIMONDS, MORTON, REID, RADCLIFFE, GUEST [1962] A.C. 1.	S.G.	Appellant (incorporated in Eire) stripped two English companies of dividend and claimed repayment of tax: *held*, s. 4 (2), Finance (No. 2) Act 1955 qualified the double-taxation agreement with Eire and disentitled the claim.
36. Wm. CORY LTD. v. C.I.R.	Stamp Duty— Moderate	C.A. (DIPLOCK diss.) rvsg. PENNYCUICK	Allowed (U.) REID, MORRIS, DONOVAN [1965] A.C. 1088	F.A. 1965, s. 90 (1) S.G.	Device of a transfer to purchasers on trust for vendors, pending exercise of oral option to purchase *held* to have successfully avoided stamp duty of £8,418.

ANNEX A—REVENUE APPEALS (133)

CASE	Subject and Degree of General Public Importance	Decisions Below	Report, Result, Speeches	Subsequent Reversal	Sui Generis, or Part of a Pattern	Epitome
37. COUPER'S TRUSTEES v. Lord Advocate	Estate Duty—Small	C.S. (i) (U.) affg. C.I.R.	Dismissed (U.) SIMONDS, MORTON, REID, 1960 S.C. (H.L.) 74	Succession (Scotland) Act 1964	S.G.	*Held*, F.A. 1894, s. 2 (1) applied to a half-share inherited by a sister, although she had not chosen to collate under the Intestate Moveable Succession (Scotland) Act 1855.
38. COUTTS v. C.I.R. (*Re* BRASSEY)	Estate Duty—Moderate	C.A. (U.) affg. ROMER	Allowed (U.) PORTER, REID [1953] A.C. 267		S.G.	*Held*, the 'Interest' of beneficiaries entitled to certain insurance policies to be maintained by premiums to be paid out of trust income, did *not* include so much of the fund as was needed to pay the premiums.
39. COUTTS C.I.R. v. (*Re* GROVES)	Estate Duty—Moderate	C.A. (DIPLOCK diss.) affg. BUCKLEY	Dismissed (U.) REID, JENKINS, GUEST [1964] A.C. 1393		P.P.	*Held*, the exemption from a second charge of duty, in F.A. 1894, s. 5 (2), applied to the subsequent passing of an interest less than that on which the first charge had been paid.
40. CYRIL LORD LTD. v. C.I.R.	Excess Profits Levy—Small	C.A. (N.I.) (U.) affg. McVEIGH	Dismissed (U.) GUEST, UPJOHN [1965] 42 T.C. 463		S.G.	The company wrote down the value of certain stock at 31 Dec. 1951 from cost to market price (about ⅓ of cost). In the next two years it found a new market and sold stock at prices higher than written-down value but still below cost. E.P.L. assessments, on the footing of 'actual profits' made on the excess of sale price over written-down value, were *upheld*.
41. DALE v. C.I.R.	Special Contribution —Great	C.A. (U.) rvsg. HARMAN	Allowed (U.) NORMAND, OAKSEY, MORTON, COHEN [1954] A.C. 11		P.P.	*Held*, an annuity, bequeathed to D. while he continued as trustee, was not 'investment income' but remuneration from an office of profit.

Case	Subject	Court below	Judges / Citation		Held
JENKINS & CO. LTD. v. Davies	Moderate	diss.) affg. STAMP	(GUEST diss.) DILHORNE, MACDERMOTT, MORRIS, UPJOHN [1968] A.C. 1097		F.A. 1953, s. 20 to a company which has ceased trading.
43. D'AVIGDOR-GOLDSMID v. C.I.R.	Estate Duty—Great	C.A. (U.) rvsg. VAISEY	Allowed (U.) SIMON, PORTER, MORTON, REID, ASQUITH [1953] A.C. 347	P.P.	Held, the beneficial interest in a life policy taken out by the deceased in 1904 and assigned to the appellant in 1934 (after which he paid the premiums) 'arose' then, and not on the death of the deceased in 1940: so no duty payable under F.A. 1894, s. 2 (1) (d).
44. DE VIGIER v. C.I.R.	Income Tax—Moderate	C.A. (U.) affg. WILBERFORCE	Dismissed (U.) REID, EVERSHED, PEARCE, UPJOHN, [1964] 1 W.L.R. 1073	P.P.	Wife lent £7,000 to trustees to enable purchase of rights issue: held on repayment of loan, s. 408 (1) and (7). I.T.A. 1952, applied to justify surtax assessment of £12,174 (£7,000 grossed up) on settlor.
45. DOWDALL, MAHONEY & CO. C.I.R. v.	Excess Profits Tax—Great	C.A. (U.) rvsg. CROOM-JOHNSON	Allowed (U.) OAKSEY, REID, RADCLIFFE [1952] A.C. 401	P.P.	Held, company resident in Eire could not deduct Irish taxes in computing profits (of two branches in U.K.) for E.P.T., as they were not '. . . expenses wholly and exclusively laid out for the purposes of its trade in U.K.' but were an application of profits when made.
46. DUPLE MOTOR BODIES C.I.R. v.	Income Tax—Moderate	C.A. (U.) affg. VAISEY	Dismissed (U.) SIMONDS, REID, GUEST [1961] 1 W.L.R. 739: 2 All E.R. 167	P.P.	Held, the 'direct cost method of valuing work in progress (labour and materials) which had been used in this business since 1924, was correct, and the 'on-cost' (labour and materials and a part of overheads) method was wrong.
47. ESCOIGNE PROPERTIES v. C.I.R.	Stamp Duty—Moderate	C.A. (U.) rvsg. VAISEY	Dismissed (U.) (REID & SIMONDS diss. on ratio (1)) SIMONDS, REID, KEITH, SOMERVELL, DENNING [1958] A.C. 549	P.P.	Executors of Vendor, paid by the purchasing co. without conveying the property, conveyed it to an associate at direction of purchasing co. Held (1) s. 32, F.A. 1930 did not exempt from stamp duty; (2) because connected with sale by Vendor s. 50 (1) (6), F.A. 1938 caught the instruments.

CASE	Subject and Degree of General Public Importance	Decisions Below	Report, Result, Speeches	Subsequent Reversal	Sui Generis, or Part of a Pattern	Epitome
48. EVANS MEDICAL SUPPLIES v. Moriarty	Income Tax—Great	C.A. (U.) rvsg. in part UPJOHN	Allowed in part (MORTON & KEITH diss.) SIMONDS, TUCKER, DENNING [1958] 1 W.L.R. 66	'Know-how' was dealt with in F.A. 1968, s. 21	P.P.	E.M.S. received £100,000 from Government of Burma for promise to divulge secret and technical information and 'know-how'. *Held*, not taxable because (1) (SIMONDS and TUCKER) this was capital, paid for a capital asset; (2) (DENNING) though this was income, it was received in the course of a new trade, begun at date of agreement.
49. FENWICK v. C.I.R.	Special Contribution —Moderate	C.A. (U.) rvsg. DONOVAN	Dismissed (U.) NORMAND [1953] 1 W.L.R. 1039		S.G.	*Held* (1) 'a full year's income' in s. 61, F.A. 1948, meant income actually received in a full year, and did not justify dividends being treated as accruing from day to day; (2) In selecting the year they had, the Special Commissioners had not exercised their discretion improperly.
50. FERGUSON v. C.I.R.	Income Tax— Great	C.S. (1) (U.) rvsg. Sp. COMRS.	Allowed (U.) REID, UPJOHN, DONOVAN, DIPLOCK [1970] A.C. 442		S.G.	Net payments of £35 paid to wife under agreement to pay them 'free of income tax' *held* not to be gross sums, taxable in her hands. *Blount v. Blount* [1916] 1 K. B. 230 overruled.
51. FINSBURY SECURITIES Bishop v.	Income Tax— Great	C.A. (DENNING diss.) affg. BUCKLEY	Allowed (U.) MORRIS [1966] 3 All E.R. 105: [1966] 1 W.L.R. 1402: 43 T.C. 591		P.P. (c.f. HARRISON)	Fifteen 'forward-dividend strips' could not reasonably be regarded as 'adventures in the nature of trade'.

No. & Case	Subject	Courts below	Decision / Citation	Cat.	Notes
52. FIRESTONE TYRE & RUBBER Co. v. Llewellin	Income Tax—Small	C.A. (U.) affg. HARMAN	Dismissed (U.), MORTON, RADCLIFFE [1957] 1 W.L.R. 464	*S.G.*	Appellants (registered in U.K.), a subsidiary of an American company, manufactured tyres for it and fulfilled orders for Europe obtained by it, etc. *Held* they were properly assessed, as its agents, as through them it exercised a trade in the U.K.
53. FRASER's (GLASGOW) BANK v. C.I.R.	Income Tax—Small	C.S. (i) (GUTHRIE diss.) affg. Sp. COMRS.	Dismissed (U.), REID 1963 S.C. 18 (H.L.)	*S.G.*	Appellant, a private bank, made £18,300 on the only sale of stocks in the bank's history (stock in the House of Fraser had been bought in 1947 'to support the market': more was added in 1952: all was sold in 1958 to reduce an overdraft). *Held.* Special Commissioners were entitled to treat this as profit of banking.
54. FRERE C.I.R. v.	Surtax—Great	C.A. (RUSSELL diss.) rvsg. WILBERFORCE	Allowed (U.), RADCLIFFE [1965] A.C. 402	P.P.	Interest paid on loans (not from a bank) for less than a year *held* not deductible in assessing F's income for surtax purposes. (Criticism by RADCLIFFE of I.T.A. s. 200 and of 'extra-statutory concessions' by the Revenue.)
55. F.S. SECURITIES C.I.R. v.	Surtax—Great	C.A. (U.) affg. UNGOED-THOMAS	Allowed (U.), REID, RADCLIFFE [1965] A.C. 631	P.P.	F.S.S. dealt in shares and dividend-stripped three companies (£927,400 net) it had bought claimed a resulting capital loss (£895,000 in all) and recovered tax under s. 341, I.T.A. 1952 (£404,000). A surtax direction was made on the ground that the dividends were investment income (i.e. not assessable under Sch. B or D), hence F.S.S. was an investment company within s. 257 (2), I.T.A. 1952. *Held*, it was: *dicta* in CENLON FINANCE corrected.
56. GARTSIDE v. C.I.R.	Estate Duty—Great	C.A. (U.) rvsg. UNGOED-THOMAS	Allowed (U.), REID, WILBERFORCE [1968] A.C. 553 · F.A. 1968, s. 39	P.P. (cf. KIRKWOOD)	The right of an object of a discretionary trust is not an 'interest' within s. 43, Finance Act 1940.

CASE	Subject and Degree of General Public Importance	Decisions Below	Report, Result, Speeches	Subsequent Reversal	Sui Generis, or Part of a Pattern	Epitome
57. GOLLAN Duckering v.	Income Tax— Moderate	C.A. (U.) rvsg. PENNYCUICK	Dismissed (U.) REID, DILHORNE, DONOVAN [1965] 2 All E.R. 115	F.A. 1967, s. 36	S.G.	Construction of a double-taxation agreement New Zealand.
58. GORDON C.I.R. v.	Income Tax— Moderate	C.S. (i) (U.) rvsg. S.C.	Dismissed (U.) TUCKER, COHEN [1952] A.C. 552	F.A. 1953, s. 24	P.P.	G. overdrew his account in London with a bank who agreed to 'transfer overdrafts' at intervals to their branch in Ceylon. *Held*, G. received advances of capital in London, not sums taxable under r. 2, Case v, Schedule D.
59. GREY v. C.I.R.	Stamp Duty— Moderate	C.A. (EVERSHED diss.) rvsg. UPJOHN	Dismissed (U.) SIMONDS, RADCLIFFE [1960] A.C. 1		P.P.	Settlor orally directed trustees of shares to hold on trusts of six settlements: a month later, trustees and settlor executed deeds of declaration of trust confirming the oral directions. *Held*: the oral directions were purported dispositions of equitable interests and invalidated by s. 53 (1) (c), Law of Property Act 1925: so the deeds were the effective dispositions, attracting *ad valorem* duty.
60. HARRISON (WATFORD) LTD. Griffiths v.	Income Tax— Great	C.A. (DONOVAN diss.) affg. DANCK-WERTS	Dismissed (REID & DENNING diss.) SIMONDS,		P.P.	H. Ltd. ceased trade as merchants with loss £13,585, altered its Memorandum to enable it to deal in shares, and did a dividend strip (net dividend £15,902) (capital loss £15,900) before

Case	Subject	Court	Statute	Decision & Citation		Notes
				MORRIS, GUEST [1963] A.C. 1		re-selling and claiming repayment of tax on the aggregate loss (£29,485). Special Commissioners held the strip transaction not an 'adventure in the nature of trade'. *Held* they could not reasonably so hold.
61. HENRY ANSBACHER & Co. C.I.R. *v.*	Stamp Duty— Moderate	C.A. (DONOVAN diss.) affg. DANCKWERTS	F.A. 1963, s. 63	Dismissed (U.) MORRIS [1963] A.C. 191	P.P.	Under sale agreement, 2nd instalment of price was to be guaranteed by a bank. *Held*, duty was 10s. on the guarantee, not *ad valorem*, because not 'the only principal or primary security for the payment . . . of money' within Sch. 1. to Stamp Act, 1891. Primary obligation was purchasing; security, the sale agreement.
62. HERDMAN C.I.R. *v.*	Income Tax— Moderate	C.A. (N.I.) (U.) rvsg. Sp. COMRS.	F.A. 1969 S.33	Dismissed (U.) REID, PEARCE [1969] 1 All E.R. 495; 45 T.C. 394	S.G.	H. transferred assets to a company in Eire, but not to avoid liability to U.K. taxation. By that transfer he gained power to enjoy income from that company. 'Associated operations', which did not effect such gain, were irrelevant: so he escaped s. 412 I.T.A. 1952.
63. HINCHY C.I.R. *v.*	Income Tax— Moderate	C.A. (U.) rvsg. in part DIPLOCK	F.A. 1960, ss. 44, 46–8, etc.	Allowed (U.) KILMUIR, REID, RADCLIFFE, KEITH [1960] A.C. 748	S.G.	H.'s return understated his Schedule D and additional assessment £14. 5s. was made. C.I.R. then sued under s. 25 (3) of I.T.A. 1952 for penalties of '£20+3× [Total Schedule E tax+£14. 5s.]' as 'treble the tax which he ought to be charged under this Act'. *Held* correct.
64. HODGE & Co. (GLASGOW) LTD. (in liquidation) C.I.R. *v.*	Profits Tax— Moderate	C.S. (i) (U.) affg. Sp. COMRS.		Allowed (U.) REID, COHEN, HODSON [1961] 1 W.L.R. 1218	S.G.	H. Ltd. got non-distribution relief in 1941–50 carrying on a business they sold then to P. Ltd. for shares in P. Ltd. (both companies electing under s. 36 (4), F.A. 1947) and traded as an investment company. In last period before liquidation H.'s net relevant distributions exceeded profits. *Held* distribution charge, in respect of the 1941–50 relief, was exigible from H. Ltd. and was not transferred by s. 36 (4) (ii) to P. Ltd.

ANNEX A—REVENUE APPEALS (133)

CASE	Subject and Degree of General Public Importance	Decisions Below	Report, Result, Speeches	Subsequent Reversal	Sui Generis, or Part of a Pattern	Epitome
65. HENRY BRIGGS Son & Co. Ltd. (in liquidation) v. C.I.R.	Profits Tax— Small	C.A. (U.) affg. UPJOHN	Dismissed (U.) REID, TUCKER, MORRIS [1961] 1 W.L.R. 68		S.G.	H.B. Ltd. held all shares in a colliery expropriated in 1947 which thereafter did nothing but finalize compensation and receive interim income payments, with which it paid dividends to H.B. Ltd. *Held* the dividends were not 'franked investment income' because the functions of the colliery did not consist wholly or mainly in the holding of investments or other property within s. 19 (4), F.A. 1937.
66. HOLMDEN C.I.R. v.	Estate Duty— Moderate	C.A. (DENNING diss.) affg. PENNYCUICK	Dismissed (U.) REID, MORRIS, HODSON, GUEST, WILBERFORCE [1968] A.C. 685	F.A. 1966 (cf. RALLI, KIRKWOOD)	P.P.	Trusts were varied under the Variation of Trusts Act 1958. *Held* estate duty not exigible under F.A. 1940, s. 43. RALLI applied, KIRKWOOD distinguished.
67. HOOD BARRS v. C.I.R.	Income Tax— Small	C.S. (1) affg. S.C.	Dismissed (OAKSEY diss.) SIMONDS, COHEN, MORTON, KEITH [1957] 1 W.L.R. 529		P.P.	H, timber merchant, paid £24,275 and £24,900 for specified numbers of tree—none then being identified. *Held* to be capital expenditure, not expense (deductible from profits) of buying stock-in-trade.
68. HOOD BARRS v. C.I.R.	Income Tax— Small	C.S. (1) affg. WALKER	Dismissed (U.) REID 1961 S.C. (H.L.) 22		S.G.	*Held* (1) in granting tax loss certificates General Commrs are performing a quasi-judicial function; so (2) certiorari lay as they granted them without giving the Inspector a right to be heard, i.e, in breach of natural justice.

69. I.T.A. & ASSOCIATED REDIFFUSION LTD. v. C.I.R.	Stamp Duty— Great	C.A. (U.) affg. WYNN-PARRY	Dismissed (U.) RADCLIFFE, COHEN, KEITH [1961] A.C. 427	P.P.	A.R. agreed under seal to provide programmes for specified annual sums to be adjusted in certain events: *held* (1) this was 'a security' and fell under 'Bond, Covenant or Instrument'; (2) *ad valorem* duty on the specified sums was payable.
70. JAMIESON C.I.R. v.	Income tax— Great	C.A. (SELLERS diss.) rvsg. PLOWMAN	Allowed (U.) REID, JENKINS, HODSON [1964] A.C. 1445	P.P.	Trustees of a settlement had power to appoint whole of the fund to one of the beneficiaries: *held*, applying COUNTESS OF KENMARE, this was power to determine the settlement, which was not, therefore, irrevocable.
71. JOHN HUDSON & Co. LTD. Kirkness v.	Income Tax— Great	C.A. (U.) affg. UPJOHN	Dismissed (MORTON diss.) SIMONDS, REID, TUCKER [1955] A.C. 696	S.G.	*Held*, the vesting of wagons in Transport Commission under Transport Act 1947 is not a sale within I.T.A. 1945, s. 17: so no balancing charge was exigible thereunder. There being no ambiguity, F.A., s. 1947 & 1948 did not assist.
72. KENMARE (Countess) v. C.I.R.	Income Tax— Moderate	C.A. (U.) affg. DANCKWERTS	Dismissed (U.) SIMONDS, REID, COHEN, KEITH [1958] A.C. 267	P.P.	Settlement by K. (not resident in U.K.) under the Law of Bermuda, with power to transfer successive parts of the fund so much as to eventually exhaust it, to the settlor, *held* to be within F.A. 1938, s. 38 (=I.T.A. s. 404).
73. KIRKWOOD, In re (Public Trustee v. C.I.R.)	Estate Duty— Great	C.A. (U.) rvsg. WILBERFORCE	Dismissed (DONOVAN diss. on 2 points.) GUEST, MORTON, UPJOHN [1966] A.C. 520	P.P.	Estate Duty *held* payable on ⅓ of settled funds, the trust having been varied by deed.
74. KORNER C.I.R. v.	Income Tax— Small	C.S. (i) (U.) rvsg. Sp. Comrs.	Dismissed (U.) F.A. 1969, GUEST, s. 15. UPJOHN, DONOVAN (1969) 45 T.C. 287	S.G.	Rates, repairs and insurance on a twenty-room 'farmhouse' occupied by Professor K. *held* allowable in full against the farming profits he made.

[341]

ANNEX A—REVENUE APPEALS (133)

CASE	Subject and Degree of General Public Importance	Decisions Below	Report, Result, Speeches	Subsequent Reversal	*Sui Generis*, or Part of a Pattern	Epitome
75. LAIDLER v. Perry	Income Tax— Great	C.A. (U.) affg. PENNYCUICK	Dismissed (U.) REID, MORRIS, HODSON, DONOVAN [1966] A.C. 16		P.P.	£10 Christmas Gift Voucher given to employees *held* assessable as emoluments under Sch. E.
76. LAND SECURITIES INVESTMENT TRUST C.I.R. v.	Profits Tax— Great	C.A. (U.) rvsg. CROSS	Allowed (U.) DONOVAN [1969] 2 All E.R. 430		P.P.	The Trust bought reversions—*held*, to be capital assets in its hands—in consideration for rent charges, so could not deduct the latter in computing its profits.
77. LAZARD INVESTMENT CO. LTD. Rae v.	Income Tax— Small	C.A. (U.) rvsg. PLOWMAN	Dismissed (U.) REID, JENKINS, GUEST, PEARCE [1963] 1 W.L.R. 555: 41 T.C. 1		S.G.	L. owned shares in American co. C which in exchange for shares in American co. B. transferred to it part of its business. C. distributed those shares to its own shareholders (incl. L.) as capital under American law: *held*, those shares in B. were capital in L.'s hands.
78. LINSLEYS LTD. Special Commissioners v.	Surtax (+Profits tax)— Moderate	C.A. (U.) affg. Div. Ct.	Allowed (U.) REID, MORTON, SOMERVELL, DENNING [1958] A.C. 569		P.P.	L., investment co., sought *mandamus* to compel surtax direction; if made, L. would elect under F.A. 1947, s. 31 (3) and then avoid £16,421 profits tax. *Held*, profits tax, having been assessed, was payable: this reduced 'actual income' to nil: hence no direction could or should be made.
79. LITTLEWOODS MAIL ORDER STORES v. C.I.R.	Stamp Duty— Small	C.A. (U.) affg. DANCKWERTS	Dismissed (U.) SIMONDS, REID [1963] A.C. 135		P.P. (cf. ESCOIGNE)	Of six instruments devised to save stamp duty, *held* (1) a voluntary assigned by L. to a subsidiary was a 'conveyance or transfer on sale' attracting *ad valorem* duty; (2) a deed of exchange was 'a conveyance or transfer of any kind not hereinbefore described' attracting 10s. duty.

[342]

80. *e contra*				
81. LITTMAN Barron *v.*	Income Tax—Great	C.A. (JENKINS diss.) rvsg. WYNN-PARRY	Dismissed (U.) SIMON, NORMAND, OAKSEY, REID, ASQUITH [1953] A.C. 96	P.P.	L. *held* entitled to set off against excess rents assessed under Schedule D, Case VI, losses in subletting (or failing to sublet) properties because they were 'transactions' within F.A. 1927, s. 27.
82. LONDON INVESTMENT & MORTGAGE CO. LTD. *v.* Worthington *v.* C.I.R.	Income Tax, Profits Tax—Moderate	C.A. (U.) rvsg. UPJOHN	Dismissed (U.) SIMONDS (REID dubitante) [1959] A.C. 199.	S.G.	*Held* value payments by War Damage Commission to property dealing co. were trading receipts for income and profits tax purposes.
83. LUKE *v.* C.I.R.	Income Tax—Moderate	C.S. (t) (U.) rvsg. G.C.	Allowed (dissents in Col. 7) DILHORNE, REID, GUEST, PEARCE [1963] A.C. 557	S.G.	Employers as owners of house let to L. (a director) spent (*A*) £256 on rates, insurance, etc. and (*B*) £694 on repairs. *Held* (1) (JENKINS & GUEST diss.) (*A*) were not part of L.'s emoluments under I.T.A., s. 161 (1)(a); (2) (JENKINS diss.) (*B*) were incurred by employers 'in the acquisition or production of an asset' within I.T.A., s. 162 (1) and were not part either.
84. MADRAS ELECTRIC SUPPLY CORP. *v.* Boarland	Income Tax—Moderate	C.A. (U.) affg. UPJOHN	Dismissed (U.) OAKSEY, MACDERMOTT, REID, TUCKER, KEITH [1955] A.C. 667	S.G.	The Crown succeeded to appellant's trade in 1947, and was *held* a 'person' within r. 11(2) Schedule D., Cases I & II, I.T.A. 1918, so appellant was liable to a balancing charge.
85. MAURICE & CO. LTD. Sec. of State *v.*	S.E.T.—Moderate	C.A. (DIPLOCK diss.) rvsg. Div. Ct.	Dismissed (U.) GUEST, DONOVAN, WILBERFORCE, PEARSON [1969] 2 A.C. 346	P.P. (cf. RELIANT TOOL)	Industrial Tribunal's finding that Maurice's work qualified for premium was mixed fact and law: could not be said to be unreasonable: so should be upheld.

ANNEX A—REVENUE APPEALS (133)

CASE	Subject and Degree of General Public Importance	Decisions Below	Report, Result, Speeches	Subsequent Reversal	Sui Generis or Part of a Pattern	Epitome
86. Mayes Hochstrasser v.	Income Tax—Great	C.A. (Parker diss.) affg. Upjohn	Dismissed (U.) Simonds, Radcliffe, Cohen, Denning [1960] A.C. 376		P.P.	ICI required M. to move, assisted him with a loan to buy a house for £1,850, again required him to move, and reimbursed his loss when he resold for £1,500. *Held* M. was *not* assessable on the £350 under Sch. E.
87. Moyse Thomson v.	Income Tax—Moderate	C.A. (U.) affg. Wynn-Parry	Allowed (U.) Reid, Radcliffe, Cohen, Denning [1961] A.C. 967		P.P. (cf. Gordon)	M. received income in U.S.A. from 'securities and possessions out of the U.K.' within cases iv and v of Schedule D; drew cheques on U.S.A. banks in favour of English banks, to whom he sold them for sterling: they collected dollars in U.S.A.: though Special Commissioners found banks acted as principals and not as his agents assessments under cases iv and v were upheld.
88. National Coal Board v. C.I.R.	Profits Tax—Moderate	C.A. (Romer diss.) rvsg. Roxburgh	Dismissed (U.) Morton, Radcliffe [1958] A.C. 104		S.G.	N.C.B. *held* not entitled to allowances on collier's dwelling-houses as 'industrial buildings likely to have little … value to the person carrying on the trade when the mine … is no longer worked' within I.T.A. 1945, s. 8(3).

Nobes—see under Chancery Lane (24)

CASE	Subject and Degree of General Public Importance	Decisions Below	Report, Result, Speeches	Subsequent Reversal	Sui Generis or Part of a Pattern	Epitome
89. North of Scotland Hydro-Electric Board v. C.I.R.	Excess Profits Tax—Moderate	C.S. (1) (U.) affg. Walker	Allowed (Keith diss.) Reid, Tucker, Hodson, Guest 1961 S.C. (H.L.) 31		S.G.	On nationalization, the appellant succeeded to the property and liabilities (incl. to E.P.T.) of a previous undertaking: *Held*, it was entitled to relief in respect of terminal expenses (under F.A. 1946, s. 37) as if the liability to E.P.T. had been its own.

Case	Subject	Court	Decision	Initials	Held
90. ORAM Mapp v. 91. à contra	Income Tax—Great	C.A. (DANCKWERTS diss). rvsg. UNGOED-THOMAS	Dismissing Appeal (U.)—Allowing Cross-Appeal (U.) HODSON, DILHORNE, UPJOHN, PEARSON [1970] A.C. 362	S.G.	Taxpayer's over-16 undergraduate son, advised by tutor, worked in a French Lycée 2½ months and spent all £150 of his earnings there. *Held* 'income' in I.T.A. s. 212 (4) meant 'income chargeable to tax' and as this wasn't, taxpayer, was entitled to full child allowance under s. 212(1).
92. OUGHTRED v. C.I.R.	Stamp Duty—Great	C.A. (U.) rvsg. UPJOHN	Dismissed (RADCLIFFE & COHEN diss.) DENNING, JENKINS [1960] A.C. 206	P.P.	Trustees by deed transferred shares in which a mother had a life interest, to her, pursuant to an agreement with the remainderman, her son. *Held,* deed was chargeable *ad valorem,* this being a transfer 'on sale' within s. 54, Stamp Act.
93. OWEN v. Pook	Income Tax—Great	C.A. (DENNING diss.) affg. STAMP	Allowed (with partial dissents) GUEST, PEARCE, WILBERFORCE [1970] A.C. 244	P.P.	O. practised at Fishguard but was on duty as obstetrician, etc. from moment of 'phone call from hospital at Haverfordwest. *Held* (1) sums he received for travelling were not emoluments (PEARSON *diss,* WILBERFORCE *dubitante*); (2) what he spent above those sums on travelling between his two places of work was a deductible expense from his salary (PEARSON & DONOVAN *diss.*)
94. PARKER v. Lord Advocate	Estate Duty—Great	C.S. (II) (U.) affg. Registrar	Dismissed (U.) SIMONDS, RADCLIFFE, COHEN, KEITH, JENKINS [1960] A.C. 608	P.P.	Three beneficiaries under a settlement were entitled (a) during settlor's life, to income of fund equally (b) on her death to ⅓ share of the fund. *Held,* on her death, estate duty payable on whole fund—F.A. 1894, s. 2 (1) (d.)
95. PARKER C.I.R. v.	Surtax—Great	C.A. (U.) rvsg. UNGOED-THOMAS	Allowed (MORTON and HODSON diss.) DILHORNE, GUEST, WILBERFORCE [1966] A.C. 141	P.P. cf. (BLOTT FISHER'S EXORS)	s. 28, F.A. 1960 and meaning of 'tax advantage' luminously explained by WILBERFORCE.

ANNEX A—REVENUE APPEALS (133)

CASE	Subject and Degree of General Public Importance	Decisions Below	Report, Result, Speeches	Subsequent Reversal	Sui Generis, or Part of a Pattern	Epitome
96. PHILIPSON-STOW v. C.I.R.	Estate Duty—Great	C.A. (HARMAN diss.) affg. UPJOHN	Allowed (RADCLIFFE diss.) SIMONDS, REID, DENNING [1961] A.C. 727	F.A. 1962, s. 28(1)	P.P.	Testator, domiciled in England devised and bequeathed residuary estate, including land in S. Africa to trustees on trust for sale, his son having a life interest. *Held* (1) Succession to immovables is ruled by the *lex situs*; (2) so S. African law applied both on his and his son's death; (3) so the land was exempt from estate duty.
97. PUBLIC TRUSTEE v. C.I.R. (The Arnholz Case)	Estate Duty—Great	C.A. (U.) affg. DANCKWERTS	Allowed (KEITH diss.) SIMONDS, RADCLIFFE, COHEN [1960] A.C. 398		P.P. (cf. SANDERSON)	Testator gave to one of the trustees of his will the income from certain shares 'during his life, so long as he shall act as executor and trustee by way of remuneration for so doing'. *Held*, the trustee's interest was in respect of his office and so on his death no estate duty was payable.
98. RACECOURSE BETTING CONTROL BOARD v. Young v. C.I.R.	Income Tax, Profits Tax—Small	C.A. (U.) affg. UPJOHN	Dismissed (U.) SIMONDS, KEITH [1959] 1 W.L.R. 813		S.G.	*Held* in computing Board's profits for income and profits tax no deductions permissible for six kinds of voluntary payment broadly aimed at assisting racecourse executives and encouraging racing.
99. RALLI BROS. LTD. v. C.I.R.	Estate Duty—Great	C.A. (RUSSELL diss.) rvsg. BUCKLEY	Allowed (PEARSON diss.) UPJOHN, DONOVAN [1966] A.C. 483		P.P.	Estate duty payable on deceased's interest in four years' income from the settled funds, not on their principal value.

[346]

100. REGENT OIL v. Strick	Income Tax— Moderate	C.A. (U.) affg. PENNYCUICK	Dismissed (U.) REID, MORRIS, PEARCE, UPJOHN, WILBERFORCE [1961] A.C. 295	P.P.	Premiums paid to garages for (tied) leases were capital not revenue, expenditure.
101. RELIANT TOOL Lord Advocate v.	S.E.T.— Moderate	C.S. (i) (U.) affg. Industrial Tribunal	Dismissed (U.) DILHORNE, MACDERMOTT GUEST, WILBERFORCE, PEARSON [1968] 1 All E.R. 162	P.P (cf. MAURICE, below)	Industrial Tribunal's finding that Reliant's designing of tools formed part of process of manufacture and so qualified Reliant for premium, *held* a question of fact (several other *rationes*).
102. RENDELL v. Went	Income Tax— Moderate	C.A. (U.) rvsg. BUCKLEY	Dismissed (U.) REID, RADCLIFFE [1964] 1 W.L.R. 650	S.G.	R., a director, was defended on a motoring charge at employers' expense. *Held*, as it had all been spent on benefiting him, it was all caught by I.T.A., s. 161 (1), and he was properly assessed on it.
103. RENNELL, Lord C.I.R. v.	Estate Duty— Moderate	C.A. (U.) affg. BUCKLEY	Dismissed F.A. 1963, (RADCLIFFE & s. 53 MACDERMOTT diss.) COHEN, JENKINS, GUEST [1964] A.C. 173	P.P.	On his daughter's marriage, settlor 'in consideration of her marriage' settled funds on discretionary trusts for her and *his five other children*. *Held*, their inclusion did not take the settlement out of s. 59 (2), F.A. 1910.
104. REYNOLDS & GIBSON Crompton v. C.I.R. v.	Income Tax, Profits Tax— Small	C.A. (U.) rvsg. ROXBURGH	Dismissed (U.) NORMAND, REID [1952] 1 All E.R. 888	S.G.	Partners in a firm of cotton brokers took over a debt, believed to be bad, from predecessors, having elected to be treated as having set up a new trade. It was paid in full. *Held* profit so accruing was not taxable under case I of Schedule D.

ANNEX A—REVENUE APPEALS (133)

CASE	Subject and Degree of General Public Importance	Decisions Below	Report, Result, Speeches	Subsequent Reversal	Sui Generis, or Part of a Pattern	Epitome
105. ROLLS-ROYCE v. Jeffrey	Income Tax, Profits Tax—Moderate	C.A. (U.) rvsg. PENNYCUICK	Dismissed (U.) SIMONDS, REID, RADCLIFFE, MORRIS, GUEST [1962] 1 W.L.R. 425	'Know-how' dealt with in F.A. 1968, s. 21(2).	P.P.	In consideration of 'capital sums' R.R. licensed foreigners to make engines and provided 'know-how'. *Held*, such receipts were of revenue, not capital, nature.
106. ROSS, HIRTENSTEIN Mitchell v. DREW, MARSHALL, TARNESBY Taylor-Gooby v. (5 appeals)	Income Tax—Great	C.A. (U.) rvsg. in part UPJOHN	Allowed (U.) SIMONDS, RADCLIFFE, COHEN [1962] A.C. 814		P.P.	Schedules D & E being mutually exclusive, *held* that five medical consultants' expenses incurred in relation to their employment but not deductible under the rules to Sch. E, could not be set off against private practice earnings, under Sch. D.
107. SANDERSON v. C.I.R.	Estate Duty—Great	C.A. (U.) affg. UPJOHN	Dismissed (U.) MORTON, RADCLIFFE [1956] A.C. 491		P.P.	In 1942 H. settled private company he controlled: in 1943 he died: *held*, s. 55(1), F.A. 1940 was simply a valuation section and applied, since by s. 2(1)(c) F.A. 1894 the shares were deemed to pass on death.
108. SAUNDERS C.I.R. v.	Income Tax—Great	C.A. (U.) rvsg. WYNN-PARRY	Dismissed (KEITH & SOMERVELL diss.) SIMONDS, REID, COHEN [1958] A.C. 285	F.A. 1958, s. 21(2) now I.C.T., s. 446 (2)	P.P.	Trustees of a settlement were empowered to apply capital for benefit, inter alia, of settlor's wife, remaining capital never to be less than £100. *Held*, this was not a power to revoke or … determine' within F.A. 1938, s. 38(2) (cf. COUNTESS OF KENMARE).
109. SAXONE, LILLEY & SKINNER C.I.R. v.	Income Tax—Great	C.S. (i) (U.) rvsg. S.C.	Dismissed (U.) REID [1967] 1 All E.R. 756: 44 T.C. 122		P.P.	Warehouse *partly* used for qualifying purposes, *held* 'in use for [those] purposes', and hence 'an industrial building'.

No. Case	Subject—Degree	Lower court	Final decision	Statute		Summary
110. SHOP & STORE DEVELOPMENT v. C.I.R.	Stamp Duty— Moderate	C.A. (U.) rvsg. PENNYCUICK	Allowed (REID & GUEST diss.) MORRIS, HODSON, WILBERFORCE [1967] 1 A.C. 472	F.A. 1967, s. 27(3)	S.G.	Narrow construction of 'consideration directly or indirectly provided' saved shareholders, on public flotation, £19,693.
111. SNEDDON v. Lord Advocate	Estate Duty— Great	C.S. (II) (MACKAY diss.) affg. C.I.R.	Allowed (KEITH diss.) MORTON, MACDERMOTT, REID [1954] A.C. 257	F.A. 1957, ss. 38	P.P.	In 1946 settlor put £5,000 in trust—a gift *inter vivos*—with which trustees bought shares which by 1948 when he died, were worth £9,250. *Held*, estate duty was payable on only £5,000.
112. SOUTH GEORGIA CO. LTD. C.I.R. v.	Profits Tax— Great	C.S. (i) (U.) affg. C.S.	Allowed (U.) SIMONDS, REID, KEITH [1958] A.C. 599		S.G.	The co. incurred trading loss £602,000, received franked investment income £272,000, and paid dividends £181,000. *Held*, liable to profits tax on £181,000=the 'gross relevant distributions' within F.A. 1947, s. 34(2).
113. SOUTHERN Ry. of PERU v. Owen	Income Tax— Great	C.A. (U.) affg. UPJOHN	Dismissed (MACDERMOTT diss.) OAKSEY, RADCLIFFE [1957] A.C. 334		P.P.	By law of Peru, the co. had to pay compensation to employees at end of their contracts. *Held*, it could not deduct against each year's profits the cost of making provision for estimated future liabilities to compensation.
114. STAFFORD COAL & IRON v. Brogan	Income Tax, Profits Tax— Great	C.A. (PEARSON diss.) rvsg. PLOWMAN	Allowed (DEVLIN diss.) REID, EVERSHED, HODSON, JENKINS [1963] 1 W.L.R. 905: 41 T.C. 305	F.A. 1964, s. 21	S.G.	S. (& other companies) paid premiums (allowed as trade expenses) to N., a mutual insurance company. On nationalization N. was liquidated and distributions of surplus assets to S. (& others) were assessed as trade receipts. *Held*, not: they were capital.

[349]

CASE	Subject and Degree of General Public Importance	Decisions Below	Report, Result, Speeches	Subsequent Reversal	Sui Generis, or Part of a Pattern	Epitome
115. SUN LIFE ASSURANCE v. Davidson PHOENIX ASSURANCE v. Logan	Income Tax— Moderate	C.A. (U.) affg. HARMAN	Dismissed (REID diss. as to brokerage) SIMONDS, MORTON, SOMERVELL [1958] A.C. 184	(I.T.A., s. 425 (4) repealed, but 'expenses of management' recurs in F.A. 1965, s. 57: now I., C.T., ss. 304, 411)		*Held*, life assurance companies, assessed on income from investments, could not deduct brokerage and stamp duty paid on changing investments as 'expenses of management' under the predecessor of I.T.A., s. 425 (4).
116. In re SUTHERLAND: Winter v. C.I.R.	Estate Duty— Great	C.A. (U.) affg. DANCKWERTS	Allowed (TUCKER & HODSON diss.) REID, BIRKETT, GUEST [1963] A.C. 235		P.P.	S. had control of co. before his death so that assets valuation applied. Co. owned five ships on which capital allowances received. After his death they were sold for sums giving rise to balancing charges of £548,318. *Held* this was a 'contingent liability' within F.A. 1940, s. 50(1) and reduced the assets valuation.
117. TATE & LYLE Morgan v.	Income Tax— Great	C.A. (SINGLETON diss.) affg. HARMAN	Dismissed (KEITH & TUCKER diss.) MORTON, REID, ASQUITH [1955] A.C. 21.		P.P.	Finding by Sp. Comrs. that cost of propaganda to oppose nationalization was 'wholly and exclusively laid out for the purposes of the company's trade and was an admissible deduction from its profits' was *upheld*.
118. THOMAS v. Marshall	Income Tax— Great	C.A. (U.) affg. DONOVAN	Dismissed (U.) MORTON [1953] A.C. 543		P.P.	Gifts of money put in Savings Bank Account in names of infant unmarried children were *held*, 'settlements' within s. 21, F.A. 1936, so father liable to tax on interest.

[350]

Case	Subject	Court below	Decision & citation		Summary
119. TOLLEMACHE SETTLED ESTATES TRUSTEES v. Coughtrie	Income Tax— Great	C.A. (U.) rvsg. UPJOHN	Dismissed (U.) KILMUIR, DENNING, MORRIS, HODSON [1961] A.C. 880	S.G.	Sandpit royalties. The actual rent (including royalties) in the year of assessment, adjusted (if necessary) to make it the true rent, *less* collection expenses, is the excess assessable under I.T.A., s. 175 (1).
120. UNION CORPORATION v. C.I.R.	Profits Tax— Great	C.A. (U.) affg. HARMAN	Dismissed (U.) COHEN [1953] A.C. 482	P.P.	'Ordinarily resident outside the U.K.' in s. 39 (1), F.A. 1947 means exclusively so: so relief under it cannot be given any company with any U.K. residence.
121. UNIT CONSTRUCTION v. Bullock	Income Tax— Great	C.A. (U.) affg. WYNN-PARRY	Allowed (U.) SIMONDS, RADCLIFFE, COHEN, KEITH [1960] A.C. 351	P.P.	Three Kenya subsidiaries of A.B. Ltd. (an English company) should have been managed by their boards in Kenya but were in fact managed by A.B. Ltd. in London. *Held,* this made them 'resident in U.K. and carrying on trade... in U.K.' so as to entitle appellant co.—another subsidiary of A.B. Ltd.—to make subvention payments to them.
122. UNIVERSAL GRINDING WHEEL C.I.R. v.	Profits Tax— Moderate	C.A. (HODSON diss.) affg. UPJOHN	Dismissed (U.) SIMONDS, MORTON, REID, COHEN [1955] A.C. 807	S.G.	By its Articles, £1 pref. shares were redeemable at 27s. *Held,* on redemption the 7s. was 'a sum applied in reducing share capital ...' within s. 36 (1), F.A. 1947, hence not a distribution liable to profits tax.
123. VANDERVELL v. C.I.R.	Surtax— Small	C.A. (U.) affg. PLOWMAN	Dismissed (REID & DONOVAN diss.) PEARCE, UPJOHN, WILBERFORCE [1967] 2 A.C. 291	S.G.	Settlement of shares on a charity misfired because procedure gave rise to resulting trust for settlor.
124. WALKER'S TRUSTEES v. Lord Advocate	Estate Duty— Small	C.S. (II) (MACKAY diss.) affg. C.I.R.	Allowed (U.) MORTON, REID 1955 S.C. (H.L.) 74	S.G.	Policies on a father's life, expressed to be within Married Women's Policies of Assurance (Scotland) Act 1880, *held* on the facts, to be within s. 2 and so non-aggregable with rest of his estate.

CASE	Subject and Degree of General Public Importance	Decisions Below	Report, Result, Speeches	Subsequent Reversal	Sui Generis, or Part of a Pattern	Epitome
125. WELFORD GRAVELS v. De Voil	Income Tax— Great	C.A. (UPJOHN diss.) rvsg. PLOWMAN	Dismissed (U.) JENKINS, GUEST [1965] A.C. 34			Land, including a gravel pit, was assessed at £8. 10s. by apportioning the Schedule A assessment of the farm of which it was previously part. On discovering it was worked, the Inspector made an additional assessment of £4,375 net. *Held,* in the circumstances, a substantially different subject came into existence and justified the revaluation.
126. WERNHER Sharkey v.	Income Tax— Great	C.A. (U.) rvsg. VAISEY	Allowed (OAKSEY diss.) SIMONDS, RADCLIFFE [1956] A.C. 58		P.P.	W. transferred horses, bred in her stud farm, to her racing stables. *Held,* their market value, not their cost of breeding, must be credited in the stud farm accounts for purposes of Schedule D tax.
127. WESTMINSTER BANK v. C.I.R.	Estate Duty— Great	C.A. (ROMER diss.) rvsg. HARMAN	Allowed (RADCLIFFE diss.) MORTON, REID, KEITH		P.P.	Settlors of paid-up policies on their lives directed trustees (a) to pay income of fund (comprising policy moneys+investments) to nephew for life, (b) to pay half to other trustees, and invest half for benefit of three younger sons: the settlors died (a) 22, (b) 18 years later. *Held,* the beneficiaries' interests on the deaths were not different from before, so no estate duty was payable.
128. WRIGHTSON v. C.I.R.		C.A. (U.) rvsg. HARMAN	Allowed (RADCLIFFE & REID diss.) [1958] A.C. 210			
129. WHITWORTH PARK COAL LTD. v. C.I.R. RAMSHAW COAL LTD. v. C.I.R. BRANCEPETH COAL LTD. v. C.I.R.	Income Tax— Moderate	C.A. (U.) affg. HARMAN	Dismissed (RADCLIFFE diss.) SIMONDS (=REID), KEITH [1961] A.C. 31	F.A. 1960, s. 39	P.P.	W.P., after nationalization, was an investment co. within predecessor of I.T.A., s. 257. It received payments of interim income from the Ministry, in respect of preceding years. *Held,* they fell within Sch. D Case III, arose in the years of receipt, and must be apportioned among the shareholders as actual income of those years.

No. / Case	Subject — Degree	Court	Decision		Counsel	Notes
130. WIGRAM SETTLED ESTATES LTD. v. C.I.R.	Surtax— Moderate	C.A. (U.) affg. VAISEY	Dismissed (U.) SIMONDS, REID [1958] 1 W.L.R. 213; 1 All E.R. 338		S.G.	On a surtax direction, under predecessor of I.T.A., s. 245, correct apportionment of actual income is according to the shareholders' rights to share it.
131. WILSON's (DUNBLANE) LTD. C.I.R. v.	Income Tax— Moderate	C.S. (i) (U.) rvsg. Sp. Comrs.	Dismissed (U.) REID, NORMAND (=SIMON) [1954] 1 W.L.R. 282; 35 T.C. 107	F.A. 1954, s. 23	S.G.	The appellant co. bought a business, including machinery at its open market price. *Held,* this prevented s. 59 (2) of I.T.A. 1945 from applying.
132. WISEMAN v. Borneman & Others	Surtax— Moderate	C.A. (U.) affg. PENNYCUICK	Dismissed (U.) REID, MORRIS, GUEST, DONOVAN, WILBERFORCE [1969] 3 All E.R. 275		S.G.	The Tribunal set up under F.A. 1960, s. 28, before considering whether there is a prima facie case, is not bound to furnish the tax-payers with a copy of the Revenue counter-statement, or to hear the parties.
133. WOOD BROS. (BIRKENHEAD) LTD. C.I.R. v.	Surtax— Great	C.A. (U.) affg. HARMAN	Dismissed (SIMONDS & KEITH diss.) MORTON, REID [1959] A.C. 487		P.P.	The co. was subject to surtax direction for its last accounting period before liquidation (I.T.A., ss. 245, 248) and was liable to a balancing charge in respect of sales of plant (I.T.A., ss. 292 (1) & 323 (4)). *Held,* the balancing charge was not part of its 'actual income from all sources' to be apportioned.

ANNEX B—RATING APPEALS (23)

CASE	Subject and Degree of General Public Importance	Decisions Below	Report, Result, Speeches	Subsequent Reversal	Sui Generis, or Part of a Pattern	Epitome
1. ARBUCKLE SMITH & CO. v. Greenock Corporation	Occupation—Great	C.S. (II) (U.) affg. GUEST	Allowed (U.) KILMUIR, REID, RADCLIFFE, KEITH [1960] A.C. 813	Unoccupied Property may now be rated—General Rate Act 1967	P.P.	Co. bought a warehouse for use as a bonded store. Before it could lawfully be so used, considerable alterations had to be made. *Held*, while they were being made, co. was not in 'actual occupation' (hence not liable to rates): 'there was no enjoyment of the value of the building *as a warehouse*' (RADCLIFFE).
2. ASH BROS. & HEATON LTD. Dawkins (V.O.) v.	Value—Moderate	C.A. (U.) affg. L.T.	Dismissed (GUEST & DONOVAN diss.) PEARCE, WILBERFORCE, PEARSON [1969] 2 A.C. 366		P.P.	*Held*, the probability that part of the respondent's hereditament would 'within about a year' be demolished by Birmingham Corporation (the actual landlords) under a road-widening scheme justified a reduction in rateable value from £3,400 to £3,050.
3. BIRMINGHAM ROYAL INSTITUTE FOR THE BLIND Almond (V.O.) v.	Rating Relief—Small	C.A. (U.) rvsg. L.T.	Dismissed (U.) REID, HODSON [1968] A.C. 37		P.P.	Respondent, a war charity and voluntary organization within Rating & Valuation (Miscellaneous Provisions) Act 1955 (hereinafter 'R.V. (M.P.) 1955') s. 9 (1) occupied, *inter alia*, a large 2-storey building. *Held*, this was a 'structure' within the section, and so exempt from valuation.
4. CAMPBELL COLLEGE, BELFAST v. Commissioner of Valuation	Rating Relief—Moderate (Northern Ireland only)	C.A. (N.I.) (CURRAN diss.) affg. Q.B.D.	Allowed (U.) REID, RADCLIFFE, UPJOHN [1964] 1 W.L.R. 912		P.P.	Hereditaments occupied by the appellant (fee-paying) school *held* exempt from rates because 'used for charitable purposes' within s. 2 of the Valuation (Ireland) Amendment Act 1854.

[354]

No. & Case	Subject	Court	Decision	Judges / Citation		Notes
5. CHURCH OF JESUS CHRIST OF LATTER DAY SAINTS v. Henning (V.O.)	Rating Relief—Small	C.A. (U.) rvsg. L.T.	Dismissed (U.)	EVERSHED, MORRIS, PEARCE [1964] A.C. 420	S.G.	Though all 75 Mormon chapels in U.K. were open to the public (and exempt under s. 7 (2) (a) R.V. (M.P.) 1955 as 'places of public religious worship') the Mormon Temple was only open to a selected class known as 'Mormons of good standing'. *Held* the Temple was *not* exempt.
6. DERBYSHIRE MINERS' WELFARE COMMITTEE Skegness U.D.C. v.	Rating Relief—Moderate	C.A. (U.) affg. Div. Ct.	Dismissed (U.)	SIMONDS, DENNING [1959] A.C. 807	See now General Rate Act 1967, s. 40 (5) (c) P.P.	The respondents managed a holiday camp (provided from funds which came from the N.C.B.) for miners on a non-profit making basis. *Held*, it was occupied 'for the purposes of an organization ... whose main objects were concerned with ... social welfare', within s. 8 R.V. (M.P.) 1955, and so was entitled to relief.
7. W. & J. B. EASTWOOD LTD. v. Herrod (V.O.)	Rating Relief—Great	C.A. (U.) rvsg. L.T.	Dismissed (U.)	REID, MORRIS, GUEST, DILHORNE [1971] A.C. 160	Rating Act 1971 P.P.	For the purpose of producing broiler chickens for sale appellants occupied 20 layer houses, a hatchery, a poultry-food mill, a packing station, 72 broiler houses (22,000 birds in each), and 1,150 acres of land (20 acres used by cockerels, the rest to grow 13% of the grain used in the mill). *Held*, these buildings were not 'used solely in connection with agricultural operations' on the land; hence were not exempt from rates as 'agricultural buildings'.
8. GAS COUNCIL Solihull Corporation v.	Occupation—Small	C.A. (U.) rvsg. L.T.	Dismissed (U.)	SIMONDS [1962] 1 W.L.R. 583	P.P.	(Facts in [1961] 1 W.L.R. 619). A Gas Board owned, and ran, a research station on behalf of the Gas Council, who (1) in fact provided the research costs (2) selected its director (3) put their name in the building and on station notepaper and applications for licences etc. *Held*, the Board, not the Council occupied the station.

ANNEX B—RATING APPEALS (23)

CASE	Subject and Degree of General Public Importance	Decisions Below	Report, Result, Speeches	Subsequent Reversal	Sui Generis, or Part of a Pattern	Epitome
9. GENERAL NURSING COUNCIL v. St. Marylebone B.C.	Rating Relief—Moderate	C.A. (U.) rvsg. DANCKWERTS	Dismissed (COHEN & SOMERVELL diss.) MORTON, TUCKER, KEITH [1959] A.C. 540		P.P.	The appellants, established under Nurses Act 1967, had to maintain a register and exercise supervisory powers. Held, they were not within R.V. (M.P.) 1955, s. 8 (1) (a). To regulate the nursing profession is not charitable or 'concerned with the advancement of social welfare'.
10. HUDSON'S BAY CO. v. Thompson (V.O.)	Rating Relief—Small	C.A. (U.) affg. L.T.	Allowed (U.) SIMONDS, REID, KEITH, DENNING [1960] A.C. 926	Industrial de-rating was abolished from 1963, by Rating & Valuation Act 1961	P.P.	Appellants' sorting and grading of skins involved great skill. Held to be 'adapting for sale' within s. 149, Factory and Workshop Act 1901; so their premises would be 'a workshop' and qualify for relief (under Rating & Valuation (Apportionment) Act 1928) if 'manual labour' was exercised on the skins.
11. IMPERIAL TOBACCO CO. v. Pierson (V.O.)	Value—Small	C.A. (U.) rvsg. L.T.	Allowed (DENNING diss.) SIMONDS, MORTON, REID, COHEN [1961] A.C. 463	Corrected Rating & Valuation Act 1961, s. 9	S.G.	Held advertising rights under s. 56, Local Government Act 1948 should be valued (a) regardless of the value of any structure involved (in this case worth £15 a year) if provided by the occupier; and (b) whether the right is exercised or not. Hence, because I.T.C. provided the structure in this case, its rateable value was reduced from £165 to £150.
12. INSTITUTE OF FUEL v. Morley (V.O.)	Rating Relief—Small	C.A. (JENKINS diss.) affg. L.T.	Allowed (U.) MORTON, TUCKER [1956] A.C. 245	Scientific Societies Act repealed, as from 1963, by Rating & Valuation Act 1961	P.P.	Held, although one of the purposes of the appellant was 'to uphold the status of members' and 'to support . . . industries and scientific research', it was 'instituted for the purposes of science . . . exclusively' within Scientific Societies Act 1843, s. 1.

13. INSTITUTE OF MECHANICAL ENGINEERS v. Cane (V.O.)	Rating Relief— Small	C.A. (U.) rvsg. L.T.	Dismissed (U.). SIMONDS, REID, RADCLIFFE, TUCKER, DENNING [1961] A.C. 696	(1843 Act repealed, see above)	P.P.	The appellants' object under their charter was 'to promote *the development of mechanical engineering . . .*'. *Held*, this included not only a science but also an art, an industry, and a profession: so exemption under Scientific Societies Act 1843 was refused.
14. JOHNSTONE & Others Glasgow Corporation v.	Rating Relief— Small	C.S. (II) (U.) rvsg. CAMERON	Dismissed (GUEST diss.) REID, EVERSHED, HODSON [1965] A.C. 609		P.P.	Respondents, congregational board of a church, owned a house, part of the church building, and required an officer-caretaker to live there (rent-free). *Held*, (1) they occupied it (U.); and (2) (GUEST diss.) it was 'wholly or mainly used for charitable purposes' within the Local Government (Financial Provisions) (Scotland) Act 1962, s. 4 (2) (a).
15. KINGSTON-UPON-HULL CORPORATION v. Clayton (V.O.)	Occupation— Moderate	C.A. (DONOVAN diss.) rvsg. L.T.	Dismissed (U.) TUCKER, GUEST [1963] A.C. 28		P.P.	Two-thirds of the hereditament—which was held by appellants on (a charitable) trust to permit its use in perpetuity as a public art gallery—was open daily to the public as such without charge. The rest was used for ancillary offices, store rooms etc. *Held* the rights of the public were not exhaustive and 'beneficial occupation' remained in the appellants.
16. L.C.C. v. Wilkins (V.O.)	Occupation— Great	C.A. (U.) affg. L.T.	Dismissed (U.). KILMUIR, JOWITT, OAKSEY, RADCLIFFE [1957] A.C. 362		P.P.	Contractors' huts, erected and standing on a building site for 18 months, *held*, capable of rateable occupation, because (a) whether chattels or not, defined sites had been appropriated for them, (b) for long enough to be 'permanent' in the context of rating.
17. LONDON TRANSPORT EXECUTIVE v. Betts (V.O.)	Rating Relief— Small	C.A. (U.) affg. L.T.	Dismissed (DENNING diss.) MORTON, REID, KEITH, SOMERVELL [1959] A.C. 213		P.P.	Appellants occupied a depot for the periodic overhauling and reconditioning of omnibuses. *Held*, it was used for 'maintenance' of their vehicles within s. 3 (2), Rating & Valuation (Apportionment) Act 1928, and was therefore not an industrial hereditament.

ANNEX B—RATING APPEALS (23)

CASE	Subject and Degree of General Public Importance	Decisions Below	Report, Result, Speeches	Subsequent Reversal	Sui Generis, or Part of a Pattern	Epitome
18. MID-NORTHANTS WATER BOARD v. Lee (V.O.)	Valuation—Moderate	C.A. (U.) rvsg. L.T.	Dismissed (U.) MORTON, RADCLIFFE, KEITH [1958] A.C. 68	(The Rating & Valuation Act 1961 introduced valuation by a new formula)	P.P.	The appellant Board, assessed on 'the profits basis' borrowed to build new works, and its precepted income from local authorities included an estimated £9,515 for loan interest. In fact interest cost only £3,365. Held, although in respect of works not yet in occupation, the whole £9,515 must be included in its gross receipts for the purposes of the assessment.
19. NATIONAL DEPOSIT FRIENDLY SOCIETY v. Skegness U.D.C.	Rating Relief—Moderate	C.A. (U.) affg. Div. Ct.	Dismissed (U.) KEITH, MACDERMOTT, DENNING [1959] A.C. 293		P.P.	The appellants, not a charity, had 700,000 members, for whose benefit it provided (and occupied) a convalescent home on a mutual basis. Held, (1) it was 'not established or conducted for profit', but (2) was not within R.V. (M.P.) 1955, s. 8 (2), because, lacking the element of altruism or public benefit, it was not 'concerned ... with the advancement of social welfare'.
20. SCOTTISH BURIAL REFORM & CREMATION SOCIETY v. Glasgow Corporation	Rating Relief—Small	C.S. (II) (WALKER diss.) affg. MILLIGAN	Allowed (U.) REID, UPJOHN, WILBERFORCE [1968] A.C. 138		P.P.	Held, a non-profit-making society running and occupying a crematorium were a charity and entitled to 50% relief under Local Government (Financial Provisions) Scotland Act 1962, s. 4 (2).
21. SHELL-MEX & B.P. LTD. v. Clayton (V.O.)	Rating Relief—Small	C.A. (U.) affg. L.T.	Dismissed (OAKSEY diss.) SIMONDS, MORTON, TUCKER, KEITH		S.G.	The Transport Commission (a) leased waste land, adjoining its Hull docks undertaking, to the appellants who built oil storage tanks on it; (b) built jetties for incoming ships to dis-

charge oil, via pipes, to the appellant's tanks. Oil was accepted from three other oil companies, on commission. *Held, not* a 'freight-transport hereditament' (three different *rationes*).

S.G.

The appellants stored petrol underground in a metal cylinder 13ft. 6in. long, 7ft. diameter, surrounded by dry sand, in a concrete & 9in.-brick container, and covered by slabs of reinforced concrete. *Held*, the cylinder was not rateable, being itself a 'tank' in structure and not part of a 'tank' comprising the whole installation.

P.P.

In 1951 a hereditament occupied by the appellant society was held, by a local valuation court, to be within the Scientific Societies Act 1843, and deleted from the then valuation list. The V.O. nevertheless entered it in the 1956 list. No change of circumstances were alleged *Held*, the V.O. was not estopped *per rem judicatam* from re-arguing the appellants' status.

22. SHELL-MEX & B.P. LTD. *v.* Holyoak (V.O.)	Rating Relief—Great	C.A. (U.) rvsg. L.T.	Allowed (KEITH & DENNING diss.) SIMONDS, MORTON, REID [1959] 1 W.L.R. 188	[1956] 1 W.L.R. 1198
23. SOCIETY OF MEDICAL OFFICERS *v.* Hope (V.O.)	Rating Relief—Great	C.A. (SELLERS diss.) affg. L.T.	Dismissed RADCLIFFE, KEITH [1960] A.C. 551	

XVI

APPEALS AND LEGISLATIVE RESPONSE

FEW doubt nowadays that judges are in some sense law-makers. (If such doubts persist in the reader's mind we would feel that our own study has failed in one of its objectives.) Judges demonstrably alter the law more often, if less comprehensively than do legislators. But is there a clear division of function, conventional or constitutional, which makes it necessary for Parliament either to step in where judges fear to tread, or to reverse the law declared by the courts?

In the context of revenue law we have already noted the relations between the Law Lords and Parliament; invariably one of the litigating parties is the Crown which has a peculiar (if unsurprising) ability to secure reversal of an adverse ruling. And a whole chapter has been devoted to discussing the role of Law Lords as active members of the legislature. Such relations need to be viewed against the broader background of generally acceptable ideas about respective law-making roles. Where does the boundary between the parliamentary function of statute-creating and judicial decisions begin and end? Lord Radcliffe, extra-judicially,[1] has asserted: 'We cannot run the risk of finding the archetypal image of the judge confused in men's minds with the very different image of the legislator', the risk being that of destroying the image of the judge as an 'objective, impartial, erudite, and experienced declarer of the law that is'. What, then, are the boundaries of parliamentary law-making where judicial decision is directly involved?

English judges operate within a constitutional framework which declares the sovereignty of Parliament, a doctrine tempered by the political reality of executive supremacy. Not only is the government of the day able to control the business of legislation, which includes the power to abrogate any court decision unacceptable to the Executive, but it is also unfettered in the legislation it proposes. Even the most creative and individualistic judge can hardly deny the recognition that an Act of Parliament is the superior source of law. As Lord Devlin has aptly observed:[2] 'In the long struggle with the Executive which established the liberty of the subject the common law and Parliament fought side by side. They fought for the supremacy of Parliament and they won. Thus the common law has put the control of the Executive into the safe

---

[1] *The Law and its Compass* (1960), p. 14.
[2] Devlin, *Samples of Lawmaking* (1964), p. 119.

keeping of Parliament. They cannot now withdraw their endorsement even if they would.' The concession by the courts of the role of supreme law-maker may not survive. A march into a European federation and the enactment of a Bill of Rights may reflect parliamentary repayment in kind to the courts for the control achieved over the Sovereign and the Executive. But until either or both events happen the judges will remain lions under the legislators' throne.

A consistent product of parliamentary sovereignty is that the courts have yielded to legislators' notions of public policy, while continuing to assert their autonomy and independence. Time and again, judges have declared themselves content to leave a particular issue to be resolved by Parliament. This dutiful deference is founded upon the belief that legislation is the more appropriate vehicle for legal declaration of social policy. And there are numerous instances of such an approach.

In *Cartledge* v. *E. Jopling & Sons Ltd.*,[1] the plaintiffs did not discover that they were suffering from pneumoconiosis until after the end of the statutory period of limitation. All the courts held that a cause of action accrues when the damage is done and not when the plaintiff first learns that he is suffering from the injury caused. Lord Reid, in dismissing the appeal, said: 'One thing at least is clear. The fact that the present law requires us to dismiss the appeal shows that some amendment of the law is urgently necessary.' Even while the case was under appeal, the Government set up a departmental committee to consider what change should be made.[2] The law was swiftly amended in the Limitation Act 1963.[3]

In *Myers* v. *Director of Public Prosecutions*[4] the majority of the House of Lords showed a marked reluctance to change the rules of evidence without the sanction of Parliament. The case concerned the sale of cars by a gang of car thieves who attempted to obliterate the identity of the cars. The evidence produced at the trial showed that it was possible to trace the manufacturer of the car, as well as its former owner, through the cylinder block number placed on the car when the chassis was built. The cards bearing the records were micro-filmed and destroyed. The workmen who moulded the engine block were unknown and could not be called to testify.

The defendant was convicted, but appealed on the ground that the manufacturer's records were wrongly admitted as hearsay evidence. Records of this type would be considered true, because of the mechanical and generally disinterested nature of entries made in the routine of duty and their constant liability, if false, to be detected. But the person who made the declaration must, by a long-standing judge-made rule, be shown to be dead before the

---

1 [1963] A.C. 758.
2 Report of the Committee on Limitation of Action in Cases of Personal Injury (1962) Cmnd. 1876.
3 Proposals to amend the Act by providing a period longer than twelve months after discovery of the injury were made by the Law Commission in 1970 (Law. Com. No. 35).
4 [1965] A.C. 1001.

evidence becomes admissible. It is not enough that the declarer is unidentifiable or untraceable. The Court of Criminal Appeal upheld the conviction saying 'that the admission of such evidence does not infringe the hearsay rule because its probative value does not depend upon the credit of an unidentified person but rather on the circumstances in which the record is maintained and the inherent probability that it is correct'.

On appeal, the House of Lords, by a majority, held that the records were inadmissible as hearsay. To allow their admission would be to change the law in such a way as to be beyond the courts' function. Lord Reid explained that 'an out-of-court statement can only operate to confirm or deny other evidence if it is assumed to be *true*, and the hearsay rule prohibits the tendering of the statement as evidence of the *truth* of the facts stated.' If the court were to extend the law, 'it must be by the development and application of fundamental principles. We cannot introduce arbitrary conditions or limitations: that must be left to legislation. . . . The only satisfactory solution is by legislation following on a wide survey of the whole field, and I think such a survey is overdue.'

Professor Jaffe has criticized this attitude, suggesting that a judge of Lord Reid's stature 'should ask whether the law of evidence is an area in which piecemeal improvements are not preferable to none at all. It is a question whether a present good should be sacrificed for the indefinite and uncertain prospect of parliamentary action'.[1] Lords Pearce and Donovan did not feel so constrained, holding that the process of improvement and evolution of the common law so as to serve the interests of justice was never complete, and it rested with the judges to mould and adapt the law to modern conditions.

Parliament responded promptly by passing the Criminal Evidence Act 1965. The Act provides that 'where direct oral evidence of a fact would be admissible, a statement in a document tending to establish that fact shall, on production of the document, be admissible as evidence of that fact.' But the legislation was directed only to the narrow issue in the Myers decision and did not encompass a 'wide survey' of the law of evidence advocated by Lord Reid. This judicial deferment to Parliament did not evoke fully the desired response. The whole of the law relating to criminal evidence (including the *Myers* legislation) is now under review by the Criminal Law Revision Committee.

The difference in judicial approach to the dual methods of law-making was reflected in the cases relating to the 'deserted wife's equity.' Ever since *Bendall* v. *McWhirter* in 1952, the Court of Appeal, following the lead of Lord Denning, had attempted by a series of decisions to give the deserted wife the protection of a roof over her head as against her owner-husband or his mortgagee. When ultimately in 1965 the House of Lords came to consider the problem in *National Provincial Bank Ltd.* v. *Ainsworth*[2] the law left the

---

[1] Louis L. Jaffe, *English and American Judges as Lawmakers* (1969), pp. 28–9.
[2] [1965] A.C. 1175. See pp. 308 ff, *ante*.

deserted wife unprotected, and the Law Lords implored the legislature to intervene. Lord Wilberforce, who sat on the appeal, subsequently in his legislative capacity pointed out that the Matrimonial Homes Bill showed 'in a rather striking and interesting way the difference, the dividing line, between cases where the law can be reformed by decisions of the courts and other cases where intervention by the legislature is concerned'.[1]

The subject of the property rights of the deserted wife was considered by the Law Commission, and remedial legislation was enacted within two years of the *Ainsworth* judgment. The Matrimonial Homes Act 1967 provides that a spouse's 'right of occupation' shall, during the subsistence of the marriage 'be a charge on the other spouse's estate or interest taking priority as if it were an equitable interest'. The charge is capable of being registered as a Land Charge Class F under the Land Registration Act. Where a charge is registered, it is a term of a contract for the sale of the dwelling with vacant possession that the vendor will have the registration cancelled before completion of the sale.

The Matrimonial Homes Act, reversing the *Ainsworth* decision, is an example of certain types of social policy where the legal issues involved may be so complex, and the implications so wide, that it is more convenient for judges to seek legislative change than to legislate themselves, though this view is held more strongly by some judges than by others. Another example, where the Law Lords bowed to Parliamentary law-making, was that of *Chapman* v. *Chapman*[2] which prompted the Variation of Trusts Act 1958. The House of Lords had held that the power of the courts to vary trusts was confined to a compromise of disputed rights, and the Court had no inherent jurisdiction to modify or vary trusts despite the fact that the variation was consented to by the interested adults and was beneficial to other parties.

Dissatisfaction with the decision was rife, particularly among those engaged in the practice of 'trust-busting' in order to avoid the penal consequences of estate duty. Once again the Law Reform Committee was pressed into service and this time its recommendations were taken up in a private Members' Bill. Where property is held on trust for various classes of infants, and unborn and incapacitated parties, the Court may now approve any arrangement of the trusts which would be for the benefit of such persons.

If judicial deference to Parliament can be defended in all these instances, much of the defence depends on prompt legislative action. If Parliament is lax, judicial intervention may become unavoidable.

In *Suisse Atlantique Société d'Armament Maritime S.A.* v. *N.V. Rotterdamsche Kolen Centrale*[3] their Lordships hinted broadly that only Parliament could deal with the scope of exemption clauses; four years later there was no sign of Parliamentary action, although the Law Commission had indicated

---

1 H.L. Debs., vol. 272 col. 44, 14 June 1966.
2 [1954] A.C. 429.   3 [1967] 1 A.C. 361.

the line of reform. In *Beswick* v. *Beswick* in 1967 the Law Lords declined to review the English law on the *jus quaesitum tertio*, even though the shackles of the doctrine of *stare decisis* had by then been removed: as yet there are no signs of remedial legislation. With the increasing legislative burden on Parliament there is a danger that the law will lag too long behind the times if the judiciary, and the Law Lords in particular, will not itself shoulder some of the legislative burden.

Professor Jaffe in his recent book, *English and American Judges as Law-makers*,[1] notes that judges

overdo the gospel of self-restraint. What is necessary is a more discriminating approach to the question of judicial creativity. . . . There is still judicial innovation in England, an awareness that there are and always will be important lawmaking jobs for the judges. These judges should be encouraged; a more positive, a more comprehensive philosophy of the judicial role should be developed.

The House of Lords displays that degree of judicial innovation Professor Jaffé invites, haltingly and sporadically. Lord Reid's argument, that whereas the courts can extend the law by the application of fundamental principles, only the legislature can introduce exceptions and limitations, may be hard to refute as an orthodox guide to the extent of the courts' capacity to change the law.[2] This orthodoxy is applied unwaveringly in the area of statutory construction, on the basis that the courts are there only to seek Parliament's intentions: if the search proves chimerical or produces unsatisfactory solutions then Parliament alone should correct its own handiwork.[3] It is in the area of the common law that the judges are prepared to be bold. *Hedley Byrne & Co. Ltd.* v. *Heller & Partners Ltd.*[4] opened up a new area of the test of negligence by embracing liability for negligent mis-statements. *Home Office* v. *Dorset Yacht Co.*[5] launched tort liability on government departments. In *Indyka* v. *Indyka*[6] the basis for the recognition of foreign decrees of divorce was substantially modified, although not all that was laid down was to the liking of the Law Commission.[7]

On the evidence we have examined, the House of Lords in its judicial capacity has been meticulously deferential to Parliament in refraining from decisions which reflect on public policy not directly involved in the instant case. Indeed, there is more than a hint here and there that judicial self-restraint is over-practised, and that the Law Lords could be bolder without seriously endangering relationships with the legislature.

Parliament responds in kind to the Law Lords' self-denying ordinance not to usurp the legislature's function. The understanding which sustains Parlia-

[1] *Op. cit.*, p. 59.   [2] [1965] A.C. 1001, 1021.
[3] *D.P.P.* v. *Bhagwan* [1970] 3 W.L.R. 501, per Lord Diplock at p. 512; *I.R.C.* v. *Parker* [1966] A.C. 141; *Shop & Store Development Ltd.* v. *I.R.C.* [1967] 1 A.C. 472.
[4] [1964] A.C. 365.   [5] [1970] A.C. 1004.   [6] [1969] 1 A.C. 33.
[7] Report on the Hague Convention on Recognition of Divorces and Legal Separations (Law Comm. No. 36) para 25, p. 11. See now the Recognition of Divorces and Legal Separations Act 1971.

mentary supremacy, at least on policy issues, has its counterpart in the understanding that the judiciary will be independent, and the integrity of legal
procedures preserved. We have already seen in Chapter x that Law Lords
react most strongly in parliamentary debate when this understanding is
breached. There is a mutual understanding that courts and Parliament must
harmonize and dovetail their respective law-making functions. A confrontation over the dual legislative roles will produce unhappy consequences.

Throughout our period, Government, with its ability to shape the parliamentary programme, has on the whole responded to the invitation from the
House of Lords to sponsor remedial legislation reversing court decisions.
From time to time it has not waited for the hint, but has referred problems to
various law reform committees. Apart from correcting erroneous statutory
constructions (or, at least, constructions which conflict with parliamentary
intentions), almost exclusively in the field of revenue law, Government and
Parliament have otherwise sensibly left the courts' decisions unsullied, save
where policy issues were involved or statutory reversal was requested.

But in three instances over the last two decades there were signs of an unhappy clash, and in one of them the judges and legislators were at loggerheads.

The exemption of trade unions from the law of the land has been a constant
politico-legal issue. The antipathy of organised labour towards the law is well
known: and the courts have not always concealed their dislike of labour's
immunity from the judicial process. These feelings were manifest when
Parliament in the Trade Disputes Act 1968 reversed in part the decision in
Rookes v. *Barnard*.[1]

The plaintiff was a skilled draughtsman in the employment of B.O.A.C. He
had for long been at odds with his union colleagues, and as a result resigned
his union membership. The office in which he worked was a closed shop, and
when he refused to rejoin the union, the union officials informed B.O.A.C.
that union labour would be withdrawn unless the plaintiff was instantly dismissed. B.O.A.C. ultimately complied under the threat of a strike. The
plaintiff brought his action against the union officials for using unlawful
means to induce B.O.A.C. to determine his contract of service.

The House of Lords supported the lower courts in their revival of an
obsolescent remedy, the tort of intimidation. The Court of Appeal thought
that, to constitute the tort, the illegal act must be something criminal or
tortious, and that the threat of a breach of contract was not enough. The Law
Lords held that a threatened breach of contract was sufficient to constitute
the wrong, which, furthermore, was not protected by s. 3, Trade Disputes
Act 1906. The reaction from trade unionists was instinctive. The prospect of a
suit for intimidation would hang over every union official contemplating
strike action. The Government, sensitive to trade union pressure, reacted with
promised and judicially-uninvited statutory reversal.

[1] [1964] A.C. 1129.

The ensuing Bill provided that an action in tort could not be brought against a person on the grounds only that he threatens to break a contract of employment, and that a person who threatens to induce someone else to break his contract of employment is protected from an action in tort. The debates on the Bill revived the simmering battle between the law and trade unionism. The Lord Chancellor (Lord Gardiner) said that judges or lawyers were ill-informed on the topic of industrial relations: 'Parliament has thought it right largely to remove the whole of this sphere from the courts.'[1] The Trade Disputes Bill was only filling a lacuna in the 1906 legislation.

The proponents of a dosage of legalism for trade unionists were less concerned with the reversal of *Rookes* v. *Barnard* than with the ability of the T.U.C. to bludgeon the Government into preserving its unique immunity. And indeed the lawyers were unperturbed. One Law Lord in *Rookes* v. *Barnard*, Lord Pearce, observed in a later case, *J. T. Stratford & Son Ltd.* v. *Lindley*,[2] that *Rookes* v. *Barnard* was more restricted than was sometimes thought:

It was suggested in argument that *Rookes* v. *Barnard* went a long way further than it was, in my opinion, intended to go. It was, for instance, suggested by counsel for the respondents that it withdrew from the protection of section 3 of the Trade Disputes Act 1906 the threats of a trade union official to the employer to call a strike in breach of the contract of employment. It certainly does not do that.

Misunderstanding abounded to the point where the legal decision was swamped in a flood of political rhetoric. The relationship between the law and industrial activity has long been a thorny issue. It cannot be said that judicial integrity was affronted by the parliamentary reversal of *Rookes* v. *Barnard*. Indeed, by implication the re-establishment of the tort of intimidation was approved. But the controversy did serve momentarily to arouse the mutual antipathies. In that climate misunderstanding is understandable.

Less understandable was the contretemps over *D.P.P.* v. *Smith*.[3] The accident of a few ill-chosen words in the single judgment of Viscount Kilmuir in the Lords' appeal created a veritable rift in legal opinion and led to statutory reversal seven years later in the Criminal Justice Act 1967.[4]

The accused was driving a car containing stolen property. While stopped at a crossing waiting for traffic directions he was told by a police officer to draw up to the kerb so that the policeman could inspect the contents of the vehicle (the accused was carrying stolen scaffolding). The accused started to obey, but then accelerated, with the police officer hanging on to the bonnet. As the car sped away with the police officer lying partially on the front, it took a sinuous path down the road. Several cars struck the police officer's body (there were no marks on the accused's car). These blows killed the police officer.

The trial judge had directed the jury that

if you are satisfied that . . . he must as a reasonable man have contemplated that grievous bodily harm was likely to result to that officer . . . and that such harm did

[1] H.L. Debs., vol. 270, col. 34, 2 August 1965.   [2] [1965] A.C. 269.
[3] [1961] A.C. 290.   [4] Section 8.

happen and the officer in question dies, then the accused is guilty of capital murder
. . . On the other hand . . . if you think he could not as a reasonable man have contemplated that grievous bodily harm would result to the officer in consequence of his activities—well, then, the verdict would be guilty of manslaughter.[1]

The standard to be followed was whether the jury thought the accused, as a reasonable man, *contemplated* that grievous bodily harm was likely to result from the actions and that *such harm did occur*. The defence pleaded the test was whether the accused had *actually* intended to kill or do grievous bodily harm. The Court of Criminal Appeal thought that the trial judge had applied an exclusively objective test for the accused's intentions, and quashed the conviction for murder, substituting manslaughter.

In the House of Lords, on the Crown's appeal, Viscount Kilmuir, delivering the only judgment, rejected the Court of Criminal Appeal's formulation: 'This purely subjective approach involves this, that if an accused said he did not in fact think of the consequences and the jury considered that that might well be true, he would be entitled to be acquitted of murder.' Such an argument was 'a departure . . . from that upon which the courts have always acted'. Once the jury had made up its mind on whether 'the accused was unlawfully and voluntarily doing something to someone . . . it matters not what the accused in fact contemplates as the probable result, or whether he ever contemplated at all, provided he was in law responsible and accountable for his actions'. The presumption, Viscount Kilmuir concluded, that a man intends the natural and probable consequence of his acts 'is merely another way of applying the test of a reasonable man'.

The decision provoked adverse academic criticism,[2] a vigorous note of dissension from a judicial body no less august than the High Court of Australia through the voice of Sir Owen Dixon[3] and a recommendation for statutory reversal by the Law Commission.[4] When the Criminal Justice Bill was being considered in 1966 by the House of Lords the Lord Chancellor moved an amendment reflecting the view of the Law Commission. Viscount Dilhorne, who was Attorney General and had conducted the case for the Crown, said that there had been no case in his lifetime 'which has been so generally misunderstood'. He observed that the House of Lords had not applied the objective test of 'whether or not there was an intent to do the act which caused the death, but that . . . you applied the objective test of the nature and quality of the act intended'.[5]

The impression that the Law Lords had applied an objective test to the accused's intent was created by the inapt (even inept) language used by

---

[1] [1960] 3 All E.R. 161, 163.
[2] 'Constructive Malice Revived', 23 M.L.R. 605, 609; (1960) and Crim. L. Rev., 766 (1960).
[3] *Parker* v. *The Queen* (1963) 111 C.L.R. 610, 632.
[4] 'Imputed Criminal Intent (*D.P.P.* v. *Smith*)', Law Com. No. 10.
[5] H. L. Debs., vol. 287, cols. 250–2, 5 June 1967.

Viscount Kilmuir. This impression was not helped by a misinterpretation of the facts. Many commentators have stated that the accused's car had 'hit three other cars', when in truth it was the police officer's prone body that felt the blows from oncoming vehicles.

If the angry ripostes to the decision of *D.P.P.* v. *Smith* were only in part justified, the temporary rift between parliamentarians and the courts was healed by the statutory provision. It was unanimously agreed that it was time that the law was put back as it was before the misunderstanding arose. Judicial honour was in this instance preserved by the timely intervention of Parliament.

The last instance of friction had no such happy ending, and the incident will not readily be forgotten. The War Damage Act 1965, which retrospectively reversed the Lords' decision in *Burmah Oil Co.* v. *Lord Advocate*[1] and abolished the right at common law to receive compensation for damage to property destroyed on authority of the Crown at war, will rank along with the Commonwealth Immigrants Act 1968 as the most inglorious of recent parliamentary actions. It was one thing to prevent any future claims, but the successful claimants in the Lords (a majority decision of 3:2) had the fruits of litigation snatched from their jaws.

The basis of the claim dated from 1942 when the oil installations in Rangoon belonging to the Burmah Oil Co. were destroyed by direction of the British Government in order to deny their use to the advancing Japanese.

A preliminary compensation policy for war losses was announced by the Government in February 1943; it provided that goods and property destroyed should be replaced or repaired as resources permitted, and that the Government would assist the territories in financing the scheme. The emphasis was placed on rehabilitation rather than on full compensation. In 1946 a Claims Commission was set up in Burma and other Far Eastern colonies to register and assess claims. However, after independence, the Burmese government declined to provide any war damage compensation. Representations to the British Government resulted in an offer of some £10 million to meet Burmese claims, and of this sum the Burmah Oil Company received just under £5 million, which represented about 16 per cent of the company's claim. There was no undertaking that the claimants should accept the money as payment in full, largely because 'it was thought undesirable to do anything which might prejudice claims which were still before Burmese Courts.'[2] In any event, the claims were rejected by the Burma High Court in 1960, on the grounds that the Military Governor had acted under military necessity in a national emergency, which gave rise to no claims in law. Burmah Oil Co. then brought

---

1 [1965] A.C. 75. Lords Reid, Pearce and Upjohn gave the majority judgment; dissent was expressed by Viscount Radcliffe and Lord Hodson.

2 Mr. Niall MacDermot, the Financial Secretary to the Treasury, H. L. Debs., vol. 262, col. 1097, 3 February 1965.

action against the Crown in the Scottish courts in 1961, the choice of court being determined by the fact that the company was registered in Scotland and the claims were not statute-barred there.

An indication that there were stormy days ahead appeared when a letter, addressed to the Burmah Oil Company and signed by the Deputy Treasury Solicitor, warned the claimants that if their claims were successful, legislation would be introduced to indemnify the Crown and its agents. The letter said in part:[1]

I have been instructed to inform you that Her Majesty's Government . . . have been advised that the claim in this action is wholly unfounded in law and that it is likely to be rejected by the courts. Her Majesty's Government are moreover satisfied that the claim made is not in any event one which ought to be met by the British tax-payer. Her Majesty's Government have accordingly decided that, in the unlikely event of your company succeeding, legislation would be introduced to indemnify the Crown and its officers, servants and agents against your company's claim.

Despite the threat, the proceedings continued, and a preliminary point of law was taken to determine the possible liability of the Government. In the Outer House of the Court of Session, the case went against the Government,[2] but the Government won on the appeal,[3] and the case was then taken to the House of Lords. The Scottish courts were critical of the letter written by the Government to the Burmah Oil Company. The trial judge, Lord Kilbrandon, said that the Government was wrong in saying that the claim was wholly un-founded in law. He had found that the claim was well-founded and was 'in accordance with the opinions which have been expressed . . . by the most re-spected jurists and civilians, starting from a time earlier than the law of Scotland as we know it now, and proceeding from those days to all intents and purposes in unanimity'. The Government had proposed to obtain relief from Parliament inasmuch as the claim was said not to be one which 'ought' to be met by the British tax-payer. 'The use of the word "ought" in this context appears to indicate that in the view of Her Majesty's Government there is some moral principle involved in their claim to indemnity which must override the common law of Scotland and the notions of justice of our forebears.'[4]

The Lord President, Lord Clyde, criticized the Government for writing directly to the Burmah Oil Company. 'It is, of course', he said, 'quite con-trary to professional etiquette in Scotland for a solicitor on one side in the course of a litigation to communicate direct with the client on the other, and we have had no explanation as to why this was done.'[5]

---

1 See H.L. Debs., vol. 264, col. 739, 25 March 1965.
2 1962 S.L.T. 347; 1963 S.C. (H.L.) 410, 421–37. Opinion of Lord Kilbrandon in the Outer House.
3 1963 S.L.T. 261; 1963 S.C. (H.L.) 420. First Division of the Court of Session, composed of the Lord President (Clyde), Lords Carmont, Sorn, and Guthrie.
4 1962 S.L.T. 347, 357; 1963 S.C. (H.L.) 410, 436.
5 1963 S.L.T. 261, 274; 1963 S.C. (H.L.) 440, 456.

The House of Lords, by a majority of three to two, reinstated the decision of the Outer House. It did not advert to the letter from the Treasury Solicitor. The judgment developed the distinction between 'battle damage' to property, for which there was no legal right to receive compensation, and 'denial damage', for which compensation must be paid. If property were taken or destroyed in the course of actually fighting the enemy, there would be no legal claim to compensation, but the demolition of the Burmah oil installations did not fall under the rubric of 'battle damage'. Viscount Radcliffe (with whom Lord Hodson agreed) wrote a strong dissenting judgment in which he said that there was no known case in which a court of law had declared that compensation of this nature was due as of right, and that no payment of compensation had been identified as having been made in recognition of a legal right to such compensation.

But it is for those who fill and empty the public purse to decide when, by whom, on what conditions and within what limitations such compensation is to be made available. After all, States lose wars as well as win them: and at the conclusion of a war that has seen massive destruction, whether self-inflicted through the medium of a 'scorched earth' policy or inflicted by the enemy, there may well be urgent claims for reconstruction priorities that make it impossible in advance to mortgage the public treasury to legal claims for individual compensation for such destruction as we have now to consider. . . . Has the law any principle for measuring compensation as a legal right when an act has been done in circumstances so special that the ordinary conceptions of property do not apply to it?[1]

There is, moreover, little to be said for a distinction between blowing up an oil refinery in the face of an advancing enemy and a successful bombing of that refinery within hours of the enemy taking possession.

Viscount Radcliffe's dissent gave support to those who claimed that the common law was believed to be otherwise than what the House of Lords said it was, although he did not speak in favour of the Bill reversing *Burmah Oil*.[2] (He has in any event not been much in evidence as a legislator.) His dissenting opinion, however, was echoed when the War Damage Bill was debated in Parliament. It was said that the object of the Bill was to restore the common law 'to the position which was generally thought to exist before the decision in the House of Lords' and to provide that cases then pending before the courts 'are disposed of on the basis of the law as it has always been thought to be'.[3] If one accepted the concept of sharing the burden of loss, it was said, an equitable scheme for distributing the compensation must be followed, with no opportunity for special groups to claim redress on a preferential scale. 'Any entitlement to compensation on an indemnity basis of common law would, in effect, give preferential treatment to those enjoying it.'[4]

[1] [1965] A.C. 75, 134.
[2] Viscount Radcliffe did not want it said that compensation or indemnity should not be provided for such loss as the appellants suffered, ibid., 1266.
[3] Mr. Niall MacDermott, H.C. Debs., vol. 262, col. 1091, 3 February 1965.
[4] Ibid., col. 1092.

In the House of Lords, the Government Chief Whip, Lord Sheppard, criticized the judgment. 'My Lords,' he said, 'Her Majesty's Government believe that the law as it now stands, after the *Burmah Oil* judgment, is utterly wrong: it is opposed to the public interest; it is opposed to any system of equitable distribution towards the war sufferers; it is imprecise; it is arbitrary and administratively unworkable.'[1]

Viscount Dilhorne, the former Lord Chancellor, supported the Government's Bill, whose purpose, he said, was to change the law as it was declared to be in the *Burmah Oil* case, and to give that change a retrospective effect.[2] Why had not legislation been introduced earlier? In 1962, he said, the Government had to consider whether to introduce a Bill barring claims of the Burmah Oil Co., and other claimants, but it was 'not all that easy' to justify introducing a Bill in Parliament when the general view was that there was nothing to be indemnified against.[3] He thought the Government was right to warn the claimants that legislation would be introduced. His sole concession to judicial criticism was to agree that it was a mistake not to send the letter to the solicitors on the other side.[4]

The opponents of the Bill based their case on general principles of law and of fair-dealing, holding that it was wrong to interfere with the judicial process in so blunt a manner. In the words of Lord McNair, the Bill raised issues which transcended party politics: 'Questions of the correct balance between the rights of the subject and the rights of the Crown; questions of the relations between the judiciary and the legislature, and certain international questions.'[5]

Lord Parker, the Lord Chief Justice, was infuriated and said he 'should not be able to hold up my head again' were he not to remonstrate as strongly as possible against the Bill,[6] which he considered to be 'about as blatant a piece of confiscatory legislation as it is possible to imagine'.[7] The more he heard in debate, the more confirmed he was 'in complete abhorrence' of the Bill.[8] The courts respected the expressed intention of the legislature, and for his part he had always hoped 'that the legislature, in turn, would respect and uphold the standards of justice adopted by the courts'.[9] He would have been more sanguine 'if the Bill had provided for some form of compensation'.[10]

One of the most amazing aspects of the proposal, Lord Parker said, was that 'a court is required to set aside the proceedings on the application of a defendant who has lost his case and who seeks to avoid the incident of that loss.'[11] The letter of warning written by the Government to the Burmah Oil Company was 'a frightening idea. We shall soon be without any laws at all. It will save legislative time. All the Executive have to do is to write a letter of warning and put them off.'[12]

[1] H.L. Debs., vol. 264, col. 734, 25 March 1965.   [2] Ibid., col. 750.   [3] Ibid., col. 756.
[4] Ibid., col. 757.   [5] Ibid., col. 762.   [6] Ibid., col. 776.
[7] Ibid., col. 777.   [8] Ibid., col. 777.   [9] Ibid., col. 778.
[10] Ibid., col. 777.   [11] H.L. Debs., vol. 265, col. 334, 13 April 1965.
[12] H.L. Debs., vol. 264, col. 778, 25 March 1965.

Lord McNair, who also opposed the Bill, said that the proposal to 'forthwith set aside or dismiss the proceedings' drove a coach-and-four through the Crown Proceedings Act 1947. The House was being asked to stop an action 'which our Appellate Committee, after deciding the law, has remitted to the Court of Session for proof of the facts and assessment of compensation, if awarded' (the case came to the Lords on an interlocutory point, whether there was liability). He did not think it right that the courts 'should be treated in this dictatorial fashion after devoting such long and careful consideration to the case'.[1] It was incorrect to say that this was purely domestic legislation, with no international impact, and he saw no reason to 'set this example to some predatory foreign Government' who might be tempted to encroach on the rights of British subjects.[2]

A poignant speech opposing the Bill was made by Viscount Slim, the Military Commander on the spot during the retreat from Burma in 1942 who actually gave the executive order for the destruction of the property. Speaking as 'an ordinary Englishman', as he put it, he said the Bill infringed on the traditional and unquestioned rights of the subject. Destruction was carried out in Burma on orders of the Coalition Government, and everyone in the House 'has inherited not only the certain responsibility for that policy but also responsibility for seeing that no injustice is done to any of Her Majesty's subjects'.[3] Any damage that took place was done on the orders of the British Government, and the demolition was carried out by civilians, 'who remained behind, at great risk to themselves, and were an example, in courage and steadfastness, in carrying out these demolitions'.[4] There had been a certain amount of smokescreening to make the dispute appear to be only a bickering between Government and big business, but he was interested in anything that affected the right to live under the law.

Viscount Slim thought that the threatening letter sent to the Burmah Oil Company 'was really inexcusable',[5] but the gravest charge against the Bill, 'a slight which must be hard to swallow', was that it overrode the judgment of the House of Lords.[6] The measure introduced things which were foreign to the country, such as the overriding of the courts, the effort to prevent people from going to court, and the retrospective effect of the legislation. 'Your Lordships' House is the last defence for some of our most cherished English liberties. Defend them!'[7]

The reversal of the *Burmah Oil* case appeared to many to have been an unnecessary exercise of legislative power, bearing the additional opprobrium of interfering crudely in the judicial process. If a new policy on compensation were required, the timing of the proposal was most awkward. A different policy on compensation could have been made earlier, in the long period of

[1] Ibid., col. 763.　　[2] H.L. Debs., vol. 265, col. 293, 13 April 1965.
[3] H.L. Debs, vol. 264, col. 766, 25 March 1965.　　[4] Ibid., col. 767.　　[5] Ibid., col. 767.
[6] Ibid., col. 768.　　[7] Ibid., col. 768.

adjustment following the war, or if such earlier opportunities were missed, it would have been more becoming for the Government to hear the final judgment of the court before proposing new legislation. The legislation itself could have included compensation, as suggested by the Chief Justice,[1] or the Government could have reopened negotiations with the Company, as suggested by Mr. Selwyn Lloyd, the former Chancellor of the Exchequer.[2]

The legislation clearly appeared to reprimand the majority of the Law Lords, a reprimand which was hardly justified even if the decision was wrong. The judgment in the *Burmah Oil* case reflected the expanding doctrine of Government responsibility for torts and the right of the subject to sue the Crown. The concept of 'denial damage' may have been novel, but it found favour with the majority of their Lordships. The final answer would seem to be that Government and Parliament should for once have anticipated judicial innovation. Instead of a threatening solicitor's letter, which has been over-criticized in the circumstances, Parliament should have legislated in advance of the litigation. It is difficult to agree with Viscount Dilhorne that it was not easy to justify introducing a Bill before the litigation got under way. The statute could simply have declared the common law doctrine that compensation was unavailable for battle damage, including denial damage. Precedents abound where statute is declaratory of the common law. Few parliamentarians could have resisted the logic of such legislation. But once committed to litigation, the Government was bound to allow the judicial process to run its course. It was not right to alter the rules of the game, once the game had started or when the Crown had lost. Statutory reversal at any stage of the legal proceedings involved inevitable opprobrium. In retrospect, it may be that the turbulent debates leading up to the War Damage Act 1965 will prove to have one salutary effect—namely, in inducing Parliament to re-examine the reality of parliamentary sovereignty in the light of modern conditions, particularly of entry into the European Economic Community.

To sum up, the courts have been dutifully deferential to Parliament, and Parliament has repaid the compliment. But Parliament may find it increasingly difficult to provide the time or the skill to reverse a judgment of the courts with the detailed concern that such an issue deserves. Lord Devlin wrote in 1962 that 'it would be beneficial if there were a small body of men who devoted the whole of their time, working perhaps with the aid of a larger body of consultants meeting from time to time, to a systematic tidying up of the law as well as to making proposals for wider reform.'[3] This has, in effect, taken place, with the creation in 1965 of the Law Commission. Professor Jaffe would apparently agree with such a procedure. Although he has argued for a more activist attitude from English judges, he has also suggested that 'there are many things that Parliament and judges can do together, and such co-operative action may be the most fruitful of all methods of lawmaking'.[4]

[1] Ibid., col. 777.   [2] Ibid., col. 765.   [3] Devlin, op. cit., p. 27.   [4] Jaffe, op. cit., p. 75.

The device of submitting special legal problems to law committees/commissions is an acceptable substitute for excessive judicial activism, on the one hand, or for excessive reliance on parliamentary intervention, on the other. Of course, the committee/commission procedure would not necessarily prevent Government from intervening in issues touching on policy which also concern the integrity of the judicial process, but if such cases should again arise the harm of this type of intervention could be clearly pointed out.

XVII

NON-ENGLISH JURISDICTION

A) SCOTTISH APPEALS

ENGLAND and Scotland were fused in 1707 into the Kingdom of Great Britain, but their distinctive legal systems remained unimpaired by the Act of Union. Even parliamentary unification (which included, or more accurately did not expressly exclude, the judicial House of Lords) did not materially affect the traditional civilian imprint of Scottish private law. But the essentially English institution of the House of Lords has over 250 years increasingly provoked suspicion that Anglicization of Scottish law would inevitably be the outcome of Scots appeals going finally to Westminster. What grounds are there for that suspicion?[1]

We are clearly in no position, being devoid of expertise in Scots law, to give anything approaching a definitive answer. And, in spite of some invaluable assistance from a Scots legal source, we do not pretend to do more than record our very English impressions of House of Lords activity in Scots appeals during the period of our study.

Scots contributions to the case-load of the House of Lords are restricted to civil appeals. No appeal has ever been competent from judgments of the High Court of Justiciary (an exclusively criminal appeal court) to the House of Lords. Lord Chancellor Cairns said in *Mackintosh* v. *Lord Advocate*[2] that 'an attempt to maintain the right of appeal from an order of the Court of Justiciary is a pure experiment altogether unwarranted by precedent, and which must fail the moment of history which I have attempted to narrate to your Lordships is looked into'. Since no criminal appeal had ever lain to the Scottish Parliament prior to Union, the English Parliament could not assume this jurisdiction. The Criminal Procedure (Scotland) Act 1887 set the seal on the finality of Scottish criminal appeals in the Court of Justiciary by providing in section 72 that 'all interlocutors and sentences pronounced by the High Court of Justiciary . . . shall be final and conclusive, and not subject to review by any court whatsoever . . .', and section 17 (2) Criminal Appeal (Scotland) Act 1926 confirmed the separate evolution of the Scottish criminal law, undiluted by any potential influence of English criminal jurisprudence.

Has Scottish criminal law benefited or suffered for its independence from

[1] A history of the Scottish jurisdiction of the House will be found at pp. 31–5.
[2] (1876) 3 R. (H.L.) 34.

English influence? We can, as a start, do no better than to cite a distinguished Scots academic lawyer writing in 1955, for a strong nationalist view. Professor D. M. Walker wrote:[1]

> The question whether Scotland could have managed without civil appeals to the House of Lords is to my mind conclusively answered by the case of criminal law. Appeal does not lie from the High Court of Justiciary to the House of Lords in any circumstances. In the Scottish criminal courts no English decision in criminal matters, of the Lords or of any other English court, is of greater than purely persuasive authority. . . . Moreover even in matters common to both countries, such as statutory offences, the Scottish court quite freely declines to follow English cases. And the fact remains that the High Court of Justiciary has built up a very satisfactory body of criminal law without the assistance of the House of Lords and with scant regard to English practice. In many respects the systems differ, and I do not think they are any the worse for it. There is no reason to suppose that the civil courts could not have done the same had they not been fettered by the appeal to London with its resultant transfusions.

With unfeigned deference to so respected an academic, we dissent from this view. English criminal law has in recent years undergone many modifications, one at least of which, the defence of diminished responsibility, was in 1957 borrowed from Scotland.[2] In recent years the performance of the Law Lords in criminal appeals has undergone marked improvement. And Parliament is increasingly legislating for both sides of the Border indiscriminately, a modern example being the Road Safety Act 1967 (the victim of much subsequent judicial interpretation).

English judges have consistently pointed (we discern no similar pronouncements from Scots judges) to the undesirability of statutes common to both countries being construed in different senses on either side of the Border.[3] Revenue cases are a prime example.[4]

In *Abbott* v. *Philbin*[5] the English Court of Appeal, with evident reluctance and out of deference to Scottish colleagues, followed a decision of the Court of Session in *Forbes's Trustees* v. *Inland Revenue Commissioners*;[6] and the House of Lords on appeal, while overruling the Scottish decision and reversing the Court of Appeal, said that the Court of Appeal adopted the proper course.[7] Lord Reid commended the propriety of the Court of Appeal's action, 'because it is undesirable that there should be conflicting decisions on revenue matters in Scotland and England'.

Statutes common to both countries are not confined to the civil law. The

---

[1] 18 M.L.R. 321, 356.

[2] See Nigel Walker: *Crime and Insanity in England* (1968) Chapters 8 and 9.

[3] *Watson* v. *Nikolaisen* [1955] 2 Q.B. 286, 296 (Adoption Act 1950); *Cording* v. *Halse* [1955] 1 Q.B., 63, 70 (Road Traffic Act 1930); *Kahn* v. *Newberry* [1959] 2 Q.B. 1 (Shops Act 1950); *Daley* v. *Hargreaves* [1961] 1 W.L.R. 487, 492 (Road Traffic Act 1930).

[4] *Wiseburgh* v. *Domville* (Inspector of Taxes) [1956] 1 W.L.R. 312, 319; *Abbott* v. *Philbin* [1959] Ch. 27, 49, and [1961] A.C. 352, 368, 373; *Westward Television Ltd.* v. *Hart* [1969] 1 Ch. 201, 212, 222.

[5] [1960] Ch. 27.   [6] 1958 S.C. (H.L.) 177.   [7] [1961] A.C. 352, 368, 373.

erroneous decision in Scotland in *Forbes's* case, which led the English courts to perpetuate the error for English taxpayers, was quickly rectified by the higher and common appeal court for both countries. It is every bit as important for the citizens in both territories to share the same criminal law as it is for them as taxpayers to pay the same taxes. A political union, unlike a federation of autonomous states, demands, at least, that in matters of law and order (and in other branches of law which are of a public character) there should be no disparity in judicial treatment.

Some Scots commentators, dissatisfied with the pronouncements of the High Court of Justiciary (and we are aware that there are some) would contend that Scots judges might handle criminal appeals more satisfactorily if there was a possibility of a further appeal to the House of Lords. We are not equipped to gauge the strength of such a view, but we would assert that if there is to be a further appellate tribunal for Scottish litigants at all, there is as great a need (if not greater) for the criminal law of the two countries to be more nearly assimilated, at least where the criminal law is prescribed by statutes common to both countries. Indeed, if anything, there is a stronger case to be made out for leaving areas of civil law, peculiar to the two systems, to develop along their own distinct, even if parallel lines. Such a conclusion stems not from any judgment of the quality of Scots criminal justice but from the extent of the role of a second appellate tribunal. Since criminal justice in Scotland has been administered indigenously, only a Scots lawyer could begin to evaluate the quality of justice purveyed. And only someone equally familiar with Scots and English law could measure the comparative quality of the two systems, differently administered and without any unifying influence, save that of Parliament. (Even here Parliament tends sometimes to legislate separately.)

But in the civil field, the existence of the jurisdiction of the House of Lords for both countries does provide some basis for evaluation of both legal systems. More particularly, we have tried to discover whether the Scots representation among the Law Lords adequately ensures the purity of Scots law in appeals from Scotland. We are aware that a question like this can be tackled only on a highly subjective basis. How does one measure 'Scottishness' in the judicial process? One might as well ask whether English Law Lords still retain their 'Englishness' in the face of redoubtable Scots legal intellects, when dealing with English appeals. If one asks whether Scots law has been Anglicized by House of Lords decisions, why should we not ask whether English law has been 'Scoticized' by Scots influence in the House of Lords? These are samples of the difficulty in approach to such issues. Nothing daunted, we venture to proffer our views on the body of Scots appeals to the House of Lords. In various sections of the present work we have dealt with appeals from Scotland alongside those from England and Northern Ireland, commenting, where necessary, upon any manifest difference. For instance, the role of Scottish

Law Lords in dealing with Scottish appeals is discussed at some length in the chapter on the Law Lords, and statistical tables, juxtaposing figures relating to Scottish and English appeals can be found in Chapter XII, as well as in the chapters on dissenting judgments and on costs.

Three questions deserve special mention here: first how many appeals come to the House of Lords from Scotland; second, how successful are they; and third, do they differ substantially in range of subject-matter from those which come from English courts? The first two questions can readily be answered by recourse to the composite table, Table 48 in Chapter XII (p. 242). This shows that 21·9 per cent of civil appeals over the whole period of study came from Scotland: there are wide annual variations, as one would expect from the small numbers involved. The years 1952, 1964, and 1967 saw a veritable feast of Scottish appeals, and each of these good harvests were followed by a year of famine.

No fewer than 47·0 per cent of all Scottish appeals were allowed wholly or in part: this compares strikingly with the success-rate of 36·1 per cent for appeals from the English Court of Appeal during the same period. The figure seems all the more remarkable if we recall that virtually all Scottish appeals lie as of right, a factor which, if anything, would lead to at least a sprinkling of hopeless appeals reaching the House of Lords and so depressing the average success-rate (though without examining in detail the work of the Court of Session itself we cannot attach too much importance to a statistic of this kind). Does the answer lie in the quality of decision-making in the Court of Session? If so, both divisions of the Inner House must be equally to blame since the success-rate from the First Division is identical with that of the Second Division.[1] Nor can the Judges of the Outer House be exonerated from any such criticism since they were reversed by the Inner House only in 39 per cent of cases which came eventually to the House of Lords, as compared with a 54 per cent reversal-rate in the English Court of Appeal. Moreover, the percentage of cases where the House of Lords restored the decision of the Lord Ordinary after it had been reversed by the Inner House (18 per cent) is almost exactly the same as the number of cases where the Lords upheld the reversal of the Lord Ordinary (17 per cent). Certainly the bare statistics do not seem to lend much support to the hypothesis that the judgments of the Court of Session are 'worse' than those of the Court of Appeal; if this is so then the rot has spread through both Divisions of the Inner House, and reached the Outer House. (Conceivably, the reduction of issues of law to mere statistics does, in this instance, more harm than good. The real question is one of substantive law, and this we will explore later in this chapter.)

[1] Seventy-two per cent of Scottish appeals to the House of Lords came from the First Division and 28 per cent from the Second Division. Both courts have a stereotyped composition and have a similar case-load, though it is customary for most 'chancery' cases to be heard in the First Division while most appeals from Sheriff courts go to the Second Division: this explains why most House of Lords appeals tend to come from the First Division.

Next we come to the question of the case-load of the House of Lords in Scottish appeals: does the distribution of cases differ significantly from that in English appeals? This question is answered by Table 49 (p. 246) which juxtaposes the relevant sets of figures for the period 1952–68. Few firm conclusions can be drawn from this table, since the numbers involved in each category are very small. But it is clear that of the two largest categories of appeal, revenue appeals come much more often from English courts than from Scottish, while the reverse is true of cases involving fault liability (which, in practice, often involve a significant element of fact). It is noticeable too that patent, copyright and trade mark appeals, which account for 7 per cent of the English case-load, are completely absent from the Scottish —and the same is true of cases involving international law and defamation.

No fewer than 15 per cent of Scottish appeals to the House of Lords originated in the Sheriff courts (where the jurisdiction is limited geographically and in some cases monetarily) as compared with 3 per cent of English appeals originating in the County Courts which have a general monetary limit on jurisdiction. The respective jurisdictions of the two courts are far from identical, but these figures may explain why some cases from Scotland involving relatively trivial subject-matter. (One cannot assume, however, that *all* cases of legal importance start life in the Court of Session.)

Interlocutory proceedings are much more common among Scottish appeals than among those from England, the figures for our period being 22 per cent and 3 per cent respectively. But interlocutory proceedings in the form of preliminary issues are common in Scotland. It is common practice for the relevancy of an averment to be tried as a preliminary point of law; cf. the English demurrer which was abolished in 1882. This is far from being indicative of triviality: *Donoghue* v. *Stevenson* and *Burmah Oil* came to the Lords by this route. This may be a partial explanation for Scottish appeals taking much less time for argument in the Lords. Nineteen per cent of Scottish appeals occupied one day (or part day) in the Lords as compared with 4 per cent of English appeals; 48 per cent of Scottish appeals took two days as compared with 26 per cent of English appeals. Only 4 per cent of Scottish appeals took more than four days as compared with 26 per cent of English appeals. As we have seen, this (coupled with the relatively lower brief fees paid in Scottish appeals) brings the average bill of costs in Scottish appeals well below that in English cases.

Finally one important 'index of triviality' should be mentioned. In a very small percentage of cases the House of Lords do not call upon the respondent to reply to the appellant's argument: this happened in 3 per cent of English appeals during our period of study, and in 8 per cent of Scottish appeals. (Again the numbers are so small as to invite caution in drawing any firm conclusion.)

Decisions in the House of Lords in Scots appeals produced their own crop of legislative reactions. In eleven cases parliamentary action resulted directly from the decisions of the Law Lords. In over half the cases—seven out of eleven—the Court of Session was upheld, so that a further appeal did not provide any added inducement to legislate against the Court's verdict. In two cases the House of Lords allowed the appeal only by a majority of 3:2; the first, *Cleisham* v. *B.T.C.*,[1] was a much criticized decision, a factor that hastened a change in the law as regards corroboration in actions for damages; the second, *Burmah Oil Co.* v. *Lord Advocate*[2] is sufficiently notorious to render further comment here supererogatory. One other appeal allowed—an estate duty case—was by a majority of 4:1.[3] In the last successful appeal[4] the statute in question, the Public Authorities Protection Act 1893, was repealed in 1954; the House of Lords in fact found that the Scottish Milk Marketing Board was not a public authority. (Annexed to this chapter is a list of legislative provisions consequent upon House of Lords decisions in Scots appeals.)

We then asked ourselves whether there had been a discernible merit in having a case finally determined by the House of Lords rather than by the Court of Session. In the absence of suitable criteria, there is no reason why we should not adopt a purely pragmatic test. On this basis the record shows that half of the Court of Session's decisions have been overturned, a significantly higher rate of success for Scots appellants than for their English counterparts. To underline this point, we can state that relatively few of the House of Lords' decisions have been criticized and several have received both professional and academic plaudits. And we sense, in our conversations with Scots lawyers, that (notwithstanding our statistics) there is a ripple, if not a wave, of discontent with much that nowadays falls from the lips of the judges of the Inner House of the Court of Session. But any disillusionment about contemporary Scots justice is very much a phase: few Scots lawyers would deny that the post-war era of Lord Cooper of Culross sitting in the chair of the First Division of the Inner House was a golden period in Scots law. Just as there are horses for courses, there are judges for courts. The present Senators of the College of Justice who sit in the Outer House will tomorrow form the two divisions of the Inner House, and the critics may once again fashion encomia on their judicial utterances.

All we are saying is that much depends on the personality and perspicacity of the judges sitting from year to year, and that goes as much for those at Westminster as for those at Parliament House in Edinburgh. It is pertinent here to note Professor Walker's comment[5] on *Walsh* v. *Lord Advocate*,[6] a case concerning a Jehovah's Witness and exemption from National Service, that

---

[1] 1964 S.C. (H.L.) 8.
[2] [1965] A.C. 75. Discussed at pp. 368–73, *ante*.
[3] *Hetherington's trustees (or Sneddon)* v. *Lord Advocate* [1954] A.C. 257.
[4] *Marshall* v. *Scottish Milk Marketing Board* 1956 S.C. (H.L.) 37.
[5] [1956] T.R. 269.   [6] [1956] 1 W.L.R. 1002.

'it would be very regrettable if an appeal in a Scottish case' (by which he meant a case involving Scots private law) 'were to be heard by a tribunal thus composed'. The court was made up of an English chancery lawyer, an English common lawyer, the Lord Chief Justice of England, the Lord Chief Justice of Northern Ireland and a Scots Law Lord. If Scots lawyers cannot always claim majority representation on a Scots appeal (in *Wilson's (Dunblane) Ltd.* v. *C.I.R.*[1] exceptionally there were three Scots Law Lords and the Lord Chief Justice of Northern Ireland) it is fair to insist that both the Scots Law Lords should sit on a Scots appeal, which they ordinarily do.[2] It is also important that the Law Lords should sit a full complement of five, particularly since the Court of Session is frequently a four-judge court. It is hardly good politics to do as was done in *C.I.R.* v. *Albion Rovers F.C.*,[3] when only three English Law Lords overruled four Lords of Session. During our period no fewer than 15 per cent of Scots appeals were heard by a three- or four-judge House of Lords, though the practice ceased after 1963.

If then the House of Lords appears to perform a useful function at the apex of the Scottish judicial hierarchy, have Scots lawyers in recent years had grounds for complaint that a peculiarly English approach has been adopted (or one which differed substantially from that of the Court of Session)? Again, our view must necessarily be impressionistic.

In some cases the approach adopted by the House of Lords will differ because the advocates' submissions have become refined upon further reflection prompted by another appeal. Or it may be that they are altered as a result of something said by a judge in the lower courts. This happened in *Baird* v. *Baird's Trustees*,[4] where some doubts expressed by Lord Sorn opened up a new train of thought fastened on to by the Law Lords. The manner in which the Law Lords tackled *Burmah Oil Co.* v. *Lord Advocate*[5] was markedly different, since it was only at that stage that it was agreed that English constitutional law, and not (as had been assumed) the law of Scotland, applied.[6]

In *Mathieson Gee Ltd.* v. *Quigley*[7] the House of Lords treated the lack of *consensus ad idem* in the law of contract in a substantially different way from that taken by the First Division and the Lord Ordinary. Not surprisingly the Court of Session's decision was reversed. Was this an Anglicizing influence at work? There was no overt sign of it.

It is, indeed, very difficult to say what constitutes a peculiarly English approach. If *Hedley Byrne* v. *Hellers Ltd.*[8] had not overruled *Candler* v. *Crane*

---

1 [1954] 1 W.L.R. 282.
2 76 per cent of Scots appeals were heard by a House of Lords containing at least two Scots Law Lords (as compared with 35 per cent of English and Northern Ireland appeals).
3 [1952] T.R. 327.   4 1956 S.C. (H.L.) 93.   5 [1965] A.C. 75.
6 The case, arguably, furnished an example of a Scots Law Lord, Lord Reid, adopting a peculiarly Scottish approach to a question of English law.
7 1952 S.C. (H.L.) 38.   8 [1965] A.C. 465.

Christmas & Co.[1] on the question of culpable or negligent misrepresentation, might not the more sensible Scottish law of *culpa* have prevailed over the English tort of negligence? But this is a stark illustration of a conflict of legal concepts that does not frequently arise. Scots law is Anglicized, if Anglicized it is, in more subtle ways.

Every appellate court, from time to time, changes the direction of the law it administers. If the House of Lords chooses to give a lead in a Scots appeal and brings the law into line with altered social conditions or modern ways of thought, and if in so doing Scots law is equated more nearly with English, can it be said that this is an example of naked Anglicization? To draw the line between a genuinely forward-looking decision and one which unashamedly foists English doctrine on Scots law is not always easy. Our impression is that the Law Lords have been deliberately circumspect not to adopt an English approach to a Scots legal problem. It is, of course, different with statutory provisions where a common approach is permissible; we have seen that there is a great striving for uniformity in construing sections in Finance Acts.

Given this commendation of English judicial tenderness towards Scottish susceptibilities, there have been three cases which fall into the category of unadulterated Anglicization.

(a) *C.I.R.* v. *Glasgow Police Athletic Association.*[2] This case, which concerned the definition of charity for tax purposes, is all too familiar to students of Scots law. The House of Lords, in a decision which cannot be faulted on legal grounds, held that the Court of Session was bound by the notorious English decision in *C.I.R.* v. *Pemsel.*[3] Lord Normand (himself a Scots lawyer) had this to say:

I will not disguise that I have a certain sympathy with the Scottish judges, who feel embarrassed at having to administer as part of the law of Scotland a difficult and technical branch of English law. For I have had, in the Court of Session, some though not a large experience of this jurisdiction, and I felt the embarrassment. Nevertheless I must say at once that there has been here a failure to exercise a jurisdiction which the Court had a plain duty to exercise. . . . The necessary effect of Pemsel's case . . . is that the English law of charity has, for income tax purposes and for them alone, to be regarded as part of the law of Scotland and not as foreign law.

(b) *Scottish Burial Reform and Cremation Society Ltd.* v. *Glasgow Corp.*[4] also involved income tax and charities.

(c) *C.I.R.* v. *Hood Barrs*[5] involved a consideration of the quite unfamiliar writ of *certiorari* by the Court of Session sitting as the Court of Exchequer.

Although the days of the ignorant and contemptuous attitude of a Lord Chancellor Cranworth or a Viscount Maugham towards Scots law have long since passed, there are still occasions when the Scots lawyer pauses to reflect on the extent of English influence: but the influence (such as it is) now is unintentional though no less significant.

---

[1] [1951] 2 K.B. 164. [2] [1953] A.C. 380. [3] [1891] A.C. 531.
[4] [1968] A.C. 138. [5] [1957] 1 W.L.R. 529.

Was it necessary in *Miller* v. *South of Scotland Electricity Board*,[1] a case concerning relevancy and foreseeability, for Lord Denning to concentrate so much on the English 'demurrer'? Certainly he has been criticized by Professor Walker[2] for so doing. In *White & Carter (Councils) Ltd.* v. *McGregor*,[3] when Lord Hodson talked about equity—'No doubt this aspect impressed the Court of Session, but there is no equity which can assist the respondent. It is trite that equity will not rewrite an improvident contract where there is no disability on either side'—was it the specialized rules of English equity (which have no counterpart in Scotland) that he had in mind? In *Coats' Trustees* v. *Lord Advocate*[4] Lord Donovan said: 'For example, in the present case the wife had *what in England* would be called a special power of appointment . . .' and 'or, as we should say in England . . .'.

One case which, on the face of it, showed a peculiarly English approach adopted by the House of Lords (but which we think did not, in fact, do so) is *Jamieson* v. *Jamieson*.[5] This was a divorce case involving consideration of what constitutes (or did then constitute) mental cruelty—the law having been altered in 1964 by the Divorce (Scotland) Act. The House of Lords, including two Scottish Law Lords, upheld an appeal from the First Division—Lord Cooper of Culross, Lord Carmont, and Lord Keith (dissenting)—and found that the pursuer's averments were relevant. In the lower court Lord Cooper said:[6] 'Whether it be that the Scottish character is of tougher fibre or of blunter susceptibilities, or that the Calvinist tradition still finds expression in a deeper sanctity of the marriage tie and its obligations, the fact remains that more than one decree on the ground of 'cruelty' has recently been pronounced in England which would not have been granted in Scotland.' The House of Lords did not agree with this (and certainly Lord Cooper's statement appears rather odd in view of the relatively permissive attitude of Scots law towards divorce in the century immediately after the Reformation when the Calvinist tradition was at its strongest), took a more liberal and humane view of what constitutes cruelty, and delivered opinions that there was no difference in principle between the law of England and the law of Scotland in regard to the kind or degree of cruelty necessary for divorce. The difference in approach in this case is not, we think, the result of English influence (although it was perhaps unfortunate that Lord Merriman relied to such an extent on English authority). It seems just as likely to have been a reflection of the differing temperaments and attitudes of the judges involved (is it without significance that Lord Cooper was a life-long bachelor and Lord Carmont a Catholic?). The debate as to what constituted mental cruelty and the uncertainty as to whether the law of England and law of Scotland were the same continued for some twelve years after *Jamieson* v. *Jamieson*.[7] The Lord Ordinary (Lord

1 1958 S.C. (H.L.) 20.   2 1958 J.R. 287.   3 [1962] A.C. 413.
4 1965 S.L.T. 145.   5 [1952] A.C. 525.
6 1951 S.C. (H.L.) 286, 292.   7 [1952] A.C. 525.

Walker), a lone dissenter on the Royal Commission on Marriage and Divorce 1956 (whose views ultimately were adopted in the Divorce Reform Act 1969) in the case of *Waite* v. *Waite*[1] (which was not appealed to the Lords) took a different view from the First Division, and the Law Lords in the English case of *Gollins* v. *Gollins*[2] adopted a standpoint irreconcilable with that taken by the Division in *Waite*. However, the different approaches taken are not in the final analysis, we think, referable to law but to temperament and personality.

In two cases involving the foreseeability of an accident, the House of Lords took a less strict view than the Court of Session, although there are no grounds for supposing that this was due to English influence. In *Hughes* v. *Lord Advocate*[3] the House of Lords, agreeing with Lord Carmont who had dissented in the First Division of the Court of Session, held that it was enough that an accident of some sort was foreseeable even although the precise type of accident which did in fact occur could not have been foreseen. As has been pointed out by Dworkin[4] it is difficult to reconcile this decision with that in the English case of *Doughty* v. *Turner Manufacturing Co.*[5] In *Miller* v. *S.S.E.B.*,[6] the House of Lords held that foreseeability of the precise chain of circumstances leading up to an accident was not necessary; and also said that it was undesirable, save in a very clear case, to dismiss an action of this type on the grounds of relevancy.

In the period under study the House of Lords has shown a definite tendency to adopt a less legalistic and more liberal approach than the Court of Session in construing the written word, whether in pleadings, dispositions (that is, deeds conveying an interest in land) or statute law. Among cases in which a less strict view of written pleadings has been taken are: *Alford* v. *N.C.B.*;[7] *Grant* v. *N.C.B.*;[8] *Miller* v. *S.S.E.B.*;[9] *Nimmo* v. *Alex. Cowan & Sons Ltd.*;[10] and in particular *Cleisham* v. *B.T.C.*[11]

The case of *Cleisham* is the only one in the period under study in which both Scottish Law Lords found themselves in the dissenting minority, and it is the case in which, it could be argued, there is most trace of English influence. W. A. Wilson, commenting,[12] said that at first sight it looked as if 'the House of Lords, having wrested from defenders the sword of relevance (*Miller* v. *S.S.E.B.*) and the shield of foreseeability (*Hughes* v. *Lord Advocate*) had now stripped them of the armour of corroboration and left them naked and defenceless before the onslaught of the jury.' He went on to show, however, that the effect of the case was not so far-reaching but that it did disclose a basic difference of opinion on the question of pleading. In fairness to the English Law Lords concerned, it should be noted that both Lord Morris of Borth-y-Gest and Lord Hodson paid particular attention to Scottish authority

---

[1] 1961 S.C. (H.L.) 266. [2] [1964] A.C. 644. [3] [1963] A.C. 837.
[4] 27 M.L.R. 344 (1964). [5] [1964] 1 Q.B. 518. [6] 1958 S.C. (H.L.) 20.
[7] [1952] 1 T.L.R. 687. [8] [1956] A.C. 649. [9] 1958 S.C. (H.L.) 20.
[10] [1968] A.C. 107. [11] 1964 S.C. (H.L.) 8. [12] 1964 S.L.T. (News) 57.

in the course of their judgments. The legislature resolved the controversy in 1968 (see Annex A at the end of this chapter which sets out the instances of statutory reversal of House of Lords decisions in Scottish appeals).

In *Hunter* v. *Fox*[1] the House of Lords, in overturning the First Division (which had itself reversed the Lord Ordinary) adopted a more liberal and, we believe, more sensible, construction of a deed. Lord Reid observed:[2] 'I can think of no stricter method of construction—and none was suggested in argument—than to ask whether a reasonable man with a competent knowledge of the English language could have any real doubt about the meaning of the provision read in its context in the disposition.'

In the important, and frequently criticized, case of *Anderson* v. *Lambie*[3] the House of Lords took a less strict view than the First Division of the effect of a recorded disposition which contained an error neither admitted nor obvious on the face of the deed. An extreme view of this case would be that it overthrew a cardinal principle of Scottish conveyancing. Their Lordships were careful, however, to argue the case on a Scottish basis and, if fault is to be found with their reasoning, it is more a matter of hard cases making bad law[4] than because of any supposed English approach. It was in this case that Lord Morton of Henryton quoted with approval Lord Dunedin's statement in the somewhat similar case of *Krupp* v. *Menzies*:[5] 'There are cases in which it would be truly a disgrace to any system of jurisprudence if there was no way available of rectifying what would otherwise be a gross injustice.'

Instances of a more liberal construction of statute are provided by *Watson* v. *Winget Ltd.*[6] where Lord Denning said: 'But if the decision of the Court of Session is correct, it means that a man may lose his right of action before he has got it. Which is absurd. So I think that there must be something wrong about it.' And there is *Gardiner* v. *Admiralty Commissioners*.[7]

One final case in which the Lords reached a very different decision from the Court of Session was *White and Carter (Councils) Ltd.* v. *McGregor*,[8] although it does not appear (despite Lord Hodson's comments on equity) that an English approach was taken. The case, a much criticized one,[9] was decided by a bare majority and the question of law involved, concerning repudiation of contract, is the same in Scotland as in England. The consequences of the case have been as important to the south of the Border as to the north.

We have devoted much space to the vexed and highly elusive question of the Anglicization of Scots law by English Law Lords. We conclude that, a few notable exceptions apart, Scots lawyers have not too much to complain of on this score. The best guarantee against any erosion of Scots law by English

1 1964 S.C. (H.L.) 95.   2 Ibid., p. 99.   3 [1954] 1 W.L.R. 303.
4 (1958) 1 Corn. Rev. 50 and 135.   5 1907 S.C. 903, 908.
6 1960 S.C. (H.L.) 92.   7 [1964] 1 W.L.R. 590.   8 [1962] A.C. 413.
9 Among the many articles critical of the House of Lords' decision, by which three Law Lords laid down the law as against the view of six judges, including two Law Lords, are those in 25 M.L.R. 364 (1962) and 78 L.Q.R. 263 (1962).

judges is a strengthened Court of Session which commands instantly respectful treatment from the House of Lords, ever sensible of its trusteeship of Scots law by virtue of its pre-eminent position in the British judicial system. There is, moreover, no evidence to suggest that the Scottish Law Lords have themselves succumbed to the process of Anglicization and forsaken their legal heritage. Indeed it might even be asserted, with some degree of confidence, that the English Law Lords have come under the compelling influence of Lord Reid. May it not be in fact that English law has become 'Scoticized'? Since this is an afterthought on our part, we have not made any study of English appeals at the hands of Scots Law Lords—a doctoral thesis, perhaps, for some comparative law student.

Before passing to our conclusion, we should make one further observation. We have alluded earlier to the desirability of a uniform approach, which can more nearly be achieved by a common final appeal court, to matters of public order. There is one other current area of transparent disparity, and that is the amount of damages for personal injuries awarded by courts in the two parts of the kingdom. It is the gravest social injustice that the 'tariff' for personal injuries, which has not yet been replaced in either jurisdiction by actuarial calculations, should vary so greatly between England and Scotland when economic and social conditions are not dissimilar. This matter has been brought to a head recently in an unhappy case of *McCallum* v. *Paterson*[1] (in which no appeal to the House of Lords was possible). The First Division held that the award of a second jury in a reparation action—the award of the first having been set aside as excessive—could be excessive even if it substantially repeated the award of the first jury. A new trial (the third) could be ordered even if that meant a succession of abortive trials. The sums twice set aside as grossly excessive were less than would have been awarded by an English court in similar circumstances by a judge sitting without a jury.

We have said enough, we feel, to suggest that so long as England retains a two-tier appeal system there is logic in keeping it for Scots appeals, including we would underline, Scots criminal law. The only qualification is that the composition of the House of Lords must cater for the Scots appeal, in particular for the appeal that features peculiarly (to English eyes) alien legal doctrines.

Any amalgamation of the House of Lords with the Judicial Committee of the Privy Council (see Chapter XIX) would have to take account of the composition of the new final appellate tribunal. The merged final appellate court would probably be infused with judges from Commonwealth countries (all of whom, except the Ceylon judges, would be common law trained); one distinguished Scots lawyer, Professor T. B. Smith, has declared himself strongly against the idea on the grounds that 'appeals to the proposed new court would presumably be to a larger body than the House of Lords virtually

[1] 1969 S.L.T. 177.

entirely manned by lawyers trained in the English legal tradition'. And that is a sober warning to English reformers of British legal institutions.

(b) APPEALS FROM NORTHERN IRELAND

The present Northern Irish jurisdiction of the House of Lords is little more than a litigious drop in the appellate bucket. Moreover, since Northern Irish law (both in its common law and in its statutory aspects) is almost identical with English law, and the Northern Irish courts are microcosms of English ones, we have tended to treat this part of the Lords' work as an extension of its English jurisdiction. There is no problem, as there is with Scottish appeals, of reconciling alien systems of jurisprudence. Even the interesting constitutional jurisdiction of the House, which gave rise to such cases as *O.D. Cars Ltd.* v. *Belfast Corporation*,[1] has been diluted by statute. We make no apology, therefore, for according this small part of the Lords' jurisdiction only a very cursory glance.[2]

During our period of study (1952–68) the House of Lords heard fifteen civil appeals from Northern Ireland (no fewer than seven of them in 1959; and none at all during the period 1952–6 inclusive). It also heard two important criminal appeals, *Attorney-General for Northern Ireland* v. *Gallagher*[3] and *Bratty* v. *Attorney-General for Northern Ireland*,[4] both of which are discussed elsewhere.[5]

All the important civil appeals from Northern Ireland are discussed in other chapters: a complete list is as follows:

McClelland v. *Northern Ireland General Health Services Board* [1957] 1 W.L.R. 594 (Allowed 3:2) C.A. 2:1.

Belfast Corporation v. *O.D. Cars Ltd.* [1960] A.C. 490 (Allowed—unanimous) C.A. reversing trial judge.

Cavanagh v. *Ulster Weaving Co. Ltd.* [1960] A.C. 145 (Allowed—unanimous) C.A. by 2:1 reversing trial judge.

McKeown v. *Thomas Burrell* (unreported) (Allowed—unanimous) C.A. reversing trial judge.

Rental Holdings Ltd. v. *Hall* (unreported) (Dismissed—unanimous).

Scottish C.W.S. v. *Ulster Farmers' Mart Co. Ltd.* (*et è contra*) [1960] A.C. 63. (Appeal allowed—unanimous; cross-appeal dismissed—unanimous).

Smyth v. *Cameron* (unreported) (Dismissed—unanimous) C.A. 2:1.

McCann v. *Attorney-General for Northern Ireland* [1971] N.I. 102 (Dismissed—unanimous).

Bill v. *Short Brothers and Harland Ltd.* [1963] N.I. 7 (Allowed—unanimous) C.A. 2:1.

Northern Ireland Hospitals Authority v. *Whyte* [1963] 1 W.L.R. 882 (Allowed—unanimous) C.A. 2:1 reversing trial judge.

---

1 This case, and the constitutional jurisdiction generally, is discussed at p. 261.
2 A history of the Irish jurisdiction can be found at pp. 35–7.
3 [1963] A.C. 349.   4 [1963] A.C. 386.
5 See chapter on Criminal Law, p. 278.

Irwin v. *White, Tomkins & Courage* [1964] 1 W.L.R. 387 (Allowed—unanimous) C.A. 2:1 reversing trial judge.

Governors of Campbell College v. *Northern Ireland Valuation Commissioners* [1964] 1 W.L.R. 912 (Allowed—unanimous) C.A. 2:1.

Cyril Lord Ltd. v. *C.I.R.* (1965) 42 T.C. 463 (Dismissed—unanimous).

O'Hagan (A.P.) v. *Northern Ireland Farmers Bacon Co. Ltd.* (unreported) (Dismissed—unanimous) C.A. reversed jury decision.

Several points emerge from an examination of these appeals, which can best be set out in a list:

(1) In every case since 1962 (when the hitherto unqualified right of appeal was curbed by statute) leave to appeal came from the Court of Appeal in Northern Ireland.

(2) All but two of the cases involved either a reversal of the trial decision by the Court of Appeal, or a dissenting judgment in the Court of Appeal, or (in three cases) both.

(3) No fewer than six involved a jury trial.

(4) In four, respondent's counsel was not called upon.

(5) All this suggests that not only the Northern Irish jurisdiction of the House of Lords is small in size, but also (with a few notable exceptions) trivial in subject-matter. In a small country the legal profession as a whole, and the judiciary in particular, is drawn from a segment of a small population. It may be that the judicial process in such a country particularly requires the guidance of a senior tribunal, even if this means that a few trifling appeals are thereby allowed to reach the House of Lords. Certainly the large percentage of Northern Irish appeals that are successful in the Lords seems to bear this out.

ANNEX A. STATUTORY REVERSALS OF HOUSE OF LORDS DECISIONS IN SCOTTISH APPEALS

Case	Subject	Outcome	Reported	Statutory reversal
C.I.R. v. Gordon	Revenue	D	[1952] A.C. 552	s. 24, Finance Act, 1953
Wilson's (Dunblane) Ltd. v. C.I.R.	Revenue	D	[1954] 1 W.L.R. 282	s. 23, Finance Act, 1954
Hetherington's Trustees (or Sneddon) v. Lord Advocate	Estate duty	A (4:1)	[1954] A.C. 257	s. 38 Finance Act 1957
Martin v. Sinclair	Wills	D	1955 S.C. (H.L.) 56	s. 31, Succession (S) Act 1964
Marshall v. Scottish Milk Marketing Board	Limitation of Action	A	1956 S.C. (H.L.) 37	Law Reform (Limitation of Action) Act 1954
British Oxygen Co. v. South of Scotland Electricity Board	Electricity tariff	D	[1956] 1 W.L.R. 1069 Note: repeal took place before case reached the House of Lords	Electricity Reorganization (S) Act 1954
Couper's Trustees v. Lord Advocate	Will	D	1960 S.C. (H.L.) 74	Succession (S) Act 1964
Cleisham v. British Transport Commission	Evidence— accident	A (3:2)	1964 S.C. (H.L.) 8	s. 9, Law Reform (Miscellaneous Provisions) (S) Act 1968
Burmah Oil Co. v. Lord Advocate	War damage	A (3:2)	[1965] A.C. 75	War Damage Act 1965
Brown v. C.I.R.	Revenue	D	[1965] A.C. 244	Solicitors (S) Act 1965
Coats's Trustees v. Lord Advocate	Marriage contract	D (3:2)	1965 S.L.T. 145	Succession (S) Act 1964 (preceded this decision)

(S) denotes that statute is exclusively applicable to Scotland.

XVIII

POSTSCRIPT: THE END OF A DECADE

THE trouble with decades is that they are labels without bottles, giving spurious significance to arbitrary periods of time. When labels are easy to handle they are frequently used. When they are not, nobody bothers to invent them. We make no excuse for labelling this period of House of Lords judicial activity. For reasons which we have alluded to throughout this study—the presidency of Lord Reid since 1962, the expanded criminal jurisdiction since December 1960, the modification of the doctrine of *stare decisis* in 1966, the experiment, introduced in 1969, of 'leapfrogging'—the 1960s may in retrospect turn out to have been a watershed in the life of the three-tier court structure. At least the 1960s were markedly different from the staid 1950s. And the year 1969 ended the decade on a high note.

We have throughout this survey pointed to the paucity of work that comes to the final court of appeal, and there is a strong case, discussed in our concluding chapter, for taking steps to increase substantially the Court's caseload: only then can the House of Lords perform its true function as befits a reviewing and supervisory court of appeal. We have made suggestions elsewhere as to how a more extensive flow of appeals might be generated, but in 1969, without any drastic procedural changes, an unprecedented number was disposed of—53, almost half as much again as the average annual case-load of the previous eighteen years, though still not, in our view, nearly enough to give Law Lords opportunity to develop the law in every area of jurisprudence. It will remain to be seen whether, with or without the stimulus of other procedural reforms, this higher rate of turnover will be sustained, and preferably augmented in the 1970s.

If the dramatic change in the case-load was scarcely a plethora, or even an elegant sufficiency, of appellate work, it did produce some significant lawmaking. Indeed the Law Lords in English civil appeals for the first time upset the decision of the courts *a quo* in more than half,[1] and in criminal appeals the results were even more startling (though hardly statistically significant) as can be seen from the following table, which shows not only that there were as many as eight criminal appeals (equalling the record established in the preceding year) but also that six of these were allowed wholly or in part.

---

[1] In 1955 they had come close to doing this by allowing fifteen out of thirty-one, and in 1964, eight out of sixteen. Those years notwithstanding, the average rate of success for appellants in English cases was one in three.

TABLE 54

House of Lords Appeals, 1969

	Appeals allowed	Appeals dismissed	Total
Criminal (all English)	$5+\frac{1}{2}$	$2+\frac{1}{2}$	8
Civil			
English	17	13	30
Scottish	3	6	9
N. Irish	$\frac{1}{2}$	$3+\frac{1}{2}$	4
	$25+(2\times\frac{1}{2})$	$24+(2\times\frac{1}{2})$	51^{a}

The figure $\frac{1}{2}$ denotes appeals allowed in part.

[a] The total number differs, due to the fact that in some appeals there was either a partial allowance, or an appeal and a cross-appeal were successful.

The criminal jurisdiction produced perhaps the more startling innovations. We have noted elsewhere how this has for long been the Cinderella of our legal system; that the House of Lords has only recently begun to put its imprint on it, and that when an appeal has gone to the House, the result has not always been satisfactory. Nineteen sixty-nine marked a sharp departure from a former lethargy and unhelpfulness towards the development of the criminal law. *Sweet* v. *Parsley*[1] (the schoolteacher whose tenants, unbeknown to their landlord, imported cannabis into the premises) firmly put a brake on the blanket imposition of strict liability, and retrieved the position adopted a year earlier in *Warner* v. *Metropolitan Police Commissioner*.[2] 'Possession' of drugs to be unlawful now requires some knowledge by the possessor that he is handling drugs. The Lords' decision, reversing decisions of the criminal courts, was, with justification, warmly and widely applauded.

Later in the year the Law Lords injected a dose of realism into the breath-alyser law. A series of decisions in the lower courts had upheld technical objections by motorists (a new breed of criminal appellant) who were quick to exploit loopholes in the Road Safety Act 1967, and the law was in such public disrepute that legislation was being strongly urged, and was seriously contemplated by the Ministry of Transport. *D.P.P.* v. *Carey*,[3] by giving flexibility to the statutory provisions relating to the administration of the breath test, restored public confidence in the law and made amending legislation unnecessary. Lord Diplock's analysis of statutory construction was, in addition, a masterly judicial exposition.

The Law Lords' taste for a forthright approach to the criminal law was marked a year later in *D.P.P.* v. *Bhagwan*[4] where a method adopted by a

[1] [1970] A.C. 132.   [2] [1969] 2 A.C. 256.
[3] [1970] A.C. 1072.   [4] [1970] 3 W.L.R. 501.

Commonwealth immigrant to avoid the restriction on entry into Britain under
the Commonwealth Immigrants Act 1962 was upheld. (This loophole was
plugged in the widely criticized Act of 1968.) Until Parliament in the 1968 Act
added to the means of achieving its policy of effectively controlling Commonwealth immigration, the courts were unable and unwilling to do the work for
legislators, but only gave effect to the existing statutory means of controlling
entry into Britain. As if that were not enough, Lord Diplock in another
illuminating judgment (all other four Law Lords formally concurred)
sounded a warning to prosecutors that the law of criminal conspiracy, under
which the prosecution in *Bhagwan* had been brought, was outmoded and
would receive a mauling from the lordly lions, if and when such a case came to
the Lords. All this is heady stuff for the English criminal lawyer. The criminal
law so long has remained unreformed at the hands of the judiciary: it has kept
pace with modern conditions only because the legislature has sporadically
been forced to modernize it. Of the other criminal appeals, *S (an infant)* v.
Recorder of Manchester[1] gathered up a good deal of driftwood accumulated
by the courts over the years and, upsetting a train of decisions, decided that a
plea of guilty may be retracted at any time before sentence. Ostensibly it was
a small piece of reform of criminal procedure, but the manner in which the
Law Lords despatched a number of earlier decisions was both refreshing and
helpful.

The rest of the criminal work involved two leading extradition cases, to
which we have alluded elsewhere, and a variety of less significant cases, one
case of only limited general application under the Road Safety Act 1967;[2] a
company fraud case in which the majority of the Law Lords construed a provision in the Companies Act 1948 in favour of the accused;[3] and a gaming
appeal which rang the death knell of roulette.[4] What came out of the appeal
was anything but the last word. In 1970, apart from *D.P.P.* v. *Bhagwan*, there
was little excitement save an excursion into the uncharted water of the extra-
territoriality of crimes in *Treacy* v. *D.P.P.*[5] Their Lordships were divided on
the issue whether a blackmailing letter posted in England to a victim in West
Germany committed an offence under the Theft Act 1968. Four judgments reflected three different approaches to the crucial question—when can punishment at home be inflicted for a crime committed abroad?

But in the space of two years, the Law Lords had begun to give the appearance that they actually relished their new found (since 1960) jurisdiction and
wished to make some sweeping innovations and to fashion jurisprudential
thought in the area of the criminal law.

If the work in English civil appeals in 1969 was less than breath-taking, it
was far from insignificant. Family law was perceptibly advanced by *Pettitt* v.

1 [1971] A.C. 481.   2 *Pinner* v. *Everett* [1971] A.C. 1.
3 *D.P.P.* v. *Schildkamp* [1971] A.C.1.
4 *Victoria Sporting Club* v. *Hannam* [1970] A.C. 55.   5 [1971] A.C. 537.

Pettitt[1] which preceded the Matrimonial Proceedings and Property Act 1970 by defining restrictively the right of spouses to a share in the ownership of the other spouse's property. The following year in *Gissing* v. *Gissing* their Lordships reaffirmed the propositions enunciated in *Pettitt* v. *Pettitt*. And the welfare of children as the paramount consideration in *all* custody proceedings was firmly entrenched in *J.* v. *C.*,[2] nearly a half-century after Parliament had apparently said as much in the Guardianship of Infants Act 1925.

Pension rights as a factor in assessing damages in personal injury cases was helpfully stated in *Parry* v. *Cleaver*.[3] In the personal injury field, some significance attaches to the unanimous decision in *Barnes* v. *Hampshire C.C.*,[4] where the local education authority was, only at the last judicial hurdle, held liable for a child killed by a lorry when she had been released from school earlier than the pre-arranged time. The Law Lords were not afraid to reverse both lower courts (Lord Denning had dissented in the Court of Appeal) on a question of inferential fact, whether premature release from educational control (the child was sent home from afternoon school five minutes earlier than usual) was negligence. The victim of a road accident was again favoured when the Law Lords, by a majority, in *Henderson* v. *Henry E. Jenkins & Son*,[5] placed the onus of proving that proper steps had been taken to ensure the safety of a lorry's hydraulic brake on the lorry owner.

The Crown received its seemingly perennial blow at their Lordships' hands in *A.G.* v. *Nissan*[6] where the defence of Act of State was held inapplicable to a claim by a British hotelier in Cyprus whose property was damaged by a British force assisting the Cyprus Government: a decision of some constitutional importance.

The Crown, in the shape of the Inland Revenue Commission, played less of a role in House of Lords appeals in this bonanza year than in any recent year. Only one in five cases involved the Revenue authority: there were seven income tax appeals, one profits tax case, and one S.E.T. case. There were two rating appeals and two Customs and Excise fights—a pools betting duty claim and one concerning a loss of Commonwealth preference on Rhodesian tobacco at the time of U.D.I. One tax appeal, *Wiseman* v. *Borneman*,[7] raised the extent to which the rules of natural justice may apply to the proceedings before the Tax Commissioners, adding a helpful gloss on, by way of confining, the doctrine laid down in *Ridge* v. *Baldwin*.[8] For the rest there was a miscellany of appeals—trade marks, town and country planning, industrial training levy and redundancy payments—as well as the annual crop of personal injury cases.

The only blots on the judicial copy-book were *McEldowney* v. *Forde*,[9] where political considerations overbore the right of free association, and

1 [1970] A.C. 777.   2 [1970] A.C. 668.   3 [1970] A.C. 1.
4 [1969] 1 W.L.R. 1563.   5 [1970] A.C. 282.   6 [1970] A.C. 179.
7 [1971] A.C. 297.   8 [1964] A.C. 40.   9 [1971] A.C. 632.

Dawkins v. *Ash Bros.*,[1] a rating appeal about the extent to which the prospect of early demolition of a building affected the valuation for rates. But, since both these rather unfortunate decisions upheld the courts *a quo*, the advocacy for only one appeal court is not advanced. We can say, with confidence, that the law of England would have been significantly the poorer in 1969 (and for years to come) without the House of Lords.

The beginning of a new decade was hardly less important in terms of the future of the House of Lords. In 1970 the case-load was less than in the previous bumper year—the total was thirty-five—but it was nevertheless a fruitful year in terms of legal development.

There were at least four seminal decisions: *Home Office* v. *Dorset Yacht Co.*[2] opened up a whole new area of tort liability in affixing legal responsibility on Government departments for the negligence of civil servants: *McPhail* v. *Doulton*[3] was the first major review of the law of trusts, in which the distinction between trusts and powers was swept away in a majestic piece of law-making: *S* v. *S*: *W* v. *W*[4] (two appeals heard consecutively) resolved the conflict in the Court of Appeal over blood tests in paternity suits in favour of ordering serological tests whenever it is in the interests of the child to ascertain parenthood: *Gallie* v. *Lee*[5] mopped up all the irreconcilable decisions over a century on the vexed doctrine of *non est factum*, and laid down the circumstances under which a signatory to a document can afterwards resile from his commitment on the grounds that he thought he was binding himself legally to something other than the document which he signed.

A number of other cases were of prime importance: *American Cyanamid Co.* v. *Upjohn Co.*,[6] the first 'leapfrog' case (see above, pp. 149 ff), dealt with the novel problem of the inclusion in patent specifications of micro-organisms used for making commercial products, in this case a pharmaceutical antibiotic called Porfiromycin. The Lords held that the exclusion from the specification of the natural elements in the product did not constitute a failure to describe the invention and the method by which it is to be performed. The Law Lords declined to rule on the wider problem whether the commercialization of natural substances can be a patentable invention: a hint was dropped in the direction of the legislature that statutory clarification would be appropriate.

International contracts and arbitrations were comprehensively considered in *Cie. d'Armement Maritime* v. *Cie. Tunisienne de Navigation S.A.*[7] and in *James Miller & Partners Ltd.* v. *Whitworth.*[8] The latter case concerned an interpretation of the R.I.B.A. standard form contract which received further judicial scrutiny in two more cases: *N.W. Metropolitan Regional Hospital Board* v. *T. A. Bickerton & Son Ltd.*[9] and *Westminster City Council* v. *J. Jarvis*

---

1 [1969] 2 A.C. 366.   2 [1970] A.C. 1004.   3 [1971] A.C. 424.
4 [1970] 3 W.L.R. 366.   5 [1971] A.C. 1004.   6 [1970] 1 W.L.R. 1507.
7 [1971] A.C. 572.   8 [1970] A.C. 583.   9 [1970] 1 W.L.R. 607.

& *Sons Ltd.*[1] The Law Lords in *W. & J. B. Eastwood* v. *Herrod*[2] gave the *coup de grâce* to the perennial argument about the exemption (or rather non-exemption) of broiler houses from rating on the basis that they are agricultural buildings. And in *B. S. Brown & Sons* v. *Craiks Ltd.*[3] one of the only two Scottish cases in the year, the Law Lords echoed what had been said a year previously about what 'merchantable quality' meant in the Sale of Goods Act.

For the rest the mixture was much the same as in the previous year. Once again revenue cases figured less prominently in the case-load. As in 1969 they formed only a fifth of the total volume and in this year the bulk of them—five out of six—came from Scotland. This trend—if trend it be—can only be welcome. Too often in the past the Law Lords seemed obsessively preoccupied with this recondite branch of law.

Our study of the House of Lords in judicial action over two decades has shown many changes, some marked, some so slight as to be imperceptible. The beginning of the new decade has prompted us to reflect upon some of these changes. If 1970 has been undramatic, we suspect that by the time of the centenary of the modern jurisdiction, in 1976, evolution will have even further transformed the Lords from the body which operated even as recently as the immediate post-war period. We can but watch and observe.

1 [1970] 1 W.L.R. 637. 2 [1971] A.C. 160; reversed by the Rating Act 1971.
3 [1970] 1 W.L.R. 752.

XIX

CONCLUSIONS: REFORM OF THE JUDICIAL HOUSE OF LORDS

THE central purpose of this study has been to subject the present judicial functions exercised by the House of Lords to careful scrutiny, to arrive at an informed evaluation of various aspects of the appellate system. To this end we have employed various methods of statistical analysis, supplemented by more impressionistic methods of assessment, to evaluate the recent performance of the House of Lords in the main areas of substantive law and to examine the virtues and shortcomings of the appellate machinery. The end-product of our labours is an accumulation of evidence selected and organized in terms of various criteria of relevance, and measured against preselected yardsticks of excellence. We outlined the philosophy of such an approach and the problems inherent in it in the opening chapter.

A two-tier appeal system is a prominent feature of the British hierarchy of courts though, as we have seen, this country is by no means unique in maintaining a system of this kind. Despite sporadic murmurings of discontent there seems to be no immediate likelihood of the House of Lords losing its jurisdiction, either wholly or partially. For one thing there is little or no immediate political capital to be made out of reforming the appellate court structure: in any case, reformers are likely to be fully occupied for several years to come with re-structuring the lower echelons of the court system. With a seize-up of the assize system affecting the lives of tens of thousands of litigants every year, a court which deals with thirty or so appeals annually tends not unnaturally to be left to its own devices. The Courts Act 1971 has now mopped up the Assize and Quarter Sessions jurisdictions and it seems likely that for a few years little else will be done by Parliament to revise the structure of the courts.

It must be remembered, however, that what the House of Lords does today, every court in the land, by virtue of the doctrine of precedent, will be doing tomorrow: for this reason the issue of reforming the appellate hierarchy is one (to adopt a phrase all too familiar in this context) of general public importance. Has our present study pointed to the need either for outright abolition of this ancient tribunal, or for drastic revision of the nature and extent of its jurisdiction, or for streamlining its procedures?

We will begin by making a categorical and *a priori* assertion, in the light of which all our more detailed conclusions must be viewed. Our study convinces us that, given the present size and complexity of our network of courts, given the present system of *stare decisis*, and given the definitive 'legalism' of our judges (and their very human fallibility), there must be a need for some institution to supervise the legal system as a whole. Since we would also broadly accept the need for an independent judiciary (while rejecting emphatically any dogmatic adherence to the wider doctrine of the separation of powers) we regard the judges as the most suitable contenders for this supervisory role, not forgetting at all the role of the Law Commission and of Parliament. We realise that these are personal viewpoints, though they would, we think, find many adherents; we plead, partly in mitigation and partly by way of explanation, that the comparatively narrow terms of reference we have set for this study have inhibited us from delving too deeply into wider constitutional matters. And there still remains unanswered the all-important question of whether or not the supervisory function should continue to reside with the House of Lords in its present form.

No doubt, if a society were to be constructed from scratch, the last place one would think of for housing a court exercising this important role would be in the second chamber of the legislature. But for the purpose of drafting our conclusions we have eschewed the wholly unreal device of pretending that the House of Lords is not there, so as to be able to devise a utopian 'ideal system'. In this context the social system is regarded as an established fact and the House of Lords, its manifest incongruity notwithstanding, is part of that fact.

Our suggestions for reform of the judicial House of Lords fall into two main categories; internal (or procedural) reforms, and external (or structural) reforms. The former are 'medicinal' in character—founded upon the premise that the House of Lords should still be retained to carry out the supervisory function essential to our legal system, but that a number of internal modifications would enable it to perform these functions more effectively. Structural reforms are 'surgical' in character, and would be necessary only under either or both of the following sets of circumstances:

(a) if it could be shown that the job which the House of Lords purports to perform is irrelevant to modern conditions (a conclusion we have rejected); *or*
(b) if it can be shown that the functions of the House of Lords could be performed with greater efficiency by another institution.

The distinction is an important one. Our suggestions for procedural reforms relate directly to our empirical findings: we have demonstrated, for example, some of the drawbacks in the machinery for determining petitions for leave to appeal. Thus we have 'hard' data upon which to found a case for reform, though ultimately our interpretation of that data and our preference for one of a number of solutions to the problem must be subjective. The question of structural reform is more open to subjectivity: our own arbitrary selection of data cannot in any sense *prove* that fundamental reforms are required in the appellate system. We have discussed many variables which form part of the total equation, but in the last analysis our opinion, although it is buttressed by a considerable body of empirical fact, is as good (or as bad) as anyone else's. Be that as it may, we have not been deterred from dipping our personal oar into the controversy by exploring other proposals for structural reform.

Of course, structural reform is closely related to procedural reform: the accumulation of a large number of relatively minor reforms may change the whole character of the institution. Thus a series of important changes in the procedure, jurisdiction and composition of the House of Lords has meant that the court of last resort in 1972 bears little resemblance to its 1876 counterpart. And if reform is needed, we feel that the surgeon's knife should be used only when the gentler arts of the physician have demonstrably failed.

We deal first with procedural reforms: many of these have been discussed. Only the more extensive proposals are considered here, though a number of lesser criticisms and suggestions will be found scattered throughout the book. To some extent procedural reforms are alternative to structural reform; but we feel that many of our suggestions would be relevant in constructing the machinery of a completely new court of last resort.

A. PROCEDURAL REFORMS

(i) *Petitions for leave to Appeal*

The problem raised by the large number of garrulous petitioners for leave to appeal appearing in person before the Appeal Committee, often seeking leave in cases which lie outside the jurisdiction of the House, was discussed at length in Chapter VII. As we have seen, any demand for this situation to be remedied was anticipated in July 1970 by the issuing of an important practice direction which eliminates any judicial hearing of petitioners whose appeals would be barred either by the rule in *Lane* v. *Esdaile*, or by statute, from taking their appeals to the House of Lords. At one stroke the greatest single anomaly in the procedure of the House was eliminated, and one can only wonder why it was allowed to remain so long.

Petitioners will no doubt continue to take advantage of their present right to appear in person before the Appeal Committee. It is difficult to estimate how many of those whose cases came within our period of study would have been eliminated by the new rule. The *Lane* v. *Esdaile* doctrine was not revived until 1960, and in any event it has not always been clear from the documents at our disposal whether in any particular case the petition was incompetent, particularly as their Lorships do not normally give their reasons for dismissing a petition and often do not make it clear whether rejection is on the grounds of lack of merit, incompetence, or both. Our estimate is, however, that at least half the petitioners in person would have been denied a hearing under the new rule.

The change of practice certainly represents a step in the right direction and even though their Lordships will still have to listen to some time-wasting non-sense, while respondents are put to trouble and expense (both usually irretriev-able) in opposing hopeless petitions, we would be loath to see the time-honoured right of litigants to conduct their own cases in person tampered with.

It is ironic that the unfortunate situation brought about by a plethora of petitioners in person could not have arisen until the passing of the Adminis-tration of Justice (Appeals) Act 1934 which, for the first time, made English appeals subject to the granting of leave. Most of the hopeless cases would have been effectively excluded from the House by the provisions of S.O.V. which compels an appellant to lodge a substantial sum of money as security for costs. If the remedy provided by the 1970 practice direction proves insufficient to stem the flood of time-wasting petitions, we would strongly urge a reversion to the pre-1934 position and permit English civil appeals to go to the House of Lords as of right, subject only to the statutory exclusion of incompetent appeals. The rules requiring security for costs and the signature of two counsel on every petition of appeal would provide an effective sieve, and the Appeal Committee would need to sit only intermittently to dispose of interlocutory matters, such as applications for further time for lodging of cases. To avoid discriminating against poor litigants we would suggest that the criteria to be applied by Legal Aid Area Committees in considering applications for Legal Aid in respect of House of Lords proceedings should be extended to cover all cases in which important points of law are involved, as suggested below (section iii).

The reversion to the pre-1934 situation would assist materially in promoting a desirable reform in respect of the current case-load of the House of Lords.

(ii) *The Case-Load of the Lords*

The problem of the size and character of the case-load of the House of Lords goes to the heart of the supervisory jurisdiction it exercises. There is much to be said for a court which can deliberate unhurriedly upon a small body of cases; but equally one must set against this the substantial drawback of a small case-load whereby the court is denied an opportunity to develop its expertise in particular areas of law. This is one of the main conclusions that we would draw from the matters discussed in Part C: only in the compara-tively esoteric field of revenue and rating appeals does the number of cases reach a level where the House can develop a coherent body of jurisprudence—and this, after all, is what the supervisory function is supposed to be about.

The effects of this can perhaps be seen most clearly in the field of criminal law (more particularly before the Administration of Justice Act 1960 extended the right of appeal) and in the law of obligations. All too often when an important case does come up there seems to be an almost audible cry of 'now is our chance': the disastrous consequences of such an an approach can often be felt for years afterwards until another comes up on the same point. There is a tendency too for individual judges (particularly the more junior) to have limited opportunities of participating in the work of the court; a larger number of cases, making even heavier demands on judge-hours, would perhaps lead to the adoption of the American practice of assigning the preparation of leading judgments on a rota basis.

We consider that it is vital that many more cases should be allowed to reach the Lords—a state of affairs which could be achieved only by a radical streamlining of its procedures. For example, much shorter oral hearings (achieved by adopting the South African system of 'heads of argument': see below, section VI) would probably enable the House of Lords to treble its case-load to about 100 cases a year (the Court of Appeal, now admittedly sitting most of the year in four divisions, hears five times this number). This would increase very considerably the range of cases considered, while preserving a case-load small enough for weighty deliberation and authoritative decision-making. Ideally we would combine this with a proposal to assign the task of writing opinions on a rota basis. Under such a system some lesser cases would inevitably come before the court; but this disadvantage would be more than offset by a widening of the court's horizons and a broadening of its range of influence in developing the law.

(iii) *Legal Aid*

Legal aid was extended to House of Lords proceedings in 1960 and the effects of this innovation have already been discussed in Chapter XI. Of 436 appellants and respondents in civil causes who went to the House of Lords during the period 1961–8, 50 (11·5 per cent) were legally aided. Of these 50, 35 were appellants, of whom 18 won their appeals: 15 were respondents, of whom 6 were successful.

To some extent this low figure can be explained by the fact that leave to appeal tends in practice to be more frequently asked for and granted to litigating public authorities and large corporations whose interests in a still predominantly capitalist society are, by and large, more likely to be regarded as being of 'general public importance' than those of the bulk of individual litigants. But there can be no doubt that the limitations in the power of Legal Aid Area Committees to grant legal aid is also an important factor.

In *Rondel* v. *Worsley*,[1] Lord Reid remarked that: '. . . the Appellant's claim was clearly as devoid of merit as it was of any prospect of success. But *in view of the importance of the question of law involved* [our emphasis] this House gave the Appellant leave to appeal.' However, notwithstanding the obvious general

1 [1969] 1 A.C. 196.

importance of this case, the Legal Aid Area Committee which had considered Rondel's application for legal aid considered itself bound to refuse the application on its merits—and its decision was upheld by the Divisional Court (see *R. v. Area Committee No. 1 (London) Legal Aid Area, ex parte Rondel*[1] discussed also in Chapter XI).

If one accepts the unique position of the House of Lords as a second-tier appellate court, one must also accept the principle that the *only* cases which should go to the House are those which involve points of legal principle of far-reaching public importance. Our common law system is based on an adversary system of justice which demands that such cases must be resolved, not as academic exercises, but by way of actual litigation between contending parties who have a direct stake in the outcome of the case. This view is supported by the dictum of Viscount Simon L.C. in *Sun Life Assurance Co. of Canada v. Jervis*.[2] In that case leave to appeal to the House of Lords was granted by the Court of Appeal subject to an undertaking by the Appellants, 'to pay the costs as between solicitor and client in the House of Lords in any event and not to ask for the return of any money ordered to be paid by this order'. In the House of Lords, Lord Simon (expressing the unanimous view that the House should decline to hear the appeal) said:

The difficulty is that the terms put on the appellants by the Court of Appeal are such as to make it a matter of complete indifference to the respondent whether the appellants win or lose. . . . I do not think that it would be a proper exercise of the authority which this House possesses to hear appeals if it occupies time in this case in deciding an academic question, the answer to which cannot affect the respondent in any way.

Provided that appeals which are *not* of general importance can be sifted out, it seems anomalous that litigants who are being employed as a pawn in the game of socio-legal development should be obliged (unless they are inordinately rich) to pay for the privilege; this applies, *a fortiori*, when a poor litigant with an important but unmeritorious appeal is excluded from the House of Lords altogether.

Our proposal is to extend the criteria for the granting of legal aid in respect of House of Lords appeals to include cases like that of *Rondel*. We should also like to see a very large increase in the income limit for obtaining legal aid in the House of Lords—or even a total abolition of such a limit, accompanied by a provision for graduated contributions up to 100 per cent for the very wealthy litigant. (Legal persons would still be excluded from the scheme.) The marginal advantage of the 'no-limit' alternative would be to obviate the need for periodic adjustments in the income ceiling to take account of inflation.

(iv) *Judgments*

At present, each Law Lord who hears an appeal ordinarily prepares a

---

[1] [1967] 2 Q.B. 482.   [2] [1944] A.C. 111.

separate speech or judgment: even when the House is unanimous in its decision it is common for five full-length speeches to be prepared. (The average is three to four per case.) If only one full opinion is delivered in a case and that opinion turns out to have been unsatisfactory, then confusion can obviously result (see the observations of Lord Reid in *C.I.R.* v. *Chancery Lane Safe Deposit and Offices Co. Ltd.*).[1] But it can be argued that confusion is even more likely to arise with the delivery of several separate assenting judgments in the same case. (Recent cases which illustrate the legal uncertainty which can result in this way have been discussed at pp. 90–3 above.)

It is not proposed to repeat our detailed criticisms of the role of assenting opinions (already discussed in Chapter v) except to say that the right to deliver a separate assenting opinion must be used circumspectly. Assenting judgments are no promoters of the cause of legal certainty.

Our proposal under this sub-heading is that House of Lords judgments should (as is the case in the Judicial Committee of the Privy Council) ordinarily be combined in a single 'opinion of the Court' the writing of which would be assigned on a rota basis, and that this single opinion would be the only authority for the decision. Although this proposal might tend, to some small extent, to discourage judicial individuality, the additional certainty in the law would be ample compensation. Moreover, we would not wish to eliminate either separate assenting or dissenting opinions by individual judges with strong views on the case. It is only that individual judgments, additional to the single opinion, would carry no authority other than the force of their own reasoning. Such a practice would obviate the practitioner's unenviable task of having to unravel the *ratio*(*nes*) *decidendi* from several assenting judgments.

(v) *The Composition of the House of Lords*

At present the composition of the House of Lords is as follows: five English Common Law Judges, two English Chancery judges, one English Divorce judge, and two Scottish judges. In addition, ex-Lord Chancellors and peers who hold or have held high judicial office (such as Lord Denning M.R., Lord MacDermott, and Lord Gardiner) are sometimes invited to sit. The Appellate Committee almost invariably these days sits as a bench of five.

It seems anomalous that a decision in a particular case might depend upon the permutation of Lords selected to sit.[2] In many areas of law uncertainty is inevitable; and judges (despite their uniformity of background and training) are bound to differ in attitude. It is not merely in the lower courts that barristers can complain that another court might have reached a different decision.

---

1 [1966] A.C. 85.
2 See Robert Stevens's suggestions about the *Hedley Byrne* decision, in 27 M.L.R. 130, which is discussed above at p. 153, n. 1, and *Jones* v. *Secretary of State for Social Services* [1972] 1 All E.R. 145, 196 per Lord Simon of Glaisdale.

Although the selection of the Court for each appeal rests with the Lord Chancellor, it is not suggested that nowadays the House is ever 'packed' for political or other reasons, although, according to Professor Heuston, the first Lord Hailsham was not averse to doing this during the 1930s in order to isolate the progressive leanings of Lord Atkin.[1]

It is interesting to reflect that, of the 466 civil appeals heard by the House of Lords during the period 1952–68, no fewer than 53 (11 per cent) were decided, one way or the other, by a majority of 3:2. With judicial opinion as finely balanced as this it is impossible to discount the composition of the court as a factor with at least some influence on the development of legal principles by the House of Lords. And we have already discussed the disquietingly high proportion of 'minority' decisions which do nothing to advance the cause of litigant satisfaction.

We consider that there is a strong argument in favour of the House of Lords sitting *en banc* (i.e. as a full court of nine or eleven):[2] this suggestion would, after all, only be a reversion to the original notion of an appellate court, and even today the courts occasionally make use of a full court procedure (see Appendix 6). However, this situation does raise serious problems: it would disrupt the work of the Judicial Committee of the Privy Council, although it could (but not very readily) be staffed by ex-Lord Chancellors and others having held high judicial office plus Lords Justices of Appeal. But if there were a merger of the two and a speed-up in the disposal of appeals, the work could be accommodated. It would undoubtedly involve a considerable additional burden on the Law Lords unless some way could be found of adjusting their work-pattern. A third objection would be that the House would be precluded from sitting simultaneously as two Appellate Committees, or as one Appellate Committee and one Appeal Committee. It would also mean that it would be more difficult for the Law Lords to cope with the heavier case-load with which we would saddle them. We, therefore, make no specific recommendation on this point, though we feel that the objections we have reviewed are essentially administrative and do nothing to weaken the argument.

(vi) *The Case and Oral Argument*

Under the present system the appellant and the respondent in a House of Lords appeal are obliged to lodge a document called the Case which contains a brief outline of the arguments which will be relied upon by the two parties, and a selection of documents, including the writ and transcripts (or reports) of the judgments delivered in the lower courts. However, unlike the U.S. Supreme Court where the elaborate printed 'briefs' form the basis of the pro-

[1] *Lives of the Lord Chancellors*, p. 531.
[2] At the time of writing there is an establishment for eleven Law Lords but only ten have been appointed. Absence would, from time to time, reduce the available number, which could be supplemented by the use of supernumeraries if it was thought necessary to maintain an uneven number on the Court.

ceedings before the court and oral arguments restricted by a time-limit are regarded merely as a supplement to the brief, the procedure of the House of Lords is geared wholly to oral argument. The Case is merely regarded as a useful preliminary statement of the issues involved. Indeed it sometimes appears that their Lordships have not even read it.

As things stand at present, too little use is made of the Case. Our proposal is to adopt the procedure of South African courts whereby counsel are bound, within four days of the hearing, to submit 'heads of argument' which contain a full précis of propositions and authorities to be relied upon. In oral argument there would still be no time-limit, but counsel would be expected to confine themselves to supplementing the material contained in the 'heads of argument' and not permitted to produce additional arguments without the leave (sparingly granted) of the court. Such a practice would obviate the need to raise a new point for the first time at the hearing of the appeal.[1]

Another undesirable feature of the present system is that counsel spend a great deal of time in reading authorities (some of them at inordinate length) to their Lordships. We feel that, notwithstanding the recent failure of a similar experiment in the Court of Appeal[2] it would be a useful innovation if the Law Lords could make it an invariable rule to read some of the authorities before oral argument begins.

It must be acknowledged that giving their Lordships a large amount of additional 'homework' could wreak havoc with the current timetable of appeals. It might be necessary, for example, for the House to have a 'reading day' once a week.[3]

(vii) 'Mumbo Jumbo'

Seven centuries of constitutional history underlie the contemporary jurisdiction of the House of Lords, and we are loath to suggest tampering with the cherished traditions of House of Lords procedure without good reason. But we feel that, for example, the present proceedings whereby the Appellate Committee must report back to the House of Lords (consisting of the same Law Lords who sat on the Committee) in order that the decision be approved by a formal vote of 'the House' is a waste of time for everyone concerned. We suggest that counsel be notified of decisions and sent the printed speeches through the Judicial Office: the decisions could then be laid on the table of the House and approved *en masse* at the end of each parliamentary session (though they would have effect from the time that counsel were notified).

---

[1] *P. & M. Kaye* v. *Hosier & Dickinson Ltd.* [1972] 1 W.L.R. 146.

[2] *Practice Statement* (*Reading Documents*) [1962] 1 W.L.R. 395.

[3] If this suggestion were ever adopted we would propose Wednesday as a traditionally suitable day. Before the war the House used to sit on Mondays, Tuesdays, and Thursdays. One Law Lord quipped that on Monday he could say he had come back from a splendid break at the week-end; on Tuesday he was looking forward to a holiday the following day, and on Thursday he could reflect both on a break in the working week and delight on the pleasures of a forthcoming long week-end!

Another procedural anachronism resulting from the constitutional position of the Judicial House of Lords as an offshoot of the legislature is its complete separation from the Supreme Court. This means that, in order to enforce a judgment of the House of Lords, counsel must go before a Master of the Supreme Court in order to obtain a formal Supreme Court order. We propose that House of Lords judgments should automatically become enforceable without the necessity for obtaining a further order.

Our third suggestion under this heading is that hearings in the Chamber of the House should be abolished. It must be confessed that this proposal is intended more for the comfort of counsel than to achieve any far-reaching benefit for the legal system as a whole.

Finally, in the interests of administrative convenience and the expeditious disposal of business, the lodging of petitions and the convening of Appeal Committees should not be dependent upon the sittings of Parliament.

(viii) *Scottish Appeals*

Notwithstanding Professor Walker's defence of the High Court of Justiciary, and in defiance of a long historical tradition, we feel that Scottish criminal appeals should lie (with the same procedure for obtaining leave as in the Administration of Justice Act 1960) to the House of Lords. In saying this we imply no criticism of the work of the Scottish courts, but feel strongly that the present position militates against the movement towards synthesizing a common body of United Kingdom law, based upon the best of Scottish and English jurisprudence. The position is becoming increasingly anachronistic with the increase in the number of statutory offences which apply equally on both sides of the Border. Scottish protests about this change are weakened by the vast improvement in the Lords' performance in criminal appeals since the dark ages of *Shaw* and *Smith*.

On the civil side, although there is no firm evidence that many (or any) Scottish appeals are unworthy of a hearing in the Lords, it is noticeable that a high proportion come from Sheriff's courts and/or involve questions, such as fault liability, with a strong element of fact. We see no reason why the Scottish litigant should not have to pass through the same sieve as the English if indeed any such sieve is needed at all (see section i): the idea of making Scottish appeals subject to leave was raised during the debates on the Administration of Justice (Appeals) Bill in 1934. Equally, we see no reason why Scots should be excluded from the benefits of the leapfrogging provisions, though no doubt they, like the rest of us, will want to see how the English experiment works out in practice.

We considered the possibility of recommending special sittings of the House of Lords in the Parliament House in Edinburgh. While this might well benefit Scottish litigants and their advisers, we feel that this would be more than offset by the cost and disruption of bodily uprooting an English-based court and transporting it like a travelling circus to deal with a handful of Scottish appeals. Moreover, any such move would detract from the role of the Lords as a centralizing institution: the evolution of a United Kingdom jurisprudence would hardly be helped by bowing to nationalistic sentiments.

(ix) *'Public Importance'*

In the course of this study we have come across a number of cases whose claim to be of public importance seems dubious: many patent appeals, for example, seem to go to the Lords only because of the vast sums of money at stake. We feel, however, that statutory exclusion is not the answer; the House of Lords, through its Appeal Committee, must be relied upon to act as its own sieve in judging issues of public importance. Indeed, some of the categories, such as bankruptcy and matrimonial causes which are at present subject to especially stringent requirements for leave to appeal, seem to have been selected somewhat arbitrarily and might well be reconsidered. A major statutory development in divorce and matrimonial property law might well call for consideration at the highest judicial level.

(x) *Law Clerks*

English barristers are accustomed to a life of professional self-sufficiency: apart from the shared services of a clerk to organize the disposal of briefs within a set of chambers, a member of the Bar has to act as his own research assistant (unless he has a devil or a particularly bright pupil) and to make his own secretarial arrangements. The same solitary tradition is maintained when the barrister becomes a judge: even in the House of Lords, some Law Lords have to make do with shared rooms and all have to share the single amanuensis.

We feel that there is a strong case for emulating the United States Supreme Court and providing their Lordships with personal 'law clerks' to undertake at least some of the basic toil of predigesting bulky documents and consulting and checking case references. Assisted by a law clerk, each Law Lord would invariably be briefed in advance of argument and time would often be saved. When it came to the writing of judgments, judicial time would not be wasted in ploughing through irrelevant references, and speeches might be sooner prepared.

Would there perhaps be a danger of law clerks exerting a pernicious influence on the decisions of the court of last resort? We think not: Law Lords are judges of long experience and considerable independence. Law clerks would be appointed from the ranks of newly qualified barristers for a period of (say) two years: but while their role would be predominantly secretarial, they would inject a breath of youth into an old-established tribunal.

We suspect that our suggestion will not be welcomed by the Law Lords themselves, though it is intended to lighten the physical side of their burden. The scheme would be more attractive if combined with our earlier proposal for allocating the writing of each judgment to a particular Law Lord.

(xi) '*Public Relations*'

The House of Lords is a 'public' institution but, like most of the superior courts—and probably to an even greater extent—it has an image of remoteness from day-to-day human activity. It is associated in the public mind with the worlds of big business, of public authorities, and of wealthy entrepreneurs: our examination of the case-load of the House shows clearly that this image is not wholly inaccurate.

One way to improve the public image of the House of Lords lies in reforms we have suggested in preceding sections—particularly, an extension of legal aid. One explanation of this problem, however, is simply the name of the institution, which not only conceals the almost total separation between the legislative and judicial functions of the House of Lords, but is also inextricably linked with notions of hereditary class privilege. In our view, the name should be changed, and, as will be seen in our next section, this would be one of the secondary consequences of our main proposal for structural reform—the merging of the House of Lords with the Judicial Committee of the Privy Council.

B. STRUCTURAL REFORMS

The major premise which underlies our study of the House of Lords is that if the House of Lords cannot be shown to function effectively as a court of supervision—laying down the guidelines for the development of legal principles by the courts—then its retention merely as a second-tier tribunal of review must be seen, at best, as a luxury. Our subjective but carefully considered judgment is that the House of Lords does perform effectively such a supervisory function. It makes mistakes; frequently it simply rubber-stamps the verdict of the court *a quo*, though this is not necessarily a waste of time; and sometimes the court *a quo* arrives at a more sensible decision than that of the House of Lords. But our survey of the appeals heard over a period of seventeen years convinces us beyond doubt that the House of Lords plays a major creative role—for better or for worse—in developing the law. The question remains, however, whether the same role could be performed more effectively if the system were radically reformed.

To abolish the House of Lords might bring at least two important benefits: the charge on public funds resulting from the retention of a third-tier court would be eliminated (though in fact the present cost to the public, and indeed to most individual litigants, is relatively small), and individual appeals would probably be disposed of more cheaply and quickly than now is the case. The four major disadvantages are:

(1) There would no longer be a supreme appellate court acting, as the House of Lords does, as a court of supervision.

(2) A vital institutional link between the legal systems of England and

Scotland would be severed and the unification of English and Scottish jurisprudence would be retarded. (There is also the question of Northern Irish appeals.)

(3) A small percentage of unsuccessful litigants in the Court of Appeal would be deprived of a judgment in their favour, and a number of cases which are now considered in great depth in the House of Lords would inevitably receive more perfunctory treatment in a first-tier Court of Appeal.

(4) To abolish the office of Law Lord would be to deprive the Judicial Committee of the Privy Council of its present permanent nucleus of senior and experienced appeal judges.

The compromise provided by the leapfrogging provisions of the 1969 Administration of Justice Act may go part of the way to solving the problem, though it remains to be seen whether the new procedure will overcome the difficulty of picking out cases suitable for 'House of Lords treatment' at an early stage in the proceedings. In any event the procedure will inevitably be used with considerable caution for some years. It would be impossible to devise reform which would eliminate the drawbacks of the present system without giving rise to regrettable side-effects. However, in the following sections we examine two schemes which would at least cushion the shock of structural reform.

A Strengthened Court of Appeal as court of supervision

This proposal is based on two main assumptions:

(1) That an appeal court with a supervisory function is an indispensable feature of our legal system.

(2) That in the interests of public economy and of individual litigants, it is preferable that supervision should be exercised within a two-tier (as opposed to the present three-tier) court hierarchy.

Provisional proposals might be as follows, though numerous variations could readily be devised:

(a) The appellate jurisdiction of the House of Lords should be totally abolished.

(b) The office of Law Lord should be retained, though the number of judges holding this office could be reduced to (say) five. As well as sitting in the Judicial Committee of the Privy Council, these Law Lords would sit in the Court of Appeal alongside the Lords Justices of Appeal, as they do on rare occasions under the present system. The normal composition of each Court of Appeal would be one Law Lord and two Lords Justices, though, of course, this ratio could be varied. The Law Lords would retain their life-peerages and the right to participate in debates in the (legislative) House of Lords so long as it survives.

(c) The existing right of appeal to the Court of Appeal should not be altered (in other words, appeals should continue to lie as of right in all final appeals). The trial judge in each case would certify (with or without application by the parties) whether the case was of sufficient importance to merit an appeal to a full Court of Appeal of five judges, at least two of whom must be Law Lords. If the judge did not consider that a full court hearing was justified it would be open to counsel representing either party (or an *amicus curiae*) to apply to the Court of Appeal for a full court to be convened. Moreover, if it became apparent during the hearing of the appeal that a full court should have been convened, then the Court of Appeal should have the discretion to reconvene itself as a full court. In the latter event, the costs of both parties in the Court of Appeal up to the time that reargument was ordered would be met out of public funds.

Decisions of the full court would be binding on the ordinary Court of Appeal, and the full court could overrule previous decisions of the latter. In general (but with the same exceptions that apply in the House of Lords under the present system) the full Court of Appeal would be bound by its own previous decisions and those of the House of Lords, though it might be desirable that a court of seven should be convened if there were any likelihood of the latter course being adopted.

(d) Scottish judges of the Inner House of the Court of Session should be attached to the Court of Appeal on a rota basis (say two judges for one year at a time). In cases which might involve a clash between English and Scottish legal principles, and in *all* cases heard by the full courts, a Scottish judge would sit on the bench. He would participate fully in argument and write an opinion, but the latter would be more in the nature of a memorandum on the Scottish aspects of the case than a formal judgment. Such an opinion would be accorded strong persuasive authority in the Court of Session. Similarly, two English judges would be seconded to the two divisions of the Court of Session on a similar basis.

The merit of this scheme lies in the combination of the advantages of total abolition with those of 'leapfrogging', with a minimum of disruption to the existing system. Moreover, the difficulties inherent in the sieving of cases coming before the supreme tribunal are greatly reduced if the entire appellate process is confined to a single institution: the safeguards outlined in paragraph (c) would minimize the risk of an important case failing to reach the full court. The present rigmarole of Appeal Committees having to decide whether or not to grant leave to appeal would be dispensed with. The status of the full court would be at least equivalent to that of the present House of Lords, and even the 'ordinary' Court of Appeal would enjoy an enhanced status with the addition of Law Lords to its current complement of judges. Furthermore, one would avoid the situation (not infrequent under the present system) where, on a count of judicial hands, a respondent in the House of Lords who loses by a majority decision can claim that he has really 'won'.

The total number of appellate judges could be cut down, but the present career structure of the judiciary need be only marginally affected. There would be much more contact between 'senior' and 'junior' appellate judges than at present. The existing links between the legal systems of England and Scotland would be maintained; indeed, the judicial interchange envisaged would, in some respects, be even more satisfactory than the present system whereby distinguished Lords of Session take up more or less permanent residence South of the Tweed. These proposals would give junior Scottish judges an opportunity to gain experience of English law comparatively early in their judicial careers (and similar opportunities would be given to English judges, who, at present, seldom have any experience of the Scottish system): there would be a healthy interaction of ideas without any danger of either legal system being 'adulterated' by the other. The final advantage of the proposal is that the Law Lords would be able to continue to make valuable contributions to technical legal debates in the House of Lords.

Of course even under the present system it is open to the Court of Appeal to sit as a full court, though it very rarely does so. The only three cases arising during our period of study were *Ward* v. *James*;[1] *Morelle* v. *Wakeling*;[2] and *Nowotnik* v. *Nowotnik*.[3] These cases, together with the twenty-seven full court decisions of the Court of Criminal Appeal during the same period, are discussed in Appendix 6. It appears that, at present, full courts are convened almost exclusively to consider previous decisions of the court concerned, and very rarely to deal with a difficult and important question of law. The present system, therefore, throws little light on the probable effects of substituting full courts in the Court of Appeal for the House of Lords.

What are the drawbacks of the proposal? While it has its attractions, it must be confessed that the reform envisaged would be little more than a disguise of the present three-tier system though it would have the prime merit of bringing some rational control into the system of appeals. But a scheme of this kind has all the marks of contrivance: it is reform for reform's sake. The question is whether the real advantages—we think that the reformers overstate them—warrant dismantling an historical tribunal. Perhaps, in the last analysis, the factor which weighs most heavily against a scheme of this kind is that the House of Lords must inevitably play a real role in maintaining the dignity of the law, which an overworked Court of Appeal dealing with a mass of trivia cannot adequately perform by itself. And there is a peculiar dignity in the House of Lords which will be preserved by retaining the 'infallible voices' of this judicial ivory tower: a House of Lords which is somewhat remote from

---

[1] [1964] 1 Q.B. 273.   [2] [1955] 2 Q.B. 379.   [3] [1967] P. 83.

the hurly-burly of the Strand yet attuned to the law-making function of Westminster.

Merger of the House of Lords and the Judicial Committee of the Privy Council
The assumptions which underlie our other choice for structural reform are diametrically opposed to those upon which the first proposal was based. They are:

(1) That a three-tier structure is a useful feature of our legal system—because a third-tier appellate court is in a better position to perform a supervisory function than a second-tier appellate court (however strongly the latter might be constituted).
(2) That the House of Lords as such has become riddled with archaisms and requires a major overhaul to bring it up to date.

The proposal (which, by virtue of its simplicity, can be stated very briefly) is as follows:
That the House of Lords be abolished and its functions transferred to the Judicial Committee of the Privy Council: the Law Lords to move into permanent occupation of the Downing Street building (in a reconstructed form) English, Scottish, Northern Irish, and Commonwealth appeals would all be dealt with on an identical basis—with Commonwealth judges sitting by invitation in United Kingdom appeals as well as in appeals from the Commonwealth courts.

The principal merit of this scheme is its simplicity: it retains the benefits of the House of Lords, but disposes of all the constitutional anachronisms of House of Lords procedure. Common facilities would be available in a single building which would be physically self-contained. The most important effect of the proposal would be to place Commonwealth appeals on an equal footing with United Kingdom appeals, thereby facilitating a unity of approach in all the legal systems involved. Moreover, with both Scots and Commonwealth judges in the Court, Scottish judges could no longer have grounds for complaining that an alien system of law was being imposed upon them by a bunch of Sassenachs and Anglicized Scots.

A further bonus might accrue from such an arrangement if the current movement towards the enactment of a Bill of Rights achieves its object. The Judicial Committee of the Privy Council has, as we have seen, a traditional role as a constitutional court in respect of the written constitutions of Commonwealth countries. If British judges ever found themselves cast in the unfamiliar role of pronouncing upon the constitutional validity of legislation they could surely have no better theatre than a reconstituted final court of appeal combining a domestic and a Commonwealth jurisdiction. Proposals for a Bill of Rights have often included provision for pre-legislative scrutiny of bills by an extra-parliamentary body (cf. the French Couseil D'État): one way of achieving this might be by adaptation of the special reference procedure provided by section 4 of the Judicial Committee Act 1833. One might even go one step further and combine such a constitutional role with the tasks of an administrative court, for example, along the lines suggested in the Conservative pamphlet 'Let Right be Done', in 1966.

But while we like the idea of an all-purpose tribunal, combining an appellate and a constitutional role in respect both of the U.K. and of the Commonwealth, it must be confessed that such a proposal belongs more to speculation than to reality.

The main drawback of the scheme is that, by itself, it does not go far enough. If this proposal is to provide a viable alternative to the present system, we consider that it should be implemented in conjunction with some of the procedural reforms discussed in previous sections—in particular, that the case-load be increased, the provision for legal aid greatly extended, and that some of the procedural anachronisms now connected with the granting of leave should not be carried across to Downing Street.

Our two choices for structural reform are put forward as a basis for discussion only. Variations on the 'strengthened Court of Appeal' theme are frequently cited in arguments about reform of the judicial hierarchy, and undoubtedly have superficial attractions. But their relevance does depend upon the premise that the House of Lords is either unfitted to retain its present judicial function, or at least that it performs its function at a prohibitive cost not commensurate with the need for much better quality than the Court of Appeal provides. The evidence for such a proposition must be carefully weighed. Ultimately the onus of proof rests squarely upon those who express discontent with the present system. Our interpretation of that evidence leads us to assert that the case for abolition falls far short of being made out: that the accumulated shortcomings of the present system do not merit an indictment, let alone our calling for the death sentence. Procedural reforms are needed, and we hope that some of our own proposals will eventually be adopted. Our proposal for a merger with the Judicial Committee of the Privy Council is essentially a procedural reform writ large, though it does entail some restructuring.

It may be deduced from our conclusions that we have ultimately adopted a conservative stance and in studying this remarkable institution have become enamoured of its workings, warts and all. We confess to an unashamed affection for this ancient tribunal which has managed to survive only by adapting itself to considerable changes which have taken place around it. But our affection has been tempered by dissatisfaction, even downright irritation, with its less lovable foibles, and sometimes even with the decisions which have emerged from it. We would sum up by saying that, while we strongly defend the House of Lords from the animadversions of abolitionists, we call loudly and clearly for a major tidying-up operation to enable it to go forward, with renewed vigour, into an era where the law through the courts will take on an ever-increasing social importance.

XX

EUROPEAN POSTSCRIPT

BRITISH entry into the European Economic Community became an imminent prospect only after the manuscript of this book had been delivered to the publishers. The event calls for a postscript.

In complying with this requirement we have been at pains not to involve ourselves in the crucial political and economic elements of the controversy about joining the European Economic Community. (Her Majesty's Government signed the Treaty of Accession on 22 January 1972, when this book was in an advanced state of readiness for publication.) We have even refrained from looking at the broad constitutional implications of signing the Rome Treaty, except for the one very narrow issue—bedevilled by semantic and definitional problems—of the extent to which commitment to the terms of the Treaty will involve any surrender of the sovereignty, or at least the autonomy, of British legal institutions.[1] More specifically, the one question we did ask ourselves was: what, if any, effect would Community law have upon the jurisdiction of British courts and, in particular, of the House of Lords?

One of the four institutions set up to carry out the various jobs entrusted to the European Economic Community was a Court of Justice[2] to ensure that 'the law is observed in the interpretation and implementation of this Treaty'.[3] Apart from its judicial control over the administrative agencies of the Community and its arbitration of disputes between member-States and of complaints by European civil servants against Community agencies, the European Court of Justice has inevitably become embroiled in national litigation to the limited extent that Community law is relevant to such litigation. Given that backcloth to the problem, how will the European Court's jurisdiction extend to the British judicial scene?

Article 177 of the Rome Treaty is the focal point of the European Court's incursion into national litigation, reflecting a need to achieve a delicate balance between the judicial sovereignty of national courts and the laudable aim of imposing implementation of European Economic Community laws uniformly throughout the member-States. The Article provides that the European Court shall have jurisdiction to give preliminary rulings concerning the interpretation of the Rome Treaty, the validity and interpretation of acts

---

[1] *Blackburn* v. *Attorney-General* [1971] 1 W.L.R. 1037; [1971] C.M.L.R. 784.
[2] Article 4, E.E.C. Treaty.   [3] Article 164, E.E.C. Treaty.

taken by Community institutions, and the interpretations of the statutes of bodies established by the Council of Ministers. Where any such question is raised before any national court or tribunal, that court or tribunal 'may, if it considers a decision on the question is necessary to enable it to give judgment, request the Court of Justice to give a ruling thereon'. That discretionary power is to be contrasted with the apparently mandatory version of the rule in relation to the final court of appeal. Article 177 (3) provides that 'where such a question is raised in a case pending before a court or tribunal of a member-State, from whose decisions there is no possibility of appeal under internal law, the court or tribunal shall be bound to refer the matter to the Court of Justice'.

Far from the exercise of this jurisdiction resulting 'in the House of Lords ceasing to be the court of last instance on all matters coming before the English courts'[1] there is, as we shall show, no intention by this provision to confer on the European Court, by way of an appeal, a direct control over the implementation of Community law by national courts.[2] Indeed a study of Article 177, and the case-law so far developed both in the European Court and in the courts of the six original member-States, discloses a collaborative forensic process in which a single purpose is achieved through a dialogue between two courts performing separate roles, the division being between *interpretation* of community laws by the supranational court and *implementation* of those laws by national courts harnessed by their States' commitment to the Treaty to the development of Community law.[3]

The precedent for Article 177 is the long-standing practice of the French courts in relation to public acts of an international character. Whenever an interpretation relating to an international treaty is raised, the French judges stay the proceedings and apply to the Executive for guidance wherever the problem before the court touches upon public international law or public international interests.[4] This is a practice not entirely unfamiliar to English lawyers, since the obtaining of an executive certificate in relation to public acts (the contents of which are binding on the court) is not uncommon.[5] Al-

[1] As suggested by Michael Niblock, *The E.E.C.: National Parliaments in Community Decision-making*, Chatham House and P.E.P., April 1971, p. 97.

[2] Pescatore, *Interpretation of Community Law and the Doctrine of the Acte Clair*, 1–6, paper delivered at the Dublin conference on Expansion of the European Communities, organized by the British Institute of International and Comparative Law in September 1970.

[3] *Costa* v. *E.N.E.L.* [1966] C.M.L.R. 172.

[4] Pescatore, op. cit., 1–21/22, and Nicole Questiaux, *Interpretation of Community Law*, paper delivered at the Dublin Conference organized by the British Institute of International and Comparative Law, September 1970, 1–34. There appears to be a difference in the practice of the various types of court. The Conseil d'Etat consults the Executive on any international treaty, whereas the ordinary courts drew a distinction between private and public international law problems, referring only the latter to a Government department. See O'Connell, *International Law*, vol. I, p. 133: 'In France the Executive may give an official interpretation of a treaty which binds the courts'.

[5] There has always been some doubt about the conclusiveness of the evidence supplied in an Executive Certificate. There are, however, certain statutory provisions which make

though there has never been a case where the English courts have sought the Executive's view on the interpretation of a treaty, there are a number of instances where the Executive, in certifying as to a particular fact, inevitably encroaches on the judicial preserve, and to that extent acceptably usurps the judicial function.[1] The rationale of this division of functions is that in matters of public policy touching on the Crown's foreign relations 'the State cannot speak with two voices . . . the judiciary saying one thing, the Executive another'.[2] (A maxim which, in an ideal world, might be applied in other legal contexts.) Hence, the handing over of the interpretation of Treaty provisions to an international court may prove not to be so alien a concept for English lawyers as it was to the five member-States (not including France) of the Community.

Article 177 seeks to impose uniform interpretation of Community law within national jurisdictions. Uniformity is sought not only in the substantive law, but also—and more importantly—in the effectiveness of Community law in national litigation.[3] A large part of the Court's work has been concerned with problems of efficacy and not of substance. A series of decisions on the direct application of Community law to national law has turned on the question of implementing treaty provisions by national courts and not on their meaning in substance. The nub of these questions has been, either expressly or implicitly, a question of fixing the precise relationship between national legislation and Community law: in some cases the court has even been asked to draw the boundaries between the two,[4] whereas in others it has had to pro-

---

any such certificate conclusive: see, e.g. s. 4, Diplomatic Privileges Act 1964 and s. 4 (4), Fugitive Offenders Act 1967.

[1] The kind of questions asked are:

(a) Whether a foreign state has been recognized by the Crown, or whether a foreign government has been recognized either de jure or de facto: Carl-Zeiss Stiftung v. Rayner & Keeler Ltd. [1967] 1 A.C. 853, 901. Re Al-Fin Corporation's Patent [1970] Ch. 160.

(b) Whether a particular territory is under the sovereignty of the Crown or some other state: Adams v. Adams (Attorney-General intervening) [1971] P. 188.

(c) What is the status of property which is the subject matter of claims by foreign states or sovereigns: The Parlement Belge (1879) L.R. 4 P.D. 129.

(d) Whether a state of war exists between the Crown and foreign states, or between two foreign states.

(e) Whether a person is entitled to diplomatic status: Engelke v. Mussman [1928] A.C. 433; R. v. Governor of Pentonville Prison, ex Parte Teja [1971] 2 Q.B. 274.

(f) The question as to the existence or extent of British jurisdiction in any foreign place, and the extent of territory claimed by the Crown: Ex Parte Mwenya [1960] 1 Q.B. 241; Post Office v. Estuary Radio Ltd. [1968] 2 Q.B. 740, 753.

(g) The question as to the status of British Allied Forces.

For the limitations on the type of question that may properly be asked, and for which an Executive Certificate is available, see Devlin J. in Bank voor Handel en Scheepvaart v. Slatford [1953] 1 Q.B. 248, 253, 266.

[2] Sir Jocelyn Simon P. in Adams v. Adams (Attorney-General intervening) [1971] P. 188, 198, citing Lord Atkin in The Arantzazu Mendi [1939] A.C. 256, 264.

[3] Van Gend en Loos v. Nederlandse Belastingadministratie [1963] C.M.L.R. 105.

[4] Wilhelm and others v. Bundeskartellamt [1969] C.M.L.R. 100, 118–19.

vide the elements of interpretation sufficient to allow the national judge to decide on the compatibility of national statutes with Community law.[1]

But whatever the nature of the cases referred for preliminary ruling, the European Court has jealously guarded the jurisdictional sovereignty of national courts. It has faithfully recognized, notwithstanding the mandatory character of Article 177 in respect of courts from which there is no appeal, that the issue whether to refer a question to the European Court is solely a matter for the national court, even to the point that the European Court has not so far accepted an objection by a party to the admissibility of questions put to it.[2] Furthermore, the European Court has resolutely declined to apply Community law to the national law.[3]

By studied judicial courtesy it has been possible to maintain mutual respect for differential judicial responsibilities. Both the European Court and the national courts, in adhering strictly to their separate functions while at the same time collaborating in the performance of complementary roles, ultimately have to display the Community spirit without which there would be no Community worth speaking of. And collaboration entails a constant dialogue between the separate courts.

Given this essential background to Article 177, we can ask the question: what are its likely effects upon the work of the House of Lords on appeals raising Common Market issues? The distillation of cases coming before the lower appeal courts is such that perhaps only a fraction of those involving Community law will ever reach the House of Lords. Or will they be cases inherently so important that an unusually high proportion will be fought through the gamut of courts? Even if there is a significant number coming to the House of Lords, there remains the distinct possibility that in their ascent of the judicial ladder reference to the European Court will have been made at some stage on the way up.

The Community's own experience to date is that quite the largest number of requests for preliminary rulings come from courts of first instance (even from administrative tribunals) or at least from intermediate courts of appeal. There is a positive virtue in an early reference, since it allows problems of Community laws to be resolved rapidly in the preliminary stages of litigation and provides the European Court with the earliest opportunity of resolving doubts for the courts of all member-States. Such a procedure reduces protracted discussions on Community rules and minimizes the risk of a whole series of

---

[1] See Pescatore, *Droit Communautaire et droit nationale selon la jurisprudence de la Cour de Justice des Communautés Européenes*, Dalloz 1969, Chroniques, pp. 182–4.

[2] *Salgoil S. p. A.* v. *Italian Ministry of Foreign Trade* [1969] C.M.L.R. 181, 185, 193.

[3] *Bosch (Robert) G.m.b.H.* v. *Kleding-Verkoopbedrijf de Geus en Uitdenbogerd* [1962] C.M.L.R. 1; *Technique Minière* v. *Maschinenbau Ulm G.m.b.H.* [1966] C.M.L.R. 357; *De Cicco* v. *Landesversicherungsanstalt Schwaben* [1969] C.M.L.R. 67, 75.

judgments given, as it may afterwards transpire, in error.[1] If this experience were to commend itself to English courts it may be rare for the House of Lords ever to be faced with the obligation to comply with Article 177.

There are, however, two situations which might tend to counteract this effect. First, presumably, any case involving the interpretation of Community law would qualify for the leapfrogging procedure established under the Administration of Justice Act 1969. Any resort to this procedure without the trial judge perceiving the Community law issue, or with him declining to exercise his discretion of referral to the European Court, might subject the House of Lords to the obligations of Article 177. Might not the Practice Direction[2] be amended so as to preclude leapfrogging where Community law is involved unless reference has already been made to the European Court? Even this would not cover cases where the Community law issue only emerges after protracted argument in the lower courts.

Second, there is the problem of determining which is the court of last resort. Article 177 (3) makes it obligatory to refer cases of interpretation and validity of Community laws 'where such a question is raised in a case pending before a court or tribunal of a member-state, *from whose decisions there is no possibility of appeal* under internal law'. If this phrasing is interpreted to be synonymous with the general status of the court, then clearly under the laws of the countries forming the United Kingdom the House of Lords is the court from whose decisions there is no possibility of appeal. Or does Article 177 (3) refer merely to the possibility of an appeal in the instant case? There are several statutory instances where the Court of Appeal is the final court of appeal:[3] and there is the general rule that, apart from Scotland, no civil appeal lies to the House of Lords, except either with the leave of the Court of Appeal or, failing that, of the House of Lords itself. If the aspiring appellant waits until the House of Lords refuses leave to appeal, it will then be too late to determine, for the purposes of Article 177, that the Court of Appeal was in practice the court of last resort.

---

[1] An example of this is provided by *De Cicco* v. *Landesversicherungsanstalt Schwaben* [1969] C.M.L.R. 67. The Sozialgericht of Augsburg referred to the European Court the meaning to be given to 'periods of insurance' in Community Regulations dealing with the social security for migrant workers. The Sozialgericht had, in an earlier case on the same point of law, been reversed by its own appellate court, the Bayrisches Landessozialgericht. The Sozialgericht referred the later case to the European Court, explaining at length its reasons for differing from its own court of appeal. In the result the lower court was upheld by the European Court. (This European tale is reminiscent of the English judge who, when told his judgment had been upheld by the Court of Appeal, said that he still thought he had been right!)

[2] Practice Direction (House of Lords: Leapfrog Procedure) [1970] 1 W.L.R. 97.

[3] In Bankruptcy (s. 108 (2), Bankruptcy Act 1914); in County Court appeals on questions of fact (s. 114, County Courts Act 1959); in appeals from the Foreign Compensation Commission, (Foreign Compensation Act 1969, s. 3 (8)); and in certain cases where the Court of Appeal declines itself to give leave on a point of law (s. 27 (2), Supreme Court of Judicature Act 1925 in divorce and nullity suits).

The choice seems to lie between (a) regarding the House of Lords as the only court with the status of a final court of appeal, and (b) treating the Court of Appeal as the final court of appeal only when theoretically there is no possibility of appeal. Mr. Andrew Martin Q.C. has expressed the view that a 'test of a theoretical possibility of appeal would not . . . be a satisfactory device' for ensuring uniform interpretation of Community law.[1] This tenable view argues even more forcibly for references to be made, if at all, at the stage of trial or of first appeal.

The latter practice would at least remove the one sensitive area of the application of Article 177—namely, the compulsory reference which is felt by some as an undignified practice for a final court of appeal exercising the ultimate in judicial sovereignty. Although, as so far interpreted, Article 177 does not in fact tamper with such judicial sensibilities, some may still regard it in an uncharitable light. That said, when, if at all, can a court of last resort decline to refer issues to the European Court?

To answer that, it is necessary to look back and consider the cases where a court, other than one of final appeal, ought, under its discretionary power, properly to refer under Article 177. Clearly where the validity of a Community law is challenged, the sooner that issue is authoritatively disposed of the better for the laws of the member-States and for the stability of Community jurisprudence as a whole. It would be unfortunate, to say the least, if litigious disputes were frequently resolved on the basis of a Community law which was much later declared invalid by the European Court, though it could be argued that any hierarchical system based on binding higher authority carries this risk. A second instance where a decision to refer might be indicated is where there were already conflicting decisions from national courts, either within a member-State or between the national courts of member-States. The only umpire is the European Court, and its verdict should be speedily sought to resolve such conflicts. The discretion of the courts whether to refer an issue or not must otherwise remain unfettered.

The lower courts have a wide discretion, but does Article 177 mean that the final court of appeal can never decline to refer? There are strong indications that the obligation stipulated in Article 177 (3) 'implies a margin of appreciation'. This idea was expressed by Advocate-General Lagrange in his submissions to the European Court in *Da Costa en Schaake N.V.* v. *Nederlandse Administratie der Belastingen*[2] and in *Costa* v. *E.N.E.L.*[3] It has been most forcibly argued in the French courts.[4] But what is meant by the 'margin of appreciation'?

[1] *The Accession of the United Kingdom to the European Communities: Jurisdictional Problems*, vol. 6, Common Market Law Review (1968), p. 44.

[2] [1963] C.M.L.R. 224.

[3] [1964] C.M.L.R. 425; see also Advocate-General Roemer's submissions in *Internationale Crediet-en-Handels-Vereniging 'Rotterdam'* v. *Ministry of Agriculture and Fisheries* [1964] C.M.L.R. 198, 209.

[4] *Re Shell-Berre* [1964] C.M.L.R. 462.

Clearly if there has already been a ruling of the European Court on a question of interpretation or the validity of a Community law, there is no need to refer the identical problem again to the Court, so long as the national court is merely applying the Court's previous interpretation of Community law.[1] Again, the compulsory reference does not apply to interlocutory proceedings; but only to decisions which conclusively settle the case,[2] though in practice it might sometimes be expedient for the parties to submit a preliminary point for determination by the national courts and invite them to refer the issue to the European Court. The other possible limitation upon the requirement to refer is the judge's appreciation of his own function in applying Community law. No one would contest the national courts' right to determine the relevance of the particular Community law to the instant case: indeed such courts must always determine whether, and to what extent, a question of Community law has a bearing on the case before the court. They alone are in a position to judge whether an argument involving a provision of Community law is relevant, and whether a preliminary ruling is essential to the resolution of the case. If Community law turns out to be incidental or subsidiary to the case, then compulsory referral could only waste the time of everyone involved.

Those considerations apart, national courts of last resort, faced with a genuine issue of Community law, must fulfil the obligation to seek a preliminary ruling. To do otherwise would be to usurp the supervisory function of the European court.

Strictly, to interpret a law is to expound its meaning or to render its meaning clear or explicit. But there is a legal doctrine, *in claris non fit interpretatio*, which (turned on its head) means that a legal rule has to be interpreted only in case of doubt: a clear rule must simply be applied without questioning its source. This distinction is of no significance so long as the functions of interpreting and applying laws are performed by one institution. It is the division of judical labour that creates the problem. Can a national judge properly say that a particular Community law is clear beyond argument (even though the parties have argued about it) and that there is no requirement to interpret, and hence no call for referral under Article 177?

The distinction, between a clear law that is readily applied and the unclear law which calls for judicial interpretation before it can be applied, is unreal in practice. And even the logic of the distinction is doubtful. It takes for granted a premise which itself is dependent on the conclusion. It is manifestly tautologous to hold that a legal rule only becomes clear after the judge has mentally expounded its meaning—which is itself an interpretative act.

The relevance of the so-called doctrine of *acte clair* is that in a related field it has been employed by the English courts, which might be tempted, by

---

[1] *Internationale Crediet-en-Handels-Vereniging 'Rotterdam'* v. *Ministry of Agriculture and Fisheries* [1964] C.M.L.R. 198.
[2] In Re *'Agfa-Optima'* (*No. 2*) [1964] C.M.L.R. 87.

analogy, to employ it in propounding the nature of the obligation under Article 177. Worse still, an innocuous tool of legal dialectics might be used as a device for influencing the jurisdiction of different tribunals in favour of national autonomy in respect of Community law.[1] It would be a pity if such a practice developed.

The main authority which prompts our misgivings is a decision of the House of Lords in *Ellerman Lines Ltd.* v. *Murray*[2] which held that, if the language of a statute is clear, no reference may be made to the treaty which prompted, or upon which was based, the domestic legislation. That rule has been adopted by Lord Justice (now Lord) Diplock in *Salomon* v. *Commissioners of Customs & Excise*[3] where he stated: 'If the terms of the legislation are clear and unambiguous they must be given effect to, whether or not they carry out Her Majesty's treaty obligations. . . . But if the terms of the legislation are not clear but are reasonably capable of more than one meaning, the treaty itself becomes relevant, for there is a prima facie presumption that Parliament does not intend to act in breach of international law.' In the same case, however, Lord Denning did not appear to draw any distinction between clear and unclear provisions: 'We ought always to interpret our statutes so as to be in conformity with international law.' More recently, in *The Banco*,[4] Lord Denning reiterated his view[5] that when an Act of Parliament is passed so as to give effect to an international convention 'we can look at the convention so as to help us construe the Act . . . and this is so even though the Act of Parliament does not mention the convention'.[6] But Lord Justice Megaw, one of the *acte clair* brigade, thought that it was necessary to look at the convention only if the statutory provision was ambiguous.[7] Lord Justice Cairns thought the convention could be looked at 'to assist construction'. Neither he nor Lord Denning alluded to the ambiguity or otherwise of the statutory provision as a prerequisite to looking at the appropriate treaty.

Nothing would sooner or more devastatingly sap the spirit of mutual confidence which must govern the relationship between the European Court and the national courts than for the latter to transplant a dubious doctrine into the field of enforcement of Article 177. Whatever may be the English rule about the non-justiciability of treaties, and reliance upon their texts only when driven to them by the uncertainties of statutory interpretations, there is every reason for confining the doctrine to its present limits.

Enough has been said, we hope, to indicate the nature and size of the problem affecting the House of Lords in relation to the European Court. We have indicated some of the factors which will, in practice, shield their Lordships from the seemingly unqualified obligation to refer cases under Article

[1] *Da Costa en Schaake N.V.* v. *Nederlandse Administratie der Belastingen* [1963] C.M.L.R. 224, 234.
[2] [1931] A.C. 26.   [3] [1967] 2 Q.B. 116, 143.   [4] [1971] P. 137.   [5] Ibid., p. 151.
[6] See also *Post Office* v. *Estuary Radio Ltd.* [1968] 2 Q.B. 740, 755, 757.
[7] Ibid., p. 345.

177 (3). But even if our prognosis is wrong about references invariably being made by the lower courts, we would observe that no disaster is likely to befall the House of Lords. It will remain in every sense the final court of appeal in a British, if not in a wider European context.

There are undoubtedly some thorny demarcation disputes on the horizon—most of them by no means peculiar to the United Kingdom. But neither they nor any entrenched Anglo-Saxon attitudes towards a two-dimensional court structure should cause even a ripple on the domestic scene. Indeed, as we have been at pains to point out, Article 177 strikes a much less discordant note in the ears of English lawyers, accustomed to courts binding themselves to facts contained in Executive Certificates, than perhaps to some Continenal lawyers. This being so, we feel no compulsion to alter our general conclusions about the role of the House of Lords as a final appeal court, though undoubtedly it will have to take its place within a wider structure of European legal institutions.

APPENDICES

APPENDIX 1

TEXT OF RELEVANT STATUTES

(i) APPELLATE JURISDICTION ACT 1876

CHAPTER 59

An Act for amending the Law in respect of the Appellate Jurisdiction of the House of Lords; and for other purposes.　　　　　[11th August 1876.]

BE it enacted by the Queen's most Excellent Majesty, by and with the advice and consent of the Lords Spiritual and Temporal, and Commons, in this present Parliament assembled, and by the authority of the same, as follows:

Preliminary

1. This Act may be cited for all purposes as 'The Appellate Jurisdiction Act 1876'. — Short title.

2. This Act shall, except where it is otherwise expressly provided, come into operation on the first day of November one thousand eight hundred and seventy-six, which day is herein-after referred to as the commencement of this Act. — Commencement of Act.

Appeal

3. Subject as in this Act mentioned an appeal shall lie to the House of Lords from any order or judgment of any of the courts following; that is to say, — Cases in which appeal lies to House of Lords.

(1) Of Her Majesty's Court of Appeal in England; and
(2) Of any Court in Scotland from which error or an appeal at or immediately before the commencement of this Act lay to the House of Lords by common law or by statute; and
(3) Of any Court in Ireland from which error or an appeal at or immediately before the commencement of this Act lay to the House of Lords by common law or by statute.

4. Every appeal shall be brought by way of petition to the House of Lords, praying that the matter of the order or judgment appealed against may be reviewed before Her Majesty the Queen in her Court of Parliament, in order that the said Court may determine what of right, and according to the law and custom of this realm, ought to be done in the subject-matter of such appeal. — Form of appeal to House of Lords.

5. An appeal shall not be heard and determined by the House of Lords unless there are present at such hearing and determination not less than three of the following persons, in this Act designated Lords of Appeal; that is to say, — Attendance of certain number of Lords of Appeal required at hearing and determination of appeals.

(1) The Lord Chancellor of Great Britain for the time being; and
(2) The Lords of Appeal in Ordinary to be appointed as in this Act mentioned; and
(3) Such Peers of Parliament as are for the time being holding or have held any of the offices in this Act described as high judicial offices.

Appointment of
Lords of Appeal
in Ordinary by
Her Majesty.

6. For the purpose of aiding the House of Lords in the hearing and determination of appeals, Her Majesty may, at any time after the passing of this Act, by letters patent appoint two qualified persons to be Lords of Appeal in Ordinary, but such appointment shall not take effect until the commencement of this Act.

A person shall not be qualified to be appointed by Her Majesty a Lord of Appeal in Ordinary unless he has been at or before the time of his appointment the holder for a period of not less than two years of some one or more of the offices in this Act described as high judicial offices, or has been at or before such time as aforesaid, for not less than fifteen years, a practising barrister in England or Ireland, or a practising advocate in Scotland.

Every Lord or Appeal in Ordinary shall hold his office during good behaviour, and shall continue to hold the same notwithstanding the demise of the Crown, but he may be removed from such office on the address of both Houses of Parliament.

There shall be paid to every Lord of Appeal in Ordinary a salary of six thousand pounds a year.

Every Lord of Appeal in Ordinary, unless he is otherwise entitled to sit as a member of the House of Lords, shall by virtue and according to the date of his appointment be entitled during his life to rank as a Baron by such style as Her Majesty may be pleased to appoint, and shall during the time that he continues in his office as a Lord of Appeal in Ordinary, and no longer, be entitled to a writ of summons to attend, and to sit and vote in the House of Lords; his dignity as a Lord of Parliament shall not descend to his heirs.

On any Lord of Appeal in Ordinary vacating his office, by death, resignation, or otherwise, Her Majesty may fill up the vacancy by the appointment of another qualified person.

A Lord of Appeal in Ordinary shall, if a Privy Councillor, be a member of the Judicial Committee of the Privy Council, and, subject to the due performance by a Lord of Appeal in Ordinary of his duties as to the hearing and determining of appeals in the House of Lords, it shall be his duty, being a Privy Councillor, to sit and act as a member of the Judicial Committee of the Privy Council.

Supplemental Provisions

Pension of Lord
of Appeal in
Ordinary.

7. Her Majesty may by letters patent grant to any Lord of Appeal in Ordinary, who has served for fifteen years, or is disabled by permanent infirmity from the performance of the duties of his office, a pension by way of annuity to be continued during his life equal in amount to the pension which might under similar circumstances be granted to the Master of the Rolls, in pursuance of the Supreme Court of Judicature Act 1873.

Previous service in any office described in this Act as a high judicial office shall for the purposes of pension be deemed equivalent to service in the office of a Lord of Appeal in Ordinary under this Act.

The salary and pension payable to a Lord of Appeal in Ordinary shall be charged on and paid out of the Consolidated Fund of the United Kingdom, and shall accrue due from day to day, and shall be payable to the person entitled thereto, or to his executors and administrators, at such intervals in every year, not being longer than three months, as the Treasury may from time to time determine.

8. For preventing delay in the administration of justice, the House of Lords may sit and act for the purpose of hearing and determining appeals, and also for the purpose of Lords of Appeal in Ordinary taking their seats and the oaths, during any prorogation of Parliament, at such time and in such manner as may be appointed by order of the House of Lords made during the preceding session of Parliament; and all orders and proceedings of the said House in relation to appeals and matters connected therewith during such prorogation, shall be as valid as if Parliament had been then sitting, but no business other than the hearing and determination of appeals and the matters connected therewith, and Lords of Appeal in ordinary taking their seats and the oaths as aforesaid, shall be transacted by such House during such prorogation. *Hearing and determination of appeals during prorogation of Parliament.*

Any order of the House of Lords may for the purposes of this Act be made at any time after the passing of this Act.

9. If on the occasion of a dissolution of Parliament Her Majesty is graciously pleased to think that it would be expedient, with a view to prevent delay in the administration of justice, to provide for the hearing and determination of appeals during such dissolution, it shall be lawful for Her Majesty, by writing under her Sign Manual, to authorise the Lords of Appeal in the name of the House of Lords to hear and determine appeals during the dissolution of Parliament, and for that purpose to sit in the House of Lords at such times as may be thought expedient; and upon such authority as aforesaid being given by Her Majesty, the Lords of Appeal may, during such dissolution, hear and determine appeals and act in all matters in relation thereto in the same manner in all respects as if their sittings were a continuation of the sittings of the House of Lords, and may in the name of the House of Lords exercise the jurisdiction of the House of Lords accordingly. *Hearing and determination of appeals during dissolution of Parliament.*

10. An appeal shall not be entertained by the House of Lords without the consent of the Attorney General or other law officer of the Crown in any case where proceedings in error or on appeal could not hitherto have been had in the House of Lords without the fiat or consent of such officer. *Saving as to fiat of Attorney General.*

11. After the commencement of this Act error shall not lie to the House of Lords, and an appeal shall not lie from any of the courts from which an appeal to the House of Lords is given by this Act, except in manner provided by this Act, and subject to such conditions as to the value of the subject-matter in dispute, and as to giving security for costs, and as to the time within which the appeal shall be brought, and generally as to all matters of practice and procedure, or otherwise, as may be imposed by orders of the House of Lords. *Procedure under Act to supersede all other procedure.*

12. Except in so far as may be authorised by orders of the House of Lords an appeal shall not lie to the House of Lords from any court in Scotland or Ireland in any case, which according to the law or practice hitherto in use, could not have been reviewed by that House, either in error or on appeal. *Certain cases excluded from appeal.*

13. Nothing in this Act contained shall affect the jurisdiction of the House of Lords in respect of any error or appeal pending therein at the time of the commencement of this Act, and any such error or appeal may be heard and determined, and all proceedings in relation thereto may be conducted, in the same manner in all respects as if this Act had not passed. *Provision as to pending business.*

Amendment of Acts

14. Whereas by the Act of the session of the thirty-fourth and thirty-fifth years of the reign of Her present Majesty, chapter ninety-one, intituled 'An Act to make further provision for the despatch of business by the Judicial *Amendment of the Act of 34 & 35 Vict. c. 91, relating to the*

constitution of
the Privy Council.

Committee of the Privy Council', Her Majesty was empowered to appoint and did appoint four persons qualified as in that Act mentioned to act as members of the Judicial Committee of the Privy Council at such salaries as are in the said Act mentioned, in this Act referred to as paid Judges of the Judicial Committee of the Privy Council:

And whereas the power given by the said Act of filling any vacancies occasioned by death, or otherwise, in the offices of the persons so appointed, has lapsed by efflux of time, and Her Majesty has no power to fill any such vacancies:

Be it enacted, that whenever any two of the paid Judges of the Judicial Committee of the Privy Council have died or resigned, Her Majesty may appoint a third Lord of Appeal in Ordinary in addition to the Lords of Appeal in Ordinary herein-before authorised to be appointed, and on the death or resignation of the remaining two paid Judges of the Judicial Committee of the Privy Council Her Majesty may appoint a fourth Lord of Appeal in Ordinary in addition to the Lords of Appeal in Ordinary aforesaid; and may from time to time fill up any vacancies occurring in the offices of such third and fourth Lord of Appeal in Ordinary.

Any Lord of Appeal in Ordinary appointed in pursuance of this section shall be appointed in the same manner, hold his office by the same tenure, be entitled to the same salary and pension, and in all respects be in the same position as if he were a Lord of Appeal in Ordinary appointed in pursuance of the power in this Act before given to Her Majesty.

Her Majesty may by Order in Council, with the advice of the Judicial Committee of Her Majesty's Privy Council or any five of them, of whom the Lord Chancellor shall be one, and of the archbishops and bishops being members of Her Majesty's Privy Council, or any two of them, make rules for the attendance, on the hearing of ecclesiastical cases as assessors of the said Committee of such number of the archbishops and bishops of the Church of England as may be determined by such rules.

The rules may provide for the assessors being appointed for one or more year or years, or by rotation or otherwise, and for filling up any temporary or other vacancies in the office of assessor.

Any rule made in pursuance of this section shall be laid before each House of Parliament within forty days after it is made if Parliament be then sitting, or, if not then sitting, within forty days after the commencement of the then next session of Parliament.

If either House of Parliament present an address to Her Majesty within forty days after any such rule has been laid before such House, praying that any such rule may be annulled, Her Majesty may thereupon by Order in Council annul the same, and the rule so annulled shall thenceforth become void, but without prejudice nevertheless to the making of any other rule in its place, or to the validity of anything which may in the meantime have been done under any such rule.

Amendment of
the Supreme
Court of Judica-
ture Acts in re-
lation to Her
Majesty's Court
of Appeal.

15. Whereas it is expedient to amend the constitution of Her Majesty's Court of Appeal in manner herein-after mentioned: Be it enacted, that there shall be repealed so much of the fourth section of 'The Supreme Court of Judicature Act 1875', as provides that the ordinary Judges of Her Majesty's Court of Appeal (in this Act referred to as 'the Court of Appeal') shall not exceed three at any one time.

In addition to the number of ordinary Judges of the Court of Appeal authorised to be appointed by 'The Supreme Court of Judicature Act, 1875',

Her Majesty may appoint three additional ordinary Judges of that court.

The first three appointments of additional Judges under this Act shall be made by such transfer to the Court of Appeal as is in this section mentioned of three Judges of the High Court of Justice, and the vacancies so created in the High Court of Justice shall not be filled up, except in the event and to the extent herein-after mentioned.

Her Majesty may by writing, under her Sign Manual, either before or after the commencement of this Act, but so as not to take effect until the commencement thereof, transfer to the Court of Appeal from the following Divisions of the High Court of Justice, that is to say, the Queen's Bench Division, the Common Pleas Division, and the Exchequer Division, such of the Judges of the said Divisions, not exceeding three in number, as to Her Majesty may seem meet, each of whom shall have been a Judge of any one or more of such Divisions for not less than two years previously to his appointment, and shall not be an ex-officio Judge of the Court of Appeal, and every Judge so transferred shall be deemed an additional ordinary Judge of the Court of Appeal in the same manner as if he had been appointed such Judge by letters patent. No Judge shall be so transferred without his own consent.

Every additional ordinary Judge of the said Court of Appeal appointed in pursuance of this Act shall be subject to the provisions of sections twenty-nine and thirty-seven of 'The Supreme Court of Judicature Act 1873', and shall be under an obligation to go circuits and to act as Commissioner under commissions of assize or other commissions authorised to be issued in pursuance of the said Act, in the same manner in all respects as if he were a Judge of the High Court of Justice.

There shall be paid to every additional ordinary Judge appointed in pursuance of this Act, in addition to the salary which he would otherwise receive as an ordinary Judge of the Court of Appeal, such sum on account of his expenses on circuit or under such commission as aforesaid as may be approved by the Treasury upon the recommendation of the Lord Chancellor.

Each of the Judges of the High Court of Justice who is in pursuance of this Act transferred to the Court of Appeal, by writing under the Sign Manual of Her Majesty, shall retain such officers as are attached to his person as such Judge, and are appointed and removable by him at his pleasure, in pursuance of 'The Supreme Court of Judicature Act 1873', and the officers so attached shall have the same rank, and hold their offices by the same tenure, and upon the same terms and conditions, and receive the same salaries, and if entitled to pensions be entitled to the same pensions, and shall, as nearly as may be, perform the same duties as if the Judges to whom they are attached had not been transferred to the Court of Appeal.

Subject as aforesaid, the provisions of the Supreme Court of Judicature Acts 1873 and 1875, for the time being in force in relation to the appointment of ordinary Judges of Her Majesty's Court of Appeal, and to their tenure of office, and to their precedence, and to their salaries and pensions, and to the officers to be attached to such Judges, and all other provisions relating to such ordinary Judges, shall apply to the additional ordinary Judges appointed in pursuance of this section in the same manner as they apply to the other ordinary Judges of the said Court.

For the purpose of a transfer to the Court of Appeal under this section, service as a Judge in a court whose jurisdiction is transferred to the High Court shall be deemed to have been service as a Judge in any one or more of such Divisions of the High Court as are in this section in that behalf mentioned; and for the purpose of the pension of any person appointed under this Act an additional ordinary Judge of appeal, service in the High Court of Justice, or in any Court whose jurisdiction is transferred to the High Court of Justice or to the Court of Appeal, shall be deemed to have been service in the Court of Appeal.

Orders in relation to conduct of business in Her Majesty's Court of Appeal.

16. Orders for constituting and holding divisional courts of the Court of Appeal, and for regulating the sittings of the Court of Appeal, and of the divisional courts of appeal, may be made, and when made, in like manner rescinded or altered, by the President of the Court of Appeal, with the concurrence of the ordinary Judges of the Court of Appeal, or any three of them; and so much of section seventeen of 'The Supreme Court of Judicature Act 1875', as relates to the regulation of any matters subject to be regulated by orders under this section, and so much of any rules of court as may be inconsistent with any order made under this section, shall be repealed, without prejudice nevertheless to any rules of court made in pursuance of the section so repealed, so long as such rules of court remain unaffected by orders made in pursuance of this section.

Regulations as to business of High Court of Justice and divisional courts of High Court.

17. On and after the first day of December one thousand eight hundred and seventy-six, every action and proceeding in the High Court of Justice, and all business arising out of the same, except as is herein-after provided, shall, so far as is practicable and convenient, be heard, determined, and disposed of before a single Judge, and all proceedings in an action subsequent to the hearing or trial, and down to and including the final judgment or order, except as aforesaid, and always excepting any proceedings on appeal in the Court of Appeal, shall, so far as is practicable and convenient, be had and taken before the Judge before whom the trial or hearing of the cause took place: Provided nevertheless, that divisional courts of the High Court of Justice may be held for the transaction of any business which may for the time being be ordered by rules of court to be heard by a divisional court; and any such divisional court when held shall be constituted of two Judges of the court and no more, unless the President of the Division to which such divisional court belongs, with the concurrence of the other Judges of such Division, or a majority thereof, is of opinion that such divisional court should be constituted of a greater number of Judges than two, in which case such court may be constituted of such number of Judges as the President, with such concurrence as aforesaid, may think expedient; nevertheless the decisions of a divisional court shall not be invalidated by reason of such court being constituted of a greater number than two Judges; and

Rules of court for carrying into effect the enactments contained in this section shall be made on or before the first day of December one thousand eight hundred and seventy-six, and may be afterwards altered, and all rules of court to be made after the passing of this Act, whether made under 'The Supreme Court of Judicature Act 1875', or this Act, shall be made by any three or more of the following persons of whom the Lord Chancellor shall be one, namely, the Lord Chancellor, the Lord Chief Justice of England, the Master of the Rolls, the Lord Chief Justice of the Common Pleas, the Lord Chief Baron of the Exchequer, and four other Judges of the Supreme Court of Judicature, to be from time to time appointed for the purpose by the Lord Chancellor in writing under his hand, such appointment to continue for such time as shall be specified therein, and all such rules of court shall be laid before each House of Parliament within such time and subject to be annulled in such manner as is provided by 'The Supreme Court of Judicature Act 1875'.

There shall be repealed on and after the first day of December one thousand eight hundred and seventy-six so much of sections forty, forty-one, forty-two, forty-three, forty-four, and forty-six of 'The Supreme Court of Judicature Act 1873', as is inconsistent with the provisions of this section.

18. Whenever any two of the said paid Judges of the Judicial Committee of the Privy Council have died or resigned, Her Majesty may, upon an address from both Houses of Parliament, representing that the state of business in the High Court of Justice is such as to require the appointment of an additional Judge, fill up one of the vacancies created by the transfer herein-before authorised, by appointing one new Judge of the said High Court in any Division thereof; and on the death or retirement of the remaining two paid Judges of the said Judicial Committee, Her Majesty may, upon the like address, fill up in like manner another of the said vacancies, and from time to time fill up any vacancies occurring in the offices of Judges so appointed.

Power in certain events to fill vacancies occasioned in High Court of Justice by removal of Judges to Court of Appeal.

19. Where a Judge of the High Court of Justice has been requested to attend as an additional Judge at the sittings of the Court of Appeal under section four of 'The Supreme Court of Judicature Act 1873', such Judge shall, although the period has expired during which his attendance was requested, attend the sittings of the Court of Appeal for the purpose of giving judgment or otherwise in relation to any case which may have been heard by the Court of Appeal during his attendance on the Court of Appeal.

Attendance of Judges of High Court of Justice on Court of Appeal.

20. Where by Act of Parliament it is provided that the decision of any Court or Judge the jurisdiction of which Court or Judge is transferred to the High Court of Justice is to be final, an appeal shall not lie in any such case from the decision of the High Court of Justice, or of any Judge thereof, to Her Majesty's Court of Appeal.

1892 P. 152 Amendment of Judicature Acts as to appeals from High Court of Justice in certain cases.

21. Whereas by section thirty-four of 'The Supreme Court of Judicature Act 1875', it is enacted that upon the occurrence of any vacancy in an office coming within the provisions of section seventy-seven of 'The Supreme Court of Judicature Act 1873', the Lord High Chancellor of Great Britain may, with the concurrence of the Treasury, suspend the making of any appointment to such office for any period not later than the first day of January one thousand eight hundred and seventy-seven, and may, if it be necessary, make provision in such manner as he thinks fit for the temporary discharge in the meantime of the duties of such office, and it is expedient to extend the said period as hereinafter mentioned: Be it therefore enacted as follows:

The said section shall be construed as if the first day of January one thousand eight hundred and seventy-eight were therein inserted in lieu of the first day of January one thousand eight hundred and seventy-seven.

Continuation until 1st January 1878 of s. 34 of 38 & 39 Vict. c. 77. as to vacancies in legal offices.

22. A district registrar of the Supreme Court of Judicature may from time to time, but in each case with the approval of the Lord Chancellor and subject to such regulations as the Lord Chancellor may from time to time make, appoint a deputy, and all acts authorised or required to be done by, to, or before a district registrar may be done by, to, or before any deputy so appointed: Provided always, that in no case such appointment shall be made for a period exceeding three months. This section shall come into force at the time of the passing of this Act.

Appointment of deputy by district registrars.

23. Whereas by 'The Vice-Admiralty Courts Act 1863', it is enacted, that 'nothing in this Act contained shall be taken to affect the power of the Admiralty to appoint any vice-admiral, or any judge, registrar, marshal, or other officer of any Vice-Admiralty Court, as heretofore, by warrant from the

Appointment of vice-admiral, judge, and officers of Vice-Admiralty Court.

Admiralty, and by letters patent issued under the seal of the High Court of Admiralty of England':

And whereas since the commencement of the Supreme Court of Judicature Acts 1873 and 1875, doubts have arisen with respect to the exercise of the said power of the Admiralty, and it is expedient to remove such doubts: Be it therefore enacted as follows:

Any power of the Admiralty to appoint or cancel the appointment of a vice-admiral, or a judge, registrar, marshal, or other officer of a Vice-Admiralty Court, may, after the passing of this Act, be exercised by some writing under the hands of the Admiralty, and the seal of the office of Admiralty, and in such form as the Admiralty from time to time direct.

Every appointment so made shall have the same effect, and every vice-admiral, judge, registrar, marshal, and other officer so appointed shall have the same jurisdiction, power, and authority, and be subject to the same jurisdiction, power, and authority, and be subject to the same obligation, as if he had been appointed before the commencement of the Supreme Court of Judicature Acts 1873 and 1875, under the seal of the High Court of Admiralty of England.

'Admiralty' in this section means the Lord High Admiral, or the Commissioners for executing his office, or any two of such Commissioners.

Repeal and Definitions

Repeal of certain sections of the Church Discipline Act and of the Supreme Court of Judicature Acts.

24. Section sixteen of the Act for better enforcing Church Discipline, passed in the session of the third and fourth years of the reign of Her present Majesty, chapter eighty-six, and sections twenty, twenty-one, and fifty-five of the Supreme Court of Judicature Act 1873, and section two of the Supreme Court of Judicature Act 1875, shall be repealed (with the exception of so much of section two as declares the day on which that Act is to commence).

Definitions:

25. In this Act, if not inconsistent with the context, the following expressions have the meaning herein-after respectively assigned to them; that is to say,

'high judicial office:'

'High judicial office' means any of the following offices; that is to say,
The office of Lord Chancellor of Great Britain or Ireland, or of paid Judge of the Judicial Committee of the Privy Council, or of Judge of one of Her Majesty's superior courts of Great Britain and Ireland:

'superior courts:'

'Superior courts of Great Britain and Ireland' means and includes,—
As to England, Her Majesty's High Court of Justice and Her Majesty's Court of Appeal, and the superior courts of law and equity in England as they existed before the constitution of Her Majesty's High Court of Justice; and
As to Ireland, the superior courts of law and equity at Dublin; and
As to Scotland, the Court of Session:

'error.'

'Error' includes a writ of error or any proceedings in or by way of error.

(ii) THE APPEAL (FORMÂ PAUPERIS) ACT 1893, s. 1
(AMENDS 1876 ACT)

1. Power to refuse appeal in formâ pauperis—wherein an appeal to the House of Lords a petition is presented for leave to sue in formâ pauperis, and the House on Report of its Appeal Committee determines that there is no prima facie case for the appeal the House may refuse the prayer of the petition.

(iii) CRIMINAL APPEAL ACT 1907, s. 1 (6)

If in any case the Director of Public Prosecutions or the prosecutor or defendant obtains the certificate of the Attorney General that the decision of the Court of Criminal Appeal involves a point of law of exceptional public importance, and that it is desirable in the public interest that a further appeal should be brought, he may appeal from that decision to the House of Lords, but subject thereto the determination by the Court of Criminal Appeal of any appeal or other matter which it has power to determine shall be final, and no appeal shall lie from that court to any other court.

(iv) ADMINISTRATION OF JUSTICE (APPEALS) ACT 1934, s. 1

The provisions of the Act in so far as it concerns appeals to the House of Lords are as follows:—

1. (1) No appeal shall lie to the House of Lords from any order or judgment made or given by the Court of Appeal after the first day of October 1934, except with the leave of that Court or of the House of Lords.

(2) The House of Lords may by order provide for the hearing or determination by a committee of that House of petitions for leave to appeal from the Court of Appeal: provided that section 5 of the Appellate Jurisdiction Act 1876[1] shall apply to the hearing and determination of any such petition by a committee of the House as it applies to the hearing and determination of an appeal by the House.

(3) Nothing in this section shall affect any restriction existing, apart from this section, or the bringing of appeals from the Court of Appeal to the House of Lords.

(v) ADMINISTRATION OF JUSTICE ACT 1960, ss. 1 and 2

An Act to make further provision for appeals to the House of Lords in criminal cases; to amend the law relating to contempt of court, habeas corpus and certiorari; and for purposes connected with the matters aforesaid.

[27th October 1960]

BE it enacted by the Queen's most Excellent Majesty, by and with the advice and consent of the Lords Spiritual and Temporal, and Commons, in this present Parliament assembled, and by the authority of the same, as follows:—

Appeal to House of Lords in Criminal Cases

1. (1) Subject to the provisions of this section, an appeal shall lie to the Right of appeal. House of Lords, at the instance of the defendant or the prosecutor,—

(a) from any decision of a Divisional Court of the Queen's Bench Division in a criminal cause or matter;

(b) from any decision of the Court of Criminal Appeal on an appeal to that court.

(2) No appeal shall lie under this section except with the leave of the court below or of the House of Lords; and such leave shall not be granted unless it is certified by the court below that a point of law of general public importance is involved in the decision and it appears to that court or to the House of Lords,

---

[1] Section 5 of the Act of 1876 specifies the quorum of Law Lords necessary for the hearing of appeals.

as the case may be, that the point is one which ought to be considered by that House.

(3) Section five of the Appellate Jurisdiction Act 1876 (which regulates the composition of the House of Lords for the hearing and determination of appeals) shall apply to the hearing and determination of an appeal or application for leave to appeal under this section as it applies to the hearing and determination of an appeal under that Act; and any order of that House which provides for the hearing of such applications by a committee constituted in accordance with the said section five may direct that the decision of that committee shall be taken on behalf of the House.

(4) For the purpose of disposing of an appeal under this section the House of Lords may exercise any powers of the court below or may remit the case to that court.

(5) In this Act, unless the context otherwise requires, 'leave to appeal' means leave to appeal to the House of Lords under this section.

Application for leave to appeal.

2.—(1) Subject to the provisions of this section, an application to the court below for leave to appeal shall be made within the period of fourteen days beginning with the date of the decision of that court; and an application to the House of Lords for such leave shall be made within the period of fourteen days beginning with the date on which the application is refused by the court below.

(vi) ADMINISTRATION OF JUSTICE ACT 1969
PART II
APPEAL FROM HIGH COURT TO HOUSE OF LORDS

Grant of certificate by trial judge.

12. (1) Where on the application of any of the parties to any proceedings to which this section applies the judge is satisfied—

(a) that the relevant conditions are fulfilled in relation to his decision in those proceedings, and

(b) that a sufficient case for an appeal to the House of Lords under this Part of this Act has been made out to justify an application for leave to bring such an appeal, and

(c) that all the parties to the proceedings consent to the grant of a certificate under this section,

the judge, subject to the following provisions of this Part of this Act, may grant a certificate to that effect.

(2) This section applies to any civil proceedings in the High Court which are either—

(a) proceedings before a single judge of the High Court (including a person acting as such a judge under section 3 of the Judicature Act 1925), or

(b) proceedings before a commissioner acting under a commission issued under section 70 of the Judicature Act 1925, or

(c) proceedings before a Divisional Court.

(3) Subject to any Order in Council made under the following provisions of this section, for the purposes of this section the relevant conditions, in relation to a decision of the judge in any proceedings, are that a point of law of general public importance is involved in that decision and that that point of law either—

(a) relates wholly or mainly to the construction of an enactment or of a statutory instrument, and has been fully argued in the proceedings and

fully considered in the judgment of the judge in the proceedings, or
(b) is one in respect of which the judge is bound by a decision of the Court
of Appeal or of the House of Lords in previous proceedings, and was
fully considered in the judgments given by the Court of Appeal or the
House of Lords (as the case may be) in those previous proceedings.

(4) Any application for a certificate under this section shall be made to the
judge immediately after he gives judgment in the proceedings:

Provided that the judge may in any particular case entertain any such
application made at any later time before the end of the period of fourteen
days beginning with the date on which that judgment is given or such other
period as may be prescribed by rules of court.

(5) No appeal shall lie against the grant or refusal of a certificate under this
section.

(6) Her Majesty may by Order in Council amend subsection (3) of this
section by altering, deleting, or substituting one or more new paragraphs for,
either or both of paragraphs (a) and (b) of that subsection, or by adding one
or more further paragraphs.

(7) Any Order in Council made under this section shall be subject to annulment in pursuance of a resolution of either House of Parliament.

(8) In this Part of this Act 'civil proceedings' means any proceedings other
than proceedings in a criminal cause or matter, and 'the judge', in relation to
any proceedings to which this section applies, means the judge or commissioner referred to in paragraph (a) or paragraph (b) of subsection (2) of this
section, or the Divisional Court referred to in paragraph (c) of that subsection,
as the case may be.

13. (1) Where in any proceedings the judge grants a certificate under Leave to appeal
section 12 of this Act, then, at any time within one month from the date on to House of
which that certificate is granted or such extended time as in any particular case Lords.
the House of Lords may allow, any of the parties to the proceedings may make
an application to the House of Lords under this section.

(2) Subject to the following provisions of this section, if on such an
application it appears to the House of Lords to be expedient to do so, the
House may grant leave for an appeal to be brought directly to the House; and
where leave is granted under this section—
(a) no appeal from the decision of the judge to which the certificate relates
shall lie to the Court of Appeal, but
(b) an appeal shall lie from that decision to the House of Lords.

(3) Applications under this section shall be determined without a hearing.

(4) Any order of the House of Lords which provides for applications under
this section to be determined by a committee of the House—
(a) shall direct that the committee shall consist of or include not less than
three of the persons designated as Lords of Appeal in accordance with
section 5 of the Appellate Jurisdiction Act 1876, and   1876 c. 59.
(b) may direct that the decision of the committee on any such application
shall be taken on behalf of the House.

(5) Without prejudice to subsection (2) of this section, no appeal shall lie to
the Court of Appeal from a decision of the judge in respect of which a certificate is granted under section 12 of this Act until—
(a) the time within which an application can be made under this section has
expired, and

(*b*) where such an application is made, that application has been deter-mined in accordance with the preceding provisions of this section.

Appeal where leave granted.

1876 c. 59.

14. In relation to any appeal which lies to the House of Lords by virtue of subsection (2) of section 13 of this Act—

(*a*) section 4 of the Appellate Jurisdiction Act 1876 (which provides for the bringing of appeals to the House of Lords by way of petition),

(*b*) section 5 of that Act (which regulates the composition of the House for the hearing and determination of appeals), and

(*c*) except in so far as those orders otherwise provide, any orders of the House of Lords made with respect to the matters specified in section 11 of that Act (which relates to the procedure on appeals),

shall have effect as they have effect in relation to appeals under that Act.

Cases excluded from s. 12.

1965 c. 72.

15. (1) No certificate shall be granted under section 12 of this Act in respect of a decision of the judge in any proceedings where by virtue of any enact-ment, apart from the provisions of this Part of this Act, no appeal would lie from that decision to the Court of Appeal, with or without the leave of the judge or of the Court of Appeal.

(2) No certificate shall be granted under section 12 of this Act in respect of a decision of the judge where—

(*a*) the decision is in proceedings other than proceedings under the Matri-monial Causes Act 1965, and

(*b*) by virtue of any enactment, apart from the provisions of this Part of this Act, no appeal would (with or without the leave of the Court of Appeal or of the House of Lords) lie from any decision of the Court of Appeal on an appeal from the decision of the judge.

(3) Where by virtue of any enactment, apart from the provisions of this Part of this Act, no appeal would lie to the Court of Appeal from the decision of the judge except with the leave of the judge or of the Court of Appeal, no certificate shall be granted under section 12 of this Act in respect of that de-cision unless it appears to the judge that apart from the provisions of this Part of this Act it would be a proper case for granting such leave.

(4) No certificate shall be granted under section 12 of this Act where the decision of the judge, or any order made by him in pursuance of that decision, is made in the exercise of jurisdiction to punish for contempt of court.

Application of Part II to Northern Ireland.

1962 c. 30.
1877 c. 57.

1965 c. 72.

1939 c. 13 (N.I.).

16. (1) In the application of this Part of this Act to Northern Ireland—

'the Court of Appeal' means Her Majesty's Court of Appeal in Northern Ireland;

'the High Court' means the High Court of Justice in Northern Ireland;

'statutory instrument' includes an instrument made under an enactment of the Parliament of Northern Ireland;

for the references in section 12 (2) to sections 3 and 70 of the Judicature Act 1925 there shall be substituted respectively references to section 5 (1) of the Northern Ireland Act 1962 and to sections 29 and 41 of the Supreme Court of Judicature Act (Ireland) 1877; and

for the reference in section 15 (2) (*a*) to the Matrimonial Causes Act 1965 there shall be substituted a reference to the Matrimonial Causes Act (Northern Ireland) 1939 or any enactment re-enacting that Act (whether with or without modifications).

(2) Nothing in this Part of this Act shall affect the operation of—

(*a*) any enactment of the Parliament of Northern Ireland having effect after the commencement of this Act by virtue of section 1 (8) or section 2 (3) of the Northern Ireland Act 1962, or

(*b*) paragraph 6 (2) of Schedule 1 to the Irish Free State (consequential 1922 c. 2. Provisions) Act 1922 (Session 2) (appeals to the Court of Appeal in Northern Ireland where validity of Acts of the Northern Ireland Parliament is involved and an appeal would not otherwise lie).

APPENDIX 2(*a*)

COMPLETE LIST OF HOUSE OF LORDS APPEALS, 1952–1968

Abbreviations:

C.A.	Court of Appeal
C.C.A.	Court of Criminal Appeal
C.S.	Court of Session
(N.I.)	Northern Ireland
In f.p.	*in formâ pauperis*
A.	Appeal Allowed
A.i.p.	Appeal Allowed in Part
D.	Appeal Dismissed

Majority decisions shown thus—(4:1) or (3:2).
The figure '½' denotes part-dissents.

* denotes Scottish appeal
† denotes Northern Irish appeal

For titles of cases we have adhered to the names used in the 'blue-lists' of cases for hearing published every term by the Judicial Office of the House of Lords, the only exception being wardship and custody cases (etc.) where we use initial letters to denote the infant parties.

The catch-phrases used in the subject-matter column are also adapted from the blue-lists.

The phrase 'minority decision' denotes that on a counting of judicial heads the final decision was arrived at by an overall minority of judicial opinion.

All English civil appeals in which the entry 'leave of the Appeal Committee' does not appear were by leave of the Court of Appeal.

CIVIL APPEALS

Judgments delivered in 1952

NAME OF CASE	REPORTED	SUBJECT-MATTER	OUTCOME	REMARKS
Alford *v.* N.C.B.	1952 S.C. (H.L.) 17	Negligence—Master and Servant—Injury to fellow servant—Ambit of master's liability—Unqualified miner arrogating to himself duties of shot firer in contravention of statutory regulations.	A.i.p.	
Barron *v.* Littman	[1953] A.C. 96	Income Tax—Charge in respect of Excess Rents under s. 15 of Finance Act 1940—Relief in respect of losses under Finance Act 1927.	D.	Reversed in C.A.
Best *v.* Samuel Fox	[1952] A.C. 716	Negligence—Personal injuries—Injury to husband resulting in impotence—Claim by wife for interference with consortium.	D.	In f.p.

NAME OF CASE	REPORTED	SUBJECT-MATTER	OUTCOME	REMARKS
C.I.R. v. Reynolds & Gibson	[1952] 1 All E.R. 888	Income Tax—Computation of trade profits of cotton brokers—trade debts taken over from predecessors—Whether capital or income profit.	D.	Reversed in C.A.
*Dundee Hospitals v. Bell's Trustees	1952 S.C. (H.L.) 78	Trust—Discretionary powers of trustees—Right of Court to interfere with bona fide exercise of discretion—Trustees disclosing grounds on which discretion exercised.	D.	Reversed in C.S.
Edwards v. Railway Executive	[1952] A.C. 737	Child trespasser on railway—Occupier's Liability.	D.	Reversed in C.A. In f.p.
General Cleaning Contractors v. Christmas	[1953] A.C. 180	Negligence—Safe system of work—Window-cleaning—Defective window—Injury to window-cleaner—Lack of precautions—Employers' liability.	D.	Leave of Appeal Committee
Gdynia Ameryka Linie v. Boguslawski	[1953] A.C. 11	International Law—Retroactive effect of recognition of new Polish Government.	D.	
*Hay v. Murdoch	1952 S.C. (H.L.) 29	Charity—Charitable Trust—Lapse—Public Bequest—Whether bequest failed—Estate left by testatrix for home for aged and infirm Shetland seamen, a surgical hospital or a convalescent hospital.	A.	Reversed in C.S.
*C.I.R. v. Albion Rovers	[1952] T.R. 327	Revenue—Income Tax—Football Club—Players' wages—Alteration of contract period—Wages for off-season charged as expenses.	A.	Reversed in C.S.
C.I.R. v. Gordon	[1952] A.C. 552	Revenue—Income Tax—Overdrafts in the United Kingdom extinguished by transfer to and payments in Ceylon.	D.	Reversed in C.S.
*Jamieson v. Jamieson	[1952] A.C. 525	Husband and wife—Divorce—Divorce for Cruelty—'Cruelty'—No physical violence—Use of contraceptives—Mental Cruelty—Divorce (Scotland) Act 1938, s. 1 (1).	A.	2:1 in C.S. In f.p.
King v. King	[1953] A.C. 124	Husband and wife—Husband's petition—Cruelty—Nagging—Matters to be taken into consideration.	D. (3:2)	Reversed in C.A. (2:1). Leave of Appeal Committee
John Lewis Ltd. v. Tims	[1952] A.C. 676	False imprisonment—Arrest without warrant—Duty of person arresting to inform person arrested of reason for arrest—Duty of person arresting to take person arrested forthwith to a justice or police officer with power to grant bail.	A.	Reversed in part in C.A. Leave of Appeal Committee

NAME OF CASE	REPORTED	SUBJECT-MATTER	OUTCOME	REMARKS
Lilley v. Harrison	(1952) 33 T.C. 344	Income Tax—Mortgage interest in arrear—Cancellation of mortgage bonds—Sum equal to arrears of interest paid thereafter.	D.	Reversed in C.A.
*Martin v. Scottish T.G.W.U.	1952 S.C. (H.L.) 1	Trade Union—Membership—Rules—Termination of Membership—Contract.	D.	Reversed in C.S. In f.p.
Royal College of Surgeons v. National Provincial Bank	[1952] A.C. 631	Charity—Will—Construction—Gift to hospital for Department of Medical School—Effect of nationalization—If hospital 'nationalized' then to Royal College of Surgeons of England.	A. (4:½)	Reversed in C.A.
*Parvin v. Morton Machine Co.	[1952] A.C. 515	Negligence—Master and Servant—Breach of statutory duty—Fencing dangerous machinery—Machine built in factory for sale and not forming part of factory equipment.	D.	
*Quigley v. Mathieson Gee (Ayrshire) Ltd.	1952 S.C. (H.L.) 38	Contract—Construction—*Consensus ad idem.*	A.	Reversed in part in C.S. (3:1)
C.I.R. v. Dowdall, O'Mahoney Ltd.	[1952] A.C. 401	Excess Profits Tax—Computation of profits of trade—Deduction of taxes imposed by legislature in Eire.	A.	Reversed in C.A.
Earl Fitzwilliam's Wentworth Estates v. Min. of H. & L.G.	[1952] A.C. 362	Compulsory Purchase—Building land —Compulsory purchase by Central Land Board—Power of Board to acquire land for disposal for permitted development.	D.	(2:1) in C.A.
Kemsley v. Foot	[1952] A.C. 345	Libel—Fair Comment—Article criticizing conduct of newspaper—Need for facts on which comment made to be stated in alleged libel.	D.	Reversed in C.A. Leave of Appeal Committee
U.S.A. v. Dollfus Mieg et cie. S.A.	[1952] A.C. 582	International Law—French subject's bar gold looted by Germans—Recovery by Allies—Deposit at Bank of England for safe custody.	A.i.p.	

Judgments delivered in 1953

NAME OF CASE	REPORTED	SUBJECT-MATTER	OUTCOME	REMARKS
Coutts & Co. v. C.I.R. (In re Brassey's Deed of Appointment)	[1953] A.C. 267	Revenue—Estate Duty—Property deemed to pass—Settlement—Policies Settlor's life purchased by settlement trustees—Payment of premiums out of trust income.	A.	
D'Avigdor-Goldsmid v. C.I.R.	[1953] A.C. 347	Revenue — Estate Duty — Property passing on death—Policy of life assurance—Claim for estate duty on value of policy—Whether an interest provided by deceased—Whether any beneficial interest arose on death of deceased.	A.	Reversed in C.A.

NAME OF CASE	REPORTED	SUBJECT-MATTER	OUTCOME	REMARKS
Fenwick v. C.I.R.	[1953] 1 W.L.R. 1039	Revenue—Special contribution—Relief—Income attributable to a period of years—More than one year's income in year of charge.	D.	Reversed in C.A.
Bray v. Colenbrander	[1953] A.C. 503	Revenue—Income Tax—Employment —Increment made abroad—Employment exercised in United Kingdom— Remuneration payable abroad.	D.	
*C.I.R. v Glasgow Police Athletic Association	[1953] A.C. 380	Revenue—Income Tax—Charity— Police Athletic Association—Profits of Annual Sports Meeting—'Established for Charitable Purposes only'.	A. (4:1)	
C.I.R. v. City of London (as Epping Forest Conservators)	[1953] 1 W.L.R. 652	Revenue—Income Tax—Statutory Duty—Payment of annual sums to charity to meet expenses—'Annual Payments'.	D.	Reversed in C.A.
Dale v. C.I.R.	[1954] A.C. 11	Revenue—Special contribution—Investment income—Annuity payable to trustee included in assessment—'Annual payment'—'Earned income'— Whether trusteeship an office of profit.	A.	Reversed in C.A.
Union Corporation v. C.I.R.	[1953] A.C. 482	Revenue — Profits Tax — Residence —Companies resident both in United Kingdom and abroad—Whether 'ordinarily resident outside the United Kingdom'—Test of dual residence— Control and Management.	D.	
Latimer v. A.E.C.	[1953] A.C. 643	Factory—Master and Servant—Floor —Flooding of factory floors by exceptional rainfall—Gangway slippery with mixture of water and escaped oil.	D.	Reversed in C.A. Leave of Appeal Committee
L.C.C. v Marks & Spencer Ltd.	[1953] A.C. 535	Town and Country Planning—Development begun before appointed day—Permission to erect buildings granted in 1938—Permission conditional on completion of work within 18 months—No reason given for condition—Validity of condition.	D.	Reversed in C.A. (2:1)
Preston and Area Rent Tribunal v. Pickavance	[1953] A.C. 562	Landlord and Tenant—Rent Tribunal —Security of tenure—Notice to quit given by landlord more than three months after decision of tribunal.	A.	(2:1) in C.A.
*Road Haulage Executive v. Elrick	[1953] A.C. 337	Transport — Nationalization — Road Haulage — Compensation — Transport undertaking—One-man business —Compulsory acquisition—Calculation of annual profits.	D.	
*Shiels v. Cruikshank	[1953] 1 W.L.R. 533	Reparation—Damages—Measure of Damages—Claim by widow for loss of support by husband.	D.	(3:1) in C.S.

NAME OF CASE	REPORTED	SUBJECT-MATTER	OUTCOME	REMARKS
Stapley v. Gypsum Mines	[1953] A.C. 663	Negligence—Causation—Breach of statutory duty—Contributory negligence—Metalliferous mine—Order by foreman to two miners to fetch down insecure roof.	A.i.p. (3:2)	Reversed in part in C.A.
Starkowski v. A.G.	[1954] A.C. 155	International law—Marriage—Validity—Retroactive foreign law—Religious ceremony invalid by Austrian law—Retroactive Austrian law validating marriage on registration.	D.	Leave of Appeal Committee In f.p.
Thomas v. Marshall	[1953] A.C. 543	Revenue—Income Tax—Infant's savings bank account—Gift by father—'Settlement'—Interest as income of settlor.	D.	

Judgments delivered in 1954

NAME OF CASE	REPORTED	SUBJECT-MATTER	OUTCOME	REMARKS
*Anderson v. Lambie	[1954] 1 W.L.R. 303	Contract—Sale of Heritage—Reduction—Error in Expression.	A.	Reversed in C.S.
Bank voor Handel v. Administrator of Hungarian Property	[1954] A.C. 584	Exemption from tax—Crown servants —Custodian of Enemy Property.	A. (3:2)	Reversed in C.A. (Minority decision)
*C.I.R. v. Wilsons (Dunblane)	[1954] 1 W.L.R. 282	Revenue—Income Tax—Profits—Deductions—Plant—Wear and Tear Allowance—Conversion of partnership to limited company.	D.	Reversed in C.S.
*Sneddon v. Lord Advocate	[1954] A.C. 257	Revenue—Estate Duty—Trust Funds —*Inter Vivos* Trust—Whether subject of gift consisted of capital transferred to Trustees or of sum of interests conferred upon beneficiaries.	A. (4:1)	(3:1) in C.S.
Arab Bank v. Barclays Bank	[1954] A.C. 495	Banking—War—Effect on credit balance—Payment to custodian of 'absentee' property—Rights of customer to recover from bank.	D.	
Briess v. Woolley	[1954] A.C. 333	Company—Sale of shares—Fraud of Director during negotiations—Sale authorized by members—Whether innocent shareholders liable vicariously to purchaser of shares.	A.	Reversed in C.A. Leave of Appeal Committee
Epsom Grand Stand Association v. Knight	Unreported (*The Times*, 12 March 1954)	Charges to Bookmakers.	A.	Leave of Appeal Committee

NAME OF CASE	REPORTED	SUBJECT-MATTER	OUTCOME	REMARKS
Hovis Ltd. *v.* Spillers Ltd.	(1954) 71 R.P.C. 234	Trade Mark—Application for Registration in respect of flour—Opposition—'Vivos' and 'Hovis'—Whether use of a miller's mark upon loaves of bread is covered by registration for flour—Relevance of likelihood of deception or confusion when so used.	D.	Leave of Appeal Committee
Chapman *v.* Chapman	[1954] A.C. 429	Trust—Scheme to avoid tax—Jurisdiction of Court to sanction.	D.	(2:1) in C.A.
*C.I.R. *v.* Barr	[1954] 1 W.L.R. 792	Revenue—Income Tax—Sale of Assets—Permanent discontinuance of business—Balancing charge.	A.	
Marshall *v.* Gotham Co. Ltd.	[1954] A.C. 360	Mines and Minerals—Gypsum mine —Fall of marl from roof—Caused by slickenside—duty of mine owners 'to make secure the roof and sides of every . . . working place so far as shall be reasonably practicable'.	D.	Reversed in C.A. In f.p.
*McGrath *v.* N.C.B.	Unreported	Negligence—Facts proved by injured workman relevant to infer negligence for which his employers are responsible—Extent of *onus* of rebutting primâ facie inference of fault—Failure of employers by evidence sufficient in law to discharge that onus.	D.	(2:1) in C.S.
Morgan *v.* Tate & Lyle Ltd.	[1955] A.C. 21	Income Tax—Profits of Trade within Case I of Sch. 'D'—Deduction in computing profits—Expenditure upon anti-nationalization campaign.	D. (3:2)	(2:1) in C.A.
N.C.B. *v.* England	[1954] A.C. 403	Coal Mining—Shot-firing—Breach of statutory duty and negligence of shot-firer—Plaintiff himself in breach of safety regulations—Liability of mine owner.	A.i.p. (3:2 × ½)	Reversed in C.A.
Shephard *v.* Cartwright	[1955] A.C. 431	Advancement—Qualified and conditional gifts—Shares registered by father in names of his children—Children not informed of transaction—Shares sold and proceeds of sale dealt with under mandates signed by children.	A.	Leave of Appeal Committee
Parke Davis *v.* Comptroller-General of Patents	[1954] A.C. 321	Patents—Application for compulsory licence within three years of grant—International Convention—Jurisdiction of Comptroller—Writ of *prohibition*.	D.	Leave of Appeal Committee
George Wimpey & Co. Ltd. *v.* B.O.A.C.	[1955] A.C. 169	Negligence—Joint tort-feasors—Contribution—Action against one tort-feasor barred—Whether that tort-feasor 'is, or would if sued have been, liable'.	D. (3:2)	(2:1) in C.A.

NAME OF CASE	REPORTED	SUBJECT-MATTER	OUTCOME	REMARKS
Yorkshire Copper Works Ltd. *v.* Registrar of Trade Marks	[1954] 1 W.L.R. 554	Trade Mark—Registration—Geographical Name—'Adapted to distinguish'.	D.	
		Judgments delivered in 1955		
Benmax *v.* Austin Motor Co.	[1955] A.C. 370	Patent—Action for Infringement—Validity—Obviousness—Patent held infringed.	D.	Reversed in C.A. Leave of Appeals Committee
Government of India *v.* Taylor	[1955] A.C. 491	Proof in liquidation—Debt for tax due to another State—Penal Law.	D.	
C.I.R. *v.* Baddeley	[1955] A.C. 572	Conveyances—Whether to Trustees of a trust established for charitable purposes only.	A. (4:1)	Reversed in C.A.
Corporation of London *v.* Cusack-Smith	[1955] A.C. 337	Town and Country Planning—Purchase Notice—'Owners' of Land—Person entitled to receive Rack Rent—Confirmation of Purchase Notice.	A. (3:2)	Reversed in C.A.
Sterling Engineering *v.* Patchett	[1955] A.C. 534	Employee's claim in action for royalties or remuneration—Employer's claim to patents—*Res Judicata*—Apportionment.	A.	Reversed in C.A. Leave of Appeals Committee
Richard Thomas & Baldwins Ltd. *v.* Cummings	[1955] A.C. 321	Factory — Dangerous Machinery — Transmission Machinery—Dangerous parts of machine—Duty to fence when 'in motion or in use'—Machine being adjusted and without electrical motive power.	A.	(2:1) in C.A.
The Stonedale (No. 1)	[1956] A.C. 1	Limitation of Liability—Wreckraising expenses—Expenses incurred by Canal Company.	D.	
A.-G. *v.* Parsons	[1956] A.C. 421	Mortmain — Lease — Forfeiture to Crown—Burdensome Covenants—Liability of Crown as Lessee—Inquisition—Whether necessary before entering on forfeiture—Landlord and tenant—Covenant—Covenants by landlord—Whether liable before entry.	A (4:1)	Minority decision
Bambridge *v.* C.I.R.	[1955] 1 W.L.R. 1329	Revenue—Income Tax—Transfer of assets to company incorporated abroad—Death of transferors—Settlement of shares in company—Liability of beneficiary to tax—'Associated operation'.	D.	Reversed in C.A.
B.T.C. *v.* Gourley	[1956] A.C. 185	Personal Injuries—Negligence—Assessment of Damages—Loss of professional earnings—Income Tax and Surtax—Whether to be considered in assessing damages.	A. (6:1)	7 Law Lords sat

NAME OF CASE	REPORTED	SUBJECT-MATTER	OUTCOME	REMARKS
Bonsor v. Musicians' Union	[1956] A.C. 104	Trade Union—Action by Member against Union—Expulsion—Right to damages for breach of contract.	A.	(2:1) in C.A. In f.p.
B. v. B.	[1955] 1 W.L.R. 557	House of Lords—Appeal to—Leave to Appeal—Matrimonial cause—Infant—Custody—Religious upbringing.	D. (Incompetent)	Reversed in C.A. Leave of Appeal Committee
C.I.R. v. Universal Grinding Wheel Co.	[1955] A.C. 807	Profits Tax—Non-distribution Relief—Redemption of Preference Shares at premium—Reduction of share capital.	D.	(2:1) in C.A.
Camille and Henry Dreyfus Foundation Inc. v. C.I.R.	[1956] A.C. 39	Income Tax—Charity—Whether Corporation incorporated in U.S.A. for charitable purposes entitled to exemption from income tax—Whether foreign objects charitable—Evidence of foreign law.	D.	
Carmarthenshire C.C. v. Lewis	[1955] A.C. 549	Negligence—Child straying from school premises on to highway—Lorry driver killed in avoiding child—Negligence of schoolmistress—Liability of School Authority to dependants of deceased.	D. (4:1)	Leave of Appeal Committee
*Corporation of Glasgow v. Central Land Board	1956 S.C. (H.L.) 1	Process—Recovery of Documents—Power of Court to order production of documents in hands of a public department—Public policy—Objection to calls in specification of documents on ground of public interest—Whether Central Land Board a department of the Crown—Whether court must give effect to a certificate by the proper minister that disclosure would not be in the public interest.	D.	
Esso Petroleum v. Southport Corporation	[1956] A.C. 218	Shipping—Nuisance—Discharge of oil—Public Navigable river—Tanker stranded in estuary—Refloating by jettison of oil cargo—Damage to foreshore by oil—Action by owners of shore against Shipowners—Claim based on trespass, nuisance, and negligence—Practice—Pleadings.	A.	Reversed in C.A. (2:1)
Edwards v. Bairstow	[1956] A.C. 14	Income Tax—Schedule 'D'—Trading Adventure—Review of Finding of General Commissioners—Dealing in Spinning Plant.	A.	
Galloway v. Galloway	[1956] A.C. 299	Infant — Custody — Divorce Court—Child born in adultery—Not legitimated by subsequent marriage of parents—Divorce—No jurisdiction to order custody—'Children the marriage of whose parents is the subject of the proceedings'—primâ facie meaning 'Legitimate Children'.	A. (3:2)	(2:1) in C.A. In f.p. Minority decision

NAME OF CASE	REPORTED	SUBJECT-MATTER	OUTCOME	REMARKS
Holdsworth & Co. (Wakefield) v. Caddies	[1955] 1 W.L.R. 352	Contract — Construction — Appointment of Managing Director—Right to restrict duties of Managing Director—Master and Servant—Whether Master obliged to provide Servant with work.	A. (4:1)	Minority decision
*Hynd v. Forrester	1955 S.C. (H.L.) 1	Writ—Authentication—Notarial execution of Will—Solicitor adding docquet and witnesses subscribing without testator's presence—Whether solemnities should be performed *unico contextu*.	D.	Reversed in C.S.
Institute of Fuel v. Morley	[1956] A.C. 245	Rates and Rating—Scientific Society —Exemption—Society to promote fuel technology—Whether instituted for scientific purposes exclusively.	A.	(2:1) in C.A.
Kirkness v. John Hudson & Co. Ltd.	[1955] A.C. 696	Income Tax—Balancing Charge under Income Tax Act 1945—Whether railway wagons vested in British Transport Commission were sold to the Commission.	D. (4:1)	Leave of Appeal Committee
Mason v. Clarke	[1955] A.C. 778	Landlord–Tenant—*Profit à prendre*— Game—'Reservation' of Game, rabbits, etc.—'Regrant' by tenant—Extermination of rabbits by gas—Reasonable operation in interests of farming—Snares set by grantee—Unreasonable and oral letting of rabbiting rights—Tainted with illegality.	A.	Reversed in C.A. Leave of Appeal Committee
*Martin v. Sinclair	1955 S.C. (H.L.) 56	Succession—Will construction—*Casus improvisus*—Common Calamity—Identical wills by two sisters—Whole estate in each case bequeathed to brother and sister equally and to survivor—Brother predeceasing both sisters—Sisters dying in common calamity—Whether estates fell into intestacy.	D.	Reversed in C.S.
Madras Electric Supply Corpn. v. Boarland	[1955] A.C. 667	Revenue—Income Tax—Succession to trade—Sale of electricity undertaking to Crown—Whether 'person [who] succeeds to any trade' includes Crown —Crown prerogative.	D.	
Qualcast Ltd. v. Thorpe	Unreported	Factory—Negligence—Failure of employer to enforce the wearing of protective clothing.	A.	(2:1) in C.A. Leave of Appeal Committee
Owner of 'Rogenaes' v. owner of 'Prins Alexander'	[1955] 2 Ll. R. 1.	Collision—Radar—Fog.	D.	Reversed in C.A.

NAME OF CASE	REPORTED	SUBJECT-MATTER	OUTCOME	REMARKS
Sharkey v. Wernher	[1956] A.C. 58	Income Tax—Profits of stud farm—Horses transferred to racing stables—Figure of credit item in stud farms accounts.	A. (4:1)	Reversed in C.A.
Stewarts and Lloyds v. Zoes	Unreported (*The Times*, 5 July 1955)	Commission agreement—Whether term of an oral contract should be construed differently from sense in which both parties understood it.	D.	Reversed in C.A. (Leave of Appeal Committee)
Sanderson v. C.I.R.	[1956] A.C. 491	Revenue—Estate Duty—Valuation—Shares—'Property deemed to pass'—Shares in company controlled by deceased—Disposition within three years of death—Method of valuation.	D.	
John Summers & Sons Ltd. v. Frost	[1955] A.C. 740	Factory — Dangerous machinery — Fencing—Grindstone—Duty to fence —Compliance with Act rendering machine unusable.	D. (4:½)	Reversed in C.A. (2:1)
Tool Metal Manufacturing Co. v. Tungsten Electric	[1955] 1 W.L.R. 761	Licence to use patent on payment of compensation if quota exceeded—Whether a penalty or unlawful restraint of trade—Whether temporary waiver of right to compensation determined.	A.	Reversed in C.A.
*Walker v. C.I.R.	1955 S.C. (H.L.) 74	Revenue—Estate Duty—Aggregation —Policies of Assurance—Estate in which deceased never had an interest —Destinations under policies of Assurance in favour of children—Whether funds under policies 'estate by itself'.	A.	(3:1) in C.S.

Judgments delivered in 1956

Morris v. West Hartlepool Steam Navigation Co.	[1956] A.C. 552	Personal injuries—Duty of shipowners to fence, guard or cover opening of 'tween-deck hatch.	A. (3:2)	Reversed in C.A. (2:1)
Staveley Iron and Chemical Co. v. Jones	[1956] A.C. 627	Negligence—Duty of care—Contributory negligence—Injury caused by fellow workman—Employer's liability —Employer's duty of reasonable care not diminished by delegation.	D.	Reversed in C.A. Leave of Appeal Committee
A.-G. v. Prince Ernest Augustus of Hanover	[1957] A.C. 436	Nationality—Naturalization—Royal Family—Naturalization of Princess Sophia and 'all persons lineally descending from her'—Whether limited to persons born in the lifetime of Queen Anne.	D.	Reversed in C.A.
Automatic Woodturning v. Stringer	[1957] A.C. 544	Factory — Circular Saw — Factory owners' duty.	A.	Reversed in C.A. Leave of Appeal Committee
et è contra			D.	ditto

NAME OF CASE	REPORTED	SUBJECT-MATTER	OUTCOME	REMARKS
*Baird v. Baird's Trustees	1956 S.C. (H.L.) 93	Liferent and fee—Ante-nuptial marriage contract—Unqualified liferent to husband—Fund provided by husband's father—Direction that on death of survivor of spouses trustees to make over fund to husband's testamentary trustees to form part of his estate and to be administered in accordance with any will or other deed executed by him—Whether provisions inferred immediate gift of fee.	A.	
*Bonnington Castings Ltd. v. Wardlaw	[1956] A.C. 613	Negligence—Master and Servant—Pneumoconiosis—Failure to provide against dust containing silica—Cause of the pursuer contracting the disease.	D.	(2:1) in C.S.
Chloride Batteries Ltd. v. Gahan	[1956] 1 W.L.R. 391	Profits of Trade—Computation for purpose of Income Tax under Schedule 'D' of Income Tax Act 1918 as later amended—Deduction of profits tax as an expense—Principal Company's notice that subsidiary's profits be treated as principal's—Subsidiary company's reimbursement of profits tax paid by principal — Whether amount payable 'by virtue of the notice' was whole profits tax paid by principal.	D.	Reversed in C.A.
C.I.R. v. Butterley Co. Ltd.	[1957] A.C. 32	Revenue — Profits tax — Separate trades—Nationalized industry—Company carrying on colliery undertaking and other separate trades—Colliery undertaking nationalized—Compensation—Interim income payments—'Profits arising from the trade or business'.	D.	Reversed in C.A.
Davis Contractors Ltd. v. Fareham U.D.C.	[1956] A.C. 696	Building Contract—Delay not due to fault of either party—Scarcity of labour—Buildings ultimately completed—Whether contractors entitled to sum in excess of contract price on *quantum meruit*.	D.	Reversed in C.A.
East Riding C.C. v. Park Estate (Bridlington)	[1957] A.C. 223	Town and Country Planning—Enforcement Notice.	D.	
The Empire Jamaica	[1957] A.C. 386	Limitation of liability—Collision—Fault or privity of owners—Ship having more than one mate—Statutory obligation that first and second mates should be certificated—Negligent navigation—Whether owners precluded from claiming limitation.	D.	

NAME OF CASE	REPORTED	SUBJECT-MATTER	OUTCOME	REMARKS
Lister v. Romford Ice and Cold Storage Co.	[1957] A.C. 555	Master and Servant—Contract of Service—Implied term—Master's right of contribution or indemnity under Act of 1935—Vicarious liability—Indemnity for servant—Joint tortfeasor—Contribution Road Traffic—Third Party Insurance—Subrogation.	D. (3:2)	(2:1) in C.A. In f.p.
L.C.C. v Wilkins	[1957] A.C. 362	Rates and rating—Rateable occupation—Building Contractors' huts—Site handed over to contractor with right of access reserved—Whether rateably occupied—Huts not affixed to ground—Whether part of hereditament chattel—Fixture.	D	
*Marshall v. Scottish Milk Marketing Board	1956 S.C. (H.L.) 37	Limitation of actions—Public Authority—Action of reparation for negligence raised more than six months after the cause of action had arisen—Whether Scottish Milk Marketing Board a public authority—Whether entitled to statutory protection in respect of exercising its power to produce cheese.	A.	
H. Millwood Ltd. v. Martin	[1956] R.P.C. 125	Patent—Infringement—Invalidity of patent—Counterclaim for revocation—Construction of amended specification—Reference to unamended specification—Anticipation—Obviousness—Insufficiency—Inutility—Ambiguity—Non-infringement.	D.	Reversed in C.A.
Nyali Ltd. v. A.-G.	[1957] A.C. 253	East Africa—Kenya Protectorate—Exemption from tolls for 'military on duty'—Whether exemption extends to all soldiers of the Queen.	D.	Reversed in C.A. One part-dissent
A. V. Pound & Co. v. M. W. Hardy & Co.	[1956] A.C. 588	Sale of Goods—f.a.s.—Effect of failure to obtain export licence where the contract is silent—Frustration—Effect of foreign law—Repudiation.	D.	Reversed in C.A.
Renton & Co. v. Palmyra Trading Corporation of Panama	[1957] A.C. 149	Shipping—Bill of Lading—Port of Discharge—Bills of Lading providing for delivery of timber at London and Hull—Strike, etc., clause—Meaning of delay—Clause permitting discharge of cargo 'at port of loading or any other safe and convenient port' such discharge to 'be deemed due fulfilment of contract'—Whether void at Common Law or under the Hague Rules.	D.	Reversed in C.A.

NAME OF CASE	REPORTED	SUBJECT-MATTER	OUTCOME	REMARKS
Shell-Mex & B.P. *v.* Clayton	[1956] 1 W.L.R. 1198	Rates — De-rating — Freight - Transport Hereditament — Installations for unshipping and storing oil—Ratepayer selling agent for oil companies—Use of hereditament for dock purposes—Occupation and use of hereditament as part of a dock undertaking.	D. (4:1)	
Smith *v.* East Elloe R.D.C.	[1956] A.C. 736	Acquisition of Land—Compulsory purchase order—Right of owner to question validity of the order in High Court proceedings on the ground of fraud by members or officers of the Local Authority.	A.i.p. (3:2)	Leave of Appeal Committee. In f.p.
Southern Railway of Peru *v.* Owen	[1957] A.C. 334	Income Tax—Schedule 'D'—Cases I and II—Deductions—Defined payments of compensation to employees leaving.	D. (4:1)	
*South of Scotland Electricity Board *v.* British Oxygen	[1956] 1 W.L.R. 1069	Electricity—Tariff—'Undue preference'—'Undue discrimination'—Lower rates charged to high voltage consumers because of reduced cost of supply—Provision for increase in rates in respect of increased cost of fuel—Uniform increase to high and low voltage consumers—Whether undue discrimination exercised against high voltage consumers.	D.	Reversed in C.S.
Vine *v.* National Dock Labour Board	[1957] A.C. 488	Action for declaration of invalidity of dismissal and damages—Delegation of quasi-judicial disciplinary powers—Declaration—Discretionary Remedy.	A.	Reversed in part in C.A. One part-dissent.
et è contra			D.	Leave of Appeal Committee
*Walsh *v.* Lord Advocate	[1956] 1 W.L.R. 1002	Statute — Construction — Regular Minister of religious denomination—Exemption from National Service—Congregation Servant and Pioneer Publisher of Jehovah's Witnesses.	D.	
W. Suffolk C.C. *v.* Rought Ltd.	[1957] A.C. 403	Compulsory Purchase—Compensation —Loss of Profit—Income Tax not deductible from compensation.	A.	
Wheeler *v.* Mercer	[1957] A.C. 416	Security of Tenure—Tenancy at will— Whether protected.	A.	Leave of Appeal Committee
Fairclough, Dodd & Jones *v.* J. H. Vantol Ltd.	[1957] 1 W.L.R. 136	Sale of goods—c.i.f.—Extension of time for shipment clause—Temporary prevention of shipment by specified clause—Effect of prohibition—Construction of clause.	A.	Reversed in C.A.

NAME OF CASE	REPORTED	SUBJECT-MATTER	OUTCOME	REMARKS
*Corporation of Glasgow v. Western Heritable Investment	[1956] A.C. 670	Housing—Promotion of construction of houses by Local Authority—Special conditions—Right of owners to sell without consent of Secretary of State.	D.	
Goodrich v. Paisner	[1957] A.C. 65	Landlord and tenant—Rent Restriction—'Separate dwelling'—Shared accommodation—Letting of rooms—Use of extra bedroom in common with landlord.	A. (4:1)	
*Grant v. N.C.B.	[1956] A.C. 649	Coal Mines—'Roof and sides of every travelling road . . . shall be made secure . . .'—Bogie derailed by stone fallen from roof.	A.	Reversed in C.S.
Hayward v. Port of London Authority	[1956] 2 Ll. R. 1	Dock worker drowned—Provision for rescue from drowning—'Means at or near the surface of the water at reasonable intervals'—Provision of ladders recessed in quay walls at intervals of 300 ft.—Usual practice of Dock owners—Lighting—'All places . . . shall be efficiently lighted'.	D.	In f.p.

Judgments delivered in 1957

NAME OF CASE	REPORTED	SUBJECT-MATTER	OUTCOME	REMARKS
Wrightson v. C.I.R. Westminster Bank v. C.I.R.	[1958] A.C. 210	Revenue — Estate duty — Property chargeable—Property deemed to pass —Settlement of Assurance Policies and cash—Cash invested under settlement—Tenant for life entitled to income from investments after specified period—Death of Settlor 9 years later —Clause for Estate Duty on life interest in policies—Finance Act 1894, s. 2 (1) (d).	A. (3:1+½)	Reversed in C.A.
A. C. Billings v. Riden	[1958] A.C. 240	Negligence—Liability of contractors —Access to building rendered dangerous—Plaintiff's knowledge of danger —Independent contractor—Work outside office building containing caretaker's flat—No safe means of access.	D.	Reversed in C.A. (2:1)
B.T.C. v. Westmorland C.C. B.T.C. v. Worcestershire C.C.	[1958] A.C. 126	Highway — Dedication — Capacity to dedicate.	D.	
R. B. Burden Ltd. v. Swansea Corporation	[1957] 1 W.L.R. 1167	Building — Contract — Certificate — Determination of contract by builders —Interim Certificates—Issue—Negligent assessment by independent surveyors.	D. (4:1)	Reversed in C.A.

NAME OF CASE	REPORTED	SUBJECT-MATTER	OUTCOME	REMARKS
*Hood Barrs v. C.I.R.	[1957] 1 W.L.R. 529	Revenue — Income Tax — Profits — Standing timber—Capital or revenue expenditure.	D. (4:1)	
*Ellis v. Designers and Decorators (Scotland) Ltd.	1957 S.C. (H.L.) 69	Emergency Legislation—Building Licence—Block Building Licence issued for work to be carried out by various contractors — Action for payment for work done by an individual contractor—Whether Architect entitled to allocate specific sums to individual contractors.	D.	
Fomento (Sterling Area) v. Selsdon Fountain Pen Co.	[1958] 1 W.L.R. 45	Construction of Patent licence — Rights and duties of auditors—Information given in confidence—'Most favoured nation' clause.	A.i.p. (4:2 × ½)	Reversed in C.A. Leave of Appeal Committee
Canadian Pacific Steamships v. Bryers	[1958] A.C. 485	Dry Dock—Several repairers contracting with shipowners—No notional occupier—Accident to shipowners' employee—Liability of shipowners—'Duties'. Persons benefited by Regulations—'Person employed'—Seaman employed as yeoman carpenter by shipowners—Work of repair on ship in public dry dock.	D.	Reversed in part in C.A. Leave of Appeal Committee
Cane (V.O.) v. Soc. of Chemical Industry	(1957) R. & I.T. 506	Rating — Exemptions — Scientific Society—'Instituted for purposes of science exclusively'—Collateral and incidental or ancillary objects—'To advance applied chemistry'.	D.	Reversed in C.A. (2:1). Leave of Appeal Committee
*Nicholson v. Atlas Steel Foundry Engineering Co. Ltd.	[1957] 1 W.L.R. 613	Master and Servant—Pneumoconiosis —Whether caused by breach of statutory duty of Employers.	A.	Reversed in C.S.
C.I.R. v. Saunders	[1958] A.C. 285	Surtax—Settlement—'Power to revoke or otherwise determine the settlement or any provision thereof'— Power to apply part of capital for benefit of class including Settlor's wife.	D. (3:2)	Reversed in C.A.
Firestone Tyre & Rubber v. Lewellin	[1957] 1 W.L.R. 464	Revenue — Income Tax — Non-resident—Trade within United Kingdom for sale of goods manufactured there —United Kingdom company assessed as agent of foreign company.	D.	

NAME OF CASE	REPORTED	SUBJECT-MATTER	OUTCOME	REMARKS
Countess of Kenmare v. C.I.R.	[1958] A.C. 267	Revenue — Income Tax — Settlement —Revocability—Residence of Settlor out of the jurisdiction—Property within the jurisdiction—Income from Settlement included in Settlor's assessment for surtax—Power from time to time to determine part of trusts— Equivalent to a power to revoke— Settlor out of the jurisdiction included.	D.	
†McClelland v. N. Ireland General Health Services Board	[1957] 1 W.L.R. 594	Contract of officer with Statutory Board—Employment expressed to be 'permanent'—Contract providing for termination of employment in certain circumstances.	A. (3:2)	(2:1) in C.A. (N.I.) Minority decision. In f.p.
Mid-Northants Water Board v. Lee (V.O.)	[1958] A.C. 68	Rates and Rating—Assessment— Rateable value—Profits' basis—Statutory Water Undertaking.	D.	Reversed in C.A.
Moriarty v. Evans Medical Supplies	[1958] 1 W.L.R. 66	Income Tax—Schedule 'D'—Profits of Trade — Whether payment of £100,000 a trade receipt—Whether, if a trade receipt, capital or income— Knowledge of secret processes.	D. (4:1)	Reversed in part in C.A.
et è contra		ditto	A. (3:2)	Reversed in part in C.A. Minority decision
Rahimtoola v. Nizam of Hyderabad	[1958] A.C. 379	Conflict of laws—Sovereign immunity —Foreign state not a party to proceedings—Impleading foreign sovereign— Money belonging to one sovereign transferred to defendant servant of another foreign sovereign—Transfer by person entitled to operate bank account—No authority to transfer— Agency—Accountability of agent to principal—Money paid to agent under mistake or wrongfully—Trust—Sole beneficiary.	A.	Reversed in C.A.
Regazzoni v. K. C. Sethia (1944) Ltd.	[1958] A.C. 301	Contracts—Illegality—Foreign prohibition—Contract for sale of Jute bags —C.i.f.—European Port—Intention that contract goods be shipped from India for resale to South Africa—Prohibition by Indian Government of export of goods to South Africa—Recognition of prohibition by English courts.	D.	Leave of Appeal Committee
Taylor v. National Assistance Board	[1958] A.C. 532	Legal Aid—Disposable income—Subject matter of dispute—Order for alimony pending suit after application but before computation by National Assistance Board.	D.	Reversed in C.A. Leave of Appeal Committee. In f.p.

NAME OF CASE	REPORTED	SUBJECT-MATTER	OUTCOME	REMARKS
Whitmorley Displays v. Multiform	(1957) R.P.C. 260	Patent—Amended specification—Proper approach to be adopted in construction—Extent to which unamended version to be taken into account—Committal for contempt of court.	A.	Reversed in part in C.A. (2:1)
*Quinn v. Cameron and Roberton	[1958] A.C. 9	Master and Servant—Pneumoconiosis —Whether caused by breach of statutory duty of Employers.	A. (4:1)	Minority decision
Sun Life Assurance Society v. Davidson	[1958] A.C. 184	Income Tax—Expenses of management—Repayment of Tax—Life Assurance Companies—Brokerage and stamp duties on purchases and sales of investments.	D. (4:½)	
National Bank of Greece and Athens v. Metliss	[1958] A.C. 509	Conflict of Laws—Universal Succession by foreign law of one foreign Company to another—Whether successor protected by moratorium imposed by foreign law.	D.	
N.C.B. v. C.I.R.	[1958] A.C. 104	Revenue — Profits tax — Allowances —Industrial buildings or structures— Dwelling-houses of colliery—Owned by mine-owners—Occupied by miners —Value 'when the mine is no longer worked'.	D.	Reversed in C.A. (2:1)

Judgments delivered in 1958

NAME OF CASE	REPORTED	SUBJECT-MATTER	OUTCOME	REMARKS
Escoigne Properties v. C.I.R.	[1958] A.C. 549	Stamp Duty—Conveyance of Transfer on Sale—Purchaser and sub-purchaser associated companies—Whether Conveyance or Transfer to sub-purchaser exempt from ad valorem duty.	D.	Reversed in C.A.
Income Tax Special Commissioners v. Linsleys (Established 1894) Ltd.	[1958] A.C. 569	Surtax—Investment Company—Profits Tax—Direction by Special Commissioners—Computation of Company's actual income—Deduction in respect of profits tax—Election exempting company from profits tax.	A.	Minority decision
Wigram Family Settled Estates v. C.I.R.	[1958] 1 W.L.R. 213	Surtax—Investment Company—Apportionment of actual income—Redeemable Preference Shares entitled to Dividend—Additional right to have part of the profits otherwise available for dividend credited to fund for redemption of the Shares.	D.	
Adamastos Shipping v. Anglo-Saxon Petroleum	[1959] A.C. 133	Charter party—Consecutive voyage charter—Paramount Clause—Effect of incorporation — Unseaworthiness — Extent of shipowners' obligations.	A. (3:2)	Reversed in C.A. Minority decision

NAME OF CASE	REPORTED	SUBJECT-MATTER	OUTCOME	REMARKS
Betty's Cafés v. Phillips Furnishing Stores	[1959] A.C. 20	Landlord and Tenant Act 1954—Business Premises (Security of Tenure)—Landlords' intention to reconstruct—Application for new tenancy—Relevant time of landlords' intention to reconstruct.	D. (4:1)	Reversed in C.A. (2:1)
Cade v. B.T.C.	[1959] A.C. 256	Meaning of 'repair' in all cases where any danger is likely to arise.	D. (4:1)	In f.p.
Carson v. Cheyney's Executor	[1959] A.C. 412	Income Tax—Schedule 'D'—Copyright royalties paid after author's death under contracts made by him—Whether assessable to income tax.	D.	
*C.I.R. v. South Georgia Co.	[1958] A.C. 599	Revenue—Profits Tax—Distribution Charge.	A.	
C.I.R. v. Wood Bros. (Birkenhead)	[1959] A.C. 487	Surtax — Company — Direction and apportionment.	D. (3:2)	Leave of Appeal Committee
Regis Property Co. v. Dudley	[1959] A.C. 370	Landlord and Tenant—Appropriate Factor.	D. (3:2)	
*Scottish C.W.S. v. Meyer	[1959] A.C. 324	Company — Winding-up — 'Just and equitable' — Alternative remedy in cases of oppression—Subsidiary company—Oppression of independent shareholder to destroy company's business.	D.	Reversed in C.S.
Smith v. Austin Lifts Ltd.	[1959] 1 W.L.R. 100	Occupier—Invitor and invitee—Invitee injured by defect on premises—Invitee aware of defect without realizing extent of danger—No warning or safeguard by occupier.	A.	Reversed in C.A.
Wintle v. Nye	[1959] 1 W.L.R. 284	Probate — Trial of action — Cross-examination—Allegation of want of knowledge and approval.	A.	(2:1) in C.A. In f.p. Appellant in person
*John Young & Co. v. O'Donnell	1958 S.L.T. (Notes) 46	Reparation — Negligence — Master and Servant—Liability of master for fault of servant—Servant working for another person.	D.	(2:1) in C.S.
Koppelman v. Kopel	Unreported	Application for appointment of Special Examiner.	A.	Reversed in C.A. Leave of Appeal Committee. Respondent in person
London Investment & Mortgage Co. v. Worthington	[1959] A.C. 199	Profits of trade within Case I of Schedule 'D'—War damage value payments—Whether receipts of trade in property dealing for income tax and profits tax purposes.	D.	Reversed in C.A.

NAME OF CASE	REPORTED	SUBJECT-MATTER	OUTCOME	REMARKS
London Transport Executive *v.* Betts (V.O.)	[1959] A.C. 213	Rates — De-rating — Industrial here-ditament—Bus maintenance depot—Whether used by occupier for the maintenance of his road vehicles.	D. (4:1)	
B. S. Lyle Ltd. *v.* Rosher	[1959] 1 W.L.R. 8	Equitable interest—Trust expressed in favour of person absolutely—Person holds on behalf of others—Purported assignment of interest by person in favour of third party or security. Competing equitable interests—Application of rule in *Dearle* v. *Hall* where assignor a trustee.	D.	
*Miller *v.* S. of Scotland Electricity Board	1958 S.C. (H.L.) 20	Negligence — Child — Live electric cable in partially demolished house—Duty of Electricity Authority.	A.	In f.p.
National Deposit Friendly Society Trustees *v.* Skegness U.D.C.	[1959] A.C. 293	Rates and Rating—'Social Welfare'—Friendly Society.	D.	
T. Oertli A.G. *v.* E. J. Bowman	[1959] R.P.C. 1	Passing off—Dishonest trading—Liability of Directors—Malicious conspiracy—Directors of Limited Company held liable for damages caused by dishonest course of trading by Company — Malicious conspiracy not proved.	D.	Reversed in C.A. Leave of Appeal Committee

Judgments delivered in 1959

NAME OF CASE	REPORTED	SUBJECT-MATTER	OUTCOME	REMARKS
Shell-Mex and B.P. Ltd. *v.* Holyoak (V.O.)	[1959] 1 W.L.R. 188	Rates—Valuation—Plant and Machinery—'Tank'—Underground petrol tank in brick and concrete compartment.	A. (3:2)	Reversed in C.A. Minority decision
Davie *v.* New Merton Board Mills	[1959] A.C. 604	Master and Servant—Liability of Master—Accident to Servant—Tool bought from reputable manufacturers —Defect due to negligence in manufacture—Defect not reasonably discoverable by employers but patent to manufacturers.	D.	Reversed in C.A. (2:1)
General Nursing Council *v.* St Marylebone Borough Council	[1959] A.C. 540	Rates and rating—Social Welfare—Health—Council required by Statute to maintain register of nurses—Claim for rating relief—Advancement of 'Social Welfare'.	D. (3:2)	Reversed in C.A.
Baldwin & Francis *v.* Patents Appeal Tribunal	[1959] A.C. 663	*Certiorari*—Opposition to grant of patent—Allowance by tribunal of Appeal against insertion of reference to Opponents Patent—Application by Opponents for Order of *Certiorari* against Tribunal.	D.	Leave of Appeal Committee

NAME OF CASE	REPORTED	SUBJECT-MATTER	OUTCOME	REMARKS
†Belfast Corporation v. O.D. Cars Ltd.	[1960] A.C. 490	Statutory Provision excluding compensation for certain planning restrictions, Planning and Housing Act (Northern Ireland) 1931—Whether applicable to refusal of an interim development application—Whether *ultra vires* the Parliament of Northern Ireland as constituting a 'taking of property without compensation' within s. 5 (1) of the Government of Ireland Act 1920.	A.	Reversed in C.A. (N.I.)
†Cavanagh v. Ulster Weaving Co.	[1960] A.C. 145	Master and Servant—Negligence—Breach of Statutory Duty.	A.	Reversed in C.A. (N.I.) (2:1). Refused leave to appeal in f.p.
Chappel & Co. v. Nestlé Co. Ltd.	[1960] A.C. 87	Copyright — Records of Musical Works—'Retail Sale'.	A. (3:2)	Reversed in C.A. (2:1)
Contract & Trading Co. v. Barbey	[1960] A.C. 244	Currency control—Bills of Exchange —Holder in due course—Resident outside Scheduled territory—No Treasury permission obtained.	D. (4:1)	
Electrix Ltd. v. Electrolux Ltd.	[1960] A.C. 722	Trade Marks—Application to register 'Electrix' for, *inter alia*, electrically driven vacuum cleaners—Opposition by proprietors of registered Trade Mark 'Electrolux'.	D.	Reversed in C.A.
Gough v. N.C.B.	[1959] A.C. 698	Coal Mining—Statutory Duty—Breach—Security of Working Place—Fall of Coal from Coal Face—Duty to make 'secure' sides of a working place.	A. (3:2 × ½)	(2:1) in C.A.
Grey v. C.I.R.	[1960] A.C. 1	Revenue—Stamp duty—Gifts *inter vivos*—Oral settlement—Settlements in favour of grandchildren—Transfer of company shares to trustees as nominees—Oral direction to trustees to hold shares on trusts of settlements— Subsequent declarations of trust by trustees—Whether voluntary dispositions liable to *ad valorem* duty.	D.	Reversed in C.A. (2:1)
*Hamilton v. N.C.B.	[1960] A.C. 633	Reparation—Negligence—Breach of Statutory Duty—Coal mine 'Properly Maintained'.	A.	(2:1) in C.S.
Hinton v. Maden & Ireland Ltd.	[1959] 1 W.L.R. 875	Income Tax—Depreciation—Investment Allowance.	D. (3:2)	Reversed in C.A.

NAME OF CASE	REPORTED	SUBJECT-MATTER	OUTCOME	REMARKS
Hochstrasser v. Mayes	[1960] A.C. 376	Sums paid or credited by employer to employee in respect of loss suffered by employee on sale of dwelling house—Whether sums 'perquisites or profits whatsoever' chargeable to Income Tax.	D.	(2:1) in C.A.
Hudson's Bay Co. v. Thompson (V.O.)	[1960] A.C. 926	Rates and rating—Industrial hereditament—Adaptation for sale—Fur sorting and auction premises—Mixed parcels of skins received from individual sellers. Sorted into auction lots of identical grade and species irrespective of ownership—Sold on commission on behalf of sellers.	A.	
*Islip Pedigree Breeding Centre v. Abercromby	1959 S.L.T. 161	Sale of cattle—Wrong cow delivered—Onus of proof.	A. (3:1)	Minority decision (only 4 judges in H.L.)
*Junor v. McNicol	Unreported (The Times, 26 March 1959)	Negligence—House Surgeon working under consultant's supervision—Misunderstanding of consultant's instructions—Duty of House Surgeon towards patient—Duty of Hospital Board to provide a system of instructing parents of child patients as to dangers inherent in treatment.	D.	(Only 3 judges in H.L.). In f.p.
*Lyle & Scott v. Scott (2 Appeals) Lyle & Scott Ltd. v. Thompson (4 Appeals) Lyle & Scott Ltd. v. Edinburgh Investment Trust (7 Appeals)	[1959] A.C. 763	Company — Private Company — Shares—Articles of Association—Preemptive right of other members to purchase shares of member 'desirous of transferring'—Purported contract for sale of shares by member to outside party.	A.	
*Mortimer v. Samuel B. Allison Ltd.	[1959] 1 W.L.R. 330	Reparation—Accident during Demolition of building.	D.	Reversed in in C.S. In f.p.
Ostime v. Australian Mutual Provident Society	[1960] A.C. 459	Double Taxation Relief (Taxes on Income) (Australia) Order 1947—Australian Life Assurance Company carrying on business in United Kingdom—Mutual trading—Basis of assessment.	D. (4:1)	
Oughtred v. C.I.R.	[1960] A.C. 206	Stamp Duty—Conveyance on sale—Transfer of shares—Shares subject to settlement—Oral agreement to exchange reversionary interest in settled shares for shares owned by life tenant—Trustees' subsequent transfer of shares to life tenant.	D. (3:2) C.A.	Reversed in C.A.

NAME OF CASE	REPORTED	SUBJECT-MATTER	OUTCOME	REMARKS
*Parker v. Lord Advocate	[1960] A.C. 608	Revenue—Estate Duty—Property passing on death—Declaration of Trust—During Trustor's lifetime income to children—At Trustor's death Trust Funds divisible amongst surviving children or issue.	D.	
Public Trustee v. C.I.R.	[1960] A.C. 398	Estate duty—Property passing on death—Bequest to trustee of income from shares of residue 'so long as he shall act as … trustee … by way of remuneration'—Duty on capital of share claimed in respect of death of trustee.	A. (3:1)	Minority decision
Pyx Granite Co. v. Min. of H. & L.G.	[1960] A.C. 260	Town and Country Planning—Development—Permission—Necessity for permission—Agreement between quarry owners and local authority as to quarrying areas scheduled to Act of Parliament.	A.	Reversed in C.A. (2:1)
†McKeown v. Burell	Unreported	Damages for negligence—Amount—Excessive and unreasonable—Setting aside verdict.	A.	Reversed in C.A. (N.I.)
Qualcast (Wolverhampton) v. Haynes	[1959] A.C. 743	Negligence—Safe system of work—General precautions—Metal moulding—Protective clothing available for workman—No orders or advice to wear it—Workman injured—Employer's liability.	A.	Leave of Appeal Committee
Racecourse Betting Control Board v. Young	[1959] 1 W.L.R. 813	Income Tax—Profits of trade of totalizator operator within Case I of Schedule 'D'—Deduction in computing profits.	D.	
†Rental Holdings Ltd. v. Hall	Unreported	Breach of covenant in lease—Forfeiture—Whether sale within two years by lessee to third party—Inferences to be drawn.	D.	
†Scottish C.W.S. v. Ulster Farmers' Mart	[1960] A.C. 63	Tort—Disturbance of a market.	A.	Allowed in part in C.A. (N.I.)

NAME OF CASE	REPORTED	SUBJECT-MATTER	OUTCOME	REMARKS
Skegness U.D.C. *v.* Derbyshire Miners' Welfare Committee	[1959] A.C. 807	Rates and Rating—'Social welfare'— Miners' welfare holiday camp—Trustees occupying premises used for 'purpose of a holiday 'centre . . . for the benefit of' coal miners, their dependants and invitees'—Provision of cost-price holidays—Organization not established or conducted for profit.	D.	
*S. of Scotland Electricity Board *v.* British Oxygen Co. Ltd.	[1959] 1 W.L.R. 587	Statute — Construction — Electricity supply — Tariffs — 'Undue preference' and 'undue discrimination'— High voltage consumers charged at a rate less than low voltage consumers— High voltage consumers averring 'undue discrimination' against them and 'undue preference' to low voltage consumers—Relevancy of cost to producer.	D. D. $(3:2\times\frac{1}{2})$	Reversed in C.S. (3:1) ditto
Unit Construction Co. *v.* Bullock	[1960] A.C. 351	Residence — Company — Income Tax—'Superior or Directing Authority'.	A.	
Whitworth Park Coal Co. *v.* C.I.R.	[1961] A.C. 31	Income Tax—Basis of assessment— Case VI—Whether payments assessable in year in which received or in respect of which they were paid.	D. (3:1)	
Bennett *v.* Rowse	(1959) 38 T.C. 476	Revenue — Income Tax — Balancing Charge—Discontinuance of Trade— Computation of Time—Fractions of a Day.	D.	Appellant in person
L.C.C. *v.* Henry Boot & Sons Ltd.	[1959] 1 W.L.R. 1069	Building — Contract — London County Council standard contract— 'Rise and fall' clause—'Rates of wages payable'—Holiday credits included in the rates of wages—Master and Servant—'Wages' Holidays with pay—Whether weekly credits 'Wages' within meaning of building contract.	A.	Reversed in C.A.
†Smyth *v.* Cameron	Unreported	Master and Servant—Verdict of jury that master was not guilty of negligence causing damage to servant— Reasonableness of verdict.	D.	(2:1) in C.A. (N.I.). In f.p. Respondent not called

Judgments delivered in 1960

Elmdene Estates Ltd. *v.* White	[1960] A.C. 528	Rent Restriction—Premium—Payment—Third party receiving benefit— Tenant required by Landlord, as condition of grant of Tenancy, to sell house, owned jointly by him and his wife, to third party at undervalue of £500—Whether Landlord liable to repay £500 to Tenant.	D.	Reversed in C.A.

NAME OF CASE	REPORTED	SUBJECT-MATTER	OUTCOME	REMARKS
Northern Fishing Co. (Hull) Ltd. v. Eddom	[1960] 1 Ll. R. 1	Limitation of liability.	D.	(2:1) in C.A.
Society of Medical Officers of Health v. Hope (V.O.)	[1960] A.C. 551	Estoppel—*Res non judicatum*—Rates and Rating—Local Valuation Court—Decision in 1951 that Society be entered on current valuation list as exempt from rates—Same question arising in 1956.	D.	(2:1) in C.A.
Abbott v. Philbin	[1961] A.C. 352	Income Tax Schedule 'E'—Purchased option to acquire shares in employer company — 'perquisite' — Whether taxable in year of purchase or year of exercise.	A. (3:2)	Reversed in C.A. Minority decision
Adams v. National Bank of Greece S.A.	[1961] A.C. 255	Conflict of Laws—Succession—Corporation — Amalgamation — Retrospective foreign legislation.	A.	Reversed in C.A.
*Arbuckle Smith v. Greenock Corpn.	[1960] A.C. 813	Rating—Liability for rates—Occupation—Alterations to premises previously unoccupied.	A.	
A. G. v. Vernazza	[1960] A.C. 965	Practice and procedure—Vexatious litigant—Matters to be taken into consideration—Pleadings disclosing cause of action—Whether Court entitled to look at whole history of matter.	A.	Leave of Appeal Committee
Barclays Bank v. C.I.R.	[1961] A.C. 509	Estate Duty—Valuation of shares—Control of company by virtue of shares held by first named of four Trustees.	D. (4:1)	Reversed in C.A.
*Bellshill & Mossend Co-op. v. Dalziel Co-op.	[1960] A.C. 832	Arbitration—Dispute between two member societies of co-operative union—Decree arbitral regulating trade competition between them—Whether arbitral award in restraint of trade—Question of arbitrators' *bona fides*—Necessity for intimation to arbitrators.	D.	Reversed in C.S.
*Bradford Property Trust v. Hunter	Unreported	Contract—Gratuitous contract—Error in Law—Whether contract reducible—Homologation.	D. (3:2)	
Henry Briggs Ltd. v. C.I.R.	[1961] 1 W.L.R. 68	Profits Tax—Former colliery company remaining in being to receive compensation under Coal Acts—Whether 'function' that of holding property.	D.	Leave of Appeal Committee
*Brown & Gracie v. F. W. Green & Co. *et è contra*	[1960] 1 Ll. R. 289	Action for damages for alleged breach of contract—Whether a contract was entered into between the parties—Interpretation of cables allegedly setting up contract.	D. D.	Reversed in C.S.

NAME OF CASE	REPORTED	SUBJECT-MATTER	OUTCOME	REMARKS
*Brown v. Rolls Royce Ltd.	[1960] 1 W.L.R. 210	Negligence—Master and Servant—Dermatitis — Workman contracting dermatitis through contact with oil—Elaborate system of precautions taken by employers—System not including provision of barrier cream commonly provided by other employers.	D.	Reversed in C.S. (3:1)
Chapman (A. P.) v. Rix	Unreported (*The Times*, 22 December 1960)	Negligence—Error in diagnosis by medical practitioner—Failure by him to communicate directly with deceased's own doctor causing latter to be misled.	D. (3:2)	Reversed in C.A. (2:1)
The Hebridean Coast	[1961] A.C. 545	Collision—Damages for detention.	D.	Leave of Appeal
*Spencer v. Brocklehurst	1960 S.C. (H.L.) 84	Damages—Breach of contract—Process—Reclaiming Motion—Failure of Reclaimer to appear or instruct Counsel—Procedure.	D.	
The Aello	[1961] A.C. 135	Shipping — Charter party — Arrived Ship—Ship awaiting cargo of maize compelled to wait in Buenos Aires Roads—Ships excluded from dock area unless cargo immediately available—Commercial area of port—Relevance of type of cargo —Roads not place where ships awaiting delivery of grain usually lay—Whether roads within commercial area of port. Shipping—Charter party—Cargo, obligation to Charterer to provide—Ship unable to become an arrived ship unless cargo immediately available.	D. (3:2) D. (4:1)	
London Clinic v. Hoare	Unreported (*The Times*, 25 March 1960)	Claim for balance of account for services rendered—Set off and counter-claim—Onus of proof on claim and counter-claim—Measure of damages for breach of contract to provide skilled nursing services—Pleadings.	A.	Reversed in part in C.A. Leave of Appeal Committee. Respondent in person
*Law v. Lord Advocate	Unreported	Revenue — Estate Duty — Intestate moveable estate—*Collatio inter haeredes*—Whether heir portioner required to collate with issue of a predeceasing sister entitled to succeed—'Competency to Dispose'—Whether competent to dispose of funds which could have been obtained on collation.	D.	

NAME OF CASE	REPORTED	SUBJECT-MATTER	OUTCOME	REMARKS
The Marinegra	[1960] 2 Ll. R.1	Collision—River—Vessel in difficulties—Duty of other vessel.	D.	(2:1) in C.A.
Fawcett Properties v. Buckingham C.C.	[1961] A.C. 636	Town and Country Planning—Development—Planning permission—Condition—Relation of condition to local planning considerations — Whether condition *ultra vires* or void for uncertainty.	D. (4:1)	Reversed in C.A.
Fischler v. Administrator of Roumanian Property	[1960] 1 W.L.R. 917	Treaty of Peace (Roumania) Order 1948—Ownership of property represented by balance held by Clearing Office on Compensation Account.	A.	Reversed in C.A. Leave of Appeal Committee
Philipson-Stow v. C.I.R.	[1961] A.C. 727	Revenue — Estate duty — Property chargeable—Immovable property situate outside Great Britain—Settlement — Testamentary disposition — Proper law of disposition.	A. (4:1)	(2:1) in C.A.
Thomson v. Moyse	[1961] A.C. 967	Income Tax Act 1918, Schedule 'D', Cases IV and V—Whether sums received in United Kingdom.	A.	(2:1) in C.A.
Tomkinson v. First Pennsylvania Banking and Trust Co.	[1961] A.C. 1007	Conflict of Laws—Contract—Discharge—Debt payable under contract —Whether discharged—Whether proper law of contract or *lex situs* of debt applicable—Conflict of laws—Contract—Renvoi—Applicability of doctrine to contract.	A.i.p.	One part-dissent in C.A.
*Watson v. Winget Ltd.	1960 S.C. (H.L.) 92	Limitation of Actions—Personal injuries—Workman injured by cement mixing machine—Time limit for action against manufacturer.	A. (3:2)	Reversed in C.S. Minority decision. In f.p.
Independent Television Authority and Associated Rediffusion Ltd. v. C.I.R.	[1961] A.C. 427	Stamp Duty—Bond Covenant Duty—Whether assessable on executory contract for services—Payments variable with interim index of retail prices—No maximum or minimum payment.	D.	
C.I.R. v. Hinchey	[1960] A.C. 748	Tax penalty for understatement of Post Office Savings Bank interest.	A.	Respondent absent
Imperial Tobacco Co. v. Pierson (V.O.)	[1961] A.C. 463	Rates and Rating—Assessments—Rateable value—Advertising right—Ratepayer granted licence to erect advertising sign—Basis of assessment.	A. (4:1)	Reversed in C.A.
Institute of Mechanical Engineers v. Cane (V.O.)	[1961] A.C. 696	Rates and Rating—Science or fine art —Exemption—Society 'to promote the development of mechanical engineering'—Supported mainly by annual subscriptions.	D.	Reversed in C.A.

NAME OF CASE	REPORTED	SUBJECT-MATTER	OUTCOME	REMARKS
		Judgments delivered in 1961		
Riverstone Meat v. Lancashire Shipping Co. Ltd.	[1961] A.C. 807	Shipping—Bill of lading—Seaworthiness—Hague Rules.	A.	
Wainright v. Symes (A.P.)	Unreported (*The Times*, 6 February 1961)	Running down action—Finding of fact by trial judge reversed—Function of Court of Appeal reviewing finding of fact by trial judge.	A.	Reversed in C.A. Leave of Appeal Committee
Wilts & Dorset Motor Services Ltd. v. Kitto	Unreported	Running down action—Finding by trial judge reversed—Function of Court of Appeal reviewing finding of trial judge.	A.	Reversed in part in C.A. Leave of Appeal Committee
*Hood Barrs v. C.I.R.	1961 S.C. (H.L.) 22	Revenue—Appeal to Court of Session as Court of Exchequer in Scotland—Procedure—Order of *certiorari*—Equivalent of Scottish procedure—Breach of natural justice—Error on face of record—Limits of jurisdiction of Court of Session—Revenue—Income Tax—Business losses—Issue of loss certificates—Function of General Commissioners—Whether administrative or judicial.	D.	One part-dissent in C.S.
Bowes-Lyon v. Green	[1963] A.C. 420	Landlord and Tenant—Meaning of 'the Landlord' in Landlord and Tenant Act 1954—Meaning of 'Reversionary Tenancy'.	D. (4:1)	Conditions of leave waived by Appeal Committee
Bank Line v. Evera	[1961] 1 Ll. R. 231	Shipping — Charterparty — 'Argentine Maritime Pensions Tax for Charterers' account'—Right of shipowners to recover from Charterers sum paid to Argentine tax authorities—Award in form of Special Case.	D. (4:1)	Reversed in C.A.
Braithwaite (Structural) v. Caulfield	Unreported (*The Times*, 5 May 1961)	Negligence — Breach of statutory duty—Spanish windlass supporting platform—Steel erector while on platform injured by windlass—Whether safe system of work—Employers' liability—Plaintiff's evidence not accepted by judge at trial—Plaintiff in person in the Court of Appeal.	D.	Reversed in C.A. (2:1) Defended in f.p. by respondent in person
*Warden v. Warden (2 Appeals)	Unreported (Referred to in later proceedings, 1962 S.L.T. 33)	Divorce—Cruelty—Credibility.	D.	Appellant in person
Brown v. N.C.B.	[1962] A.C. 574	Mines—Breach of statutory duty—Roof and sides—Fall of stone from roof following fall of girder—Duty to keep road and working place secure.	D.	

NAME OF CASE	REPORTED	SUBJECT-MATTER	OUTCOME	REMARKS
I. & H. Caplan Ltd. *v.* Caplan	[1962] 1 W.L.R. 55	Landlord and Tenant—Business Tenancy—Date for determination of extent of holding.	A.	Reversed in C.A. Leave of Appeal Committee
Collco Dealings Ltd. *v.* C.I.R.	[1962] A.C. 1	Income Tax—Double taxation relief—Whether Irish company a person entitled under any enactment to an exemption from Income Tax.	D.	
Ching Garage *v.* Chingford Corporation	[1961] 1 W.L.R. 470	Highways — Means of access — obstruction of—Highways Act 1959.	D.	Reversed in C.A. Leave of Appeal Committee
Close *v.* Steel Co. of Wales	[1962] A.C. 367	Factory — Dangerous machinery — Duty to Fence—Hand drill—Breaking of revolving bit—Fragments flying out and causing injury—Danger not foreseeable in ordinary course of events.	D.	
*Dingwall (A.P.) *v.* J. Wharton Ltd.	[1961] 2 Ll. R. 213	Personal injuries to person unloading ship—Weight of evidence—Invitor's liability.	A.	Reversed in C.S.
*Gardiner (A.P.) *v.* Motherwell Machinery & Scrap	[1961] 1 W.L.R. 1424	Reparation — Negligence — Master and Servant—Industrial diseases—Dermatitis—Whether contracted in course of his employment.	A.	Reversed in C.S.
†McCann *v.* Attorney-General for Northern Ireland	[1961] N.I. 102	Betting and Lotteries Act (Northern Ireland) 1957—Provision prohibiting bookmaking in premises without a license—Termination of existing business including lawful credit betting—Whether *ultra vires* the Parliament of Northern Ireland as constituting a 'taking of property without compensation' within s. 5 (1) of the Government of Ireland Act 1920—Finance (No. 2) Act (Northern Ireland) 1957—Retrospective legislation giving compensation.	D.	
*I.R.C. *v.* J. B. Hodge (Glasgow)	[1961] 1 W.L.R. 1218	Revenue—Profits Tax—Distribution Charge—Reconstruction of Company —Joint election by transferor and transferee companies—Effect of joint election on liability of transferor and transferee companies to distribution charge.	A.	
Hull Corporation *v.* Clayton (V.O.)	[1963] A.C. 28	Rating — Rateable occupation — Art Gallery—Hereditaments for use by the public as an art gallery—Exclusion of public from parts of hereditament—Whether any beneficial occupation.	D.	Reversed in C.A. (2:1)

NAME OF CASE	REPORTED	SUBJECT-MATTER	OUTCOME	REMARKS
Longhurst v. Guildford Water Board	[1963] A.C. 265	Factory — Definition— Pumping station—'Altering' or 'cleaning' an article—Water—Whether an 'article' —Whether pumping station 'factory'.	D.	
Mitchell v. Ross etc. Taylor-Gooby v. Tarnesby, etc. (5 appeals and 5 cross-appeals in all)	[1962] A.C. 814	Revenue — Income Tax — Medical Specialist — Part-time appointment under National Health Service— Whether appointment an office and, if so, whether expenses not allowable under Schedule 'E' may be deducted under Schedule 'D'.	A. D.	Reversed in part in C.A. ditto
Ostime v. Duple Motor Bodies	[1961] 1 W.L.R. 739	Revenue — Income Tax — Work in progress—Method of valuation—Whether 'on cost' or 'direct cost' method to be applied—Whether any principle involved.	D.	Leave of Appeal Committee
Verdin (Tolle-mache Trustees) v. Coughtrie	[1961] A.C. 880	Revenue—Income Tax—Excess Rents —Land—Royalties of Sandpit—Whether actual or notional receipts taken in making assessment—Whether royalties part of rent.	D.	Reversed in C.A.
Plato Films Ltd. v. Speidel	[1961] A.C. 1090	Libel — Pleading — Evidence in mitigation of damages—Plea of Justification—Intention of Defendant to adduce evidence as to character of Plaintiff.	D.	Reversed in part in C.A Leave of Appeal Committee
*Potec v. Edinburgh Corporation	1964 S.C. (H.L.) 1	Negligence—Master and Servant— Safe system of work—Reasonable care —Failure to provide guard rail on working platform. Evidence—Sufficiency—Opinion evidence of export— Whether corroboration necessary.	D.	Reversed in C.S.
Rye v. Rye	[1962] A.C. 496	Landlord and Tenant—Agreement— Writing—Whether necessary—Lease of three years or under—Freehold owned by two tenants in common— Whether competent for freeholders to grant lease by parol to themselves— 'Conveyance'.	D.	Reversed in C.A. Leave of Appeal Committee
*North of Scotland Hydro-Electric Board v. C.I.R.	1961 S.C. (H.L.) 31	Revenue—Excess Profits Tax—Right of relief in respect of repairs deferred by wartime conditions—Transfer of the rights and liabilities in respect of Excess Profits Tax of electricity undertaking—Whether transfer includes right of relief in respect of deferred repairs.	A. (4:1)	Minority decision

NAME OF CASE	REPORTED	SUBJECT-MATTER	OUTCOME	REMARKS
Scruttons Ltd. v. Midland Silicones	[1962] A.C. 446	Shipping—Bill of Lading—Discharge —Hague Rules—Limitation of liability—Stevedores engaged by carrier—Action against stevedores for admitted negligence—Whether entitled to protection of limitation — Contract—Construction—Implied term—Benefit to third party — Enforcement by third party — Bailment — Bailor or sub-bailment.	D. (4:1)	
Tsakiroglou v. v. Noblee Thorl G.m.b.H.	[1962] A.C. 93	Sale of Goods (c.i.f.)—Non-performance—Alleged frustration due to closing of Suez Canal—Whether shipment prevented by force majeure—Meaning of 'shipment'—effect of finding of fact by I.O.S.A. Board of Appeal that performance via Cape of Good Hope 'was not commercially or fundamentally different' from performance via Suez Canal.	D.	
*White and Carter (Councils) Ltd. v. McGregor	[1962] A.C. 413	Contract — Repudiation — Sum payable under Contract—Whether can be recovered as a debt or only damages at large—Penalty or genuine pre-estimate of damage.	A. (3:2)	Minority decision
Winter v. C.I.R. Re Sutherland dec'd	[1963] A.C. 235	Revenue — Estate Duty — Valuation —Shares—'Contingent liabilities'—Control of company by deceased—Company in receipt of capital allowance in respect of assets leaving expenditure unallowed—Sale by company of assets after death of deceased giving rise to balancing charges—Balancing charges resulting in additional assessments to income tax and profits tax.	A. (3:2)	Minority decision

Judgments delivered in 1962

NAME OF CASE	REPORTED	SUBJECT-MATTER	OUTCOME	REMARKS
Amp Inc. v. Hellermann	[1962] 1 W.L.R. 241	Patent—Application by Plaintiffs in action for infringement to amend Specification.	A. (3:2)	Reversed in part in C.A. Minority decision
Bridge (A.P.) v. Campbell Discount	[1962] A.C. 600	Hire Purchase—Penalty—Minimum payment clause—Termination of hiring by a hirer—No breach of contract —Whether sum payable on exercising option to terminate—Whether hiring was a penalty.	A.	Reversed in C.A.
Glinski (A.P.) v. McIver	[1962] A.C. 726	Malicious prosecution — Reasonable and probable case of prosecution—Lack of honest belief—Appellant's guilt — Evidence — Proper Question —Effect of jury's verdict—Malice—Whether jury's verdict perverse.	D.	Reversed in C.A. Originally granted in f.p.

NAME OF CASE	REPORTED	SUBJECT-MATTER	OUTCOME	REMARKS
Ross Smith v. Ross Smith (A.P.)	[1963] A.C. 280	Nullity — Jurisdiction — Celebration of marriage in England.	A. (5:1)	Reversed in C.A. 7 Law Lords sat
Associated Newspapers v. Dingle	[1964] A.C. 371	Libel and slander—Damages for libel —Libel published elsewhere—Irrelevance—Mitigation—Reputation—No settled bad character—Defamatory matter in Select Committee Report— Subsequent newspaper article—Damages—Joint tortfeasors.	D.	Reversed in part in C.A.
†Bill v. Short Bros. and Harland Ltd.	[1963] N.I. 7	Master and Servant—Negligence— Breach of statutory duty—Knowledge of danger.	A.	(2:1) in C.A. (N.I.)
Br. Commonwealth International Newsfilm Agency Ltd. v. Mahany	[1963] 1 W.L.R. 69	Revenue — Income Tax — 'Annual payments'—Covenant to pay sum equal to company's trading deficit— Tax deducted from sum paid—Whether an 'annual payment'—Profits of trade—Covenant—Payments thereunder to supplement trading receipts —Case I or Case III?	D.	
B.T.C. v. Compensation Appeals Tribunal	Unreported (The Times, 22 February 1962)	Certiorari—Claim for compensation for diminution of emoluments—Reference to Compensation Appeal Tribunal—Correctness of review by Compensating Authority upheld by Compensation Appeal Tribunal.	D.	
Cenlon Finance Co. v. Ellwood	[1962] A.C. 782	Income Tax—Profits of trade—Dividends—Exclusion—Capital profits dividend—Dealer in stocks and shares— Whether dividend taxable as profits.	D.	Reversed in part in C.A.
Central Electricity Generating Board v. Halifax Corporation	[1963] A.C. 785	Limitation of Actions—Action to recover fund transferred on nationalization of electricity undertakings—Decision by Minister on disputed question of fact—Whether time runs from vesting date or from Minister's decision.	D.	Reversed in C.A.
Compania Naviera Aeolus S.A. v. Union of India	[1964] A.C. 868	Shipping—Bill of Lading—Demurrage —Strike after expiration of laydays— Exception of strikes in Centrocon Strike Clause incorporated into Bill of Lading—Effect of Centrocon Strike Clause.	A. (3:2)	Minority decision
C.I.R. v. Littlewoods Mail Order Stores et è contra	[1963] A.C. 135	Revenue — Stamp Duty — Conveyance or transfer on sale—Deed entitled 'Deed of Exchange'—No evidence of preceding contract of sale— Stamp duty—Conveyance or Transfer on Sale—Voluntary Disposition— Ar-	D. D.	

NAME OF CASE	REPORTED	SUBJECT-MATTER	OUTCOME	REMARKS
		rangement between freeholder and leaseholder and wholly-owned subsidiary of leaseholder—New lease from freeholder to leaseholder, to wholly-owned subsidiary.		
C.I.R. v. Henry Ansbacher & Co.	[1963] A.C. 191	Revenue — Stamp duty — Agreement for Sale—Guarantee of part of purchase price—Whether guarantee 'mortgage, bond, debenture, covenant . . . (1) Being the only or principal or primary security . . .'.	D.	(2:1) in C.A.
Rolls Royce Ltd. v. Jeffrey	[1962] 1 W.L.R. 425	Income Tax—Excess Profits Tax—Profits Tax—Excess Profits Levy—Capital or income receipt—Sale of 'know-how'—Lump sum receipts—Whether receipts of a capital nature.	D.	Reversed in C.A.
*Duchess of Argyll v. Duke of Argyll	1962 S.C. (H.L.) 88	Divorce—Amendment of Record.	A.	(2:1) in C.S.
Griffiths v. J.P. Harrison (Watford) Ltd.	[1963] A.C.1	Income Tax — Dividend-stripping — Business of merchant till 1953-4—Loss to carry forward—Purchase of shares in company—Dividend received from subsidiary—Loss on sale of shares—Whether trade of share-dealing carried on.	D. (4:1)	(2:1) in C.A.
*McWilliams (A.P.) v. Sir William Arrol & Co. Ltd.	[1962] 1 W.L.R. 295	Negligence—Master and Servant—Whether breach of duty caused accident—Duty to provide safety belts—Liability of employer—Duty to ensure safety — Whether breach of duty caused accident—Provision of safety belts.	D.	
Moore v. Lea	Unreported	Landlord and Tenant—Lease—Forfeiture—Writ claiming possession—Service of Writ—Whether irrevocable election to determine tenancy—Whether judgment in case necessary—Whether proof of breach necessary—Assignment of Lease or guarantee for rent—Defence of non est factum—No representation—Innocent misrepresentation.	D.	Leave of Appeal Committee. Appellant in person
Pilkington v. C.I.R.	[1964] A.C. 612	Trusts—Power of advancement—Exercise of power—Statutory power—fund held on trust for beneficiary for life and after his death for such of his children or remoter issue as he should appoint—Settlement for the benefit of infant child of beneficiary—Advance-	A.	Reversed C.A.

NAME OF CASE	REPORTED	SUBJECT-MATTER	OUTCOME	REMARKS
		ment of moiety of infant's expectant share on trusts of new settlement—Avoidance of death duties—Perpetuity Rule—Power of advancement—Power used for resettlement—Application of perpetuity rule.		
Fairweather v. St. Marylebone Property Co.	[1963] A.C. 510	Limitation of Action—Recovery of land—Squatters' title—Title acquired against lessee—Surrender of Lease—Merger of lease in freehold—Whether freeholder entitled immediately to re-enter.	D. (3:1)	Reversed in C.A. (2:1)
Knoll International v. Parker-Knoll	[1962] R.P.C. 265	Trade Mark—Passing-Off—Form of Injunction.	D. (3:2×½)	Reversed in part in C.A. One partial dissent
S.W. Gas Board v. Hickin	Unreported	Compensation to officers of former gas undertakers — 'retiring age' — 'expectation of pension'—loss of employment—loss or diminution of pension rights—substantive and residual compensation.	A.	One part dissent in C.A.
Sparrow v. Fairey Aviation Co. Ltd.	[1964] A.C. 1019	Factory—Dangerous machinery (fencing)—Tool held by operator—contact with—Whether duty to fence against —Operator injured by tool coming into contact with machine.	D. (4:1)	(2:1) in C.A.
*Thompson (A.P.) v. Glasgow Corporation	1962 S.C. (H.L.) 36	Process – Amendment – Competency – Reclaiming motion—Motion for leave to amend record.	D.	
*Thomson v. Thomson	1962 S.C. (H.L.) 28	Succession — Will — Construction — Nomination to share in partnership—Universal bequest to widow.	D. (4:1)	(3:1) Reversal in C.S.
Wigley (A.P.) v. British Vinegars	[1964] A.C. 307	Window cleaner—Factory—Whether secure foothold and handhold provided by ladder.	D.	Reversed in C.A.
Solihull Corporation v. Gas Council	[1962] 1 W.L.R. 583	Rating—Rateable occupation—Gas research station—Area gas board conducting research for Gas Council.	D.	Reversed in C.A. Leave of Appeal Committee

Judgments delivered in 1963

NAME OF CASE	REPORTED	SUBJECT-MATTER	OUTCOME	REMARKS
N. V. 'Amsterdam' v. Union of India	[1963] 2 Ll. R. 336	Carriage of goods by sea—Hague Rules—Whether due diligence exercised to make ship seaworthy—Lloyds continuous survey—Nature of obligation—Court of Appeal—Power to reverse Trial Judge's findings of fact.	A.	Reversed in C.A. (2:1)

NAME OF CASE	REPORTED	SUBJECT-MATTER	OUTCOME	REMARKS
Associated Newspapers *v.* Registrar of Restrictive Trading Agreements	[1964] 1 W.L.R. 31	Restrictive Trade Practices—Court—Jurisdiction—Termination of Agreement before Reference.	D.	(2:1) in C.A.
*Boyd *v.* Cole-Hamilton	1963 S.C. (H.L.) 1	Reparation—Title to sue—Action of damages for personal injuries at instance of cedent and assignee. Reparation—Collision between motor car and motor cyclists—Assignation of passenger's claim to car owner upon payment—Subsequent action by cedent and assignee against motor cyclist.	A.	
*Cleisham *v.* British Transport Commission	1964 S.C. (H.L.) 8	Evidence—Corroboration—Evidence of pursuer alone.	A. (3:2)	Reversed in C.S. Minority decision
C. H. W. (Huddersfield) Ltd. *v.* C.I.R.	[1963] 1 W.L.R. 767	Revenue — Surtax — Company — Subsidiary Company—Sale of Shares three days before end of accounting period—Shares sold to two companies—Direction that company's income be treated as original members' income—Whether a 'subsidiary company'.	A. (4:1)	Minority decision
Cartledge (A.P.) *v.* E. Jopling & Sons Ltd.	[1963] A.C. 758	Limitation of action—Negligence—Injury caused by acts outside statutory period—Injury first discovered within statutory period—When cause of action accrues—Whether damage must be ascertainable—pneumoconiosis.	D.	
Church of Latter-Day Saints *v.* Henning	[1964] A.C. 420	Rating—Religion—Places of 'public religious worship'—Exemption—Mormon temple certified as place of religious worship—Entry restricted to selected class of worshippers—public not admitted to building—Whether building a 'church hall, chapel hall or similar building used in connection with . . . place of public religious worship'.	D.	Reversed in C.A.
C.I.R. *v.* Coutts & Co.	[1964] A.C. 1393	Revenue — Estate Duty — 'Surviving spouse' exemption—derivative settlement—Duty paid on death of first life tenant — Subsequent settlement of limited interests in settled estates—Passing of limited interests on death.	D.	(2:1) in C.A.
C.I.R. *v.* Jamieson	[1964] A.C. 1445	Surtax—Settlement—Special power to appoint whole fund to one of class of beneficiaries absolutely.	A.	Reversed in C.A. (2:1)

NAME OF CASE	REPORTED	SUBJECT-MATTER	OUTCOME	REMARKS
C.I.R. v. Lord Rennell	[1964] A.C. 173	Estate Duty — Gift *inter vivos*—Settlement made on marriage of Settlor's daughter — Discretionary trusts for large class including daughter and family — Whether settlement 'made in consideration of marriage'.	D. (3:2)	Conditions of leave waived by Appeal Committee
East Coast Amusement Co. v. British Transport Commission	[1965] A.C. 58	Landlord and Tenant—Business premises (security of tenure)—Terms of new tenancy—Rent—Effects of improvements.	D.	(2:1) in C.A.
Essex C.C. v. Essex Incorporated Congregational Church Union	[1963] A.C. 808	Town Planning—Purchase notice by owner—Prescribed limit—Church affected by highway control line—Valuation list entry 'exempt'—Counter-notice—Grounds of objection—no allegation that claimant's interest did not qualify for protection—No jurisdiction in Lands Tribunal to determine point of law.	Declined jurisdiction	
Faramus (A.P.) v. Film Artistes' Assn.	[1964] A.C. 925	Trade Union—Membership—Rules—Restraint of Trade—no person 'convicted in a Court of Law of a criminal offence' eligible for membership—Conviction in Jersey in 1948 discovered in 1958.	D.	Reversed in C.A. (2:1)
*Frasers (Glasgow) Bank v. C.I.R.	1963 S.C. (H.L.) 18	Revenue — Income Tax — Director's emoluments—Schedule 'E'—Benefits in kind—Director in occupation of Company's house—Repairs carried out by the Company.	D.	(2:1) in C.S.
Gill (A.P.) v. Donald Humberstone	[1963] 1 W.L.R. 929	Building — Safety Regulations — 'Working Place'—Meaning—Ladder—Workmen using interlocked ladders to paint roof—No guard rails or toe boards—Workman's fall from roof while stepping off ladder.	D.	Reversed in C.A.
Gollins (A.P.) v. Gollins (A.P.)	[1964] A.C. 644	Divorce—Cruelty—Indirect conduct—Husband's failure to maintain his family and involving wife in debts—Conduct not actuated by desire to injure wife—Not amounting to cruelty in normal sense of the word.	D. (3:2)	Reversed in C.A. (2:1)
Hedley Byrne & Co. v. Heller & Partners	[1964] A.C. 465	Negligence—Duty to take care—Statements—References given by bank honestly but without due care—No special relationship between inquirer and bank giving rise to duty of care—Whether bank liable for negligent reference—Whether duty owed by bank to take reasonable care—Effect of reference given without responsibility.	D.	

NAME OF CASE	REPORTED	SUBJECT-MATTER	OUTCOME	REMARKS
*Hughes (A.P.) v. Lord Advocate	[1963] A.C. 837	Negligence — Liability — Foreseeability of accident—Whether accident and injuries of a type which could reasonably be foreseen. Trespasser—Open manhole in road covered by shelter tent—Boys entering tent and letting fall paraffin lamp in manhole causing explosion where one boy injured.	A.	(3:1) in C.S.
*Luke v. C.I.R.	[1963] A.C. 557	Revenue — Income Tax — Director's Emoluments—Schedule 'E'—Benefits in kind—Director in occupation of Company's house—Repairs carried out by the Company.	A. (4:1)	Reversed in C.S.
†N. Ireland Hospitals Authority v. Whyte	[1963] 1 W.L.R. 882	Contract—Construction—Incorporation of document in common form.	A.	Reversed in C.A. (N.I.) (2:1)
Official Solicitor v. K. (A.P.)	[1965] A.C. 201	Infant—Ward of Court—Evidence—Confidential reports—Statements by guardian *ad litem*—Official Solicitor—Disclosure—Whether parties entitled to disclosure.	A.	Reversed in C.A.
Rae v. Lazard Investment Co. Ltd.	[1963] 1 W.L.R. 555	Income Tax—Share held in overseas company—Distribution by overseas company of shares in another overseas company—Whether income arising from overseas possessions.	D.	Reversed in C.A.
Ridge (A.P.) v. Baldwin	[1964] A.C. 40	Power of Watch Committee to dismiss Chief Constable for misconduct—Whether power to be exercised in accordance with natural justice.	A. (4:1)	Leave of Appeal Committee Minority decision
*Robertson v. John White & Son	1963 S.C. (H.L.) 22	Negligence—Master and Servant—Fault of fellow workmen—Whether evidence of facts and circumstances sufficient to corroborate pursuer's evidence.	A.	Reversed in C.S.
Rubber Improvements v. Associated Newspapers	[1964] A.C. 234	Libel and slander—Justification—Suspicion of crime—Statement that Fraud Squad inquiring into affairs of limited company—Ordinary meaning of words admitted to be defamatory, but justified—Proof of Police inquiry in progress at date of report—Whether justification—Whether words reasonably capable of meaning plaintiffs guilty of fraud.	D. (4:½)	Reversed in C.A.

NAME OF CASE	REPORTED	SUBJECT-MATTER	OUTCOME	REMARKS
Simpson's Motor Sales (London) v. Hendon Corporation	[1964] A.C. 1088	Compulsory purchase—Compulsory Purchase order—Notice to treat—Validity — Changed circumstances — Order for acquisition of land 'for purposes of . . . Part V of Housing Act 1936'—Specific plan for development of owner's site—Provisional compensation agreed at current values —Delay in completion.	D.	Reversed in C.A.
Staffordshire Coal & Iron v. Brogan & C.I.R. (2 Appeals)	[1963] 1 W.L.R. 905	Revenue—Income tax—Capital or income receipt—Insurance premiums repaid—Mutual insurance company—Liquidation—Distribution of accumulated premiums to members—Whether taxable as income.	A. (4:1)	Reversed in C.A. (2:1)
*Stirlingshire and Falkirk Water Board v. Grangemouth	1963 S.C. (H.L.) 49	Statute — Construction — Meaning of 'Burgh' — Water Supply — Water Board excluded from 'Burgh of . . . '.	D. (4:1)	
Vizor v. Multi-Spring	Unreported	Appeal—Master and Servant—Trial by Judge alone—Demonstration by Plaintiff of method of working—Finding by Judge (a) as to what Plaintiff was doing and (b) that Defendants negligent—Power of Appellate Court to reverse both findings—Test of reasonable foreseeability of accident.	D.	Reversed in C.A. Leave of Appeal Committee
Welford Gravels v. De Voil	[1965] A.C. 34	Income Tax—Schedule 'A'—Part of farm including a gravel pit sold—Gravel pit more intensively exploited —Additional Schedule 'A' assessment in respect of part of farm sold—Whether fresh separate valuation or apportioned part of annual value of whole farm for preceding year.	D.	Reversed in C.A. (2:1)
H. West & Sons v. Shephard (A.P.)	[1964] A.C. 326	Damages—Personal injuries—Loss of amenities—Knowledge of loss—Incapacity to enjoy damages—Loss of happiness—Permanent brain injury—Slight degree of consciousness—bias of assessment.	D. (3:2)	
Williams (A.P.) v. Williams (A.P.)	[1964] A.C. 698	Husband and Wife—Cruelty—Insanity as defence—M'Naughten Rules.	A. (3:2)	(2:1) in C.A. Minority decision
Cape of Good Hope Motor Ship Co. Ltd. v. Ministry of Agriculture, Fisheries and Food	[1963] A.C. 691	Shipping — Charter Party — Cargo—Alternative cargo—Loading of intended cargo delayed—Duty of charterer to exercise alternative cargo option—Burden of proving that alternative cargo could have been shipped—Demurrage—Exceptions Clause—	A.i.p.	One part-dissent in C.A.

NAME OF CASE	REPORTED	SUBJECT-MATTER	OUTCOME	REMARKS
		Charterer excused if loading of the cargo or the intended cargo delayed by *force majeure*—strikes or any other hindrance of whatsoever nature beyond the charterer's control—Strike at nominated port.		
		Judgments delivered in 1964		
Dorman Long (Steel) *v.* Bell	[1964] 1 W.L.R. 333	Master and servant—Personal injuries caused to servant in course of employment by tripping or slipping on objects on floor—Causation and contributory negligence.	D.	Leave of Appeal Committee
*Kelly (A.P.) *v.* Cornhill Insurance	[1964] 1 W.L.R. 158	Motor car insurance for benefit of third party—Enforceability by third party after death of insurer.	A. (3:2)	Minority decision (3:6)
*Fairfield Shipbuilding & Engineering *v.* Hall	[1964] 1 Ll. R. 73	Negligence—Master and Servant— Breach of Statutory Duty—All floors to be kept free from any obstruction and from any substance likely to cause persons to slip.	A. (3:2)	Minority decision (3:6)
*McCutcheon (A.P.) *v.* David Macbrayne Ltd.	[1964] 1 W.L.R. 125	Contract — Carriage — Ship —Condition of Carriage excluding carrier's liability — Evidence that consignor knew that conditions applied but was ignorant of their purport.	A.	Reversed in C.S.
†Irwin *v.* White, Tomkins and Courage Ltd.	[1964] 1 W.L.R. 387	Master and servant—Negligence— Breach of Statutory Duty.	A.	Reversed in C.A. (N.I.) (2:1)
English Electric *v.* Musker & C.I.R. (2 Appeals)	(1964) 41 T.C. 556	Sales of manufacturing technique whether lump sums, capital or income —Whether trading receipts of Appellant Company's trade.	D.	
*Hunter *v.* Fox	1964 S.C. (H.L.) 95	Land and heritages — Servitude of Prospect — Reservation in recorded Disposition.	A.	Reversed in C.S.
*Burmah Oil Co. *v.* Lord Advocate (4 Appeals) *Lord Advocate *v.* Burmah Oil Co. (4 Cross-Appeals)	[1965] A.C. 75	Compensation — War — Royal Prerogative—Denial of private property to the enemy by order of commanding officer in pursuance of Government scorched-earth policy—Limitation of actions.	A. (3:2) D.	Reversed in C.S. ditto
*Gardiner *v.* Admiralty Commissioners	[1964] 1 W.L.R. 590	Negligence—Master and Servant— Safe means of access and safe place of employment.	A.	(2:1) in C.S.

APPENDICES

NAME OF CASE	REPORTED	SUBJECT-MATTER	OUTCOME	REMARKS
C.I.R. v. Binns	(1964) 41 T.C. 598	Profits tax—Non-distribution relief—Grouping Notice—Dividend paid by subsidiary company—Direction dividing period of account into two chargeable accounting periods.	A.	Reversed in C.A.
Rendell v. Went	[1964] 1 W.L.R. 650	Income Tax — Income — Perquisites or profits of office or employment—ring expense on defence of director on criminal charge—Payment made primarily for company's benefit—Payment in excess of what director would have paid if defending out of his own resources—Whether whole expenses to be treated as taxable perquisite.	D.	Reversed in C.A.
Ross (A.P.) v. Associated Portland Cement Manufacturers Ltd.	1964 S.C. (H.L.) 102	Factory—Occupiers held negligent and in breach of statutory duty—Whether deceased workman's contributory negligence extinguishes widow's claim.	A.	Leave of Appeal Committee
Chertsey U.D.C. v. Mixnam's Properties	[1965] A.C.735	Town Planning—Caravan site—Conditions of licence—Limitation on local authority's power to impose—Site licence issued subject to 'conditions of tenancy' relating, inter alia, to site rents and security of tenure of caravan dwellers—Whether ultra vires—Whether reasonable—Whether void for uncertainty.	D. (4:½)	Reversed in C.A. One partial dissent
*Waugh (A.P.) v. James K. Allan Ltd.	1964 S.C. (H.L.) 102	Negligence—Accident to pedestrian on pavement—inference to be drawn from proved facts.	D.	(2:1) in C.S.
C.I.R. v. F.S. Securities Ltd.	[1965] A.C. 631	Revenue—Surtax—Controlled Company—Dealer in stocks and shares—Purchase of shares for dividend-stripping—Whether dividends 'investment income'.	A.	
Commissioners of Customs & Excise v. J. & C. Moores	[1964] 1 W.L.R. 817	Revenue—Purchase tax—Valuation of goods—Football pool coupons—Copyright—Tax on the wholesale values of goods in the open market—Only one possible buyer—Whether 'open market' limited by the particular factors of the sale—Copyright—Licence — Statutory licence —Agreement between licensee and owner of copyright—Payment of royalty by licensee—Printing by third party of copyright material under statutory licence.	D.	

NAME OF CASE	REPORTED	SUBJECT-MATTER	OUTCOME	REMARKS
*Douglas (A.P.) v. Cunningham (A.P.)	1964 S.C. (H.L.) 112	Process—Jury trial—Motion for new trial.	A.	Reversed in C.S. (2:1)
C.I.R. v. Frere	[1965] A.C. 402	Revenue — Surtax — Total income— 'Short' interest payments—Whether deductible from total income.	A.	Reversed in C.A. (2:1) Leave of Appeal Committee
*Brown v. C.I.R.	[1965] A.C. 244	Income Tax—Earned Income Tax Relief—Solicitor—Client's money placed on deposit receipt—Interest bearing loan of client's money to other clients —Interest retained by Solicitor— Whether interest derived from carrying on of profession.	D.	
De Vigier v. C.I.R.	[1964] 1 W.L.R. 1073	Surtax — Settlement — Settlor's wife a Trustee—Payments to Trustees by settlor's wife to acquire shares—Cross payments by Trustees.	D.	Leave of Appeal Committee
Haley (A.P.) v. London Electricity Board	[1965] A.C. 778	Nuisance—Statutory undertaker, liability of—Highway—Electric undertaking—Excavation in pavement pursuant to statutory powers—Excavation guarded by sloping handle of punner-hammer—Guard sufficient for sighted person—Duty to blind person tripped up by handle and injured— Fall into hole in pavement—Adequately guarded for others.	A.	Leave of Appeal Committee
Imperial Chemical Industries v. Shatwell	[1965] A.C. 656	Negligence—Breach of Statutory Duty —Vicarious Liability—Contributory negligence—Quarry—Testing detonators—Failure by two workmen of equal status to comply with Regulations and written Rules—Both men injured by explosion.	A.	One part dissent in C.A.
†Campbell College v. N.I. Valuation Commissioner	[1964] 1 W.L.R. 912	Valuation—School premises occupied for charitable purposes.	A.	(2:1) in C.A. (N.I.)
Ladbrokes (Football) v. William Hill (Football)	[1964] 1 W.L.R. 273	Copyright—Action for infringement— Literary work—Substantial part— Compilation.	D.	Reversed in C.A. (2:1)
Rookes (A.P.) v. Barnard	[1964] A.C. 1129	Intimidation—Ingredients of tort— Threat to break a contract—Whether criminal or tortious act—Trade dispute—Act harming plaintiff—Threat by members of union to strike unless	A. (Cross-Appeal on damages allowed)	Reversed in C.A.

NAME OF CASE	REPORTED	SUBJECT-MATTER	OUTCOME	REMARKS
		plaintiff fellow-worker removed from employment — Threat to withdraw labour in breach of contracts of employment—Whether defendants protected by Trade Disputes Act 1906—Exemplary damages.		
J. T. Stratford & Son Ltd. v. Lindley (A.P.)	[1965] A.C. 269	Trade dispute—Conspiracy—Predominate motive—Intimidation—Right to strike—Interference with contracts other than contracts of employment.	A.	Reversed in C.A. (2:1)
Godfrey (A.P.) v. Godfrey	[1965] A.C. 444	Husband and Wife—Connivance at Wife's adultery—Husband's genuine desire for reconciliation following the adultery—Reconciliation not achieved —Wife's subsequent adultery with same man—Effect of earlier connivance.	D.	(2:1) in C.A.

Judgments delivered in 1965

NAME OF CASE	REPORTED	SUBJECT-MATTER	OUTCOME	REMARKS
Pfizer Corporation v. Ministry of Health	[1965] A.C. 512	Patent—Crown, use by—'Make, use and exercise'—'Services of the Crown' —Drug—Uses of invention for National Health Service—Charges to out-patients and private in-patients— Whether vending.	D. (3:2)	Reversed in C.A.
*Glasgow Corporation v. Johnstone	[1965] A.C. 609	Local Government—Rating—Exemption from rates—Church Officer's house adjacent to Church—'Occupied by . . . a charity and . . . wholly or mainly used for charitable purposes'.	D. (4:1)	
Davy v. Leeds Corporation	[1965] 1 W.L.R. 445	Housing—Clearance area—Compulsory Purchase Order—Compensation —Assessment—House on part only of clearance area being acquired—'No clearance area' basis—Whether regard should be had to increase of value by clearance of rest of area.	D.	Reversed in C.A.
National Provincial Bank v. Ainsworth (A.P.)	[1965] A.C. 1175	Husband and wife—Matrimonial home—Desertion by husband—Mortgage subsequently—Wife in occupation — Registered land — Whether wife's right an over-riding interest.	A.	Reversed in part in C.A. (2.:1)
Regent Oil Co. v. Strick (2 Appeals)	[1966] A.C. 295	Capital or revenue expenditure—Trading profits of oil company—Payments to secure exclusive sales stations— Sub-leases — Lease arrangements — Whether payments under arrangement for permanent assets.	D.	Leave of Appeal Committee

NAME OF CASE	REPORTED	SUBJECT-MATTER	OUTCOME	REMARKS
A. E. Farr v. Ministry of Transport	Unreported	Contract—I.C.E. Conditions of Contract—Standard Method of Measurement of Engineering Quantities issued by the Institute of Civil Engineers (1953)—Additional excavation carried out by contractor to provide working space during construction of road underpass—Bill of Quantities providing that additional excavation for working space etc. would be paid for under separate items.	A. (3:2)	Reversed in C.A.
Henriksen v. Tallon Ltd. *et è contra*	[1965] R.P.C. 434	Patent infringements—obviousness—Inutility.	A. (4:1) D.	Part reversed in C.A. One partial dissent ditto
Public Trustee v. C.I.R.	[1966] A.C. 520	Revenue — Estate duty — Property passing on death—Similar interest before and after death—Property held on discretionary trusts for life—Deed of variation executed by reversioner for benefit of same discretionary class for life of mother or seven years, whichever was longer.	D. (4:1)	Reversed in C.A.
Westminster Bank Ltd. v. Zang	[1966] A.C. 182	Bill of Exchange—Unindorsed cheque paid by customer into company's account—Whether cheque delivered 'for collection' — Permission to draw against uncleared effects—Whether bank gave value for cheque.	D.	Reversed in C.A.
B. W. Nobes Ltd. v. C.I.R.	[1966] 1 W.L.R. 111	Revenue — Income Tax — Annual payment—Deduction of tax—Whether payment made out of taxable profits or gains or out of capital—Taxable income insufficient to pay both dividends and annual payment—Taxpayer's right to attribute payments to particular income source.	D.	Reversed in C.A.
*J. G. Stein v. O'Hanlon	[1965] A.C. 890	Reparation — Negligence — Breach of Statutory Duty—Clay Mine—Duty on Manager—Whether duty upon manager to provide supports to roadway before firing and subsequent trimming to guard against after effects of shot firing and subsequent trimming.	D.	Reversed in C.S.
Wm. Cory & Son Ltd. v. C.I.R.	[1965] A.C. 1088	Stamp Duty—Conveyance sale—Option agreed.	A.	Reversed in C.A. (2:1)
Minister of Housing and Local Government v. Hartnell	[1965] A.C. 1134	Town Planning—Caravan Site—Conditions of Licence—Existing use rights—Application for site licence—Permission subject to conditions specifically limiting number of caravans on site—Whether derogating from existing rights—Whether conditions valid.	D.	

NAME OF CASE	REPORTED	SUBJECT-MATTER	OUTCOME	REMARKS
*Coats v. C.I.R.	1965 S.C. (H.L.) 45	Husband and wife—Marriage contract—Rights on dissolution of marriage—Divorce—Subsequent remarriage of innocent party—Effect of remarriage on income of marriage contract funds—whether divorce equivalent to predecease.	D. (3:2)	(3:1) in C.S.
Laidler v. Perry	[1966] A.C. 16	Income Tax—Schedule 'E'—Voucher given to employee at Christmas—Whether a benefit in kind.	D.	
Duckering v. Gollan	[1965] 1 W.L.R. 680	Income Tax—Double Taxation—Relief—Change in basis of assessment of overseas tax—New Zealand income tax—Alteration from previous year's to current year's basis—Tax not chargeable on income for last year of old basis.	D.	Reversed in C.A.
British South Africa Co. v. Varty	[1965] A.C. 381	Income Tax—Stock in trade—Investment company's option to subscribe for shares.	A. (4:1)	Reversed in C.A. (2:1)
Deere & Co. v. Harrison, McGregor & Guest Ltd.	[1963] R.P.C. 217	Patent infringement—omnibus claim —Construction.	D.	(2:1) in C.A.
J. Rosenthal & Sons v. Esmail	[1965] 1 W.L.R. 1117	Sale of Goods (c.i.f.)—Description— Rejection—Goods shipped, in one vessel, under two sets of documents each covering half total quantity— Whether buyers entitled to reject goods under one set of documents yet accept goods under other set.	D.	
† Cyril Lord Ltd. v. C.I.R.	(1965) 42 T.C. 463	Excess Profits Levy—Computation of Profits—Value of Stock-in-Trade— Actual Profits arising in the chargeable accounting period.	D.	
Chancery Lane Safe Deposit and Offices Co. Ltd. v. C.I.R.	[1966] A.C. 85	Whether payments of interest made out of taxable profits or out of capital.	D. (3:2)	Reversed in C.A.
Ralli Bros. Ltd. v. C.I.R.	[1966] A.C. 483	Revenue — Estate duty — Settlement —Life interest with grandsons of life tenant absolutely entitled in reversion —Assignment by grandsons of income of fund to life tenant until her death or a specified date whichever later— Death of life tenant before specified date.	A. (4:1)	Reversed in C.A. (2:1)
East Ham Corporation v. Bernard Sunley & Sons	[1966] A.C. 406	Certificate — Whether conclusive — Building contract—R.I.B.A. form— Architects' certificate to be final and conclusive evidence as to sufficiency of	A. (3:2)	Reversed in C.A.

NAME OF CASE	REPORTED	SUBJECT-MATTER	OUTCOME	REMARKS
		work save as regards defects and insufficiencies which 'reasonable examination' would not have disclosed —Defects revealed after end of defects liability period—Whether arbitrator entitled to reopen certificate.		
Cramas Properties v. Connaught Fur Trimmings Ltd.	[1965] 1 W.L.R. 892	Landlord and Tenant—Business premises (security of tenure)—Transitional effect of Act of 1954—Compensation—Order for new tenancy precluded—Assignment of underlease—Assignor's business carried on at premises for eleven years—Assignees carrying on same type of business as assignors—No assignment of goodwill —Termination of tenancy by landlord 18 months after assignment.	A.	(2:1) in C.A.
*M'Glone (A.P.) v. British Railways Board	1966 S.C. (H.L.) 1	Negligence—Failure to take reasonable care—Injury to child climbing electric transformer on property of British Railways Board.	D.	Reversed in C.S.
		Judgments delivered in 1966		
Bishop v. Finsbury Securities	[1966] 1 W.L.R. 1402	Income Tax—'Forward Stripping'— Dealer in shares and securities—Purchase of shares in companies—Price, payable by instalments, to depend on dividends received—Special dividend rights exhausting assets of companies —Tax repayment claim by dealer in respect of loss in value of shares.	A.	(2:1) in C.A.
Vandervell v. C.I.R.	[1967] 2 A.C. 291	Revenue — Surtax — Settlement — Gift of Shares to college subject to option to purchase—Benefit of option granted to trustee company acting as trustee of family settlement — No direction to hold on express trust.	D. (3:2)	
*Smith v. Colvilles Ltd.	Unreported	Negligence — Master and Servant — Cause of accident—Evidence—Sufficiency.	A.	Reversed in C.S. One part-dissent
*Scottish Omnibuses v. Wyngrove (A.P.)	1966 S.C. (H.L.) 47	Negligence — Omnibus — Bus travelling with door open—No central pillar on platform of Bristol Lodekabus— Passenger falling out while bus in motion.	A.	(2:1) in C.S.
*A. & W. Hemphill Ltd. v. Williams (A.P.)	1966 S.C. (H.L.) 31	Reparation — Negligence — Master and Servant—Vicarious liability— Lorry driver taking devious and unauthorized route when accident occurred—Liability of employers.	D.	(3:1) in C.S.

NAME OF CASE	REPORTED	SUBJECT-MATTER	OUTCOME	REMARKS
Minister of Social Security v. Amalgamated Engineering Union	[1967] 1 A.C. 725	Industrial Injury—Medical Appeal Tribunal — Jurisdiction — Scope of Jurisdiction—Finding by statutory authority (Deputy Commissioner) on claim for injury benefit that injured workman suffered personal injury caused by accident—Subsequent application by workman for disablement benefit.	D. (4:1)	Reversed in C.A. (2:1)
Central & District Properties v. C.I.R.	[1966] 1 W.L.R. 1015	Stamp Duty—Acquisition of shares in the capital of a company—Requirement that not less than 90 per cent of the consideration for the acquisition consists of shares in the capital of the acquiring company—Whether 'consideration for acquisition limited to consideration given by or moving from acquiring company'.	D.	Reversed in C.A.
Boardman v. Phipps	[1967] 2 A.C. 46	Trusts—Remuneration of trustee— Special expert work—Complex transaction in company's shares by solicitor to trust and beneficiary—Profit by self-appointed agents—Accountability to beneficiary for profit—Whether agents entitled to remuneration for work done.	D. (3:2)	
Shop & Store Developments v. C.I.R.	[1967] 1 A.C. 472	Stamp Duty—Transfer of Property from one associated company to another in return for fully-paid shares of transferee—Shares then sold to issuing house for cash.	A. (3:2)	Reversed in C.A. Leave of Appeal Committee
Churchill Gear Machines v. National Broach	[1967] 1 W.L.R. 384	Patents—Confidential Information— Practice—Pleading—Scope of inquiry as to damages—Obligation on patent licensee to disclose to licensor 'improvements developed' by licensee— Licensor's right to patent licensee's developments.	D.	Reversed in part in C.A.
Carl-Zeiss-Stiftung v. Rayner & Keeler (Original Appeal) Rayner & Keeler v. Courts (Cross-Appeal)	[1967] 1 A.C. 853	Trade Mark—Passing Off—Carl Zeiss —Existence of plaintiff in East Germany—Res judicata—English Court not bound by perverse foreign judgment. International law—Recognition —Effect—Action begun by English solicitors on behalf of East German organization—Solicitors instructed by governing body of organization— Governing body authorized by government not recognized by H.M. Government—Unrecognized government set up by de jure government.	A. D. (as 'unnecessary')	Reversed in C.A. ditto

NAME OF CASE	REPORTED	SUBJECT-MATTER	OUTCOME	REMARKS
Fluffon v. William Frost & Sons Ltd.	[1968] R.P.C. 508	Preliminary issue—Construction of a licence agreement.	D.	Reversed in C.A. Leave of Appeal Committee
C.I.R. v. Parker (2 Appeals)	[1966] A.C. 141	Revenue — Surtax — Company — Capitalization of accumulated profits —Issue of bonus debentures redeemable after seven years—Redemption— Meaning of 'tax advantage'.	A. (3:2)	Reversed in C.A.
Wheat (A.P.) v. E. Lacon & Co.	[1966] A.C. 552	Occupier's Liability—'Occupation'— Inn—Manager employed by owners of inn—Manager's wife's allowed to take in paying guests in private part of premises—Paying guest killed by fall on staircase in private part.		
Tophams Ltd. v. Earl of Sefton	[1967] 1 A.C. 50	Restrictive Covenant—Construction —'Permit'—Covenant by purchaser, T. Ltd., not to 'cause or permit' land to be used otherwise than for horse-racing, etc.—Covenant binding only during life of vendor and limited so that T. Ltd. not liable for breach after parting with land—Vendor retaining no land capable of being benefited— Contract for sale by T. Ltd. to third party with intention, known to T. Ltd., of using land for housing. Tort— Inducement of breach of contract— Purchase of land for use in breach of restrictive covenant not binding on land—Vendor had covenanted, as purchaser knew, not to cause or permit land to be used otherwise than for horse-racing, etc.	A. (3:2)	(2:1) in C.A.
Bates v. C.I.R.	[1968] A.C. 483	Revenue — Surtax — Settlement — Trust fund—Shares in trading company—Payments by company to settlor of capital sums—Whether company a 'body corporate connected with the settlement'—Reasonable part of company's income distributed in relevant years.	D.	Reversed in C.A.
James v. Secretary of State for Wales	[1968] A.C. 409	Town Planning—Caravan site—'Existing site' application for site licence —Scope and effect of prior grant of planning permission—Whether site licence application thereby excluded— Whether application abandoned— Meaning of 'development'—Material change of use—Caravan site—Increase from one to four caravans—Form of Enforcement notice.	A. (4:1)	One part-dissent in C.A. Leave of Appeal Committee

NAME OF CASE	REPORTED	SUBJECT-MATTER	OUTCOME	REMARKS
Duke of Buccleuch v. C.I.R.	[1967] 1 A.C. 506	Revenue — Estate Duty — Valuation —Land—Real and leasehold property —Large estate comprising diverse holdings—Statutory assumptions to arrive at price which property would fetch in open market 'at the time of the death'.	D.	(2:1) in C.A.
Tradax Export v. Compania Naviera	[1966] 1 Ll. R. 566	Shipping—Charter party—Ship unable to berth through congestion— Subsequent delay by tides—Special Clause in Charter party—Whether time counts during delay by tides.	D.	Reversed in C.A. (2:1)
*Albacora S.R.L. v. Westcott and Laurence Line	1966 S.C. (H.L.) 19	Shipping—Bill of Lading—Delivery of Cargo in damaged condition— Damage due to excessive temperature during voyage—Liability of Ship-Owner/Carrier.	D.	Reversed in C.S.
†O'Hagan (A.P.) v. N. Ireland Farmers Bacon Company	Unreported	Master and Servant—Duty to provide plant and equipment.	D.	Jury reversed in C.A. (N.I.) Refused leave in f.p.
Suisse Atlantique Sociéte d'Armement Maritime S.A. v. N.V. Rotterdamsche Kolen Centrale	[1967] 1 A.C. 361	Charter party—Consecutive voyages —Detention—Delays by charterers in loading and discharging cargoes preventing vessel performing more voyages in charter time—Whether shipowners entitled to damages (less demurrage payments) for loss of further freights—Effect of deliberate breach by charterers.	D.	Leave of Appeal Committee
Coathew Investments Ltd. v. C.I.R.	[1966] 1 W.L.R. 716	Surtax—Investment Company—Controlled investment company—Actual income from all sources—Deductions —Payments to charity under seven-year covenant.	D. (4:1)	
McClelland, Pope & Langley v. Howard	Unreported (noted at [1968] 1 All E.R. 569)	Board of Trade Inquiry under s. 165 (b), Companies Act 1948—Certiorari to quash report—Prohibition— Compellable and non-Compellable witnesses—Incriminating questions— Necessity to answer questions.	D.	Leave of Appeal Committee
Hepburn v. A. Tomlinson (Hauliers)	[1966] A.C.451	Insurance — Bailee — Carrier's insurance under goods in transit policy— Policy describing goods as property of I., in transit, and including loading and unloading—Insurance pursuant to agreement by carrier with I. to effect full comprehensive insurance—Goods stolen after carrier's vehicle arrived at	D.	Leave of Appeal Committee

NAME OF CASE	REPORTED	SUBJECT-MATTER	OUTCOME	REMARKS
		I's premises but before unloading—No negligence by carrier—Whether goods still on risk—Whether carrier could recover in respect of owner's proprietary interest.		
Blyth v. Blyth	[1966] A.C. 643	Divorce—Condonation by husband—Isolated act of sexual intercourse as condonation—Transitional effect of Matrimonial Causes Act 1963—Wife's adultery—Terminated by wife without resumption of cohabitation.		

Judgments delivered in 1967

NAME OF CASE	REPORTED	SUBJECT-MATTER	OUTCOME	REMARKS
*C.I.R. v. Saxone, Lilley & Skinner	[1967] 1 W.L.R. 501	Revenue — Profits — Deductions — Allowances—Industrial building or structure—Building used for storage of shoes.	D.	Reversed in C.S.
*Milne (A.P.) v. Gerard Ltd.	Unreported	Fatal Accident—Fall by deceased down well of hoist shaft—Failure to fit gate within the meaning of the Regulation—Proof of causation.	A.i.p.	(2:1) in C.S.
*C.I.R. v. Brebner	[1967] 2 A.C. 18	Revenue — Tax advantages — Bona fide commercial transaction — Company—Financial arrangements to defeat threatened takeover bid—Purchase of company by group of shareholders—Transaction financed by bank loan—Subsequent reduction and repayment of capital to meet obligations to bank.	D.	
Cleary v. C.I.R.	[1968] A.C. 766	Whether or not tax advantage obtained under s. 28 of the Finance Act 1960.	D.	
Yorkshire Electricity Board v. Naylor	[1968] A.C. 529	Measure of Damages—Loss of expectation of life—Matters relevant to assessment—Man aged twenty with real prospects of successful and happy life killed instantaneously—Change in value of money since earlier decisions.	A.	Reversed in C.A. (2:1)
Davies Jenkins & Co. v. Davies	[1968] A.C. 1097	Income Tax—Discontinuance of trade—Company subvention agreement between associated companies—Associated Company ceasing to trade.	A. (4:1)	(2:1) in
Indyka (A.P.) v. Indyka (A.P.)	[1969] 1 A.C. 33	Divorce—Foreign decree—Wife domiciled Czechoslovakia — Husband domiciled England—Decree granted wife in Czechoslovakia January 1949—Czechoslovakian decree recognized in England?	D.	Reversed in C.A. (2:1) Leave of Appeal Committee
Price (A.P.) v. Claudgen Ltd.	[1967] 1 W.L.R. 575	Building—Safety regulations—Neon lighting signs—Fixed to cinema—Repair.	D.	

NAME OF CASE	REPORTED	SUBJECT-MATTER	OUTCOME	REMARKS
Britiish Railways Board v. Liptrot	[1969] 1 A.C. 136	Factory — Dangerous Machinery — Mobile crane—Failure to fence—Gap between rotating body and wheel—Injury to workman trapped in gap—Whether mobile crane was machinery.	D.	Reversed in C.A. (2:1)
Garnac Grain Co. Inc. v. Faure & Fairclough Ltd.	[1968] A.C. 1130	Agent—Creation of agency—Agency for entering into contract—Circle of contracts made on same day whereby A. sold goods and subsequently re-bought the goods from another purchaser further down the chain of buyers—Transaction designed by A. for financial reasons—Contracts genuine, not shams.	D.	Reversed in C.A.
*Chalmers Property Investment Co. v. Robson	Unreported	Heritable Property — Servitude — Aqueduct—Identification of subject matter of grant—'Spring or Well'—'Adequate water pipes'.	D.	
Smith v. N.C.B.	[1967] 1 W.L.R. 871	Mines — Railway sidings — Material near track—Material (colliery dirt stack) less than 3 feet from railway line —Duty of manager to see that employee 'required' to pass on foot over material or between it and line can do so safely—Shunter required to uncouple railway wagons at reservoir—Killed by train while walking to reservoir along route beside line.	A.i.p. (3:2×½)	Reversed in C.A. (2:1)
S. v. S.	1967 S.C. (H.L.) 46	Parent and child—Divorce—Access—Access for paternal grandparents.	D.	
Donaghey (A.P.) v. Boulton & Paul	[1968] A.C. 1	Building—Roof work—Sloping surface—Protection against falling down and off roof but not against falling through hole in roof under construction—Liability of contractors to servants of sub-contractors—Employee of sub-contractors falling through gap between purlins of roof—Crawling boards provided but not used—Foreman of sub-contractors present but did not ensure that crawling boards used.	A.	Reversed in C.A.
Beswick (A.P.) v. Beswick (A.P.)	[1968] A.C. 58	Contract—Stranger to contract—Annuitant—Widow of deceased owner of business—Sale of business by deceased on terms under which widow was to be paid weekly sum—Charge on business ancillary to other clauses of contract—Widow not party to contract—Death of deceased.	D.	Reversed in C.A. Leave of Appeal Committee

NAME OF CASE	REPORTED	SUBJECT-MATTER	OUTCOME	REMARKS
*Campbell v. Mackay	1967 S.C. (H.L.) 53	Contract—Specific implement—Sale of heritage together with moveables—Action for implement of sale of heritage only.	D.	
*Nimmo v. Alexander Cowan & Sons Ltd.	[1968] A.C. 107	Factory—Safe place of work—"So far as is reasonably practicable"—Onus of proof.	A. (3:2)	(3:6) Minority decision
*O'Donnell (A.P.) v. Murdoch, McKenzie & Co.	1967 S.C. (H.L.) 63	Negligence—Breach of statutory duty —Duty to provide suitable and sufficient scaffolds—Whether breach of duty caused accident.	A. (3:2)	(3:6) Minority decision
*Scottish Burial Reform and Cremation Society Ltd. v. Glasgow Corporation	[1968] A.C. 138	Charity—Cremation—Remission of rates.	A.	(3:1) in C.S.
White Ltd. v. Tarmac Ltd.	[1967] 1 W.L.R. 1508	Indemnity clause in Contract for hire of plant—Notional transfer of services of Plant operator to hirer of plant—Liability of hirer for negligence of plant operator.	A.	Reversed in part in C.A. Leave of Appeal Committee
et è contra			D.	Reversed in part in C.A.
Koufos v. C. Czarnikow Ltd.	[1969] 1 A.C. 350	Damages — Shipping — Charterparty —Delay in Delivery—Fall in Market —Measure of damage.	D.	Reversed in C.A. (2:1)
Rondel v. Worsley	[1969] 1 A.C. 191	Negligence—Barrister—As advocate —Whether action for negligence lies at suit of client—Basis of barrister's immunity — Solicitor — As advocate—Whether liable to client—Basis for immunity. Public Policy—Whether immunity extends to advisory work unconnected with proceedings in court.	D.	Leave of Appeal Committee
C.I.R. v. Holmden	[1968] A.C. 685	Revenue — Estate Duty — Settlement —Discretionary trust of income terminable on death of named member of discretionary class—Order under Variation of Trusts Act 1958 extending or purporting to extend period of 'discretionary trust during life of that member or 21 years whichever should be the longer—Death of that member within three years—Whether duty payable.	D.	(2:1) in C.A.

NAME OF CASE	REPORTED	SUBJECT-MATTER	OUTCOME	REMARKS
Gartside v. C.I.R.	[1968] A.C. 553	Estate duty — Settlement — Discretionary trust of income—accumulation of surplus income to capital—on death of named member of discretionary class trust of capital and income to his children—Advancement of children 16 months before death.	A.	Reversed in C.A.
Owners 'Miraflores' v. Owners 'George Livanos'	[1967] 1 A.C. 826	Shipping — Collision — Apportionment of Liability—Collision partially consequent grounding of third Ship—All three Ships negligent—Individual assessment of liability of each vessel involved.	A.i.p.	(2:1) in C.A.
Esso Petroleum v. Harper's Garage (Stourport)	[1968] A.C. 269	Restraint of trade—Agreements with oil companies for sale of petrol—Mortgage of garage irredeemable for 21 years with sales tie—Whether agreements in unlawful restraint of trade—Whether reasonable—Whether categories closed — Restrictions falling within doctrine—Whether applicable to covenants in mortgage.	A.i.p.	Reversed in C.A. Leave of Appeal Committee
Almond (V.O.) v. Birmingham Royal Blind Institution	[1968] A.C. 37	Rating — Health — Exempt structure — 'Structure' — Institution for the Blind — Hereditament comprising main building and workshops—Hereditament used as hostel and technical training centre for blind.	D.	Reversed in C.A.
Dietz v. Lennig Chemicals Ltd.	[1969] 1 A.C. 170	Fatal Accident Acts—Practice—Consent order—Acceptance by widow of lump sum on behalf of herself and infant—Widow's remarriage before order drawn up.	D.	Leave of Appeal Committee
*Lord Advocate v. Reliant Tool Co.	[1968] 1 W.L.R. 205	Selective employment payments — Selective Employment Premium — 'Activities falling under any of the minimum list headings shown in the Standard Industrial Classification'.	D.	Statutory requirement of leave: granted by Appeal Committee

Judgments delivered in 1968

NAME OF CASE	REPORTED	SUBJECT-MATTER	OUTCOME	REMARKS
Harper J. Ransburg v. Aerostyle	[1968] R.P.C. 287	Patent—Infringement—Electrostatic spraying—Construction of claim—Whether claim novel method of operation infringed by combination of novel with known integers.	A.	Reversed in C.A.
et è contra			D.	
Padfield v. Minister of Agriculture, Fisheries and Food	[1968] A.C. 997	Agricultural Marketing — Milk Marketing Scheme—Complaint to Minister of Agriculture, Fisheries and Food —Duty of Minister.	A. (4:1)	Reversed in C.A. (2:1)

NAME OF CASE	REPORTED	SUBJECT-MATTER	OUTCOME	REMARKS
Conway (A.P.) v. Rimmer	[1968] A.C. 910	Appeal — Practice — Discovery — Production of documents—Claim of Crown Privilege—Documents withheld from production.	A.	2:1 in C.A.
Rodi & Wienenberger v. Henry Showell	[1969] R.P.C. 367	Patent — Infringement — Expanding Wristwatch Bracelet—Mechanical equivalents — Pith and marrow — Patent valid and infringed.	D. (3:2 × ½)	Reversed in C.A.
Henry Kendall & Sons v. William Lillico & Sons Ltd. v. (3 Appeals) Reported as Hardwick Game Farm v. Suffolk Agricultural Poultry Producers Association	[1969] 2 A.C. 31	Sale of Goods—Implied warranty of suitability—Whether applicable to feeding stuffs for pheasants and partridges—Whether applicable only to specific article sold in original state—Meaning of 'poultry'—Passing of property—Fitness for purpose—Implied condition — Merchantable quality — Contract—Implied term from course of dealing—Whether conditions printed on contract notes sent to buyers in previous dealings could be impliedly incorporated into contract although buyers had never read those conditions.	D. (4:1 × ½)	Reversed in part in C.A. (2:1)
Bersel Manufacturing Co. v. Berry (A.P.)	[1968] 2 All E.R. 552	Company—Life Director—Power to remove other directors—Joint power conferred on two permanent Life Directors—Construction of Articles of Association—Power not conferred by way of joint confidence but for securing the interests of the Life Directors—Whether power exercisable by survivor.	A.	Leave of Appeal Committee. Reversed in C.A. (2:1)
G. W. Thornton & Sons Ltd. v. Parks-Cramer & Co. Ltd.	Unreported	Patent — Infringement — Cleaning devices for textile machinery—Mechanical equipments—Obviousness.	A.	
*I.R.C. v. Carron Company	1967 S.C. (H.L.) 47	Revenue — Income Tax — Profits — Deductions—Application for Supplementary Royal Charter to replace absolute Charter—Actions by Shareholders to delay application for Supplementary Royal Charter—Whether sums spent in compromising litigation obtaining supplementary Royal Charter 'wholly and exclusively expended' for company's trade.	D.	
*University of Strathclyde v. Carnegie Trustees	1968 S.C. (H.L.) 27	Charitable and Educational Trusts—Universities—Trust Fund for benefit of scientific study and research in the Universities of Scotland.	A.	Reversed in C.S.

NAME OF CASE	REPORTED	SUBJECT-MATTER	OUTCOME	REMARKS
Pharmaceutical Society of G.B. *v.* Dickson	[1970] A.C. 403	Corporation—Powers — Professional body—'Safeguard and promote the interests of the members' of professional body—Restrictions on trade activities of members—Restraint of trade—Professional body—Pharmacists—Use of powers to restrict trade activities of members—Non-contractual relationship.	D.	
Gloucestershire C.C. *v.* Richardson (A.P.)	[1969] 1 A.C. 480	Building Contract — Damage —Subcontract—Nominated suppliers—Defective materials supplied—Undetectable defect—Whether main contractor warrants impliedly the fitness of materials supplied by nominated supplier—R.I.B.A. form of contract.	D. (4:1)	Reversed in C.A. (2:1)
Young & Marten Ltd. *v.* McManus Childs Ltd.	[1969] 1 A.C. 454	Building Contract—Breach of Contract—Fitness of materials—Sub-contract for Work and Materials—Defective materials supplied—Materials specified by Contracts, manufactured only by one manufacturer—Specified material obtained, but having undetectable defects, due to faulty manufacture, rendering it unfit for its purpose.	D.	Reversed in C.A.
Branwhite (A.P.) *v.* Worcester Works Finance	[1969] 1 A.C. 552	Hire Purchase—Agency—Payment of deposit to dealer—Whether received by dealer as agents for Finance company—Whether credit given by Finance company to dealer for deposit of sale of vehicle by dealer to Finance company means that Finance company has received deposit.	A.	
Pickering *v.* John Tye & Sons Ltd.	[1968] F.S.R. 563	Patent—Infringement—Obviousness —Plastic sachets.	D.	Leave of Appeal Committee
Campbell *v.* C.I.R.	[1969] 1 A.C. 77	Income Tax—Payment of annual sums to charitable trust—Understanding that sums to be used for purchase of covenantors business—Whether 'annual payments'—Whether applied for charitable purposes only.	D.	Leave of Appeal Committee
Onassis *v.* Vergottis *et è contra*	[1968] 2 Ll. R. 403	Contract — Option — Shares in ship —Whether partly provided money by way of loan or for purchase of shares in ship.	A. (3:2) D.	Reversed in C.A.
Barclays Bank *v.* Quistclose Investments	[1970] A.C. 567	Company—Winding up—Voluntary liquidation—Loan to company for specific purpose of paying dividend—Money paid into separate account at bank—Company's liquidation before payment of dividend—Bank's claim to set off—Payment in of sum borrowed specifically to pay dividend.	D.	Reversed in C.A.

NAME OF CASE	REPORTED	SUBJECT-MATTER	OUTCOME	REMARKS
Whishaw v. Stephens (Re Gulbenkian's Settlements)	[1970] A.C. 508	Trusts—Void for uncertainty—Unascertainable class—Power to appoint to 'persons with whom G. may be residents'—Validity—Power of appointment—Power or trust.	D.	Leave of Appeal Committee. Reversed in C.A.
Avais (A.P.) v. Hartford Shankhouse and District Workingmen's Social Club and Institute Ltd.	[1969] 2 A.C. 1	Gaming — Gaming machine—Guarantee of earnings—Owner of machines agreed to let them at weekly rental to club—Guaranteed that yearly earnings of the machines should not be less than £1,900.	A.	Reversed in C.A. (2:1)
Anisminic Ltd. v. Foreign Compensation Commission	[1969] 2 A.C. 147	Crown Practice — Certiorari — Foreign Compensation Commission—Determination — Construction of Order in Council—Whether error going to jurisdiction — Tribunal's power to determine but not to enforce the liability—Ouster of jurisdiction of court — Statute — Determination by statutory commission—Not to 'be called in question in any court of law'.	A. (3:2)	Reversed in C.A.

CRIMINAL APPEALS

NAME OF CASE	REPORTED	SUBJECT-MATTER	OUTCOME	REMARKS
		Judgments delivered in 1952		
Harris v. D.P.P.	[1952] A.C. 694	Evidence — System — Joinder of charges—Eight counts alleging similar offences of office-breaking—Acquitted on first seven counts—Defence of coincidence on eighth count—Application for separate trials—Admissibility by the court of evidence on other counts.	A. (4:1)	
		Judgments delivered in 1954		
Davies v. D.P.P.	[1954] A.C. 378	Murder—Fight between groups of youths — Evidence of system — Whether applicable.	D.	L.C. presided
Bedder v. D.P.P.	[1954] 1 W.L.R. 1119	Homicide — Provocation — Woman jeering at accused's impotence—Whether disability to be taken into account.	D.	L.C. presided
		Judgments delivered in 1957		
B.O.T. v. Owen	[1954] A.C. 602	Conspiracy to commit a Common Law Misdemeanour, to defraud, and to utter forged documents.	D.	Reversed in part in C.A.
		Judgments delivered in 1958		
D.P.P. v. Head	[1959] A.C. 83	Unlawful carnal knowledge of mental defective—Invalidity of detaining order.	D. (4:1)	Reversed in C.C.A.

NAME OF CASE	REPORTED	SUBJECT-MATTER	OUTCOME	REMARKS
		Judgments delivered in 1959		
De Demko v. Home Secretary	[1959] A.C. 654	Jurisdiction — Criminal cause or matter—Fugitive offender—Habeas corpus.	D.	
		Judgments delivered in 1960		
D.P.P. v. Smith	[1961] A.C. 290	Homicide—Intention to kill or cause grievous bodily harm—Presumption of intention—Extent of application— Test of reasonable man.	A.	Reversed in C.C.A.
Welham v. D.P.P.	[1961] A.C. 103	Fraud—Intent to defraud—Forgery— Uttering forged documents with intent to defraud—Whether economic loss necessary.	D.	C.C.A. sat with five
		Judgments delivered in 1961		
Payne v. Bradley	[1962] A.C. 343	Whether tombola 'for purposes other than purposes of private gain'.	D. (3:2)	From Div. Ct.
†Bratty v. Attorney-General (N.I.)	[1963] A.C. 386	Defence of automatism—Evidence— Psychomotor epilepsy.	D.	
Sykes v. D.P.P.	[1962] A.C. 528	Misprision of felony—Existence of offence—Whether active concealment a necessary constituent.	D.	Sentence reduced by C.A.A.
Shaw v. D.P.P.	[1962] A.C. 220	Obscene libel—Conspiracy to corrupt public morals—Living off immoral earnings.	D. (4:1 × ½)	Reversed in C.C.A.
†Attorney-General (N.I.) v. Gallagher	[1963] A.C. 349	Murder—Defence of insanity—M'-Naghten rules—Defect of reason from disease of the mind—Psychopath with tendencies of violence—Whether voluntary consumption of intoxicating liquor contributory to outburst of violence relevant evidence of insanity.	A.	Reversed in C.A.A. (N.I.) Leave of Appeal Committee
		Judgments delivered in 1962		
Chandler v. D.P.P.	[1964] A.C. 763	Evidence — Admissibility — Official Secrets Act 1911.	D.	
Rumping v. D.P.P.	[1964] A.C. 814	Evidence—Admissibility of letter to wife—Privilege.	D. (4:1)	Leave of Appeal Committee
Schtraks v. Govt. of Israel	[1964] A.C. 556	Habeas Corpus—Extradition Act 1870 —What constitutes offence of a political character—Jurisdiction of magistrate in committing fugitive offender to await return.	D.	From Div. Ct.
Zacharia v. Republic of Cyprus	[1963] A.C. 634	Fugitive offender — Jurisdiction — Whether court entitled to take cognisance of political character of application for return of offender—Fugitive Offenders Act 1881, s. 10.	D. (4:1)	Leave of Appeal Committee. From Div. Ct.

NAME OF CASE	REPORTED	SUBJECT-MATTER	OUTCOME	REMARKS
Cox v. Army Council	[1963] A.C. 48	Military Law—Civil offence committed abroad—Driving without due care and attention in Germany—Whether civil offence within meaning of Army Act.	D.	From C.M.A.C.
Jones v. D.P.P.	[1962] A. C. 635	Murder—Admissibility of evidence.	D.	

Judgments delivered in 1963

Fisher v. Raven *et é contra*	[1964] A.C. 210	'Obtaining' credit by fraud—Intent to perform service—Debtors Act 1869—Bankruptcy Act 1914.	A. D.	Reversed in part in C.C.A. ditto

Judgments delivered in 1964

Vane v. Yiannopoullos	[1965] A.C. 486	Licensing—Whether knowledge of servant can be imputed to master.	D.	Leave of Appeal Committee (From Div. Ct.)
Connelly v. D.P.P.	[1964] A.C. 1254	*Autrefois acquit*—Issue estoppel. Murder conviction quashed—Recharged with robbery.	D.	Sentence reduced in C.C.A.
Midland & Low Moor Iron and Steel Co. Ltd. v. Cross	[1965] A.C. 343	Factory—Duty to fence—Whether construction of machine and material a danger—Dangerous Machine (Fencing).	D.	Reversed in Div. Ct.
Myers v. D.P.P.	[1965] A.C. 1001	Hearsay—Manufacturers' evidence—Admissibility of evidence.	A. but proviso applied (3:2)	
Rosenbaum v. Burgoyne	[1965] A.C. 430	Gaming—One-arm bandits—Multiple stakes—Fruit Machine—Betting and Gaming Act 1960.	A.	Leave of Appeal Committee from Div. Ct.
Metropolitan Police Commissioner v. Hammond	[1965] A.C. 810	Habeas corpus—Fugitive offender—Jurisdiction of Magistrate in respect of endorsement of warrants from Ireland.	D.	From Div. Ct. (2:1). Leave of Appeal Committee

Judgments delivered in 1965

Murdoch v. Taylor	[1965] A.C. 574	Criminal Evidence Act—Character—evidence of co-accused—Right to cross-examine—True construction of words 'has given evidence against'—Criminal Evidence Act 1898.	D. $(4:1 \times \frac{1}{2})$	From Div. Ct.
Hammond v. Hall & Ham River Ltd.	[1965] A.C. 1049	Road Traffic — Goods vehicle — Licence—'C' carrier's licence—Sand and gravel operators—Necessity to fill in excavated pit—Rubbish obtained from builders—Payment by builders for removal of rubbish from building site—Rubbish carried in 'C'	D.	From Div. Ct.

NAME OF CASE	REPORTED	SUBJECT-MATTER	OUTCOME	REMARKS
		licence vehicle — Whether rubbish 'goods . . . used . . . in the course of a trade or business' carried on by the operators — Whether 'carriage of goods for hire or reward'.		
Smith v. Desmond	[1965] A.C. 960	Criminal Law—Verdict—Alternative offence—Indictment for robbery with violence—Whether alternative verdict of simple larceny permissible.	A.	Reversed in part in C.C.A.
Toohey v. Metropolitan Police Commissioner	[1965] A.C. 595	Magistrates — Summary trial — Election of trial by jury—Assault on police constable in execution of his duty—Whether accused entitled to claim trial by jury.	A.	Leave of Appeal Committee
Swain v. D.P.P.	[1965] A.C. 591	Definition of 'affray'—Whether 'public place' essential—Precedent.	D.	L.C. presided
Armstrong v. D.P.P.	[1965] A.C. 1262	Gaming—Lottery conducted by club-Postal bingo—Possibility of members choosing numbers on joining club—Choice of numbers confirmed after joining—Draw taking place in private room of club premises—Supervision of draw by Chartered Accountants—Subsequent broadcast as though draw taking place.	D.	From Div. Ct. Leave of Appeal Committee

Judgments delivered in 1966

NAME OF CASE	REPORTED	SUBJECT-MATTER	OUTCOME	REMARKS
Commissioners of Customs & Excise v. Harz and Power	[1967] 1 A.C. 760	Evidence — Confession — Admission tending to establish guilt—Admissibility—Whether oral admission made in consequence of a threat to prosecute for a statutory offence should be received in evidence.	D.	Reversed in C.A. (2:1)
J. & F. Stone Lighting & Radio v. Haygarth	[1968] A.C. 157	Factory—Repairs carried out in shop —Whether premises a factory.	D.	From Div. Ct.
Toohey v. Woolwich Justices	[1967] 2 A.C. 1	Magistrates—Election of trial by jury —Assault on police punishable summarily.	D.	From Div. Ct. Leave of Appeal Committee
Verrier v. D.P.P.	[1967] 2 A.C. 195	Length of sentence for conspiracy.	D.	
Armah v. Government of Ghana	[1968] A.C. 192	Fugitive offender—Whether "strong or probable presumption" offence committed.	A.	From Div. Ct.

Judgments delivered in 1967

NAME OF CASE	REPORTED	SUBJECT-MATTER	OUTCOME	REMARKS
Churchill v. Walton	[1967] 2 A.C. 224	Crime—Conspiracy to commit absolute offence—*Mens rea* and requisite knowledge for agreement to do unlawful act.	A.	

NAME OF CASE	REPORTED	SUBJECT-MATTER	OUTCOME	REMARKS
Athanassiadis v. Govt. of Greece	[1971] A.C. 282	Extradition—Final judgment in default—Conviction in absence after service of process—Whether contrary to natural justice—Relevance—Whether conviction for contumacy—Anglo-Greek Extradition Treaty.	D.	From Div. Ct. Leave of Appeal Committee

Judgments delivered in 1968

NAME OF CASE	REPORTED	SUBJECT-MATTER	OUTCOME	REMARKS
Adcock v. Wilson	[1969] 2 A.C. 326	Whether all the persons playing the first hand of a Bingo Session in each of about 500 Bingo Clubs could in law be playing at the same time a game of Bingo with each other.	D.	From Div. Ct.
Crickitt v. Kursaal Casino	[1968] 1 W.L.R. 53	Unlawful gaming—Roulette—Contrary to s. 32 (4) of the Betting, Gaming and Lotteries Act 1963.	A.	Quashed by Div. Ct.
Selvey v. D.P.P.	[1970] A.C. 304	Evidence — Cross-examination — Discretion of judge to admit previous record—Whether discretion unfettered—Whether general rule limiting exercise against defence—Defendant's refusal to admit or deny previous record—Whether tantamount to admission—No warning to jury that record not formally proved.	D.	
Fox v. Adamson	[1970] A.C. 552	Gaming—Amusements with prizes—Premises where gaming lawfully conducted—Additional gaming facilities after grant of permit—Whether grant of permit imposition of separate code.	D.	Leave of Appeal Committee
Warner v. Metropolitan Police Commissioner	[1969] 2 A.C. 256	Drugs—Defendant in possession of box which he knew contained something—Whether defence that he did not know it contained drugs—Drugs (Prevention of Misuse) Act 1964, s. 1 (1).	D.	
S. of S. for Defence v. Warn	[1970] A.C. 394	Military Law—Navy—Civil offence—Gross indecency between men one under 21—Whether civil offence within meaning of Naval Discipline Act 1957—Consent of Director of Public Prosecutions to proceedings—Whether procedural requirement or complete nullity.	D.	Reversed by C-M.A.C.
D.P.P. v. Ottewell	[1970] A.C. 642	Crime — Sentence — Extended sentence — Imprisonment — 'Extended term of imprisonment'—Treatment of offenders—Release on licence.	A.	Reversal in part by C.A. (Crim. Div.)

NAME OF CASE	REPORTED	SUBJECT-MATTER	OUTCOME	REMARKS
Cronin v. Grierson	[1968] A.C. 895	Gaming—Machine on premises in respect of which permit granted by local Authority—Games playable by insertion of coin or token into machine—Machine operating at random but winning of jackpot enabling player to win further similar jackpots at odds favouring player on same machine for same stake.	A.	From Div. Ct. Leave of Appeal Committee
McCollom v. Wrightson	[1968] A.C. 522	Gaming—Bingo—Licensed premises —Free bingo—No stake hazarded and free prizes—Whether 'gaming' taking place on premises—Whether members of public playing for 'winnings' in currency or money's worth.	D.	From Div. Ct. Leave of Appeal Committee

APPEALS WITHDRAWN, ABANDONED etc.

Note:

THESE cases appear in the House of Lords Journals as having been presented for appeal but did not reach the stage of a hearing by the Appellate Committee. One can only speculate as to why some of them did not proceed beyond the point of presentation: in some cases (particularly where the Journal indicates that the appellant had been refused leave to appeal *in formâ pauperis*) we may assume that pecuniary resources were inadequate to sustain the heavy cost of appealing. In some instances the parties may have settled out of court and in others the optimism which sustained the appellant in his original application for leave to appeal may have evaporated as the day for setting down the appeal drew near. The word 'abandoned' merely denotes that the entries in the Journals relating to an appeal came to an abrupt halt without discernible cause.

Abbreviations:

In f.p.	*in formâ pauperis*	*	denotes Scottish Appeal
A.C.	Appeal Committee	†	denotes Northern Irish Appeal
A.P.	Assisted Person		

Presented

29 Jan. 1952   Abbott *v.* L.C.C.—Proceedings stayed—Abandoned.

1952   Allmanna Svenska Electrisca Arktieboleget *v.* Burntisland Shipbuilding Co. Ltd.

10 June 1952   D. C. Thomson & Co. Ltd. *v.* Deakin—Abandoned.

*29 Jan. 1952   Webb-Bowen *v.* Burn-Murdoch (*et è contra*)—Abandoned.

*29 Jan. 1952   Macdonald *v.* Burn-Murdoch—Abandoned.

22 Oct. 1951   Portland Plastics Ltd. *v.* Mayor etc. of Dover—Withdrawn by leave 15 May 1952.

20 Oct. 1953   Finnegan *v.* Cementation Co. Ltd.—Given leave to appeal in f.p. then abandoned.

25 Nov. 1952   Lloyd *v.* Aveling—Set down 19 Feb. 1953—Withdrawn by leave 3 Nov. 1953.

2 Dec. 1952   May *v.* C.I.R.—Abandoned.

*28 Apr. 1954   Haldane *v.* C.I.R.—Proceedings stayed until judgment in Walker's Trustees *v.* Lord Advocate—Withdrawn.

27 Apr. 1954   Mulhens *v.* R. J. Reuter Co. Ltd.—Set down 19 Oct. 1954—Abandoned.

Feb. 1955   Solomons *v.* Edwards—A.C. gave conditional leave to appeal and leave to appeal in f.p. 11 Jan. 1955. Set down 19 Apr. 1955—Withdrawn by leave 17 Oct. 1955.

4 Oct. 1955	Bowaters Lloyd Pulp and Paper Mills Ltd. *v.* Compania Naviera Maropan S.A.—Abandoned.
9 June 1955	British Fondants Ltd. *v.* Vigon—Abandoned.
12 Sept. 1956	Midland Bank Executory & Trustee Department *v.* C.I.R.—Stayed until after judgment in Westminster Bank *v.* C.I.R.—12 Sept. 1956—Withdrawn.
*12 Sept. 1956	Mitchell *v.* Temple—Refused leave to appeal in f.p. 24 Oct. 1956—Abandoned.
*13 Mar. 1956	Pullar *v.* Window Clean Ltd.—Refused leave to appeal in f.p. (no prima facie case) 26 Mar. 1956—Abandoned.
17 July 1956	Treseder-Griffin *v.* Co-operative Insurance Society Ltd.—Set down 8 Oct. 1956—Withdrawn by leave 22 Jan. 1957.
*31 July 1956	Wilson *v.* Keenan Ltd.—Abandoned.
2 July 1957	Adrema Werke Gesellschaft Mit Beschrankter Haftung *v.* Campbell—Set down 13 Nov. 1957—Withdrawn by leave 13 Feb. 1958.
†26 Feb. 1957	Borough Building Society *v.* Moley—Abandoned.
4 June 1957	Branhills Ltd. *v.* Town Tailors—Stayed till after judgment in Betty's Cafe *v.* Phillips f.s. 7 June 1957—Withdrawn.
1 May 1957	Earl of Shrewsbury *v.* C.I.R.—Abandoned.
*22 Jan. 1957	Hay *v.* Duthie—Refused leave to appeal in f.p. (no prima facie case) 18 Feb. 1957—Abandoned.
Mar. 1955	B. *v.* B.—Leave to appeal given by A.C. Feb. 1955—Heard 5 Apr. 1955 when Appellate Committee ruled that it had no jurisdiction.
Oct. 1955	L.C.C. *v.* Knight (Valuation Officer)—Proceedings stayed until one month after result of appeal in L.C.C. *v.* Wilkins—Withdrawn.
*2 Oct. 1958	Heggie *v.* Edinburgh & Leith Window Cleaning Co. Ltd.—Refused leave to appeal in f.p. (no prima facie case) 4 Nov. 1958—Abandoned.
Oct. 1958	Lyle & Scott Ltd. *v.* Thompson etc. (11 appeals)—Judgment given in accordance with the ruling in Lyle & Scott Ltd. *v.* Scott 19 Oct. 1959.
*21 July 1959	Diack *v.* Kilgour & Walker—Refused leave to appeal in f.p. 18 Apr. 1959—Abandoned.
*23 Mar. 1959	Jenkins *v.* B.T.C.—Refused leave to appeal in f.p. 16 Apr. 1959—Abandoned.
13 Jan. 1959	Kinder (Inspector of Taxes) *v.* Jennings—Stayed till after result in Hochstrasser *v.* Mayes—Abandoned.
†4 May 1959	Mount *v.* Electricity Board for N. Ireland—Refused leave to appeal in f.p. 9 June 1959—Abandoned.
11 Oct. 1960	Beal *v.* Surface Silos Ltd.—A.C. gave leave 28 July 1960—A.C. refuse to restore appeal after numerous petitions for further time 18 Apr. 1962.
23 May 1961	Compagnie des Compteurs *v.* G. Kromschroder Aktien Gesellschaft—Abandoned.

21 June 1960	Flack (A.P.) *v.* Withers—Joint Petition, that judgment be given in agreed terms granted, order discharged 20 July 1961.
*5 Oct. 1959	Lambert *v.* Lambert—Refused leave to appeal in f.p. 14 Oct. 1959—Abandoned.
2 June 1960	Lucbor Dealings Ltd. *v.* C.I.R.—Stayed till after judgment in Collco Dealings Ltd. *v.* C.I.R.—Withdrawn.
†14 June 1960	Thompson *v.* Baird—Abandoned.
28 July 1960	Unity Theatre Co. Ltd. *v.* Speidel—A.C. gave leave to appeal—Stayed until after judgment in Plato Films Ltd. *v.* Speidel—Abandoned.
13 Feb. 1961	Alfred etc. *v.* Henning (Valuation Officer)—Abandoned.
17 Oct. 1961	Daniels *v.* Lincoln—Direction for payment out of costs—Abandoned.
*7 Oct. 1961	Hester *v.* Molne—Abandoned.
1 May 1961	Packaging Centre Ltd. *v.* Poland St. Estate Ltd.—Set down 24 July 1961—Withdrawn by leave 8 Nov. 1961.
31 July 1961	Tableau Holdings Ltd. *v.* Williams—Stayed till after judgment in Cenlon Finance Co. Ltd. *v.* Ellwood—Withdrawn.
31 Oct. 1961	Abbott *v.* Refuge Assurance Co. Ltd.—Abandoned.
*6 Feb. 1961	Breigans *v.* Provost etc. of Alloa—Abandoned.
19 Mar. 1962	Coward *v.* Motor Insurers Bureau—Set down 22 July 1963—Abandoned.
26 June 1962	Kaye *v.* Wise—Withdrawn by leave—28 Feb. 1963.
*	Lind *v.* Lind.
*25 Jan. 1962	McMillan *v.* B.P. Refinery (Grangemouth) Ltd.—Abandoned.
Oct. 1962	Spencer, etc. *v* C.I.R. (2 Appeals)—Stayed till result in C.H.W. Ltd. *v.* C.I.R.
June 1962	C.I.R. *v.* Wills—Decided on result of C.I.R. *v.* Jamieson.
July 1962	Essex County Council *v.* Essex Incorporated Congregational Church Union—Appellate Committee ruled that it had no jurisdiction 17 Jan. 1963.
4 Mar. 1963	Archdale *v.* Russell—Abandoned.
2 May 1963	Boulting *v.* Association of Cinematograph, T.V. and Allied Technicians—Withdrawn by leave 11 Feb. 1964.
*14 Jan. 1964	Beveridge *v.* Beveridge (A.P.)—Abandoned.
22 Jan. 1964	Earl of Iveagh, etc. *v.* Min. of H. & L.G. (*et è contra*)—Set down 13 Apr. 1964—Withdrawn by leave 18 June 1964.
*21 Jan. 1964	Ferguson *v.* N.C.B.—Abandoned.
*26 May 1964	Morrison's Associated Companies Ltd. *v.* James Rome & Son—Abandoned.
*31 July 1964	Motherwell Bridge & Engineering Co. *v.* R. & J. Dempster Ltd.—Abandoned.
*27 July 1964	N. British Steel Foundry Ltd. *v.* MacDonald—Abandoned.
2 Oct. 1963	Younghusband *v.* Coutts & Co. (*et è contra*)—Abandoned after 8 petitions for further time on appeal and 5 on cross-appeal.

5 Oct. 1965	Aurora Corporation *v.* Costin—Appeal Committee gave leave to appeal 28 July 1965—Abandoned.
19 Jan. 1965	Every *v.* Miles—Restored 2 Feb. 1965—Abandoned.
*15 June 1965	Greig *v.* Sir Wm. Arrol & Co.—Abandoned.
23 Feb. 1965	Hull and Humber Investment Co. *v.* Hull Corporation—Abandoned.
†5 Oct. 1964	J. H. A. Swinson & Co. *v.* Dossor—Abandoned.
17 June 1965	Leather *v.* Kirby (A.P.)—Judgment given in terms requested 21 Oct. 1965.
Apr. 1965	C.I.R. *v.* Parker (2 Appeals)—Decided on result in C.I.R. *v.* Parker.
†16 Mar. 1966	Chalfant *v.* Cavendish Furniture Co. Ltd.—Respondents given leave to present Appeal without giving security 23 Feb. 1966—Further time 27 Apr. 1966.
28 Feb. 1966	Denman (A.P.) *v.* Arthur Gibson & Son (A.C. having given leave to appeal 15 Feb. 1966)—Abandoned.
*9 Dec. 1965	Hutchison *v.* Todd—Respondent's petition praying that the appeal be dismissed as incompetent referred to Appeal Committee 13 Jan. 1966—Abandoned.
†17 Jan. 1966	Taylor *v.* Flinn—Abandoned.
13 Apr. 1967	A. King & Sons Ltd. *v.* Liberian Shipping Corporation—Set down for hearing *ex parte* (after 6 petitions for further time by Appellant) 22 Jan. 1968—Withdrawn by leave 19 June 1968.
*18 Apr. 1967	British Insulated Callender Construction Co. Ltd. *v.* McGilivray (A.P.)—Abandoned.
*23 May 1967	C.I.R. *v.* Graham—Further proceedings stayed pending judgment in C.I.R. *v.* Brebner.
13 June 1967	Macsaga Investment Co. Ltd. *v.* Lupton (Inspector of Taxes)—Set down for hearing *ex parte* (after 3 petitions for further time)—Appeal withdrawn by leave on agreed terms 4 July 1968.
23 May 1967	Perren *v.* C.I.R.—Proceedings stayed pending judgment in Cleary *v.* C.I.R.
17 Apr. 1967	Snook (A.P.) *v.* London and West Riding Investments Ltd.—Abandoned.
*23 May 1967	Truscon Ltd. *v.* Byrne—Abandoned.
11 Mar. 1968	Chic Fashions (West Wales) Ltd. *v.* Jones (A.C. having given leave to appeal 5 Mar. 1967)—Abandoned.
*20 Feb. 1968	Grenfell *v.* Lorimer—Abandoned.
29 Apr. 1968	Jacobs *v.* Chaudhuri—2 petitions for further time—Abandoned.
23 Nov. 1967	Kerr (A.P.) *v.* National Coal Board—Withdrawn by leave 30 Apr. 1968.
19 Mar. 1968	Leek *v.* C.I.R.—Appellant given leave to prosecute appeal without giving security 25 Mar. 1968—Abandoned.
7 Oct. 1967	Morgan (A.P.) *v.* Fry—Abandoned.

APPENDIX 2(c)

PETITIONS FOR LEAVE TO APPEAL REJECTED BY THE APPEAL COMMITTEE AND PETITIONS IN WHICH LEAVE WAS GRANTED BUT THE APPEAL WAS NOT PURSUED

THE years given refer to the Parliamentary sessions in which each petition was presented: this appendix has been adapted from the annual lists in the House of Lords Journal.

Cr.   Denotes criminal appeal.

G.   Denotes petition in which leave was granted but the appeal was not pursued.

*   Denotes petition presented in person.

(A.P.) Denotes assisted person.

P.A.   Denotes petition dismissed in the petitioner's absence.

1951–2

Abbott v. Sullivan
G. Ebbs v. James Whitson & Co. Ltd.
Grove v. Eastern Gas Board
  * Gurtner v. Morny Ltd. (2 petitions)
Higgs (Inspector of Taxes) v. Olivier
Isaacs v. Hoenig
  * Lewis v. Reeves
Manchester Corporation v. McIntosh (Inspector of Taxes)
Ross v. Arab Bank Ltd.
  * Sarbah v. Taylor
Sayce v. Ameer Ruler Sadiq Mohammad Abassi Bahawalpur State
  * Siepmann v. Siepmann
  * Westley v. Matthews
G. Bauman v. Fussell
China Clay Freeholds Ltd. v. Gill
  * Cooper v. Cooper
Danegoods (London) Ltd. v. Duncan Brothers (Liverpool) Ltd.
David Taylor and Son Ltd. v. Barnett

  * Fry v. London Transport Executive
James Shaffer Ltd. v. Findlay Durham and Brodie
Prince v. Mayor, etc. of Borough of Barnstaple
  * Russell v. Shephard
Ryder v. Loudon
  * Thomas v. Rose
  * Tomlin v. Naerger
  * Walker v. Lloyds Bank Ltd.
Wright Anderson and Company Ltd. v. Pryde

1953–4

Anglo-Dal Ltd. v. Heisler
Barnett v. Campbell Mostyn (Provisions Ltd.)
Bravery v. Bravery
  * Cockell v. A. Waddington and Son Ltd.
Cole v. Wormald
Hawksley v. Fewtrell

* Hibbert *v.* Coulsdon and Purley Urban District Council
* Holt *v.* Davies
* Holt *v.* Hay's Wharf Cartage Company Ltd.
P.A. Huddleston *v.* The Official Receiver
Jayson *v.* Belne and Jackson Ltd.
* Lawley *v.* Rochester and Southwark Diocesan Trust
* Miller *v.* Ministry of Agriculture and Fisheries
* Musiel *v.* Barclays Bank Ltd.
Nigerian Farmers' and Commercial Bank Ltd. *v.* The London Directory Company Ltd.
Palmer *v.* Bray
Roe *v.* Ministry of Health
* Tyrrell *v.* Field
* Vandiyar *v.* Kenneth Brown, Baker, Baker
* Walters *v.* Nichols
Weightman *v.* Weightman

1954–5

Alvion Steamship Corporation of Panama *v.* Galban Lobo Trading Company S.A. of Havana
Daniels *v.* Ford Motor Company Ltd.
* Fromhold *v.* Fromhold
* Halstead *v.* The Public Trustee
Herraghty *v.* Riley and Neate Ltd.
* Nickolls *v.* Ministry of Health
Rands *v.* McNeil
Smith *v.* Port Line Ltd.
Sonotone Corporation *v.* Multitone Electric Company Ltd.

1955–6

A. Green (Spinster) *v.* Guinness Trust (London Fund)
A. Lewis & Company (Westminster) Ltd. *v.* Lyle-Mellor
* Ali *v.* Indian L'Orient Restaurant
Barclays Bank Ltd. *v.* Frish Ltd.
* Bilainkin *v.* Bilainkin
Birmingham Sound Reproducers Ltd. *v.* Collard Ltd.

* Blackburn *v.* Attorney-General
* Blackburn *v.* The Law Society
Buckingham *v.* Daily News Ltd.
Bullock *v.* G. John Power (Agencies) Ltd.
Compania Uruguaya de Fomento Industrial de Sociedad Anonima *v.* Mentmore Manufacturing Company Ltd.
* Fleet *v.* Fleet
Greenslade *v.* World's Press News Publishing Company Ltd.
* H.R.H. The Princess Alexandria Albertina Palmer Dinizulu *v.* Debenhams Ltd. (Proprietors of Marshall and Snelgrove)
* Hatherly *v.* Crofts
* Hibbert *v.* Board of Trade
Hick Hargreaves & Company Ltd. *v.* Gregson
Hills (Patents) Ltd. *v.* Board of Governors of University College Hospital
* Holt *v.* Taberner
Huyton-with-Roby Urban District Council *v.* Hunter
* Iger *v.* Daily Mirror Newspapers Ltd.
* Lloyd *v.* Sir Robert McAlpine & Sons (South Wales) Ltd.
* Millbank *v.* Millbank
G. Morcom *v.* Campbell-Johnson
Perry *v.* Kendriks Motor Transport, Ltd.
Pietryga *v.* Shannon
* Price *v.* Price
* Reynolds *v.* Dennison
Rhys Jones *v.* Attorney-General (3 petitions)
Richley *v.* Mann
* Thompson *v.* Manor House Hospital Management Committee
* Tomlin *v.* Official Receiver
P.A. Vandiyar *v.* Church Commissioners for England

1956–7

A. Glasser (suing as a firm) *v.* Holstein
* Boaks *v.* Reece

* Dunn *v.* Commissioners of Inland Revenue

* Golmick *v.* Steven

H. L. Bolton (Engineering) Company Ltd. *v.* T. J. Graham & Sons Ltd.

Indo-British Industries Ltd. *v.* Govindram Brothers Ltd.

* L. Brooks & Co. *v.* R. A. Brand & Company Ltd.

* Lall *v.* O'Leary

* Macmichael *v.* Commissioners of Inland Revenue

Needham *v.* Needham

Newman Industries Ltd. *v.* Indo-British Industries Ltd.

Pelton *v.* Griffith

* Reynolds *v.* Mayor etc. of County Borough of West Ham

* Ritchie *v.* T. G. Irving

Samrose Properties Ltd. *v.* Gibbard

* Walters *v.* Attorney-General

1957–8

Ambassador Hotel Ltd. *v.* Hammond

* Andrews *v.* Devnelle Flats Ltd.

P.A. Arnold *v.* Musicians' Union

* Arnold *v.* Rent Tribunal for Paddington and St. Marylebone

* Carlish *v.* Commissioners of Inland Revenue

* Fromhold *v.* Church Commissioners for England.

* Gush *v.* Holt

* Harris *v.* Williams

* Korda *v.* Korda

Koyo Siko Kabushki Kaisha *v.* Skefco Ball Bearing Company Ltd.

* Lawrence *v.* West Ham Borough Council

* Lear *v.* Charlesworth

Lyons *v.* Central Commercial Properties Ltd.

Marchioness of Winchester *v.* Fleming

G. R. E. Glanville and Sons (Bovey Tracy) Ltd. *v.* Rutherford

Société Française Bunge *v.* Leeds Shipping Company Ltd.

Taylor *v.* John Summers and Sons Ltd.

G. Thomas Robinson Sons & Co. Ltd. *v.* Wilts United Dairies Ltd.

* Thompson *v.* Thompson

* Vandiyar *v.* Tregeser

1958–9

Ballantyne Stewart and Company Ltd. *v.* George Ballantyne and Son Ltd.

British Petroleum Company Ltd. *v.* Amyer Abdullah

* Carlish *v.* Official Receiver

Daintifyt Brassiere Company Ltd. *v.* English Rose Ltd.

G. L. Baker Ltd. *v.* Medway Building and Supplies Ltd.

* Ghosh *v.* High Commissioner for India

* Gray *v.* Ralli

H. L. Savory and Company Ltd. *v.* Welbeck Way Holdings Ltd.

* Hunt *v.* Allied Bakeries Ltd. (2 petitions)

McCullie (Infant) *v.* Butler

* Maynard *v.* Jones

Mayor *v.* Ribble Motor Services Ltd.

Regina Fur Company Ltd. *v.* Bossum

* Richmond *v.* Twining

Ryan *v.* Redpath Brown & Co. Ltd.

* Tannock *v.* Ministry of Works

Velleman *v.* Ralph's Stores (Carshalton) Ltd.

* Vine *v.* National Dock Labour Board

1959–60

Ackroyd & Son *v.* Hasan

* Acland *v.* Acland

* Allan *v.* Martin

* Arnold *v.* Marrinan

Ballantyne Stewart and Company *v.* George Ballantyne and Son Ltd.

Bieber *v.* Registrar of Solicitors

Bramwell *v.* Jacksons Industries Ltd.

* Brazdzionis *v.* Prudential Assurance Company Ltd.
* Carlish *v.* Commissioners of Inland Revenue
Collyer *v.* British Transport Commission
* Crisp *v.* Daily Herald (1929) Ltd.
Davies *v.* Manchester Ship Canal Company
* Gill *v.* Gill
* Gush *v.* Co-operative Building Society
* Harris *v.* Great Grimsby Co-operative Chemists Ltd.
P.A. Harris *v.* Harris
* Holt *v.* Church Commissioners for England
Hood Barrs *v.* Commissioners of Inland Revenue
* Jedral *v.* Jedral
P.A. Killick *v.* Thomas
Lloyds Permanent Building Society *v.* Registrar of Building Societies
* Mackinlay *v.* Attorney-General
* MacMichael *v.* Combe
* { Matthews *v.* Pillon
  { Matthews *v.* Wardle
Messier Société Anonyme (incorporated under the law of the French Republic) *v.* Armandias
* Millington *v.* Ford
* Munday *v.* Munday
* Odufuwa *v.* McKechnie
* Routh *v.* Central Land Board (2 petitions)
S. Simpson Ltd. *v.* Kidax Ltd.
* Solanke *v.* Posnett
Spanish Holiday Tours (London Ltd. *v.* Cook

1960–1

* Acland *v.* Acland
* Barritt *v.* Raymond Kerry Ltd.
* Broadsmith *v.* McCubbin
Cr. Caldough *v.* Governor of Brixton Prison (Habeas Corpus)
Chalmers Property Investment

Company Ltd. *v.* Rubery (Valuation Officer)
Cook *v.* National Coal Board
Credit Enterprise Ltd. *v.* Woodcocks Sussex Ltd.
* Daniels *v.* Lord Keyes
Davies *v.* Elsby Brothers Ltd.
Duffy *v.* Ministry of Labour and National Insurance for Northern Ireland
Cr. Duke *v.* Director of Public Prosecutions (from the Court of Criminal Appeal)
* Dunster *v.* Dunster
* Fisher *v.* Brandt
* Fletcher *v.* Collins
Cr. Gelberg *v.* Miller
* Ghosh *v.* Mukherjee
* Gush *v.* Holt
* Hamilton *v.* Hall (Town Clerk) acting and representing Halifax County Borough Council
Harrison *v.* D. W. Curtis Ltd.
* Hinds *v.* Attorney-General
Hoare *v.* Trustees of the London Clinic Ltd.
Cr. Holmes, Kenneth Edward
Hotchkiss (A.P.) *v.* S. & C. Walmsley Ltd.
J. A. Jones Construction Company (trading as Derbendi Khan Contractors *v.* Alliance Assurance Company Ltd.
Jenkinson (Inspector of Taxes) *v.* Freedland
Julian Praet et Cie Société Anonyme *v.* Poland (suing on behalf of himself and all other underwriting members of the Syndicate of K. G. Poland and others
* MacCarthy *v.* Chairman and Councillors of London County Council
* McKay *v.* Attorney-General
* Odufuwa *v.* Crisp
Owen (A.P.) *v.* Yeoman Credit Ltd.
* Privetsky *v.* Menell
* Rasbash *v.* Rasbash
Richard Abel and Sons Ltd. *v.* Peacock
Richard Thomas & Baldwins Ltd. *v.* Williams

*{ Russell v. Cresswell
Russell v. Stuperski
Russell v. Wanstall
* Sleeman v. Barlow Lyde and Gilbert
* Sobiye v. Odunjo
* Tyacke v. Tyacke (A.P.)
* Ware-Lane v. Drewery
* White v. Commissioners of Inland Revenue

1961–2

* Ackrill v. Ackrill
Airports Restaurants Ltd. v. Mayor etc. of the County Borough of Southend-on-Sea
* Arwas v. Forte
* Buck v. Attorney-General
* Cullinane v. Sturdy
* de Havilland v. Taylor
Cr. Director of Public Prosecutions v. Clayton (from the Court of Criminal Appeal)
* Fletcher v. Collins
* Garbett v. T. W. Bates (Aggregates) Ltd.
* Ghosh v. D'Rozario
Gilbert v. Mousley
* Gosling v. Mayor, etc. of Mansfield
* Hinds v. Home Office
* Horne v. Horne
Ispahani Ltd. v. Compagnie Continentale d'Importation Zürich S.A.
* Johnson v. Jewitt (Inspector of Taxes)
Langan v. W. & C. French Ltd.
* Langton v. Lloyds Bank Ltd.
* Lermitte v. Lermitte
* Maggiora v. Maggiora
* Majid v. Broadstone Mills Ltd.
Metro Metal Traders Ltd. v. Vereinigte Metallwerke Ranshofen-Berndorf A.G.
Miller-Mead (trading as Coventry Cars and Caravans) v. Warwick Rural District Council
* Mousley v. Dyer
* Munday v. Stohr (widow)

* Norman v. Commissoners of Inland Revenue
Patterson v. Hall
* Russell v. Burrows
Shaw v. Shaw (A.P.)
* Smith v. Wentworth
* Sobiye v. Odunjo
* Stone v. Association of Official Shorthandwriters
* Stone v. Jones
Symonds (A.P.) v. Symonds
* Tannock v. Attorney-General
Cr. Thompson v. Director of Public Prosecutions (from the Court of Criminal Appeal)
* Waddington v. Turner
* Walters v. Meade-Miles
* Ward v. Clonmany Estates Ltd.
* Ward v. Medway Oil and Storage Company Ltd.
Weait (A.P.) v. Jayanbee Joinery Ltd.
* White v. Commissioners of Inland Revenue
White Window and General Cleaning Company v. Baker (A.P.)
Wick Films Incorporated v. Associated Rediffusion Ltd.
* Wilson v. Midland Bank Ltd.
Woodman & Son (Builders) Ltd. v. Charles E. Ware & Son
* Yates v. Commercial Purchase Ltd.

1962–3

* Adams v. Attorney-General
* Allan v. Martin
Anglo Auto Finance Company Ltd. v. James (A.P.)
* Boaks v. South London Press Ltd.
Cr. Brown etc. v. Dowling (3 petitions)
Commissioners of Inland Revenue v. West Hertfordshire Main Drainage Authority
* Dennis v. Hamerton
* Dennis v. Heaton-Ward
* Dennis v. Norfolk County Council
Cr. Director of Public Prosecutions v. Straker
* Dunster v. Dunster

Cr. Enahoro *v.* Federation of Nigeria

Cr. Enahoro *v.* Home Secretary

Cr.* Enahoro *v.* Home Secretary

Fairman *v.* Driver

Fidelitas Shipping Co. Ltd. *v.* V/O Exportchleb

Financings Ltd. *v.* Baldock

Foster and Mulholland *v.* Attorney-General

* Gohoho *v.* Guinea Press Ltd.

* Harris *v.* Bristow

* Hart *v.* Ministry of Pensions and National Insurance

Henley *v.* Orion Property Trust Ltd.

Hilling (Widow and Administratrix of the Estate of Dennis Hilling deceased) *v.* Ferris

* Holder *v.* C. & J. Hirst & Sons Ltd.

Cr. Jordan *v.* Burgoyne

* Langton *v.* Lloyds Bank Ltd.

Lennon *v.* Renishaw Iron Company Ltd.

* Linklater *v.* Daily Telegraph Ltd.

* London *v.* London County Council

* Long *v.* Official Solicitor

Lord Mayor, etc. of City of Manchester *v.* North Western Gas Board

Mersey Ports Stevedoring Company Ltd. *v.* Henry

* Moore *v.* Buchanan

* Mousley *v.* Dyer

* Odufuwa *v.* Fleming

Penn-Texas Corporation *v.* English Transcontinental Ltd.

* Sproston, Trading as Tickets & Co. *v.* Sowden & Co. Ltd.

* Stone *v.* Association of Official Shorthandwriters Ltd.

U.G.S. Finance Ltd. *v.* National Mortgage Bank of Greece

Cr. Webb *v.* Commissioner of Police of the Metropolis

1963–4

* Anderson *v.* Hills' Automobiles (Woodford) Ltd.

* Bailey *v.* Bailey

Bamfords Ltd. *v.* C. van der Lely N.V.

Cr. Boal *v.* Director of Public Prosecutions

* Burns *v.* Burns

C.H.T. Ltd. *v.* Ward

Cr.* Chandler *v.* Commissioner of Police of the Metropolis

Cutner *v.* Acceptance Company Ltd.

* Diment *v.* Sanctuary and Son

Duerdin-Dutton and another *v.* Berkhamsted Rural District Council

* Fairhead *v.* Norfolk News Company

Cr. Field etc. *v.* Director of Public Prosecutions (2 petitions)

Foreign Compensation Commission *v.* Anisminic Ltd.

* Ghosh *v.* Harvey Lemon and Company

Hammill *v.* Camborne Water Company Ltd.

Herbert *v.* Haines

* Hopkins *v.* Hopkins

Howell *v.* Sunbury on Thames Urban District Council

* Jennings (Administratrix of Estate of John Harold Jennings deceased) *v.* Prescott

* Langton *v.* Lloyds Bank Ltd.

Lappin (A.P.) *v.* Dorman Long (Steel) Ltd.

* Morton *v.* London Transport Board
Morton *v.* Ministry of Public Building and Works

Motor Insurers' Bureau *v.* Hardy

Oliver *v.* Oliver

Overseas Aviation Ltd. *v.* Ellis Air Tours Abroad Ltd.

Painter *v.* Townsend (A.P.)

Petrotim Securities Ltd. (formerly Gresham Trust Ltd.) *v.* Ayres (Inspector of Taxes)

* Rosen *v.* Golomb

* Russell *v.* Hardern

* Schenk *v.* Schenk

Soul *v.* Boyles (Inspector of Taxes)

* Soul *v.* Commissioners of Inland Revenue

* Soul v. Irving etc. (Inspectors of Taxes) (5 petitions)
Taylor-Gooby (Inspector of Taxes) v. Harrods (Buenos Aires) Ltd.
Vickers (A.P.) v. British Transport Docks Board
Weisz v. General Medical Council
Cr. Wells v. Hardy
* Zoernsch v. Waldock

1964-5

* Adams v. Executors of the late W. J. Johnson
* Anderson v. Stadium Finance Ltd.
Automatic Telephone and Electric Company Ltd. v. Registrar of Restrictive Trading Agreements
* Buck v. Attorney-General
* Bush v. Lord Chief Justice of England
* Carson v. T. Wall & Sons (Meat and Handy Foods) Ltd.
Cementation Company Ltd. v. McCarron (A.P)
* Chamberlain v. Chamberlain
Cr. Creamer v. Director of Public Prosecutions
Fidelitas Shipping Company Ltd. v. V/O Exportschleb
G. C. Dobell & Company Ltd. v. Steel Brothers & Company Ltd.
Gordon Hotels Ltd. v. British Railways Board
* Gott v. National Union of Teachers (4 petitions)
Halifax Tool Company Ltd. v. Williams (Widow and Administratrix of the Estate of Richard Williams deceased)
* Harris v. Bremner
Harris v. Wallis Tin Stamping Company Ltd.
* Harvey v. Darby & Sons
* Jonescu v. Board of Governors of Royal Free Hospital
Kemp v. Pearce & Sons
* Kennedy v. Fortes & Co. Ltd.
Litherland v. Litherland
* Mabry v. Schneider

Mayor, etc. of Borough of Wednesbury and others v. Ministry of Housing and Local Government
Cr. Mitten v. Huntley
* Morton v. Jordine
* Morton v. Ministry of Public Building and Works
Owners of Motor Vessel 'Crystal Jewel' v. Owners of Steam Tankship 'British Aviator' (The 'British Aviator')
* Patel v. Lord Mayor, etc. of City of Birmingham
Photo Centre Ltd. v. Grantham Court Properties (Mayfair) Ltd.
* Russell v. Hardern
Saul (A.P.) v. St. Andrew's Steam Fishing Company Ltd. (The 'St. Chad')
* Shine v. Odhams Press Ltd.
* Sitkowski v. Baldessare
* Stone v. Widgery
* Strand Securities Ltd. v. Caswell
* Tannock v. Clerk of the Crown
Tarkin v. Board of Governors of Middlesex, Hospital.
* Underwood v. Mathews
Venner Ltd. v. The Shannon Ltd.
* Watson v. Smith
Cr. White v. Hamer
Whiting v. Barenz (Inspector of Taxes)
William Brandts Sons & Co. Ltd. v. Chippendale's Workshop Ltd.

1965-6

A. L. Wilkinson Ltd. v. Brown
Amp Incorporated v. Hellerman Ltd.
Astaire v. Campling
Re C. (M.A.) (an infant)
* Cogswell v. Taylor
* Constantinou v. Frederick Hotels Ltd.
Esdell Caravan Parks Ltd. v. Hemel Hempstead Rural District Council
* Fletcher v. Adamson, Re H., infants

* Jones v. Dunmow Flitch Bacon Company Ltd.
Cr. Kronenberg v. Federal Republic of West Germany
* March v. March
Montres Buler S.A. v. Bulova Watch Company Ltd.
* Morton v. Electronics Crosfield Ltd.
Cr. Okai v. Governor of Brixton Prison
* Paton v. Croxon
Peachey Property Corporation Ltd. v. Mayor, etc. of City of Westminster
Peachey Property Corporation Ltd. v. Morley (Valuation Officer)
Cr. Pugh v. Chief Constable, Glamorgan County Constabulary
* Schenk v. Schenk
Shute (A.P.) v. Clay
Cr. Shuter v. Director of Public Prosecutions
* Sterman v. Bendall
Cr. Wibberley v. Thorne
Cr. Williams v. Chief Superintendent, Lancashire Constabulary
Cr. Yeandel (A.P.) v. Fisher

1966–7

* Adams v. Attorney-General
P.A. Arnold v. Musicians' Union
Aschaffenburger Zellstoffwerke A.G. (a company incorporated in accordance with the laws of the German Federal Republic) v. Barclays Bank Ltd.
* Bawden v. Morris
* Becker v. Home Office
Bergsagel (A.P.) v. Henderson (A.P.)
* Blank v. Robophone Facilities Ltd.
Bristol Laboratories Ltd. v. Beecham Group Ltd.
Broll v. Westmore
Chris Foodstuffs Ltd. v. Nigerian National Shipping Line Ltd.
Copydex Ltd. v. Seager

Crampsie (A.P.) v. Unit Construction Company Ltd. (Northern Ireland)
* Durrant v. Blown
Elliot v. Chiew
Fine Fare Ltd. v. F. & G. Sykes (Wessex) Ltd.
* Garrod v. Buckingham County Council
* Garrod v. Marsham Tyre Co. Ltd.
P.A. Gracie v. Beaton (Scotland)
P.A. Gracie v. Clark (two petitions)
Hawkins v. Morris Motors Ltd.
* Hayball v. Quick
Cr. * Holmes v. The Registrar, as agent for the Court of Criminal Appeal
Hood Barrs v. Howard (Valuation Officer)
* Imhof (widow) v. Whittaker, Williams & Co.
* Ingham v. Hinds
Johnson v. Stanton and Staveley Ltd.
Lambert (trading as St. Michael's Garage) v. Baxter
* Langton v. Attorney-General
Lawson (Inspector of Taxes) v. Hosemaster Machine Company Ltd.
* Long v. Official Solicitor
* Long v. Shute (Northern Ireland)
Lyons v. Alfred F. Beckett Ltd.
* Marshall v. Marshall
* Moore v. Attorney-General
* Moore v. Buchanan (2 petitions)
* Moore v. West Park Hospital, Epsom, Surrey
Cr. Moore v. Buchanan
* Morton v. Martin
Newton v. Farmer
North Devon Hospital Management Committee v. Cozens (A.P.)
Odhams Press Ltd. v. Morgan
O'Keefe v. British Railways Board
* Oliver v. R. M. Bull and Company
* Padwick v. Lockyer
Paton v. Croxon (A.P.)
Pilbrico Company Ltd. v. Foster Wheeler Ltd.
R. V. Ward Ltd. v. Rothschild and Sons
* Radivojevic v. Leslie

Cr. * Rakshit *v.* Clarke
* Richards *v.* Richards
* Sammy-Joe *v.* Milton
* Soul *v.* Caillebotte (Inspector of Taxes)
* Spanglett *v.* National Provincial Bank Ltd.
Cr. Suidan *v.* Federal Republic of Germany
* Thomson *v.* Thomson
* Watts *v.* Monmouthshire County Council
* Wenlock *v.* Shinwell
* Wheeler *v.* Somerfield
* White *v.* Thomas Borthwick & Sons Ltd.
Wilson *v.* Taylor
Wragg *v.* Grout
Cr. Wright *v.* Ford Motor Company Ltd.

1967–8

Alfred Wood (trading as Alfred Wood and Co.) *v.* Provan (Inspector of Taxes)
* Beg *v.* Wingate
* Burden *v.* Cleveland Petroleum Co. Ltd.
Button (A.P.) *v.* Button (A.P.)
G. Chic Fashions (West Wales) Ltd. *v.* Jones
Chumley (the administrator of the estate of Robert Chumley deceased) *v.* Cutts (married woman, wife of Thomas Larry Cutts)
Clyde Crane and Booth Ltd. *v.* Robinson (A.P.)
Cole *v.* Hucks (married woman)
Commissioners of Inland Revenue *v.* Hague (married woman)
* Conway *v.* Williams
Cr. Cox *v.* Griffin
* De Costa *v.* Home Office
Denmark Productions Ltd. *v.* Boscobel Productions Ltd.
* Dhargalkar *v.* Area Committee of No. 14 (London West) Legal Aid Area

* England *v.* Public Trustee
Fenn *v.* Standard Motor Company Ltd.
* FitzPatrick *v.* FitzPatrick
* Francois *v.* Cope's Pools Ltd.
* Garrod *v.* Marsham Tyre Co. Ltd.
Glick *v.* Butcher
* Glick *v.* Hinchcliffe
P.A. Glick *v.* Law Society (2 petitions)
Gloria (femme sole) *v.* Sokoloff
Cr. Goswami *v.* Commissioners of Customs and Excise
P.A. Gracie *v.* Toms
* Gush *v.* Beresford
P.A. H.R.H. The Princess Dinizulu *v.* Registrar General
Cr. Hillyer *v.* Taylor
* Howard *v.* Rowe Bros. & Co. Ltd.
Hunter (A.P.) *v.* W. Thompson & Sons (Leeds) Ltd.
* Imhof *v.* Barclays Bank
Cr. Ingram (A.P.) *v.* Percival
Kennedy, a minor, by Samuel Kennedy, her father and next friend *v.* Smyth and another (trading as James McKillop) (Northern Ireland)
Kirk *v.* North
* Lampart-Barczynski *v.* Massey-Ferguson Perkins Ltd.
* Lampart-Barczynski *v.* Shakespeare
* Lincoln *v.* Titan International Ltd.
Mallett *v.* Hanyet Securities Ltd.
* Masters *v.* Bishop & Sons' Depositories Ltd.
Moore *v.* Buchanan
Poole *v.* Series
Reid-Jamieson *v.* Williams
Cr. Ross-Munro *v.* Aubrey-Fletcher
* Savundra *v.* Merchants and Finance Trust Company
* Steel *v.* Prothero
* Tannock *v.* Chief Associate of Court of Appeal
Teece *v.* Joseph Sankey and Sons Ltd.
Tajendrasingh *v.* Simpson
* Thorne *v.* Odhams Press Ltd.
Cr. Thorpe *v.* Director of Public Prosecutions

HOUSE OF LORDS STANDING ORDERS

(a) STANDING ORDERS OF THE HOUSE OF LORDS (PUBLIC BUSINESS)

JUDICIAL BUSINESS

77.—(1) For the purposes of its appellate jurisdiction, the House shall have Appellate and Appeal Committees, of which all Lords qualified under the Appellate Jurisdiction Acts 1876 and 1887 shall be members. *(margin: Appellate and Appeal Committees. 20 May 1970.)*

(2) These Committees shall be:

(*a*) two Appellate Committees, which shall hear any cause or matter referred to them and shall report thereon to the House;

(*b*) two Appeal Committees, which shall consider any petition or application for leave to appeal that may be referred to them and any matter relating thereto, or to causes depending, or formerly depending, in this House, and shall report thereon to the House.

(3) In any criminal matter, or in any matter concerning extradition, an Appeal Committee may take decisions and give directions on behalf of the House.

(4) The Lord Chancellor if present, or in his absence the senior Lord of Appeal in Ordinary present, shall take the chair in any Appellate or Appeal Committee.

(5) For the purposes of the preceding paragraph, seniority shall be determined by reference to the date of first appointment to the office of Lord of Appeal in Ordinary without regard to rank in the Peerage.[1]

(6) For the purposes of section 8 of the Appellate Jurisdiction Act 1876, any Appellate Committee may sit and act while Parliament is prorogued.

(b) STANDING ORDERS OF THE HOUSE OF LORDS REGULATING JUDICIAL BUSINESS, MADE IN PURSUANCE OF THE APPELLATE JURISDICTION ACT 1876 AND SUBSEQUENT ENACTMENTS

In the inner margins:

The italicised dates (*round bracketed*) are those of the original Standing Orders prior to 1876.

The dates [square bracketed] are those of the original Standing Orders made in pursuance of the Appellate Jurisdiction Act 1876.

The dates unbracketed are those of the last substantial amendments.

[1] See text, p. 179.

(*13 December 1661*)
[14 August 1876]
26 February 1959

I. Ordered, that no petition of appeal be received by this House unless the same be lodged in the Parliament Office for presentation to the House within the period of three months from the date of the last order or interlocutor appealed from.

Time limited for presenting appeals.

[24 October 1935]
3 March 1966

II. Ordered, that, in all Appeals from the Court of Appeal, the Court of Appeal in Northern Ireland or the Court of Session in Scotland in which the leave of the House is required under the provisions of any Act of Parliament, a petition for leave to appeal be lodged in the Parliament Office within one month from the date of the last order or judgment appealed from, and that such petition be referred to an Appeal Committee to consider whether such leave should be granted.

Leave to appeal from the Courts of Appeal.

15 December 1969

III. Ordered, that, in all cases where application is made for leave for an appeal to be brought direct to the House from the High Court of Justice in England and Wales or from the High Court of Justice in Northern Ireland—

Leave to appeal from the High Court.

> (*a*) a petition for such leave, together with the certificate granted by the High Court under section 12 of the Administration of Justice Act 1969, be lodged in the Parliament Office within one month from the date of the grant of such certificate or within such extended time as in any particular case the House may allow;
>
> (*b*) any such petition, and any application for extension of time or other incidental matter, be referred to an Appeal Committee for their consideration and report.

Appeals to be signed and certified by counsel.

(*3 March 1967*)
[14 August 1876]
18 February 1959
3 March 1966

IV. Ordered, that, except in cases where leave to appeal has been granted under the provisions of any Act of Parliament, all petitions of appeal be signed, and the reasonableness thereof certified by two counsel.

[14 August 1876]
26 February 1959

V. Ordered, that the 'order of service' issued upon the presentation of an appeal for service on the Respondent or his solicitor be returned to the Parliament Office, together with an affidavit of due service entered thereon, within the time limited by Standing Order No. VII. for the Appellant to lodge his Cases, unless within that period all the Respondents shall have lodged their Cases; in default the appeal to stand dismissed.

Order of Service.

(*20 November 1680*)
[14 August 1876]
12 April 1962

VI. (1) Ordered, that in all Appeals the Appellants do give security for costs either—

Security for costs.

> (*a*) by payment into the House of Lords Security Fund Account of the sum of one thousand pounds, such sum to be subject to the Order of the House in regard to the costs of the Appeal; or
>
> (*b*) by payment of the sum of five hundred pounds into the House of Lords Security Fund Account, and by entering into a recognizance, in person or by substitute, to the amount of five hundred pounds; or
>
> (*c*) by procuring two sufficient sureties, to the satisfaction of the Clerk of the Parliaments, to enter into a joint and several

bond to the amount of five hundred pounds, and by entering into a recognizance, in person or by substitute, to the amount of five hundred pounds.

ORDERED, that all payments of money into the Security Fund Account be made within one week of the presentation of the Appeal.

ORDERED, that the names of sureties or substitutes, with a certificate of sufficiency signed by the Agents for the Appellants, be lodged in the Parliament Office within one week of the presentation of the Appeal, two clear days' previous notice of the names so proposed for the bond and the recognizance having been given to the Solicitors or Agents for the Respondents.

(2) ORDERED, that, in the event of the Clerk of the Parliaments requiring a justification of the sureties or substitute, the Agents for the Appellants do, within one week from the date of official notice to that effect, lodge in the Parliament Office an affidavit or affidavits by the proposed sureties or substitute, setting forth specifically the nature of the property in consideration of which they claim to be accepted, and also declaring that the property in question is unencumbered and that, after payment of all just debts and liabilities, such sureties or substitute are each well and truly worth the sum required under the bond or the recognizance respectively.

ORDERED, that, in the event of the proposed sureties to the bond not being deemed satisfactory by the Clerk of the Parliaments, the Appellants do, within four weeks of the date of official notice by the Clerk of the Parliaments to that effect, pay into the Security Fund Account the sum of five hundred pounds, to be subject to the Order of the House with regard to the costs of the Appeal; and that, in the event of the proposed substitute to the recognizance not being deemed satisfactory by the Clerk of the Parliaments, the Appellants do enter into the usual recognizance in person.

(3) ORDERED, that any such bond and the recognizance (whether entered into by the Appellants or by a substitute) be returned to the Parliament Office duly executed within one week from the date of the issue thereof to the Solicitors or Agents for the Appellants.

On default by the Appellants in complying with the above conditions, the Appeal to stand dismissed.

15 December 1960

(4) This Standing Order shall not apply to Appellants who have been granted legal aid. *Legal Aid.*

(*12 July 1811*)
[14 August 1876]
26 February 1959

VII. (1) ORDERED, that the Case and the Appendix thereto be lodged in the Parliament Office within six weeks from the date of the presentation of the appeal to the House; and the appeal be set down for hearing on the first sitting day thereafter (or as soon before, at the option of either party, as all the Cases and the Appendix shall have been lodged); on default by the Appellant, the appeal to stand dismissed. *Time for lodging Case.*

25 March 1964

(2) ORDERED, that in all appeals from Scotland the Appellant alone, in his Case or in the Appendix thereto, shall lay before this House a copy of the record as authenticated by the Deputy Principal Clerk of Session or a Clerk of Session delegated by him; together with a supplement containing an account, without argument or statement of other facts, of the further steps which have been taken in the *Case in Scottish Appeals.*

cause since the record was completed, and containing also copies of the interlocutors or parts of interlocutors complained of; and each party shall in his Case lay before the House a copy of the case presented by him to the Court of Session, if any such case was presented there, with a short summary of any additional reasons upon which he means to insist; and if there shall have been no case presented to the Court of Session then each party shall set forth in his Case the reasons upon which he founds his argument, as shortly and succinctly as possible.

(19 April 1698) (3) ORDERED, that the Case be signed by one or more Counsel, who shall have attended as counsel in the Court below, or shall purpose attending as Counsel at the hearing in this House. — Case to be signed by Counsel.

(8 March 1763) 14 August 1876 — VIII. ORDERED, that all cross-appeals be presented to the House within the period allowed by Standing Order No. VII. for lodging Cases in the original appeal. — Cross appeals.

[14 August 1876] IX. ORDERED, with regard to appeals in which the periods under Standing Orders Nos. V., VI., VII. and VIII. expire during the recess of the House, that such periods be extended to the third sitting day of the next ensuing meeting of the House. — Expiry of time during recess.

[15 December 1960] X. ORDERED, that where a party to an appeal has applied to a Legal Aid Committee, and the decision of the Committee has not been announced before the expiration of the periods of time limited by Standing Orders Nos. II., VI. or VII., such periods of time shall be extended until one week after the refusal of the application or the issue of a Certificate. — Legal Aid.

[12 August 1884] 26 February 1959 — XI. ORDERED, that in the event of abatement by death or defect through bankruptcy, an appeal shall not stand dismissed for default under Standing Orders Nos. V., VI. or VII., provided that notice of such abatement or defect be given by a letter from the Appellant's Agent addressed to the Clerk of the Parliaments and lodged in the Judicial Office prior to the expiration of the period limited by the Standing Order under which the appeal would otherwise have stood dismissed. — Abatement or defect.

ORDERED, that all appeals marked on the Cause List of the House as abated or defective shall stand dismissed unless, within three months from the date of the notice to the Clerk of the Parliaments of abatement or defect, if the House be then sitting, or, if not, then not later than the third sitting day of the next ensuing sittings of the House, a petition shall be presented to the House for reviving the appeal or for rendering the same effective. — Revivor etc.

(20 March 1823) ORDERED, that when an appeal has abated or become defective after the Cases have been lodged, and it is subsequently revived or rendered effective, a Supplemental Case shall be lodged by the Appellant setting forth the Order or Orders made by the House reviving the appeal or rendering the same effective. — Supplemental Case.

The like rule shall be observed by the Appellant and Respondent respectively, where any person or persons shall, by leave of the House, upon petition or otherwise, be added as a party or parties to the said appeal after the Cases in such appeal shall have been lodged.

[14 August 1876]

XII. ORDERED, that when any petition of appeal shall be presented to this House from any interlocutory judgment of either division of the Lords of Session in Scotland, the counsel who shall sign the said petition, or two of the counsel for the party or parties in the Court below, shall sign a certificate or declaration, stating either that leave was given by that division of the judges pronouncing such interlocutory judgment to the Appellant or Appellants to present such petition of appeal, or that there was a difference of opinion amongst the judges of the said division pronouncing such interlocutory judgment.

Certificate of leave or difference of opinion in Scottish Appeals.

(3 April 1835)
[7 August 1877]
2 June 1959

XIII. (1) ORDERED, that the Clerk of the Parliaments shall appoint such person as he may think fit as Taxing Officer, and in all cases in which this House shall make any order for payment of costs by any party or parties in any cause, the amount thereof to be certified by the Clerk of the Parliaments, the Taxing Officer shall tax the Bill of the Costs so ordered to be paid, and ascertain the amount thereof, and report the same to the Clerk of the Parliaments or Clerk Assistant: And it is further Ordered, that the same fees shall be demanded from and paid by the party applying for such taxation for and in respect thereof as is now charged or shall be fixed by any resolution of this House; and such fee shall be added at the foot of the said Bill of Costs as taxed. And the Clerk of the Parliaments or Clerk Assistant may give a certificate of such costs, expressing the amount so reported to him as aforesaid, and in his certificate, as well as in the Taxing Officer's report, regard shall be had to any sum that has been paid in to the Security Fund Account of the House, as directed by Standing Order No. VI.; and the amount in money certified by him in such certificate shall be the sum to be demanded and paid under or by virtue of such order as aforesaid for payment of costs.

Taxation of costs.

[14 August 1919]

(2) ORDERED, that when the payment of costs is so ordered to a successful Appellant in an appeal in *formâ pauperis*, the Taxing Officer shall not, on taxation, allow the fees of the House nor the fees of Counsel, but shall allow to the Solicitor his costs out of pocket, with a reasonable allowance (such allowance to be taken as three eighths of the Solicitor's charges in 'Divers' Appeals, other than out-of-pocket costs) to cover office expenses, including clerks, &c.

Poor Persons' Appeals (Northern Ireland).

[10 March 1902]

XIV. ORDERED, that in lieu of the fees heretofore charged, the fees contained in the Schedule hereto be taken in this House on the documents specified in the said Schedule, except in the case of parties petitioning for leave to sue in *formâ pauperis*, and that, except in such cases, none of the said documents be issued from or received at the Parliament Office, unless it shall have been endorsed by the Accountant and Receiver of Fees with the date of lodgment and the fee paid.

Fees.

SCHEDULE OF FEES

		£
1 January 1922	Lodgment of Petition of Appeal	4
	Entering Appearance	1
26 March 1970	Issue of Order of Service	4
	Return of Recognizance	4
	Lodgment of Petition not referred to Appeal Committee	4
	Lodgment of Joint Petition, from each Party thereto	2
	Lodgment of Petition referred to Appeal Committee (including report thereon)	6
	Application for Order on consent in lieu of Petition	2
	Lodgment of Case, including laying Case on the Table, entering Appeal on Cause List, Bar fee, and Counsel attending	26
	Application to set down for Hearing	4
	Issue of Final Judgment	6

THE LORD CHANCELLOR'S STATEMENT ON PRECEDENT, 26 JULY 1966

JUDICIAL PRECEDENT

BEFORE judgments were given in the House of Lords to-day (Tuesday, 26 July 1966) the Lord Chancellor made the following statement on behalf of himself and the Lords of Appeal in Ordinary:

'Their Lordships regard the use of precedent as an indispensable foundation upon which to decide what is the law and its application to individual cases. It provides at least some degree of certainty upon which individuals can rely in the conduct of their affairs, as well as a basis for orderly development of legal rules.

Their Lordships nevertheless recognize that too rigid adherence to precedent may lead to injustice in a particular case and also unduly restrict the proper development of the law. They propose therefore to modify their present practice and, while treating former decisions of this House as normally binding, to depart from a previous decision when it appears right to do so.

In this connection they will bear in mind the danger of disturbing retrospectively the basis on which contracts, settlements of property and fiscal arrangements have been entered into and also the especial need for certainty as to the criminal law.

This announcement is not intended to affect the use of precedent elsewhere than in this House.'

Since the House of Lords decided the English case of *London Street Tramways* v. *London County Council* in 1898, the House have considered themselves bound to follow their own decisions, except where a decision has been given *per incuriam* in disregard of a statutory provision or another decision binding on them.

The statement made is one of great importance, although it should not be supposed that there will frequently be cases in which the House thinks it right not to follow their own precedent. An example of a case in which the House might think it right to depart from a precedent is where they consider that the earlier decision was influenced by the existence of conditions which no longer prevail, and that in modern conditions the law ought to be different.

One consequence of this change is of major importance. The relaxation of the rule of judicial precedent will enable the House of Lords to pay greater attention to judicial decisions reached in the superior courts of the Commonwealth, where they differ from earlier decisions of the House of Lords. That could be of great help in the development of our own law. The superior courts of many other countries are not rigidly bound by their own decisions and the change in the practice of the House of Lords will bring us more into line with them.

The Lord Chancellor understands that the Law Commission and the Scottish Law Commission welcome the change which would not preclude either Commission from considering the question of precedent in relation to other courts or tribunals.

APPENDIX 5

WORK-LOADS AND MANPOWER OF BRITISH APPELLATE COURTS

WHILE it is far from our purpose to embark upon a detailed analysis of the work of appellate courts other than the House of Lords we have attempted throughout our study to view the work of the final appellate court in relation to other institutions, and in particular to the various courts *a quo*. Thus it is germane to our argument to show how the work-load of appellate business is distributed among the courts in the hierarchy, and to say something about the distribution of manpower between them.

The figures in the first table serve to illustrate the comparative rarity of appeals to the House of Lords, a fact which can be related to one of our central arguments: that the small case-load of the House of Lords enables it to deal with problems in depth but by hearing only a small number of appeals in each subject category the

continued at p. 520

Appeals heard by Appellate Courts in the United Kingdom.[a]

Year	House of Lords	Judicial Committee of the P.C.	Court of Appeal (Civil)	Court of Appeal Criminal Division (formerly Court of Criminal Appeal)	Court of Session (Inner House)	Q.B.	Divisional Courts Ch.	P.D.A.[b]	Court of Appeal in N. Ireland	Court of Criminal Appeal in. N. Ireland[y]
1952	39	28	623	199	114	209	34	208	17	25
1953	27	52	645	171	152	201	39	141	21	12
1954	19	38	618	156	143	189	25	159	22	33
1955	36	50	517	169	138	180	31	108	22	13
1956	34	35	533	163	139	225	36	11	24	19
1957	31	45	515	208	146	165	25	94	31	14
1958	26	28	490	192	133	161	18	43	26	27
1959	58	29	441	295	101	137	21	55	20	27
1960	38	42	566	288	168	208	28	111	23	19
1961	50	52	660	424	132	156	24	76	20	37
1962	45	38	615	492	113	226	30	139	22	14
1963	43	36	527	430	136	166	69	130	27	41
1964	42	59	460	391	111	150	76	73	15	40
1965	40	42	529	440	93	158	72	81	22	47
1966	35	30	576	472	87	187	72	113	34	42
1967	38	38	521	575	83	267	81	97	34	48
1968	33	26	679	833	105	292	84	89	40	84

(*N.B.* There may be slight discrepancies between the figures in col. 1, which are derived from the Civil Judicial Statistics, and those appearing elsewhere in the text, since we have computed the figures on a different basis.)

[a] i.e. disposed of after a judicial hearing rather than abandoned or withdrawn.

[b] Appeals from courts of summary jurisdiction in matrimonial proceedings.

[y] Including applications for leave to appeal.

Full-time Judicial Manpower available for Appellate Work

Office Held	Number (1 Jan. 1971)	Statutory Maximum	Extent of Participation in Appellate Business
Lord Chancellor	1	1	*Ex officio* president of the Court of Appeal, but never sits there. Occasionally presides in the House of Lords.
Master of the Rolls	1	1	*De facto* president of the Court of Appeal. Rarely sits *ex officio* in the Lords.
Lord Chief Justice	1	1	Presides in Criminal Division of Court of Appeal and in the Divisional Court of Queen's Bench Division. Sometimes sits at first instance. Very rarely sits *ex officio* in the Lords.
President of the P.D.A.*	1	1	Presides in Divisional Court of P.D.A.* and sits at first instance in that division.
Lord President of the Court of Session	1	1	Presides in First Division of the Inner House of the Scottish Court of Session.
Lord Justice Clerk	1	1	Presides in Second Division of the Inner House of the Court of Session.
Lord Chief Justice of Northern Ireland	1	1	Presides in Court of Appeal and of Criminal Appeal in Northern Ireland. Occasionally sits *ex officio* in the Lords.
Lords of Appeal in Ordinary	10	11	Sit in the House of Lords and in the Judicial Committee of the Privy Council. Sometimes, asked to sit in the Court and (very rarely) at first instance.
Lords Justices of Appeal	13	14	Sit in the Court of Appeal (Civil and Criminal Divisions) and can be required to sit at first instance. Qualified to sit on Judicial Committee of the Privy Council but are seldom asked to do so.
Lords Ordinary	15	20	The six most senior senators of the College of Justice sit in the two divisions of the Inner House of the Court of Session under the presidency of the Lord President and the Lord Justice Clerk respectively. The other Lords Ordinary sit in the Outer House at first instance.
Lords Justices of Appeal in Northern Ireland	2	2	Sit in the Court of Appeal in Northern Ireland and sometimes at first instance.
English puisne judges	66	75	Can be required to sit in the Court of Appeal (Civil and Criminal divisions). Queen's Bench judges sit frequently in the Criminal Division. Also sit in the Divisional Court of the Division in which they sit.
Northern Irish puisne judges	4	4	Can be required to sit in the Courts of Appeal for Northern Ireland and in Divisional Courts. Mostly at first instance.

* Now the Family Division of the High Court.

N.B. in addition, on 1 January 1971 there were ten retired Lords of Appeal who, technically, could sit (by invitation) in the House of Lords. The Judicial Committee of the Privy Council has in recent years issued an increasing number of invitations to Commonwealth judges to sit.

These figures take no account of the fact that some judges of all ranks are absent from the courts for long periods while undertaking other official business such as chairmanship of Royal Commissions or of committees of enquiry.

House is hampered in its attempts to develop a coherent body of jurisprudence. These figures also suggest that if the House of Lords were to be deprived of its judicial functions (a course which we do not advocate) then, in purely numerical terms, the proportionate impact on the case-load of already busy appellate courts, which would have to convene full courts more frequently than at present (see Appendix 6), would be small.

The second table shows the judges who are available to man the various appellate courts, clearly demonstrating that there is a reserve of mobility between the different courts. This too is an important factor to be borne in mind in discussing possible reforms.

APPENDIX 6

THE USE OF FULL COURTS IN THE APPELLATE PROCESS[1]

THE structure of the English court system is like a pyramid. When a piece of ligitation—civil or criminal—is launched, its future progress can invariably be predicted by reference to two factors: the type of court in which proceedings were begun and the subject-matter of the case. There is one hierarchy for criminal proceedings tried summarily, another for trials on indictment, another for revenue proceedings, another for interlocutory proceedings, yet another for proceedings started by motion in the Divisional Court of the Queen's Bench Division, and so on. The apex of each is either the House of Lords or (in cases such as bankruptcy proceedings where appeals to the Lords are proscribed or restricted by statute)[2] the Court of Appeal. Not surprisingly the bulk of litigation goes no further than the court of first instance: the litigant frequently does not wish, or thinks it unwise, to appeal. And sometimes the right of appeal—even to the Court of Appeal—is subject to statutory limitation.[3] Thus judicial hierarchy is of practical significance only in a minority of cases, though its theoretical significance to students of the judicial process is considerable.

The existence of identifiable court-hierarchies is part of the order which is a feature of all legal systems. Another manifestation of legal order is to be found *within* the hierarchies: it takes the form of a predictable progression in the *sizes* of courts at different levels. A ligitant at first instance will always[4] be faced by a trial judge sitting alone (or with a jury); his first appeal will almost invariably be to three judges; and if he wishes, and is permitted to appeal to the House of Lords his appeal will be heard by five Law Lords. There are logical reasons for this arithmetic progression. First, our appellate system is based upon a general philosophy of 'good, better, best'; not only are appeal judges *promoted* (i.e. moved up the hierarchy on the basis of merit and seniority);[5] they also present a phalanx of combined expertise

[1] The authors are greatly indebted to Mr. Michael Knight, Lecturer in Law, Queen's University, Belfast, for allowing them to make use of his hitherto unpublished research on the use of full courts in the Court of Criminal Appeal. This appendix is adapted from an article by the present authors entitled 'The Use of Full Court in the Appellate Process', 34 M.L.R. 364–76 (1971).

[2] e.g. Bankruptcy Act 1914, s. 108 (2) (a); Supreme Court of Judicature (Consolidation) Act 1925, s. 27 (2); Foreign Compensation Act 1969, s. 3 (8).

[3] e.g. appeals from rulings of judges in chambers in interlocutory proceedings.

[4] This is not, of course true, in the case of summary trials before a lay bench. And we are excluding cases in which proceedings are begun in statutory tribunals since our concern is with the commencement of *judicial* proceedings.

[5] Although Law Lords are, slightly better paid than judges of the Supreme Court of Judicature, Lords Justices of Appeal receive the same pay as puisne judges. While the judicial system is founded upon a sense of hierarchy there still prevails a notion that judicial minds should be wholly unconcerned with financial reward (witness the outcry over the resignation of Fisher J. to take up an appointment in the City, *The Times*, August 1970) and, a *fortiori*, that there should be no sense of financial competition between judges on the rungs of the promotion ladder.

numerically sufficient to overrule the judgment below. In one sense the larger size of the higher court is a face-saver for trial judges who are found to have fallen into error; though more does not necessarily mean better.

The hierarchy of courts is reinforced by that aspect of the doctrine of *stare decisis* which makes the decisions of higher courts binding upon the lower courts. This can lead, as we have seen, to the alarming phenomenon of a House of Lords' judgment being a final decision based upon an overall minority of judicial opinion; technically it would be possible for the combined opinions of a three-judge Divisional Court, a three-judge Court of Appeal and two dissenting Law Lords to be overridden by the votes of only three Law Lords. Although 'minority' decisions are by no means rare,[1] this ultimate score of 3:8 has, so far as we can tell, never yet been achieved: such a possibility is one of the perils of judicial hierarchy. The existence of this ostensibly alarming phenomenon proves very little: the courts at different levels have a different role in the judicial process, which makes a straightforward counting of judicial heads a pointless exercise. More specifically, the House of Lords is able to overrule precedents established by the Court of Appeal (or even, since 1966, previous decisions of itself) which are binding upon the lower courts.

Another principle which plays a part in determining the size of a court is the desirability of clear-cut decisions; this means that, wherever possible, courts should consist of an uneven number of judges.[2] It is rare but by no means unheard-of for a two-judge Court of Appeal[3] to be evenly divided, in which case the appeal is decided upon the principle, *semper praesumitur pro negante*.[4] Up to 1963 the House of Lords sometimes sat with four Law Lords, but we have no record of any such cases in recent years, until January 1971 when Lord Upjohn's death resurrected the problem of an equally divided Appellate Committee. The only case under judgment at the time of his death which led to any difficulty[4a] was *Kennedy* v. *Spratt*[4b] (the Law Report contains a background note on the problem, prepared by the Judicial Office). Lord Upjohn had written a speech and would have voted with Lords Reid and Diplock in dismissing the appeal. In the result Lord Reid read Lord Upjohn's speech as part of his own[4c] and in accordance with the principle *semper praesumitur pro negante* the appeal was dismissed. Had Lord Upjohn been in favour of allowing the appeal, the application of the principle would have produced a disgruntled appellant whose victory had been snatched from under his nose: it may well be that such manifest injustice would have led to the case being reargued before a reconstituted Court.[5]

[1] It happened in no fewer than 7·3 per cent of House of Lords appeals during the period 1952–68, see pp. 192–5 above.

[2] s. 1 (2) of the Criminal Appeal Act 1907 prescribed a Court of Criminal Appeal with at least three, an uneven number of judges. Curiously, s. 2 (2) of the Criminal Appeal Act 1966 which established the criminal division of the Court of Appeal, followed the pattern of the civil division and said nothing about an uneven number. This situation has been remedied by s. 9 of the Administration of Justice Act 1970.

[3] Except in interlocutory proceedings the Court of Appeal can sit with two judges only by consent of the parties.

[4] e.g. *Packer* v. *Packer* [1954] P. 15 (Denning and Morris L.JJ.)

[4a] Another consequence of Lord Upjohn's death was that the Appellate Committee, due to start the hearing of an adoption appeal, *Re W (An infant)* [1971] A.C. 682, had to be reconstituted at short notice with the Lord Chancellor presiding. See H.L. Debs., vol. 314, col. 82, 26 January 1971.

[4b] [1971] 2 W.L.R. 667.   [4c] Cf. *Ross Smith* v. *Ross Smith*, below.

[5] The principle *semper* etc. . . . appears first in the House of Lords in *R.* v. *Millis* (1844) 10 Cl. and F. 534, 907, although the background note to *Kennedy* v. *Spratt* [1971] 2 W.L.R. 680 refers to an earlier, unreported case in 1773. In *Eastern Steamship Co.* v. *Smith* [1891]

The minimum size of appeal courts is laid down by statute, but as a rule, the legislature has imposed no upper limit except by restricting number of judges qualified to sit in a particular court. Both the Court of Appeal and the House of Lords normally sit with more than a bare quorum of judges: the former with three Lords Justices (the quorum is two) and the latter with five Law Lords (the quorum is three). But in certain circumstances both courts sometimes sit with more judges than is usual—as a full court: and it is the function of these full courts which is the central theme discussed here.[1]

In our period of study there were only two instances [1a] where the House of Lords has sat with more than five judges: the cases were *B.T.C.* v. *Gourley*[2] and *Ross Smith* v. *Ross Smith*.[3] (Both these cases are discussed elsewhere in the text.) The former involved an important question of the extent to which future liability to tax should be taken into account in assessing damages payable for loss of earnings, and led the House to reconsider and overrule a decision of the Court of Appeal.[4] Originally the appeal was argued before a five-judge Appellate Committee in July 1954; but after two days of argument their Lordships decided to convene a full court, and the case was fully argued the following October before seven Law Lords. *Ross Smith* concerned the rules governing the jurisdiction of the courts in nullity proceedings—a question which had been determined by the House a century before in the much criticized decision in *Simonin* v. *Mallac*.[5] In the result the latter case was rather indecisively overruled (in part at least) by the full court: one Law Lord dissented,[6] and two were content merely to confine the scope of the earlier decision. The unsatisfactory nature of the decision (or, perhaps more accurately, indecision) in *Ross*

A.C. 310, 316, the principle was laid down that where the House of Lords is evenly divided, two for reversing and two for affirming the decision of the court *a quo*, the ancient rule of law *semper praesumitur pro negante* applies and the appeal is dismissed, but usually without costs. The same principle was applied in *Paquin Ltd.* v. *Beauclerk* [1906] A.C. 148, 168 by Lord Chancellor Loreborn. But in his autobiography Lord Macmillan tells of a rather different outcome in another appeal presided over by Lord Loreburn, *Colquhoun* v. *the Faculty of Advocates*, 1908 S.C. (H.L.) 10, in which Macmillan appeared as counsel for the appellant. At the conclusion of argument the four Law Lords went away to write their opinions, but it was soon found that their views were evenly divided. Nothing daunted, the Lord Chancellor who (according to Lord Macmillan) had shown himself to be in favour of the appellant's case, ordered a re-hearing before seven Law Lords. In the result the Appellant (and, perhaps one might add, the Lord Chancellor) was successful by four to three. (*A Man of Law's Tale*, p. 117.) *Quaere*, whether the rule applies in questions of costs, *Anderson* v. *Morice* (1876) 1 App. Cas. 713, 750–751.

1 Full courts are not unknown to the Scottish courts. The effect of various 19th Century enactments is to enable the Court of Session to sit 5 (or more usually 7) or as the whole Court: where the judges are equally divided, or in cases of difficulty, or where the importance of the case renders it expedient. Such courts can resolve conflicting decisions, overrule earlier decisions of the Inner House and define the scope of an Act of Parliament which a previous decision has rendered doubtful.

1a There have been two further instances: *Jones* v. *Secretary of State for Social Services* [1972] 1 All E.R. 145 and *Cassell & Co. Ltd.* v. *Broome*, heard in December 1971.

2 [1956] A.C. 185.

3 [1963] A.C. 280.

4 *Billingham* v. *Hughes* [1949] 1 K.B. 643.   5 (1860) 2 Sw. & Tr. 67.

6 In fact both Lord Hodson and Lord Merriman prepared dissenting speeches, but Lord Merriman died on the morning that judgment was to be delivered and his speech was adopted by Lord Hodson as part of his own. Cf. Lord Donovan's posthumous judgment in *Ealing London Borough Council* v. *Race Relations Board*, [1972] 2 W.L.R. 71, 74.

Smith was subsequently criticized in a scholarly judgment by Simon P. in *Padolecchia* v. *Padolecchia*.[1]

Full courts have become curiosities in the House of Lords, and neither *Gourley* nor *Ross Smith* is particularly persuasive advertisement for their extended use. Five dimensions of diverse reasoning are confusing enough without adding further elements of confusion. Technically there is nothing to prevent all the Law Lords from being convened simultaneously to hear an appeal—and the House could still call upon the judges of the Queen's Bench Division to assist in their deliberations, though this has not happened since 1898.[2] Now that the House is empowered, in limited circumstances, to review its own previous decisions we doubt whether there will be any further occasion for courts larger than the usual five, unless the House of Lords were to adopt the practice of sitting *in banc*. It is surprising that there is a glimmer of a suggestion that reversal of an earlier decision—particularly one recently handed down—will be effected only by a full court.[3]

In the lower appeal courts the role of full courts is quite different and, as we shall see, on the criminal side they have been employed quite frequently. In the (civil) Court of Appeal, notwithstanding recent statements to the contrary by Lord Denning M.R.,[4] it is quite clear that the Court is bound by the self-imposed fetter of its decision in *Young* v. *Bristol Aeroplane Co.*,[5] which permits it to depart from its own previous decisions only in very limited circumstances.[6] The tariff of exceptions laid down in that case does not include any power of a full court to overrule decisions reached by ordinary sittings of the Court, and full courts in the civil Court of Appeal are almost as rare as those in the House of Lords.

In the Court of Criminal Appeal (now the Criminal Division of the Court of Appeal) there has been a general practice of following previous decisions[7]—though there is no unequivocal authority on the matter. The criminal law, unlike most civil law, rests largely upon social *mores* which are in a perpetual state of flux: hence it may be argued that the criminal courts should be flexible, particularly as criminal proceedings often involve both rigorous social stigma and severe penal sanctions. But, equally, the reverse may be true: it can be argued that for the same reasons

[1] [1968] P. 314.

[2] *Allen* v. *Flood* [1898] A.C. 1. See also R.F.V. Heuston, *Lives of the Lord Chancellors*, pp. 119–22.

[3] Following upon the decision to convene a full court in *Jones* v. *Secretary of State for Social Services*, *ante*, the House of Lords issued on March 18, 1971, the following addition to Judicial Direction 12(1) which is concerned with the preparation of Cases (Practice Direction [1971] 2 All E.R. 159): if the parties intend to invite the House to depart from one of its own decisions this must clearly be stated in a separate paragraph of the Case, to which special attention must be drawn. The intention must also be restated as one of the Reasons. The combined implications of *Jones* v. *Secretary of State for Social Services* and of this Direction are not yet clear but they may indicate an intention by the House to convene full courts to reconsider previous decisions or perhaps only one of recent vintage or of those in which members of the present Court were involved. Cf. *Cassell & Co. Ltd.* v. *Broome* heard by 7 Law Lords in December 1971.

[4] *Gallie* v. *Lee* [1969] 2 Ch. 17: and *Hanning* v. *Maitland (No. 2)* [1970] 1 Q.B. 580. The principle, as enunciated by Lord Denning, was discussed on a different level in *Broome* v. *Cassell and Co. Ltd.* [1971] 2 W.L.R. 853, namely, to what extent may the Court of Appeal decline to follow a binding decision of the House of Lords itself.

[5] [1944] K.B. 718.

[6] (1) It can resolve two conflicting decisions of its own; (2) it can reject a decision which cannot stand with a subsequent decision of the House of Lords; (3) it can reject a decision reached *per incuriam*.

[7] See R. Cross, *Precedent in English Law* (2nd ed.), pp. 110 ff.

(stigma and punishment) the criminal law should be clearly and firmly stated by the courts so that potential deviants can ascertain precisely where they stand. The former principle seems to have prevailed to the extent that the Court of Appeal (Criminal Division) has never laid down a 'Bristol Aeroplane doctrine', and, as we shall show later, it is far freer than its civil counterpart in convening full courts—mainly for the purpose of reconsidering previous decisions of its own.

Full courts are not just curious mutations from the ordinary evolutionary order of courts, they have an important bearing upon the more general problem of the appellate hierarchy. Proposals for the abolition of the House of Lords are invariably accompanied by a suggestion for revising the procedure of the Court of Appeal which would thereby be elevated to the status of final Court of Appeal. If the Court of Appeal were confronted with an appeal which merited the fullest consideration by the highest court in the land, so the suggestion runs, the ordinary three-judge court might be re-constituted as a full court of five judges, simulating the deposed Law Lords (perhaps even including them among its membership).

It is not easy to assess the effectiveness of such a change in saving time and money. If the Court of Appeal were to reconstitute itself in such a way for *all* the cases that would ordinarily have gone to the House of Lords, there would be less merit in the proposal than if the Court were to reserve the full-court procedure for only a proportion of the cases that would otherwise have been taken to the top of the court ladder, or if the initial proceeding before the 'ordinary' Court of Appeal were briefer than at present. But by what criteria would cases deserving of 'House of Lords treatment' be selected? If the wishes of the litigants were relevant, presumably the Court would adopt the full-court procedure in cases where currently it grants leave to appeal—and that would provide a case-load little less than the House of Lords now undertakes. (Of course its criteria in considering applications might be more liberal than at present in borderline cases, since it would no longer be able to shift the responsibility for granting leave on to the Appeal Committee.)

If there is merit in the full-court procedure it is difficult to understand why it has not been used more frequently to stem the tide of aspiring appellants to the House of Lords. There is no prohibition in the Rules of the Supreme Court on use of the procedure, but only very occasionally has it been employed. In the period 1951–66 three cases were so disposed of by the (civil) Court of Appeal: *Morelle Ltd.* v. *Wakeling*,[1] *Ward* v. *James*,[2] and *Nowotnik* v. *Nowotnik*.[3] And the latter case was severely criticized, if not reversed, in a later *three*-judge Court of Appeal decision, *Hanning* v. *Maitland (No. 2)*.[4]

Morelle Ltd. v. *Wakeling* was a complicated case involving the doctrine of mortmain. When the case came on before a court of three judges, it was adjourned to give the Attorney-General, on behalf of the Crown, which had a vital interest in the appeal, an opportunity to attend as *amicus curiae*. On the re-hearing a five-judge court was constituted, mainly (it seems) to deal with the difficulty of a previous authority in the Court of Appeal decision in *Morelle Ltd.* v. *Waterworth*.[5] Since the Court granted the losing party leave to appeal, there was clearly no desire on the part of the Court of Appeal to prevent the House of Lords finally determining the law, though in fact the parties declined to take the case to the Lords.[6]

Ward v. *James*, on the other hand, represented an attempt both to consider an earlier five-judge decision and to bring finality to an issue of adjectival law—namely,

[1] [1955] 2 Q.B. 379.   [2] [1966] 1 Q.B. 273.   [3] [1967] P. 83.
[4] [1970] 1 Q.B. 580.   [5] [1955] 1 Q.B. 1.
[6] A parallel case going through the courts at that time, *Attorney-General* v. *Parsons* [1956] A.C. 421, was in fact reversed by the House of Lords.

the circumstances in which a party to a personal injury action could properly ask for trial by jury. At the original hearing, Lord Justice Sellers said (at p. 278): 'It is said that they [a number of recent decisions] are in conflict with a decision of this Court in *Hope* v. *Great Western Railway Co.*[1] That case was a decision of the full court, and this particular problem has not been reconsidered by a full court since that date.' The defendant in that case, who needed to obtain leave to appeal to the Court of Appeal (because the issue was an interlocutory one), agreed not to prosecute his appeal to the House of Lords were he to fail in his appeal in the Court of Appeal.

Nowotnik v. *Nowotnik* received the 'full-court' treatment for no better reason than that it raised a complicated issue arising out of the Legal Aid Act 1964 and it was the first case under the Act. No authorities were cited, so that the Court had no precedent to bind its decision. The case was one of pure (or impure?) statutory construction. Leave to appeal was refused to the losing party and there the case rested. And ultimately, in *Hanning* v. *Maitland* (*No. 2*), the statutory construction favoured only four years earlier was declared wrong by a three-judge court. Certainly *Nowotnik* is intrinsically no more important than numerous cases heard annually by an ordinary three-judge court.

We feel that there is nothing positive to be learnt from this trilogy of 'full court' appeals. Clearly, while the House of Lords remains the court of last resort, the Court of Appeal will be likely to use the 'full court' procedure sparingly. A rational use of the procedure would be to deal with previous awkward decisions of the Court of Appeal where the amount involved or the importance of the case would not warrant a second appeal. On that basis *Ward* v. *James* is explicable; *Morelle Ltd.* v. *Wakeling* is in part understandable, although the use of a full court was rendered unnecessary by the grant of leave to appeal: *Nowotnik* v. *Nowotnik* is, however, totally inexplicable.

Continuing our search for a hypothesis for the use of the full-court procedure, we turned to the practice of the Court of Criminal Appeal, particularly since, until the Administration of Justice Act of 1960, that court was effectively the final appellate court in criminal matters. (Certainly, the Court itself had no control over further appeals to the House of Lords: allowable only on the fiat of the Attorney-General and this, very seldom granted.)

We approached the material with two hypotheses in mind: (1) that the cases which received the full-court treatment involved *predominantly* important points of substantive, evidential or adjectival law; and (2) that these cases were of greater importance than run-of-the-mill criminal appeals. If these assumptions proved correct, one might expect the civil Court of Appeal, in the absence of a higher appellate court, to adopt a similar policy in the use of full courts. If the assumptions proved false, one would have no reason to suppose that the civil appeal court, thrust into an unaccustomed role as court of last resort, would be any more successful in formulating a coherent policy towards the full court procedure which would accord with the public interest in having a tribunal in which important points of law can be fully and comprehensively argued out.

During the period 1951–66[2] there were, so far as we have been able to discover, 27 full court decisions out of 476 reported decisions of the Court of Criminal Appeal

---

[1] [1937] 2 K.B. 130. In *Ward* v. *James* the Court of Appeal purported not to reverse *Hope* but to 'reinterpret' the decision: a piece of sophistry clearly intended to side-step the *Bristol Aeroplane* doctrine, above.

[2] Since 1966 there have so far been only three instances of the criminal division of the Court of Appeal sitting with five judges—*R.* v. *Newsome* and *R.* v. *Browne* [1970] 2 Q.B. 711 below. See also Gavin Drewry, 'Full Courts', 120 New L.J. 759 (13 August 1970); *R.* v. *Locker*, [1971] 2 Q.B. 321; and *R.* v. *Szulimowski* (1971) unreported, Criminal Appeal No. 3984/c/70.

(5·6 per cent). (Annexed is the list of these cases—Annex A—all but one of which is reported: and there is a brief reference in *Anderson and Morris*[1] to the one unreported case, *Smith*, 6 November 1961.) We have broken down the period into two parts: (a) 1951–60, the period when criminal appeals to the House of Lords were very rare and leave to appeal depended upon the fiat procedure; and (b) 1961–6 when there were considerably more appeals to the House of Lords.

At the outset we should repeat that the Court of Criminal Appeal normally followed its own previous rulings on points of law but was not absolutely bound by them: it could and did overrule them if it felt it was desirable to do so. The usual procedure when an earlier statement of law was to be seriously questioned, was to summon a full court of five or more judges, the classic example being *Taylor*.[2] This was not, however, the invariable practice: to quote Mr. Michael Knight, 'it is not unknown for a normal division of three judges in no way specially summoned to state in a later case the exact contrary of an earlier three-judge ruling and yet not expressly overrule it.'[3]

Over the whole period, 1951–66, the full Court was regularly used, not predominantly to deal with cases involving particularly difficult points of law but primarily because the Court was confronted with an awkward precedent it wanted to bypass or overrule. In 11 out of the 27 full court cases (41 per cent) it was clear that awkward precedents were the reason for the composition of a five-judge court: indeed in two cases *McVitie*[4] and *Hallam*[5] this is given explicitly as the reason for a full court; and in another case—*Vickers*[6]—although the point of law involved was important, the reason given for having a full court was that there had been an irreconcilable conflict when the case came before the three-judge court originally.

The eleven cases, chronologically from 1951, clearly indicate the purpose in having a full court:

1. *Hallam* (1957) 41 Cr. App. R. 111	Considered and overruled *Dacey* (1931) 27 Cr. App. R. 86.
2. *McVitie* (1960) 44 Cr. App. R. 201	Distinguished *Hyde* (1934) 24 Cr. App. R. 149.
3. *Flynn* (1961) 45 Cr. App. R. 268 ⎱ 4. *McBride* (1961) 45 Cr. App. R. 262 ⎰	A number of earlier cases were overruled, distinguished or explained.
5. *Evans* (1961) 45 Cr. App. R. 59	Studied, but did not follow the reasoning in, an unreported case in 1960 (McCarthy).
6. *Amos* (1961) 45 Cr. App. R. 42	Overruled *Jones* [1960] 1 W.L.R. 812 and *Longstreet* (1960) unreported.
7. *Golder, Jones & Porritt* (1961) 45 Cr. App. R. 5	Firmly distinguished the earlier cases of *White* (1922) 17 Cr. App. R. 160 and *Harris* (1927) 20 Cr. App. R. 144.
8. *Patterson* (1962) 46 Cr. App. R. 106	Overruled *Ward* [1915] 3 K.B. 696; (1915) 11 Cr. App. R. 284.

---

[1] (1966) 50 Cr. App. R. 216. (Hereafter the notation '*R. v.*' is omitted for the sake of brevity).

[2] [1950] 2 K.B. 368; (1950) 34 Cr. App. R. 138.

[3] 'The Court of Criminal Appeal and Binding Precedent', 113 L.J. 589 (13 September 1963).

[4] (1960) 44 Cr. App. R. 201.   [5] (1957) 41 Cr. App. R. 111.

[6] (1957) 41 Cr. App. R. 189.

9. *Box* (1963) 47 Cr. App. R. 284	Explained *Symes* (1914) 10 Cr. App. R. 284.
10. *Anderson and Morris* (1966) 50 Cr. App. R. 216	Explained two, possibly conflicting, earlier cases.
11. *Assim* (1966) 50 Cr. App. R. 224	Expressly did not follow *Phillips* (1731) 2 Stra. 921 and *Leigh and Harrison* [1966] 1 All E.R. 687.

In some of the remaining sixteen cases, while there was no awkward precedent, seemingly standing in the path of modern attitudes to the criminal law, to be over-ruled, distinguished or to have its reasoning doubted or explained, there was a morass of case law on the point. A full court was decreed ostensibly to speed the flow of a sluggish tributary of law by gathering up the accumulated driftwood, (e.g. *Cook*[1] and *Whybrow*[2]). For the rest, with the exception of *Vickers* which needed a five-judge court to resolve the three-judge impasse (one judge in private had declared his tentative dissent), a full court was summoned simply because of the intrinsic importance of the case. The criteria for 'intrinsic importance' seemed to be (1) repercussion on the future law of a comparatively straightforward point of law: *Murtagh and Kennedy*;[3] (2) difficulty in the point of law: *Podola*;[4] or (3) seriousness of charge, e.g. capital murder, coupled with a novel point of law, e.g. diminished responsibility: *Matheson*.[5] On these criteria it is a little hard to explain why three cases—*Mitchell*,[6] *Michalski*[7] and *Fisher*[8]—were thought worthy of the full court procedure.

If the 27 cases are broken up into the two periods, it is interesting to note that in the period before the coming into force of the Administration of Justice Act 1960, most of the 15 cases were on important points of law, whereas, post-1960, out of 11 reported and one unreported cases, 8 were concerned with awkward precedents. Can this be interpreted as a change in policy whereby important criminal cases are left for possible determination by the House of Lords, leaving the Court of Criminal Appeal (and now its successor the Court of Appeal Criminal Division) to convene full courts to deal only with awkward precedents? Clearly, the double test prescribed by the 1960 Act for granting leave to the House of Lords—that the case raises a point of law of general public importance and that it ought to be determined by the House of Lords—indicates a call for less use of the full court procedure where the case may be destined for further appellate treatment.

A recent statement concerning the use of full courts is to be found in the judgment of Widgery L.J. in the twin appeals *Newsome* and *Browne*: the criminal division of the Court of Appeal sat with five judges for the first time since the Court was instituted in 1966, to resolve conflicting decisions on a matter of sentencing policy. His Lordship said: 'We are satisfied that, if a court of five is duly constituted to consider an issue of discretion and the principles upon which the discretion should be exercised, that court ought to have the right to depart from an earlier view expressed by the court of three, especially where that earlier view is very recent and especially where the court did not have the opportunity of argument on both sides. Accordingly, within that restricted sphere—we take the view that a court of five can and should depart from an earlier direction in the exercise of a judge's discretion if satisfied that the earlier direction was wrong.' He added, with particular reference to

[1] (1959) 43 Cr. App. R. 138.	[2] (1951) 35 Cr. App. R. 141.
[3] (1955) 39 Cr. App. R. 72.	[4] (1959) 43 Cr. App. R. 220.
[5] (1958) 42 Cr. App. R. 145.	[6] (1952) 36 Cr. App. R. 79.
[7] (1955) 39 Cr. App. R. 22.	[8] (1965) 49 Cr. App. R. 116.

the present appeals, that where a court was not following an earlier decision it was important to see that the individual suffered no injustice in the result.

Taken as a whole, the full court process is rather a nonentity, even in the Criminal Appeal courts where it all but died out after 1966. (And the cautious remarks of Widgery L.J. in *Newsome* hardly herald the dawn of a new era of full courts in the Criminal Division.) It has chiefly been used to disentangle the law from the awkwardness of precedent; in few cases was the intrinsic importance of the case the governing factor in convening full courts. Even a slight change of heart post-1960 hardly upgrades the process from its unimportant part in the criminal appellate process.[1]

We are convinced that there are literally dozens of reported cases in the period 1951–66 on topics as important as, if not more important than the cases given the full court treatment. We attach a list (Annex B) of some cases which we would think, on the grounds of importance, merited the full court procedure. A third of them were pre-1960. None of the others (post-1960 cases) in fact went on to the House of Lords. Our view is of course highly subjective, but we venture to think that most criminal lawyers would agree on a high proportion of our examples.

We conclude from this study that if it is left to the first-tier appeal courts alone to determine whether the full court procedure should be employed, a number of important points of law will not get the special treatment afforded by a more thorough review, and that a full court will tend to be used primarily whenever the Court of Appeal wants to reverse its own previous decisions. If, however, litigants were able to apply for a full court hearing, in much the same way as they now apply for leave to appeal to the House of Lords, the full court procedure would be likely to be used at least as often as appeals are now heard by the House of Lords.

If a larger court is used merely as a substitute for a first appeal to all ordinary three-judge courts, then any benefit of a second appeal derived from a saving of judicial man-hours is, at one blow, lost. If full courts are combined with a modified two-tier system, with a first hearing before three judges, who refer the case to a larger court, then the system has gained nothing. The only lesson to be learned from the examination of the use of full courts in recent years is that they are used sparingly and in restricted circumstances—and they hardly provide a model system which might replace the House of Lords. This is not to say that a full court might not be employed as the court of last resort, but it would have to be something a great deal more high-powered and purposive than the anaemic specimens produced in recent years. If this story has produced nothing more exciting than re-affirmation of the value of a three-tier system of courts, it is as well to remind oneself that proving a negative, if somewhat dampening to the ardour of a reformer, has a useful function in clearing away the dead wood of ill-considered reforms.

[1] The total disappearance of full courts post-1966 and pre-*Newsome*, may reflect not only the fact that the House of Lords has continued to expand its activities in the field of criminal law, but also that the Criminal Division of the Court of Appeal now includes Lords Justices who can perhaps reconsider more authoritatively previous decisions (especially those of the old Court of Criminal Appeal) in a three-judge court while leaving important points of law to be determined by the House of Lords.

ANNEX A: REPORTED FULL COURT DECISIONS 1951–1966

Whybrow (1951) 35 Cr. App. R. 141.
Harrison-Owen (1951) 35 Cr. App. R. 108.
Mitchell (1952) 36 Cr. App. R. 79.
Murtagh and Kennedy (1955) 39 Cr. App. R. 72.
Michalski (1955) 39 Cr. App. R. 22.
Sparkes (1956) 40 Cr. App. R. 83.
Hopkins and Collins (1957) 41 Cr. App. R. 231.
Vickers (1957) 41 Cr. App. R. 189.
Hallam (1957) 41 Cr. App. R. 111.
Matheson (1958) 42 Cr. App. R. 145.
Green (1958) 42 Cr. App. R. 77.
Podola (1959) 43 Cr. App. R. 220.
Cook (1959) 43 Cr. App. R. 138.
Evans (1959) 43 Cr. App. R. 66.
McVitie (1960) 44 Cr. App. R. 201.
Flynn (1961) 45 Cr. App. R. 268.
McBride (1961) 45 Cr. App. R. 262.
Spurge (1961) 45 Cr. App. R. 191.
Evans (1961) 45 Cr. App. R. 59.
Amos (1961) 45 Cr. App. R. 42.
Golder, Jones and Porritt (1961) 45 Cr. App. R. 5.
Patterson (1962) 46 Cr. App. R. 106.
Box (1963) 47 Cr. App. R. 284.
Fisher (1965) 49 Cr. App. R. 116.
Anderson (1966) 50 Cr. App. R. 216.
Assim (1966) 50 Cr. App. R. 224.

The one unreported full-court decision:
Smith (6 November 1961), discussed *Anderson* (1966) Cr. App. R. 216.

ANNEX B: IMPORTANT THREE-JUDGE COURT CASES
1951–1966

THE JURY

Owen (1952) 36 Cr. App. R. 16.
Wilson (1957) 41 Cr. App. R. 226.
Davis (1960) 44 Cr. App. R. 235.
McKenna (1960) 44 Cr. App. R. 63.
Davey (1960) 45 Cr. App. R. 11.
Thompson (1962) 46 Cr. App. R. 72.
Young (1964) 48 Cr. App. R. 292.
Gearing (1966) 50 Cr. App. R. 18.

REPRESENTATION OF ACCUSED

Howes (1964) 48 Cr. App. R. 172.
Sowden (1965) 49 Cr. App. R. 32.
Lacey and Wright (1966) 50 Cr. App. R. 205.

RIGHTS OF UNREPRESENTED PRISONER
Carter (1960) 44 Cr. App. R. 225.

FRESH EVIDENCE AVAILABLE
Jordan (1956) 40 Cr. App. R. 152.
Parks (1961) 46 Cr. App. R. 29.
Flower, Siggins and Flower (1966) 50 Cr. App. R. 22.

DIMINISHED RESPONSIBILITY
Dunbar (1957) 41 Cr. App. R. 182.
Spriggs (1958) 42 Cr. App. R. 69.
Walden (1959) 43 Cr. App. R. 201.
Byrne (1960) 44 Cr. App. R. 246.
Terry (1961) 45 Cr. App. R. 180.
Jennion (1962) 46 Cr. App. R. 212.
Ahmed Din (1962) 46 Cr. App. R. 269.
Gomez (1964) 48 Cr. App. R. 310.
King (1965) 49 Cr. App. R. 140.

BURDEN OF PROOF
Lobell (1957) 41 Cr. App. R. 100.
MacPherson (1957) 41 Cr. App. R. 213.
Head and Warrener (1961) 45 Cr. App. R. 225.

PROVISO TO SECTION 4 (1)
Wallwork (1958) 42 Cr. App. R. 153.
Sparrow and Friend (1962) 46 Cr. App. R. 288.
Oliva (1962) 46 Cr. App. R. 241.
Slinger (1962) 46 Cr. App. R. 244.
Johnson (1961) 46 Cr. App. R. 55.
Trigg (1963) 47 Cr. App. R. 94.

SUBSTITUTION UNDER SECTION 5 (2)
Caslin (1961) 45 Cr. App. R. 47.
Smith (1962) 46 Cr. App. R. 277.
Scaramanga (1963) 47 Cr. App. R. 213.

JUDGE'S BEHAVIOUR
Clewer (1953) 37 Cr. App. R. 37.

WIFE AS WITNESS
Boucher (1952) 36 Cr. App. R. 152.

RIGHT OF APPEAL

Robinson (1953) 37 Cr. App. R. 95.
Hinds (1962) 46 Cr. App. R. 327.

HOME SECRETARY'S REFERENCE

Caborn-Waterfield (1956) 40 Cr. App. R. 110.

INDICTMENTS

Seymour (1954) 38 Cr. App. R. 68.
Hammersley, Heath, Bellson (1958) 42 Cr. App. R. 207.
Dawson and Wenlock (1960) 44 Cr. App. R. 87.
Martin (1961) 45 Cr. App. R. 199.
Harden (1962) 46 Cr. App. R. 90.

PROCEDURAL REQUIREMENTS ON PUNISHMENT, IMPORTION OF

Evans (1956) 40 Cr. App. R. 165.
Long (1960) 44 Cr. App. R. 9.
Chapman and Pidgley (1960) 44 Cr. App. R. 115.

HOSTILE WITNESS

Oliva (1965) 49 Cr. App. R. 298.

SUMMING-UP

Attfield (1961) 45 Cr. App. R. 309.

SELECT BIBLIOGRAPHY

THE following list of relevant books is highly selective: the lists of articles and official publications that follow it are even more eclectic. To attempt anything approaching a comprehensive bibliography of works on the judicial process and appellate courts would require a separate volume and would duplicate readily accessible lists compiled by others. We would, in particular, refer our readers to the excellent bibliographies in J. Gillis Wetter's *The Style of Appellate Judicial Opinions* and in Henry J. Abrahams, *The Judicial Process* (below).

BOOKS

ABEL-SMITH, BRIAN, and STEVENS, ROBERT, *In Search of Justice*. London: Allen Lane at the Penguin Press, 1968.

ABEL-SMITH, BRIAN, and STEVENS, ROBERT, *Lawyers and the Courts*. London: Heinemann, 1967.

ABRAHAMS, HENRY J., *The Judicial Process*. London: Oxford University Press, 1962.

ALLEN, C. K., *Law in the Making*. Oxford: Clarendon Press, 7th edition, 1964.

AMOS, SIR M. S., and WALTON, F. P., *Introduction to French Law* (revised by F. H. Lawson, A. E. Anton, and L. Neville Brown). London: Oxford University Press, 3rd edition, 1967.

ARCHER, P., *The Queen's Court*. Harmondsworth: Pelican, 2nd edition, 1963.

AUBERT, V. (ed.), *Sociology of Law: Selected Readings*. Harmondsworth: Penguin, 1969.

BAADE, HANS W. (ed.), *Jurimetrics*. New York: Basic Books, 1963.

BAGEHOT, WALTER, *The English Constitution*. London: Fontana Books, 1962 (originally published 1867).

BAKER, H. E., *The Legal System of Israel*. London: Sweet & Maxwell, 1961.

BALDWIN, J. F., *The King's Council in England During the Middle Ages*. Oxford: Clarendon Press, 1913.

BENTWICH, N., *Privy Council Practice*. London: Sweet & Maxwell, 3rd edition, 1937.

BROMHEAD, P. A., *The House of Lords in Contemporary Politics*. London: Routledge & Kegan Paul, 1958.

CARDOZO, BENJAMIN N., *The Nature of the Judicial Process*. New Haven: Yale University Press, 1921.

CECIL, HENRY, *Tipping the Scales*. London: Hutchinson, 1964.

CORNISH, W. R., *The Jury*. Harmondsworth: Pelican, 1971.

CROSS, RUPERT, *Precedent in English Law*. Oxford: Clarendon Press, 2nd edition, 1968.

DAVID, RENÉ, and BRIERLEY, JOHN E. C., *Major Legal Systems in the World Today*. London: Stevens, 1968.

DERRETT, J. DUNCAN M. (ed.), *An Introduction to Legal Systems*. London: Sweet & Maxwell, 1968.

EDWARDS, J., *The Law Officers of the Crown*. London: Stevens, 1964.

ENSOR, R. C. K., *Courts and Judges in France, Germany and England*. London: Oxford University Press, 1933.

EVERSHED, LORD, *The Court of Appeal in England*. London: Athlone Press, 1950.

FRANK, JEROME, *Courts on Trial*. Princeton, N.J.: Princeton University Press, 1950.

FRIEDMANN, W., *Law in a Changing Society*. Harmondsworth: Pelican, abridged edition, 1963.

GARDINER, GERALD, and MARTIN, ANDREW (eds.), *Law Reform NOW!* London: Gollancz, 1963.

GOODHART, A. L., *Essays in Jurisprudence and the Common Law*. Cambridge: Cambridge University Press, 1937.

GROSSMAN, JOEL B., and TANENHAUS, JOSEPH, *Frontiers of Judicial Research*. New York: John Wiley, 1969.

GUTTERIDGE, H. C., *Comparative Law*. Cambridge: Cambridge University Press, 2nd edition, 1949.

HAHLO, H. R., and KAHN, E., *Union of South Africa*. (Vol. 5 of the series *British Commonwealth—The Development of its Laws and Constitutions*.) London: Stevens, 1960.

HALDANE, LORD, *An Autobiography*. London: Hodder & Stoughton, 1929.

HANBURY, H. G., *English Courts of Law* (4th edition prepared by D. C. M. Yardley). London: Oxford University Press, 1967.

HARDING, ALAN, *A Social History of English Law*. Harmondsworth: Pelican, 1966.

HEUSTON, R. F. V., *Lives of the Lord Chancellors, 1885–1940*. Oxford: Clarendon Press, 1964.

HOLDSWORTH, SIR WILLIAM, *A History of English Law*. Vol. 1. London: Methuen, 7th edition, 1956.

HYDE, H. MONTGOMERY, *Norman Birkett*. London: Hamish Hamilton, 1964.

JACKSON, R. M., *The Machinery of Justice in England*. Cambridge: Cambridge University Press, 5th edition, 1967.

JAFFE, LOUIS L., *English and American Judges as Lawmakers*. Oxford: Clarendon Press, 1969.

JUSTICE, *Proposal for a Suitors' Fund*. March 1969.

KALVEN, H., and ZEISEL, H., *The American Jury*. Boston: Little, Brown, 1966.

KARLEN, DELMAR, *Appellate Courts in the United States and England*. New York: New York University Press, 1963.

KILMUIR, THE EARL OF, *Political Adventure*. London: Weidenfeld and Nicolson, 1964.

KILRAFY, A. K., *The English Legal System*. London: Sweet & Maxwell, 4th edition, 1967.

KNIGHT, MICHAEL, *Criminal Appeals*. London: Sweet & Maxwell, 1970.

MCILWAIN, C. H., *The High Court of Parliament*. New Haven, Conn.: Yale University Press, 1910.

MACKENZIE, KENNETH, *The English Parliament*. Harmondsworth: Pelican, revised edition, 1968.

MACMILLAN, LORD, *A Man of Law's Tale*. London: Macmillan, 1953.

MCWHINNEY, E., *Judicial Review in the English Speaking World*. Toronto: Toronto University Press, 2nd edition, 1961.

MAYERS, LEWIS, *The American Legal System*. New York: Harper, 1955.

MILSOM, S. F. C., *Historical Foundations of the Common Law*. London: Butterworths, 1969.

MONTROSE, J. L., *Precedent in English Law and Other Essays* (edited by H. G. Hanbury). Shannon: Irish University Press, 1968.

MURPHY, WALTER F., and PRITCHETT, C. HERMANN, *Courts, Judges and Politics*. New York: Random House, 1961.

PATON, G. W., *Commonwealth of Australia*. (Vol. 2 of the series *British Commonwealth—The Development of its Laws and Constitutions*.) London: Stevens, 1952.

PHILIPS, O. HOOD, *Constitutional and Administrative Law*. London: Sweet & Maxwell, 4th edition, 1967.

PHILLIPSON, N. T., 'The Scottish Whigs and the Reform of the Court of Session, 1785–1830'. Unpublished Doctoral Thesis, University of Cambridge.

PIKE, LUKE OWEN, *A Constitutional History of the House of Lords*. London: Macmillan, 1894.

POWELL, J. ENOCH, and WALLIS, KEITH, *The House of Lords in the Middle Ages*. London: Weidenfeld & Nicholson, 1968.

RADCLIFFE, LORD, *The Law and its Compass*. London: Faber, 1960.

REYNOLD, FREDERIC, *The Judge as Lawmaker*. London: MacGibbon & Kee, 1967.

ROBSON, J. L., *New Zealand*. (Vol. 4, of the Series *British Commonwealth—Development of its Laws and Constitutions*.) London: Stevens, 2nd edition, 1967.

SAMPSON, ANTHONY, *The New Anatomy of Britain*, (Ch. 18: 'Law'). London: Hodder & Stoughton, 1971.

SAWER, GEOFFREY, *Law in Society*, Oxford: Clarendon Press, 1965.

SCHMIDHAUSER, J. R., *The Supreme Court: Its Politics, Personalities and Procedures*. New York: Holt, Rinehart & Winston, 1960.

SCHUR, EDWIN M., *Law and Society*. New York: Random House, 1968.

SCHUBERT, GLENDON, and DANELSKI, DAVID, J. (eds.), *Comparative Judicial Behaviour*. London: Oxford University Press, 1969.

SHKLAR, JUDITH N., *Legalism*. Cambridge, Mass.: Harvard University Press, 1964.

SMITH, S. A. DE, *Judicial Review of Administrative Action*. London: Stevens, 2nd edition, 1968.

SMITH, T. B., *Scotland*. (Vol. 11 of the series *British Commonwealth—The Development of its Laws and Constitutions*.) London: Stevens, 1962.

SMITH, T. B., *Studies Critical and Comparative*. Edinburgh: W. Green & Son Ltd., 1962.

STEVENS, R. B., and YAMEY, B. S., *The Restrictive Practices Court: A Study of the Judicial Process and Economic Policy*. London: Weidenfeld & Nicolson, 1965.

WALKER, D. M., *The Scottish Legal System*. Edinburgh: W. Green & Son Ltd., 1959.

WASSERSTROM, RICHARD A., *The Judicial Decision*. London: Oxford University Press, 1961.

WETTER, J. GILLIS, *The Styles of Appellate Judicial Opinions*. Leyden: A. W. Sijthoff, 1960.

ARTICLES

ANDERSON, Q.C., JAMES, 'On the Appellate Jurisdiction of the House of Lords from the Courts of Scotland'. *Transactions of the N.A.P.S.S.* 239 (1860).

ANON., 'Appeals to the House of Lords'. (1957) Crim. L.R. 566.

ASQUITH, LORD, 'Some Aspects of the Work of the Court of Appeal'. 1 J.S.P.T.L. (N.S.) (1947–1951) 350.

ATKIN, LORD, 'Appeal in English Law'. 3 C.L.J. 1 (1929).

BEVAN, THOMAS, 'The Appellate Jurisdiction of the House of Lords'. 17 L.Q.R. 155 and 357 (1901).

BLOM-COOPER, L. J., and DREWRY, G. R., 'House of Lords: Reflections on the Social Utility of Final Appellate Courts'. 32 M.L.R. 262 (1969).

BLOM-COOPER, L. J., and DREWRY, G. R., 'The Use of Full Courts in the Appellate Process'. 34 M.L.R. 364 (1971).

BORRIE, G., 'Judicial Conflicts of Interest in Britain'. 18 *American Journal of Comparative Law* 697 (1970).

BRAYBROOKS, E. K., 'The Authority of the House of Lords in New Zealand Courts'. 32 *New Zealand L.J.* (1956).

CARPENTER, WILLIAM L., 'Courts of Last Resort'. 19 *Yale L.J.* 280 (1910).

CARSON, 'Great Dissenting Opinions'. 50 *Alb. L.J.* 120.

COHEN, LORD, 'Jurisdiction, Practice and Procedure of the Court of Appeal'. 11 C.L.J. (1951).

COWPER, F. 'The Judicial Jurisdiction of the House of Lords'. *Burke's Peerage*, p. cxxvii (1953).

CROSS, RUPERT, 'Three tier or two tier?' 59 *Law Society's Gazette* 587 (1962).

DAVIS, A. G., 'Judicial Precedent in New Zealand: House of Lords and the Privy Council'. 31 *New Zealand L.J.* 42 (1955).

DENNING, LORD, 'New Work for an Old Hand'. *The Oxford Lawyer* (Trinity Term 1958), p. 7.

DIPLOCK, LORD, 'The Lords as Legislators', *The Holdsworth Club of the University of Birmingham* (1965).

DOUGLAS, WILLIAM O., 'The Dissent: A Safeguard of Democracy'. 32 *Journal of American Judicature Society* 104 (1948).

DREWRY, GAVIN, 'Judges in Parliament'. 119 N.L.J. 431 (8 May 1969).

DREWRY, GAVIN, 'One Appeal Too Many?—An Analysis of the Functions of the House of Lords as a Final Court of Appeal'. 19 *British Journal of Sociology* 445 (1968).

DREWRY, GAVIN, 'Ex-Officio Law Lords'. 119 N.L.J. 524 (5 June 1969).

DREWRY, GAVIN, 'Leapfrogging to the Lords'. 118 N.L.J. 1084 (14 November 1968).

DREWRY, GAVIN, and MORGAN, JENNY, 'Law Lords as Legislators'. *Parliamentary Affairs* (July 1969), p. 226.

DWORKIN, G., '*Stare Decisis* in the House of Lords'. 25 M.L.R. 163 (1962).

FAIRLIE, JOHN A., 'The Doctrine of *Stare Decisis* in British Courts of Last Resort'. 35 *Michigan L.R.* 946 (1935).

GODDARD, LORD, 'The Working of the Court of Criminal Appeal'. 2 J.S.P.T.L. (N.S.) 1 (1952).

GOODMAN, SIR VICTOR, 'The Judicial Business of the House of Lords'. 18 *Journal of the Society of Clerks-at-the-Table in Empire Parliament* 112 (1949).

HEUSTON, R. F. V., 'Liversidge *v.* Anderson in Retrospect'. 86 L.Q.R. 33 (1970).

HEUSTON, R. F. V., 'Who was the third Lord in Rylands *v.* Fletcher?' 86 L.Q.R. 160 (1970).

HOLDSWORTH, SIR W., 'The House of Lords, 1689–1783'. 45 L.Q.R. 307 and 432 (1929).

HOWARD, COLIN, 'Australia and the House of Lords—Parker *v.* The Queen' (1963) Crim. L.R. 675.

JUSTICE, 'Report of Winter Conference 1962'. 6 *The Lawyer* 43 (1963).

KNIGHT, MICHAEL, 'The Court of Criminal Appeal and Binding Precedent'. 113 L.J. 589 (1963).

MACDERMOTT, LORD, 'The Supreme Court of Northern Ireland, Two Unusual Jurisdictions'. 2 J.S.P.T.L. (N.S.) 201 (1952).

MACMILLAN, LORD, 'Lords of Appeal in Ordinary'. 97 L.J. 541 (10 October 1947).

MCWHINNEY, EDWARD, 'Judicial Concurrences and Dissents: A Comparative View of Opinion-writing in Final Appellate Tribunals'. 31 *Canadian Bar Review* 595 (1953).

MEGARRY, R. E., 'Decisions by Equally Divided Court as Precedents'. 70 L.Q.R. 318 and 471 (1954). See also rejoinder by Glanville Williams, ibid., p. 469.

MILLER, Q.C., ALEXANDER EDWARD 'On the Constitution of a Supreme Court of Appeal for the British Empire'. *Transactions of the N.A.P.S.S.* 213 (1874).

MILLER, Q.C., ALEXANDER EDWARD 'Supreme Court of Judicature Act (1873) Amendment Bill, No. 2, So far as relates to Appeals'. *Sessional Proceedings of N.A.P.S.S.* 239 (1864–5).

MOORHEAD, R. DEAN, 'Concurring and Dissenting Opinions'. 38 *American Bar Association Journal* 821 (1952).

NEWARK, F. J., 'On Appealing to the Lords'. 8 *Northern Ireland Legal Quarterly* (1949) 102.

PARKER OF WADDINGTON, LORD, 'The Criminal Division of the Court of Appeal'. (Riddell Lecture to Institute of Legal Executives, February 1969). Abridged version in the *Law Guardian*, No. 47, March 1969, p. 11.

PURPOOLE, PATRICK, 'Appellate Committee'. 118 N.L.J. 1160 (5 December 1968).

SIMPSON, A., 'Dissenting Opinions'. 71 *University of Pennsylvania L.R.* 205 (1923).

SOMERVELL, LORD JUSTICE, 'Acts of Attainder'. 67 L.W.R. 306 (1951).

STEPHENS, RICHARD B., 'The Function of Concurring and Dissenting Opinions in Courts of Last Resort'. 5 *University of Florida L.R.* 394 (1952).

STEVENS, ROBERT, 'The Final Appeal: Reform of the House of Lords and Privy Council 1867–76'. 80 L.Q.R. 343 (1964).

STEVENS, ROBERT, 'The Role of a Final Appeal Court in a Democracy: The House of Lords Today'. 28 M.L.R. 509 (1965).

UPJOHN, LORD, 'Twenty Years On'. (Address to 1968 National Conference of the Law Society.) 65 *Law Society's Gazette*, No. 11, p. 657 (November 1968).

WALKER, D. M., 'Some Characteristics of Scots Law'. 18 M.L.R. 321 (1955).

OFFICIAL PUBLICATIONS

Hansard. Parliamentary Debates:
   3rd Series 1830–91
   4th Series 1892–1908
   5th Series (Official) 1909–date.

House of Lords Journals. Published every Session.

The Standing Orders of the House of Lords Relating to Public Business, 1970. H.L. 4 (1970–1).

House of Lords: Form of Appeal, Directions as to Procedure and Standing Orders Applicable to Appeals from: The Court of Appeal in England; The Court of Session in Scotland; and the Court of Appeal in Northern Ireland (1970).

Civil Judicial Statistics (formerly *Judicial Statistics*). Published annually as a Command Paper 1858-date. (During the Second World War publication was suspended for reasons of economy.)

Civil Judicial Statistics (Scotland). Published annually as a Command Paper.

Criminal Statistics. Published annually as a Command Paper.

Committee Appointed to inquire into the Causes that retard the Decision of Suits in the High Court of Chancery. 1810–11, H.L. Sessional Papers, vol. 3.

Committee to inspect the Lords' Journals:
   1st Report, XLIV H.L. Sessional Papers 45 (1811).
   2nd Report, XI H.L. Sessional Papers 343 (1812).

Select Committee on the Appellate Jurisdiction of the House of Lords. Report, X. H.L. Sessional Papers (1823).

Royal Commission on the Judicature. (Chairman: Lord Cairns). 1st Report, XXV Parliamentary Papers (1868–9).

House of Lords Select Committee on the Appellate Jurisdiction. Report and Minutes of Evidence, H.L. Sessional Papers (July 1872).

Committee on Appeals from Courts of Summary Jurisdiction. (Chairman: Sir W. F. K. Taylor). Report, Cmd. 4296 of 1933.

Business of Courts Committee (Chairman: Lord Hanworth M.R.):
  1st interim report, Cmd. 4265 of 1933.
  2nd interim report, Cmd. 4471 of 1934.
  Final report, Cmd. 5066 of 1936.

Committee on Legal Aid and Legal Advice (Chairman: Lord Rushcliffe). Report, Cmd. 6641 of 1945.

Committee on Supreme Court Practice and Procedure (Chairman: Lord Evershed M.R.):
  1st interim report, Cmd. 7764 of 1949.
  2nd interim report, Cmd. 8176 of 1951.
  3rd interim report, Cmd. 8617 of 1952.
  Final report, Cmd. 8878 of 1953.

Committee on Jury Trial in Scotland (Chairman: Lord Strachan). Report, Cmd. 851 of 1959.

Interdepartmental Committee on the Business of the Criminal Courts (Chairman: Mr. Justice Streatfeild). Report, Cmnd. 1289 of 1961.

Departmental Committee on Jury Service (Chairman: Lord Morris of Borth-y-Gest). Report, Cmnd. 2627 of 1965.

Interdepartmental Committee on the Court of Criminal Appeal (Chairman: Lord Donovan). Report. Cmnd. 2755 of 1965.

Reform of the House of Lords (White Paper). Cmnd. 3799 of 1968.

Royal Commission on Assizes and Quarter Session: (Chairman: Lord Beeching). Report, Cmnd. 4153 of 1969.

Committee on the Supreme Court of Judicature in Northern Ireland (Chairman: Lord MacDermott). Report. Cmnd. 4292 of 1970.

Royal Commission on Assizes and Quarter Sessions 1968–69: Special Statistical Survey (by G. N. G. Rose). H.M.S.O. 1971.

INDEX OF CASES

* Where a case is cited by year only, it is unreported.

INDEX OF STATUTES

SUBJECT INDEX

In order to reduce the extent of an already bulky index we have not included separate page references to judgments of individual Law Lords where these are alluded to only in the form of tabular lists of cases in the text (e.g. the annexes of revenue and rating appeals at pp. 327–359).